Personal Names, Hitler, and the Holocaust

Personal Names, Hitler, and the Holocaust

A Socio-Onomastic Study of Genocide and Nazi Germany

I. M. NICK

LEXINGTON BOOKS
Lanham • Boulder • New York • London

Published by Lexington Books
An imprint of The Rowman & Littlefield Publishing Group, Inc.
4501 Forbes Boulevard, Suite 200, Lanham, Maryland 20706
www.rowman.com

6 Tinworth Street, London SE11 5AL, United Kingdom

British Library Cataloging in Publication Information Available

Library of Congress Cataloging-in-Publication Data

Names: Nick, I. M.
Title: Personal Names, Hitler, and the Holocaust : A Socio-Onomastic Study of
    Genocide and Nazi Germany / I. M. Nick.
Description: Lanham : Lexington Books, 2018. | Includes bibliographical references.
Identifiers: LCCN 2018043243 (print) | LCCN 2018044972 (ebook) |
    ISBN 9781498525985 (electronic) | ISBN 9781498525978 (cloth : alk. paper)
Subjects: LCSH: Names, Personal—German—Political aspects. | Names, Personal—
    Jewish—Political aspects. | World War, 1939-1945—Jews.
Classification: LCC CS2325 (ebook) | LCC CS2325 .N53 2018 (print) |
    DDC 929.408943—dc23
LC record available at https://lccn.loc.gov/2018043243

for Günter . . .

Contents

Preface

I was twenty-six years old when the United States Holocaust Memorial Museum (USHMM) first opened its doors. For years, the Beltway had been abuzz with talk about the newest museum due to hit the Plaza. It seemed like every week there were reports on the nightly news or in the local press about the ground-breaking architectural design or the stunning collection of artifacts that had been gathered directly from Europe just for this exhibit.

As a German major with a specialization in Holocaust Studies, I was elated when I heard that the museum had finally been finished and visitors would now be allowed in. Initially, the crowds were so great that it was impossible to get inside. Everyone knew that the interest in the museum was tremendous but this was something altogether different. From all across the nation and beyond, survivors and their families traveled to Washington, DC, to view the museum.

Having lived in the DC area for years, my mother and I knew that it was best to arrive early for new exhibits. So, we made sure to be there several hours before the museum opening hours in hopes of being among the first to be in line. As we rounded the corner from our parking spot, we were shocked to see that a large crowd had already formed outside of the museum. But unlike other excited crowds for popular events like the "King Tutankhamun" exhibition at the National Gallery of Art in 1976–1977, the people who had gathered here in front of the USHMM were almost entirely silent.

As the minutes ticked on, and new people came, each one of them was solemnly greeted with a simple nod of the head. The tension was unbearable. Grandchildren and parents rubbed the shoulders and backs of grandparents in an attempt to prepare them for what they would see and remember. And there were tears, so many tears, so many silent tears. I whispered to my mother that I thought it would be better if we came another time. It did not seem right to go now. This was a private time for families directly touched by the Holocaust and

I did not want to take the space of someone who needed to be here. My mother agreed and we quietly, gently, stepped out of line. I remember the crowd, shifting graciously to let us pass by, as the next huddled family inched their way forward.

Many, many months later, we ventured to the museum again. The lines were just a bit shorter and the mood was just a bit lighter. It seemed to me that the crowd was also just a bit younger on that day. There were more parents with their adult children who had come to see for themselves what they had only heard about in fractured stories. As the doors opened, I remember how startled we all were by the booming voice of a security guard, shouting at us to make a single file. Like a flock of birds, we all instinctively bristled at the sudden, unexpected loudness. As those of us who were younger laughed a bit, embarrassed by our reaction, the few elderly men and women on that day stiffened in a way I will never forget.

It was an involuntary movement. A sudden straightening of their backs with a flash of deep anger. "You don't have to yell like that!" I heard one woman say, as she walked past him. The young guard, taken aback, immediately apologized. It had only been his intention to make himself heard over the large crowd. He had forgotten that in this place, in this space, loud voices had a completely different meaning.

As we filed slowly into the museum, I remember feeling a nourishing and deep sense of comforting unity within our group. Somehow, we had arrived as strangers but now, as we walked across the threshold, we had become connected with one another. That feeling did not end as we walked through the museum. In fact, it intensified as we moved past the exhibits slowly, ever so slowly, trying to balance out the desire to see everything and the need to protect one's self from being completely overwhelmed. We did not speak together about what we saw or our reactions. It was enough to look deeply into someone's eyes or touch someone lightly on the shoulder when it became too much.

At that time, one of the features of the museum was a special machine that gave tiny slips of paper with the name of someone who had experienced the Holocaust. As one moved through the museum, it was possible to check in at various stations and learn what had happened to that person over the years. I remember viscerally the shock I felt when the person my mother had been assigned died almost immediately. Somehow in that brief period of time, I had automatically associated that woman's name with my mother. When we learned of her sudden death, I could not help but think of all of those daughters who had lost their mothers just that suddenly, just that unexpectedly.

As we continued to move through the museum and found ourselves crowded into smaller and smaller spaces, I felt even more deeply the emotional waves of physical reactions that continued to ripple through our group. Many of us were weeping, others were trying to console, some of us had withdrawn completely, deep into a space beyond anyone's reach. And I can still remember the jolt, as one by one, the people whose names we had been holding were arrested, deported, interned, murdered. And as we passed from one station to the next, my dread increased as I read what happened to the person whose name I carried with me.

Suddenly, we rounded the corner and I realized that we were near the end of the exhibit. I remember being startled but elated. There was only one station left and the person whose name I carried was still by some miracle still alive. Just one more stop, and then it would finally be over: but the final update left me in shock. The status of that person was unknown. I remember turning to my mother and asking, "What does THAT mean? Is she DEAD?" My mother looked at me in a way that only mothers do when they know that their child has just discovered some horrible life truth. "It means, Sweetheart" my mother began, "it means that we just don't know what happened. . . . Maybe she survived. Maybe she made it and she's living with her family somewhere happy and safe."

I remember bursting into tears and walking instinctually back toward what I later learned was called the "Hall of Reflection." The room was open and flooded with warm light. I don't remember how long I sat in that space. I don't remember when I stopped crying. What I do remember is how an older woman with soft, snow white hair offered me a Kleenex. I accepted it gratefully and she smiled down at me with an expression on her face which I will never forget. She did not say a word. She simply nodded and patted me gently on the shoulder.

When I left the museum that day, I did so with a sense of purpose. It simply could not be that we do not know what happened to people during the Holocaust. We have a responsibility to them, to us, and to all of the people who come after us. And it begins with the names.

*****

When neo-Nazis came to our dormitory in the small village of Dudweiler in the Saarland, no one noticed anything unusual at first. Just a small group of young men who met outside of our building and were waiting for someone to let them in. When no one came, they decided to break in the door—no small feat considering the fact that our door had a thick steel frame that held two impossibly heavy panes of glass with wire meshing in between. Somehow, they summoned enough hatred to kick an opening through the door with their steel-tipped leather boots. And then, something very odd happened. They walked very calmly over to the row of metal mailboxes and quietly studied all of the names. Finding one that sounded foreign, they noted the floor and the apartment number and then quietly walked up the staircase.

When they located the room they were looking for, they rang the doorbell and waited as if they were there to deliver a package. A few seconds later, a young exchange student from Africa opened her door. Within less than an instant, they attacked in an orgiastic frenzy of punches and kicks and screams using words that none of us understood back then. It did not take long before a neighboring exchange student came from his dorm room to see what was going on. Another foreigner. More yelling, more punching, tearing, and stomping of boots on flailing hands and broken faces. Soon more students were coming, running to help.

The neo-Nazis, now outnumbered, thundered down the staircase, past the shattered glass of our dormitory and into the neighboring town. The police did come. I can't say that they did not show up. They did talk to a few people about what they had seen. And arrests were made. It did not take long to locate the rabble-rousers. They were well-known in town. Good boys, who were bored and had gotten into a bit of trouble, the townspeople said. No need to press formal charges though. That would go too far. After all, the police had given them a good talking to about the mess they had made at the international dorm. Their parents would be required to pay for all that broken glass.

I remember what it felt like to have to walk by that door each day to and from the university. I remember even months afterward you could still find shards of glass crushed down into the grass or wedged into a tight forgotten corner of the entrance way. I remember staring at the mailboxes and reading through the names listed there trying to see what they had seen. Sure enough, if you read through the names it was pretty easy to make a good guess at which of us might be a foreigner. My friends, also US Americans, asked me why I kept staring at those boxes. I pointed out that in among all those names, their names—with their German-American roots—blended right in, but my name was different. It stood out. I stood out.

A few days later as I came down the stairs, (somehow, we always took the stairs back then, and never the elevator—that would have been uncool), I saw my best friend standing in front of those mailboxes reading through the names as I had done so many times before. When she saw me, she smiled sadly back: "Look, your name is only a few boxes away from hers [the young woman who had been attacked]." "Yeah, I know," I said. After a few minutes, she said, "To me you're not any different, you know. I don't see you as any different. You're just 'Iman' to me. *My* Iman." "And you're my Annie," I whispered. But we knew the world saw us very differently.

I used to ask my mother why she had given me this strange name. Why couldn't she have named me something "normal?!?" I used to complain. "What's normal?" she would reply, annoyed but curious to hear how I would answer. "*Normal* like . . . Mary or *Robyn* . . . I LOVE the name Robyn! When I grow up, I'm gonna change my name," I declared. "I gave you that name, Iman. It is my gift to you. It is to remind you of who you are, of who we are, and where we come from. . . . One day you will understand."

*****

This book is an exploration of names and naming immediately before, during, and after the Holocaust. In researching this book, I searched through the city, state, and national archives throughout Germany and examined hundreds of original records. As a scientist, I know that there are readers who will immediately bristle when they read the word "hundreds." What is the exact number? And so, let me take this opportunity to say now that this book is NOT about the numbers. My purpose was <u>not</u> to provide an objective statistical analysis of the most significant diachronic trends in the morphophonological features isolated in a nationally representative sample of personal nomenclature used by twentieth-century German residents whose individual biographical profiles were found to match a pre-selected set of demographic characteristics. Although I have great appreciation for such empirical research on names and naming and have throughout my career published work that relies on statistical analyses, I nevertheless decided that I did not want this work to be about the numbers. As Holocaust researchers, Vera Schiff and Jeff McLaughlin write:

> A number like six million dead may give you the historical result but does not tell you any of the story; it does not give you the meaning or the significance as much as the number "one." One individual. If we can put a name to that number one; if we can tell you about the love, the life, the courage of that person; if we can share with you who they were, what they experience, what they did, what they chose, and what was imposed upon them, then you will better understand the enormity of what happened.[1]

My decision against providing a quantitative analysis here came from my profound respect and concern for the millions of people who had their identities and names stolen and replaced with serial digits during the Holocaust. It is also out of profound respect and concern for the people today whose lives have been, are, or will be threatened by a different genocide.

The purpose of this book, then, is twofold: commemoration and prevention through awareness-building of the significance of names and naming in genocide. And in my opinion, one of the best ways to achieve this goal is through telling the personal stories of the people behind the names. As Shoah scholar and genocide researcher Daniel Jonah Goldhagen explained, at the end of the day, the key to getting the international community to take decisive action to prevent genocide is identification with the victims, "to think of each one as if he or she were your daughter or son, your sister or brother, your mother or your father."[2] To reinforce that human connection and promote a deep understanding, it is important to engage both the heart and the mind. For this reason, this book does provide empirical information, but only to augment, buttress, or contextualize the personal namestories presented.

Accordingly, the namestories shared here are embedded within a historical examination of naming laws, policies, and practices that were significant for the preparation and execution of the atrocities perpetrated during the Holocaust. In addition, this work examines the ways in which similar naming practices have been used in several contemporary genocides.

Whenever possible, the original historical records were utilized for this investigation. For the reader's ease, I have provided English translations of this material. Great care has been taken to preserve not only the literal meaning but also the accompanying style and sentiment of the original texts. For readers who are interested in reading the German language originals, detailed source notations have been included throughout the text. However, the reader is cautioned that many of the archives visited did not use a comprehensive or consistent system of recording within their files. It is not unusual, for example, to find that within a single file, a succession of different archivists had marked through and changed the notations of their predecessor. As a result, it is often extremely difficult to identify the best, most recent, or most accurate catalogue codes.

Chapter 1 introduces readers to the governmental use of personal names for identifying, monitoring, and tracking individuals and groups within the United States. As will be shown, the widespread collection and distribution of name-based data have become an integral part of modern law enforcement and government regulation. On the one hand, the information that can be gleaned via personal name-analysis is essential to quickly and accurately identify individuals and groups who may pose a serious threat to public safety. On the other hand, that very same intelligence can be used to infringe upon or directly violate personal liberty.

Chapter 2 examines precisely this historical tension in Europe. This chapter begins by providing a brief historical survey of the emergence, promotion, and spread of stable personal names, including inheritable surnames. Initially, the adoption of this naming system by Jewish communities was read as a positive sign of sociocultural assimilation and growing national cohesion. Before long, however, this positive interpretation reversed. Against the background of anti-Semitism, the inability to differentiate between Jews and Gentiles was increasingly considered a threat to national security. Regulations to significantly restrict the ability of Jewish residents to legally alter or exchange their personal names were consequently introduced. Once the National Socialists came to power, even more radical naming laws were implemented to simultaneously stigmatize and unambiguously identify residents of Jewish lineage.

Chapter 3 examines the naming patterns that were adopted by the Nazis to mark both their racial and ideological identification with their Aryan status and their chosen leader, Adolf Hitler. To illustrate these patterns, particular focus is placed upon the innermost circle of the Nazi elite, the SS. In particular, detailed information is given on the naming practices promoted within the Lebensborn society and its clandestine program to promote the birth of Aryan children considered to embody the highest of racial standards. Information is also provided on how the Nazis used names to systematically change and conceal the identities of thousands of children who were kidnapped by the Nazis as a part of the Lebensborn program. The chapter ends with a personal namestory provided by an adult Lebensborn child interviewed during my research.

Chapter 4 turns the attention back to the Jewish residents of Europe who were finding it increasingly difficult to survive under National Socialism. As will be shown here, the government-sanctioned hunt for Jews in the Reich was greatly facilitated by the introduction of discriminatory name policies. The obligatory use of the prescribed personal names *Sara* and *Israel* was not only insulting. Under the Nazis' expanding network of constant surveillance, the presence of stigmatized names on each and every form of identification required for even the most mundane activities meant relentless exposure to persecution. These name markers not only impacted upon the daily lives of individuals, as this chapter illustrates. They were also integral to the system of identifying, tracking, deporting, and murdering of the millions. Through case after case drawn from the archival records, the real-life effects of this system are illustrated from its disturbing start to its lethal crescendo.

Chapter 5 focuses on the first two decades immediately after the war as the Allied Forces assumed control over the vanquished Reich. Information is provided here about the Allies' attempts to reverse the decades of discriminatory naming policies that had been instituted by the National Socialists. As this chapter demonstrates, however, there is a significant difference between changing policies and changing practices. This discrepancy is made abundantly clear in both the postwar persecution of Shoah survivors and the protection of Holocaust perpetrators who went from being the hunters to being the hunted after the war. Once again, personal names played a key role here—from the search for relatives lost during the war to the pursuit of war criminals who sought refuge in the chaos of the postwar period. The chapter ends with the first major acts of legislation introduced by the fledgling West German government: amnesties for criminals living under assumed names.

Chapter 6 examines the efforts of Nazi war criminals to create new names and identities for themselves in the new Democratic Republic of Germany. Despite the diversity of aliases that were chosen by the Nazis on the run, as this chapter illustrates, there are also many patterns that can be discerned. Perpetrators' choices in alias often not only had a direct impact upon their ability to remain undetected but also revealed a great deal about the personalities and predilections of their carriers, both past and present. Indeed, a successful change in name was rarely accompanied by a commensurate change in character.

Chapter 7 maintains the same theme as chapter 6. However, the focus is different. This chapter specifically examines the names used by female war criminals on the run. This gender segregation is important, for as has been shown time and time again, it simply can't be assumed that what is true for men is also true for women. The names and naming patterns utilized by female perpetrators were indeed quite different than those displayed by their male criminal counterparts. These differences are due in large measure to the differential naming laws that are routinely applied to men and women living within the same society. As this chapter illustrates, these differences in naming regulations have significantly complicated the ability of authorities to identify and prosecute women who committed atrocities under National Socialism.

Chapter 8 shifts focus back once again to Shoah victims and survivors. In comparison to the other chapters, however, this chapter presents these unique and moving experiences in the very own words of the people who lived them. In the series of namestories shared in this chapter, Shoah survivors recount how they were able to use the introduction of name laws in Nazi-controlled Europe to survive under new identities. Their stories then are not only histories of shocking persecution and devastating loss. They are also inspirational messages of hope that remind us how, even in the most desperate of times, there are still those who are willing to risk their lives to save someone else's. Each of these stories is dedicated to loved ones lost but never forgotten.

Chapter 9 is devoted to the ongoing struggle of researchers to recover and preserve the names and identities of those whose lives were destroyed during the Holocaust. Information is provided about international efforts to recover the names of both the victims and the perpetrators. Interviews with independent scholars as well as leading researchers in Holocaust memorial institutions such as Yad Vashem and the USHMM are presented. As is addressed here, the struggle to recover the names is not limited to logistical and legal obstacles. Sociopolitical trends favoring the denial and dismissal of the Holocaust have also posed a significant barrier. Joining the international fight against this Holocaust denial are another group of people who know all too well just how dangerous willful ignorance fueled by intolerance, fear, and hatred can be—the direct descendants of the perpetrators of the Holocaust. In interviews conducted with the author, the children and grandchildren of prominent Nazis address why they have chosen to speak publicly against National Socialism and add their voices to those dedicated to ensuring that the horror of the Holocaust is neither forgotten nor repeated.

The push to keep the memory alive is not one which is always appreciated, however. There are many who feel that it is high time that the world does precisely the opposite. Just recently, for example, in the final months of writing this book, on June 2, 2018, the leader of the German right-extremist party, Alternative for Germany [Alternative für Deutschland (AfD)], spoke before a national assembly of junior politicians in the former East German state of Thuringia. During his speech, he pronounced that Hitler and National Socialism were nothing more than a speck of "bird shit in comparison to the 1,000 years of successful German history."[3] Although the speech received broad condemnation, it is also undeniable that for a certain portion of the society, the politician had simply expressed what so many others have felt but been reluctant to say so openly. With each and every passing day, however, this inhibition has eroded. The result has been a measurable increase in anti-Semitism.

In the fall of 2017, for example, some 1,000 demonstrators marched down the streets of Berlin, past the Spandau Prison. The date was August 19, the thirtieth anniversary of the death of Rudolf Hess. The former deputy of Adolf Hitler was the last remaining Nazi war criminal in Spandau prison. In commemoration of his death, the marchers carried black and white banners emblazoned with the words "I regret NOTHING!"[4] On the one hand, one might say that the hate-speech of radicals cannot be construed as representing the opinions of the mainstream, and I would wholeheartedly agree. It is imperative not to over-generalize or lose sight of those people whose hearts and minds are not filled with bigotry. On the other hand, it is equally important that we remain vigilant to potentially dangerous societal trends.

It is not insignificant, for example, that in a nationally representative 2015 survey conducted in Germany by the Bertelsmann Stiftung,[5] it was determined that 81 percent of those polled stated that they felt it was time to stop discussion of the Holocaust and leave the past behind.[6] As Germany's Federal Agency for Civic Education [Bundeszentrale für politische Bildung] reports, anti-Semitic attitudes are not a monopoly held by the political right.[7] Across the ideological spectrum, there are many who take the position that the Holocaust happened so many years ago that it is finally time to let bygones be bygones.[8]

Personally speaking, I have always found this opinion to be both repugnant and baffling. In so-called cold cases where a child is kidnapped, tortured, and murdered, the public reaction in Germany is one of relief and vindication when the murderer is finally caught. The fact that law enforcement refused to give up until the culprit was finally brought to justice has always been applauded as a sign that our justice system is intact. The families of the victims are supported with heart-warming vigils, and speeches are made with private citizens and public officials alike promising to implement policy changes to ensure that nothing like this will ever happen again in the future. And, depending on the circumstances of the case, it is not unusual to hear public discussions resurface over the re-institution of the death penalty, if only for this one deviant offender. Why is it then that the reaction is so different when the offender who committed the crime was an avowed National Socialist who murdered not one but dozens, or even thousands of people. Why is it that the officials who dedicate their lives to bringing these criminals to justice are so often ridiculed for wasting the tax-payers' time and money? Why is that the surviving victims who summon up the strength and the courage to testify before an open court of law and confront their tormentor face-to-face are so often condemned as merciless, malevolent, contemptuous, spiteful, and unforgiving. And why is it that even before the evidence has been heard, one can hear people asking "When we will finally be allowed to forget?"

In my opinion, one of the best answers to this question comes from Nobel Peace Prize winner, human rights activist, and Shoah survivor Elie Wiesel. In speaking about the necessity of bearing witness to the Holocaust, Wiesel reminded that testifying to the truth is a duty "for the dead and for the living. . . . To forget would be not only dangerous but offensive; to forget the dead would be akin to killing them a second time."[9] This is a point which was made repeatedly during the many interviews I conducted for this book. Again and again, people independent of one another stressed that an essential part of honoring the victims, survivors, and descendants of the Holocaust is working to protect future generations against new acts of genocide. This book, therefore, concludes with an examination of other genocides. More specifically, this segment explores the ways in which names and naming have been used to engineer modern-day atrocities with the hope of helping to detect dangerous trends in society before the killing begins.

Notes

1. Vera Schiff and Jeff McLaughlin. *Bound for Theresienstadt: Love, Loss, and Resistance in a Nazi Concentration Camp.* (Jefferson, NC: McFarland and Co., 2017), 10.

2. Daniel Goldhagen, "Genocide Worse than War," Public Broadcasting Service (1:40:42). http://www.pbs.org/wnet/worse-than-war/the-film/about/the-film-about-the-film/17/.

3. *Zeit Online*, "Bundesregierung bezeichnet Gauland-Äußerung als beschämend" https://www.zeit.de/politik/deutschland/2018-06/afd-bundesregierung-alexander-gauland-hitler-nationalsozialismus-vogelschiss.

4. Austin Davis, "Anti-Semitism is still alive in Germany as Jews face 'disturbing' discrimination." *USA TODAY*, (December 21, 2017). https://eu.usatoday.com/story/news/world/2017/12/21/anti-semitism-germany-jews-discrimination-muslims-right-wing-nationalists/962383001/.

5. Bertelsmann Stiftung, "Deutschland und Israel heute: Verbindende Vergangenheit, trennende Gegenwart?" (2015), 21. https://www.bertelsmann-stiftung.de/fileadmin/files/BSt/Publikationen/GrauePublikationen/Studie_LW_Deutschland_und_Israel_heute_2015.pdf.

6. This finding was by no means a fluke but is a part of disturbing trend. Already in 2014, the same opinion poll found that 58 percent of the respondents agreed that it was time to finally draw the line and that far less attention should be given to the persecution

of the Jews during the Holocaust. Among adult survey-takers without a university degree, the percentage of people with this opinion was even higher at 71 percent. Bertelsmann Stiftung, *Deutschland und Israel heute: Verbindende Vergangenheit, trennende Gegenwart?* (2014). https://www.bertelsmann-stiftung.de/fileadmin/files/BSt/Publikationen/Graue Publikationen/Studie_LW_Deutschland_und_Israel_heute_2015.pdf.

7. Daniel Kilpert, "Antisemitismus von links" (Bundeszentrale für politische Bildung, 2006), para. 5. http://www.bpb.de/politik/extremismus/linksextremismus/33604/antisemitismus-von-links?p=all.

8. This opinion is by no means isolated to Germany. In 2018, the Conference on Jewish Material Claims Against Germany commissioned a comprehensive national study of Holocaust awareness and knowledge in the United States. The investigation revealed that 70 percent of US Americans polled agree with the statement that "fewer people seem to care about the Holocaust as much as they used to." The Holocaust Knowledge and Awareness Study (Schoen Consulting, 2018), 1. http://cc-69bd.kxcdn.com/wp-content/uploads/2018/04/Holocaust-Knowledge-Awareness-Study_Executive-Summary-2018.pdf.

9. Kate Reilly, "Action is the only remedy to indifference: Elie Wiesel's most powerful quotes." *Time* (July 2, 2016). http://time.com/4392252/elie-wiesel-dead-best-quotes/.

Acknowledgments

As with any labor of love, this work would not have been possible without the support of a great many people at every stage of this incredible, often harrowing, journey. This work represents the culmination of an incredible circle of love and faith and humanity: three virtues that have become all the more sacred, all the more dear, in these troubling times.

There were many times during this process that I felt completely and utterly overwhelmed by the list of depravity I discovered, day after day, year after year. There were weeks when I could not write a single word, when I was sure that if I read another story of horror, either my heart or my psyche would break. I felt, at times, that if I was not careful, I would begin to scream and would never stop until everything that I ever was shattered into a million fractured pieces.

Over time, I began to feel overwhelming guilt for telling one person's story and not someone else's. Until it hit me one day, as I found myself buried in a mound of files, that it was simply impossible for me to tell everyone's story. And, so I asked forgiveness of those whose stories I was unable to tell and gave them my promise that I would not forget them, who they were, and what they might have lived to become.

This work then is dedicated to all those people whose names have yet to be recovered, whose stories have yet to be told. This work is gratitude to all of those incredible people who so generously and graciously shared the story of their lives and names with me. It has been my profound honor to share these namestories here. And this work is also for all of those who will come after us; may you have the strength to live your lives in honor, with kindness, forbearance, and truth. May you always find the courage to protect and cherish those around you as they protect and cherish you. May your own namestory be one filled with tolerance, bravery, honesty, and grace.

German WWII Military Ranks and US Equivalents

German Military Ranks	US Equivalents
Hauptmann	Captain
Generalfeldmarschal	General
Generalleutnant	Major General
Generalmajor	Brigadier General
Generaloberst	General
Gefreiter	Private First-Class
Grossadmiral	Fleet Admiral
Hauptscharführer	First Sergeant
Hauptsturmführer	Master Sergeant
Kapitän	Captain
Kapitánleutnant	Lieutenant
Leutnant	Second Lieutenant
Major	Captain
Matrose	Seaman
Oberleutnant	First Lieutenant
Oberscharführer	Staff Sergeant
Oberschütze	Senior Rifleman
Oberst	Colonel
Oberstleutnant	Lieutenant Colonel
Obersturmführer	First Lieutenant
Scharführer	Sergeant
Sturmbannführer	Major
Sturmführer	Second Lieutenant

Unteroffizier	Sergeant
Unterscharführer	Corporal

SS

Reichsführer	Field Marshall
SS-Brigadeführer	Brigadier General
SS-Gruppenführer	Major General
SS-Hauptsturmführer	Captain
SS-Oberführer	Colonel
SS-Obergruppenführer	Lieutenant-General
SS-Oberstgruppenführer	General
SS-Obersturmbannführer	Major
SS-Obersturmführer	First Lieutenant
SS-Standartenführer	Lieutenant-Colonel
SS-Sturmbannführer	Captain
SS-Untersturmführer	Second Lieutenant

Abbreviations and Acronyms

AfD	Alternativ für Deutschland (Alternative for Germany)
BDM	Bund Deutscher Mädel (League of German Girls)
BfV	Bundesamt für Verfassungsschutz (the domestic intelligence service of the Federal Republic of Germany)
BND	Bundesnachrichtendienst (the foreign intelligence service of the Federal Republic of Germany)
BRD	Bundesrepublik Deutschland (Federal Republic of Germany)
CDU	Christlich Demokratische Union (Christian Democratic Union of Germany)
CNI	Central Name Index
CTC	Counterterrorism Center
DANAT	Därmstädter und Nationalbank (Darmstadt and National Bank)
DHS	Department of Homeland Security
DP	displaced persons
FDP	Freie Demokratische Partei (Free Democratic Party)
HICOG	US High Commission for Occupied Germany
IMT	International Military Tribunal
IRTPA	Intelligence Reform and Terrorism Prevention Act
KdF	Kanzlei des Führers (Chancellery of the Führer)
LAFFN-1	Law for the Alteration of Family and First Names-1
LAFFN-2	Law for the Alteration of Family and First Names-2
Napola	Nationalpolitische Erziehungsanstalten (National Political Institutes of Education)
NPD	Nationaldemokratische Partei Deutschlands (National Democratic Party of Germany)

NS	Nationalsozialismus (National Socialism)
NSDAP	Nationalsozialistische Deutsche Arbeiterpartei (National Socialist German Workers' Party)
NSEERS	National Security Entry-Exist Registration System
NSF	Nationalsozialistische Frauenschaft (National Socialist Women's League)
NSU	Nationalsozialistischer Untergrund (National Socialist Underground)
NSV	Nationalsozialistische Volkswohlfahrt (National Socialist Social Welfare Organization)
OIG	Office of the Inspector General
OSI	Office of Special Investigation
OSCE	Organization for Security and Co-operation in Europe
RGBl	Reichsgesetzblatt (Reich Law Gazette)
RMBLiV	Reichsministerialblatt der inneren Verwaltung (Reich Law Gazette of the Ministry of Interior)
RMK	Reichsmusikkammer (Reich's Music Bureau)
RuSHA	Rasse- und Siedlungshauptamt (Race and Settlement Bureau)
SA	Sturmabteilung (Storm Troops)
SED	Sozialistische Einheitspartei Deutschlands (Socialist Unity Party of Germany)
SRP	Sozialistische Reichspartei (Socialist Reich Party of Germany)
SS	Schutzstaffel (Protective Squad)
TIDE	Terrorist Identities Datamart Environment
TSDB	Terrorist Screening Database
UGIF	Union générale des israélites de France (Union of French Jews)
USHMM	United States Holocaust Memorial Museum
WJC	World Jewish Congress
WMP	World Memory Project
WVHA	Wirtschafts- und Verwaltungshauptamt (Main Economic and Administrative Bureau)
UCK	Ushtria Çlirimtare e Kosovës

CHAPTER 1

Names, Naming, National Security, and Personal Liberty in the United States

Whether traveling by air, land, or sea, the excitement and anticipation of modern travel are often marred by the aggravation, anxiety, and pure exhaustion amassed during the long lines of security checks. Aside from the personal inconvenience and public concerns over the possible short- and long-range health risks, the growing government arsenal of increasingly invasive biometric screening methods—from iris scans, vein matching, and digital face imaging to full body scanning—also raises legitimate ethical questions.[1] Precisely what information is being collected? How is it being stored? How long will it be kept? Who is privy to all this personal data? The answers to these and other questions have been a continual source of contention among human rights and security experts.

For all the controversy surrounding the collection of biometric data, surprisingly little attention has been given to the widespread collection of one of the most powerful pieces of biographical information: personal names. Indeed, despite the growing availability and accuracy of biometric techniques, people's individual names still remain one of the most commonly used methods "to identify an individual, especially in border control measures, criminal investigations, and intelligence analysis."[2] There are many reasons for the popularity of using personal names for identity verification.

Aside from the simple fact that most people on the planet have an official name—in comparison to many biometric features such a person's size, weight, and coloring, all of which may radically change overtime either naturally or intentionally—personal names tend to be fairly stable and when they do change, they often leave behind a discernible official trail. Even in countries where the laws governing name changes are comparatively liberal, even minor changes such as alterations in spelling or punctuation frequently require the name-bearer to first obtain permission from and then give notification to administrative authorities, both large and small. The ensuing bureaucratic nightmare not only tends to discourage people from frivolously and repeatedly altering their names but also rather ingeniously ensures that government officials can easily continue to track people via their names.[3] The combined ubiquity, stability, and accessibility of personal names explain why they are one of the most popular and powerful tools for personal identification and authentication.

Nevertheless, most travelers do not even think twice about giving their names to authorities when they pass through a security check. Instead, the majority of us are far more preoccupied with trying to figure out whether we really have to remove our shoes and socks; and if really ALL of our small change has been removed from our pockets. In the meantime, the documents containing our names are surreptitiously registered and compared against unseen computerized "watchlists" containing the names of individuals who have been identified by governmental agencies as potential subjects of interest.

In the United States, part of the legislative mandate for the establishment of these automated name-check systems came from the impressively named post-9/11 anti-terrorism legislation: "Uniting and Strengthening America by Providing Appropriate Tools Required to Intercept and Obstruct Terrorism Act of 2001"—a.k.a. the "US Patriot Act." As a part of this historic legislation, both the Secretary of State and the Attorney General were given the conjoint responsibility of developing technological standards for investigating the identity of individuals either applying for a US visa or wishing to enter the United States pursuant to a visa.[4] To help accomplish this goal, a revolutionary computer-automated data-system was needed that was capable of rapidly storing and processing large-scale name lists and accompanying records[5] filled with relevant biometric (i.e., fingerprinting and photography) and biographical data (e.g. personal names, addresses, date of birth, place of birth, etc.).[6] With this new computerized repository, it would be possible to keep better track of the names of individuals or groups known or believed to be involved with or linked to "activities constituting a threat to homeland security, and/or activities that are preparatory to, or facilitate or support such activities."[7] That was the plan.

*****

To increase the efficiency of data-sharing, the newly envisioned data-system would essentially need to fuse together the preexisting independent data banks already being used by the various law enforcement and intelligence agencies. On its surface, this fusion may seem relatively straightforward, if not downright simple. However, interagency differences in the type as well as the manner in which biographical information was entered, stored, and retrieved—to say nothing of the sheer volume of the records involved—made for an arduous task. To illustrate these challenges, consider the following records kept by fictitious agencies.

Table 1.1 Sample Records of Biographical Data from Three Fictitious Agencies

AGENCY 1

ID#	DOB	LAST NAME	FIRST NAME	RACE	ETHNICITY	ID CODE
AG1A	May 25, 1945	McDougal	Pat	Mixed	Non-Hispanic	2Ag1
AG2A	September 17, 1976	Jimenez	Miguel	White	Hispanic	2Ag2
AG3A	June 6, 2000	Roehr	Christina	White	Hispanic	2Ag3
AG3A	February 9, 1984	Lee	Huang	Asian	no	2Ag4

AGENCY 2

SURNAME	FIRST NAME	MIDDLE NAME	AGE GROUP	SEX	BIRTH YEAR
Jimenez-Rodriguez	Miguel	Jorge	Adult	M	1976
MacDougal	Patricia	Ann-Margaret	Senior	F	1945
Lee	Huang	XXXXX	Young Adult	M	1984
Canete	Christina	Rohr	Teenager	F	2000

AGENCY 3

NAME	MARITAL STATUS	NATIONALITY	ANCESTRY	DOB	RECORD NO.
Tina Cañete-Röhr	Single	American	Filipino	06.06.00	645127
Huang Lee	Single	Canadian	Chinese	02.09.84	255561
Peggy McDougal	Divorced	UK	Black British	05.25.45	188760
George Rodríguez	Married	American	Cuban	09.17.67	817723

As can be seen in table 1.1, there is considerable conceptual overlap in the categories of information used by each of the respective agencies. However, there is also a great deal of variation in the way in these categories are labeled and the manner in which the data is recorded, and missing data is indicated (e.g. 9999 vs. XXXX). Such interagency variation is often the result of differences in the information needs, duties, and authorization levels of data-users. For example, the officials in fictional AGENCY 2 may only need to generate basic statistics on the age groups of persons registered in their system at their date of entry. By comparison, AGENCIES 1 and 3 may be charged with tracking large volumes of individuals over time. For disambiguation and verification purposes, these two agencies may then require the exact birth date of the people listed in their systems.

Despite this common purpose, the manner in which AGENCIES 1 and 3 record this biographical information clearly differs. Again, such variance could be accounted for by the different sets of users accessing each respective databank. For example, the records kept by AGENCY 3 might be exclusively used by US officials. For this reason, the institution employs the purely numerical six-digit mm/dd/yy format customarily used in the United States. By comparison, the records maintained by AGENCY 1 may be used by authorized officials within both the United States and Germany. To avoid possible confusion and error between the US mm/dd/yy and the German dd/mm/yy conventions, the policy-makers responsible for AGENCY 3's databank may have opted for an alphanumerical format where the month is written out in its entirety and the numbered days and months are visually separated from one another.

Alongside such inconsistencies in the recording of the demographic data (e.g., date of birth, gender, race, ethnicity, ancestry), the three fictitious agencies also demonstrate a number of glaring discrepancies in the recording of personal name data. While AGENCY 1 only records first and last names, AGENCY 2 maintains data on first, middle, and last names. AGENCY 1 does not allow for double last names but AGENCIES 3 and 2 do, albeit one with hyphenation and the other without. Such variations may seem merely cosmetic and therefore inconsequential but linguistic markers such as hyphenation can be invaluable aides in record disambiguation tasks.

To clarify this point, consider the following sets of personal names: *Patricia Ann-Margaret McDougal* and *Patricia-Ann Margaret MacDougal; Miguel Santiago Rodriguez* and *Miguel Santiago-Rodriguez.* A record-entry policy which requires the consistent recording of markers such as hyphenation can provide officials with important clues about whether two names that look almost identical may actually belong to two different people. Without such markers, the likelihood that officials consider this possibility may diminish appreciably. What is true for hyphenation is also true for letters which are commonly found in different script systems. An "o" is simply not identical to an "ö," "ô," "å," "ò," "ó," "ō," or an "ø." These letters may not only represent different pronunciations and historical derivations but also reflect different languages, nationalities, and ethnicities.

In view of these differences, to create one centralized databank for interagency use, it would first be necessary to develop a single, unified policy concerning the type and manner of data to be entered. In instances where the decision is made to maintain the original databanks used by the individual agencies <u>alongside</u> a new shared interagency system, strategies for consistently recognizing and "translating" deviations must also be developed. Only after such structural decisions have been made is it possible to compare records across each database and identify possible matches.

Going back then to the fictitious agencies in table 1.1, during fusion, inconsistencies in the manner in which data is recorded can lead to considerable confusion. Is the "*Peggy McDougal*" who was recorded by AGENCY 3 truly the same person as the "*Pat McDougal*" or the "*Patricia Margaret MacDougal*" listed in the files of AGENCIES 1 and 2? Is the White Hispanic male "*Miguel Jimenez*" contained in AGENCY 1's records identical to the married Cuban-American "*George Rodríguez*" recorded by AGENCY 3 or the "*Miguel Jorge Jimenez-Rodríguez*" listed by the officials of AGENCY 2? In order to determine the likelihood that the name records in the respective databanks are a "true match," a "possible match," or "no match," comparisons are systematically and automatically made across all of the data fields of every record in each of the relevant databases, with more weight being given to those informational attributes considered to be the most significant and allowances being made for possible errors in data entry.

Through this reiterative processing, possible matches are brought into sharp relief against the "noise" of irrelevant data. The process of identifying and consolidating person-related data that has been recorded in either multiple data silos or a single silo but in multiple locations is commonly referred to as "identity resolution" or "entity resolution." The accuracy and reliability of identity resolution is directly linked to the timeliness, credibility, completeness, and correctness of the data contained in each of the respective databases. The record-matching and linking process is also obviously complicated by inconsistent, faulty, or missing data as well as by the respective sizes of the databanks that are to be fused. As Peter Christen, senior lecturer at the Research School of Computer Science at the Australian National University, explains in his book, *Data Matching*, "If the quality of the input data is low, then the output generated is normally not of high quality or accuracy either."[8]

With regard to the specific task of name-matching, the identity resolution process is further complicated by an additional set of factors. Aside from the theoretically limitless store of personal names around the world, there is also a daunting degree of variation found in the forms personal names take. Some of the common types of form variation include the following: (1) order and composition ([FIRST NAME:LAST NAME]; [LAST NAME:FIRST NAME]; [FIRST NAME: FAMILY LAST NAME:CLAN NAME:TRIBAL NAME]); (2) spellings (*Tomas* vs. *Thomas*; *Geoffrey* vs. *Jeffrey*; *Rebecca* vs. *Rebekah*; *Hailey* vs. *Hayley* vs. *Haley*; *Husain* vs. *Huseyin* vs. *Hassan*; *Siobhan* vs. *Shevaun* vs. *Shavonne*); (3) separation and punctuation (*MacAllister* vs. *Macalister*; *OBrian* vs. *O'Brian*; *Sinclair* vs. *St. Clair*; *Sal-al-Din* vs. *Saladdin*; *Muñoz* vs. *Munoz*); and (4) transliteration across different scripts and alphabets (*Mueller* vs. *Müller*; *Aiko* vs. 愛子; *Fang* vs. 芳, 方 ; *Larisa* vs. Лариса; *Sarah* vs. שׂרה; *Hamed* vs. حامد).

The investigatory importance of such variation was repeatedly addressed in the 9/11 Commission Report[9] and was then taken up again in the "Intelligence Reform and Terrorism Prevention Act" (IRTPA). Enacted on December 18, 2004, the IRTPA authorized the introduction of sweeping changes to remedy systemic deficiencies in the intelligence community's response to international terrorism. Section 7205 of the IRTPA specifically addressed the real-life consequences of not having a single, unified system of standards for translating Arabic names, for example. As detailed in the US Congressional findings outlined in the IRTPA, the name policy deficit made it possible for "some of the 19 hijackers of aircraft used in the terrorist attacks . . . to vary the spelling of their names to defeat name-based terrorist watchlist systems and to make more difficult any potential efforts to locate them."[10] As detailed in the 9/11 Commission Report, rather than exclusively relying upon aliases with little or no resemblance to their original names, many of the Al-Qaeda hijackers simply used slight variants of their original names (e.g., *Abu Bara al Yemeni* vs. *Abu al Bara Taizi*; *Ramzi Binalshibh* vs. *Ramzi al Sheiba*; *Alhazmi* vs. *al Hazmi*).[11] Such minor name changes were enough to allow them to slip by US security undetected. In light of this fact, in order to be effective, the newly envisioned consolidated databank mandated by the US Patriot Act would have facilitated the reliable detection of such name permutations.

Importantly, the challenge of name permutations to high-quality record-linkage is not limited to names that are comparatively new or foreign to a nation's core name stock. In the United States, for example, there are many names that can function as either forenames or surnames (*Thomas, Riley, Mackenzie, Hamilton, Macauley, Anderson, Stewart*). For that reason, the sequence of names cannot be automatically assumed by their appearance. Is the proper listing *Anderson Cooper* or *Cooper Anderson*? Just eye-balling these two names is not enough to determine which sequence is correct or even likely. It is also not unusual for US residents to use nicknames either instead of or even alongside their formal names (*Patricia* → *Pat(ty)* or *Trish*; *Margaret* → *Maggy, Peggy*). Residents may also use cross-linguistic variants of their names depending on the linguistic context they find themselves in (*Jorge* → *George*; *Miguel* → *Michael*). All of these variations and more may be used instead of or in addition to official names recorded on official documentation.

People may also vary their name with the perceived formality of the communicative situation (e.g., *Jonathan Raymond Gimble* vs. *Johnny-Ray Gimble* vs. *J. R. Gimble* vs. *Jay-Ray*). When one considers all of these factors, it becomes clear that even in cases where data fusion involves comparatively few records, data-matching remains highly complex and time-consuming, with considerable potential for error. This challenge then provides some insight into the enormity of the Patriot Act mandate: namely, the integration of dozens of agency databases,[12] each with millions of records, to create one centralized system with an unlimited record capacity that could be simultaneously used by thousands of authorized law enforcement and intelligence officials with differing levels of security clearance to obtain reliable, up-to-date, comprehensive intelligence on specific individuals or groups. And all that, as Peter Christen reminds, "in (near) real-time,"[13] that is, within the time it takes to scan a passport or run a driver's license.

Despite the enormity of this task, the operative mandate was met. The resulting "interoperable" databank which was finally created might best be described as an information reservoir with a bi-directional flow of intelligence. This principle of bi-directionality is key. On the one hand, authorized agencies may make formal nominations to the FBI to include the names and records of investigative subjects who may present a "reasonable investigatory interest."[14] On the other hand, law enforcement agencies may also use the centralized databank to generate name lists of people to be added to their in-house watchlists of persons targeted for heightened surveillance. Two examples of such agency-level watchlists are the "No Fly List": a roster of individuals who are prohibited against flying from, to, or over US territory; and the "Selectee List": a name list of persons who are to be singled out for additional questioning and inspection before being allowed to fly to, from, or over US territory.

In the United States, the routine and widespread use of governmental "watch-listing" has been generally accepted by the domestic intelligence community as being crucial to protecting national security. What's more, the routine sharing of the information on a need-to-know basis with select foreign and international law enforcement and intelligence agencies has become standard procedure for combating crime on a global scale. In a perfect world, these practices would seem to be indispensable for the pre-emptive protection of national and international security interests. However, as we all know, the world we live in is far from perfect. Even with the best of intentions, the practice of governmental watchlisting remains highly problematic for both ethical and practical reasons. Ironically, the validity of these concerns became particularly salient in the wake of 9/11.

On June 6, 2002, nine months after the 9/11 attacks, Jay B. Stephens, the US Attorney General under President George W. Bush, announced the introduction of a "Special Registration" to help monitor the US entry and exit of all foreign nationals originating from four countries: Iran, Iraq, Libya, and the Sudan.[15] The term "originating" is important here as the registration requirement was not only imposed on citizens of these nations but also used to monitor individuals with other nationalities who had been born in one of these four countries but later obtained citizenship from another country not designated for the Special Registration (e.g., an Iranian-born woman who later took on British citizenship after permanently relocating to the United Kingdom).

Popularly known by the acronym "NSEERS," the "National Security Entry-Exist Registration System" authorized the collection of both biometric and biographical data (complete personal names, addresses, date of birth, etc.). One of the touted advantages of this watchlisting surveillance program was that it would make it, for example, easier for authorities to track non-immigrants who had legally entered the United States on a tourist or student visa but had then remained in the country after their visa expiration date.[16] Part of the impetus for this surveillance strategy lies in the fact that the personal names of at least three of the hijackers involved in the 9/11 attacks (*Nawaf al Hazmi, Salem al Hazmi,* and *Khalid al Mihdhar*) were in database systems kept by the intelligence community. Therefore, as the official *9/11 Commission Report* concluded, "Had they been watchlisted, their terrorist affiliations could have been exposed either at the time they applied for a visa or at the point of entry."[17] NSEERS was originally conceived as a means for thwarting such fatal security lapses in the future. Against that background, it should come as no surprise that the initial support for NSEERS was great.

During the time of its enforcement, the list of countries targeted for this registration was eventually expanded to include twenty-five different nations: Afghanistan, Algeria, Bahrain, Bangladesh, Egypt, Eritrea, Indonesia, Iran, Iraq, Jordan, Kuwait, Lebanon, Libya, Morocco, North Korea, Oman, Pakistan, Qatar, Saudi Arabia, Somalia, Sudan, Syria, Tunisia, the United Arab Emirates, and Yemen.[18] As Louise Cankar[19] points out, from an intelligence perspective, this assemblage of countries was puzzling:

> Although at times government officials stated that the countries whose citizens and nationals were required to register were selected because of Al-Qaeda presence, countries with no proven Al-Qaeda presence were included, and countries with known Al-Qaeda presence, such as Germany and England, were excluded.[20]

The common denominator of the above list seems to have been the fact that all have comparatively large Muslim communities. For this reason, the NSEERS program was broadly criticized as being blatantly discriminatory.

This criticism was compounded by the fact that many individuals who had willingly registered with the NSEERS soon found themselves being subjected to unscheduled visits by FBI agents,[21] unlawful arrests, detentions, and removal proceedings.[22] In the face of these civil liberty violations, concerns about the NSEERS program extended relatively quickly beyond the United States. More than once, the United Nations' Committee on the Elimination of Racial Discrimination[23] urged the US government to stop the NSEERS program as it "encouraged the racial profiling of Muslims, Arabs, and South Asians since September 11th, 2001" and to desist from instituting counter-terrorism measures that "discriminate on the grounds of race, color, descent, or national or ethnic group."[24] National and international criticism was also based on the fact that names of persons gathered via NSEERS were being widely and systematically shared across governmental and law enforcement agencies, thereby multiplying the potential for harassment.

This intelligence-sharing was precipitated by the 2002 creation of the Department of Homeland Security which subsumed no less than twenty-two different federal agencies, including the US Immigration and Customs Enforcement and the US Citizenship and Immigration Services. This interagency cooperation meant that the placement of a person's name on the NSEERS list could (and often did) lead to that person's name being included on watchlists maintained by local, state, national, and international authorities. The result was a dramatic increase in the number of personal names flagged for special governmental surveillance. Rather than creating concern, this expansion was initially seen by many in law enforcement and intelligence as a positive development: the general philosophy seeming to be: "the more the merrier!" Consequently, in just a few years, watchlists that had begun with a few hundred names had bloated to contain hundreds of thousands.

On December 6, 2001, for example, the "names of more than 300,000 'alien absconders' [non-citizens who resided in the US despite previous deportation or removal orders] were added into the FBI's National Crime Information Center database."[25] Five months later, on April 11, 2002, Attorney General John Ashcroft gave the order to have the names of thousands of "known or suspected" terrorists added to the government's law enforcement databases, including those used by police officers nationwide when making routine arrests or traffic stops.[26] To many outside observers, governmental watchlisting had begun to take on Orwellian proportions. There was even concern among those who agreed that maintaining name lists of persons known or suspected to be a danger to the community was crucial to national security. If left unchecked, the proliferation of this practice could ultimately become counter-productive.

On October 29, 2011, a formal request was filed with the Department of Justice, the FBI, and the Immigration and Naturalization Service to release the names of people who had been collected as a part of NSEERS and other programs. Governmental compliance with that request revealed that many of the names of law-abiding residents who had willingly, even eagerly, registered themselves out of a deep, heartfelt sense of allegiance to the United States had been subjected to intense interrogation and subsequently placed on deportation lists.[27] By May 2003, some 1,100 non-citizens had been detained as a part of the Department of Justice's "Absconder Apprehension Initiative" and by the end of 2003, another 2,870 more had been detained.[28]

Tragically, not a few of these individuals had been enthusiastic supporters of the US government's anti-terrorism measures, out of a combined sense of loyalty to their new homeland and hatred for the terrorist regimes under which they and their family members had suffered in their countries of origin. The fact that these voluntary acts of patriotism had not only been ignored but also been abused led to widespread feelings of fear and resentment within the Muslim/Arab communities both inside and outside of the United States. According to concerned observers, the predictable backlash had helped to increase rather than decrease the nation's security risk. Added to this dangerous side-effect was the failure of the registry to uncover the anticipated cache of terrorists. These combined deficits eventually caused even the most ardent supporters of the NSEERS program to publicly question whether the documented drawbacks of the registry far outweighed its predicted promises. As James W. Ziglar, former Commissioner of the Immigration and Naturalization Service (before it was subsumed by the Department of Homeland Security), admitted in a 2004 interview with *The New York Times*,

> This project was a huge exercise and caused us to use resources in the field that could have been much better deployed. . . . To my knowledge, not one actual terrorist was identified. But what we did get was a lot of bad publicity, litigation and disruption in our relationships with immigrant communities and countries that we needed help from in the war on terror.[29]

Despite these very serious concerns, the US government continued to stockpile names as a part of the NSEERS program until April 28, 2011,[30] when the registry was officially suspended. The reason offered to the public for the discontinuance of the program was operational redundancy. According to the Department of Homeland Security, NSEERS had ultimately been made obsolete through the introduction of several "new automated systems that capture arrival and exit information on nonimmigrant travelers to the United States."[31]

> In light of the development of and improvements to the Department's information collection systems and international information sharing agreements, the Secretary [of State] has determined that subjecting nationals from designated countries to a special registration process that manually recaptures data already collected through

automated systems is redundant and does not provide any increase in security.[32]

In other words, the government was not ending its practice of watch_isting: it was just getting started.

*****

After Congress passed the *Homeland Security Act* in November 2002, the **D**epartment of **H**omeland **S**ecurity (DHS) became a stand-alone cabinet-level administrative division of the government.[33] Less than a year later, in September 2003, "Presidential Directive 6" called for the establishment of a centralized, consolidated terrorist watchlist to improve the government's ongoing efforts to identify, screen, and track down individuals either known or suspected to be engaged in terrorist activities. This legislative mandate was further strengthened by the issuance of Executive Order 13354[34] by President George W. Bush and the passage of IRTPA of 2004. These pieces of legislation collectively served as the foundation for the substantive reformation of the US intelligence community and the establishment of the **N**ational **C**ounterterrorism **C**enter (NCTC).[35]

As its name implies, the express mission of the NCTC is to "lead and integrate the national counterterrorism effort by fusing foreign and domestic counterterrorism information."[36] With an eye toward fulfilling this ambitious albeit somewhat diffusely articulated goal,[37] the NCTC is charged with maintaining a centralized computer "repository for all known or suspected international terrorists and their networks of contacts and support."[38] This classified repository is formally called the "**T**errorist **I**dentities **D**atamart **E**nvironment" or TIDE. According to the NCTC,[39] TIDE is a name-based database which, as of February 2017, contained information on approximately 1.6 million people. Of this number, the NCTC estimates that about 16,000 constitute "US Persons (both citizens and lawful permanent residents)."[40] There are two basic types of records housed in TIDE: (1) Terrorist and (2) Non-terrorist. Included in this second type are records on alien spouses, children, and other relatives, both with or without US American citizenship, "who have a close relationship to a KNOWN or SUSPECTED international terrorist."[41] Also stored are records on any individual with a "possible nexus to terrorism."[42]

Conceived as a knowledge reservoir, the information contained in TIDE is both classified and unclassified in nature. While the classified intelligence may only be accessed by a select circle of authorized counterterrorism professionals on a need-to-know-basis, the unclassified segments of TIDE are regularly channeled into another centralized name-based repository, the "**T**errorist **S**creening **D**atabase" (TSDB). The intelligence contained in TSDB is available to the DHS and its respective agencies to achieve their counter-terrorism, law enforcement, border security, and inspection missions. The TSDB itself, however, is maintained at the **T**errorist **S**creening **C**enter (TSC) of the Department of Justice's FBI.

Explained briefly, the TSDB is the authoritative terrorist watchlist for the United States.[43] The original basis of the TSDB was composed of the separate watchlists that had been maintained by the different agencies of the federal government. Since then, terrorist-related information can be obtained by the respective agencies of the Department of Justice (the Bureau of Alcohol, Tobacco, and Firearms; the Federal Bureau of Prisons; the Drug Enforcement Administration; etc.) for their day-to-day operations. In a 2012 interview with CBS News, Timothy Healy, the former TSC Director, described how this information-sharing works using the example of a police officer who stops a driver for a minor traffic violation.[44] If the officer decides to run a check on the driver's license, the name appearing on the ID will be automatically compared against the names on the TSC watchlists. "So if you are speeding, you get pulled over, they'll query that name" and if there is a name-match, a flag "will pop up and say call the Terror Screening Center."[45] According to Healy, these encounters are then used to gather additional intelligence on known or suspected terrorists: "[The] location of where the guy's going. What he's doing [and] additional associates that the subject is hanging around."[46] This flow of information to and from the field is an excellent example of the previously mentioned concept of bi-directionality. In the case of the TSDB, those same agencies which access the databank may also make formal suggestions for the addition of new records and names.

Fairly quickly, this steady stream of nominations resulted in the databank's perpetual expansion. By 2008, just five years after its inauguration, the TSDB, which is updated daily, already contained approximately 1 million name records on some 400,000 individuals.[47] The numerical disparity between records and names is due to the fact that for each individual recorded, any and all known names for that person are also included in that record. According to an official statement made by Greg Wellen, the Assistant Administrator of TSA's Office of Transportation Threat Assessment and Credentialing, the TSDB averages just over two records for every individual.[48] Today, it can be reasonably assumed that the number of name records is far greater given the rising number of official requests or "nominations" made to add names and aliases to the watchlist each year.[49] In the year 2009, for example, there were approximately 227,000 nominations made. By 2013, that number had more than doubled to reach just under 469,000 nominations. During this time period, the number of accepted nominations remained above 98 percent.[50]

On the surface, the growth of the TSDB may be interpreted positively: the more names and records the system contains, the higher the likelihood that a potential terrorist will be included. However, even more important than the size of a databank is the quality of the data it contains. Inconsistent, inaccurate, incomplete, obsolete, and redundant data are all obstacles to successful data-bank management. In addition, there are also specific challenges posed by the storage, search, and retrieval of name data. As the Assistant Administrator to the Transportation Security Administration's Office of Transportation Threat Assessment and Credentialing explained before the 2008 Congressional Hearing on "Cleaning up the Nation's Watchlists," the problem faced is not the size of a watchlist. "The real issue is how to match actual passenger names against those very important names that are on the TSC Watchlist."[51] To illustrate some of the difficulties of name-matching, consider the following hypothetical example.

In a major international airport, a Mr. Jonathan Allan Smith presents his airplane ticket and identification papers to the clerk at the check-in desk. The clerk swipes the ticket-holder's identification (ID) card through the scanner and the passenger name "Jonathan Allan Smith" is checked against the airline's watchlist. This watchlist contains an entry for a "Mr. John Allen Smythe." However, as the automated system has been set to identify <u>only exact name matches</u>, the passenger is allowed to proceed to the gates. Before boarding, our hypothetical passenger is required to go through yet another security check. Although the same watchlist and name-matching program is used here, this time, the software has been set to flag all <u>similar names</u>, including those with standard variations in spelling, order, and form (*John Allen Smith, John Allan Smythe, Johnnie Allen Smythe, Allen John Smith*, etc.). Typographical variants that might have been produced via data-entry errors are also flagged (e.g., *Jonh Allen Smythe, Johnn Allen Smythe, John Allen MSythe*) as well as cross-linguistic and/or phonological variants (e.g., *Juan, Johann, Eoin, Jan, Jean, Sean*). As a result, during this second scan, the name "Jonathan Allan Smith" is flagged and the passenger is submitted to heightened security questioning wherein the biographical and biometric details contained in the traveler's documents are more carefully compared against the intelligence records linked to the watchlisted name "Mr. John Allen Smythe." If no further matches are found, Mr. Jonathan Allan Smith may be allowed to proceed to boarding. If, however, additional matches are identified, he may be further detained for additional, more intensive, questioning.

Enthusiastic supporters of governmental watchlisting might take the above scenario as evidence for the elegance and expediency of this approach. Although it is not fool-proof, no security measure ever is. Even biometric data, which is often considered to be the "gold standard" of identification and surveillance technologies, is not infallible.[52] So, although the gradual introduction of large-scale biometric-based entry-exit-security systems quite often seems promising to some security proponents, there is no escaping that the human factor will always introduce an inescapable level of error. Moreover, the exorbitant costs and unnerving array of technological challenges related to reliably gathering, storing, and mining biometric data still make this route prohibitive in comparison to traditional name-based systems.

It is presumably for these reasons that the *9/11 Commission* concluded that biometric identifiers can <u>help</u> improve (inter)national security measures, but it will nevertheless take years before an affordable, highly reliable bio-surveillance system could be implemented. In the meantime, name-matching is and will continue to be the primary tool for intelligence and law enforcement identification/verification purposes.[53] The goal then, watchlisting supporters argue, is to continually refine and improve the protocols, personnel, and technology. In the past few years, many new, sophisticated techniques have been applied to name-matching (e.g., natural language processing, artificial intelligence, and machine learning). These techniques have significantly improved the speed and accuracy of name-matching for databases containing millions of records.[54] Nevertheless, the criticism continues.

To be sure, most skeptics of watchlisting would agree that focusing on a select group of targets is clearly more efficient than spot-checking random samples of people and more reasonable (and acceptable) than attempting to thoroughly interrogate every single traveler.[55] However, critics would also remind that it is irrefutable that serious mistakes have been and are being made where persons who should have been targeted for heightened surveillance were not; and completely innocent individuals have been unnecessarily detained. Moreover, there is the ethical questionability of treating an entire group of people like potential criminals merely because they coincidentally share a feature (be it a name or otherwise) that the government has identified as being suspect. Watchlisting, by its very nature, opponents add, makes a mockery of one of the most sacred principles of the Anglo-American criminal justice system: every individual is to be considered innocent until proven guilty. Although some might be tempted to discount such arguments as nothing more than leftist belly-aching, it is undeniable that the US government has had a history of using name lists to violate the civil rights of residents in the name of public safety. The groundwork for many of these modern abuses was unwittingly laid several hundreds of years ago.

*****

In the late eighteenth century, President John Adams signed legislation allowing the detainment, apprehension, internment, imprisonment, or deportation of non-citizen residents deemed or suspected to be a danger to the security and peace of the United States. Over a century later, the Alien Enemies Act of 1798 was codified and amended such that any native, citizen, or subject, male or female, aged fourteen years or older, who was of a nation or government deemed hostile to the United States, could be "apprehended, restrained, secured, and removed" as an "alien enemy" during times of war or potential foreign invasion.[56]

On the basis of this legislation, President Franklin D. Roosevelt issued Presidential Proclamations 2525, 2526, and 2527 that respectively declared US residents of Japanese, German, and Italian ancestry to be dangerous alien enemies subject to "summary apprehension."[57] Two months later and ten weeks after the attack on Pearl Harbor, President Roosevelt signed Executive Order 9066 which authorized the Secretary of War to remove any and all resident aliens and citizens from military areas as deemed desirable or necessary. The entire West Coast of the United States was subsequently redefined as a military area and declared off-limits for all enemy aliens. Part of the ideological justification for this historic action was expressed in a summary report issued by General De Witt on February 14, 1942:[58]

> The Japanese race is an enemy race and while many second and third generation Japanese born on United States soil, possessed of United States citizenship, have become "Americanized," the racial strains are undiluted. . . . The very fact that no sabotage has taken place to date is disturbing and confirmation that such action will be taken.[59]

By the late spring of 1942, this ideologically driven legislation was being used to forcibly "relocate" more than 110,000 US residents of Japanese ancestry to barbed-wire encircled "assembly centers" located in remote areas around the nation. The forced internment of thousands of US residents with German and Italian heritage was soon to follow. The speed and efficiency with which these relocations took place could be explained in part by the fact that the US government, in anticipation of war, had begun as early as World War I to compile custodial detention name lists of persons considered potentially dangerous to US security.[60] These comparatively rudimentary lists could not, however, explain the sheer volume of people the government had located with such pinpoint accuracy within such a short period of time. It did not take long before private citizens and elected officials were asking how such accurate and expansive name lists could have been compiled so quickly.

Almost immediately, suspicion fell upon the US Bureau of Census. Having just completed its decennial survey of the nation's population just two years earlier, it was clear that the Bureau would have had ready access to such fine-grained information. However, Census officials vehemently denied supplying the Department of War with such sensitive individual-level data. The reason for this defensive stance is explained below in a Bureau report issued in May 1988:

> By law—no one—neither census takers nor any other Census Bureau employee—is permitted to reveal identifiable information about any person, household, or business. Thus, when the United States entered World War II and the War Department wanted to relocate Japanese Americans living on the West Coast in 1942, it could not obtain their names and addresses from the 1940 Census.[61]

For decades, as Bureau Directors came and went, this position was adamantly maintained until unassailable evidence to the contrary was finally uncovered.

Thanks to the US Freedom of Information Act, documents were discovered which revealed that Census authorities had in fact provided the US Secret Service with detailed name lists of US residents. In a candid interview given to *Scientific American*, long-time former US Census Bureau Director, Kenneth Prewitt, conceded that the evidence revealed by Dr. Margo Anderson and Dr. William Seltzer, two of the nation's leading experts in population statistics, was damning.

"At the time," Prewitt explained, "available evidence (and Bureau lore) held that there had been no release of microdata . . . That can no longer be said." Moreover, based on the evidence, Prewitt goes on further to state that it appears that the US Census may have repeatedly released such information to the US Secret Service between March 1942 and August 1942, when the confidentiality restrictions were relaxed by virtue of the Second War Powers Act passed (Title XIV, Section 1402).[62] On the basis of this evidence, Prewitt admitted in a now-famous email sent to Census staff on March 24, 2000, that the "historical record is clear that senior Census Bureau staff proactively cooperated with the internment, and that Census tabulations were directly implicated in the denial of civil rights to citizens of the United States"(16).[63] According to Professor Anderson, one of the greatest history lessons to be learned from this grievous ethical breach is the "power of the government to use its data capabilities to harm the very citizens it was supposed to protect."[64]

Twenty years before this admission, on August 10, 1988, the US Congress passed Public Law 100–383 which officially acknowledged and apologized for "the fundamental injustice of the evacuation, relocation, and internment of United States citizens and permanent resident aliens of Japanese ancestry during World War II."[65] Ironically, two years before this apology was issued, the now defunct "Alien Border Control Committee" of the Department of Justice proposed a secret contingency plan to construct a detention camp in the state of Louisiana for "alien undesirables" pending their deportation. The persons to be rounded up for detention and expulsion were from the following countries: Algeria, Jordan, Lebanon, Libya, Morocco, Syria, and Tunisia.[66]

Once the story of the contingency plan broke, public outrage was great. In its defense, government officials stressed that no concrete steps had ever actually been taken to implement the idea. However, as David Sadd, the then Executive Director of the National Association of Arab-Americans, stated in an interview with *The New York Times*, the very existence of this scheme provided evidence that "ethnic internment," if left unchecked, would be "right around the corner."[67]

*****

Despite the continuing (if not increasing) dangers of such misuse and abuse, many US residents ironically accept governmental intrusions into their personal lives "as the price of freedom": the underlying premise seeming to be that national security and personal liberty are naturally and unalterably at odds with one another. In order to safeguard one, it is necessary to curtail the other. What is comparatively rarely discussed in the public sphere, however, are the real-life consequences of falsely identifying an individual as a threat to national security (a false positive); or, the reverse, failing to identify an individual who poses a clear and significant risk to public safety (a false negative).

In a 2008 Congressional Hearing before the US Sub-Committee on Transportation Security and Infrastructure Protection, Texas-native Ms. D. Robinson provided testimony regarding her own personal experience with the false-positive phenomenon. The object of the government attention was not she herself, however, but her at-the-time five-year-old son. According to Ms. Robinson, the coincidental similarity between her boy's name and the name of an absolute stranger who had been watchlisted as a security risk meant that every time her family attempted to travel, they were stopped and questioned by authorities. Repeated attempts by Ms. Robinson to finally have her son's name removed from the governmental name lists had been rejected. As the mother explained in her testimony:

> it is obvious he is not a security threat now, but when he is a teenager in his early twenties and he is traveling on his own domestically, and particularly internationally, he could encounter problems. So I am here to get him off [the watchlists] now.[68]

The necessity of addressing such procedural lapses sporadically captures public attention when the media publishes the names of some of the people who have been placed on governmental watchlists. For example, Noble Peace Prize winner Nelson Mandela,[69] Senior US Statesman Ted Kennedy, Former Air National Guard Brigadier General James Robinson, Fox News contributor and journalist Stephen Hayes, and Alyssa T., a six-year-old girl from Ohio, have all had their names placed on watchlists for known or suspected terrorists.

The scope of these false positives has been repeatedly addressed by the US courts in cases where US citizens have brought suit for being wrongfully placed on the "No-Fly" watchlist. In *Latif v. Holder*, the US District Court of Oregon made the following observation about such cases:

> In theory, only individuals who pose a threat to civil aviation are put on the No-Fly and Selectee Lists, but the Justice Department has criticized TSC [Terrorist Screening Center] for its "weak quality assurance process." . . . Tens of thousands of travelers have been

misidentified because of misspellings and transcription errors in the
nomination process, and because of computer algorithms that imper-
fectly match travelers against the names on the list.[70]

The deficits noted above have been identified during official government audits
issued by the Department of Justice's Office of the Inspector General (OIG).
In 2009, for example, the OIG found that the FBI had "failed to nominate many
subjects in the terrorism investigations . . . did not nominate many others in a
timely fashion, and did not update or remove watchlist records as required."[71]
Eight years later, in a 2017 OIG audit of the Department of Justice's watchlisting practices for known or suspected terrorists, many of the same deficits were
identified. Once again, not only were inconsistencies found in the evaluation,
verification, and application of the nomination processes, the OIG also found
that the FBI's use of incomplete, inaccurate, and outdated information evidence
meant that in all likelihood "the FBI did not perform the assessment . . . as
required, which raises questions about the adequacy of the FBI's assessments
themselves."[72] As a result, Eileen Lawrence, the Director of the Government
Accountability Office's Home and Security and Justice team, testified before a
2007 Field Hearing of the Committee for Homeland Security: tens of thousands
of people have been "stopped, questioned, and sometimes searched . . . because
their names were 'a close match to someone actually on the list or because com-
puters cannot match names exactly.'"[73] Although one might argue that, though
admittedly regrettable, such incidents do not pose a true risk to national security,
the same cannot, however, be said with respect to false negatives.

One of the most spectacular cases involving this type of error involves
the would-be-suicide-bomber, Umar Farouk Abdulmutallab. On December
25, 2009, the twenty-three-year-old Nigerian was among the 271 passengers
onboard Northwest Airlines Flight 253 from Schiphol Airport in Amsterdam.
As the plane was making its final descent to the Detroit Metropolitan Wayne
County Airport, Abdulmutallab unsuccessfully attempted to detonate a chemical weapon he had concealed in his underwear. Shockingly, Abdulmutallab
had been able to pass undetected through airport security checks conducted by
not one but three different nations (Nigeria, the Netherlands, and the United
States). An intensive investigation conducted by the Senate Select Committee on
Intelligence[74] revealed fourteen points of human, technological, and systemic error.[75] Among those mistakes was the fact that the CIA Counterterrorism Center
(CTC) had run a "limited name search" that "failed to uncover the key reports
on Abdulmutallab" such as the fact that his father, Alhaji Umaru Mutallab, had
contacted US embassy officials and Nigerian authorities weeks before the event
to warn them about his son's dangerous radicalization.[76] The failure to link that
intelligence with other records ultimately meant that his name was not placed
on the TSDB, the Selectee List, or the No-Fly List.[77]

Aside from those times when incidents like these take front and center of the
media's attention, the real-life ramifications of the false positives and false nega-

tives rarely enter the public consciousness. Instead, when people think about the importance of safeguarding their personal names, it is more often than not with respect to white-collar crime such as identity theft and identity fraud. Without doubt, there seems to be no limit to the ingenuity criminals can summon when devising methods to first steal and then misuse the names of their unsuspecting victims. Once in the hands of an adroit offender, these ill-gotten monikers can often be combined with real or fictitious personal identifiers such as date of birth or social security numbers to create fake or synthetic identities.[78] Either way, it is often only a question of time before other criminal acts follow. From the fraudulent use of credit cards, tax rebates, and health benefits to money laundering, smuggling, and drug and sex trafficking, there is almost no limit to the financial, social, and psychological harm that identity thieves can cause their victims.[79]

According to an official report by the US Bureau of Justice Statistics, in the year 2014 alone, an estimated 17.5 million US residents experienced some form of identity theft, two-thirds of whom reported a direct financial loss. Three years later, despite increasing public awareness about the importance of vigilantly protecting one's names against unauthorized use, the problem had gotten worse, not better. It is estimated that in 2017, the total financial losses due to identity theft and fraud in the United States exceeded 15 billion US dollars.[80] The losses may be even greater for fraud involving the creation of "synthetic identities" (i.e. artificial identities that are created using a blend of fake and real personal identifiers such as personal names stolen from a hacked database). In a 2017 expert panel convened by the Comptroller General of the United States, it was stated that "banks can lose an estimated $50–$250 million in a year from SIF [stolen identity fraud] related unpaid debt. . . . Panelists also described instances where SIF criminals funded terrorism through money laundering."[81] Taken altogether, the potential danger of identity crime is both significant and real, for both the private citizen as well as the society. Personal names not only are effective for creating false identities but also are quite useful for gleaning private information about the real identities of the people who carry them.

*****

Even without biographical details, a surprising amount of information can be discerned about people by analyzing their names; and it does not take an expert to do it. Consider, for example, the following list of entirely fictitious names in table 1.2.

Which of the names in table 1.2 would you wager belong to a male, a female, a Hispanic, an African-American, an Asian-American, someone from the Deep South or the California Coast, a senior citizen older than seventy or a person younger than thirty? Let's go one step further. If you were presented with the name list above, which ones would you suspect had been chosen by parents who were science fiction fans? If you had to guess, which names would you say belonged to someone who was married or divorced, well-to-do or living below the poverty line, working as a professor at an exclusive ivy-league university or slaving in the porn

Table 1.2   List of Fictitious Names

1. Mohammed Ahmadi	14. Martina Lopez
2. Liam Alexander, III	15. Susie Lust
3. Khaleesi Anderson	16. Michael MacCallaghan
4. Harold Marvin Benson	17. Patrick McKinney
5. Vaishnavi Chakrabarti	18. Ms. J. T. Norman
6. Do-Yeong Chung	19. Carlos Ortega-Garcia
7. Hannah Cohen	20. Amira Sayed
8. Rachel Dee-Light	21. Hyram Shapiro
9. Hunter Fitzpatrick	22. Arya Smith
10. Sheryl Hanson	23. Anakin Taylor
11. Malik Jones	24. Lakeesha Washington
12. Broccoli Lawrence	25. Buba Ray Williams
13. Liu Lee	

industry under an assumed alias? And if you were forced to make a choice, which names would you pick out as belonging to a Protestant, a Catholic, a Muslim, or a Jew? Just how powerful these inferences are as a source of information came to light recently in the United States when news reports broke that in at least six different locations, federal immigration agents had asked employees of the hotel chain "Motel 6" to provide the names of all those guests who had a "Latino-sounding name." Those name lists were then used by Immigration and Customs Enforcement agents to investigate the guests' resident status. It has been estimated that information may have been provided on over 9,000 Motel 6 guests, without either their knowledge or permission.[82] Incidents have been reported in several states (Washington, Arizona, Texas, and California). But wait, you might say, at the end of the day, you can't know <u>for sure</u> what group(s) people identify as or with by merely looking at their names. All you can do is guess and many of those guesses are based on stereotypes. That is completely true.

<u>However</u>, that does not change the fact that the names we carry are surprisingly sensitive to a host of sociocultural, linguistic, economic, political, and historical factors. Consequently, many surnames have very strong differential ethnoracial distributional patterns. For example, according to data collected as a part of the 2010 US Census, some 93 percent of the survey-takers with the last name *Smalls* self-identified themselves as Black or African-American; 94 percent of those with the surname *Begay* selected the category American Indian or Alaskan Native; and 96 percent of the respondents who indicated that their family name was *Mueller*

Table 1.3 US Surnames that Display Strong Ethnoracial Clustering

AMERICAN INDIAN/ ALASKAN NATIVE		ASIAN/ PACIFIC ISLANDER		BLACK/ AFRICAN AMERICAN		HISPANIC		WHITE (NON-HISPANIC)	
NAME	%	NAME	%	NAME	%	NAME	%	NAME	%
Silago	100.00	Kanumuri	100.00	Akingbade	100.00	Barrita	100.00	Biedenbach	100.00
Badonie	99.10	Behera	99.65	Adeyeye	99.56	Alejandres	99.76	Burkemper	99.81
Bowekaty	99.03	Daoheuang	99.52	Adedokun	99.52	Gallarzo	99.69	Stepanov	99.80
Declay	98.80	Namburi	99.26	Osho	99.47	Ruballos	99.58	Chernyak	99.77
Notafraid	98.61	Voong	98.82	Ajibola	98.97	Rojel	98.98	Rabkin	98.97
Clitso	98.57	Zhuo	98.32	Okpala	98.92	Guadarama	98.98	Weipert	98.96
Littlewind	98.48	Tonnu	98.26	Jimale	98.92	Tepoz	98.96	Banasik	98.88
Cayaditto	98.02	Xu	98.25	Belayneh	97.91	Liguez	97.92	Demeuse	98.87
Hollowhorn	97.50	Qiu	98.21	Olayinka	97.40	Silvalopez	97.88	Ashbeck	97.99
Zunie	97.46	Qiang	97.40	Anokye	97.31	Carrizalez	97.87	Leonelli	97.98

Table 1.4 Common US Surnames that Display Strong Ethnoracial Clustering

AMERICAN INDIAN/ ALASKAN NATIVE		ASIAN/ PACIFIC ISLANDER		BLACK/ AFRICAN AMERICAN		HISPANIC		WHITE (NON-HISPANIC)	
NAME	%	NAME	%	NAME	%	NAME	%	NAME	%
Lowrey	4.5	Xiong	98.1	Washington	87.5	Barajas	96.5	Yoder	97.8
Hunt	4.2	Zhang	98.1	Jefferson	74.2	Zavala	96.1	Friedman	96.1
Sampson	3.9	Huang	97.1	Booker	65.2	Velazquez	96.0	Krueger	96.0
Jacobs	3.8	Truong	96.9	Banks	54.5	Avalos	95.8	Schwartz	95.9
Moses	3.2	Yang	96.8	Joseph	54.2	Orozco	95.8	Schmitt	95.7
Lucero	2.9	Li	96.8	Mosley	53.2	Vazquez	95.8	Mueller	95.7
James	2.6	Vang	96.7	Jackson	53.0	Juarez	95.7	Weiss	95.6
Proctor	2.4	Huynh	96.7	Charles	53.0	Meza	95.5	Novak	95.5
Ashley	2.4	Vu	96.6	Dorsey	52.2	Huerta	95.5	OConnell	95.4
Cummings	2.3	Nguyen	96.5	Rivers	50.9	Ibarra	95.3	Klein	95.4

chose the ethnoracial classification White. In table 1.3, several surnames that show similarly strong ethnoracial ties are displayed. More specifically, surnames are shown in which over 90 percent of the 2010 US Census participants who carried them also indicated that they belonged to one and the same ethnoracial classification. For example, 98.3 percent of the 2010 Census respondents who had the surname *Zhuo* also classified themselves as being Asian or Pacific Islander.

If many of the names listed in table 1.3 appear to be unfamiliar, there is a reason. The overall national incidence of each of these names is comparatively small. For example, the surname *Badonie* ranks only 148,347 among the last names recorded for the 2010 Census. At least some of the extreme ethnoracial homogeneity demonstrated by these and other names may be due to the underlying fact that a good portion of the persons with these surnames are members of the same underlying sociocultural grouping. For example, although the surname *Badonie* is relatively uncommon for the United States as a whole, it is fairly common among the Navajo. Even among more common surnames, however, interesting ethnoracial clustering can still be identified. Table 1.4 is drawn from the top 1,000 surnames in the United States. For each ethnoracial category, surnames with comparatively large clusterings (by percentage) are presented. For example, 98.1 percent of US Census respondents from 2010 who had the surname *Xiong* classified themselves as Asian or Pacific Islander; and 96.5 percent of people with the last name *Barajas* categorized themselves as Hispanic.

In marked contrast to the above examples, the 2010 US Census also revealed other surnames that were more evenly distributed across the major ethnoracial groupings. While 97 percent of the survey respondents with the last name *Li* categorized themselves as Asian-American/Pacific Islander, only 42 percent of the 2010 Census-takers who had the homophonic surname *Lee* placed themselves into this identity category. Other respondents named *Lee* indicated that they were White (35 percent), Black/African-American (16 percent), and American Indian/Alaskan Native (1 percent). Among those people who said that their family name was *Rodriguez*, 94 percent indicated that they were Hispanic, whereas only 5 percent described themselves as being non-Hispanic White. For the surname *Rogers*, however, precisely the opposite pattern was found. Less than 3 percent of Census-takers with the last name *Rogers* self-identified as Hispanic and 75 percent with this family name selected the ethnoracial designation "White non-Hispanic." Given such patterns, it is possible to make predictions concerning the likely sociocultural identity of a single individual (or a group of people) on the basis of a personal name:

However, the more fine-grained the assignments are expected to be, the less accurate the name-classification will most likely be. It is far easier, for example, to accurately assign the surname *Yang* to one of the broad sociocultural categories of "Asian" or "non-Asian" than it is to predict whether that name belongs to the sub-groups of Chinese, Korean, or Taiwanese. The difficulty in making such distinctions is linked in part to the degree of cultural heterogeneity found within the targeted populations and the concomitant mingling of personal names. In addition, certain naming practices such as women taking on the surnames of their marital partners can pose considerable challenges when attempting to predict ethnoracial identity. It might be reasonably inferred in the United States, for example, that the name *Anna Barajas* belongs to a woman of Hispanic ethnicity. However, that prediction might change if experts were to discover that *Barajas* is actually the woman's marital surname and *Wong* is her birth name.

Similar obstacles are posed by marriage and adoptions involving people from different ethnoracial groupings with different name patterning. Consider, for example, an African-born, naturalized US citizen who marries a US-born Chinese-American with Korean ancestry. The fact that the family's surname is *Yang* would only give limited information about this family's rich cultural heritage. These examples not only illustrate some of the difficulties involved in extrapolating social identity from name data but also demonstrate the potential utility of gathering comprehensive name data about a person of interest and his/her familial relations as well. Indeed, the more reliable relevant biographical information is gathered, the more reliable and relevant the resulting predictions can become. What is true for analyses concerning single individuals is also true for groups.

Aside from identification and authentication, name-analyses can also be used to gather information about otherwise difficult-to-detect large-scale diachronic changes in a society. For many decades now, the US Bureau of Census has been charged with investigating the relative distribution of the surnames in the United States to monitor shifts in the nation's demographic composition. The results of this ongoing research almost invariably make for eye-catching newspaper headlines and heated political debates over the "future direction of the nation." Such is the case each time the Bureau announces its official list of the most common surnames in the United States. Table 1.5 shows the Census's list of the top fifteen last names over the past thirty years.[83] Bolding is used to highlight those names that made their first appearance to the roster. For instance, in the year 2000, there were four last names that made the top fifteen listing for the very first time.

One of the most striking developments evident in the above table is the progressive increase in frequency of surnames common within the Hispanic community. Despite the steady dominance of the names *Smith, Johnson,* and *Williams,* during the same time period, the proportion of last names that are frequently carried by people with Hispanic ethnicity (e.g., *Garcia, Rodriguez, Martinez, Lopez*) has demonstrated a remarkable increase.

Importantly, as Joshua Comenetz, the Assistant Chief of the Population Division's Population Geography staff and manager of the US Census Bureau's

Table 1.5   Fifteen Surnames with the Highest Frequency for Census Years 1990, 2000, and 2010

RANK	1990	2000	2010
1.	Smith	Smith	Smith
2.	Johnson	Johnson	Johnson
3.	Williams	Williams	Williams
4.	Jones	Brown	Brown
5.	Brown	Jones	Jones
6.	Davis	Miller	Garcia
7.	Miller	Davis	Miller
8.	Wilson	*Garcia*	Davis
9.	Moore	*Rodriguez*	Rodriguez
10.	Taylor	Wilson	Martinez
11.	Anderson	*Martinez*	Hernancez
12.	Thomas	Anderson	*Lopez*
13.	Jackson	Taylor	*Gonzalez*
14.	White	Thomas	Wilson
15.	Harris	*Hernandez*	Anderson

"Surnames Project," points out, the rise of "Hispanic names" is related in part to the comparatively low level of surname diversity within this ethnic group. The relatively high degree of surname clustering for this ethnic group means that large numbers of people share the same last names and that in turn pushes the popularity of those names higher up on the list. According to Comenetz, "twenty-six surnames cover a quarter of the Hispanic population and 16 percent of Hispanic people reported one of the top Hispanic names."[84] By comparison, 239 different surnames accounted for a quarter of the people who fell into the category non-Hispanic White. However, name clustering is not the only reason for the progressively high incidence of names such as *Garcia, Rodriguez, Martinez, Hernandez, Lopez,* and *Gonzalez*. This linguistic phenomenon is also directly related to the significant demographic growth in the number of US residents who self-identify as Hispanic.[85]

Despite the media attention given to this particular ethnolinguistic development, the gains made by other minorities in US American society are even more dramatic. As reported in a 2016 *New York Times* article, "most of the surnames increasing fastest among the highest-ranking 1,000 are Asian (Zhang was up 111 percent, followed by Li, Ali, Liu, and Khan)."[86] While the names *Liu* and *Khan* demonstrated a change in frequency of approximately 65 percent, *Li* showed a 93.4 percent surge and *Zhang* an astounding 111.2 percent increase in frequency from the Census year 2000 to 2010.[87] Such dramatic changes not only are of interest from a linguistic point of view, but also point to important societal shifts within the nation. That being the case, the study of personal names can provide much valuable and sensitive information about individuals and group identities.

*****

The scientific discipline that is devoted to the scholarly examination of names and naming is called "onomastics," and the specific branch that is focused upon the investigation of personal names and naming is "anthroponymy." Traditionally, anthroponymists have concentrated on studying the historical origin and development of personal names used the world over. In many countries, for example, personal names routinely contain linguistic elements that indicate the name-bearer's and/or giver's gender, marital status, place of origin, nationality, occupation, clan, and/or socioeconomic standing.

The traditional naming system in Wales, for example, contained the linguistic elements *map* and *mab* which functioned in much the same way as *mac* or *mc* in Gaelic.[88] Meaning "son," these elements were once routinely placed between a son's name and his father's name to mark the bearer's patrilineage. The Welsh names *Owain mab Evan* and *Dafydd map Richard*, for instance, basically meant "Owain, the son of Evan" and "Dafydd, the son of Richard." Through this system of nomenclature, it was once possible for Welshmen to recall, honor, and preserve their paternal lineage over multiple generations. Over time, however, with the influence of the English and their language, this traditional Celtic naming system was altered and gave rise to new anglicized forms (*Owain mab Evan → Owain ab Evan → Owen Bevan; Dafydd map Richard → Dafydd ap Richard → David Pritchard* or *David Richards*).[89] Onomastic experts who are familiar with such historical linguistic developments are able to extract important information about the ancestral heritage of a name-bearer and the identities of his/her possible progenitors.

Similar insights may also be won through the investigation of more contemporary naming traditions. Within many modern Spanish-speaking communities, a child's last name may be formed by compounding the patrilineal and matrilineal surnames within his/her family. Traditionally, the first family name of the child's father may be placed before the first family name of the mother. Armed with this information, it is possible to discern that a person with the last name *Rodriguez Juarez* (or *Rodriguez y Juarez*) may have a paternal grandfather with the last name *Rodriguez* and a maternal grandfather with the last name *Juarez*.

A completely different system is used among Russian speakers. In these language communities, the personal name is typically made up of three parts: (1) a first name; (2) a second name that is composed of the father's first name and a gendered ending (suffix) such as *-ovna* and *-evna* for "daughter of" and *-ovich* or

-*evich* for "son of"; and (3) a family name which may also have a gendered suffix. *Mikhail Nikolayevich Pushkin* and *Yulia Nikolayevna Pushkina* could be names given to the son and daughter of a man called *Nikolai*.

An even more complex naming system is found within Arabic-speaking communities where personal names may be composed of multiple elements and sub-elements that differ by national, religious, and regional grouping. The five basic elements are the following: (1) the "kunya" which basically corresponds to "father of" (*abu*) or "mother of" (*umm*); (2) the "ism" that is simply a given or first name; (3) the "nasab" which is the basic equivalent to "son of" (*ben, bin, ibn*) or "daughter of" (*bint, bent, ibnat*); (4) the "laqab" is a positive personal characteristic of the name-bearer, often religious in nature; and (5) the "nisba" that is the equivalent to a family or last name. Through both the diachronic and synchronic comparison of personal name patterns found within and across languages, cultures, and times, it is possible to identify defining characteristics in the prototypical composition, pronunciation, spelling, meaning, and usage of names. These characteristics can, in turn, be used by onomasticians and other social scientists to make informed predictions concerning the origins of a particular name and, by extension, its name-bearer.

Although not a perfect science, name-analysis has been successfully used for many decades now as a popular tool for extrapolating information about the probable identity/identification of not just individuals, but also surprisingly large groups of people—from families, neighborhoods, districts, states, regions, nations, to continents—in the past, present, and the future. Generally speaking, the prerequisite for conducting such large-scale automated name-analyses is a list of personal names gathered from a separate, independent, reference population that closely matches the desired targeted population on the feature(s) of interest (e.g., ethnoracial classification, nationality, age, gender). Once the reference list is obtained, analyses can be conducted to determine the frequency with which each of the personal names on the list occurs within a social group of interest. These findings can then be used to assign a social classification to the matching personal names of people whose official classification is unknown. The accuracy of these assignments is directly related to the degree of cultural, geographical, and temporal similarity between the reference list of names and the target list of names; the method of assignment used; the level of specificity desired in the social classifications to be made; and the size and accuracy of the sociocultural classifications in the original reference list.

To help maximize the accuracy and efficiency of large-scale ongoing electronic identity-matching activities, Section 202 of the Enhanced Border Security and Visa Entry Reform Act of 2002 authorizes the US government to utilize "commercially available technology" for the development of a centralized interoperable database that is searchable by name elements.[90] One of the undisputed global leaders in developing state-of-the-art name-analysis software has been IBM. For many decades now, the company has consistently pioneered highly accurate and efficient hardware and software for the rapid analysis of large stores of name-based data for both commercial and governmental usage. The indirect determination of biographical factors on the basis of name data is a multi-billion-dollar business which has helped encourage the development of other software programs and companies (e.g., Nam Sor, Ethnic Seer, Ethnea).

To be sure, these automated systems can and often are used for the public good. For example, in large-scale health population studies, name-based analysis can be used to help determine whether certain segments of the society may be over- or under-represented in groups diagnosed with particular diseases. Name-based analysis has also been frequently and successfully used to monitor whether goods and services are truly being equitably distributed throughout the society. However, as with every innovation, in the wrong hands, this very same technology can also be used to cause widespread harm. By carefully analyzing the family names found within certain neighborhoods, for example, predictions concerning residents' identities and probable voting behavior can be made and electoral districts can be strategically manipulated to give a particular candidate or party a clear political advantage.

Given this incredible potential for harm, public fears over the unauthorized use of their personal names for illegal purposes are more than warranted. For that reason, many US residents only (knowingly) release their full name for "official purposes." Still, when you stop to think about it, that means that most people's full names can be found on a surprisingly large number of official documents. Birth and marriage certificates, library cards, arrest records, credit cards, passenger lists, driver's licenses, phone books, church rosters, prison files, military records, visa forms, school and university transcripts, utility bills, insurance papers, political party membership lists, hospital records, tax forms, bank accounts, and voter registration cards are just a few of the documents where residents' full names are to be found. Of course, official agencies that collect and store such documentation are subject to stringent legal regulations designed to safeguard the privacy and confidentiality. In 2008, for example, the George W. Bush administration released the "Privacy Policy Guidance Memorandum" which established eight Fair Information Practice Principles or FIPPS for data management at the Department of Homeland Security: (1) transparency; (2) individual participation for accessing, correcting, and seeking redress;[91] (3) purpose specification; (4) data minimization; (5) use limitation; (6) data quality and integrity; (7) security; and (8) accountability and auditing. Failure to adhere to these and other federal standards can carry severe penalties.[92]

Presumably operating upon the assumption that adherence to governmental regulations like FIPPS is sufficient to protect the public interest, data-gathering efforts by the US government have continued to expand. During President Barack Obama's administration, for example, data-gathering efforts were significantly increased.[93] Beginning in 2012, a new two-step intelligence project was initiated with the purpose of harnessing the perpetual store of digital information that is being continuously generated by the general public data worldwide. By dredging through this reservoir of "big data," the plan was to create an unclassified "data lake" called "Neptune" that would continually be fed by multiple streams of digital information.[94] To help ensure that the quality of information contained in Neptune was not sullied by an uncontrolled build-up of dirty-data, the repository was to be continuously filtered.[95] This filtration system would also be used to tag information which authorities deemed more appropriate for a secondary system of classified data. This second reservoir was given the name "Cerberus."[96] Once again, one of the primary types of biographic data collected in both Neptune and Cerberus are personal names.

The unprecedented collection of data for surveillance and intelligence purposes, of course, immediately triggered deep concerns over potential abuse, beginning with widespread violations of personal privacy. To help allay these fears, the US government periodically analyzes and then reports on the "privacy impact" of its data use and information technology program. The need for protecting people's right to privacy was also the subject of a 2013 report on the governmental data-gathering practices. Interestingly, instead of presenting civil liberties and national security as antithetical to one another, the administration was careful to cast both objectives as complementary equals. As President Obama declared, "as Americans, we reject the false choice between our security and our ideals. We can and we must and we will protect both."[97] Given such governmental policies and personal assurances, most US residents probably feel relatively safe in providing government officials with our full name. But are we really?

To a certain extent, the fact that so few of US residents stop to ponder this question is completely understandable. Although mistakes have been made in the past and will no doubt continue to be made in the future, the United States has, by and large, enjoyed a remarkably resilient democracy with a long-standing and treasured tradition of checks and balances. But what would happen if that same prized democracy were infiltrated by a subversive totalitarian faction led by a charismatic, maniacal leader bent on destroying any and all opposition? Just how safe would all those official documents containing millions upon millions of names be? Just how safe would we be?

Notes

1. In addition to these standards, the FBI continues to develop databanks for the next generation of identification (NGIs). The Bureau's Biometric Center of Excellence has pioneered image-based matching systems for everything from scars, marks, and tattoos (SMT) to genetic markers stored in a forensic system called CODIS (Combined DNA Index System). "Image-Based Matching Technology Offers Identification Intelligence Prospects," *Criminal Justice Information Services Link* 14, no. 3 (2012), https://www.fbi.gov/services/cjis/cjis-link/image-based-matching-technology-offers-identification-and-intelligence-prospects.

2. Mazin Al-Shuaili and Marco Carvalho, "Personal Identity Matching," *Computer Science and Information Technology* (2016): 31–43. For more on this topic, see Bertrand Lisbach and Victoria Meyer, *Linguistic Identity Matching* (Wiesbaden, Germany: Springer, 2013).

3. For example, the 2008 Fair, Accurate, Secure, and Timely Redress Act, which amends the Homeland Security Act of 2002, stipulates that legal name changes must be properly reflected in any terror watchlist or databases to ensure the most accurate lists for identifications possible. It also indicates that these name changes are to be shared among federal agencies and entities for this purpose. "Fair, Accurate, Secure, and Timely Redress Act," HR 110–686. 110th Cong., 2nd Sess., (June 19, 2008).

4. Lisa Seghetti and Stephen Viña, "US Visitor and Immigrant Status Indicator Technology (US-VISIT) Program," *Congressional Report Service* [CRS], Report for Congress (February 23, 2005).

5. To create an official record, the Department of Homeland Security has established a minimum number of unique biographic elements for information exchange throughout the department. Among these core elements are the following: first name, last name, middle name, translated names, date of birth, country of birth, gender, and country of citizenship. Half of these elements include name-based data. Department of Homeland Security. DHS, *Privacy Impact Assessment for the Watchlist Service* (July 14, 2010).

6. For more than a half a century, the US Attorney General has been given authorization to impose special regulations and registration of several types of aliens. The Immigration and Nationality Act of 1954, Public Law 414, HR 5678, 82nd Cong. (June 27, 1952), chapter 7.

7. US Department of Homeland Security, Notice, "Privacy Act; Office of Intelligence and Analysis Enterprise Records System, doc. no. E8–10888," *Federal Register* 73, no. 95 (May 15, 2008): 28128–28135.

8. Peter Christen, *Data Matching: Concepts and Techniques for Record Linkage, Entity Resolution and Duplicate Detection* (London: Springer Verlag, 2012), 38.

9. Thomas Kean and Lee Hamilton, *The 9/11 Commission Report: Final Report of the National Commission on Terrorist Attacks Upon the United States* (New York: St. Martin's Press, 2004).

10. US Congress, *Intelligence Reform and Terrorism Prevention Act of 2004*, Public Law 108–458, 108th Cong. (December 18, 2004).

11. Kean and Hamilton, *9/11 Commission Report*, 178, 272, 492.

12. Single agency databanks that form a part of this computer-automated database include the Consular Lookout and Support System (CLASS), the Treasury Enforcement Communications System (TEC), and the Known or Appropriately Suspected Terrorists file (KST). American Civil Liberties Union, "US Government Watchlisting: Unfair Process and Devastating Consequences," 2014, https://www.aclu.org/sites/default/files/assets/watchlist_briefing_paper_v3.pdf.

13. Christen, *Data Matching*, 14.

14. US Department of Justice, Office of the Inspector General, "Audit of the US Department of Justice Terrorist Watchlist Nomination Process" (March 2008), https://oig.justice.gov/reports/plus/a0816/final.pdf.

15. The introduction of this registration was pursuant to Section 265(b) of the Immigration and Nationality Act that provides that the "Attorney General may in his discretion, upon ten days' notice, require the natives of any one or more foreign states, or any class or group thereof, who are within the United States and who are required to be registered" and "prescribes special regulations and forms for the registration and fingerprinting" of aliens of "any class not lawfully admitted to the United States for permanent residence." Immigration and Naturalization Service, Notice, "Registration of Certain Nonimmigrant Aliens from Designated Countries, doc. no. 02–32045," *Federal Register* (December 18, 2002), https://www.federalregister.gov/documents/2002/12/18/02–32045/registration-of-certain-nonimmigrant-aliens-from-designated-countries.

16. In governmental parlance, persons falling into this category may be referred to using the rather antiquated term "alien absconders" or the more recent term "overstays." According to a 2016 report issued by the Department of Homeland Security, there were 50,437,278 non-immigrant admissions to the United States. Of this number an "in-country overstay rate" of 1.25 percent or 628,799 was suspected. Fiscal Year 2016 Entry/Exit Overstay Report. Department of Homeland Security, https://www.dhs.gov/sites/default/files/publications/Entry%20and%20Exit%20Overstay%20Report%2C%20Fiscal%20Year%202016.pdf.

17. Kean and Hamilton, *9/11 Commission Report*, 563.

18. According to statistics maintained by the Department of Homeland Security, by September 30, 2003, people from 150 different countries had already "complied with the NSEERS registration for a total of 290,526 registrations," Department of Homeland Security, "Homeland Security Fact Sheet" (December 1, 2003), http://www2.gtlaw.com/practices/immigration/news/2003/12/01a.pdf.

19. Louise Cankar, "Post 9/11 Domestic Policies Affecting US Arabs and Muslims: A Brief Review." *Comparative Studies of South Asia, Africa and the Middle East* 24, no. 1 (2004): 245–48.

20. Cankar, "Post 9/11 Domestic Policies," 246.

21. Samira Afzali, "How 'Comprehensive' is the Comprehensive Immigration Reform Bill?" *Hamline University's School of Law and Policy* 35, no. 2 (2014): 296–329.

22. Arab American Institute, "National Security Entry-Exit Registration System," http://www.aaiusa.org/nseers.

23. "The Persistence, in the United States, of Discriminatory Profiling Based on Race, Ethnicity, Religion and National Origin," US Submission to the United Nation's *Universal Periodic Review* (November 2010), 1–12, http://lib.ohchr.org/HRBodies/

UPR/_layouts/15/WopiFrame.aspx?sourcedoc=/HRBodies/UPR/Documents/session9/
US/USHRN_UPR_USA_S09_2010_Annex19_Racial%20Profiling%20Joint%20Rep
ort%20USA.pdf&action=default&DefaultItemOpen=1.

24. "The Persistence," 2.

25. Michelle Mittelstadt, Burke Speaker, Doris Meissner, and Muzaffar Chishti, "Through the Prism of National Security: Major Immigration Policy and Program Changes in the Decade Since 9/11," *Migration Policy Institute* (August 2011), 5, http://www.migrationpolicy.org/research/post-9–11-immigration-policy-program-changes.

26. Migration Policy Organization, "Chronology of Events Since September 11, 2001 Related to Immigration and National Security," http://www.migrationpolicy.org/sites/default/files/source_charts/FE-post911-chronology-2002.pdf.

27. "About 83,000 men came forward, and nearly 13,000 were placed in deportation proceedings. Many (the actual number is unknown) were, in fact, deported for minor immigration violations, but none was charged with crimes related to terrorism." Bill Ong Hing and others, "The Administration of Immigration Law," in Bill Ong Hing, *Immigration Law and Social Justice* (New York: Wolters Kluwer, 2018), 166.

28. Natsu Taylor Saito, "Internments, Then and Now: Constitutional Accountability in Post-9/11 America." *Duke Forum for Law and Social Change* 2, no. 71 (2010): 72–101.

29. Rachel Swarns, "Program's Value in Dispute as a Tool to Fight Terrorism," *The New York Times*, December 21, 2004, http://www.nytimes.com/2004/12/21/us/programs-value-in-dispute-as-a-tool-to-fight-terrorism.html.

30. Despite running on a liberal pro-immigration platform, President Obama "earned the title of 'Deported-in-Chief' for deporting more migrants than any president, ever." Jamil Dakwar, *Not So safe and Sound*, 51.

31. US Department of Homeland Security, Notice, "Removing Designated Countries from the National Security Entry-Exit Registration System (NSEERS), doc. no.: 2011–10305," *Federal Register* 76 (April 28, 2011), https://www.federalregister.gov/documents/2011/04/28/2011–10305/removing-designated-countries-from-the-national-security-entry-exit-registration-system-nseers.

32. US Department of Homeland Security, "Removing Designated Countries from the National Security Entry-Exit Registration System (NSEERS), doc. no.: 2011–10305."

33. Even before this governmental initiative, there was broad recognition of the fact that there must be an increase in information-sharing between intelligence and law enforcement. Under the auspices of the State Department's Bureau of Intelligence and Research, the CIA, NSA, and the FBI created a consolidated database to collect and share sensitive information to help combat terrorism. The name of the computerized forerunner was called TIPOFF. The program began in 1987. Another analogous early database system for border security was the Consular Lookout and Support System (CLASS) which contained over 13 million visa records in 2004. For more, see: US Department of State, "The Fiscal Year 2004 Performance Plan," Washington, DC (March 2003), http://www.state.gov/m/rm/rls/perfplan/2004/.

34. Executive Office of the President, Executive Order no. 13354, "National Counterterrorism Center," *Federal Register* 69 (August 27, 2004): 53589–53592.

33

35. National Counterterrorism Center (NCTC), "Who We Are," https://www.dni.gov/index.php/nctc-who-we-are.

36. NCTC, "Who We Are," para. 2.

37. NCTC, "How We Work," https://www.dni.gov/index.php/nctc-how-we-work.

38. NCTC, "How We Work," para. 4.

39. NCTC, "Terrorist Identities Datamart (TIDE)," https://www.dni.gov/files/NCTC/documents/features_documents/TIDEfactsheet10FEB2017.pdf.

40. NCTC, "TIDE," 2.

41. NCTC, "Watchlist Guidance" (March, 2013), 23.

42. NCTC, "Watchlist Guidance," 24.

43. As of July 2010, the Department of Homeland Security implemented a new system of intelligence-sharing, the Watchlist Service (WLS). The WLS maintains a regularly updated, synchronized copy of the TSDB that is shared with authorized components of the DHS. For more, see: https://www.dhs.gov/sites/default/files/publications/privacy-pia-027-E-uscis-wlsfdnsds-may2016.pdf.

44. Bob Orr, "Inside a Secret US Terrorist Screening Center," *CBS News*, October 12, 2012, https://www.cbsnews.com/news/inside-a-secret-us-terrorist-screening-center/.

45. Orr, "Inside a Secret," para 12.

46. Orr, "Inside a Secret," para 14.

47. United States Congress, "Ensuring America's Security: Cleaning Up the Nation's Watchlists," Hearing before the Subcommittee on Transportation Security and Infrastructure Protection of the Committee on Homeland Security House of Representatives, 110th Cong., 2nd Session, Serial No. 110–35, September 9, 2008, 17, https://www.gpo.gov/fdsys/pkg/CHRG-110hhrg47173/pdf/CHRG-110hhrg47173.pdf.

48. "Ensuring America's Security," 4.

49. Jerome Bjelopera, Bart Elias, and Alison Siskin, "The Terrorist Screening Database and Preventing Terrorist Travel," *Congressional Research Service*. https://fas.org/sgp/crs/terror/R44678.pdf.

50. Bjelopera, Elias, and Siskin, "The Terrorist Screening Database," 7.

51. "Ensuring America's Security," 9.

52. David Gray and Stephen Henderson, eds., *The Cambridge Handbook of Surveillance Law* (Cambridge: Cambridge University Press, 2017).

53. Kean and Hamilton, *9/11 Commission Report*, 565.

54. Christen, *Data Matching*, 10.

55. Daniel Steinbock, "Designating the Dangerous: From Blacklisting to Watchlist," *Seattle University Law Review* 30 (2006): 65–118.

56. See: Section 21, Title 50 of the US Code [11 F.C.A., tit. 50, §21.

57. President, Proclamation, "Alien Enemies—Japanese, No. 2525," http://www.foitimes.com/internment/Proc2525.html; President, Proclamation, "Alien Enemies—Germans, No. 2526," http://www.foitimes.com/internment/Proc2526.html; President, Proclamation, "Alien Enemies—Italians, No. 2527," http://www.foitimes.com/internment/Proc2527.html.

58. After the war, it was determined that the Japanese government had indeed planted spies in the United States. However, as a general rule, these agents were primarily White

and not of Japanese ancestry. Thomas McDonnell, "Targeting the Foreign Born by Race and Nationality: Counterproductive in the 'War on Terrorism,'" *Pace Law Faculty Publications* 16, no. 19 (2004): 20–63.

59. Commission on Wartime Relocation and Internment of Civilians, "Personal Justice Denied: Report of the Commission on Wartime Relocation and Internment of Civilians," Washington, DC: US Government Printing Office, 1982. https://www.arc hives.gov/files/research/japanese-americans/justice-denied/summary.pdf.

60. The Commission on Wartime Relocation and Internment of Civilians, Summary Report, https://www.archives.gov/files/research/japanese-americans/justice-denied/sum-mary.pdf

61. US Bureau of Census, *Census Confidentiality and Privacy: 1790–2002*. https://ww w.census.gov/prod/2003pubs/conmono2.pdf.

62. J. R. Minkel, "Confirmed: The US Census Bureau Gave Up the Names of Japanese-Americans in WWII," *Scientific American*, March 30, 2007, https://www.sci entificamerican.com/article/confirmed-the-us-census-b/.

63. US Bureau of Census, *Census Confidentiality*, 16.

64. Margo Anderson, "Public Management of Big Data: Historical Lessons from the 1940s," *Federal History* 15 (2015): 19.

65. *The Civil Liberties Act of 1988*, Public Law 100–383, 100th Cong., H.R. 442, Sect. 1 (1–2), (August 10, 1988).

66. This secret INS-strategy was entitled the "Alien Terrorists and Undesirables: A Contingency Plan." For more, see: Berta Hernández-Truyol, "Nativism, Terrorism, and Human Rights," *Columbia Human Rights Law Review* 31 (2000): 521–59; Saito, "Internments, Then and Now," 72–101; David Cole, "Secrecy, Guilt by Association, and the Terrorist Profile," *Journal of Law and Religion* 25 (2000): 267–88; David Cole and James Dempsey, *Terrorism and the Constitution: Sacrificing Civil Liberties in the Name of National Security* (New York: The New Press, 2006): 45–46.

67. Stephen Engelbart, "Greater Access to Terrorism Data is Sought for Immigration Agency," *The New York Times*, February 5, 1987. http://www.nytimes.com/1987/02 /06/us/greater-access-to-terrorism-data-is-sought-for-immigration-agency.html.

68. "Ensuring America's Security," 43.

69. Caitlin Dewey, "Why Nelson Mandela was on a Terrorism Watch List in 2009," *The Washington Post*, December 7, 2013, https://www.washingtonpost.com/news/the-fix/wp/2013/12/07/why-nelson-mandela-was-on-a-terrorism-watch-list-in-2008/?utm_term=.792f4be51234.

70. *Latif, et al. v. Holder, et al.* United States District Court, D. Oregon, August 28, 2013, No. 3:10-CV-00750-BR, *American Civil Liberties Union*, March 13, 2015, https://www.aclu.org/legal-document/latif-et-al-v-holder-et-al-opinion-and-order.

71. US Department of Justice, Office of the Inspector General, "The Federal Bureau of Investigation's Terrorist Watchlist Nomination Practices, Audit Report." May 9–25, 2009, iv, https://oig.justice.gov/reports/FBI/a0925/final.pdf.

72. US Department of Justice, Office of the Inspector General, "Audit of the Department of Justice's Handling of Known or Suspected Terrorists Admitted into the Federal Witness Security Program," September 4, 2017, https://oig.justice.gov/reports/2017/a17 34.pdf.

73. US Department of Homeland Security, *The Progress and Pitfalls of the Terrorist Watchlist*, 11.

74. Senate Select Committee on Intelligence (SSCI), "Unclassified Executive Summary of the Committee Report on the Attempted Terrorist Attack on Northwest Airlines Flight 253" (May 18, 2010).

75. SSCI, "Attack on Northwest Airlines," 2.

76. SSCI, "Attack on Northwest Airlines," 2.

77. SSCI, "Attack on Northwest Airlines," 5.

78. On the basis of a study of 300 million accounts, it was estimated that approximately 90 percent of fraudulent bank accounts opened in the United States involved synthetic identities. Christen, *Data Matching*, 15.

79. Erika Harrell, "Victims of Identity Theft," US Department of Justice, Bureau of Justice Statistics (September 2015), https://www.bjs.gov/content/pub/pdf/vit14.pdf.

80. Bob Sullivan, "Identity Theft Hit an all-time High in 2016," *USA Today*, February 13, 2017, https://www.usatoday.com/story/money/personalfinance/2017/02/06/identity-theft-hit-all-time-high-2016/97398548/.

81. *Highlights of a Forum: Combating Synthetic Identity Fraud*. Comptroller General of the United States. U.S. Government Accountability Office. GAO-17–708SP. July 2017. http://www.gao.gov/assets/690/686134.pdf

82. Eli Rosenberg, "Motel 6 Gave Lists to ICE Agents Looking for 'Latino-Sounding' Names, Lawsuit Alleges," *The Washington Post*, January 3, 2018.

83. US Census Bureau, "Hello My Name Is: Top 15 Most Popular last names in the US by Rank," December 15, 2016. https://www.census.gov/content/dam/Census/library/visualizations/2016/comm/cb16-tps154_graphic1_surnames.pdf?eml=gd.

84. Joshua Comenetz, "Frequently Occurring Surnames in the 2010 Census," *United States Bureau of Census*, October 2016. https://www2.census.gov/topics/genealogy/2010surnames/surnames.pdf.

85. Care is taken here to avoid labels such as "Hispanic name" as bearers of these surnames need not necessarily self-identify as Hispanic.

86. Sam Roberts, "Hispanic Surnames on the Rise in the US as Immigration Surges," *The New York Times*, December 2016, https://www.nytimes.com/2016/12/15/us/census-data-hispanic-surnames.html.

87. Comenetz, "Frequently Occurring Surnames in the 2010 Census," 7.

88. George Redmonds, Turi King, and David Hey, *Surnames, DNA, and Family History* (Oxford: Oxford University Press, 2011).

89. Redmonds, King, and Hey, *Surnames, DNA, and Family History*, 53.

90. The Enhanced Border Security and Visa Entry Reform Act of 2002, House Amendment, HR 1885, 107th Cong., 2nd sess., (March 12, 2002), 14.

91. Before the Subcommittee on Transportation Security, it was stated that since its establishment in 2007, the Department of Homeland Security (DHS) "has received and processed more than 185,000 redress requests." DHS, Safeguarding Privacy and Civil Liberties while Keeping and our Skies Safe (September 18, 2014).

92. Privacy Policy Guidance Memorandum 2008–1: The Fair Information Practice Principles. (December 29, 2008), US Department of Homeland Security. https://

www.dhs.gov/sites/default/files/publications/privacy-policy-guidance-memorandum-20 08–01.pdf

93. Jamil Dakwar, "Not So Safe and Sound," *The SUR File on Migration and Human Rights* 13, no. 23 (2016): 49–60.

94. US Department of Homeland Security, *Privacy Impact Assessment Update for the DHS Data Framework: Unclassified Use.* [DHS/ALL/PIA-046(e)]. October 6, 2017. https://www.dhs.gov/sites/default/files/publications/privacy-pia-dhswide-dhsdfunclass ifieduse-october2017.pdf

95. US Department of Homeland Security, *Privacy Impact Assessment for the Neptune Pilot.* [DHS/ALL/PIA-046–1]. September 25, 2013. https://www.dhs.gov/sites/default/ files/publications/privacy-pia-dhs-wide-neptune-09252013.pdf

96. US Department of Homeland Security, *Privacy Impact Assessment for the Cerberus Pilot.* [DHS/ALL/PIA-046–3]. https://www.dhs.gov/sites/default/files/publications/pr ivacy-pia-dhs-cerberus-nov2013.pdf

97. "Guidance for Implementing Section 5 of EO 13636: Privacy and Civil Liberties Protections," June 10, 2013. https://www.dhs.gov/sites/default/files/publications/NS S%20Guidance%20on%20Section%205%20implementation_0.pdf. Explained briefly, Executive Order 113636 directs federal departments and agencies to improve cybersecurity critical to protecting US infrastructure.

CHAPTER 2

The National Socialist Policy of Onomastic Apartheid

Across the German-speaking world, the convention of possessing a relatively fixed, first and last name is quite commonplace. However, from a historical perspective, this onomastic pattern is comparatively new. First achieving popularity among the European aristocracy in the twelfth century, this two-name system did not take hold in the general population until some six hundred years had passed. Even after the pattern became widely and well established in European society, it was not at all unusual for people to alter one or both of their names to mark a significant change in their profession, residence, or status. The freedom to select and alter one's name without impediment by a governing body was a carryover from Roman law which stipulated that a change in name or *mutatio nominis* was permissible, as long as the motivation for the alteration was not for fraudulent purposes.

By the start of the nineteenth century, however, regional governments throughout what is now Germany and Austria began to enact legislation requiring the fixation of surnames. For example, on December 18, 1810, Ludwig, the Grand Duke of Hessia, announced that it had come to his attention that many of his subjects were in the habit of rather frequently altering their first and family names. According to the Duke, all this onomastic fickleness not only posed a problem for private business dealings between subjects but also caused considerable confusion and disorder in the administration of the state, especially with regard to conscription and taxation. For this reason, the Duke declared that from that date forward, no subject would be allowed to alter his/her first name, surname, or baptismal name without obtaining prior permission. Those who violated this ruling would be required either to pay a penalty of five gilders or, in the case of destitution, serve a prison sentence of no less than five days. The Grand Duchy was not the only site of this new onomastic restriction. Throughout the nineteenth century, similar legislation was enacted throughout the respective states of Germany and Austria.

Initially, this legislation was almost exclusively applied to citizens of the various German states and exempted long-term residents without citizenship such as non-assimilated Jewish residents. However, as time wore on, these exceptions began to fall under attack. Before the nineteenth century, Central European Jews, in contrast to Christians, were largely without surnames. Instead, "they bore only a forename, to which, if further clarification was necessary, the father's forename was added: for instance, 'Joseph (ben) Nathan.'"[1] In the past, the government had largely tolerated or ignored this onomastic tradition. However, with the gradual introduction of legislation designed to regulate personal naming, new policies began to appear which required the male heads of Jewish households to adopt hereditary surnames.[2]

As of July 1787, Austrian Jews were forced to take on the last names chosen for them by a special state commission. In Germany, similar edicts were successively passed by each of the separate states (e.g., Hessia 1812,[3] Bavaria 1813, Wuerttemberg 1828).[4] In some instances, anti-Semitic Christian officials often took great delight in assigning Jewish residents offensive, injurious, or otherwise disparaging family names.[5] Reported examples include *Afterduft* "anal smell," *Eselkopf* "donkey head," *Galgenstrick* "hangman's noose," *Geschwur* "abscess," *Gottlos* "godless," *Schweissloch* "sweat pit/hole," and *Trinker* "drunkard."[6] It has also been attested that corrupt officials in isolated districts of Prussia and Austria (especially Galicia) used these new policies to blackmail Jewish families for exorbitant sums of money. Those who either refused to or were unable to pay the onomastic ransom were summarily punished with particularly humiliating family names.[7]

Two years after Ludwig's proclamation, the historic Emancipation Edict of 1812 or *Judenedikt* was issued. In short, this piece of legislation granted state citizenship to all Jewish residents of Prussia who took on permanent first names and hereditary last names which were then to be registered on official governmental lists. Among optimists, the Edict appeared to be a revolutionary step toward integrating Jewish inhabitants into Prussian society. Much of the strongest support for this legislation consequently came from liberal politicians who reasoned that the adoption of a universal naming system would help bring an end to the stigmatization and discrimination which many Jewish residents were subjected to at the very mention of their names. Among skeptics, the fact that the offer of citizenship was made contingent upon forsaking a sacred part of their Jewish heritage was an insultingly high entrance fee to be recognized as a member of a society to which they already belonged. When the number of Jewish applicants for Prussian citizenship remained comparatively low, what began as an offer transformed into a requirement. In many districts, Jewish residents who "failed" to register found themselves being the repeated target of official chicanery and police brutality.

Importantly, the push for onomastic assimilation encompassed the adoption of not only surnames but also forenames. In Horchheim, a small township located directly outside of Worms, an 1809 report on the Jewish community indicated that twenty-two individuals had applied for and been granted a name change. A few examples of the name alterations contained in this listing include the following: *Aaron Salm → Adam Jacobi; Simon Jacob → Simon Jacobi; Rainge Feidel → Rosalie Feidel; Feidel Jacob → Mathias Jacobi; Buhla Feidel → Marie Anna Jacobi; Henle Gumbel → Jeanne Hirsch; Sorla Jacob → Sara Jacobi; Jendle Fiedel → Claire Jacobi.*[8] These name exchanges poignantly reflected the complex political situation of the region at the time.

In 1797, the city of Worms was annexed by France, making French the language of administration. In 1807, leading members of the Jewish community met with representatives of the French government to negotiate new terms of protection and legal equality. During these deliberations, the Jewish representatives officially declared their unreserved loyalty to France and in so doing were granted emancipation along with their Christian neighbors. The surrender of Yiddish and Hebrew names (e.g., *Henle, Baierge, Lewel, Rainge, Feidel, Aphron*) for nondescript French names (*Jeanne, Barbe, Leopold, Rosalie, Adolphe, Philippe*) clearly mirrors these sociopolitical developments. The irony is, of course, that less than ten years later, Worms once again fell under the control of the Grand Duchy of Hesse, a member state of the German Confederation.[9] Although the initial rights afforded to the Jewish residents in this area were initially respected, the rabid anti-French sentiment of the new German government soon became omnipresent. In such a Francophobic environment, having the name *Jeanne* or *Philippe* would have been a decided disadvantage.

In this case and countless others, the promised protections of a personal name change were as short-lived as the governmental assurances that inspired them. In view of this fact, the increasing institutional pressure placed on Jews to abandon their onomastic traditions did not go without resistance. In the 1909 edition of the *Deutsche Reich*, a Berlin-based newspaper published by the Central Society of German Citizens of the Jewish Faith [Centralverein deutscher Staatsbürger jüdischen Glaubens], featured an admonishing editorial which warned the German Jewish community against the individual and collective dangers of onomastic assimilation:

> The wonderful vitality of the Jewish community is due in large measure to the fact that the vast majority of Jews have remained true to themselves, open for any cultural advance but continuing to cultivate their ancient language as well as the traditions of their fathers such as the preservation of their names. Whenever Jews have attempted to conceal their lineage and betray their Jewishness, even if only through

> trading in the Old Testament names which they once carried with
> pride for Germanic first names, the result has been ruination.[10]

What many ultra-conservative Jews considered to be the preservation of their cultural heritage, arch-conservative Gentiles often interpreted as an insulting and inflammatory rejection of Germany's core values. Following this logic, Jewish residents who refused to adopt the two-name system of the Christian majority were often seen as displaying willful deviance and cultural incorrigibility. In view of this hostility, despite appeals from conservative leaders of the Jewish community to remain steadfast against the combination of persuasion and coercion launched by government officials, the number of Jewish residents who eventually capitulated and officially relinquished their ancient onomastic traditions gradually rose. There is clear statistical evidence of this development. In the forty-year period between 1812 and 1851, for example, only sixty-five Jewish inhabitants had registered themselves with a fixed last name in exchange for Prussian citizenship. In comparison, between 1912 and 1919, over 950 applications were made.[11]

In some principalities such as Hessen, Bavaria, and Mecklenburg-Schwerin, Jewish residents were relatively free to select their family surnames.[12] In other areas, local and regional authorities placed severe restrictions upon the selection of surnames possible for the Jewish sub-population (e.g., Baden and Austria).[13] In all regions, however, the government reserved the right to determine which personal names would be accepted or rejected.

No sooner had the majority of the German-speaking Jewish community adopted the traditional naming customs of the majority population, did accusations begin to surface that the Jews had shamelessly plundered the Germanic heritage by taking on names that did not belong to them. The result, they claimed, was the defilement of countless Germanic names which had been passed down from one generation of Christians to the next. To help put an end to what many considered to be an egregious affront, policies were progressively introduced which forbade Jews from taking on names which were popularly considered to be the exclusive cultural birthright of Christians. These prohibitions were directed at last names and first names.

One of the most pivotal cases of this onomastic segregation came in the summer of 1816. On August 17, Markus Lillie, a successful Jewish businessman, sent a letter to King Friedrich Wilhelm III of Prussia in which he respectfully requested permission to name his sixth-born son after the German monarch. In 1992, Bering published a translation of this original letter:

> We venture the most humble request that Your Majesty will graciously permit . . . our son born on the 14th inst. . . . to be consecrated to religion, and to give him the names Friederich Wilhelm,

with which such high thoughts, such marvelous feeling and such powerful incentives for goodness are connected.[14]

Less than two weeks later, the royal response came. In somewhat convoluted nineteenth-century German, it was declared that no unbaptized Jewish child [Judenkinde] could be allowed to take on the king's name. It was further decreed from that day forward that no unbaptized Jewish child would be allowed to take on any Christian name.

A careful reading of this edict reveals that the primary objection was not ethnoracial. Judaism was considered a religion, not a race as it would later be redefined. Accordingly, Jewish residents who converted to Christianity were not only allowed but also strongly encouraged to adopt new names. Indeed, in 1822, King Friedrich Wilhelm III expressly authorized the Minister of the Interior to automatically grant a name change to any Jewish applicant who could provide official documentation to verify conversion to Christianity (e.g., a certificate of Baptism or a letter of recommendation from a local clergy member). The king considered each conversion to be a sacred victory for Christianity and ordered that everything possible be done to encourage as many Jews as possible to embrace what he considered to be the one true faith. Despite the high priority which the king assigned this mission, on the whole, local and regional governments demonstrated an increasing resistance to granting an official name change given the administrative difficulties they posed in levying taxation and enforcing conscription. On July 6, 1836, for instance, a circular was sent out to German synagogues and cultural ministries. The order strictly prohibited any Jew from taking on a Christian first name.[15]

September 25, 1903, even saw the official repeal of residents' automatic right to change their name to mark a religious conversion. This change in policy meant that name changes in Germany and Austria were only to be granted in exceptional cases where petitioners could demonstrate that their name had caused undue personal distress, financial hardship, and/or social embarrassment. In theory, this law was to be applied to all residents, irrespective of their religion. In practice, the authorities often displayed obvious bias in how they applied this regulation.

In cases involving non-Jewish German citizens, officials tended to grant applicants' name changes if at least one of the above criteria could be fulfilled. An excellent case in point comes from an application made on April 10, 1920.[16] On this date, a typesetter named *Mr. Schwein* [Mr. Pig] petitioned the court to have his surname officially changed to *Schiller*. In the petition, he wrote: "The reason for my petition is that the name 'Schwein' makes a bad impression everywhere. I have never been convicted, have not yet been under investigation, and I can guarantee that no other reasons have led me to change my name."[17]

According to the official court records, the Minister of Justice forbade Mr. Schwein from adopting the last name of the famous German writer *Schiller*. However, the minister expressed that he would be amenable to granting the unhappy typesetter permission to adopt a less lofty surname such as *Schwender*, a composite of **Schwein** and *Schneider*, another surname found in the petitioner's family line. As a possible alternative, the Minister suggested another onomastic invention: *Schwenbach*, a name inspired by the petitioner's original surname and the name of his hometown, Ram**bach**. After many letters were sent back and forth, on October 19, 1920, an agreement was reached: the unhappy Mr. Schwein would be allowed to change his surname to *Schroeder*. In this case, the officials responsible took great pains to ensure that the new name selected was as agreeable to the applicant as it was acceptable to the court.

In cases involving non-Jewish residents without German citizenship, the court could be similarly accommodating. In an internal memo from 1906, attention was given to the name-change petitions of Polish workers residing in Germany.[18] According to the directive, applications to Germanize the surnames of these individuals should not be dismissed as insignificant. They had great potential social importance. Such name changes, the memo explained, represented a complete break with the Polish culture and traditions, and helped to ensure that the future children and grandchildren of the original petitioners would lose any and all connection to Poland.[19] To facilitate this assimilation process, these petitions should be expeditiously and, whenever possible, positively handled. Here one sees clearly the institutionalized agenda of using names and naming policies as a tool for engineering German identity. This mindset is important when considering the differential approach taken to Jewish name-change applicants.

An excellent illustration of this difference can be seen in a petition placed by a Jewish inhabitant of Sonnenberg, a district outside of Wiesbaden, just a few miles away from where the former Mr. Schwein resided. On February 25, 1920, a Mr. A. Cohn respectfully requested an official surname change on behalf of his wife and their three children. In his letter, Mr. Cohn gave the following motivation for his family's request: "we . . . are often forced to suffer derogatory names that ridicule Jewish customs and Jewish characteristics." Although Mr. Cohn's request was also granted, he was forced to supply the court with written proof of citizenship as well as a police report certifying that neither he nor any of his direct family members had a criminal record. Only after this documentation had been provided was the *Cohn* family granted permission to alter their surname to *Cramer*. Thus, while the court was willing to accept Mr. Schwein's word that he had no criminal intentions, the Cohn family was considered guilty until proven innocent. Such institutional mistrust was in no small measure due to the government's desire to progressively restrict Jewish access to German names.

More evidence of this restrictiveness is illustrated in the next case identified in the archives. In the summer of 1917, a Christian convert residing in the southwestern German state of Baden applied to have the spelling of his family surname changed from *Berliner* to *Berling*. Along with his request, the applicant provided evidence that he had converted from Judaism to Christianity and had accordingly raised all of his children in the Christian faith as well. Now that his sons had plans to join the military, the father worried that anti-Semitic reactions to the family name might thwart his sons' career aspirations and lead to their being ostracized by their fellow soldiers. Although conversion to Christianity on its own was no longer accepted as sufficient grounds for a name change, the applicant obviously fulfilled other prerequisites (i.e., financial disadvantage, social embarrassment, and personal distress). Despite this fact, Mr. Berliner's petition was flatly denied.

In the official ruling issued on July 13, 1917, the court grounded its decision by questioning the legal relevancy of an "Israelite's" conversion to Christianity for such an important administrative change. According to the court, the real motivation for such conversions usually had far less to do with religion and far more to do with greed. Furthermore, the court declared that the petitioner's assertion that an individual's career could be negatively affected by the sound of a surname and presumed origins was at best dubious.

This ruling is remarkable for several reasons. First, by referring to the petitioner as an "Israelite," the administrator effectively rejects the legitimacy of the applicant's Christian identity and thereby discounts the rightfulness of granting a name change to mark a religious conversion, despite the fact that for decades this had been a widespread legal practice. The administrator's acerbic rejection of the petitioner's claim of discrimination is particularly ironic given the fact that he displays the very same institutional anti-Semitism which he vehemently denied being in existence. It is important to stress once again that the bureaucrat's tirade was in response to the applicant's request to <u>slightly</u> alter the spelling of the family name from *Berliner* to *Berling*.

The striking incongruity of this ruling is made all the more poignant when contrasted against countless other cases where Christian applicants were routinely allowed to <u>entirely</u> alter their names to avoid the stigma, prejudice, and disdain which increasingly came with carrying a name perceived as being typically or even potentially Jewish. An excellent case in point comes from a petition lodged on June 20, 1919, by a law professor who asked to have his surname officially changed from *Lewin* to *Kundler*. According to the applicant, in his native city of Wiesbaden, he had rarely encountered difficulty with his surname as his family enjoyed a certain prominence and prestige in Hessia. However, during World War I, the unsuspecting petitioner was ordered to serve in the Reich's Department of Commerce [Reichswirtschaftsministerium] in Berlin. Once, there, Mr. Lewin soon discovered that his once so cherished surname earned him a very different kind of social reception. As he explained:

> Here in Berlin my name has caused me many unexpected difficulties. Because of it, strangers regularly mistake me for a Jew. . . . This erroneous assessment of my person not only offends my religious, but also my racial sensibilities [Rasse-Empfinden][20]. Were that not bad enough, it has also come to my attention that this misidentification by others has disadvantaged me in my work as a lawyer, a profession which already presents its own challenges in terms of opportunities for advancement. . . . This situation is made all the more bitter given my personal aversion to the Jewish nature. The similarity between my name and the names of the Russian communist Dr. Levin and Dr. Levine,[21] who thanks to their recent illegalities in Munich have sadly achieved much public attention, has made my desire for a name change that much more urgent.[22]

While the applicant Mr. Lewin may well have been a familiar VIP in provincial Wiesbaden, the Russian-born Jewish émigré Eugen Leviné was internationally recognized as one of the leading members of the German Communist Party, along with other influential intellectual leftists (e.g., Rosa Luxemburg, Leo Jogiches, Clara Zetkin, and Franz Mehring). By the time his Wiesbaden doppelganger arrived in Berlin, Leviné had already made quite a public name for himself by, for example, helping to organize mass anti-war demonstrations throughout Berlin. In the spring of 1919, some five months after the discovery of the brutalized bodies of Rosa Luxemburg and Karl Liebknecht, Leviné was arrested and executed for high treason for his participation in a sweeping series of Communist uprisings throughout Bavaria. Paul Levi, a German Jewish leftist lawyer from Stuttgart, took over the political helm of the German Communist Party. After reviewing Mr. Lewin's petition, the German authorities declared that the fact that the German Christian applicant shared not only a similar surname but also the same profession was reason enough to grant a complete name change.

One factor which doubtlessly influenced the decision-making in both the Lewin and Berliner cases is the fact that the applications were filed during the terrific sociopolitical unrest of the post–WWI period. Even before the war's end, a not insignificant portion of the German population had come to believe that Jewish treachery was to blame for the international hostility they felt Germany was unfairly made to suffer. At the end of the war, that anti-Semitism fueled widespread accusations that Jewish-led war-profiteering was ultimately responsible for Germany's spectacular defeat, the crippling financial depression, and the mounting social unrest which plagued Germany's alltag. This wholistic scapegoating is exemplified in a newspaper article from the *Ostdeutsche Rundschau*, which appeared on June 25, 1919:

> The Jews have put our winning streak to an end and robbed us of the spoils of what would have been our victory. The Jews have taken an ax to the throne and chopped the laws of our monarchy to bits. The Jews have destroyed the middle class and spread racketeering and usury over the nation like the plague. They have turned the cities against the countryside, the workers against the government, and incited hatred across our Fatherland. The Jews have brought us the Revolution, and if we now, after the lost war, also lose our peace, then Juda will have had more than his fair share of the blame. German Volk, above and before everything else, do this: free yourself from the tyranny of the Jew![23]

In such a climate of naked anti-Semitism, Christian applicants who had what an increasing number of authorities considered to be the misfortune of having Jewish-sounding names were automatically granted onomastic refuge. By contrast, Jewish applicants who were made to suffer the same or worse mistreatment in response to their names were, more often than not, abandoned to their fate. The official reason given for this difference in practice was the protection of the nation's security. According to many government officials, the mere presence of Jews posed a clear and present danger to the national peace and should, therefore, be kept under close surveillance. To make that possible, it was essential that they be readily identifiable.

Internal government directives repeatedly warned officials to remain wary when Jewish applicants requested a name change, no matter how seemingly minor. Failure to do so could allow subversive Jewish forces to take root. Officials were repeatedly instructed to remain vigilant and report any incident in which a Jewish resident had used a name change to perpetrate a crime. The feedback received from local administrators must have been disappointing to security experts hoping to uncover tangible evidence of a large-scale Jewish conspiracy. Even in a city like Wiesbaden, with a rather sizeable Jewish community with roots going back to the fourteenth century, local officials reported on December 8, 1921, that there had not been even one single case uncovered in which a Jewish resident had in any way misused a newly changed name for the purposes of committing a crime.[24]

In a similar report from the Burgermeister of Hagenbach in the Pfalz, the following report was filed: "After the careful examination of the city records, it has been determined that Jewish residents have indeed changed their family names at an unusually high rate. However, the new names which they have taken on are all, without exception, Jewish."[25] Despite such findings, the belief that the sole reason for Jewish residents to alter their names was to conceal a past or future crime remained resilient and widespread. In a 1920 issue of *The Sentinel*, an article entitled "Jews Forbidden to Adopt Gentile Names" chronicled this prejudice. In the Prussian Parliament, Deputy Mumm reportedly stated that the courts must take all measures "to prevent Jews from changing their names" as "such a tendency among the Jews was obvious, and constituted a 'menace.'"[26] Another example of such institutionalized prejudice can be seen in the following ordinance issued on November 15, 1921, from the Prussian Minister of the Interior, Adolf Köster:

> Based on the edict issued by the Prussian government on the 3rd of November 1919, scores of applicants bearing foreign names have successfully applied for the alteration of their name into German-sounding ones. The primary reason given for these petitions is that the applicant, despite having German identity, is subject to multiple acts of hostility and disadvantages as a consequence of carrying a foreign name. Up until now, such petitions have been regularly taken into consideration. . . . Given the fact, however, that this opportunity can be abused by certain elements who use such applications to conceal their foreign lineage for the purpose of better concealing their anti-German activities, I hereby formally request that thorough investigations be conducted to determine whether there is any reason to suspect that a proposed name change could be used for subversive activities aimed against the German society.[27]

Köster was not alone in his mission. There were many within the National Socialist Workers' Party (NSDAP) who held similar views. In the Reichstag elections of May 1924, the newly organized party managed to secure thirty-two seats. Less than a year later, in December 1924, another fourteen seats were added to the list. Once in the Parliament, the delegates wasted no time in introducing a wave of venomous proposals designed to address what they felt was the largest threat to the nation's security: the secret infiltration of "the Jew." This was precisely the subject of the proposal introduced by representative Ernst Graf zu Reventlow[28] on June 26, 1929. Speaking on behalf of the NSDAP, the northern German marine officer turned publicist, took the floor before a crowded Reichstag and delivered a fiery declaration of hatred:

> Over the past few years, we have been demanding the forced deportation of all JEWS who have immigrated to Germany since 1914. Unfortunately, the current conditions in Germany are not yet such to allow the implementation of this measure. In the meantime, however, the sensibility of the German Volk to the alien and destructive nature of the Jewish Volk has continued to deepen and spread. . . . A former

Justice Minister once declared before a Jewish alliance that both he
and the cabinet at the time considered everyone who possessed German citizenship to be a German. . . . We condemn in the strongest
terms possible the fallacy that a naturalized Jew is a German![29]

In reaction to this declaration, the NSDAP representative was forced to temporarily pause given the eruption of jeers from the parliamentarians representing
the Communist Party. After waiting a few moments for the opposition to quiet
down, he resumed his speech and demanded that the German Volk be made
aware of the "Jewish invasion" that threatened to take over the country. From
the average doormen to Ministers of Parliament, the nation was being infiltrated
at every level of society. Shouting over the rising cacophony of jeers, taunts, and
calls to sit down, the sea captain continued his tirade and delivered his Party's
solution to the "nation's infestation." "WE DEMAND THE PUBLIC IDEN-
TIFICATION OF EVERY SINGLE JEW IN GERMANY!"[30]

Amid the riotous calls of indignation from the left, the NSDAP leader
was greeted with a calamitous ovation of support from the right. Spurned on
equally by the condemnation as from the applause, the representative repeated
the Party's demands, clearly enunciating each word, before going on to declare
what form that identification should take: "Until the day comes that the Jew
is removed from every single public office," Reventlow declared, "his name
must be marked with his proper racial affiliation!" To make sure that his tirade achieved the maximum insult and injury, he pressed on with a series of
examples: "The JEW MINISTER OF FINANCE HILFERDING! The JEW
UNDERSECRETARY BAD!! The JEW REICHSTAG REPRESENTATIVE
BERNHARD!!!"[31]

With this the opposition exploded. "This is simply OUTRAGEOUS!," one
representative declared! "How about 'the JEW Reventlow!,'" another parliamen-
tarian jeered in a failed attempt at sarcasm. "How about 'the PSYCHOPATH
REVENTLOW!,'" a colleague offered instead. On the other side of the house,
Reventlow's speech was being frenetically received with congratulatory cheers of
"BRAVO!" At the pinnacle of the political kerfuffle, Reventlow uttered one last
prophetic sentence before taking his seat: "THAT would be a step towards our
final goal: the removal of the cuckoo from the German nest!" The perfidious
ingenuity of this zoological analogy is explained in the nesting behavior of this
species.

Cuckoos are said to lay their eggs in the nests of other birds, forcing other
species to feed their young. Over time, as the baby cuckoos grow larger and
stronger, they kick their fellow hatchlings out of the nest, one by one, pushing
them over the edge to their deaths. For this reason, the analogy of the cuckoo
was a powerful and common one among the Nazis when describing Jewish
residents. In one word, they were able to allude to the hidden danger of so-called

strangers sitting in their midst, profiting from their labors, and endangering the lives of their defenseless children.

For all of the vitriol, outrage, acrimony, and indignance expressed on that day, the very next day, on June 27, 1929, the Reichstag returned to business as usual. There was much on the agenda that day. There was the debate over changing the sugar tax, the discussion of the nation's mill industry and the processing of domestic grains, and there were adjustments to be made in the tariff on German beer. But nowhere on the agenda was there a single word mentioned about the NSDAP plans announced the day before. That, as Reventlow prophesized, would simply have to wait a bit longer, but the time was drawing near.

On December 23, 1932, the Reichskommissioner, General Kurt von Schleicher, issued an updated set of name-change guidelines.[32] Within this document, an entire segment (section 6) was devoted to the names of Jews. Government officials were once again warned that many Jewish name-change petitioners had as their single purpose the concealment of their ancestry, and such identity fraud could not be tolerated. Officials were therefore instructed to reject all applications made by Jewish residents that could be used to conceal their identity.[33] The only exceptions to be made were cases in which Jewish petitioners could demonstrate that their name provoked truly exceptionally negative reactions. As examples, the surnames *Itzig* and *Schmul* were given. In such rare cases, the applicant's petition could be (but needn't be) granted under the double proviso that the new surname was phonologically similar to the original name; and the new surname could be readily identified as belonging to a Jew.[34] The practical result of this policy was clear: regardless of their religion, citizenship, standing, or predicament, persons with Jewish parentage were to remain readily, onomastically identifiable.

On April 3, 1933, an internal government memorandum from the Ministry of the Interior issued yet another restriction regarding name-change applicants. It was decreed that name-change petitioners with Jewish or Jewish-sounding names could only have their application approved if they could provide birth certificates to verify that neither they nor their parents or grandparents were of Jewish heritage. Only in this way, the memorandum stated, was it possible to determine if the applicant was truly a Christian.[35] Taken together, these policy directives reflect a radical departure from years of onomastic policies. No longer were the constructs of Christianity and Judaism to be treated as categories of individual religious choice. Instead, they were to be re-constructed as socio-biological classifications of racial inheritance (i.e., Aryan and non-Aryan). In line with this ideological shift, on September 6, 1934, the Prussian Minister of the Interior issued a directive that officials should remain positively predisposed to all applications requesting the Germanization of a foreign name, except, that is, in cases where there was reason to believe that the petitioner was "not of Aryan mindset."[36] These anti-Semitic governmental directives reflected the significant changes occurring at the grassroots level all across the nation.

What began as a personal aversion soon developed into a national obsession. All around the Reich, public officials and private citizens fixated upon expunging non-Aryan names from daily life. The inanity and extremity of the attempt is illustrated in a citizen's complaint sent to government officials in Rostock on March 22, 1933.[37] "In view of the national turnaround that has taken place in Germany," A. J. Schliemann wrote, "I am personally of the opinion that it is completely inappropriate to feature Jewish names like David, Nathan, and Samuel in the alphabet code printed in the telephone book. I would assume that there are suitable German names that could be identified. I hope that in the next printing my suggestion will be taken into consideration."

The code to which the concerned Berlin resident referred was a standardized list of names that the government recommended telephone-users resort to when static on the line made comprehension extremely difficult and it became necessary to spell out single words or phrases. For example, instead of saying the word "medal," which might be confused with the near homophone "metal," a caller was encouraged to say: "I said medal . . . M as in Mary, E as in Edward, D as in David, A as in Anna, and L as in Larry." To expedite this system of communication, telephone books were printed with a standardized set of names that the government had extensively tested for maximum clarity and familiarity. According to Schliemann, many of the names on that list were, however, no longer acceptable for a loyal National Socialist. Although considerable time and money had been invested in developing this nationwide list, the officials in Rostock decided it was best to alert the regional office about this complaint. That office in turn contacted those responsible in the Reichstag. After careful investigation, a final decision was reached: the list of names must be Aryanized.

In fact, the government authorities decided to make changes even more radical than the original complainant had suggested and altered 47 percent of the original list.[38] The Biblical names *Zacharias, Samuel, Nathan, Jakob,* and *David* were all expunged and replaced with *Zeppelin*, the surname of Count Ferdinand von Zeppelin who pioneered Germany's fleet of hydrogen dirigibles; *Siegfried*, the name of the protagonist in Richard Wagner's opera, "die Nibelungenlied"; *Nordpol*, German for "North Pole"; *Jot*, the tenth letter of the German alphabet; and *Dora*, the future name of an underground forced labor camp which would claim the lives of approximately 11,000 people. In addition, *Yspilon*, the name of the German letter "y," was also replaced with *Ypern*, the name of the Belgian city in which the German military used poisonous gas for the very first time during World War I.

Although there seems to have been widespread agreement over the necessity of eliminating names which might offend National Socialists' sensibilities, exactly which names could truly be considered "Jewish" seems to have been a point of contention among the responsible policy-makers. As one official argued on March 25, 1933:

> The complainant seems to have failed to recognize the fact that these male names originated from the Old Testament and have been subsequently borne by not only Jews but also by exceedingly well-respected men of the Christian faith. The removal of these names from the code would certainly, at this moment in time generate considerable annoyance among the Jewry. It would also find little agreement among members of the Protestant and Catholic religions. Moreover, this action might also result in attacks from abroad, a consequence that would hardly be conducive to the national movement here in Germany.[39]

The discussion over whether to make these onomastic changes was further complicated by an unforeseen obstacle. One of the NS decision-makers happened to have the forename *Jakob* himself and took considerable umbrage at the suggestion that his name was "Jewish." As Reich Lieutenant Sprenger wrote, "The first name Jakob, a name which I have the honour of carrying myself, cannot be considered Jewish in today's times. . . . One has to consider the tens of thousands of people who would be grossly insulted through such a decree."[40] Despite this personal appeal, *Jakob* was eliminated along with all of the other names. This case indicates how quickly and unexpectedly one could find oneself having the "wrong name." The mad scramble among residents to exchange names that they or others perceived as sounding "un-German" could be clearly detected in the archival records, as one application after another was filed by citizens seeking to Aryanize their names.

On March 12, 1931, for example, a police sergeant by the name of *F. Langowsky* submitted a petition to have his family surname changed to "something more German." According to his accompanying personal letter of explanation, the police sergeant explained that his current Polish name was the source of great personal distress not only because he, his father, and his father's father were all Prussian citizens, but also because of the political tensions between Germany and Poland.[41] In the event that his name could not be Germanized, the sergeant requested that he be allowed to take on the maiden name of his deceased mother: *Schmidt*. Not surprisingly perhaps, the petitioner's request to adopt his mother's last name was granted. In this case, the officer's name change was initiated by the name-bearer himself. Just ten years later, the state would make name changes mandatory for all members of law enforcement with surnames that had easily discernible Slavic origins. In a 1941 internal directive issued by the Ministry of the Interior,[42] the following instructions are given:

The political and cultural challenges that are being faced by our Volk in areas which were wrested from the East thanks to superior German weaponry now demand that a hard line be taken with reference to the German culture and that a clear and sharp delineation be maintained between us and the foreign peoples who populate these areas. It is of the utmost importance that each and every German, wherever members of foreign peoples are encountered, maintain a stance that leaves no question open as to his inner and outer allegiance to the German Reich. This directive is of particular importance for police officials who are in the most visible position of power and who, as representatives of the German governmental authority, will come in constant close contact with those populations. This being the case, it can prove counterproductive when a family name with Polish, Czech, or Russian origins is mistakenly read as either a sign of either belonging to or being sympathetic with said foreigners. It is therefore desired that the bearers of Polish, Czech, or Russian family names who are employees of the police force within the Reich change their names as is prescribed by both the law which came into effect on the 5th of January 1938 (RGBl. I. Pg. 9) as well as the Ministerial Directive issued on the 8th of January (RMBLiV. Pg. 69). . . . The same is expected of employees who work for fire departments, however, with the interim codicil that this directive first be applied to those employees who work in areas with Polish or Czech sub-populations.[43]

In the accordance with the above directive, on January 3, 1942, police lieutenant *R. Rosnowski* of the Trier Police Department applied to have his family's surname changed. Despite the above-mentioned directive, applicants for such name changes were still required to submit a large number of documents to complete the process. In addition to completing the required official form, the police officer submitted the following documentation: (1) certification of Aryan ancestry; (2) verification of Rosnowski's Aryan lineage by the police force; (3) the birth certificates of each of the Rosnowski family members; (4) the marriage certificate of Mr. and Mrs. Rosnowski; (5) a letter of support from the Koblenz police department; (6) a letter of support from the Lord Mayor; (7) a personal declaration of agreement from each member of the Rosnowski family; (8) certification of approval from the Koblenz district court; and (9) an extract from the local judicial record on each member of the Rosnowski family.[44] Less than a month after submitting this mountain of paperwork, the petition was granted and the family's surname was officially changed to *Roden*.

The hunt for Aryan names not only was open for natural-born citizens but also extended to would-be naturalized Germans who wished to join the Reich. In a directive issued by the Reich Ministry of the Interior, state officials were informed that foreign nationals deemed suitable to hold German citizenship also had the right to carry a German name. For that reason, officials were instructed to suggest that applicants with non-German names complete the paperwork for a name change before the naturalization process had been completed. Interestingly, the ordinance also explicitly stated that officials were not, however, to apply force.[45] In other words, the right to bear a German name was to be treated as a privilege, an honor, a birthright reserved for those with the desired lineage.

Name-change petitions filed by Aryans with non-German heritage typically had a good chance of being granted. However, officers often insisted that the newly adopted name allow a direct link to be made between the applicant's new and original name. This link was often achieved through translation. For example, according to the archival records, in early December 1932, officials granted a name change for a German miner from the Mengede district of Dortmund. The petitioner's original surname was *Orlowski*, a derivative of the Polish word *orzel* meaning "eagle."[46] The miner was officially given permission to adopt the German last name *Adler* which also means "eagle."[47] A similar case was identified involving a petitioner living in Kassel. According to the applicant, his whole life, he had suffered ridicule and humiliation because of his Polish last name, *Zbikowski*. For example, in school, whenever he made the smallest grammatical mistake, he immediately received the stinging rebuke: "Of course, what do you expect from a Pollack?!" As a young man, he found it impossible to find permanent employment as a trained hairstylist. Despite being an excellent worker, his employers refused to take him on permanently with the explanation: "It simply wouldn't work. I could only refer to you by your first name. Imagine if I used your surname? My clients would never allow a Pole to style their hair!" Evidently unable to find gainful, permanent employment as a civilian, the young Zbikowski looked forward to finally being able to prove himself as a soldier. However, he worried that he would once again be rejected by his peers, once they heard his name. For that reason, before signing his letter with an emphatic, "Heil Hitler!," the desperate applicant plead that his petition be granted so that he might proudly join the Wehrmacht with his new German moniker. According to the records, Zbikowski's wish was granted and his name was officially changed to *Spieker*.[48]

Ridicule in reaction to names that were considered "non-German" was not limited to the private sphere, of course. In public discourse, such rants were also commonplace, as the next case identified in the archives demonstrated. In 1930, the winner of the Miss Germany beauty contest was crowned at the Kaiserhof luxury hotel in Berlin. The first place was awarded to a stunning ebony-haired actress and fashion model named *Dorit Ritnokowski*. Along with cosmetics, flowers, modeling contracts, and a chance to compete in the Miss Universe contest, Miss Ritnokowski was also the recipient of boundless hate-mail from enraged National Socialists. In response to the AP news story about the beauty queen's victory, a Dr. Gattelmair wrote the following incredulous message: "A '**Dorit**

Ritnokowski' is Miss Germany 1930?! That is a slap in the face for everyone with a deep sense of patriotism."[49] Although Miss Germany did not succumb to outside pressures to alter her name, at the same time that she was accepting her crown, another young woman gladly and enthusiastically traded in her name in hopes of capturing the undisputed title: The First Lady of the Third Reich.

*****

Johanna Maria Magdalena was born on November 11, 1901, in Berlin-Kreuzberg.[50] As the illegitimate daughter of a poor housemaid, she originally carried the surname of her mother Auguste Behrend.[51] A short time after her birth, however, her mother married Dr. Oskar Ritschel, the wealthy engineer in whose home her mother had previously worked as a house servant. During the three-year marriage, Dr. Ritschel developed a close relationship with Johanna or "Magda" as everyone called her. He even made sure that Magda received an excellent education in a strict Catholic school in Vilvoorde, Brussels.[52] However, he did not formally adopt her. In 1906, after her divorce from Dr. Ritschel, Magda's mother met and married a well-to-do Jewish businessman, Richard Friedländer. Judging from the fact that Dr. Ritschel attended his ex-wife's wedding and the two newlyweds moved to Brussels shortly after the ceremony, it seems safe to assume that there was little or no animosity within the small patchwork family— aside, that is, from a good-natured male rivalry between Friedländer and Ritschel who often vied for Little Magda's affection. There is no indication, however, that she suffered from the push and pull. Instead, she seemed to enjoy the power and attention this masculine competition brought, and whether knowingly or unknowingly, she would repeat this configuration throughout her life.

In 1914, when German troops invaded Belgium during World War I, Magda, her mother, and her stepfather fled back to Berlin, leaving much of their belongings and wealth behind them. The conditions for the civilian population in the German metropolis were catastrophic thanks not only to the war but also a disastrous series of crop failures. The result was crushing unemployment and widespread starvation. For city dwellers, the average caloric input was only about 1,000 per day.[53] With classic Berlin sarcasm, the city residents summed up their dire predicament saying: there was too much food to finally die, but still too little to truly live. To help feed his family, the once prosperous Friedländer worked long hours as an assistant waiter in a luxury hotel in Berlin.[54] Slowly but surely, he managed to rebuild a bit of his former life but his marriage was shattered. In 1914, Auguste filed for her second divorce. In a show of support to the man who had always been such a loving father, Magda changed her last name from *Behrend* to *Friedländer*. She did not retain that surname for long, however.

By 1920, she met the fabulously wealthy, recently widowed industrialist Günther Quandt. The family dynasty had made its initial fortune in the manufacture and sale of military uniforms during World War I. On the basis of this capital, immediately after the war, Günther Quandt invested heavily and successfully in the armament industry. After his children took over the business, the family continued to amass more wealth in the automotive industry through such globally recognized names as BMW and Daimler-Benz.[55] Today, the Quandts remain one of the most affluent families in Germany with an estimated wealth of over 30 billion Euros.[56]

One of the keys to that family success has been the capacity to accurately assess the possible gains against the potential risks. When the widowed father met the remarkably cultivated young Magda, the potential benefits of taking on such an intelligent, attractive, and vivacious wife twenty years his junior were more than obvious. However, the union would not come without risk. In the end, the tycoon offered Magda his hand in marriage upon two non-negotiable conditions: (1) she convert to Protestantism and (2) she give up her Jewish-sounding surname *Friedländer* and take on the last name of her mother's first husband, Dr. Ritschel. Magda consented. On July 15, 1920, at the age of nineteen, she was officially registered as the lawful daughter of Dr. Oskar Ritschel and became *Fraulein Johanna Maria Magdalena Ritschel.* This was the first but not the last time that Magda would betray her stepfather for her own personal gain.

On January 4, 1921, Magda married one of the richest men in all of Europe in a luxury hotel in Bad Godesberg, Germany. To her wedding, the young bride wore a swank black silk designer dress adorned with a white silk lace scarf draped stylishly about her shoulders and tucked neatly about her cleavage. The resulting décolleté of the Belgian-raised bride did not reveal more than a promise, but for the stilted Prussian industrialist it was precisely this penchant to flirt with social disaster that had made him question whether he had made the right choice. Approximately eleven months later, the new Mrs. Günther Quandt gave birth to her first son, *Harald.* What could have been a joyous time was anything but for the young bride and new mother. Her husband, it seems, was still mourning the unexpected death of his first wife. Antonie Ewald, had been one of nearly 40 million people to die between 1918 and 1920 in an outbreak of the Spanish flu.[57] Many years later, Günther Quandt described his feelings after his wife's death: "I was of the opinion that a person can only give and receive true love once in a lifetime."[58] As far as the multimillionaire was concerned, with the death of his first wife, his time for true love had come and gone.

Thus, while the tycoon's twelve-year marriage to his "Toni" seems to have been very happy and loving,[59] his marriage to Magda was anything but. Indeed, the main reason for his proposal seems to have been far less romantic than pragmatic. Quandt needed a mother for his two pre-teen boys, *Hellmut* and

Herbert. Upon meeting the energetic young lady whom their father brought home one day, the boys even suggested themselves that he hire the pretty girl as a housekeeper or nanny.[60] When the sons learned that his father intended to marry the attractive Fräulein, they were surprised but positive. They readily took to their young stepmother, as did their Aunt Elisabeth Quandt or "Ello." The wife of Günther's brother, Ello also had had her difficulties fitting into the Quandt family. She and Magda immediately hit it off and became life-long friends.[61] Ironically, the only person who did not seem to take to Magda was her husband, Günther. As Ello later recounted in an interview after the war, despite her elegance and charm, Magda could never measure up to her brother-in-law's memory of his beloved first wife, Antonie.

What began for the capricious starry-eyed bride as an incredible fairytale soon mutated into a personal nightmare, as her relationship to her husband went from painfully awkward to hopelessly estranged to openly contemptuous. Despite the mutual disappointment, for Quandt, fear of a scandal meant divorce was out of the question. Magda had no such scruples. If her husband would not give her a divorce, she would wrest it from him. Her first strategy was to try to infuriate her husband by engaging in a series of affairs.[62] When that strategy did not work she tried another: blackmail. After locating a secret assortment of letters that had been written to her husband from young women whom he had "entertained" before their marriage, Magda confronted her husband with the correspondence and offered him a deal: her freedom for the letters. Quandt immediately acquiesced. In the end, she was able to obtain not only the divorce she so desperately wanted but also a monthly alimony of about 4,000 RM; a stipend of 50,000 RM to decorate her luxurious apartment; a fund of 20,000 RM for emergencies; and the freedom to use the Quandt family estate, Severin, whenever she liked.[63]

At the age of twenty-eight, she had managed to box her way out of a relationship with a man who had demanded that she deny her faith, give up her name, and betray her family. Just two years later, she would meet her second husband who would make those very same demands and more. For her next lover, she would have to immediately break off any and all ties with her stepfather, Friedländer. Her mother, Auguste, would also have to relinquish the surname *Friedländer* and revert back to her original maiden name, *Behrend*.[64] And she had to promise to completely disavow and repudiate all professional and personalties with anyone of Jewish ancestry, including her first love, Chaim Arlosoroff.

When faced with these conditions, Magda did precisely what she had always done: she followed the path that promised the most power; and if nothing else, her new lover had that in abundance. Indeed, what her fiancé may have lacked in attractiveness, he more than made up for in charisma and ambition. When it came to achieving his goals, there was no price too high. Magda, it seems, had finally met her match. On December 19, 1931, in the same wedding dress and scarf she had worn eleven years earlier, she officially took on the name under which she would become infamous: *Frau Magda Goebbels.*

Seven years later, on June 15, 1938, a little over a month after Magda had given birth to her sixth child *Hedwig Johanna*, her long-forgotten stepfather Richard Friedländer was transferred to the Buchenwald Concentration Camp in Weimar, Germany. Once there, the fifty-seven-year-old man was assigned to one of the hardest work details in the camp, the rock quarries. After only a few months, the SS issued a final report that the "shiftless Jew" Friedlander, prisoner number 5927, had died at 7:15 from pneumonia and heart failure.[65] The date was February 18, 1939, three days after his fifty-eighth birthday.[66]

It was an unspoken rule that the name *Friedländer* was never to be mentioned in the Goebbels home. A compulsive diary writer, the propaganda minister never mentioned the name *Friedländer* in any of his entries. The Jewish connection to the first lady of the German Reich might have been completely lost forever had it not been for a few scattered documents recovered in German archives. Only in recent years, as public and scholarly interest in the wives of the Nazi elite has increased, was the story of Richard Friedländer unearthed. In the attempt to piece together the personal fragments of the woman named *Behrend, Friedländer, Ritschel, Quandt,* and *Goebbels,* some researchers have concluded that among the many perverse secrets the Reichsminister's wife held about the party and its dealings with the "Jewish question," she may have also been hiding a disturbing personal secret of her own.[67]

The man whom she allowed to die in the stone pits of the Buchenwald Concentration Camp may not have been her stepfather at all but her real biological father.[68] As horrible as this thought is, it is certainly not incongruent to think that a mother who was able to directly participate in the murder of six of her seven children[69] would also allow her father, be he biological or not, to be murdered in a Nazi concentration camp.

It has not escaped notice that all of Magda's children were given names that began with the letter "H." Although one might be tempted to assume that this choice reflected her obsession with Adolf Hitler, this explanation is far too simple. The "H" pattern actually began many years before she even met Herr Hitler with her step-sons *Helmut* and *Herbert* Quandt, whom she had no part in naming. Her decision to name her first-born son *Harold* may have been made in an effort to fit in with the Quandt family tradition. Later on, during her marriage to Joseph Goebbels, this naming pattern was continued. However, the decision to give all of the Goebbels children names beginning with the letter "H" was not solely Magda's choice. On February 10, 1938, Goebbels wrote the following in his diary:

> Chatted with Magda, Mother. . . . The children are so sweet and so
> adorable. Holde [nickname for *Holdine*] is so lovely and delicate and

does honour to her name [Holdine: derived from the Old High German name "Holda" meaning femininity] Magda is doing well. We're looking for a name for our next child: Hartmann or Harder [both Germanic names meaning hard, strong, and powerful]. With hope, this next one will be a boy![70]

As it happened, none of the Reichsminister's wishes were granted. After *Holdine Kathrin*, the next child born into the Goebbels family was a girl whom they named *Hedwig Johanna* and the child after that was also a girl, *Heidrun Elisabeth*. *Helmut Christian*, the couple's third child together, would remain the only son Goebbels would have with Magda. It is interesting that precisely this child had been given nearly the same name as Günther Quandt's first son, *Hellmut Quandt*.[71] According to many accounts, Madga had been <u>extremely close</u> with her stepson and had mourned his loss long after his sudden death from sepsis.

What is of particular importance in the diary entry above, however, is the fact that Goebbels's own personal name choices also began with the letter "H." Whether or not the couple's love of H-names was ideologically motivated must remain speculation. However, as the party grew in strength, so too grew the desire to select a name that openly demonstrated one's allegiance to the Third Reich and its principles.

Of course, this was not true for everyone. There were also people who, despite being were classified as "Aryan," neither identified with nor were supportive of National Socialism. A legendary example comes from the members of the Weiße Rose [*White Rose*], a group of activists centered at the University of Munich who were horrified at how the values of their nation had become so contorted and twisted that acts that once would have been broadly condemned as criminal and immoral were now being publicly celebrated and exalted by the masses. Four of the group's founding members, Christoph Probst, Willi Graf, Alexander Schmorell, and Hans Scholl, had all been conscripted to serve as medics on the Eastern Front.[72] It was there that they saw first-hand what the Nazi slogan "blood and honor" truly meant. The carnage had to stop.

In impassioned fliers, the group called for the people of Germany to rise up and resist the fascist government that had taken over their country and brought with it injustice, immorality, and death. "[I]f the German youth do not finally take a stand" they warned, "[t]he name of Germany will forever remain disgraced."[73] What began as a small group of friends and family in the summer of 1942 became a tightly knit, well-organized, underground network of resistance. By the winter of 1943, their fliers could be read as far away as Berlin. Their success caught not only the attention of supporters, however. By February 1943, the Gestapo had been able to locate three of the group's leaders: Christian Probst and the Scholl siblings, Hans and Sophie. On February 22, 1943, all three were beheaded. Other arrests and beheadings followed: Alexander Schmorell, July 13, 1943; Willi Graf, October 1943; Professor Kurt Huber, July 13, 1943.

In the case of the White Rose, part of the strength of their group came from their love for one another as long-time confidants and relatives. In other cases, "Aryans" who refused to follow along with the NS program found themselves being betrayed by their family. Precisely this happened to movie actress Olga Schaub.[74] As Ms. Schaub reported in an interview she provided for the Nuremberg Trials, although she had never been interested in politics, the Nazis' anti-Semitism repulsed her. In the official English translation of her transcribed testimony, she explained why: "I could never be in accord with the program of the NSDAP . . . and was in no way willing to give up my relations with my Jewish friends at home or abroad." Her step-brother, SS-Obergruppenführer Julius Schaub, was an adjutant to Hitler and found her resistance to be an unacceptable liability. In an attempt to distance himself from her, he insisted that she stop using her real name and only use her stage name, *Jeannette Madlon*.

By 1939, his sister's nonconformity had turned into active resistance. She began to use her passport to travel back and forth from Germany to England. On her journeys, she secretly transported the belongings of her Jewish friends who hoped to make their escape to the United Kingdom. Schaub's activities did not go unnoticed, however. By 1940, she was placed under arrest. According to her testimony, she was informed by the police authorities that she was to be transferred to a camp as punishment for espionage. She was also informed that effective immediately, she had been assigned a new surname: *Schubert*. Should she ever use her real name *Olga Schaub* again or should it ever be discovered that she had mentioned her real name to another person, she would be immediately shot. After receiving these instructions, she was sent to Ravensbrück Concentration Camp.[75]

Once there, her "Aryan" classification afforded her certain privileges. For example, instead of being forced to perform hard manual labor, she was ordered to perform clerical work for the camp medical staff. Her duties included helping to prepare the final name lists of the prisoners whom the camp staff had deemed to be too ill or injured to work. As she recounted, "Many prisoners came in on their knees and beged [*sic*] the doctor to take them off the list but he refused." After a period of sixteen months, she was finally released from the camp with the warning that she would remain under surveillance and would be immediately returned to the camp if she attempted to re-establish contact with her racially undesirable associates, disclose any information about what she had witnessed, or use her birth name. No sooner had the war ended did she provide a detailed account of everything she had witnessed during her time in Ravensbrück: medical experiments, beatings, lethal injections, selections, the gas chamber, and the secret incineration of the countless bodies. At the end of her report, she declared that she hoped that she would finally be able to locate her Jewish friends. Maybe some of them had managed to survive. She signed her deposition *Olga Schaub*.

*****

The desire to establish a clearly defined legal line of demarcation between Aryans and non-Aryans did not come from government officials alone, but also from private citizens. In a 1934 letter written to the Reichsministerium, a Bochum-based lawyer sent in a proposal to protect German residents with Jewish-sounding names. Having the last name *Coblenzer*, the solicitor explained that he was all too aware of the fact that many Jewish residents also happened to carry surnames based on place names. This onomastic coincidence meant that countless German citizens like himself were repeatedly forced to defend themselves against public suspicion and ridicule. To end this untenable situation, the solicitor proposed that Germans be given special permission to affix the letter "D" to their names as an unambiguous marker of their German heritage [Deutschstämmigkeit]. In addition to this onomastic privilege, Coblenzer went on to propose that anyone of non-German heritage who deigned to use this onomastic marker should be made to face criminal charges. Although the idea of implementing a system which would allow the immediate differentiation of Jews and Aryans was positively received by the fascist members of the government, the suggestion that Germans should be the ones to either relinquish or alter their names was, for many, entirely unacceptable. Clearly, another solution had to be found.

On June 15, 1936, Hans Pfundtner, the State Secretary of the Reich's Ministry of the Interior and later lead designer of the infamous Nuremberg Race Laws, received a letter from the Head of the Reich's State Secret Police, **Geheim Staatspolizei** or GESTAPO, Heinrich Himmler. In that letter, Himmler indicated that the Fuehrer himself had ordered the introduction of formal legislation to once and for all prohibit Jews from taking on Aryan names such as *Siegfried* or *Thusnelda*. The law should, according to Hitler, also force Jews who already bore such names to immediately relinquish them.[76] To facilitate this onomastic segregation, the Fuehrer, according to Himmler's communique, had ordered the creation of an official registry of names which only Jews would be allowed to carry, such as *Lewi* or *Jakob*.

The difficulty in executing this directive was a familiar one: namely, drawing a clear dividing line between Jewish and Christian names. Rather than enter into long and contentious debates over rightful onomastic ownership, Pfundtner came up with what he felt was a brilliant strategy. While non-Jews would be free to continue using the German language variants of such contested Biblical names like *Josef* and *Johannes, Maria,* and *Elisabeth*, all Jews would be required to use the Hebraic equivalent (e.g., *Yosef* and *Yehochanan; Miryam,* and *Elisheva*).[77] In those cases where a matching Hebrew name did not exist, Jews would be forced to adopt an additional personal name from a governmental roster. Although this strategy seemed to provide an effective solution to the notorious problem of segregating Jewish and German names, it had three major drawbacks. First, the success of the Pfundtner proposal was largely predicated on a governmentally approved registry of Jewish names. However, no such national registry existed and was unlikely to be created in the near future. The second major obstacle was logistical. Requiring millions of people, both Jewish and Gentile, to alter their names would overwhelm administrators who already had their hands full implementing the many other segregationist policies introduced by the Nazis. Even if these administrative obstacles could be overcome, there was still the third hurdle: the Olympic Games.

*

In 1931, the International Olympic Committee (IOC) announced that both the winter and summer Games of 1936 would be held in Germany. The pronounce- ment generated immediate controversy. Supporters of the decision argued that the Games could offer Germany an excellent opportunity to rejoin the international community. Protesters countered that recent government actions undertaken by the NSDAP government such as barring non-Aryans from Ger- man sports clubs and restricting membership on Germany's Olympic teams to Aryan athletes should have automatically disqualified Germany as a potential host nation. To protest the IOC's decision and draw attention to the injustices being perpetrated in the Reich, for the first time in Olympic history, there was serious talk of boycotting the Games.

Support for the protest came from both sides of the Atlantic, with the United Kingdom, France, the Netherlands, and the United States leading the fight. However, after a series of negotiations, Nazi officials agreed to make a few key concessions such as reinstating a _few_ previously barred Jewish athletes to the German Olympic teams. For their part, the Olympic dignitaries who had been lavishly wined and dined during their pre-game inspections of Germany finally agreed not to support the boycott. However, the agreement between the IOC and the Nazi government was tenuous at best. Among the members of the Ger- man National Olympic Committee who had worked to broker the negotiations for the 1936 Games was none other than State Secretary for the Ministry of the Interior, Hans Pfundtner.

Sensitive to just how difficult it had been to reach an agreement, Pfundt- ner along with the rest of the Ministry of the Interior lobbied to postpone the introduction of any legislation that might ruffle more international feathers. To stop that from happening, on April 18, 1936, Pfundtner's office argued for a postponement in the onomastic legislation.[78] The naming policies could wait a bit longer. In the meantime, attention should be given to making sure that the Führer shone as the supreme and sovereign leader of the glorious Third Reich. The Games, it was reasoned, presented an unparalleled propaganda opportunity to put right the negative image that had been portrayed in the world press. After all, for the first time in Olympic history, the Games would also be televised. This milestone offered the Nazi Propaganda machine and its engineer, Joseph Goebbels, a historic opportunity to place the Führer and the National Socialists at the very center of the world stage. With that goal in mind, the potentially inflammatory naming legislation was put on hold and the Party attention and resources were focused on making the Olympic Games of 1936 an international success. Judging from the media reports issued during and immediately after the event, that goal was more than met. For sixteen days, Nazi Germany presented itself as the perfect host. As soon as their guests left, however, the regime quickly returned to business as usual: persecution, intimidation, torture, and mass murder. Helping the lethal machine run was the long-awaited naming legislation.

On January 5, 1938, the first *Law for the Alteration of Family and First Names* LAFFN-1 [Gesetz über die Änderung von Familien- und Vornamen] came into effect. In paragraph 7 of this law, it was decreed that any and all name-changes granted before January 30, 1933, could be revoked if the alteration was deemed "undesirable." In such cases, the petitioner and all those persons whose names changed along with him/her (e.g., children, spouses, siblings) would be required to re-assume their original name.[79] Importantly, the law did not indicate what conditions would make the reversal of a previously granted name change "desirable." Instead, it was simply stated that all such decisions were to fall under the discretionary power of the Minister of the Interior, Wilhelm Frick. This lack of definition not only meant that it was nearly impossible for residents to effectively protest such actions but it also meant that with one fell swoop Jewish residents who had sought or even found onomastic refuge from the Reich's mounting anti-Semitism were left vulnerable again. The only people who were able to find some modicum of refuge were those few with political or financial influence. One Jewish banker in Berlin, for example, was able to persuade German authorities to allow him to change his surname from *Levy* to *Hagen* on the condition that he pay 100,000 in gold marks.[80] For the vast majority of Jews residing in the Reich, however, this was clearly not an option.

For all of its menacing power, the LAFFN-1 had one major drawback. In theory it had made it possible to neatly repeal literally hundreds of years of name changes and expose countless numbers of Jewish residents. In practice, this strategy was entirely impracticable as it created a tremendous backlog of inquiries from nervous citizens and officials alike, all seeking clarification. For example, on October 12, 1938, the Burgermeister of Leimersheim, a small town in the Rhenish Palatinate, was confronted with just such an inquiry.[81] During the implementation of this regulation, the Leimersheim officials came across a Jewish family whose ancestors had been permitted to change their name to *Behr*. The question was whether or not this name change would also have to be revoked. In reviewing the case it was decided that it would be superfluous to do so, as the "new" surname was only borne by Jews in the area and was, as such, readily identifiable as Jewish. The same decision was reached in the neighboring town of Hagenbach, where the review of all the historical name changes that had been granted to Jewish residents only involved switches from one Jewish family name to another.[82] Before decisions in these and other cases could be reached, however, a mountain of paperwork had to be reviewed. Aside from the bureaucratic headaches this legislation was causing government workers, the LAFFN-1 had another major drawback. It only targeted Jewish residents who had formally undergone a name change and utterly failed to address the vast majority of the Jewish population who had never done so. What was needed then, the Nazis realized, was an additional policy which would make it possible to force all persons of Jewish heritage to clearly identify themselves as such.

One of the most popular suggestions involved requiring Jews to affix a stigmatized onomastic marker to their surname. For example, in 1936, Martin Bormann, the then personal secretary to Rudolf Hess, suggested that all Jews be required to affix the word "Jew" [Jude] to their surname.[83] Bormann's idea was by no means original. It was already common practice within anti-Semitic circles to preface any reference to the name of a Jewish person, be it in speech or in text, with this label. Joseph Goebbels, for example, almost exclusively used this pejorative form of address in his contributions to the fascist German publication, *Der Angriff*. Even in his private diaries, he maintained this convention in his frequent tirades (e.g., *der Jude Weiß, der Jude Wahlburg, Der Jude Frankfurter, der Jude Harry Bauer Beethoven*).[84] On April 24, 1936, Goebbels even had a directive released to the press via the Reich's Propaganda Ministry.[85] Effective immediately, the press was to preface the names of all leading Jewish Soviet officials and politicians with the label "der Jude" [the Jew].[86] Bormann's suggestion not only would help to further institutionalize this party practice; it would also transform what had commonly been considered a mark of uncultured, vulgar speech into standard formal parlance.

In an effort to add even more insult to the intended injury, other officials suggested that pejorative onomastic slurs be used for the affixation instead. Two popular candidates were "Jud(d)," which roughly translates into "Yid," and "Itzig," the name commonly given to Jewish characters in anti-Semitic jokes. Another suggested variant of this policy was to require all Jews to affix a hyphenated capital letter "J" to the end of every Jew's surname. According to the Ministry of the Interior, despite their simplicity and popularity, all of these suggestions would present authorities with a number of significant problems.[87]

Setting aside the exorbitant amount of money, personnel, and time which implementing these name policies would necessitate, German name law had long eschewed the widespread use of hyphenated double surnames which frequently led to unwanted inconsistencies in cataloging and had resulted in some families inheriting long chains of surnames. Alongside these drawbacks, the implementation of the name policies would also have the unwanted effect of marking residents with partial or complete Aryan ancestry. For example, according to the long-standing German naming traditions and laws, brides were obliged to take on the last name of their respective grooms. The introduction of an onomastic policy that targeted Jewish family surnames would mean that Aryan women married to Jewish men would also by default be required to carry the stigmatized surname. The same would be true of any children (both biological and adopted) resulting from such Jewish-Aryan marriages. Although this prospect did not deter ardent anti-Semites, at the time when these plans were initially being lain, there were still powerful party members who were hesitant to accept legislation which would automatically place people with partial (e.g., *Halbjuden* [half-Jewish] or *Vierteljuden* [quarter-Jewish]) or even complete Aryan ancestry on par with those who had complete Jewish ancestry (i.e., *Volljuden*). To avoid such unwanted side-effects, a different strategy was needed.

For better or worse, the onus of finding this legislative solution largely fell to an introverted lawyer from Stuttgart by the name of Hans Josef Maria Globke. A natural-born follower who had quickly caught the attention of his superiors for being able to write sleek legislation that was relatively free of unforeseen loopholes, Globke was given the task of developing new onomastic codes which would immediately and differentially identify people with Jewish lineage. After studying the problem for some time, Globke decided upon an entirely new approach.

Instead of requiring Jews to alter their pre-existing surnames, he proposed they be forced to take on a second, pre-selected, gendered first name. For Jewish women, the compulsory personal name put forward was *Sara*,[88] and for Jewish men, *Israel*. According to Globke's plan, the only ones who would be exempted from this regulation were Jews who either were under the age of fifteen or had a first name so conspicuously Jewish that no additional second name was needed for identification. Ever the perfectionist, Globke saw to it that there was an official listing of these prototypical Jewish first names. This listing was developed by the Reich's Department for Ancestral Research [Reichstelle für Sippenforschung].[89] Three successive versions of the list of Jewish names were drawn up between the autumn and the winter of 1938.

During that time, the list of names was repeatedly expanded to include new entries. Just a small sampling of the male and female names that were added between February and October of 1938 version includes the following: *Absalom, Amon, Ehud, Barak, Elihu, Herodes, Jehuda, Mordeschaj, Sered,* and *Zeruja;* and *Abigail, Bela, Jezabel, Rebekka, Reha, Zilla.* At the same time that many names were being added to the list, a few select names were stricken and reclassified as Aryan. Examples here include *Blume, Deborah, Geisel, Heilchen, Glückchen,*

Glückel, Golde, Heilchen, Heinde, Kendel, Lilith, Male, Michle, Thamar, Traune, Veilchen, Vögelche, and *Ziper.* A careful examination of these Aryanized names revealed no clear linguistic pattern. Instead, it seems that the decision was made purely on the personal tastes of the reviewer: Adolf Hitler. Table 2.1 presents the final list of male and female names which was released in August 1938.[90]

There are two aspects that are particularly striking when reviewing these lists. The first concerns the names that were conspicuously missing: a point sarcastically commented upon in the August 29, 1938 issue of *The Palestine Press.* As staff reporters working there and elsewhere remarked, the decision about what was and was not Jewish seemed far more to do with politics than linguistics.

> It is pointed out that certain names like Peter, Mary, Julius, although of foreign origin, have been absorbed in the German language and therefore are not regarded as Jewish. The first name of the notorious anti-Semitic Leader Streicher is Julius. The names of Joseph and Jacob also do not appear in the list. Both Dr. Goebbels, the Minister for Propaganda and Dr. Buerckel the Reich Commissioner in Austria are named Joseph, while many Nazi leaders bear the name of Jacob.[91]

Just as striking as the names that were absent from the list were those names that were included. In a secret diary devoted to documenting the Nazis' use of language,[92] the philologist Victor Klemperer detailed the reaction of the largely assimilated German-speaking Jewish population to this onomastic assembly. According to him, the names left to the Jews by the National Socialists either sounded completely alien to the German ear or were so ridiculously stereotypical as to invoke feelings of embarrassment. Only a tiny fraction, he lamented, possessed the "dignity of the Old Testament names."[93] The fact that so many German Jewish residents perceived so many names on the list as being outright ridiculous to irredeemably repugnant was, to be certain, not a disadvantage in the eyes of many a Nazi.[94] However, Globke's reasoning for having settled upon this set of names may have been quite different, yet equally perfidious. The names featured on the list of exemptions were extremely rare within the culturally assimilated Jewish population of Germany. At the time that the Globke list was released, the most common names among Jewish residents in Germany were also extremely popular within Gentiles. The top ten names for German-born Jewish females during this period were: (1) *Rosa*; (2) *Bert(h)a*; (3) *Johanna*; (4) *Else/Elsa*; (5) *Frieda*; (6) *Mart(h)a*; (7) *Gertrud/Gertraud*; (8) *Anne/Anni/Anne*; (9) *Margaret(h)e/Margaret(h)a*; (10) *Hedwig.* And the top ten names for males were: (1) *Max*; (2) *Julius*; (3) *Her(r)man*; (4) *Alfred*; (5) *Joseph*; (6) *Han(n)s*; (7) *Si(e)gfri(e)d*; (8) *K/Curt*; (9) *Jac/kob*; and (10) *Ernst.*[95]

Table 2.1   Forenames Initially Designated as Posing an Exemption to the LAFFN-2

MALE NAMES	
A	Abel, Abieser, Abimelech, Abner, Absalom, Ahab, Ahasja, Ahasver, Akiba, Amon, Anschel, Aron, Asahel, Asaria, Ascher, Asriel, Assur, Athalja, Awigdor, Awrum
B	Bachja, Barak, Baruch, Benaja, Berek, Berl, Boas, Bud
C	Chaggai, Chai, Chajin, Chamor, Chananja, Chanoch, Chaskel, Chawa, Chiel
D	Dan, Denny
E	Efim, Efraim, Ehud, Eisig, Eli, Elias, Elihu, Eliser, Eljakim, Elkan, Enoch, Esau, Esra, Ezechiel
F	Faleg, Feibisch, Feirel, Feitel, Feiwel, Feleg
G	Gad, Gdaleo, Gedalja, Gerson, Gideon
H	Habakuk, Hagai, Hemor, Henoch, Herodes, Hesekiel, Hillel, Hiob, Hosea
I	Isaac, Isai, Isachar, Isboseth, Isidor, Ismael, Israel, Itzig
J	Jachiel, Jasse, Jakar, Jakusiel, Jecheskel, Jechiel, Jehu, Jehuda, Jehusiel, Jeremia, Jerobeam, Jesaja, Jethro, Jistach, Jizack, Joab, Jochanan, Joel, Jomteb, Jona, Jonathan, Josia, Juda
K	Kainan, Kaiphas, Kaleb, Korach
L	Laban, Lazarus, Leew, Leiser, Levi, Lewek, Lot, Lupu
M	Machol, Maim, Malchisua, Maleachi, Manasse, Mardochai, Mechel, Menachem, Moab, Mochain, Mordeschai, Mosche, Moses
N	Nachschon, Nachum, Naftali, Nathan, Naum, Nazary, Nehab, Nehemia, Nissim, Noa, Nochem
O	Obadja, Orew, Oscher, Osias
P	Peisach, Pinchas, Pinkus
R	Rachmiel, Ruben
S	Sabbatai, Sacher, Sallum, Sally, Salo, Salomon, Salusch, Samaja, Sami, Samuel, Sandel, Saudik, Saul, Schalom, Schaul, Schinul, Schmul, Schneur, Schoachana, Scholem, Sebulon, Semi, Sered, Sichem, Si-ach, Simson
T	Teit, Tewele
U	Uri, Uria, Uriel
Z	Zadek, Zedekia, Zephania, Zeruja, Zewi

(Continued)

Table 2.1 (Continued)

FEMALE NAMES	
A	Abigail
B	Baschewa, Beile, Bela, Bescha, Bihri, Bilha, Breine, Briewe, Brocha
C	Chana, Chawa, Cheiche, Cheile, Chinke
D	Deiche, Dewaara, Driesel
E	Egele
F	Faugel, Feigle, Feile, Fradchen, Fradel, Frommet
G	Geilchen, Gelea, Ginendel, Gittel, Gole
H	Hadasse, Hale, Hannacha, Hitzel
J	Jachet, Jachewad, Jedidja, Jente, Jezabel, Judis, Jyske, Jyttel
K	Keile, Kreindel
L	Lana, Leie, Libsche, Libe, Liwie
M	Machle, Mathel, Milkele, Mindel
N	Nacha, Nachme
P	Peirche, Peßchen, Pesse, Pessel, Pirle
R	Rachel, Rause, Rebekka, Rechel, Reha, Reichel, Reisel, Reitzge, Reitzsche, Riwki
S	Sara, Scharne, Scheindel, Scheine, Schewa, Schlämche, Semche, Simche, Slowe, Sprinze
T	Tana, Telze, Tirze, Treibel
Z	Zerel, Zilla, Zimle, Zine, Zipora, Zirel, Zorthel

Of these names, 80 percent were also among the top 100 most popular personal names in Germany during the 1930s.[96] By selecting a set of names which were exceedingly infrequent within the German-speaking Jewish communities of Western Europe, it was possible to minimize the number of Jews who were eligible to exempt out of adopting one of the two gendered compulsory onomastic markers.

In practice, this meant that, much to Hitler's satisfaction, Globke's plan could specifically and effectively target precisely those Jews whose names had made them virtually indistinguishable from their Aryan neighbors. Take, for example, the names *Anne Müller* and *Joseph Schmidt*. Before the Globke plan, it would have been impossible for officials to determine whether the name-bearer was Jewish or not. After the Globke plan, this task became child's play. *Anne Müller* and *Joseph Schmidt* were not Jewish and *Anne **Sara** Müller* and *Joseph **Israel** Schmidt* were.

Considering their nefarious purpose, the names *Sara* and *Israel* were relatively inoffensive, particularly in comparison to the motley assembly of names which other high-ranking officials had previously suggested. The selection of such pleasant-sounding names was by no means accidental. Before drawing up his final proposal, Globke had reportedly even made a point of initially consulting with leading members of the Berlin Jewish community to determine which compulsory personal names would be the most palatable for the majority of the Jewish population.[97] This step was in all probability less motivated by personal sympathy than it was by legal expediency. As an expert in constitutional law, Globke would have been all too well aware of the fact that the imposition of demonstrably degrading names would have posed a direct violation to preexisting naming laws and therefore risked encountering stiff resistance by lawmakers. If for no other reason because the imposition of blatantly offensive names would by default have forced non-Jewish citizens to use these monikers as well. By contrast, by requiring Jewish residents to adopt traditional personal names with neutral to positive associations, the Globke plan artfully circumvented these potential roadblocks.[98] The Führer agreed. Globke's plan had artfully fulfilled his vision. On August 17, 1938, the Nazis long-awaited updated version of the LAFFN-2 came into effect:

(§1)   Jewish residents of the Reich are only allowed to carry those first names that have been designated as appropriate by the Reich's Ministry of the Interior.

(§2.1) Jewish residents who carry a forename other than those prescribed by the Ministry of the Interior are required to apply to have the compulsory name *Sara* or *Israel* added to their name.

(§2.2) All Jewish residents who are required to carry the names *Sara* and *Israel* must also apply to have their new official names added to their marriage certificates as well as their residency permits. They must also formally register in writing themselves with their new official names with the police department.

(§3)   Jewish residents must present their official names with the obligatory forenames *Sara* and *Israel* in all official business where it is customary to present one's name.

(§4)   Whosoever purposefully disobeys the regulations outlined above will receive a prison sentence of up to six months. In cases of negligence, a prison term of no more than one month is to be imposed.[99]

Initially, the only major exemption to the above regulations was for those few people whose forename appeared on the list of onomastic exemptions.[100] However, government officials were also given the prerogative of insisting upon name changes for residents bearing these names as well. Before the January deadline had been reached, however, the internal policy had altered and officials were instructed that no exceptions to this regulation were permissible under any circumstance. As with the LAFFN-1, full compliance with the LAFFN-2 was mandatory and punishment for resistance was guaranteed.

It is no coincidence that just a month before the Globke's plan was made into law, a new policy was instituted which required all Jewish residents to possess an official ID card, containing their photograph, fingerprints, place of residence, occupation, and full name. Introduced on July 1938, the ID cards or "Kennkarten" were to be produced in duplicate. One copy was to be filed with the police authorities. The second was to be carried by the Jewish resident at all times. Despite Globke's enthusiasm for the creation of a nationwide ID card system, there seems to have been considerable variation across local and regional districts in the time and personnel allocated to this ambitious project.

For example, in Mainz, a city with a very large, extremely well-integrated Jewish population, there seems to have been a great deal of administrative support for this project. In a 1938 memo written on August 15, the chief of police roundly praised Globke's plan as an essential step in finally being able to track Jews across the Reich. The Chief's praise, he explained, was based on his own positive experiences in Mainz. According to him, an early review of the operating practices of the police department had uncovered that officers had no way of accurately determining "who was a Jew and who was not." Although the local Gestapo did have an internal name list of Jewish residents, the police department in Mainz was not authorized to access this intelligence. The decision was consequently made to implement an independent Jewish tracking system for the Mainz Police Department. As of January 1, 1936, a full three years before the introduction of the nationwide system of ID cards, the department had implemented its own Jewish identity card system. According to the police chief, the information contained in this system was shared among all of the respective police stations in the city, as well as the municipal officials working within the civil registry office and the passport office. The innovative system, the police chief crowed, had proven to be a major success "despite the fact that not all parties had initially recognized its necessity."[101]

The nationwide ID system was to work in much the same way as the provincial system in Mainz. To help ensure that all this intelligence was shared broadly, Jewish residents were required to immediately produce their ID cards in all official dealings. Failure to do so was punishable with a fine and up to a year of imprisonment. This regulation not only made it possible for authorities to tailor their responses to the person before them. It also surreptitiously forced Jewish residents to facilitate the interagency intelligence-sharing and surveillance network. As with all NSDAP legislation, failure to comply would result in severe punishment: a monetary fine and/or up to twelve months in a Nazi-run prison. Despite this threat, numbers of applications for the compulsory names and the ID cards were initially rather low. The increasing frequency of anti-Semitic violence made people understandably wary of any measure that would make them more visible and vulnerable. Best to keep a "low profile" in times like these. Ironically, it was the cataclysmic eruption of violence that may have caused many Jewish residents to change this survival tactic.

Just three months after the ratification of the LAFFN-2, anti-Jewish discrimination and violence reached new levels. Each night after sunset from November 9 to November 13, 1938, across Germany, Austria, and the Sudetenland[102], hundreds of synagogues were desecrated or completely destroyed; over 7,000 businesses were vandalized; nearly 100 Jewish residents were murdered; and approximately 30,000 Jewish men and adolescents were arrested by the police and transferred to Dachau, Buchenwald, and Sachsenhausen. On November 13, 1938, *The Palestine Post* carried an article entitled "Jews Hiding in the Berlin Woods: Reports of Torture and Murder." Below is an excerpt from that report:

> Mass arrests of Jews are still the order of the day in Berlin and other German towns. It is estimated that several thousand Jews were arrested in Berlin, while thousands, according to a report received here, are hiding in the woods round Berlin. . . . In addition to the demonstrations which took place on Tuesday, Wednesday and Thursday, it is now learned according to reports receive here, that the worst disorder occurred in small towns where the entire population took part in smashing and looting Jewish shops. Warnings were published in the local newspapers that anybody who failed to take part would be regarded as an enemy of the regime. . . . TORTURED TO DEATH A leading personality who witnessed some of the scenes in Berlin . . . stated that no Jewish business was left intact and many Jewish houses were damaged and looted. Scores of Jews, according to him, were not only beaten but literally tortured to death.[103]

Before those horrific nights of shattered glass, the Jewish community had hoped that it would only be a matter of time before reason and the rule of law returned. After Kristallnacht, many came to believe that the only real hope lay in escape. G. Adler, a Shoah survivor who witnessed Kristallnacht in Berlin, described what it was like in the city immediately afterward. According to Adler, all that the adults talked about was how to get out and where they could go:

> more and more families were starting to leave and the kids were talking already. "We're going to Israel!" "We're going to Palestine!" . . . all of the sudden [that was] the latest talk that was coming up in Berlin. . . . 'Where do we go?' 'Australia?' or 'Shanghai?' . . . 'Cuba?' These were names that I as a youngster heard in Berlin, yet still going to the parades on the Charlottenburger . . . I mean it was strange but I was only ten years old at that time.[104]

Receiving permission to emigrate, however, was by no means an easy task. Even if one had the financial wherewithal, the amount of paperwork required by both the country of destination and the country of origin was formidable. Birth certificates, marriage licenses, school transcripts, military service records, passports—all documents that required the applicant's full official name.

On December 11, 1938, a month after Kristallnacht, Mrs. E. May sent a letter from Heilbronn to the police department in Worms to inquire whether it was still necessary for both her and her husband to apply for ID cards [Kennkarten] given their imminent plans to leave Germany. A week later, the Worms authorities replied that the couple would indeed need to apply for the cards if they had not left the country by the end of the month. Furthermore, the police warned, if they failed to apply for the compulsory names *Sara* and *Israel* by the deadline on January 31, 1939, they would automatically be prohibited from leaving the country and would face criminal charges in Germany.[105] It is important to point out that the police were aware of the fact that the May family had not yet sent in their LAFFN-2 applications. Throughout the nation, state employees had been instructed to send in regular updates on which residents had complied with the LAFFN-1/2 regulations and which ones had not. These updates took the form of name lists including the addresses of the offending persons. For example, on July 1940, authorities from Ober-Klingen, a township outside of Darmstadt, reported that Sophie W., Elias M., Emma W., and Isidor W. had all failed to comply. The report included not only each resident's address and full name, but also the name of his/her spouse, and their wedding date.[106]

While these families had obviously chosen to try to avoid or postpone complying with this regulation, others did all they could to follow the latest regulation. In 1939, for example, a letter was sent to the registry office of Kirchhain from a former resident, Herr H. Kramer. In that correspondence, the letter-writer informed the authorities that he had taken on the name *Israel* as required. Just in case the officials had any follow-up questions or concerns, he made sure to include his current address in Amsterdam.[107] From the vantage point of today, both sets of stories are heartbreaking for they illustrate the horrific catch-22 so many people found themselves in.

Those who decided to try their luck elsewhere were forced to have the markers of *Sara* and *Israel* placed on all of their official identification, lest they be prohibited from leaving or returning one day. Those who decided to try to wait out the storm at home were also forced to adopt the hated markers lest they find themselves facing the Gestapo. No matter what choice one made, the end was always the same. With the introduction of the LAFFN-1 and the LAFFN-2, the state had made it nearly impossible to avoid being classified, tagged, registered, tracked, and hunted.

Notes

1. Dietz Bering, *The Stigma of Names: Antisemitism in German Daily Life, 1812–1933* (Ann Arbor: University of Michigan Press, 1992), 27.

2. Bering, *The Stigma of Names*, 12.

3. In 1809, an official edict released in Frankfurt expressly prohibited residents from using the names *Abraham, Moses,* and *Elias* as last names. This prohibition had a significant and negative impact upon the naming patterns of Jewish residents in the area. Stadtsarchiv Frankfurt am Main, "Fürstl. Primatische Behodern Gedrückte Bekanntmachungen un Ordnungen 1806–1810," Magistratsakten Zugang: 47/69; Signatur: 5.847; Nr. 72.

4. Max Levy, *Der Napoleonische Erlass von 1808: Wegen der Vor- und Zunamen der Juden und seine Ausführung in Worms* (Worms: Buchdruckerei Eugen Kranzbühler, 1914), 3.

5. Over time, such isolated cases seem to have become a part of urban legend and have been greatly over-generalized. Empirical studies have demonstrated that the preponderance of Jewish surnames is neither pejorative nor offensive in nature. While such last names do exist, they are not isolated to members of the Jewish faith but are to be found among Christians as well. Part of the reason for the resilience of the notion that Jews have a disproportionately high frequency of disparaging surnames may come in part from the plethora of anti-Semitic jokes featuring characters with ludicrous surnames. Such jokes were particularly popular in National Socialist circles. For more, see Bering, *The Stigma of Names*; Konrad Kunze, *Vor- und Familienname im deutschen Sprachgebiet* (Munich: Deutsche Taschenbuch Verlag, 2004).

6. Bering, *The Stigma of Names,* 12.

7. Robert Rennick, "Offensive Names," *Verbatim* 29, no. 4 (2004): 21–26.

8. Stadtarchiv Worms, *Etat Nominatif du Recensement de la population des Israelites, habitants de la commune de Horchheim: le deuxieure du mois d. Septembre 1809*, Abt. 42, Nr. 374.

9. Nils Roemer, *German City, Jewish Memory: The Story of Worms* (Lebanon, NH: Brandeis University Press, 2010).

10. Centralverein deutscher Staatsbürger jüdischen Glaubens, *Deutsche Reich,* 1909.

11. Michael Wagner-Kern, *Staat und Namensänderung* (Tübingen: Mohr Siebeck, 2002), 183.

12. Wagner-Kern, *Staat und Namensänderung,* 43.

13. Wagner-Kern, *Staat und Namensänderung,* 50.

14. Bering, *The Stigma of Names*, 47.

15. Wagner-Kern, *Staat und Namensänderung,* 62.

16. Marbug Staatsarchiv, Rambach, April 10, 1920, Abt. 469/33; Nr. 121–30.

17. Marbug Staatsarchiv, Rambach, April 10, 1920, Abt. 469/33; Nr. 125.

18. Landeshauptarchiv Koblenz, "Burgermeisterei Monzingen Acta Generalia. Namensänderungen," Abt. B. Fach 16, Nr. 6 Heft, 1.

19. Landeshauptarchiv Koblenz, "Namensänderungen von polnischen Arbeitern," December 20, 1906, Abt. B, Fach 16, Nr. 6, Heft 1.

20. It is striking that, in 1919, decades before the Nazis had assumed power, the petitioner was using vocabulary that is today considered a hallmark of the NSDAP. Here one sees again that the Nazis did not invent European anti-Semitism but harnessed it.

21. The Russian-born Jewish émigré and ardent communist Eugen Leviné led a Communist revolt in Bavaria which ended in the execution of eight hostages on April 29, 1919 by the Red Guards. After armed engagement, the German Army put down the insurrection. Leviné was eventually arrested, found guilty, and executed by firing squad in Stadelheim Prison, Munich, Germany.

22. Hessisches Hauptstaatsarchiv Wiesbaden, "Gesuch um Namensänderung; an den Herrn Regierungspräsidenten in Potsdam," June 20, 1919, 469/33 Nr. 223.

23. Peter Wulf, "'Juda ist überall': Antisemitismus in Schleswig-Holstein in der Zeit der Weimarer Republik," *Ausgegrenzt-verachtet-vernichtet: Zur Geschichte der Juden in Schleswig-Holstein, Landeszentrale für Politische Bildung* (Kiel: Landeszentrale für Politische Bildung, 1994), 71–81.

24. Frankfurter Stadtarchiv, "Standesamt Namensänderung," Akten des Magistrats der Stadt Frankfurt am Main, 1921, Dokument 38, Magistratsakten R1231.

25. Landesarchiv Speyer, "Akten des königlichen Bezirksamtes Germersheim," H34 Nr. 661.

26. *The Sentinel*, "Jews Forbidden to Adopt Gentile Names," February 2, 1920.

27. Hessisches Hauptstaatsarchiv Wiesbaden, "Brief an alle Herrn Oberpräsidenten, Regierungspräsident (für Oppeln Verwaltungsstelle Breslau) sowie an den Herrn Polizeipräsidenten in Berlin," November 15, 1921. 180 Hersfeld Nr. 3169.

28. Ernst Graf zu Reventlow was born on August 8, 1869, in Husum, Germany. After serving in the Navy from 1888 to 1899, he became a journalist and publicist. In 1920, he founded "Der Reichwart" and became a leading member of the Deutschvölkischer Freiheitspartei (DFVP). Seven years later, he left the DVFP and joined the NSDAP, after having been aggressively courted by both Joseph Goebbels and Adolf Hitler. www.bundesarchive.de/aktenreichskanzlei/1919–1933/0000/adr/adrmr/kap1_6/para2_86.html

29. Reichstag, 96. Sitzung (June 26, 1929), 278–79.

30. Reichstag, 96. Sitzung (June 26, 1929), 278–79.

31. Reichstag, 96. Sitzung (June 26, 1929), 278–79.

32. Marburg Staatsarchiv, 180 Gelnhausen, Nr. 6355, IZ 47/32.

33. On February 14, 1923, the German Ministry of Justice declared that the local police must be sent an official report on every individual who was granted any name change. This report was to include the applicant's previous name(s), place of birth, current residence, and religious affiliation. Hessisches Hauptstaatsarchiv Darmstadt, "Allgemeine Verfügung vom 14. Februar 1923 über die Veröffentlichung von Namensänderungen," January 30, 1923, Nr. 92, Bestand (G11), Nr. (26/1).

34. An excellent example comes from a petition placed by a Jewish resident of Darmstadt who petitioned in the summer of 1938 to have his surname altered from *Jud*. The applicant's request was granted and his last name was officially changed to *Jung*. Darmstadt Staatsarchiv, G15 Nr. 271: 116/24.

35. Marburg Staatsarchiv, IZ Allg. 16/33.

36. Stadtarchiv Flensburg, ID 01706.

37. Clemens Schwender, *Wie benutze ich den Fernsprecher? Die Anleitung zum Tele-fonieren im Berliner Telefonbuch 1881–1996/97* (Frankfurt am Main: Peter Lang Verlag, 1997).

38. Schwender, *Wie benutze ich den Fernsprecher*, 310.

39. Schwender, *Wie benutze ich den Fernsprecher*, 307.

40. Schwender, *Wie benutze ich den Fernsprecher*, 307–8.

41. Hessisches Hauptstaatsarchiv Wiesbaden, HHStaW: Abt 469/33 Nr. 33.

42. Hamburg Staatsarchiv, File:113–5_DVA1.

43. By the spring of 1942, the city of Hamburg received notice that officials were no longer to process new applications for name changes placed by police officials with Polish-sounding names. After consultation with Hamburg Chief Police Inspector Lönbel, it was decided, however, that the city should finish processing the fifteen remaining requests which had been made before that date. Hamburg Staatsarchiv, File, O-VuR. PBG. 4209/41.

44. Landeshauptarchiv Koblenz, "Antrag auf Namensänderung des Revierleutnants der Schutzpolizei R. Rosnowski," January 1942, Best. 517 Nr. 152.

45. Landesarchiv Speyer, "Namensänderung bei Einbürgerungen" Berlin, June 7, 1939. Id 69 III/38 Best. H34 Nr. 661.

46. Flensburg Stadtarchiv, Signatur: ID 01706 (1933–1975), Zu IZ 48/32

47. Flensburg Stadtarchiv, Signatur: ID 01706 (1933–1975), Zu IZ 48/32

48. Staatsarchiv Marburg, May 25, 1938, Bestand 180 Ziegenhain Nr. 7051, Dok. 3.

49. Landesarchiv Koblenz, "Die schönste der deutscher Frauen," February 1, 1930, Mappe: 627 Heft 7 Best. 100, 145.

50. Carlos Widmann, "Gefährtin des Bösen," *Der Spiegel* (September 24. 2001), http://magazin.spiegel.de/EpubDelivery/spiegel/pdf/20184307.

51. Anna Maria Sigmund, *Die Frauen der Nazis I* (Vienna: Überreuter, 1998), 73.

52. Anja Klabunde, *Magda Goebbels: Annäherung an ein Leben* (Berlin: Bertelsman, 1999), 15.

53. Wolfgang Eckart, "Erster Weltkrieg 1914–1918: Hunger und Mangel in der Heimat." *Deutsche Ärzteblatt* 112, no. 6 (2015): A-230–2.

54. Widmann, "Gefährtin des Bösen," 215.

55. Florian Diekmann and Philipp Seibt, "Wer sind die Quandts?" *Der Spiegel*, August 6, 2015. http://www.spiegel.de/wirtschaft/unternehmen/quandt-clan-wer-sind -die-bmw-erben-und-woher-kommt-ihr-reichtum-a-1046996.html.

56. Today, this is roughly the equivalent of 35.4 billion US dollars.

57. Jörg Vögele, Ulrich Koppitz, and Hideharu Umehara, "Epidemien und Pandemien in Historischer Perspective." *Epidemics and Pandemics in Historical Perspective*, eds. Jörg Vögele, Stefanie Knöll, and Thorsten Noack, 3–34 (Wiesbaden: Springer Verlag, 2016), 8.

58. Rüdiger Jungbluth, *Die Quandts: Ihr leiser Aufstieg zur mächtigsten Wirtschaftsdy-nastie Deutschlands* (Berlin: Campus Verlag, 2002), 46.

59. Günther Quandt and Antonie Ewald had known each other for several years before they married and their families were very closely acquainted. During their long courtship, Quandt sent regular love letters to his "Toni" in which he referred to her as the "tender, soft

and quiet love" whom he held in his heart. Rüdiger Jungbluth, *Die Quandts: Deutschlands erfolgreichste Unternehmerfamilie* (New York: Campus Verlag, 2015), 41.

60. Joachim Scholtyseck, *Der Aufstieg der Quandts: Eine deutsche Unternehmerdynastie* (Munich: C. H. Beck, 2011).

61. Hans-Otto Meissner, *Magda Göebbels: ein Lebensbild* (Munich: Blanvalet Verlag, 1978).

62. Meissner, *Magda Goebbels*, 46.

63. Widmann, "Gefährtin des Bösen," 209.

64. Sigmund, *Die Frauen der Nazis,* 85.

65. International Tracing Service, "Stiefvater von Magda Goebbels" 1.1.5.3/5893549, *ITS Digital Archive.* Bad Arolsen.

66. His ashes were reportedly buried in Weisensee, a Jewish cemetery in Berlin. Volker Koop, *Wer Jude ist, bestimmte ich: Ehrenarier im Nationalsozialismus* (Cologne: Böhlau Verlag, 2014), 81.

67. Oliver Hilmes, *Berlin 1936: Sechzehn Tage im August* (Münich: Siedler Verlag, 2016), 46.

68. At the time of the Goebbels' wedding, a popular Communist newspaper "Rote Fahne" [Red Flag] carried a biting piece about the minister having married a "Jewess." Widmann, "Gefährtin des Bösen," 215.

69. Just how horrific this final scene must have been is hinted at by the forensic evidence. Based on the reported markings on Helga's body, it is assumed that she fought violently against her parents who forced the lethal capsule down her throat. Widmann, "Gefährtin des Bösen," 216.

70. Ralf Georg Reuth, ed. *Joseph Goebbels Tagebücher 1924–1945* (Munich: Piper Verlag, 1999), 1206.

71. Jungbluth, *Die Quandts*, 159.

72. Bundeszentrale für politische Bildung, "Widerstand der Weißen Rose: Flugblätter gegen Hitler," http://www.bpb.de/geschichte/nationalsozialismus/weisse-rose/61028/flugblatt-vi.

73. Bundeszentrale für politische Bildung, "Sophie Scholl und 'die Weise Rose': Flugblatt VI," http://www.bpb.de/geschichte/nationalsozialismus/weisse-rose/61028/flugblatt-vi.

74. "Experience Report of Concentration Camp Inhabitant Olga Schaub," Donovan Nuremberg Trials Collection, Cornell University Library/Law Library, http://lawcollections.library.cornell.edu/nuremberg/catalog/nur:00424.

75. Approximately 132,000 women, adolescent girls, and children as well as some 20,000 men were registered as prisoners in Ravensbrück between 1939 and 1945 (www.ravensbrueck.de).

76. Wagner-Kern, *Staat und Namensänderung*, 294.

77. From the Nazis' perspective, another potential drawback of this proposal might have been that it would have increased rather than decreased the visibility of Jewish residents within Europe.

78. Wolfgang Benz, "The Legend of German-Jewish Symbiosis," *The Leo Baeck Institute Year Book* 37, issue 1 (1992): 95–102.

79. Original text to be found here: http://alex.onb.ac.at/pdfs/ONB_09CB.pdf.

80. Bering, *The Stigma of Names*, 182.

81. Landesarchiv Speyer, "Akten des königlichen Bezirksamtes Germershem," H34. 661.

82. Landesarchiv Speyer, "Akten des königlichen Bezirksamtes Germershem," H34. 661.

83. Cornelia Schmitz-Berning, *Vokabular des Nationalsozialismus* (Berlin: Walter de Gruyter, 2000), 329.

84. Ralf Georg Reuth, ed., *Joseph Goebbels Tagebücher 1924–1945*. Munich: Piper Verlag, 1999.

85. This was not the first time that Goebbels' Ministry played a role in developing anti-Semitic onomastic policy. In October 1935, the Propaganda Ministry under his direction issued a general prohibition against Jews being allowed to use artistic pseudonyms or stage names [Kunstlernamen]. Uwe Dietrich Adam, *Judenpolitik im Dritten Reich* (Düsseldorf: Droste, 2003), 94.

86. Schmitz-Berning, *Vokabular des Nationalsozialismus*, 329.

87. Ever the pragmatist, in response to each of these suggestions, Globke sent detailed replies explaining why the proposed system of onomastic demarcation was impracticable, undesirable, imprudent, or all of the above. Years later, when seated on the bench of the accused during the Nuremberg Trials, Globke would attempt to use this series of rejections as evidence for his resistance to the NSDAP. The legitimacy of Globke's claim that he was a part of a clandestine opposition remains questionable. Nevertheless, Frick's initial frustration and final fury with Globke for repeatedly failing to produce a policy for differentially labelling Jewish inhabitants are well-documented.

88. Although the original ordinance regarding the compulsory adoption of the onomastic markers uses the spelling *Sara,* the alternative variant *Sarah* may also sometimes be found as well in the official documentation. In a governmental report from October 4, 1946, for example, civil servants working in and around the city of Montabaur were ordered to expunge the obligatory names *Israel* and *Sara(h)* from the municipal records. Landesarchiv Koblenz, Bestand: 655, 256; Nr. 138.

89. According to Seibert, it did not take long for the administrators at the Reich's Department of Ancestral Research to determine if it would be impossible for them to provide a satisfactory list of the names by the specified deadline. Disappointing the Führer was also, however, not an option either. The solution was appropriating a preexisting list of Jewish names that had been produced several years earlier by a Professor Gerhard Kessler. Kessler was a prominent economics scholar who had, at one time, investigated the names of Jewish residents of Eastern European ancestry who were residing in Berlin. Kessler published his findings in 1935 under the title "Family names of the Jews" [Familien Namen der Juden]. Seibert's comparison of Kessler's original listing and the roster eventually released by the NSDAP as a part of the LAFFN-2 demonstrates a significant degree of overlap. There is more than a bit of irony in the fact that the Nazis decided to use Kessler's work, as the professor was a vehement and outspoken opponent of the NSDAP. Kessler was eventually forced to flee Nazi Germany and re-settle in Turkey where he, along with other prominent exiled German academics, was awarded a professorship in economics at the University of Istanbul. For more on Kessler and his list of Jewish names, see Winfried Seibert, *Das Mädchen, das nicht ESTHER heißen durfte: Eine*

exemplarische Geschichte (Leipzig: Reclam Verlag, 1996), 242–64. For more on the fate of Kessler and other exiled German intellectuals during the Third Reich, see Klemens Wittebur, *Die Deutsche Soziologie im Exil 1933–1945: Eine Biographische Kartographie* (Hamburg: LIT Verlag, 1991).

90. Ministerial-Blatt des Reichs- und Preußischen Ministeriums des Inneren, Nummer 35 on August 24, 1938.

91. *The Palestine Post,* "Official List of Names for Jews," August 29, 1938.

92. Aware that both he and his wife, Eva, could be executed for his writings, during the war, Professor Viktor Klemperer referred to his diary using the cryptic letters "LTI," which stood for *Lingua Tertii Imperii* or the *Language of the Third Reich.* In 1940, Klemperer and his wife were forced to leave their homes and relocate to a "Judenhaus": ramshackle, overcrowded housing where Jewish residents were forced to live until they received official orders of deportation to a concentration camp. Shortly after Eva and Viktor received their deportation notification, the city of Dresden underwent heavy bombing from the Allied Forces. In the chaos which erupted, the Klemperers made their escape and survived the war. In 1947, Viktor published his diary, *LTI.* Victor Klemperer, *LTI: Notizbuch eines Philologen* (Halle a. S.: Niemeyer, 1957 Reprinted. 23rd edition. Stuttgart: Reclam Taschenbuch, 2007).

93. Klemperer, *LTI,* 108.

94. In his private diaries, Victor Klemperer relates the story of a former non-Jewish university colleague who, despite being a loyal member of the NSDAP, successfully petitioned to retain his last name *Israel* after convincing authorities that his name originally derived from the sixteenth century name "Oesterhelt." Klemperer, *LTI,* 101.

95. Data on the most common names among German Jews between 1860 and 1938 is taken from Michael Wolffsohn and Thomas Brechenmacher, *Deutschland, jüdisch Heimatland: Die Geschichte der deutschen Juden von Kaiserreich bis heute* (Munich: Piper Verlag, 1996), 60.

96. Data on the most common names in Germany during the 1930s were taken from https://www.beliebte-vornamen.de/3766–1930er-jahre.htm.

97. Erik Lommatzsch, *Hans Globke (1898–1973): Beamter im Dritten Reich und Staatssekretär Adenauers* (Frankfurt am Main: Campus Verlag, 2009), 77.

98. *DDR-Justiz und NS Verbrechen: Sammlung ostdeutscher Strafurteile wegen nationalsozialistischer Tötungsverbrechen: Das Urteil gegen Hans Josef Maria Globke.* Einzelausfertigung des Urteils des OG von 23.07.1963, 1 ZST (I) 1/63) Band III, Lfd. Nr. 1068. http://www1.jur.uva.nl/junsv/pdf/globke.pdf.

99. Original text to be found here: http://alex.onb.ac.at/cgi-content/alex?apm=0& aid=dra&datum=19380004&seite=00001044&zoom=2.

100. Paragraph 3 of the LAFFN-2 lists one other minor exception. As of August 17, 1938, this new law exempted commercial businesses. By December 1938, Globke had already informed government officials that no exceptions to the LAFFN-2 were to be accepted. For an outstanding in-depth discussion of the legal intricacies involved in this policy implementation, see Wagner-Kern, *Staat und Namensänderung,* 223–343.

101. Stadtarchiv Mainz, ZGS/E3, 15.

102. The term "Sudetenland" refers to the segment of Czechoslovakia wh.ch had a significant population of ethnic Germans. The districts in this border area include Bohemia, Czech Silesia, and Moravia. Immediately after the war, millions of ethnic Germans living throughout Eastern Europe were forcibly expelled. For more see Tony Judt, *Postwar: A History of Europe Since 1945* (New York: Penguin Books, 2005).

103. http://jpress.nli.org.il/Olive/APA/NLI/?action=tab&tab=search#panel=document.

104. G. Adler [Interview code: 40288] https://3c-bap.web.de/mail/client/dereferrer?redirectUrl=http percent3A percent2F percent2Fvhaonline.usc.edu percent2Flogin.aspx.

105. Stadtarchiv Worms, Abteilung 13, Nummer 1984.

106. "Brief an Herrn Landrat des Landkreises Dieburg," July 4, 1940, Stadtarchiv Darmstadt G15 Nr. 271 aufbewahrungsort: 116/24.

107. Marburg Staatsarchiv, Bestand:330 Kirchhain, Nr. 2319, Spezialakten, Dok. 70/71.

CHAPTER 3

National Socialist Practices for Naming the Power Elite

On the one hand, life had taken a decided turn for the better. Karoline Diehl, an opera singer and widow of the theatre director Oskar Diehl,[1] had managed to seduce and convince a considerably younger SS officer, Sigmund Rascher, to marry her. On the other hand, even before the happy odd couple could begin planning their wedding, they received the crushing news that Reichsführer Heinrich Himmler had refused to grant them permission to marry. Being married to an older woman himself, Himmler indicated that the reported six-year age difference between the two was untenable as Ms. Diehl was in all likelihood long past her child-bearing years. Himmler's proclamation must have come as a shock to the singer. Since the earliest days of the Party when she had cared for a wounded Himmler during the 1923 Bürgerbräu-Putsch in Bavaria, "Nini" had been a trusted member of Himmler's inner circle,[2] regularly providing the Gestapo with secret information about persons of interest.[3]

The stinging embarrassment of the Reichsführer's rejection must have been made all the more intolerable for the blonde diva each time another member of the Nazi elite triumphantly announced the birth of yet another child. Although the nation as a whole continued to have a negative birthrate, the fecundity of the top NS wives was quickly becoming the stuff of legends. There was the Propaganda Minister's wife Magda Goebbels who, by that time, had already had five children (*Harald*, 1921; *Hildegard*, 1934; *Helmut Christian*, 1935; *Holdine Kathrin*, 1937; and *Hedwig "Hedda" Johanna*, 1938). There was Martin Bormann's wife, Gerda, who by then had had seven children, including a set of twin girls (*Adolf Martin*, 1930; *Ilse* and *Ehrengard*, 1931; *Rudolf-Gerhard*, 1934; *Heinrich Hugo*, 1936; and *Eva Ute*, 1938). And the thirty-six-year-old Reichsfrauenführerin, Gertrud Scholtz-Klink, whom Adolf Hitler described as the "perfect Nazi woman."[4] Between the two of them, she and her husband, SS Obergruppenführer August Heißmeyer, had a total of ten children. Even the Field Marshal's wife, forty-five-year-old Emmy Göring, whom no one had seriously believed would ever produce a child, had triumphantly announced the birth of a healthy baby girl, *Emma.*

So far, Karoline's young lover had proven surprisingly loyal. It had not hurt, of course, that thanks in no small measure Nini's close connections with Himmler, Sigmund had managed to leave his unpaid university assignment in Munich[5] and take on an exciting position in the Reichsführer's medical research team.[6] But, how long would it be before he would either chose to or be forced to seek another bride? Clearly, something had to be done. If she could not produce a child through pregnancy, she would simply have to find another option: thievery. Admittedly, as any would-be criminal can attest, there is a significant difference between successfully planning a crime and executing one. After several failed attempts, Diehl realized that she was going to need help. She turned to her favorite cousin, Julie "Lulu" Muschler,[7] who quickly demonstrated an unexpected knack for kidnapping.

In no time at all, Lulu proudly announced that she had been able to trick an indigent single mother into allowing her to babysit her son while she went to work. All that was left now was to wait for Sigmund to return from one of his prolonged research trips and convincingly present him with the story of how she had heroically given birth to their first son all alone. Somewhat bewildered but overjoyed, Dr. Rascher proudly announced to Himmler that the couple were the proud parents of a healthy baby boy, *Peter Heinrich Diehl.*[8] Himmler dutifully sent congratulations on this truly unexpected good news. However, he remained firmly against the couple's marriage.

For Karoline, the key to overcoming this resistance was simple: another child would have to be found to demonstrate that Peter had not been a fluke. Once again, she elicited the help of her cousin, Lulu, who stole yet another male infant while Rascher was away on assignment in North Africa.[9] On April 19, one day before the Führer's birthday, the young doctor returned home to discover that Karoline had given birth to yet another son, *Volker Sigmund.*[10] Despite being exceedingly premature, the boy was astoundingly alert and surprisingly well developed: no doubt due to his superior breeding, the doctor may have explained to surprised friends and family. Rascher sent Himmler a second birth announcement, along with a photograph of Nini radiantly nursing their second infant son. The SS Reichsführer sent the mother and child a congratulatory gift of cognac, chocolates, coffee, fresh apples, and figs. In her thank letter to the family benefactor, Diehl exclaimed:

> What incredible joy you have given us once again! So many and such wonderful gifts! For a long time to come the children's baby-food

will be especially nourishing. <u>Heinrich Peter</u> . . . guessed immediately who had sent the package.[11] (emphasis added)

It is intriguing that Diehl, in her attempt to further ingratiate herself to Himmler, not only mentions the name of the child who had been partially named after the SS Reichsführer. She also inadvertently switches the order of the boy's fake name, placing the name *Heinrich* first. After the second successful pregnancy, Himmler's initial misgivings seem to have dissipated. To the couple's relief, the Reichsführer finally acquiesced and granted the two permission to marry. In July 1941, Karoline became Frau Dr. med. Rascher.[12] She had finally reached her goal.

If she had stopped there, she might have gotten away with the kidnapping. But like most serial offenders, restraint was not among her dominant personality traits. As far as she was concerned, she and Lulu had developed the perfect plan, replete with an excellent contingency. Whenever a mother became too impatient or threatened to go the police, they simply returned her child and stole another to replace him. On November 25, 1942, the couple announced the birth of their third son: *Dieter Gerhard Rascher*.[13] From Nini's perspective, things couldn't be better. But, Lulu was starting to get cold feet. Eventually, the fear of being caught appears to have become too great for the cousin and she refused to participate in any further baby-heisting. By mid-December 1943, Julie Muschler was officially reported missing. Her corpse was later found near the Raschers' private mountain cabin in the spring of 1944.[14]

Aside from Lulu's suspicious death, which raised more than a few eyebrows, everything continued to go remarkably well for the Raschers. Dr. Rascher was in the middle of a series of research experiments involving concentration camp prisoners who, after being shot multiple times, were administered "Polygal," a new blood-clotting agent the Nazis hoped to use on the front.[15] In the meantime, Mrs. Rascher was busy making preparations for what would be their fourth son. Without her cousin's assistance, though, she made several grave errors: she returned the wrong baby to an insistent mother; and she made arrangements to "take on" a non-Aryan infant. Her fatal mistake came though during a pre-arranged pick-up at the Munich main train station. Thanks to her odd appearance and panicky behavior, she frightened off the targeted mother who refused to hand-over her son to the would-be-babysitter and contacted the police, instead. The subsequent kidnapping alert roused the attention of both the local newspapers and Himmler's Gestapo.[16] It did not take long before the Munich police arrived at the Rascher home.

Although Mrs. Rascher had reportedly just given birth to her fourth son, the officers discovered that the mother was not at home. Instead, they found Dr. Rascher alone and aggressive. The police carefully examined the child whom Dr. Rascher presented as his newborn son, *Rainer*. The child was clearly older than the doctor indicated. When the police returned again for additional questioning, they discovered that the child whom they had last examined was no longer present and had been replaced by another child whom the Raschers insisted was *Rainer*. In March of 1944, the couple was placed under arrest. The investigation was held by the chief of the Munich police, Officer Freiherr von Eberstein.[17] Soon the entire sordid story began to unravel.

Initially, Dr. Rascher insisted that he had known nothing about his wife's baby-snatching activities. The police insisted that surely, he as a doctor—especially one who had devoted part of his career to researching fertility[18]—must have noticed that his wife's pregnancies were feigned. Did he really expect them to believe that he had never noticed that "his" sons had undergone such dramatic changes in appearance? Whether in a state of denial or fear over his losing his career—to say nothing of his life—the medical doctor stubbornly asserted that he had known nothing about his wife's criminal activities. Although he did admit that he had noticed changes in the boys' looks after one of his research trips, he explained that he had simply reassured himself that it was normal for young children to undergo dramatic growth spurts.

During the course of the interrogation, Dr. Rascher was also asked if he knew anything about Lulu's sudden, unexplained disappearance. He again emphatically denied any knowledge of her whereabouts or any wrongdoing. Mrs. Rascher gave the same answer. Before the Raschers' arrest, Lulu's death had been officially ruled a suicide. However, given the new turn of events, there was strong reason to believe that one or both of the Raschers might have murdered the young woman in an effort to silence her. Having lived and worked in the Rascher home, she would have known all about the family secrets. Now, so many of these secrets were starting to come out.

While Dr. Rascher remained uncooperative throughout the questioning, his wife seemed to be quite willing to tell her story, starting with the fact that she was not six years older than her husband, as she had always contended, but nearly sixteen.[19] She explained how, after faking several miscarriages, she had grown desperate and realized that she would have to somehow come up with a child if she wanted to keep her younger lover.[20] Through the information she provided and several witness statements, the police were able to piece together how over the years, Mrs. Rascher had induced desperate pregnant women and single mothers to surrender their infant sons with the promise of high-quality childcare. She then changed the boys' names and presented them as her own, occasionally exchanging one child for another when a mother demanded her son's return. As a result, to the best of her recollection, there had been at least two *Peters* and two *Volkers*, three *Dieters*, and two *Rainers*.[21] Precisely which child had belonged to which birth mother was nearly impossible for her to remember. She and her cousin had always attempted to return the right child to the right mother, but mistakes had most likely been made.

Without today's DNA testing, it was impossible for the police to correctly pair all of the boys with their mothers. The blood tests performed could ultimately only determine who was NOT the mother of the "Rascher" children. However, according to a 1944 report issued by the police, some progress was made in determining the original birth names of four stolen children.[22] *Peter Heinrich,* whom the Raschers indicated had been born on November 25, 1939, was actually *Johann Schneider,* born on June 10, 1939. The son known as *Volker Sigmund* was not born on April 19, 1941, but on March 12, 1941. His real name before being kidnapped was *Franz Josef Malovetz. Uto Lamparski,* the third child to be presented as the Raschers' son, was born on October 6, 1942. In the Rascher household, he had been one of the stolen boys given the name *Dieter Gerhard.* Finally, one of the many *Rainer Raschers* was in fact *Wilhelm Baranjai.* His real birthday was the day before Valentine's Day 1944 and not March 20, 1944, as listed on the falsified birth certificate Frau Rascher had managed to procure.

The discrepancy between the actual children's birthdays and the day upon which Mrs. Rascher supposedly gave birth is shockingly great and completely undermines Dr. Rascher's insistence that he had not recognized his wife's deception. Otherwise, one would have to believe that a doctor had mistaken a one-month-old child for a premature infant; or, as was the case with "Peter," a six-month-old baby with a newborn. This means that from the very first child, the doctor must have either realized that something was amiss or he was a part of the scheme from the very beginning. Another point of interest concerns the boys' names. The fact that the first names assigned to the stolen children had no obvious connection to their birth names comes as no surprise. However, what was somewhat unexpected is the fact that, other than the surname *Schneider,* the boys' last names seemed to have hinted at "non-Aryan" ancestry (e.g., *Malovetz* and *Lamparski*). The same observation was made by the officers investigating the case. According to the official police report, one of the children the Raschers had presented as Rainer, *Wilhelm Baranjai,* had even been found to have a Sinti[23] mother.[24]

When Himmler received the complete police dossier, he was livid. Rather than seeking revenge, however, his primary aim seemed to be swift damage control. He immediately ordered both of the Raschers be sent to separate concentration camps. Dr. Rascher was stripped of all his titles and professional duties and was sent to the Buchenwald Concentration Camp. Curiously, he was not charged with any crimes connected with the kidnapping. Instead, on February 14, 1945, he was charged with illegally transacting business with concentration camp prisoners.[25] Approximately three months later, he was transferred from police custody to his final place of incarceration. On April 26, 1945, he arrived in the Dachau Concentration Camp, where ironically, just a short time before, he had performed many of his fatal sadistic medical experiments.[26] Before the camp was liberated, Himmler gave the order for Rascher's execution.

The SS Reichsführer had a similar fate in mind for the woman he had once called "Nini." Unlike her husband who seemed resigned to his fate, Mrs. Rascher continued to try to devise ways out of this situation. When her letters imploring Himmler's forgiveness did not work, she switched tactics. During the long police transport to a concentration camp, she informed the guards that they had the wrong woman. She claimed that while they weren't looking the real Frau Rascher had forced her to exchange clothing and then had made her escape. As unbelievable as the story must have seemed, her delivery was very convincing. Could it be that the woman they had in custody was not Frau Rascher but *Frau Dörfler*, as the prisoner claimed?[27]

Karoline Rascher knew all too well what awaited her in the concentration camp. She had served, many years, as her husband's laboratory assistant during his deadly medical experiments on concentration camp prisoners. Armed with that information, she probably gave one of the best performances of her entire life during that prison transport. But to no avail. The records were quickly double-checked and her name and identity were confirmed. In November 1944, she arrived in Konzentrationslager Ravensbrück.[28] In that same year, the camp was outfitted with a provisional gas chamber. Between January and April 1945, approximately 5,500 prisoners met their end there.[29]

Initially, Himmler ordered that the new inmate be given preferential treatment. Her hair was not shorn, for example, and she was allowed to read books. However, that leniency evaporated when she reportedly attacked a female guard. Shortly thereafter, Himmler gave the order for her execution. As the Raschers' story demonstrates, during National Socialism, kidnapping, identity fraud, and murder were considered the exclusive domain of the state.

*****

In a private memorandum sent to Reichskanzler Adolf Hitler, Heinrich Himmler addressed what was broadly agreed within the Party to be two of the most significant threats to expanding and securing the geopolitical power of the Reich. Since the end of World War I, Germany had continued to experience a negative birthrate.[30] Even more worrying to the fascist elite, however, was the fact that the percentage of "undesirables" born within the Reich remained unacceptably high.

To adjust this racial imbalance, a two-part strategy was devised. The first part called for the systematic identification, relocation, concentration, and ultimate extermination of all those deemed unworthy of life. To complement this solution, in the winter of 1933,[31] the second part of the Nazi stratagem was initiated. The purpose of this eugenic plan was to stimulate the establishment of a master race to re-populate and rule over the newly won German territories or "Lebensraum." The name of the organization dedicated to this purpose was "Lebensborn" or "The Spring of Life."

Initially, the Lebensborn program focused upon providing gynecological and obstetric clinics for select Aryan mothers and their offspring within Germany. The first of these clinics, Hochland, officially opened in August 1936. By the end of World War II, eight other Lebensborn facilities had been opened within Germany: "Harz" in Wernigerode (September 1937); "Kurmark" in Klosterheide (September 1937); "Friesland" in Hohehorst (May 1938); "Pommern" in Bad Polzin (May 1938); "Taunus" in Wiesbaden (November 1939); "Schwarzwald" in Nordrach (November 1942); "Sonnenwiese" in Kohren-Salis (November 1942); and "Franken" in Schalkhausen (summer of 1944). For the pregnant wives of German officers, being accepted into the program was considered a high honor. For the unmarried German mistresses who found themselves pregnant, acceptance into a Lebensborn facility was often considered to be a stroke of incredible luck as many offered not only temporary shelter and childcare, but also employment until such time that the single mothers were able to care for themselves and their children. These measures were taken to discourage racially desirable mothers from aborting. As an added incentive, Lebensborn officials routinely went to extraordinary lengths to keep the paternity and identity of Lebensborn children secret. Often located in majestic villas, these seemingly idyllic homes were often in reality maximum-security maternity wards in which the movements of all personnel and patients within the clinics were meticulously monitored.

Almost every minute of the mothers' days was planned with military-like precision. Even the so-called recreation period was filled with obligatory activities. According to eye-witness reports and facility records, the mothers in the program were required to complete courses in cooking, cleaning, childbirth, and childcare.[32] In addition, as of June 1938, all of the facilities were ordered to begin offering a special regime of ideological activities to mold the mothers' thinking or "Weltanschauung" such that it conformed with the National Socialist ideals. From evening sing-a-longs to group discussions of assigned chapters of *Mein Kampf*, mothers were offered a regular diet of Nazi propaganda.[33] Along with these duties, the mothers were expected to take part in regular exercise routines and were served special diets. Even such intimate activities as the frequency and duration mothers nursed or played with their children were regulated and recorded by officials. These records were sent on to Himmler, who took it upon himself to offer the mothers and staff admonishment, advice, or praise. For example, in the middle of the war, he took the time to enthusiastically congratulate a Lebensborn mother, Anni O., for having produced a record amount of breast milk.[34]

Alongside Himmler, a Chief Medical Director was appointed to ensure that all Lebensborn residents and staff adhered to the prescribed regime. Given the importance of this position, one might have expected that a leading gynecologist or obstetrician would have been chosen for this coveted post. Instead, the position was given to a small-town Bavarian general practitioner, Dr. Gregor Ebner. A long-time member of the Nazi Party and self-professed expert on "racial hygiene," Ebner was a former fraternity brother and personal family physician to Heinrich Himmler. In 1937, Ebner closed his private practice and began his Lebensborn career. From the very beginning, the doctor pursued his duties with a single-minded ruthlessness.

Chilling evidence can be seen in the case of "Baby Rosemarie."[35] In a letter sent to Himmler on July 17, 1940, Ebner reported the birth and sudden death of a "defective" female infant who had been born on April 30 in the Kurmark facility. According to Ebner's report, the child had several birth defects, including a club foot, a misshapen ear, a cleft palate, and a complex heart deformity—a diagnosis which presumably was confirmed after careful dissection. In response to Ebner's medical report, Himmler demanded that every step be taken to determine whether the mother or father was to blame for the child's deformities. Once this determination had been made, Himmler ordered the responsible parent(s) to be immediately sterilized and ejected from the Lebensborn program.[36]

An ardent supporter of negative eugenics and an uncommon sycophant, there is every reason to believe that Ebner followed Himmler's directives to the letter, not only in this case but in all other instances where Lebensborn children were deemed "defective." In cases where Lebensborn mothers gave birth to children with mental and/or physical disabilities, the same procedure seems to have been followed. The mothers were quickly and quietly removed from the premises; their membership in Lebensborn was permanently revoked; and their children, if still living, were transferred to a local medical facility which soon thereafter issued a death certificate for the new arrival.

One clinic which was charged with disposing of unwanted Lebensborn children is the Psychiatric Clinic of Brandenburg-Goerden or "Brandenburgische Psychiatrische Landesanstalt Görden." Under the helm of psychiatrist Dr. Hans Heinze (1895–1983), hundreds of children and adolescents were registered, gassed, and dissected there by medical researchers. Between 1938 and the end of the war, it has been estimated that some 1,264 minors were murdered in the Brandenburg-Goerden Clinic.[37] On October 28, 1940 alone, some fifty-eight children were murdered in the clinic's onsite gas chamber. The brains of thirty-seven of these children were delivered to the Kaiser Wilhelm Research Institute where they became a part of Professor Julius Hallervorden's special collection. This was only one of several special deliveries made to Hallervorden and his colleagues. According to a postwar statement issued by the professor, "There was wonderful material to be found among those brains: idiocy, deformity, early-childhood infirmities." To optimize the delivery and distribution process, the Professor went on to describe how he took the pedagogical initiative and provided an instructive dissection tutorial for the delivery staff on how to properly dissect, prepare, and pack the fresh cerebral material for transport. After that, the pathological orders were delivered smoothly and efficiently, in much the same fashion, Hallervorden boasted, as a "delivery truck from a furniture store."[38] For both sides of the delivery chain, the arrangement was a classic win:win situation. The academic staff of medical and psychiatric institutes around the Reich received a regular supply of biological specimens for their teaching and research agendas and the Lebensborn administrators had a means for disposing of unwanted "ballast."

With this goal in mind, the Lebensborn leadership routinely utilized the "medical services" of Görden for "processing" disabled Lebensborn children. For example, in the spring of 1942, under the direction of Maximillian Sollman, the Acting Director of Lebensborn, Inge Viermetz[39] processed the paperwork which sent "Jürgen W.," a disabled Lebensborn child, to his death in the Görden psychiatric clinic.[40] Such cases exemplify one of the undeniable truths of Lebensborn. Officially, the program was dedicated to protecting the welfare of mothers and children. In reality, the organization participated in the systematic destruction of thousands of lives. To help keep the clinics' on-goings secret, special care was taken in selecting the locations of the clinics.

An excellent example comes from the Wienerwald facility in Austria. Originally this unit was home to an exclusive medical clinic devoted to treating one of the deadliest diseases of the twentieth century—tuberculosis. The clinic was established in 1904 by two internationally renowned Jewish specialists for pulmonary disorders, Dr. Arthur Baer and Dr. Hugo Kraus. Having invested their personal savings into this joint project, the doctors soon transformed an abandoned farmland into a world-famous rehabilitation center, which offered patients state-of-the art examination rooms and a fully operational surgical theatre. With its lavishly decorated reading room, manicured gardens, elegant music room, and a palatial dining hall, the clinic was more reminiscent of a turn-of-the-century grand hotel than a medical facility. Within a just few years of its inauguration, the Wienerwald Sanatorium had earned a reputation as premiere rehabilitation center for pulmonary patients. Among its exclusive clientele were the two-time elected Austrian chancellor, Ignaz Siepel (1876–1932), and the melancholy literary genius, Franz Kafka (1883–1924). All that changed, however, in the spring of 1938, when Austria officially joined the German Reich.

On April 21, 1938, the Gestapo arrived on the sanatorium grounds. Dr. Kraus, in a panic, attempted to hide in a storeroom but was soon discovered and taken into custody. A few days later, the Gestapo reported that the medical expert had died in a local hospital from injuries related to a botched suicide attempt. In the meantime, Dr. Baer was formally summoned to Vienna, where he was subjected to intensive interrogation by the Gestapo. Dr. Baer was finally allowed to leave Austria to return to his native Czech Republic, after he had agreed to forfeit his right to the Sanatorium and its surrounding grounds. In the autumn of 1938, the Wienerwald Sanatorium officially reopened as a Lebensborn facility.

What no doubt attracted the Lebensborn officials to seizing Wienerwald was not only the clinic's preexisting superior medical facilities, but also its secluded location. Situated some 70 miles outside of Vienna, it offered just the right amount of privacy and secrecy. To help maintain this seclusion, Wienerwald, like all of the Lebensborn facilities, was assigned its very own civil registry or "Standesamt-L." Here, all of the records of Lebensborn marriages, births, and deaths were maintained. Upon Himmler's express orders, none of the information contained in these files was to be released to any other department or official of the Reich without express permission from his office. Punishments for violation of this order were particularly severe with reference to the residents' identities. As Himmler understood, the success of the program was dependent upon parental anonymity.[41]

During the 1930s and the 1940s, an unmarried German woman who found herself pregnant or, worse yet, a married woman who was suddenly with child while her husband was away fighting for the Fatherland, was subject to extreme social ostracization and legal sanctions (e.g., the loss of employment, divorce, disinheritance, reduction of social services).[42] Rather than face this public disgrace, many selected suicide or abortion. Although the official constitution of the Lebensborn society did not explicitly address this subject, Himmler placed special emphasis on attracting what he and the Party considered to be racially superior, pregnant, single women to secure their offspring for the purposes of National Socialism.[43] In an internal memo written on August 26, 1936, for the officials of the Party's **R**asse **u**nd **S**iedlungsha**u**ptamt (RuSHA) [Central Bureau for Race and Settlement], it was explicitly stated that Lebensborn should solicit the trust of unmarried mothers to prevent them from aborting and reinforcing the nation's population decline.[44]

The negative consequences of modern birth control and abortion upon the German population was a popular topic among Nazis. In a lecture held on June 26, 1931 and printed in a 1932 issue of the NSDAP monthly journal, the *Nationalsozialistische Monatshefte*, Dr. Hermann Boehm concluded that the artificial stoppage of pregnancy and the increasing usage of birth control were the primary causes for Germany's catastrophic birthrate. The horrendous loss of life sustained during war was overlooked, however.[45] During the Nazi period, the expenditure of healthy Aryan life away from the battlefield was treated as an unforgiveable criminal offense. Between the years 1933 and 1942, almost 30,000 women were accordingly prosecuted for having obtained an illegal abortion. Such cases were investigated under the direction of Himmler and the Center for the Prevention of Homosexuality and Abortion [Reichzentrale zur Bekämpfung der Homosexualität und der Abtreibung].[46]

Although Nazi officials preferred children to be born within wedlock, their primary concern was the production of robust Aryan offspring. For that reason, the Party often treated crimes which ended in the birth of a healthy Aryan child with uncommon leniency. For example, in the 1940s, a German court convicted a fifty-year-old farmer for having impregnated his fifteen-year-old niece. The Nazis overturned this decision on August 8, 1942, on the grounds that the farmer's infertile wife had given him permission to rape the girl in hopes that it would provide the couple with a healthy child.[47] As Himmler declared in regular memorandums written to the members of the SS, under the Nazi regime, marriage, sexuality, divorce, engagement, and childbirth were far from being private affairs. They were matters of state to be defined, monitored, rewarded, or punished as the Party saw fit. In the case of the SS who were considered to represent the very best of the Aryan bloodline, Himmler regularly reminded his men that reproduction was a sacred duty to their ancestors and Volk.[48] An example of such correspondence is illustrated in the following memorandum sent on June 21, 1943, to SS Hauptsturmführer A. Arnold:

> Dear Arnold!
>
> To my knowledge, you are your parents' only son. It is my opinion that you should have long since attended to your duty to take a wife and ensure that the family line Arnold does not die out. I expect a response to this letter.
>
> Heil Hitler!
>
> Your Commander, H. Himmler.[49]

Such letters were not considered friendly fatherly advice but a direct order. Officers who failed to take heed soon discovered that there were professional repercussions. During one of his regular reviews of the employment records, Himmler came across the file of a SS Hauptsturmführer Schwarz. Upon discovering that the forty-four-year old had neither married nor produced a child, Himmler sent the officer a stern letter warning him that he would be immediately removed from the SS if he did not take immediate action to correct his genetic dereliction.[50] Himmler did not content himself with letter-writing and circulars. He also offered special financial incentives.

On July 9, 1943, he even went so far as to order the week-long rental of several Bavarian guest houses for the officers of the Nederland Division and their wives for a romantic getaway. Perhaps anticipating a negative reaction to this unusual step, Himmler justified his actions, thusly: "I am intentionally supporting the coming together of married men and their wives. Otherwise, we can hardly expect that the desired and necessary children will be born from these marriages."[51] According to the statistics, it seems that these attempts at stimulating the SS birthrate were not entirely unsuccessful. By late 1938, there were 741 unmarried SS officers who had sired 811 children out-of-wedlock.[52] Although those numbers were probably cause for some jubilance, the Reichsführer was careful to remind his men that great care should be taken to only impregnate racially superior women. In cases where an officer failed to exercise the proper restraint, it was his ethical duty as a member of the SS to see to it that the young lady was properly provided for in accordance with her racial classification. Children whose mothers did not meet the superior racial and ideological standards of the SS would not be accepted into the Lebensborn society.[53]

To be officially accepted into the SS's bloodline, both prospective parents had to undergo a stringent screening process in which their family lineage was meticulously examined across several generations. In addition, adult applicants were subjected to a series of tests to ensure that they met the physical, behavioral, and political standards set for the future progenitors of the Aryan elite. The pregnant wives and mistresses of SS officers and other high-ranking officials of the Nazi aristocracy were generally given special preference among the Aryan applicants. In addition to the racial purity criterion, all Lebensborn parents were also required to pledge that their children would be raised to uphold all of the Party principles. Official affirmation of this pledge took place during the *Namensgebung*: a special "naming ceremony" for Lebensborn children.

A detailed description of the romanticized history of this ritual can be found in the foreword of the 1939 baby name book, *Die deutschen Vornamen*, printed by the "Blut und Boden" [Blood and Soil] publishing house. The societal importance of the name-giving ceremony for the National Socialist ideology is described as follows:

> The Nordic man does not live life as a solitary individual in isolation, without duty or responsibility. Rather, his life first attains its true meaning through his deepening and expanding relationship to his racial clan. The Germanic tribesmen first became a full member of their clan through the celebratory name-giving ceremony which was led by the chieftan as the leader of the tribe. For that reason, the naming ceremony was not a gathering of unrelated individuals who selected a name on the basis of frivolous tastes or trifling fads. These ceremonies were always intimately connected with and subordinate to the tribal traditions, laws, and customs of the clan.[54]

The author of this introduction was none other than Richard Walther Darré. A close protégé of SS Reichsführer Heinrich Himmler, Darré was one of the founders of the SS's RuSHA, the administrative home of the Lebens-born program.[55] With a degree in agricultural science and a specialization in animal husbandry, Darré was a fiery proponent of creating a master race through the carefully controlled selection and propagation of Nordic peoples.[56] The Namensgebung, in his opinion, was an essential rite of passage, marking an Aryan infant's official tribal initiation into the SS blood brotherhood.

For the indoctrination event, a special room was brightly decorated with flower bouquets, and traditional black, red, and white Nazi flags emblazoned with the Swastika. Candles were lit and the alter was adorned with photographs of Adolf Hitler and his mother Clara. The parents, guardians, and invited Nazi dignitaries were traditionally seated directly before the SS-altar upon which the child was laid for the induction ceremony. The pinnacle of this clandestine politico-onomastic spectacle came when the director of the clinic placed an SS dagger over the child's forehead and proclaimed: "Herewith, I place you under the protection of our ancestral order and bestow upon you the name. . . . Carry this name with honor!"[57]

The unmistakable similarity between the Lebensborn ceremonial name-giving and a traditional Christian baptism was not accidental. In copying the sacred religious ritual, the Lebensborn officials sought to replace and thereby undermine the Church's authority. SS parents were strongly discouraged from baptizing their children. In a letter written to the Director of the Hochland facility on May 6, 1940, Dr. Ebner stressed the importance of thwarting Leb-ensborn mothers from christening their children in addition to or even instead of the Namensgebung ceremony. Doing so, he said, constituted an affront to the sacredness of the SS ritual.[58] The importance which the SS placed upon this onomastic induction ceremony is indicated in the reports which facility directors were required to file about the exact procedures followed during the event.

Thanks to an unusually detailed two-page report sent to SS-Oberführer Dr. Gregor Ebner, we now have a meticulous account of the Namensgebung ceremonies conducted at the Kurmark facility.[59] According to the report, the ceremony traditionally opened with a festive song sung by the local chapter of the Hitlerian League of German Girls, "Bund Deutscher Mädel" (BDM). After the recital, the Kurmark director gave a short opening speech about the necessity of preserving the purity of the German bloodlines for the future of the German race and to honor the Aryan ancestors. Another rousing song was then sung by the BDM. Afterward, the most solemn component of the SS ritual began. The Director addressed the attendees with a speech tailor-made for each individual ceremony. In the case of a single mother, for example, the Director reportedly took great care to lavish praise upon her for her uncommon bravery in providing the German Reich with a child, despite not having the protection of a husband or a family.

The Director's speech concluded with the following question: "German mother, are you prepared to raise your child to believe in Adolf Hitler?" After answering with an enthusiastic "Jawohl!," the mother was expected to shake the hand of the Director. The Director then turned his attention to the child's designated guardian(s) and asked the following question: "Guardian, are you prepared to sacrifice your life for this child and his/her mother in the battle of life?" Upon receiving another hearty "Jawohl!," the Director recited a proverb taken from one of the Führer's many writings or speeches. Finally, the Director placed an SS dagger over the child's forehead and made the following pronouncement: "Long shall you lead, [NAME]." The ceremony ended with more music and refreshments.

In her personal recollection of her time in Lebensborn, Dr. Ebner's wife gave a similar description of the many Namensgebung ceremonies she had attended. According to her, the events were particularly festive events with cake, coffee, music. "It was," she exalted, "what you could call a real SS-Party!"[60] Once again, the levity surrounding this event was in all likelihood designed to increase the likelihood of parental participation. Although the SS naming ceremony was never made mandatory, it was expected of loyal Party members. As the Party grew in strength, the pressure placed on Lebensborn mothers to participate in this ceremony seems to have increased as well. According to the statistics collected by German historian Georg Lilienthal,[61] in April 1939, only 48.9 percent of the single mothers residing in a Lebensborn facility decided to have their child go through the Namensgebung.[62] Just three years later, that percentage had risen to 72.1 percent. This significant increase is further evidence of the importance placed on this event by the SS leadership.[63] As such, the personal names selected for the ceremony were not taken lightly. Lebensborn parents who agreed to this induction ceremony were expected to select names befitting this hallowed act. As a general rule, the only names that Lebensborn officials deemed appropriate were German, or better yet, inspired by the ancient Germanic tribes.

*****

Based on the onomastic evidence gathered from inscriptions etched on archaeological artifacts and ancient writings (e.g., the Negru Helmet and Ulfila's fourth-century Bible translation), it has been determined that the personal naming system of the Germanic tribes was governed by a complex system of grammatical and stylistic rules. Almost without exception, these ancient tribal monikers were composed of two thematic elements, usually adjectives and/or nouns. The choice of the first element appears to have been comparatively flexible (e.g., *adal-* "noble," *diet-* "people," *ger-* "lance," *sieg-* "victory"). However, the selection of the second was conscribed by the biological gender of the name-bearer.

While elements with a masculine grammatical gender (e.g., -*bert* "bright," -*fried* "protection," -*hart* "powerful," -*mar* "famous") were principally reserved for building male personal names, elements with feminine grammatical gender (e.g., -*heid* "manner," -*lind(e)* "gentle," -*trud* "power," -*run* "secret/wisdom") were primarily utilized for female personal names. Accordingly, the combinations *Adelbert*, *Dietmar*, *Gerhart*, and *Siegfried* are male names, while *Adelheid*, *Dietlinde*, *Gertrud*, and *Siegrun* are female names. Along with these regulations, names in which either the first or final sounds of the two conjoined elements were homophonous were assiduously avoided. Accordingly, combinations such as **Gergund* and **Baldbert* or **Muthart* and **Barmar* would have been rejected.

In addition to these formation rules, the personal names of the Germanic tribesmen had a high incidence of themes relating to weapons of war (e.g., shields, helmets, spears), revered predatory animals (e.g., wolves, bears, eagles, and ravens) as well as desired physical characteristics and personal attributes (leadership, wisdom, strength, bravery, and victory). According to the early writings of Tacitus, the choice of these themes was not coincidental. Despite their many intergroup differences, the Germanic tribes were all warriors with a complex system of beliefs and rituals. Names were far from being aesthetic markers of reference, but were most probably imbued with mystical powers.[64] As such, it is generally believed the tribes bestowed personal names to protect, inspire, and/ or honor the name-bearer.

As the Germanic tribes were progressively vanquished, scattered, and assimilated by other peoples, the collective knowledge of and adherence to the original system of naming began to erode. Evidence of this disintegration can be seen not only in the declining frequency and popularity of these names, but also in the appearance of names which violated the aforementioned formation rules. Examples include the oxymoronic composition *Friedgund* "peace:battle" or the redundant *Hildegund* "battle:battle."[65] The gradual disintegration of the ancient Germanic naming system might well have resulted in complete extinction had it not been for several momentous non-linguistic events.

Starting with the establishment of the German Empire in 1871, at the turn of the century, Germany underwent a series of extraordinary events: the onset of World War I in the summer of 1918 which Kaiser Wilhelm II erroneously predicted would end in Germany's victory within a few months; Germany's spectacular defeat in the winter of 1918; the signing of the 1919 Versailles Treaty which required Germany to forfeit 10 percent of its former territory and pay approximately $12.5 billion in war reparations—the equivalent to nearly half of the Great Britain's GDP;[66] the death of some 3 million civilians and 2 million soldiers; the return of 4 million wounded veterans who brought with them a grisly assortment of physical and psychological injuries; a crushing unemployment rate and astronomical inflation which saw the price of a single egg rise from the already ridiculously high price of 7.20 Reichsmarks in the summer of 1922 to 30 Reichsmarks by the winter of that same year;[67] widespread hunger and the proliferation of deprivation-related diseases (e.g., tuberculosis, rickets, and typhus). Confronted with such a depressing alltag, the seduction of escaping to a highly romanticized vision of Germany's ancient glory-days seems to have become irresistible to many. Already during the Weimar Republic, a resurgence could be seen in the public's interest in the legendary rites and rituals of the Germanic tribes, including their name-giving practices.

The increased incidence of traditional and ancient German personal names had therefore already begun with the founding of the German Empire.[68] Once the National Socialists seized power, however, this fascination grew into a national obsession. To feed this onomastic hunger, publications began to appear on the market that romanticized the Germanic tribes and their ancient naming customs. Particularly popular during this time were specialty guidebooks to help fascist parents find just the right Germanic name for their National Socialist newborn. An excellent example comes from the 1934 publication by Bogislav von Selchow. In the introduction, Selchow provides the following orgiastic description of the Germanic tribes' onomastic legacy:

> In the first names of our own blood, one can hear the clanging of swords and see the blitz of lances. One can still discern the whisper of fame, the crashing of the ocean waves, the howling of the Winter storm, and the magic of ancient secret wisdom.[69]

The influence of such baby name books was not limited to parents-to-be. They were also regularly consulted by parents who had long since named their children but wanted to make sure that their choices were in line with Party expectations. In a case from December 18, 1937, a Wilma and Willy G. filed to have the name of their ten-month-old daughter changed from *Ruth*. According to their petition, they had chosen the name without knowing that it came from the Bible. Upon making what for the NS parents was apparently a horrifying discovery, it became clear to them that the name was entirely inappropriate and therefore "respectfully requested" that the name "be stricken from the birth registry" and "replaced with the name Elke." The letter was dutifully signed: "Heil Hitler!"[70]

A few years later, in 1939, another popular baby naming book appeared on the market, *Give your Children German Names!* [Gebt den Kindern deutsche Namen!]. As the extortive title foreshadows, this guide also praises the beauty and rich tradition of the personal names once used by the ancient Germanic tribes.[71] Along with this praise, however, comes a condemnation: namely, the unusually named author, F. Khull-Kholwald, sharply criticizes Germans for their unhealthy addiction to adopting the onomastics customs of foreign countries.

The result was, according to him, the creation of ugly, absurd, and at times completely unintelligible names for German children, while foreigners availed themselves of the melodious onomastic treasures of the German language. To stop this onomastic miscegenation, Khull-Kholwald demanded Germans select exclusively German names for their children. In doing so, German parents publicly proclaim their connection to their own Volk, "a people who" Khull-Kholwald declared "had not only produced greatness in the past, but were also destined to do so again in the future." While this naming guide appealed to fascist parents' sense of racial pride, other authors attempted to trigger feelings of guilt or outrage in their readers.

This same strategy was employed in a 1939 naming guide *Deutsche Ruf-namen!* [Give German First Names].[72] In the introduction, the author Ernst Christmann details his motivation for his publication:

> Whenever I stroll along the cemetery of our homeland, a feeling of shame washes over me again and again as I am forced to read on the graves of German children the first name "Margot." The now withered human souls were born during or shortly after the French attempted to systematically destroy Germany and brought their oppression upon the left-side of our Rhinish homeland. Why must it be that a German child is given a French name? Are we really to believe that our culture is so bereft of German names? How can parents turn to the enemy, the oppressor, the tormentor of our people, at a time of our deepest degradation and humiliation and take such markers of shame from our foe?[73]

Two years later, in the 1942 baby naming guide *Wie heißt du?* [What is your Name?], a similar argument is given but with a different enemy. The author Hermine Lettau also begins her work by lavishing praise upon the naming system of the Germanic tribes. For Lettau, the names yielded from this tradition served as a constant reminder of the ancestral purity, honor, warrior mentality which all Germans desire for their children. Then, like her colleagues, Lettau also warns parents-to-be against selecting foreign names, even those from related Germanic languages. "Just as Nannette should remain in France," she reasons, "Sven should stay in Sweden." This simple xenophobia turns into unbridled hatred when the subject of "Hebrew naming" is addressed. Readers are told to, "avoid at all cost Hebrew personal names." According to Lettau, the names *Gabriel, Nathan, Simon*, and *Jakob, Anne, Hanna, Elisabeth*, and *Lilli* are entirely unacceptable for a German child; whereas the names *Diethelm, Eginhard, Willibald*, and *Hugwald, Brunhilde, Erdmuthe, Fredegunde, Siegberta*, and *Wolfhilde* are all praised as beautiful and noble. To help her readers clearly differentiate between the two groups, Lettau marks each Jewish name with a star.

As Lettau and her fellow NS writers agreed, only a German name was acceptable for a German child. Not even Germanic names from one of the Nordic languages (e.g., Swedish, Norwegian, or Danish) were good enough for the next generation of National Socialist.[74] The Head of the Department for the Protection of German Blood and Racial Culture [Blutpflege und Rassenkultur], SS-Brigadefuehrer Dr. Wilhelm Kinkelin, could not have agreed more. On February 12, 1937, after his official inspection of the Hochland Lebensborn facility, the Director complained bitterly about the number of parents who had chosen a Scandinavian name to be given to their child during the naming ceremony.[75] To avert what in his opinion was a shameless bastardization of the sacred ceremony, Kinkelin recommended the introduction of strict regulations requiring all Lebensborn parents to give their children exclusively German names.[76] Kinkelin was not alone in his rejection of Scandinavian names.

In an edict issued by the Reich's Ministry of the Interior on February 18, 1939, Nordic names from Scandinavian countries were officially designated as "non-German" and therefore inacceptable for Aryan children. According to paragraph 2 of the edict, the reason given for this prohibition was that such names neither easily nor readily conformed to the German language. Examples given of such inacceptable names included *Bjorn*, *Sven*, and *Ragnhild*.[77] However, as always, there were exceptions to this regulation. In the edict from August 18, 1938, it was decreed that non-German names that had been a part of the German onomastic store for centuries and were consequently no longer viewed as foreign were to be placed on par with native German names. The edict then went on to give examples of such Germanized names: *Hans*, *Joachim*, *Peter*, *Julius*, *Elisabeth*, *Maria*, *Sofie*, and *Charlotte*.[78]

Another author of a popular baby naming guide was no doubt extremely mindful of such legislation when composing his rabid guide for the NS parent-to-be. The title given this onomastic playbook was simple and to the point: *Deutschen Kinder—Deutsche Namen!* [German Children—German Names!]. The author of this political exhortation was Ludwig Fahrenkrog. In the 1942 edition, Fahrenkrog, like his aforementioned colleagues, also sharply criticizes what he describes as a "flood of non-German personal names," which he claims had "sullied the Aryan name pool." Included on Fahrenkrog's list of condemned names are many which modern speakers would classify as being prototypically German (e.g., *Klaus*, *Peter*, *Achim*, *Jürgen*, *Hannelore*, and *Rosemarie*). According to Fahrenkrog, the true National Socialist was without a doubt also an anti-Semite for whom no Jewish name was acceptable. An Aryan child had a natural right, he insisted, to carry a pure, German name. On his list of acceptable German names, Fahrenkrog offered special praise for those related to the name *Adolf*. According to him, this noble onomastic root was used by the ancients to describe someone whose body was well formed and healthy; whose mind was of superior intellect, emotional balance, and nobility; whose entire being was so impeccable that it formed the genetic foundation upon which the Germanic bloodline should be propagated.[79] Obviously, this description has nothing to do with objective scientific analysis.[80] As German historian Volker Koop observed, "once the National Socialists came to power, scientific reasoning was defeated by racial insanity."[81]

The market for NS inspired ideological baby name books was clearly influenced by Hitler's political ascendancy. However, the laws stating that German children should have recognizably German names actually came several decades before the Nazis came to power. On March 27, 1899, for example, the Upper House of the German Parliament or Bundesrat decreed that whenever possible German children should be given German names. By the time the Nazis took power, their horde of legal strategists effectively utilized such language policies to fortify the Party's segregationist politics while undermining the authority of other competing institutions like the Church.

*****

Lebensborn parents were strongly discouraged from naming their children according to the traditions of the Christian Church. The widespread practice of naming children after saints and martyrs was particularly frowned upon. During a Namensgebung ceremony held on April 17, 1940, in the Hochland Lebensborn facility, the Clinic Director sharply criticized this widespread tradition:

> There was a time when the only names people could give their children were of men and women who, since the beginning of Christianity, had based their entire lives upon self-denial, and whose ultimate goal was the defilement and castigation of their bodies.[82]

Rather than name their children after such religious leaders, the Director reportedly called upon Lebensborn parents to follow the example of the Germanic peoples. Male children, he said, should be given German names connected with heroic battle, courage, bravery, victory, and ferocity; and female-children should receive German names related to chastity, honor, feminine pride, and dignity. Only such names, he declared, could serve as perpetual reminders that the newest members of the SS should devote their lives to bringing honor to the Party and their Führer.[83]

In the absence of knowledge about the phonological, syntactic, and morphological rules of the Germanic tribes' personal naming system, many Party members began to generate an increasingly odd assemblage of pseudo-ancient names. Even the highest members of the Nazi aristocracy could not resist the temptation of trying their hand at creating a Germanic name. In a letter written on August 19, 1939,[84] Heinrich Himmler responded to a family friend,

SS Oberführer Dr. Hans Deutschl, who had made a formal request to have his wife's name changed from the marked name *Sara*, the name that had been designated by the Nazis as an official and compulsory marker of Jewish identity.

> Dearest Hansi!
>
> Thank you ever so much for your letter. I find it very appropriate and right that your good wife is to receive a new name. Of course, I never found it agreeable that a German woman like your wife would be called 'Sara' But why don't you make it a bit easier on yourselves. Simply drop the letter 'S'. This would yield the doubtlessly Germanic name of 'Ara'. Naturally, I also have nothing against your plan of renaming your wife 'Sigrid'.
> Warm greetings from our house to yours.
>
> Heil Hitler!
>
> Your old friend, HH[85]

Whether Herr and Frau Deutschl took Himmler's advice is not known. What is known is that they were not alone in their effort to avoid names that might be considered Jewish. On August 18, 1938, the Jewish newspaper, *The Sentinel*, reported on a court case in which an underage boy was granted permission to change his first name *Joshua*. According to the paper, the Court's explanation for the ruling was as follows:: "Joshua is not a good name for a good Nazi . . . because it 'sounds Jewish.'"[86] What made the case particularly unusual was the fact that the name change was granted although the boy's father had been against it because *Joshua* had been handed down in the family for generations.

Aryans who refused to follow the onomastic Party line could expect to become the target of social pressure and physical threat. In another news item featured in a 1939 edition of *The Sentinel*, it was reported that the official newspaper of the SS, the *Schwarze Corps*, had harassed Aryan cigar merchant *F. Israel*, for "refusing to change his name in defense to the Nazi anti-Jewish campaign."[87] This was not the only case of such resistance identified during the course of this investigation.

*

On September 11, 1938, Pastor Friedrich Luncke and his wife Luise proudly looked on as their first-born child was baptized *Esther Luncke*.[88] What normally would have been a wholly joyous celebration was marred by a recent declaration from the local authorities. Almost exactly a month to the day of the baptism, the Lunckes had been informed that they would not be permitted to name their daughter *Esther*. They would have to select a different name, a name that was more appropriate for a German child, a name that was less Jewish. The fact then that Luise and Friedrich had nevertheless christened their daughter with the name *Esther* was an act of open defiance: and one that they knew would most Lkely have very serious repercussions. But, there again, this was not the first time that the Lunckes had chosen their faith over politics; and it most certainly would not be the last. Looking back, it would not be correct to say that the Lunckes had chosen this fight for the sake of simply being obstreperous, although many Party loyalists would accuse them of being so. In fact, just the opposite appeared to be the case. It had taken no time at all for the newlyweds to make a name for themselves in the tiny parish of Spenge[89] for their compassion, generosity, and kindness. Of course, during the Third Reich, those very qualities were not always appreciated. In fact, Pastor Luncke had been politely asked to leave his first parish after church-authorities had witnessed him rush up to an elderly woman he'd seen struggling to push a wheelbarrow through the cobblestones streets. "I'm going the same way you are. Let me get that for you!," he'd said as he cheerfully came to the woman's aid. The powers that be had deemed such behavior unseemly for a man of the cloth. It was clear, the Pastor would have to leave.

The people of Wattenscheid, a small coal mining community located ouside of the city of Bochum in North Rhine Westphalia, welcomed the kindly cleric and his family into their community. The Lunckes would soon need that support. It did not take long before the local authorities learned of the recent baptism in the Pastor's family, hardly surprising given the fact that the Lunckes had placed an official announcement of Esther's christening in the local newspaper. As far as the Lunckes were concerned, they had nothing to hide. They had put a great deal of thought into selecting a name for their little girl. A child's name should not be chosen lightly. It was a symbol, a guide, a declaration of one's beliefs. On this point, the authorities could not agree more. As far as the state was concerned, the Luncke child would remain nameless until such time that the parents selected an acceptable name.

The Lunckes refused to acquiesce and appealed. Initially, the local authorities appeared to see reason and granted the family the right to name their daughter *Esther*. However, an official complaint lodged by the Lord Major led to a reversal in the decision and the entire process began again.[90] At a time when representatives of the church and state were expected to take a personal oath of unquestioned allegiance to Adolf Hitler, such obstinacy was broadly read as unpatriotic, subversive, and dangerous. Pastor Luncke, however, was a member of the Confessional Church, a German Protestant movement that staunchly resisted the attempts of the NSDAP to unite all of the churches together under one umbrella organization, the Protestant Reich Church.[91] According to Winfried Seibert, a German legal scholar who has researched the Luncke case extensively, it was no accident that the Lunckes selected the name *Esther*.

In the Old Testament, it was Esther who uses her intellect to put a stop to Haman's plot to slaughter the Jews. Thanks to her bravery and benevolence, it is Haman who is executed in the end for his own treachery. Based on personal notes which Seibert discovered in the Pastor's personal Bible, Seibert postulates that the Lunckes saw clear parallels between Haman and Hitler.[92] Their selection of their daughter's name was a public declaration of the system of beliefs. Emboldened by their faith, the Lunckes pursued their case, until a panel of three judges was appointed to make a final decision. After reviewing the entire case file, the judges issued their verdict. The name *Esther* was not permissible for a German child. The crux of judgment was based on their scathing interpretation of the child's would-be Biblical namesake:[93]

> A figure the likes of Esther, who played such a prominent role in history—and not for her transparent and fair dealings but for her cunning, trickery, deception along with her misuse of her female wiles and her social position—such a lawless harlot of the Jewish race cannot have any meaning for German women in our times; and German parents may not be permitted to have such a figure serve as the name-sake for their daughter.[94]

The decision, the judges concluded, was ultimately in the best interests of the child who would suffer immeasurably from carrying the burden of such an ill-chosen name in National Socialist Germany. The Lunckes had now exhausted all of their appeals and were instructed to select another name for their daughter. The name the Lunckes selected was *Elisabeth*.

News of the legal defeat was not only covered in Germany, but also reached as far away as the United States. On December 5, 1938, page 19 of *The Dayton Herald* carried a story entitled "Nazis Ban Esthers." That same month, more articles covering the story appeared in newspapers around the United States (e.g., *The Philadelphia Inquirer* and *The Carlisle* in Pennsylvania; *The Baltimore Sun* in Maryland; *The Capital Journal* in Salem, Oregon; *The Salt Lake Tribune* in Utah; *The Daily News* in New York; *The Detroit Press* in Michigan; and *The Austin American* in Texas)[95]. For the Luncke family, the legal defeat also marked the beginning of many personal disasters, the first and foremost being the successive deaths of the couple's two sons. Then, in 1943, the Pastor was called up for military service and forced to leave his grieving wife behind.

On the battlefield as in civilian life, the Chaplain immediately made a name for himself. Only this time it was not for his gentle, affable manner, but for his fire and brimstone sermons in which he unabashedly questioned the legitimacy of a society which seemed to put such great stock in making sure that the trappings of power were immaculate and pristine, while so many of the nation's finest were left to rot in putrefying mass graves. Miraculously, Pastor Luncke survived not only World War II, but also the Nazis. By the end of 1945, he returned home to his family in Wattenscheid.

As the Allied Forces took over command of what was left of Nazi, Germany and repealed the laws of the Reich, Pastor Luncke lost no time and submitted a special request. On May 25, 1946, he and his wife received word that their petition had been granted. Their daughter's name would be officially changed from *Elisabeth* to *Esther*. After losing so many battles, the couple had finally won their personal war. What makes this case all the more remarkable is the fact that by the time name change was granted, tragedy had struck the Luncke home again. On March 16, 1941, five years before their name petition was finally granted, the Luncke's beloved daughter had contracted a fatal case of scarlet fever and diphtheria.[96] In a remarkable demonstration of resistance, her grieving mother and father made sure that their little girl's death certificate read: *Esther Luncke*.

*

During this investigation, onomastic resistance among residents with the classification of Aryan was extremely unusual. For the most part, there was great willingness to conform to the Party expectations. Be it to avoid dangerous reprisal or to display personal allegiance, the public hunger for names that conformed with the National Socialist agenda seemed insatiable at times.

Not all Aryans could warm up to the sound of the ancient Germanic monikers, however. For those who preferred more modern alternatives, there was another name source available. NS parents could simply borrow the names of a fellow Party member in good-standing. This was the strategy followed by Gerda and Martin Bormann when facing the challenge of naming their six children. Their sons' names (*Adolf Martin, Rudolf-Gerhard, Heinrich Hugo*) were strategically chosen to honor the Führer, Heinrich Himmler, Rudolf Heß, and their father. Two of their daughter's names (*Gerda* and *Ilse*) were also inspired by prominent women in the Führer's intimate circle (i.e., their mother and *Ilse Heß*).[97] The Bormanns' strategy offered the double advantage of publicly demonstrating one's loyalty to the Party and currying favor with potentially useful allies. However, this practice was not without danger, as the Bormanns discovered.

In May 1941, immediately before the Nazis' planned invasion of the Soviet Union, Rudolf Heß flew to Glasgow to meet with British officials. In a secret, completely unauthorized mission, he hoped to broker a peace agreement and bring an end to the war. When the Führer learned of the action, he immediately stripped Heß of all of his offices and declared his former confidant to be a psychopathic traitor. In the wake of the Führer's wrath, anyone and everyone who had had a close association with the Heß family was automatically suspected of treason. This turn of events spelled disaster for the Bormann family for Rudolf Heß was not only Martin Bormann's immediate superior, he and his wife were also the godparents and namesakes of two Bormann children. In a public declaration of their unquestioned loyalty to the Führer and unconditional contempt for the Heß's, the Bormann's announced that, effective immediately, their children would no longer be called *Ilse* and *Rudolf-Gerhard* but *Eike* and *Helmut Gerhard*.[98] The onomastic reboot worked. Hitler was duly impressed and the Bormanns' position within the Führer's coveted inner circle was reaffirmed.[99]

*

In their search for the perfect Nazi name for their newborn, some Party loyalists demonstrated a disturbing degree of creativity, especially when devising names for their daughters. Two particularly striking coins include *Fricklinde* and *Goebbelen*, inspired by the Reich's Miniter of the Interior, Wilhelm Frick, and Propaganda Minister, Joseph Goebbels, respectively. What makes these choices especially striking is that rather than selecting already well-established feminine versions of the Nazi leaders' first names (i.e., *Joseph* → *Josephine* or *Wilhelm* → *Wilhemine*), the parents used the politicians' surnames to create new, presumably unique female first names. In this way, they showed an exceptional level of ingenuity, and unambiguously demonstrated their political affinity.

After all, the namesake of a *Wilhemine* might have been anyone but the inspiration for *Fricklinde* was unmistakable. Moreover, in the case of *Goebbelen*, this invention had the added advantage of circumventing the name *Joseph* which was increasingly stigmatized as being Jewish. For all this ingenuity, it is a matter of historical irony that the parents' petition to use these names was ultimately rejected on the basis of a law signed by both Goebbels and Frick. Passed on May 19, 1933, this legislation prohibited the public abuse of national symbols, including the names of National Socialist leaders.[100] Of course, Goebbels and Frick were not the only leaders whose names garnered the attention of enraptured Party parents-to-be.

On April 7, 1933, the NSDAP regional office in Duesseldorf received a special request from a Party member asking permission to name his daughter *Hitlerine* in honor of the Führer.[101] Although the member was warmly praised for his loyalty, his request was denied on the grounds that the Führer's name was "far too noble and sacred to allow it to be misused for such national clichés . . . if a National Socialist desires to name his son or daughter after our Leader, he has the opportunity to give the child the first name of *Adolf* or *Adolfine*."[102] Just how sacred the Führer's name was held is expressed in an essay "Eine mythische Blutsverbundenheit" [A Mythic Blood Tie] written by the anti-Semite Professor

Dr. Johann von Leers. In this essay, von Leers describes the mystical importance of the Führer's name for the National Socialist movement:

> There is so very much behind it . . . it is like a mythical blood tie between the warrior and the Führer . . . just as it most likely was in ancient times when the warriors of the nomadic Nordic peoples, who before plunging themselves forward to meet their certain deaths— roared the names of their leaders who now lay buried in anonymous graves! That is what makes this movement so unique and almost completely inscrutable to the outsider—just as the members of this movement greet one another with the name of the Führer, so too will they die with his name on their lips.[103]

The public's adoration for the Führer was not limited to names given to people. On May 27, 1932, a F. Dittrich respectfully requested permission to bring two new products onto the German market: a *Hitler-Cigarette* and a *Hitler-Cigar*.[104] In anticipation of being granted permission to proceed with what he believed would be a lucrative business, Dittrich was careful to stress in his letter that he alone would be the sole owner of the brand name. A similar request was issued on August 1, 1933 by B. Koch. The avid gardener enthusiastically reported that he had successfully created a high-quality strawberry which he respectfully asked to name the *Hitlerberry*.[105] In another letter from March 7, 1933, the rose horticulturalist Karl Robert K. requested permission to name one of his best breeds after the Führer before marketing it worldwide.[106] On October 26, 1934, the tiny church parish of Dannenwalde in Brandenburg inquired whether they might be allowed to name their new bell the *Adolf Hitler Bell* in honor of the Reichskanzler.[107] And, in that same year, at least two insects were named after the Führer: the now nearly extinct, blind, brown, acid spraying cave beetle,[108] *Anophthlamus hitleri*;[109] and the *Rochlinga hitleri*, a flying insect fossil (paleodictyoptera)[110] named after both the Führer and Hermann Röchling, a coal and steel industrialist who built an empire on slave labor in the Saarland before being convicted of war crimes.[111]

In most instances, the Reich Chancellery's response to such requests was a more or less polite "No!" with the rather incredible explanation that the Führer did not allow his name to be used for propagandistic and/or commercial purposes. However, in the case of the church parish, permission was granted. The explanation given for this exception was that the bell had apparently already been completed. In the case of the cave beetle, the new chancellor appears to have been rather pleased by the idea. He event went so far as to send a letter of thanks to the name-giving entomologist Oskar Scheibel.[112] These reactions seem to have been rather unusual, however. In fact, the Fuehrer's often office responded with icy indignation, when it was discovered that the chancellor's name had been used without permission: a fact which pastry chef Bruno U. discovered.

On April 20, 1933, the hopeful entrepreneur received an incensed letter from the NSDAP district office of East Prussia lambasting him for producing an *Adolf-Hitler-Torte* and, in so doing, abusing the Führer's name for his personal economic gain. In his response, the pastry chef assured the authorities that he had immediately removed the offending cake from his assortment. In his attempt to explain the offending baked-good, the chef stressed that he was a long-time, loyal Party member and that his only intention in creating the gateau had been to satisfy his many NSDAP customers who had repeatedly asked why his establishment served a *Hindenburg Cake,* but did not offer a delicacy to honor the Führer.[113]

Given the unrelenting number of requests to use the Fuehrer's name for personal or professional purposes, the government felt compelled to take definitive legislative action. In a telegram sent on July 3, 1933 from the Office of the Reich Chancellery, it was explained that in the past the German courts had allowed citizens to give their children such names as *Bolschewika* and *Stahlhelmine.*[114] That being the case, it was understandable that the public might assume that first names such as *Hitler* for boys and *Hitlerine* or *Hitlerike* for girls would also be deemed permissible. However, such names were to be strenuously discouraged as the Reichskanzler himself had expressed extreme displeasure in his name being so abused.[115] There could be only one *Adolf Hitler.*

*****

The pressure to find an acceptable name was especially great for parents whose children happened to be born on October 7, the Reichsführer's birthday. As per tradition, all racially valuable Lebensborn children born on this day were automatically eligible to be designated his godchild. In addition, Himmler also often agreed to serve as a guardian for the children of high-ranking officials. As a result, there are scores of Germans who knowingly or unknowingly have Himmler as their godfather.[116] Table 3.1 presents a small sampling of these children's first names and birth years (BY).

Not surprisingly, many of the male names displayed in table 3.1 follow the onomastic pattern of the Germanic tribes (e.g., *Dernhard, Friederum, Hartmut, Reinhard, Siegfried,* and *Ulf*). A strong preference for the personal names of leading Party members is also evident. The Führer's first name, *Adolf,* for example, appears with the highest frequency. Overall, 17.33 percent of the male children in this sample had this name either alone or in combination (e.g., *Adolf-Ferdinand, Adolf-Horst,* and *Adolf-Rudolf*). Among the hyphenated names, the most popular combined the first name of the Führer

Table 3.1 First Names (FN) and Birth Years (BY) from a Selection of Himmler's many Godchildren

FN	BY	FN	BY	FN	BY	FN	BY	FN	BY
1. Dagmar	1937	26. Gertrude	1944	51. Horst	1942	76. Heinrich	1943	101. Roland	1935
2. Gisa-Dagmar	1943	27. Gerda	1936	52. Thea	1939	77. Karl	1938	102. Gustav	1934
3. Hans	1943	28. Reinhold	1938	53. Peter	1942	78. Bernhard	1942	103. Adolf-Hermann	1936
4. Günther	1937	29. Veronika	1944	54. Peter	1941	79. Astrid	1939	104. Heinrich	1934
5. Dieter	1938	30. Adolf	1935	55. Werner	—	80. Waltraud	1944	105. Adolf-Heinrich	1933
6. Heinrich	1944	31. Adolf	1935	56. Anneliese	1943	81. Reinhard	1936	106. Adolf-Horst	1935
7. Ulf-Elmar	1938	32. Jürgen	1943	57. Horst	1941	82. Arnold	1944	107. Adolf-Heinrich	1935
8. Detlef	1930	33. Dieter	1941	58. Antje	1939	83. Edeltraut	1942	108. Adolf-Rudolf	1935
9. Heinrich	1940	34. Walter	1941	59. Reinhard	1942	84. Manfred	1939	109. Adolf	1927
10. Manfred	1942	35. Friederum	1940	60. Rolf	1942	85. Ingomar	1937	110. Hermann	1935
11. Liselotte	1936	36. Adolf	1935	61. Horst	1936	86. Sigrid	1941		
12. Renate	1941	37. Brigitte	1942	62. Gerlinde	1938	87. Uwe	1944		
13. Helge	1943	38. Wolfgang	1940	63. Karl-Wolff	1940	88. Hartmut	1941		
14. Walter	1943	39. Wilfried	1939	64. Heinrich	1939	89. Jorg	1940		
15. Jürgen	1939	40. Adolf	1939	65. Ingeborg	1939	90. Iris	1941		
16. Eveline	1939	41. Heinrich	1938	66. Arno	1938	91. Brigitte	1939		
17. Roland	—	42. Luise	1939	67. Adolf	1939	92. Heinrich	1947		
18. Helga	1941	43. Arnd	1944	68. Siegfried	1944	93. Siegfried	1939		
19. Adolf-Ferdinand	—	44. Irmgard	—	69. Freia	—	94. Dieter	1940		
20. Erna	1936	45. Heinrich	1943	70. Helga	1943	95. Elfriede	1937		
21. Kurt	1938	46. Karl	1937	71. Wolfgang	1937	96. Siegfried	1939		
22. Heinrich	1942	47. Eike-Gertrud	1941	72. Adolf-Hermann	1941	97. Helga	1936		
23. Hildegard	1944	48. Heinz	1942	73. Karl-Heinz	1942	98. Helga-Anna	1940		
24. Ella	1939	49. Sibylle	1939	74. Kai-Jasper	1939	99. Heinrich	1942		
25. Hermann	1944	50. Hans	1941	75. Dietlinde	1941	100. Heinrich-Adolf	1941		

with the first name either of Reichsmarschall Hermann Göring or Reichsführer Heinrich Himmler (i.e., *Adolf-Heinrich* and *Adolf-Hermann*, respectively). Not unexpectedly, the second most common male first name was
Heinrich, alone or in combination (e.g., *Adolf-Heinrich* or *Heinrich-Adolf*).

The popularity of *Adolf* and *Heinrich* as names for Himmler's godsons is
particularly striking when one considers the fact that neither ever reached the
top-twenty list in Germany between 1930 and 1949. One can only specu-
late, of course, over the reason(s) for this difference in onomastic tastes. Perhaps the parents of Himmler's godsons felt especially entitled or obligated
to pick these names, whereas the rest of the population felt too intimidated
to do so. In other respects, the onomastic choices of these parents were remarkably similar to the general population. Many of the boys' names which
were chosen for Himmler's godsons were also extremely popular within the
general German society during the 1930s and 1940s. For example, *Dieter,
Hans, Günt(h)er, Karl,* and *Horst* all appeared on the top-ten list for this
period of time.

Similar observations were made for the names selected for Himmler's
goddaughters. As with the boys' names, a core segment of the girls' names
also mirrored the onomastic stock of the Germanic tribes (e.g., *Dietlinde,
Edeltraut, Freia, Gertrude, Gerlinde, Helga, Hildegard,* and *Waltraut*). In ad-
dition, many of the girls' names were also extremely popular in the general
German population. However, unlike the boys' names, several of the names
chosen for Himmler's goddaughters were directly in contradiction to the
SS naming philosophy in that they were modern, Christian, and/or non-
German (*Anneliese, Antje, Astrid, Brigitte, Ella, Eveline, Iris, Liselotte,* and
Veronika).[117]

This finding is especially interesting in view of the fact that onomastic
research has consistently shown that parents tend to be far more conservative when naming their sons than when naming their daughters.[118] The
reason most often advanced for this gender difference is that parents (un)
consciously assume that a young man with a traditional name will have
good career chances, whereas, a young woman is better served by pleasant
yet unusual name. This reasoning seems a rather plausible explanation for
the relative creativity and modernity found in the names chosen for the SS
goddaughters examined here. These naming patterns went directly against
the SS philosophy, however.

The maniacal purpose of the Lebensborn program was not only to create
a pure Aryan bloodline for the future preservation of the Reich, but also to
resurrect many of the sacred rituals of the ancient Germanic tribes. With that
combined purpose, the fanatical Lebensborn leadership placed great stock in

the preservation of traditional names for the German offspring born to form the Aryan master race. That was the theory. In practice, this philosophy did not seem to have much sway with the many of Lebensborn mothers when it came time to name their children. In table 3.2, the names and birth years of forty-eight Lebensborn children born from 1937 to 1945 are provided.[119]

As can be seen in this list, several of the names conformed to the official expectation that all Lebensborn children carry traditional German(ic) names (e.g., *Dieter, Diethelm, Dietlind, Gebhard, Guntram, Helmut, Hiltrud, Hildegard, Siegfried, Sigrun, Ute, Wilfried*). However, there were also many names that directly contradicted the official expectation in that they were Christian (*Paul* and *Anne*), foreign (*Jürgen* and *Kerstin*), and/or modern (*Rita* and *Gisela*). As before, quite a few of these onomastic violations appear on the list of girls' names (e.g., *Antje, Anne, Brigitte, Eva, Gisela, Inge, Karin, Rita*). The tendency of Lebensborn parents to gravitate toward popular names, especially when naming their daughters, seems to have been a constant thorn in the eye of many Lebensborn administrators. In a report sent to the Department for Racial Research and Family Studies, on July 2, 1942, the following observation was made:

> For the girls' names, the military marching songs seem to be especially significant. The popularity of the names *Erika* and *Monika, Marie-Luise*, and *Rosemarie* all have these songs to thank for their popularity. . . . On a positive note, foreign names have significantly decreased, albeit not nearly enough. *Margot* and *Marion* are entirely superfluous and in no way more beautiful than *Magret* or *Margrit* and *Marie!*[120]

The assertion that Lebensborn parents were being influenced by popular music in selecting their newborns' names may well have some validity. At the time, many recording artists featured women's names either in their lyrics or song-titles. An example excellent from this period comes from the critically acclaimed sextet, "The Comedian Harmonists." Inspired by the US American quartet "The Revellers," many of their greatest hits featured a girl's name in the title or the refrain. Three examples are "Marie, Marie" (January 19, 1931); "Schöne Isabella aus Kastilien" [Beautiful Isabella from Castile] (June 1, 1932); and, of course, "Veronika, der Lenz ist da!" [Veronika, Spring is here!] (August 22, 1930).[121]

No sooner did the group reach international fame, did the individual fates of the six gifted singers radically turn. The winter of 1933 saw the formation of the Reichsmusikkammer (RMK), a regulatory institution which set as one of its primary goals the purification of the German music industry via the elimination

Table 3.2   First Names (FN) and Birth Years (BY) of German-born Lebensborn Children

MALE

FN	BY		FN	BY
1. Ulrich	1938		17. Hermann	1945
2. Gebhard	1938		18. Helmut	1940
3. Karl	1940		19. Guntram	1939
4. Roland	1940		20. Dieter	1941
5. Udo	1940		21. Jürgen	1942
6. Alko	1940		22. Bernhard	1943
7. Hans-Jürgen	1940		23. Hans	1942
8. Walter	1941		24. Diethelm	1943
9. Paul	1945		25. Herbert	1944
10. Horst	1938		26. Rudolf	1937
11. Paul	1938		27. Wilfried	1945
12. Gerd	1939			
13. Heinz	1938			
14. Siegfried	1939			
15. Ortwin	1942			
16. Hermann	1942			

FEMALE

FN	BY		FN	BY
1. Antje	1939		17. Brigitte	1941
2. Anne	1940		18. Karin-Ursula	1940
3. Margret	1940		19. Bärbel	1941
4. Inge	1938		20. Rita	1942
5. Eva	1940		21. Dagmar	1943
6. Gisela	1939		22. Erna	1939
7. Renate	1945			
8. Hiltrud	1937			
9. Sigrun	1938			
10. Herta	1941			
11. Helga	1941			
12. Ute	1942			
13. Hildegard	1942			
14. Kerstin	1943			
15. Dietlind	1942			
16. Ursula	1942			

of non-Aryan elements. Performers whose names did not appear on the approved list were not allowed on stage. This regulation spelled doom for the sextet and its three founding Jewish members. The Comedian Harmonists played their last concert on March 25, 1934.

At the same time that the RMK destroyed the lives of non-Aryan performers, it was also instrumental in building the careers of Party members. One of the Party's chosen few was Ferdinand Frederich Hermann Nielebock or *Herms Niel*. The wounded World War I veteran and long-time NSDAP member soon caught the attention of Propaganda Minister, Joseph Goebbels. With the Minister's backing, Niel's military marching band music was soon being played on radios and record-players throughout the Reich. Favorites among Niel's fans were songs that told the story of a valiant soldier whose loyal Aryan fiance awaited his victorious return to the Heimat. In each of these songs, the name of girl featured prominently. The only surviving son raised in a household with seven sisters, Niel's supply of girls' names seemed never-ending. *Ursula Rosalinde, Renate, Margarethe, Mara, Marie, Ingeborg, Antje, Annemarie, Edeltraut, Elisabeth, Gerda, Hannelore, Leonore,* and *Erika*[122] were just a few of the names featured in his music that no doubt inspired legions of National Socialist parents-to-be.

*****

Hartmut Wolf was a master tailor who lived at the turn of the century with his wife *Lara* nee *Gottlieb* in the city of Magdeburg. The Wolfs were a very traditional Protestant family who lived a relatively simple, hard-working middle-class life. They were neither active nor even particularly interested in politics. Their focus was solely fixed on caring for their ever-expanding family. By 1897, Lara Wolf had already had eight children and in 1898, the ninth and last was on the way. They named her *Amelie*.

As soon as Amelie was old enough, she followed in her father's footsteps and learned the sewing business. While her father worked with the customers in the front of the shop, Amelie, who had a very good head for numbers, worked in the back doing the book-keeping. No sooner had the horrible Great War ended, did talk begin that another might start any day. From the customers in the shop to her parents at home round the dinner table, there was only one topic of conversation. Another great war was coming. During this period, Amelie left her parents' business and went to work at the local confectioners where she soon was given the post as departmental director. It was in this position that Amelie met someone who would change the course of her life forever.

Not much is known about the charismatic stranger who stole Amelie's heart. The way he moved, the color of his hair, the sound of his voice, the books he read, the dreams he may have had . . . even his name remains a mystery. The only two pieces of information that we have of him today is that he was an SS officer who had been temporarily stationed in the area; and in no time at all, Amelie was pregnant.

Although the Reichsführer had repeatedly stated that every healthy child born of pure-blooded Aryan parents was a gift for the nation and the Führer as far as Amelie's small town was concerned, an unmarried pregnant woman was a disgrace to herself and scandal for her family. A solution had to be found. That solution came from Amelie's lover, who was able to use his connections and secure Amelie a place in a Lebensborn home in northern Germany. Located some 260 kilometers away from Magdeburg, the Friesland facility must have felt like a godsend. Not only would the two lovers be able to keep their romance a secret, but Amelie would be able to give birth to their child in a secure and safe environment.

So, with a small suitcase in hand, Amelie said goodbye to her parents, friends, and colleagues, and made her way to the city of Bremen. A few months later, she gave birth to a healthy little girl. Despite the fact that Lebensborn mothers were encouraged to give their children names reflective of their pure Aryan heritage, the new mother chose a rather modern non-Germanic name. Her daughter would be called *Amelie-Lara*, after Amelie's mother and herself.

Flaunting another Lebensborn regulation, Amelie also saw to it that her daughter was baptized—Protestant: Just like she had been, and her mother before her. It is not known whether Amelie informed the SS about that baptism or in which church it took place. Almost everything about her daughter was kept a secret. Indeed, as far as most of Germany was concerned, the child had never even been born.

Several months later, once she had properly regained her strength and the tell-tale signs of pregnancy had disappeared, Amelie returned home to Magdeburg. She left her baby girl behind to be cared for by the trained nursing staff of Friesland. In the meantime, Amelie devoted her every waking moment to preparing a new life for herself as a single mother. There would be no father for Amelie-Lara. Sometime after securing the placement in the Lebensbornheim, the SS officer had received orders to leave Magdeburg. It is unclear whether he was ever informed by a Lebensborn official that he had become the father of a healthy baby girl. His name does not appear on any of the surviving Lebensborn records. Amelie was on her own.

Two years after leaving the home, in 1942, the new mother was finally ready to bring home her daughter. It is not known what story she invented to explain the little girl's sudden appearance. Did she perhaps tell people that she was taking care of an orphaned child from a distant relative who had died in the war? Did she say that the little girl was a foundling? The people who have the answers to those questions have all passed away. All that we know is that Amelie brought her daughter home and, somehow, thanks to fierce ingenuity and uncommon luck, both mother and daughter survived the war. In that two-person home, Amelie, like her parents before her, never discussed politics, not even when their hometown of Magdeburg became a part of East Germany and politics were ever present. Nor did Amelie ever speak about the man in uniform who had come to their town so many years ago. For the single mother, her daughter knew all that she needed to know: Amelie-Lara had been conceived in love and raised in love. In 1987, Amelie Wolf died. She never married.

After her mother's death and the collapse of the German Democratic Republic, Amelie-Lara slowly began to search for the missing pieces of her life. She had one word to go on: Lebensborn. Eventually, she was able to locate a support group made up of other adult Lebensborn children who were also searching for their roots. After a meeting in 2005, that small group founded an official Society named "Traces of Life" [Lebenspuren]. Since then, the organization has grown substantially. Its members primarily include adult Lebensborn children, many of whom are now in their eighties and nineties. It also includes historians, therapists, and social workers who attempt to help them heal the deep scars that Himmler's program left behind.

According to the now seventy-nine-year-old Amelie-Lara, her wounds come from the many questions that she never dared to ask while her mother was alive and may never find the answer to now that her mother has died. In reflecting upon her parents—the mother whom she knew so well and the father she never met—she is certain: "The relationship between my parents was pure love. It had nothing to do with politics and certainly NOTHING to do with wanting to provide Hitler with a child!" Having researched the history of the Lebensborn society, she is also aware of the fact that her experience is by no means "typical." But, as she is careful to stress, that very difference underscores a very important all too often forgotten fact. There is no one, universal, Lebensborn experience. Although all of the facilities were under one umbrella organization, the staff, the residents, and the daily routines varied greatly from one home to the next.

In comparison to other Lebensborn children, Amalie-Lara considers herself to be extremely lucky. "I never went through the pain that so many Lebensborn children had to endure." At the same time, it would be inaccurate to say that she escaped unscathed for she, like so many other Lebensborn children, is forced to live with so many unanswered questions. Who was her father? What did he do during the war? Did he survive? Does she have brothers and sisters? Who were her grandparents? Where did they come from? Did any of them know about her? Did they ask questions about her like she still asks about them today?

The history of the Lebensborn facility where *Amelie-Lara* was born actually begins thousands of miles away in the US city of Brotherly Love. In the late nineteenth and early twentieth century, the port city of Philadelphia was home to some of the world's largest and most innovative confectioneries—much to the consternation of France's premier bonbon and chocolate-makers. In 1854, the thirty-one-year-old Pennsylvania entrepreneur Stephen F. Whitman introduced the world's first pre-packaged candy boxes to the confectionery market: "Whitman's Choice Mixed Sugar Plums." That trademarked creation became the forerunner to another sweet sensation, the now famous "Whitman's Sampler." Protected by a revolutionary cellophane wrapping, Whitman's box of assorted candies promised its customers fresh, high-quality chocolates.[123] The product soon became a best-seller throughout the United States. In recognition of Whitman's culinary and marketing genius, in 1878, the American Quaker was given an award for "product excellence" at the Paris International Exposition.

The cornerstone of Pennsylvania's award-winning candy industry was the production of refined sugar. Alongside its labyrinth of confectionaries, the metropolitan seaport was also the business address of numerous small, medium, and giant sugar refineries. In the year 1870, there were no less than fifteen different sugar manufacturers operating in Philadelphia. One of those sugar refineries was owned and operated by the German immigrant Reinert Ficken. In his personal rags to riches story, *Reinert* changed his name to *Richard* and started the Philadelphia-based company "Ficken & Williams Steam Sugar Refiners" with his partner, Fielding L. Williams. In 1867, the duo pioneered and patented a procedure for cleaning and purifying "bone-black," a form of charcoal produced when heating animal bones for use as a decolorizing and purifying agent in the manufacture of sugar. According to the patent, the Ficken and Williams method made it possible to efficiently collect large quantities of bone-black without "the nuisance and injury to surrounding property which takes place when the dust is allowed to escape into the atmosphere."[124] Their invention was a gold mine.

At the turn of the century, when mavericks like Milton Hershey, Gail Borden, and D. L. Clark were establishing US American candy-dynasties, self-made millionaire Richard Ficken found his attentions drifting back to the homeland he had left behind. In 1868, he purchased a sizeable patch of land in the picturesque countryside of northern Germany, outside of the German seaport of Bremen. A year later, he ordered the construction of a spacious family residence called "Schloss Hohehorst." However, it was not until a rather odd turn of events that he made the final leap and returned to his Hanseatic roots.

On the evening of February 14, 1870, a group of teenage boys were out delivering Valentine's Day letters. Whether Ficken knew the teens or thought they were up to no good is unclear. All that is known is that when the young men approached his home, Ficken produced a pistol and shot one of the boys in the leg. The bullet caused considerable damage and left the fourteen-year old with a septic wound that threatened to leave the teenager severely disabled. Public interest in the crime involving the famous sugar refiner was great. Even thousands of miles away on the West Coast, the papers carried the strange story of the Valentine's Day shooting. Two weeks after the event, *The Sacramento Daily Union* published an update on the case. Under the sensationalistic headline "Shot for leaving a Valentine," the California-based reporter informed readers that the young victim remained "feverish and in a restless condition" and that the shooter had, "expressed his regret at the occurrence, and his willingness to bear the expense attending the injury."[125]

After the shooting, Ficken was initially placed under arrest but then quietly released on bail upon the condition that he agree to return to court for a formal hearing. However, when Ficken's court date arrived, he was nowhere to be found in Philadelphia or Pennsylvania or even the United States for that matter. He was on his way back to Germany where his brand-new mansion awaited him. When news of Ficken's escape emerged, the public outcry was great. Even a year later, the Philadelphia paper, *The Daily Evening Telegraph*, carried a story which lambasted the Philadelphia justice system for allowing a man to, "escape the consequences of crime because he is able to command a greater amount of wealth than his neighbors."[126] The reporter's prediction that Valentine's Day in Philadelphia would forever be tied to this crime did not come to fruition, however. Eventually public outrage shifted to other injustices and Ficken was never made to stand trial for the shooting. However, in a freak riding accident, just three years after the mysterious shooting, Ficken suffered a serious leg injury himself and died from complications. In 1883, the surviving Ficken family sold the estate to another wealthy German entrepreneur, Christian Leberecht Lahusen, exporter and importer of fine furs and leathers.[127]

The Lahusen family significantly extended the original grounds and held the property over three generations. By the fourth generation, the family's wealth and influence had exponentially expanded and they were known throughout Europe and North America among the super wealthy. Although the family remained true to its textile roots, over the years it had switched from furs to wool and was the owner and operator of Nordwolle [Norddeutsche Wollkammerei und Kammgarnspinnerei Norddetusche]: the largest textile company in Europe and one of the world's biggest single-producers of wool products. In 1921, the fourth generation of the Lahusen family took over the business. Along with the change in leadership, the guiding strategy of the business altered as well—from parsimony to decadency.[128] Unfortunately, the new owners' eye for fine details did not extend to financial markets. Aside from a temporary upswing in 1927, the price for wool followed a stubborn downward trajectory for many years.[129] Despite this fact, the new patriarchs of Nordwolle, G. Carl and Heinz Lahusen, continued to expand their stores of wool in the vain hope that the market would eventually turn around. At the same time the brothers' penchant for borrowing the company's revenues to finance their extravagant lifestyles took on megalomaniacal proportions.[130]

In 1928, the family tore down the Ficken's "Schloss Hohehorst" and replaced it with a grandiose 107-room Victorian villa adorned with the finest marble, mahogany, crystal, silk, and ivory company money could buy. More than 100 servants were employed to maintain the lavish villa with the surrounding forest, hunting grounds, fountains, stables, ponds, and sculpture gardens. Although only intended as a summer residence, the transformation of the villa cost an estimated 3.5 million Reichsmark. Seven different architects, eight master sculptors, and ten artists worked day and night to create the architectural masterpiece. Incredibly, the Lahusens demonstrated an even greater appetite for modernization and growth where their global business interests were concerned. Soon the personal financial capital needed to feed this insatiable hunger was exhausted. The Lahusen brothers then used their family name and influence to borrow even more funds to pay their mounting bills and created even more debt. To keep the credits flowing, the new family patriarchs constructed an elaborate web of lies and fraud.

An unexpected audit by one of their primary creditors, the Darmstädter und Nationalbank (DANAT), eventually revealed the unthinkable. The Lahusen's were not simply in financial trouble: they were utterly and completely bankrupt. The extent of the fraud was astronomical, even by today's standards. The family owed in excess of 800 million Euros or 970 million US dollars.[131] The financial tsunami caused by the collapse of Nordwolle was catastrophic. In addition to thirteen different banking institutions in Germany, the death of Nordwolle directly threatened the existence of eighteen foreign banks that had also loaned the family-owned dynasty millions.[132] When news of the financial fraud hit the press, there was a run on the banks, as customers large and small attempted to rescue their savings from the impending implosion. Through the intervention of the German government, some, but by no means all, of the bad banks were saved. DANAT, the second largest bank in Germany at the time, was destroyed, however. It alone had loaned the family 45 million Reichsmarks in credit.[133]

In view of the damage wrought, G. Carl Lahusen, the family patriarch principally responsible for the debacle, received a surprisingly lenient sentence of five-year imprisonment and a 50,000 RM fine.[134] Among the wealthy and powerful who intervened on behalf of the Lahusens was none other than Hermann Göring.[135] For many in the landed gentry, the Lahusen's had already paid the highest price: they suffered not only the irrevocable ouster from Europe's high society but also the humiliating forfeiture of their coveted properties, including the just completed architectural triumph, "Hohehorst." The regional bank of Bremen took possession of the country residence, auctioning off whatever it could to recover at least some of the horrendous losses.[136]

On September 4, 1937, the SS purchased the residence for a total of 60,000 Reichsmark, one tenth of the true property value. Under the direction of SS Untersturmführer, Otto Bachschneider, the estate was re-modeled to suit its new residents. The lavish residence was outfitted to accommodate approximately thirty mothers and forty children. On May 1, 1938, the residence was reopened under the official name *Heim Friesland* but was also informally referred to as *Heim Hohehorst* or simply *Hohehorst*. Even before the facility had officially opened, the first Lebensborn mother of Heim Friesland gave birth on April 25, 1938. According to the SS officials, the home seemed to be off to an excellent start. During the rest of that year, another ten children were born. In 1939, the number of births jumped to 86; and in 1940, a total of 116 children were delivered in Heim Hohehorst.[137] In table 3.3, the official daily schedule devised for mothers in the Friesland facility is presented.[138]

The curator of the Hohehorst Lebensborn Archive, Hans-Werner Liebig, has conducted numerous interviews with mothers and the now adult children who once lived in Hohehorst. Despite the rigid routine, not a few of the former residents look back fondly on their time in the home. Some even stated that the comradery, friendship, and acceptance they experienced there made that time one of the best of their lives. No doubt, the relative comfort and beauty offered by the tranquil surroundings of the luxurious villa with its expansive manicured gardens, finely decorated rooms, and high-tech modern conveniences played a role in this assessment. The same is probably true for the round-the-clock security offered by the SS officers sworn to give their lives to protect the Aryan women and children living in the home. For all its idyllic appearance, it is important to remember that the Lebensborn facility had one single purpose: the propagation of the Aryan race.

With that purpose in mind, naming ceremonies were regularly held in Hohehorst to formally induct the children into the SS fold. On August 16, 1939, an official report was written to SS Oberführer Dr. Ebner detailing the ceremony that had taken place the day previous.[139] According to the report, five members of the SS military unit "Bremen" volunteered their time to provide musical accompaniment for the service, and roughly twelve SS officers served as godfathers for the child inductees. Among the SS godfathers was Gunter D'Alquen, the Chief Editor of the SS weekly newspaper, *Das Schwarze Korps* [The Black Corps]. After a short speech about the importance and meaning of the ceremony, thirteen children were given their official SS names.

In alphabetical order, these children's names were *Anna-Luise, Christa, Dietrich, Gesche, Gerhard, Gisela, Heidrun, Heinrich, Hella, Inge, Johanna, Karin,* and *Ulrike*. Even in this short list, a few interesting patterns are seen. Along with

Table 3.3   Daily Schedule of Lebensborn Mothers in the Friesland Facility

TIME ALOTTED	ACTIVITY
5:00–6:00	Breast-feed
6:00–6:30	Bring sleeping quarters in order
6:30–7:00	Drink coffee
7:00–8:00	Bathe
8:00–9:00	Breast-feed
8:30–9:00	Eat breakfast
9:00–10:45	Change child's diapers and perform housework
11:00–11:30	Eat lunch
12:00–13:00	Breast-feed
13:00–14:45	Nap
14:45–15:15	Drink Coffee
15:15–16:25	Breast-feed
16:15–17:45	Change child's diapers and perform housework
17:45–18:15	Eat dinner
18:15–19:30	Recreation
19:30–20:30	Breast-feed
21:00	Retire to sleeping quarters: LIGHTS OUT

the expected traditional German(ic) names (i.e., *Dietrich, Gerhard, Heidrun,* and *Heinrich*), the parents also selected names typical of northern Germany (e.g., *Gesche*, a Frisian variant of *Gertrud*). In addition, the list contains several names that were relatively dispreferred by Lebensborn officials due to the unwanted influences of foreign (albeit Nordic) countries (*Karin, Inge*); fashion-trends (*Anna-Luise*); and Christianity (*Christa*). The naming ceremonies performed in Heim Hohehorst were typically held in the main hall, with a bust of Adolf Hitler placed on the fireplace, large bouquets of flowers, candlelight, and a large SS flag draped over the marble mantelpiece. Hung on either side of the fireplace were two framed plagues with SS maxims written in calligraphy: (1) "man and woman are the foundation of the future"; and (2) "for those bound by common blood belong to a united Reich."

In 1940, the SS purchased another 3.5 hectares of land around the villa which the mothers, children, and staff enjoyed during their daily regime of sports. However, once the Allies radically intensified their air raid attacks upon Bremen, the authorities deemed that the premises had become far too danger-ous. On January 9, 1941, the residents and staff were temporarily evacuated to the Bavarian Lebensborn facility "Heim Hochland." According to the official records, the transport consisted of forty-nine Lebensborn children and ten nurs-ing mothers who were airlifted on Heinrich Himmler's own private plane from

Bremen to Bavaria. It would take another three years before the Hohehorst Heim was reopened.

During this period of time, some of the Hohehorst staff members went on to work in other Lebensborn facilities. Such was the case of Fraulein Ilse B. After assisting with the Hohehorst evacuation to Bavaria, the seventeen-year old began work in Heim Steinhörig outside of Munich. She was then transferred to an entirely new facility, this time in Eastern Europe. Located approximately 50 kilometers outside of the Polish city of Lodz, the "clinic" was situated in the town of Zduńska Wola which the Nazis renamed *Freihaus* after the 1939 invasion of Poland. In marked contrast to the Hohehorst and Steinhörig facilities, the conditions at Freihaus were anything but luxurious. The specialization of the clinic was so-called ethnic Germans, a tiny fraction of whom, in the demented eugenicist logic of National Socialism, had potentially salvageable Aryan blood despite partial contamination through exposure to inferior races. Children and mothers who did not meet this racial criterion were either to be used as slaves to serve the Aryan race for the rest of their lives or were to be immediately disposed of as biological ballast.

In 1944, the Hohehorst villa reopened its doors. As the Allies reclaimed Scandinavia, children in Norwegian-based Lebensborn facilities were sent down South to the Friesland facility. In total, between 1944 and 1945, Hohehorst housed thirty-three Norwegian-born Lebensborn children.[140] The following forenames are among those recorded for this group: *Ansbjörn, Anne Brit, Bjarne Walter, Bruner, Bruno, Erik, Ester, Fridjof, Fritz, Georg, Gerd, Gudmund, Heinz, Helmut Werner, Ingar, Jan, Jan Erik, Kari, Karl Sigfrid, Karl Herbert, Klaus Dieter, Lauritz, Margarete, Per, Rolf Arne, Rudi, Sven,* and *Turi*. This collection of names clearly reflects the children's German and Scandinavian background.

After the war, efforts were made by relief agencies such as the Red Cross to repatriate the Lebensborn children in Norway. However, the Norwegian government rejected the requests. In a desperate attempt to find the infants new permanent homes, a deal was made with Swedish adoption agencies. All of the children would first have to be given new new names and identities; only then, would they be put up for adoption by Swedish parents.[141] According to the curator of the Hohehorst Archive in Bremen, the majority of these children are still searching today to discover the real names and identities.[142]

*****

Just what lengths the Lebensborn staff went to conceal the identity of their exclusive clientele is illustrated by the case of Juul op ten Noord, Director of the Hejthuijsen Reich School for Girls in Holland. Despite having been born and raised in the Netherlands, op ten Noord still possessed German citizenship. As such, she was eligible to take part in the Lebensborn program. In a detailed letter from September 15, 1943,[143] Himmler enthusiastically invited the pregnant Director to check into one of the Lebensborn facilities in Germany one to two months before her due date. Once there, she would be free to give birth to her child in peace and comfort. After she had fully recuperated, she would be free to leave the facility and resume her life as if nothing had ever happened. In the meantime, her child would be fastidiously cared for by the Lebensborn staff. Once a safe period of time had transpired, she could then apply to the facility to adopt her very own child. Whether or not she later decided to reveal her child's true parentage, Himmler explained, would be entirely her decision. As a Lebensborn mother, she would also be given the freedom to select her child's surname. She could either use her own surname or that of the child's father, whichever name she preferred. Whatever choice she made, the necessary documentation would be supplied by the Lebensborn civil registry under the careful supervision of the Lebensborn legal consultant, Dr. Günther Tesch.

It is unclear today precisely how many Dutch(-German) children were a part of the Lebensborn program or its affiliated competitor, the Nationalsozialistische Volkswohlfahrt (NSV), a fascist organization also dedicated to "the preservation and promotion of racially valuable German stock."[144] What is clear is that both Hitler and Himmler identified the Dutch as being a potentially desirable source of Aryan blood. In the hopes of establishing the first of many Lebensborn facilities in the Netherlands, a representative was sent to The Hague to begin negotiations with sympathetic Dutch authorities. That representative was Inge Viermetz.

Fairly quickly after her arrival, a Jewish-owned piece of property was identified and confiscated for the first Dutch Lebensborn facility. According to the initial plans, this facility would be called "Gelderland." It was scheduled to begin operation in the summer of 1943.[145] However, due to the lackluster support of Dutch officials, the facility never opened. In fact, despite the best efforts of the German authorities, Lebensborn was never really able to gain a solid foothold in the Netherlands. In other Western European countries, however, Lebensborn was quite successful in establishing a network. One of the best examples is Norway.

In the winter of 1940, Himmler met with Lebensborn Acting Director Max Sollman and SS-Obergruppenführer Wilhelm Rediess, the commander of the Waffen-SS in Norway. The topic of discussion was the establishment of Lebensborn facilities in Norway. With approximately 6,000 German troops stationed in Norway, the officials reasoned that in no time at all a large selection of highly desirable "supply" of "German-sired" children would be available. Himmler was anxious to take advantage of this unique opportunity and directed Ebner and Sollman to begin making plans immediately. In a letter to Rediess, Himmler reportedly stated that he was overjoyed with the thought of all the racially superior children who would soon be arriving from Norway. A clear indication of Himmler's enthusiasm was the enormous amount of money set aside for this project.

For the first year alone, Lebensborn allocated a budget of no less than 2.3 million Reichsmarks for the establishment of the first Norwegian facilities. By the end of the war, this yearly budget had grown to reach 6.2 million Reichsmarks. With this constant influx of money, between the summer of 1941 and the spring of 1945, a total of twelve different Lebensborn facilities had opened their doors for operation in Norway. One of the Lebensborn administrators who worked with Norwegian officials to establish this network of SS-run facilities was Inge Viermetz. Whereas the mothers in the Lebensborn facilities in Germany and Austria received training on how to be a superior National Socialist, the education program in the Norwegian facilities focused on transforming the mothers and their children into good Germans. This meant that mothers were expected to take courses in traditional German cuisine, dress, holidays, and language. In addition to these intensive courses, the Norwegian mothers were also introduced to the basics of National Socialist ideology. Finally, as the future mothers of German children, they were also made to solemnly pledge to raise their children to be loyal members of the SS-fold.

According to historical records and eye-witness accounts collected by historian Kåre Olson,[146] mothers in the Norwegian facilities were therefore also strongly encouraged to take part in a SS Namensgebung for their newborns. Much like the ceremonies held in Germany, the naming ceremonies in the Norwegian facilities were also held in a festively decorated room, with rousing music and invigorating political speeches about the momentousness of the occasion. As with the Namensgebung in Germany, the naming ceremonies in Norway also marked the infants' official entry into the SS fold. Based on Olson's research, between November 1941 and May 1942, around sixty children went through this onomastic induction process. After 1942, the frequency of Namensgebung ceremonies in many of the facilities seemed to wane. The last induction ceremony held in "Hurdal Verk," the oldest and one of the largest Lebensborn facilities in Norway, took place in May 1942. By comparison, the Klekken facility in Hønefoss continued to perform these onomastic services until as late as February 1945. Olson speculates that the reason why Klekken continued to hold Namensgebung ceremonies so much longer than the other facilities is that this institution was reserved for Norwegian mothers who had been identified as having the most valuable bloodlines. Despite these internal rankings, as a group, the Norwegian mothers were only valued by Lebensborn officials for their birthing potential. Once their babies were delivered, their importance for the Reich radically diminished. Therein lies an important national difference. The German and Austrian Lebensborn mothers were generally encouraged to keep their children.

By comparison, many of the Norwegian mothers were pressured into giving their children away. Such was the case with Solveig Wighus, a young Norwegian woman who found herself carrying the child of a twenty-seven-year-old German machine-gun operator, Otto Ackermann. In February 1945, Ackermann fell during combat in Lettland. In her desperation, Solveig agreed to have her son, *Otto Wighus*, sent to a foster family until she could provide for the two of them. Unbeknownst to her, the Lebensborn officials changed her son's name to *Otto Ackermann* and placed him for adoption in Germany. The Dollingers, a German family residing in a rural Bavarian village, renamed their newly adopted son *Johann Baptist Alexander Dollinger*. It was not until "Hannes" was fifteen that he learned that he was adopted. It was then that his personal saga to reclaim his original identity began. The key to unlocking the mystery of his identity was the long line of names that had accompanied him on his journey. "Hannes" or "Otto" was in luck for all of his name changes had been relatively well documented via the Lebensborn Civil Registry Office.[147] Following the successive chain of name changes eventually led him back to his original birthplace and birth mother. Many other Lebensborn children have not been so lucky. For the vast majority of Lebensborn children, their onomastic trails leading back to their original identities were often purposefully destroyed.

*****

On May 27, 1942, Obergruppenführer Reinhard Heydrich's car was ambushed while on route to a meeting with Hitler. The partisan bomb exploded in the rear-end of the automobile, shattering part of Heydrich's rib-cage, perforating his diaphragm, puncturing his lung; and sending shrapnel and car-seat upholstery deep into his spleen. Heydrich was rushed to the local hospital where an emergency operation was performed. To decrease the chance of infection, the decision was made to remove his spleen. The day after the surgery, Heydrich was examined by Professor Dr. Karl Gebhardt, a top surgeon from Berlin. Gebhardt reported to Berlin that Heydrich was in relatively good spirits and would no doubt make a full recovery. Gebhardt's prognosis proved wrong, however. Just a few days after the surgery, sepsis set in and Heydrich slipped into a coma. On June 4, a little over a week after the bombing, Heydrich was pronounced dead. On June 9, Hitler called an emergency meeting with Himmler and other high-ranking officials from the Bohemian and Moravian territories to decide upon the Reich's revenge for Heydrich's assassination. Hitler's initial ideas for exacting revenge were to have 10,000 Czechs shot or to eject several million Czechs from their homes. After careful deliberation, a compromise was reached.

In the late evening hours of June 10, lines of trucks rolled into a small Czech village. The women and children were herded into trucks and driven to an undisclosed location. The remaining 173 male villagers were sent to gather at a local farm. The next morning, shortly after sunrise, the men were instructed to place mattresses against a stone wall, as execution squads took their position. The purpose of the mattresses was to protect the murderers from ricocheting bullets. The shooting went on without pause for approximately two hours. After the last villager had been murdered, the bodies were placed in neat rows and photographs were taken to document that the Führer's orders had been carried out. The executioners then ransacked the now empty houses, taking with them livestock, food, radios, and bicycles. On Himmler's and Hitler's explicit instructions, the entire community was to be so obliterated that not even the name of the village would be remembered. In the end, precisely the opposite occurred. Long after the war, the atrocities committed in that small community are immortalized by the village name, "Lidice."

While the bullet-ridden bodies of their menfolk bloated in the sun, the women and children of Lidice were separated into two groups. The first group was made up of women and infants who were sent to the Ravensbrück Concentration Camp. The second group was made up of children and young teens who were to be examined by a team of "racial experts." On the basis of these examinations, eighty-two children were immediately labeled "unworthy" and transported to the Chelmo death camp. For the remaining handful of children who were classified "worthy," an odyssey of torture, horror, and fear began. These children had been chosen for possible inclusion in Himmler's clandestine re-germanization program.

According to Nazi ideology, the bloodlines of the Germanic tribes had been progressively sullied through generations of interbreeding with racially inferior peoples. Despite this fact, it was believed that a few select children had a sufficiently high proportion of Aryan blood to warrant their "re-patricization" in the Fatherland. The purpose of this plan was two-fold: (1) to critically weaken the enemies of the German Reich by harvesting or destroying their greatest natural resource—their children; and (2) to substantially increase the size and strength of the German Reich through the infusion of new blood. According to Himmler's initial projections, this plan could yield 1 million new members of the German Reich. To make this nightmare a reality, Himmler declared that it was his solemn intention to rob and steal Aryan blood wherever it was to be found in the world.

As the Nazis extended their power into Central, Northern, and Eastern Europe, tens of thousands of children were stolen from occupied territories. In many villages like Lidice and Ležáky, the "racially desirable" children were wrested away from their parents who were summarily executed. In other cases, unsuspecting children were snatched from streets, hospitals, orphanages, playgrounds, and schools. In still other cases, parents were sent official summons instructing them to bring their children to a designated address for a mandatory health inspection. This strategy was commonly followed, for example, in Poland.

Parents whose children were classified as racially valuable were told that their sons and daughters would have to be kept temporarily for additional tests. Despite these reassurances, many parents remained suspicious and took special precautions. For example, in her research on Polish children stolen by the Nazis for Aryanization, historian Ines Hopfer[148] uncovered the story of Anna K. When Anna's mother received the news that her daughter had been selected for the Nazis' medical examination, she gathered what little money she could and had her daughter photographed. Then she carefully cut a tiny hole in the seam of her little girl's winter coat and hid a miniscule piece of paper containing her daughter's full name, address, and the contact details of her relatives. She then sewed the seam shut and reminded her daughter to always keep her coat with her, so that she would never forget who she was. As Anna K. later recalled, although she was so small that she could neither read nor write at the time, she never forgot her mother's words. What neither realized at the time, was that all of the children who were accepted into the program were forced to remove all of their clothing and put on German attire. Anna K. became one of Poland's "lost children."

Once it became clear that the German officials had lied, many parents did whatever they could to recover their stolen children. In most cases, however, it was too late. The children had already been sent to central assimilation centers for further anatomical, psychological, and cognitive tests. The purpose of the tests was to determine the children's suitability for "germanization." Children who either failed or resisted this testing were sent to concentration camps. Of those few children who were deemed suitable, two different groups were formed. Younger children between the ages of approximately two and six were frequently sent directly to a Lebensborn facility for immediate adoption. Older pre-teen children were sent to special training facilities where they were drilled in the German language and values of the National Socialist Party. Assisting in this culling process was, yet again, Inge Viermetz. For those children who satisfactorily completed this training, a special ceremony was conducted to mark their official acceptance as a bona fide National Socialist. Once again, the highlight of this indoctrination ceremony was the bestowal of a new name.

According to survivor accounts, during the ceremony the children were assembled and a required to stand at attention. A visiting Nazi dignitary then delivered a formal speech in which the children were told that their countries of birth were doomed and their families had long since either forsaken or forgotten them. This, according to the officer, was no reason to despair, however, as they would soon be returning to their rightful ancestral homeland where they would live to serve their beloved Führer and the Fatherland. As Aryanized children, they would each be assigned a new German family who would adopt them as one of their own. After this speech, the officer read the original Polish name of each child. Upon hearing their name, the children were expected to step forward. Into each child's hand, the officer placed a paper scroll containing the child's date of birth and new official German name. With this renaming act, the children's past identies were symbolically buried and their new identities as life-long members of the Reich were born.

As per the official RuSha policy, all Aryanized children were to receive their new official German name before being transferred to a Lebensborn facility for adoption. As was the case for most of the activities organized by the Nazis, extremely strict, formal guidelines were established for the development of the children's new German names. According to a directive issued by the RuSha Chief on September 17, 1942, the new names were not to deviate significantly from the children's original birth names. In cases where it was not possible to Aryanize the preexisting names, the indoctrinated children were to be issued commonly used German names. The guidelines warned officials, however, against using names which either carried strong religious associations or had a "pronounced Nordic character." Following these instructions, Polish boys with the names *Ryszard, Jan, Bogdan, Slawomir,* and *Henryk* were given the new German names *Richard, Otto, Karl, Johann,* and *Heinrich*; and four Polish girls *Wiesława, Wacława, Bogumiła,* and *Halinka* were renamed *Wilhelmine, Waltraud, Erna,* and *Helene*.[149]

In an official medical report prepared for the Adoptions Department and addressed to Dr. Ebner, detailed information about several clandestine adoptions involving stolen children is provided. According to this document, a child born on April 29, 1937, with the original first name *Kazimierz* was renamed *Klaus*; a Romanian child, born on January 21, 1936, was to receive the name *Hermann*; and *Zygmunt,* who was born on August 17, 1936, was to be renamed *Sigmund*. In two other cases listed in the report, nearly identical German variants of the children's original names were used. As a result, a little girl born on March 27, 1935, and a small boy reportedly born on January 15, 1938, were given the names *Helene* and *Alexander* respectively.[150]

Along with the first names, the surnames of these and other kidnapped children were also similarly altered. In cases where a similarly sounding German surname could be identified, this name was selected. Accordingly, *Bukorzyck* became *Buechner; Czanogorski* became *Scharnweber;* and *Zeslowski* became *Zallinger*. In other instances, the original name was translated. Thus, two children with the surnames *Ogrodowczyk* and *Mlznarczyk* had their last names translated into *Gartner* and *Mueller*. Another common method used by the Nazis involved altering the spelling of the children's original surnames by clipping and/or adding non-German elements. Thus, *Hanfová, Rostocka, Adamiak, and Antczak* were altered into *Hanf, Rost, Adams,* and *Antzinger*.[151]

It is unclear why such care was taken to maintain such close ties to the children's original names. One reason could of course have been the hope that the similarity between the original and forced names would increase the children's ability and/or willingness to retain their new identities. Another potential motivation for selecting such similar-sounding names might have been to decrease the chance of raising undue suspicion if the children inadvertently uttered the "wrong name." Alternatively, the policy may have been instituted for record-keeping purposes. Given the Nazis' notorious obsession for keeping lists of names, Party officials may have reasoned that it would be easier to keep track of the whereabouts of the stolen children by using names which were readily traceable. Supporting this theory is the fact that upon their arrival in the Lebensborn facility, the children were recorded by both their Germanized aliases and original names. Although the children were never referred to using their original names once the Namensgebung had taken place, given the complexity of the deception involved in maintaining this large-scale international kidnapping ring, following pre-determined name-changing strategies would most likely have been an invaluable identity-tracking aid.

Increasing the level of onomastic subterfuge even more, Lebensborn officials routinely invited prospective adoptive parents to alter the names (and even birthdates) of the stolen children. This additional name change would have made it that much harder for foreign officials to discover the children's true identities. All such name changes were processed with the legal guidance of Dr. Günther Tesch in conjunction with the Lebensborn's own civil registry office, Standesamt-L. Although not all of the parents who adopted Lebensborn children availed themselves of this offer, many did. In the following excerpt, a future parent writes a letter to Heinrich Himmler, expressing his gratitude and excitement over the upcoming adoption of a Lebensborn child called Wilhelm:

> 14th of March 1943
>
> My dearest Heinrich,
>
> On the 1st of March, my wife and I were in the ideally situated, wonderfully functionally decorated, Lebensborn facility Sonnenwiese in the town of Kohren/Salis. It was there that we picked out our future son. . . . All that we know about him is that he is the child of brutally murdered ethnic Germans. . . . We want to name the boy *Haymo Heinrich. Haymo* is an old Bavarian name which is hardly even recognized today . . . and the name *Heinrich* is in memory of you—a gesture which has become heartfelt matter of honour.[152]

Based on what we know today, the chances are rather high that the little boy's parents were indeed "brutally murdered." However, the person who gave execution order was in all likelihood not some partisan rebel as the adoptive parents had been led to believe but the very person whom they had chosen as a namesake for their adopted son: Heinrich Himmler.

*****

During the Nuremberg Trials, fourteen members of RuSHA were prosecuted. Of the accused, four members of the Lebensborn program were put on trial: Acting Program Director, Maximillian Sollman; Chief Medical Director, Dr. Gregor Ebner; Chief Legal Advisor, Dr. Günther Tesch; and Lebensborn Division A Co-director, Inge Viermetz. All four were charged with having committed crimes against humanity; being a member of a criminal organization; and perpetrating war crimes.

The prosecution argued that the accused had participated in an international criminal network. Within that organization, they had not only knowingly stolen properties of Jewish citizens, but had also participated in the murder of children deemed unworthy of life; cooperated in the mass murder of civilians; and kidnapped thousands of foreign children who were tortured, brainwashed, and forced into foreign-adoptions under assumed names. To support its charges, the prosecution produced several former Lebensborn employees who testified about the abuses they had seen or experienced first-hand. In addition, the prosecution called to the stand several victims of the Lebensborn program. One of them was fifteen-year-old *Maria Dolezalova*.[153] One of the few surviving children of the Lidice massacre, Ms. Dolezalova detailed how after her father's murder, she had been forcibly separated from her mother and made to take on a German identity under the false name of *Ingeborg Schiller*.

In view of the damning evidence, the defense was forced to concede that "mistakes" had been made during the war. Nevertheless, the defense contended, Lebensborn was in principle a charitable organization. When placed on the stand, the accused testified that Lebensborn had rescued thousands of orphaned children by providing them with food, clothing, an education, and in some cases even adoptive parents. The new names which the Lebensborn officials had devised for the children had only been to facilitate their successful integration into their newly provided homes, the accused argued.

Incredibly, the Court sided with the defense. After nearly a year of hearing evidence, the court ruled that there was only sufficient evidence to convict Ebner, Tesch, and Sollman on the charge of being a member of a criminal organization, the SS. Viermetz was found innocent of all four charges. All four were released for time-served. Several years later, in 1950, a German court, re-tried the case and, after reviewing the evidence, came to a completely different conclusion: namely, that the Lebensborn program was far from a charitable organization. It was a criminal organization that had played a key role in the Nazis' atrocities.

Notes

1. Volker Koop, *Dem Führer ein Kind schenken: Die SS Organisation Lebensborn e.V* (Cologne: Böhlau Verlag, 2007), 15.
2. Julien Ritzenstein, *Himmlers Forscher: Wehrwissenschaft und Medizinverbrechen im "Ahnenerbe" der SS* (Paderborn: Ferdinand Schönigh Verlag, 2014), 36.
3. Koop, *Dem Führer ein Kind schenken*, 15.
4. "'Perfect Nazi Woman' in London," *The Sydney Morning Herald*, March 9, 1939. From *rove* (online archive), National Library of Australia, https://trove.nla.gov.au/newspaper/article/17583379/1172693.
5. Ritzenstein, *Himmlers Forscher*, 36.
6. Koop, *Dem Führer ein Kind schenken*, 15.
7. Anna Maria Sigmund, *Die Frauen der Nazis II* (Munich: Wilhelm Heyne Verlag, 2002), 271.
8. Michael Kater, *Das 'Ahenenerbe' der SS 1935–1945: Ein Beitrag zur Kulturpolitik des Dritten Reiches* (Munich: R. Oldenbourg Verlag, 2006), 239.
9. Kater, *Das 'Ahenenerbe' der SS*, 239.
10. Kater, *Das 'Ahenenerbe' der SS*, 240.
11. Kater, *Das 'Ahenenerbe' der SS*, 241.
12. Sigmund, *Die Frauen der Nazis II*, 274.
13. Kater, *Das 'Ahenenerbe' der SS*, 241.
14. Wolfgang Benz, "Dr. med. Sigmund Rascher: Eine Karriere." Medizin im NS-Staat: Täter, Opfer, Handlanger. *Dachauer Hefte* 4 (Munich: deutscher Taschenbuch Verlag, 1992), 194.
15. Benz, "Dr. med. Sigmund Rascher," 212.
16. Sigmund, *Die Frauen der Nazis II*, 279–80.
17. Kater, *Das 'Ahenenerbe' der SS*, 239.
18. Paul Weindling, *Victims and Survivors of Nazi Human Experiments: Science and Suffering in the Holocaust* (New York: Bloomsbury, 2015), 54.
19. Koop, *Dem Führer ein Kind schenken*, 15.
20. Benz, "Dr. med. Sigmund Rascher," 213.
21. Sigmund, *Die Frauen der Nazis II*, 280.
22. Sigmund, *Die Frauen der Nazis II*, 281.
23. During this period of time in Germany, the Roma and Sinti people were referred to as "gypsies."
24. Kater, *Das 'Ahenenerbe' der SS*, 423.
25. Benz, "Dr. med. Sigmund Rascher," 213.
26. Koop, *Himmlers Germanenwahn: Die SS Organisation Ahneneerbe und ihre Verbrechen* (Berlin: be.bra verlag, 2012), 206.
27. Kater, *Das 'Ahenenerbe' der SS*, 242.
28. Benz, "Dr. med. Sigmund Rascher," 213.
29. www.ravensbrueck.de.
30. After World War I, Germany "exhibited the sharpest birthrate decline in Europe, reaching an unprecedented low in 1933 of fewer than one million live births."

Larry Thompson, "Lebensborn and the Eugenics Policy of the Reichsführer-SS," in *The Nazi Holocaust*, ed. Michael Robert Marrus (Munich: De Gruyter, 1989), 601.

31. In that same year, the Nazis began to pass a series of laws designed to progressively hinder and then ultimately prohibit non-Aryans from practicing medicine. For more, see Robert Lifton, *The Nazi Doctors* (New York: Basic Books, 1986).

32. For more, see Kathrin Kompisch, *Täterinnen: Frauen im Nationalsozialismus* (Cologne: Böhlau, 2008); Georg Lilienthal, *Das "Lebensborn e. V.": Ein Instrument nationalsozialistischer Rassenpolitik* (Frankfurt am Main: Fischer Verlag, 2003); Thomas Bryant, *Himmlers Kinder* (Wiesbaden: Matrix Verlag, 2011).

33. Georg Lililenthal, "Medizin und Rassenpolitik: Der Lebensbornder SS." In *Deutsches Ärzteblatt*. B. 85. 1988: 2128–34.

34. Marc Hillel and Clarissa Henry, *Lebensborn e.V.: Im Namen der Rasse* (Hamburg: Paul Zsolnay Verlag, 1975), 74.

35. Bundesarchiv (BArch), NS 19/1159, 3.

36. BArch, NS 19/1159, 3.

37. Ernst Klee, "Verschonte Medizinverbrecher: Die Professoren Heinze und Hallervorden," *Dachauer Hefte 13: Gericht und Gerechtigkeit* (December, 1997), 142–52.

38. Klee, "Verschonte Medizinverbrecher," 146.

39. Viermetz began her career with Lebensborn as one of the Program's many stenographers. Through her unusual initiative and ambition, she was repeatedly promoted until she finally reached the powerful position of co-director of *Hauptabteilung A*. This division was responsible for the selection, registration, and placement of foreign-born Lebensborn children placed in foster care homes and adopted families in the Altreich (i.e., Germany and Austria).

40. For more, see Thomas Beddies, *Dokumente zur Psychiatrie im Nationalsozialismus* (Berlin: be.bra Verlag, 2003); Andrea Böltken, "Inge Viermetz: Eine weibliche Karriere im Dritten Reich," in *Historische Rassismusforschung: Ideologen, Täter Opfer*, ed. Barbara Danckwortt, Thorsten Querg, and Claudia Schöningh (Berlin: Argument Verlag, 1995), 179–207; Dorothee Schmitz-Köster, *Deutsche Mutter, bist du bereit: Alltag im Lebensborn* (Berlin: Aufbau Verlag, 2002).

41. In cases of illegitimate children, the SS did much to protect the anonymity of the biological fathers. On October 19, 1938, for example, Führeradjutant Brueckner sent a scathing letter to the Reich's Ministry of Justice ordering the immediate exoneration of an unmarried mother who had been sentenced to one month in prison for refusing to name the father of her illegitimate child. At the same time, the SS went to great lengths to uncover the family lineage of its members. Applicants were required to demonstrate that their family had been free of Jewish ancestry since January 1, 1800. In one case, an officer was ejected from the SS, after it was discovered that one of his fourteenth-century ancestors had been Jewish. According to Himmler, although this progenitor was several generations away, his duty to future generations of Aryans compelled him to root out all Jewish contamination of the SS bloodline. For more, see Beatrice Heiber and Helmut Heiber, *Die Rückseite des Hakenkreuzes: Absonderliches aus den Akten des Dritten Reiches* (Munich: dtv Verlag, 1993), 204.

42. Kampisch, *Täterinnen*, 32.

43. Lilienthal, *Der "Lebensborn e. V.,"* 45.

44. Lilienthal, *Der "Lebensborn e. V.,"* 46.

45. Hermann Boehm, "Nationalsozialistische Gedanken zum Paragraphen 218," *Nationalsozialistische Monatshefte* 24 (Munich: Alfred Rosenberg Verlag, 1932), 126.

46. Kampisch, *Täterinnen*, 26.

47. Helmut Heiber, *Der ganz normale Wahnsinn unterm Hakenkreuz: Triviales und Absonderliches aus den Akten des Dritten Reichs* (Munich: Deutscher Taschenbuch Verlag, 2001), 295.

48. BArch NS19 3973 F1.

49. Helmut Heiber, *Reichsführer! Briefe an und von Reichsführer Himmler* (Munich: deutscher Taschenverlag, 1970), 271..

50. Heiber, *Reichsführer!*, 302.

51. Heiber, *Reichsführer!*, 276.

52. Peter Longerich, *Heinrich Himmler: Biographie* (Berlin: Panthenon, 2010), 391.

53. BArch, "Bemerkungen des Reichsführer-SS zum Vortrag 'Zwei Jahre Lebensborn Arbeit.'" NS/48 fol. 1 Signatur:1817.

54. Erwin Metzer, *Die deutschen Vorname* (Goslar: Blut und Boden Verlag, 1939).

55. Lilienthal, *Der "Lebensborn e.V.,"* 19.

56. Lilienthal, *Der "Lebensborn e.V.,"* 19.

57. The original text: "Der Heimleiter hält den SS-Dolch über das Kind, berührt es damit und spricht: 'Ich nehme dich hiermit in den Schutz unsere Sippengemeinschaft auf und gebe dir den Namen. [...] Trage diesen Namen in Ehre'" (Dorothee Schmitz-Köster qtd. in Koop, *Dem Führer ein Kind Schenken*, 125.

58. BArch, NS 048/000029, Doc. 6.

59. Located in Klosterheide, a small town situated approximately sixty miles outside of Berlin, Kurmark was one of the most lavish facilities in the Lebensborn chain. With room for only twenty-three mothers, the facility cost over half a million Reichsmarks and was in operation between 1937 and 1944.

60. Hillel and Henry, *Lebensborn e.V.*, 72.

61. Lilienthal, *Lebensborn*, 2003.

62. Even among those parents who chose to participate in the Namensgebung, several still elected to have their children baptized as well. In 1938, for example, there are several entries in the local church records where mothers from the Steinhoerig Facility had their children baptized either instead of or in addition to the Lebensborn naming ceremony. For more, see Hillel and Henry, *Lebensborn e.V. [. . .]*.

63. Nevertheless, there seems to have been a general resistance to completely forsaking Christian ceremonies such as christenings and baptisms. It was not unusual for parents to have their children participant in both NS and Church ceremonies—much to the consternation of SS officials. In a letter written on February 2, 1941 by an SS Oberscharführer to district leaders in Hamburg, the official complained that in the suburb of Elmsdorn, it was unclear whether a scheduled ceremony for children would actually take place because several parents had decided to send their children to confirmation. According to the incensed SS officer, this trend was a slap in the face of any self-respecting SS man as it undermined all the work to spread the National Socialist ideology to the next generation. For more, see Hamburg Staatsarchiv: File: 614–2/5_k12.

64. For more, see Wilfried Seibicke, *Die Personennamen im Deutschen* (Berlin: de Gruyter, 2008).

65. Nicole Arndt, *Die Geschichte und Entwicklung des familienrechtlicher. Namensrechts* (Munich: Herbert Utz Verlag, 2004), 159.

66. *The Economist*, "A Nation of Immigrants," December 23, 1999.

67. Frederick Taylor, *Inflation: Der Untergang des Geldes in der Weimarer Republik und die Geburt eines deutschen Trauma* (Hamburg: Siedler Verlag, 2013).

68. Arndt, *Die Geschichte und Entwicklung*; Juergen Gerhards, "Politischer Regimewechsel und der Aufstieg und der Fall der deutschen Vornamen," in *Die Moderne und ihre Vornamen: Eine Einladung in die Kultursoziologie*, ed. Juergen Gerhards (Berlin: Springer Verlag, 2003).

69. Bogislav von Selchow, *Das Namenbuch: Eine Sammlung sämtlicher Deutscher, Altdeutscher, und in Deutschland gebräuchlicher fremdländischer Vornamen mit Angabe ihrer Abstammung und ihre Deutung* (Leipzig: K. F. Köhler, 1935).

70. Stadtsarchive Bremen, "An das Landesrat <u>Osterholz</u>," December 18, 19376, 6/5–89.

71. These tribal groups include the Franks, the Goths, and the Visigoths. The English term "Germanic" also technically refers to the languages, cultures, and peoples who descended from these original tribes. These descendants include the English, Germans, Austrians, Swedish, Norwegians, Danes, and so on. However, in this passage, Ferdinand clearly is making reference to the Germanic tribes and not to names from Germanic languages.

72. Ernst Christmann, *Deutsche Rufname! Eine deutsche Forderung auf Grund einer Untersuchung der Verhältnisse im Saarpfälzischen Raum Kaiserlautern* (Kaiserlautern: Pfälzische Gesellschaft zur Förderung der Wissenschaften, 1939).

73. Christmann, *Deutsche Rufname!*, 4.

74. There is evidence that the names chosen for Lebensborn children were often taken from the infant's appointed guardians who were expected to be SS members in good-standing. Dorothee Schmitz-Köster and Tristan Vankann, *Lebenslang Lebensborn: Die Wunschkinder der SS und was aus ihnen wurde* (Munich: Piper Verlag, 2012).

75. Stadtarchiv Flensburg (STaFl): ID 01706 (1933–1975).

76. BArch 2/276.

77. Stadtsarchiv Flensburg (STaFL), "Runderlass der Reichsminister der Interior," August 18, 1938, ID 42X/38–5501b.

78. STaFl, "Runderlass der Reichsminister der Interior." [Edict of the Reichs' minister of the Interior. February 18, 1938), ID 113–5501b.

79. The German original: "Die Vereinigung des guten Wuchs, Gesundheit, geistigen Hochstand, seelischer Ausgeglichenheit, vornehmer Denkweise . . . zum *Adel* gehört außer dem makellosen lieb-seele Erbgut . . . der Grund und Boden auf dem das Geschlecht sich fortpflanzen soll." Rolf Ludwig Fahrenkrog, *Deutschen Kindern—Deutsche Namen* (Berlin: Fritsch Verlag, 1939), 36–37.

80. As Koop aptly notes, once the National Socialists came to power, scientific reasoning was defeated by racial insanity. *Himmlers Germanenwahn: Die SS-Organisation Ahnenerbe und ihre Verbrechen* (Berlin: be.bra Verlag, 2012), 49.

81. Koop, *Himmlers Germanenwahn*, 49.

82. BArch, NS 048/000029 fol.1.

83. BArch, NS 048/000029 fol.1.

84. Heiber, *Reichsführer!*, 80.

85. Heiber, *Reichsführer!*, 80.

86. *The Sentinel,* "Joshua Not Good Name for Nazi, Court Rules," August 18, 1938.

87. *The Sentinel,* "Israel will not Later Name," February 23, 1939.

88. For a detailed examination of this case, see Winfried Seibert, *Das Mädchen, das nicht ESTHER heißen durfte: Eine exemplarische Geschichte* (Leipzig: Reclam Verlag, 1996).

89. Pastor Luncke was reportedly enormously popular amongst his largely working class congregation. When it became known that church authorities had blocked Pastor Luncke from taking over the parish permanently, a massive demonstration erupted in protest. For more, see: Seibert, *Das Mädchen,* 36.

90. Willi Neuhoff, "Die Tochter darf nicht Esther heissen," *Wattenscheid: 600 Jahre Freiheit!* (Wattenscheid, 2017), 42. http://www.wattenscheider-hbv.de/Bilder/600Jahre.pdf.

91. Prominent clerical members of this movement included Martin Niemöller, Dietrich Bonhoeffer, and Otto Dibelius.

92. Annette Wilmes, "Das Mädchen, das nicht Esther heißen durfte: Der KKolner Rechtanwalt Winfried Seibert erinnert an eine Beschluß des Berliner Kammergerichts." (Radio Kultur: Menschen und Paragraphen, November 23, 1998, Sender Friees Berlin/Ostdeutscher Rundfunk Brandenburg).

93. One of the reasons why the judges may have chosen to place so much emphasis upon the negative character of the Biblical figure Esther as opposed to the etymological derivation of the name itself may have been to avoid the unpleasant coincidence that the daughter of one of the presiding judges happened to have been named *Ruth.* For more, see Neuhoff, "Die Tochter," 42.

94. Seibert, *Das Mädchen,* 181.

95. These and other articles covering this story were identified in the online archive: https://www.newspapers.com/.

96. During the time of Esther's lethal illness, Germany was experiencing a significant increase in the number of cases of diphtheria infections. While in 1926 there were reportedly 30,000 cases, by 1943 that number has jumped to reach 300,000 cases. Along with the increase in infection rate, there was a sharp rise in morbidity as well. In 1938, approximately 3.7 percent of those infected died from the disease. Four years later, that percentage had reached 5 percent. For more, see Winfried Süß, *Der 'Volkskörper' im Krieg: Gesundheitspoltik, Gesundheitsverhältnisse, und Krankenmord im nationalsozialistischen Detuschland 1939–1945* (Munich: Oldenburg Verlag, 2003).

97. The Bormann's seventh child was given the very Germanic name of *Irmgard.* Sigmund, *Die Frauen der Nazis III,* 24.

98. Sigmund, *Die Frauen der Nazis III,* 25.

99. In April 1945, Martin Bormann joined Hitler in the infamous Bunker in Berlin. As one of the Führer's most loyal members, Bormann was asked to serve as one of the witnesses at the wedding of Adolf Hitler and Eva Braun before the two committed suicide. Immediately afterward, Bormann unsuccessfully attempted to escape Berlin to reach the newly established seat of government in Flensburg, Germany. On October 1,

1946, he was sentenced to death in absentia by the IMT. His death was confirmed in 1973. For more, see www.dhm.de/lemo.

100. The formal German name of this law was *Gesetz zum Schutz nationaler Symbole* (RGB1 I, 285). Arndt, *Die Geschichte und Entwicklung des familienrechtlichen Namensrechts*.

101. Similarly denied was the name a daughter *Hitlerike*. Arndt, *Die Geschichte und Entwicklung des familienrechtlichen Namensrechts*, 164.

102. The German original: "Da uns Nationalsozialisten der Name unseres Führers viel zu hehr und heilig ist, als dass wir ihn dem Missbrauch nationale Klitsches ausliefern lasse. . . . Wenn ein Nationalsozialist seinen Sohn oder seine Tochter nach unserem Führer benennen will, so hat er ja die Möglichkeit, dem Kinde den Vornamen 'Adolf' oder 'Adolfine' beizulegen." Heiber and Heiber, *Die Rückseite des Hakenkreuzes*, 121–22.

103. Original: "Dahinter aber steht mehr—es ist wie eine mythische Blutsverbundenheit der Kämpfer mit dem Führer—so mögen in Urzeiten die Krieger der wandernden nordischen Völker ihren Herzögen zu gejubelt haben, so mögen sie mit seinem Namen, den heut ein namenloses Steinzeit-Grab deckt, sich dem Tod entgegengeworfen haben! Das ist es, was diese Bewegung so eigenartig und für den Fernstehenden fast unverständlich macht—wie sie sich mit dem Namen des Führers grüßen, so sterben sie mit seinem Namen auf den Lippen" qtd. from Leon Poliokov and Joseph Wulf, *Das Dritte Reich und seine Denker* (Munich: K. G. Sauer Verlag, 1978), 58.

104. Other products which private citizens requested to market using the Führer's name include cigarette filters and handkerchiefs. Henrik Eberle, *Briefe an Hitler: Ein Volk schreibt seinem Führer* (Cologne: Bastei Lübbe Verlag, 2007), 999.

105. Heiber and Heiber, *Die Rückseite des Hakenkreuzes*, 132.

106. Heiber and Heiber, *Die Rückseite des Hakenkreuzes*, 119.

107. Heiber and Heiber, *Die Rückseite des Hakenkreuzes*, 13.

108. Oskar Scheibel, "Ein neuer Anophthalmus aus Jugoslawien," *Entomologische Blätter* 33, no. 6 (1937): 438–40.

109. May Berenbaum, "ICE Breakers," *American Entomologist* 56, no. 3 (2010): 132–33, 185.

110. Ruth Elkins, "Fans Nearly Exterminate 'Hitler' Beetle," *The Independent*, August 19, 2006. http://www.independent.co.uk/news/world/europe/fans-exterminate-hitler-beetle-6232054.html.

111. For more on Hermann Röchling, see Dieter Gräbner, *Wer war Hermann Röchling?* (St. Ingbert, Saarland: Conte Verlag, 2014); Partrycja Grzebyk, *Criminal Responsibility for the Crime of Aggression* (London: Routledge, 2010), 180–82.

112. Berenbaum, "ICE Breakers," 133.

113. Heiber and Heiber, *Die Rückseite des Hakenkreuzes,* 124.

114. As this legislation indicates, such devotional naming was by no means an invention of the Nazi Period. Already in the nineteenth century, first names such as *Bismark, Genisenauette, Blücherine, Sedaine, Katzbachine,* and *Zeppeline* were attested (Arndt, *Die Geschichte und Entwicklung des familienrechtlichen Namensrechts*; Wolfgang Fleischer, *Die deutschen Personennamen* [Berlin: Akademie-Verlag, 1968]).

115. Heiber and Heiber, *Die Rückseite des Hakenkreuzes*, 131–32.

116. Marc Hillel and Clarissa Henry, *Lebensborn e.V. [. . .].*

117. Another gender difference which was apparent in this set was the incidence of double names. While only three of the girls in this set had a hyphenated name (i.e., *Elke-Gertrude, Gisa-Dagmar,* and *Helga-Anne*), 16 percent of the boys in this group had a hyphenated double name. The two most common second names among the boys were *Heinrich* and *Horst*.

118. L. Allen, V. Brown, L. Dickinson, and K. C. Pratt, "The Relation of First Name Preferences to their Frequency in the Culture," *The Journal of Social Psychology* 14 (1941): 279–93; Timothy Anderson, "Unique and Common Names of Males and Females," *Psychological Reports* 57, no. 1 (1985): 204–6; Marc Levine and Frank Willis, "Public Reactions to Unusual Names," *The Journal of Social Psychology* 134, no. 5 (1994): 561–68.

119. Schmitz-Köster, *Deutsche Mutter.*

120. Bundesarchiv Berlin (BArch), Bestandssignatur: R/1509; Archivsignatur: 1817; Reichssippenamt Rep. 309: Nr. 817.

121. Immediately thereafter, the Jewish members of the original group—Joseph Cycowski (baritone), Erich Abraham Collin (tenor), and Heinrich Frommerman (tenor)—went into exile. The remaining Aryan members formed a new choral group under the name *Meistersextett*. However, after lukewarm to miserable reviews, they eventually disbanded.

122. Also called "Auf der Heide blüht ein kleines Blümelein, Erika" [In the heather, there blooms a tiny blossom, Erika!], this song is generally considered to be Niel's greatest hit. Written originally for the SS, this military march is one of the few surviving Niel's songs which can still be heard on occasion in Germany today.

123. Russell Stover Chocolates, *Whitman's History,* https://www.russellstover.com/whitmans-history.

124. *Treating Bone Black*, US Patent Office. Reference Number (US62537). Issue date: March 5, 1867.

125. "Shot for leaving a Valentine," *Sacramento Daily Union* 38, no. 5904, February 28, 1870. California Digital Newspaper Collection. https://cdnc.ucr.edu/cgi-bin/cdnc?a =d&d=SDU18700228.2.20.

126. *The Evening Telegraph,* "Ficken's Anniversary." February 13, 1871.

127. Hans-Werrner Liebig, *Historie von Gut Hohehorst,* December 2013. http://loe hnhorst-online.de/hohehorst/HOHEHORST-HISTORIE.pdf.

128. Dietmar von Reeken, *Lahusen: eine Bremer Unternehmer Dynastie 1916–1933* (Bremen: Edition Temmen, 1996).

129. von Reeken, *Lahusen,* 82.

130. von Reeken, *Lahusen,* 83.

131. Judith Lutteroh, "Als ein deutscher Wollbaron die Welt erschütterte," *Spiegel,* December 2, 2011, http://www.spiegel.de/einestages/bankenkrise-1931-als-ein-deutsch er-wollbaron-die-welt-erschuetterte-a-947408.html.

132. Lutteroh, "Wollbaron," n.p.

133. Liebig, *Historie von Gut Hohehorst,* 13.

134. His brother, Heinz Lahusen received a prison sentence of two years and nine months, and a fine of 20,000 Reichsmarks. Liebig, *Historie von Gut Hohehorst,* 17.

135. von Reeken, *Lahusen,* 82.

136. Detlef von Horn, *Lebensborn-Standesamt Hohehorst*, Bremen: Hohehorst Archiv.

137. This period marked the birthing peak of the Hohehorst Heim. It is estimated that during the years of its operation, some 217 children were born in the Friesland facility. Liebig, *Historie von Gut Hohehorst*, 32.

138. Thomas Bryant, *Himmlers Kinder: Zur Geschichte der SS-Organisation, "Lebensborn e.V." 1935–1945* (Wiesbaden: Marix Verlag, 2011), 197.

139. Hohehorst Archiv Bremen.

140. SS Kastellholm Passagierliste für Flüchtlingstransport nach Malmö vom Sammellager des Zivilschutzes in Lübeck July 25, 1945. Hohehorst Archiv Bremen.

141. The names of the Norwegian children were retrieved from the official passenger list of the ship, the SS Kastellholm which sailed from Lübeck, Germany to Malmö, Sweden on July 25, 1945. In addition to the names of Lebensborn children on their way to begin new lives in Sweden, the passenger list also provides the names of non-Aryan children who had managed to survive the horrors of the war and were facing their own uncertain future in a new homeland.

142. Liebig, *Historie von Gut Hohehorst*, 19.

143. Heiber, *Reichsführer!*, 296.

144. English translation of a Führer Erlaß published on July 28, 1942. See Monika Diederichs, "Stigma and Silence: Dutch Women, German Soldiers and Their Children," in *Children of World War II: The Hidden Enemy Legacy*, eds. Kjersti Ericsson and Eva Simonsen (Oxford: Berg, 2005), 154.

145. Lilienthal, *Das "Lebensborn e. V."*

146. Kåre Olson, *Vater: Deutscher: Das Schicksal der Norwegischen Lebensbornkinder und ihre Mütter von 1940 bis heute* (Frankfurt am Main: Campus Verlag, 2002).

147. For the full story, see Annegret Lamey, *Kind unbekannter Herkunft: Die Geschichte des Lebensbornkindes Hannes Dollinger* (Augsburg: Wißner-Verlag, 2008).

148. Ines Hopfer, *Geraubte Identität: Die gewaltsame, Eindeutschung' von Polnische Kindern in der NS-Zeit* (Graz: Böhlau Verlag, 2010).

149. Hopfer, *Geraubte Identität*, 294–99; Roman Hrabar, Zofia Tokarz, Jacek Edward Wilczur, *Kinder im Krieg—Krieg gegen Kinder: Die Geschichte der Polnischen Kinder 1939–1945* (Hamburg: Rowohlt Verlag, 1981).

150. BArch, NS 48/000030, Dok. 59.

151. Hrabar, Tokarz, and Wilczur, *Kinder im Krieg—Krieg gegen Kinder*.

152. Hopfer, *Geraubte Identität*, 261.

153. United States Holocaust Memorial Museum, *War Crimes Trials: RuSHA Case; Justice Case Sentencing*. Film. Accession Number: 2001.358.1; RG-60.2986. Nuremberg Trials. https://collections.ushmm.org/search/catalog/irn1000383.

CHAPTER 4

The Hunt for Sara(h) and Israel

In an apartment in Berlin-Wilmersdorf, a little over a week after the Kristallnacht, the police discovered a female corpse.[1] The body was later identified as that of a seventy-six-year old, H. Jastrow, a former school principal and Jew. The official cause of death recorded in the police report was poisoning by "Leuchtgas." A toxic mixture of nitrogen, hydrogen, methane, and carbon monoxide gases, Leuchtgas or "coal gas" was commonly used in the nineteenth and twentieth centuries for illuminating street lamps, driving engines, fueling ovens, and committing suicide. The popularity of this suicide method was no doubt due not only to the relative availability of the poisonous gas, but also to the widespread misconception that it resulted in a relatively painless death. In point of fact, coal gas poisoning could produce a torturous demise. Common symptoms before exitus included heart palpitations, severe nausea, uncontrolled muscle spasms, vomiting paired with possible asphyxiation, and involuntary emptying of the bladder and bowel.[2] The reason why Ms. Jastrow summoned the will to take this lethal path can also be found in the official police record. In fastidiously neat, conspicuously small handwriting, a single word is entered in the space to enter probable motive: "Glaubensverfolgung" or [religious persecution]. As shown below, the note discovered at the death scene described in detail the exact nature of that persecution:

> This is neither an accidental death nor a case of melancholy. This is about someone leaving this life; a person whose family, for over 100 years, has had German citizenship after taking and keeping an oath of allegiance. For 43 years, I have taught German children and helped them through every tribulation. Even longer still, I have volunteered in charities to serve the German people in times of war and peace. I no longer want to live without a Fatherland, a homeland, a home, or civil rights—despised and insulted. I want to be buried with the name that my parents both gave and bequeathed me, a name which

135

is entirely untarnished. I do not want to wait until my name is defiled with a mark of shame. Every petty criminal, every murderer, is
allowed to retain his own name![3]

As expressed in the letter above, for Frau Jastrow, the public indignity of being
forced to carry a name of shame was the final straw in a long list of private humil-
iations and public injuries. When it came to devising demeaning naming laws
to isolate and demean the Jewish population, the creativity of the Nazis knew
no limits. In some jurisdictions, officials even insisted that the LAFFN-2 regulation be applied posthumously. In Duisburg, for example, Jewish families were
required to add the names *Sara* and *Israel* to the gravestones of their deceased
relatives.[4] Whether Ms. Jastrow's grave was later engraved with the name she
found so objectionable could not be determined at the time of this writing.

In comparison to the other discriminatory laws that were progressively
introduced to restrict, reverse, or rescind the civil rights of Jewish residents,
the requirement to take on an identifying name is sometimes described, when
mentioned at all, as an odd imposition. As shown by the case of Ms. Jastrow,
however, the effect of this legislation had dramatic and dire consequences for the
name-bearers. Through the institution and enforcement of the LAFFN 1 and 2,
it became possible to easily and efficiently identify, isolate, and then directly target Jewish residents for genocide. The yellow star of David could be removed or
hidden during face-to-face interactions; and in writing or over the telephone, the
tell-tale star could not be seen. But, in all of these interactions, when an official
personal name had to be supplied for identification or verification purposes, it
became nearly impossible to avoid revealing one's racial identity. And increasingly, even the accomplishment of the most mundane tasks such as buying food
or clothing required residents to present some form of official identification with
their signature and name. Under such circumstances, the compulsory affixation
of *Sara* and *Israel* meant Jewish residents were relentlessly exposed to discrimination. Each time a birth certificate, library card, military record, utility bill, bank
account statement, club membership card, marriage license, university transcript, school record, voter registration card, insurance paper, hospital record,
or some other form of identification was required, their racial classification was
exposed. Further compounding this vulnerability was the wide array of physical
spaces where people's names were routinely put on public display (e.g., store
fronts, mailboxes, grave stones).

To prevent Jewish residents from intentionally circumventing this exposure,
the NSDAP regularly instituted policies which required them to prominently
display their names and racial identities for all to see. In September of 1939,
for example, the residents of an apartment building in Hamburg were required
to prominently display their names on a list outside the building. When it was

discovered that two of the residents, a married Jewish couple, had entered their names on the list without the compulsory markers of *Israel* and *Sara,* the authorities were notified. In defense of the omission, the husband explained that in this case, he had not deemed it necessary to include the two names as their religious affiliation appeared next to each of their names. Despite this fact, on January 25, 1940, the couple was found guilty of violating the law and were ordered to pay a fine of 20 RM.[5]

That same month, another Jewish resident of Hamburg, Paula F., was also charged for violating the LAFFN-2 regulation. It seems that in the signature she had placed on her food ration card, she had also neglected (or elected) to include the name *Sara*. The omission was discovered and Paula was forced to appear before the authorities for attempting to conceal her race. On January 3, 1940, she was found guilty as charged and sentenced to pay a fine of 20 RM and serve a prison sentence of four days.[6] Although one might be tempted to think that the prison sentence was relatively light, when one stops to consider how frequent rape, torture, and murder took place in the NS prison system and how infrequently prisoners were sent home on their scheduled release date (if set free at all), the severity of this punishment becomes readily apparent. In these two cases, the number of people who would have been made privy to the residents' racial status was comparatively small.

This was not always the case, however. The Nazis also instituted name policies that allowed far larger audiences access to this sensitive information. For example, as of March 1940, all Jews residing within the Reich were required to see to it that their personal names appeared in their local telephone book with the onomastic markers of *Sara* and *Israel*, irrespective of whether the listing was for a private or business telephone line.[7] In some localities, the telephone company later used this information to segregate their listings, relegating Jewish entries to the end of the telephone book before eliminating them all together.[8] This practice meant that by simply looking through the local telephone book, it became possible for the Aryan general public to easily identify, avoid, or taunt Jewish residents. It also meant that NS officials had easy access to a regularly updated, alphabetized listing containing the telephone numbers, addresses, and names of a large segment of Jewish population living within their jurisdiction.

*****

Rather than requiring the state to automatically add the new onomastic markers to the names of all Jewish residents, the LAFFN-2 required the Jewish residents themselves to formally apply to have the names *Sara* and *Israel* added to all of their identification documents (i.e., birth certificates, marriage certificates, passports, residence permits, etc.). In the absence of a comprehensive nationwide registry of Jews, it was reasoned that it would be prohibitively laborious for German officials to attempt to identify all residents with Jewish ancestry. By requiring the populace to self-identify under penalty of law, officials were spared this search and could concentrate their efforts upon tagging the names of all those Jews who came forward. The deadline for compliance was set for January 31, 1939. The strict enforcement of this deadline also meant that extreme pressure was also placed on local officials to ensure that the vital records of all Jewish residents had been appropriately updated. In a martial pyramid of threat, administrators on the national, regional, and municipal levels were instructed to report on their progress in tracking and tagging the Jews living in their communities. While most local leaders were careful to file the required progress reports, others appeared to be far less cooperative. This failure to comply spelled real trouble for everyone in the direct chain of administrative command. In frustration over not having been sent the required progress reports from his subordinates, on December 19, 1939, an irate District Commissioner sent a final letter of warning to the remiss area civil servants in his district:

> I am demanding now for the 4th time that I be given a report on the progress being made in adding the forenames Israel and Sara to the birth and marriage records of the persons applicable. . . . In view of this fact, I will see myself forced to resort to more severe measures if I do not receive a complete report within the next few days.[9]

In the face of such threats, local government officials labored to make the required notations by the specified deadline. In small rural localities where the number of Jewish residents was comparatively small, full compliance was just about manageable. However, in larger metropolitan cities this administrative task was immense.

Spying a golden financial opportunity, an enterprising print shop owner by the name of W. König invited government officials to purchase one or more sets of his pre-printed name-change forms for the special price of 80 Rpf [cents]. According to the Munich-based businessman, his forms enabled officials to gather all of the required information in a single solitary step "with the highest possible level of perfection and efficiency." In a city the size of Hamburg, Munich, or Berlin where thousands of Jewish residents lived, a proactive printer could stand to make quite a tidy profit through the sale of these pre-made identification forms.

Where the state was concerned, however, there seems to have been some confusion over whether residents should be charged for applying for the compulsory name change. According to the §3 (1) of the LAFFN-1, officials had been allowed to charge between 5 and 2,000 Reichsmark for altering a family name and between 5 and 500 Reichsmark for making a change involving a forename.[10] However, for the LAFFN-2, there was some concern that exacting a fee might decrease the willingness of Jewish residents to comply with the new ordinance. For this reason, officials were frequently discouraged from charging a processing fee for the compulsory name change. In an internal memo sent to civil servants in Koblenz, for example, it is specifically stated that no fee was to be imposed for the application to adopt the compulsory name change.[11] Nevertheless, in archive after archive, evidence was still identified that municipalities routinely charged Jewish residents a processing fee for adding of the compulsory names. Furthermore, in cases where this name affected persons other than the primary applicant (e.g., children, spouses, parents, siblings), additional charges were also routinely levied.

Despite the financial burden and personal insult, the archives are filled with petitions from Jewish residents "requesting" the obligatory amendment. To help deal with the onslaught of requests, jurisdictions with large Jewish populations commonly provided standard forms that only required applicants to fill in their personal biographical data. In areas with smaller Jewish communities, residents were more often required to send in a personal letter to file their request. For example, on December 28, 1938, a Frau F. Rosenstock from the small town of Gladenbach in Hessia sent in a letter containing the following statement: "As required by law, I herewith announce that as of January 1, 1939, I will adopt the additional forename of SARA."[12] Such phrasing was found in the vast majority of the thousands of "applications" located during this research.

On January 15, 1939, the Ministry of the Interior sent notice to all heads of higher regional courts and state prosecutors. This circular indicated that all persons of Jewish heritage whose birth or marriage had been registered by a German governmental official were required to present evidence that they had officially adopted the compulsory personal names *Israel* or *Sara*.[13] It was not enough to assume that Jewish residents had formally adopted the onomastic marker; officials were warned that it was their personal professional duty to see to it that all Jews living within their jurisdiction properly identified themselves as such in all dealings involving Aryans. Officials who were found to be either lackluster or remiss in their enforcement of this identification system risked punishment for dereliction of duties. Consequently, local officials often responded quickly and severely to even the most minor or unintentional violation in policy.

On the exact same day that the above notification was issued, the Worms Police Department received an official letter written on behalf of a Miss L. Rawinsky of Ludwigshafen. According to the letter, the house servant expressed her regret that she had missed the deadline to apply for the formal addition of the name "Sara" to her official name. As the reason for her tardiness, she cites exhaustion from overwork. The letter ends with an NS stamp featuring the name of Miss Rawinsky's workplace: the Lichtenberg Concentration Camp.[14]

Located in the Northeast German state of Saxony-Anhalt, Lichtenberg was one of the very first camps to be erected by the National Socialists. The sixteenth-century castle–turned penitentiary was converted into a medium-sized camp in the late spring, early summer, of 1933. By September of 1933, the Nazis had already filled the dilapidated fortress with over 1,500 men. Four years later, the remaining 1,275 prisoners were transferred to a new camp designed to hold tens of thousands of inmates at a time: Buchenwald. In the meantime, the vacated Lichtenberg facility had become a temporary holding station for female prisoners, one of whom was the *Miss L. Rawinsky*. According to archival records,[15] the thirty-eight-year-old was arrested and sent to a prison facility in Darmstadt on August 13, 1937. Soon thereafter, she was transferred to a detention facility outside of Ulm before being transferred again to Lichtenberg. In the middle of May 1939, the Nazis closed the Lichtenberg facility and moved the surviving women, northward, to the specially designed female concentration camp, Ravensbrück. It was there on June 12, 1942, that Miss Rawinsky's name was added to the growing list of the dead.

The Rawinsky case demonstrates just how far-reaching the LAFFN-2 was. All Jewish residents of the Reich were expected to immediately apply for and then use the compulsory onomastic markers. Even those who were already imprisoned were expected to comply. In those cases where the Jewish resident was a ward of the state, his/her guardian was expected to apply for the addition of the compulsory name. Following this directive, on December 29, 1938, an official petition was completed and sent on behalf of forty-four-year-old J. Jonas, a patient at the Eichberg State Sanatorium [Landesheilanstalt Eichberg]. In a form letter sent to the Office of the Burgermeister in Gladenbach, Germany, the Director of the Sanatorium formally requested that the name *Israel* be added to Mr. Jonas's birth certificate.[16] Neither the reason for Jonas's original admission nor the details of his treatment in the clinic could be discerned. However, during the period of time he was a patient in Eichberg, the clinic served as a central station for forced sterilizations. Starting in January 1941, regular transports of patients began to be sent from the sanitarium in Gladenbach to another clinic in Limburg-Weilburg, some 70 kilometers southeast. The name of that facility was Hadamar. From January 13 to August 24, 1941, more than 10,000 people were systematically murdered in this center as a part of the NS-Euthanasia program. According to the records kept at Yad Vashem, this is precisely what happened to J. Jonas.

*

On June 22 of 1938, the State Secretary for the Reich's Ministry of the Interior issued a decree addressing what it described as the "deplorable state" of health institutions in the Reich which failed to prevent sexual contact between Jewish and Aryan patients. To remedy this problem and eliminate all danger of defiling the Aryan race, the edict called for the immediate physical separation of all Jewish and Aryan patients.[17] On April 15, 1940, the Ministry of the Interior, in cooperation with the Gestapo, demanded that health care facilities provide a name list of all Jewish patients suffering from mental illness or "feeblemindedness."[18] In the southwest of Germany, this information was used to coordinate a large-scale operation involving forty-one different states, churches, and privately operated clinics. Disabled Jewish patients whose names had been placed on lists for "special treatment" were transported from these clinics and taken to the Hadamar Sanatorium. Shortly after their arrival, their names were re-checked and their clothes were stripped. After a perfunctory examination, the naked patients were then murdered and incinerated in the facility's onsite gas chamber and crematoria between February 4 and 15, 1941. Several weeks later, the surviving relatives were issued pre-fabricated death certificates which falsified the date, place, and manner of death. Today, all that remains of most of those victims is a list of their names.

*****

In Germany, it is permissible to give children more than one forename. However, parents must officially designate the one forename by which the child will be called [Rufname]. On April 13, 1940, the office of the Police Inspectorate in Oranienburg sent a terse letter to the administrative offices of the Sachsenhausen Concentration Camp to determine why Jewish prisoner number 13129 had apparently been allowed to use the name *Josef* and not *Ludwig*, the forename listed on his birth certificate as his official Rufname.[19] As the letter-writer explained, the prisoner's failure to identify himself using his Rufname was in clear violation of German law and tantamount to falsifying his true identity.[20] Perhaps in anticipation of a Sachsenhausen administrator dismissing this charge as a trivial infraction, hardly worth the time and effort needed to investigate, the letter-writer stressed the importance of proper and consistent identification for monitoring the Jewish population. The prisoner in question, Josef H. (or Ludwig), was a Jewish salesman who first came to police attention in 1938, when he attempted to escape Nazi, Germany.[21] According to the official interrogation transcript recorded on March 14, 1940, Josef had traveled from his hometown of Westerburg, Austria.[22] His goal was to escape to Israel. Unfortunately, Josef was intercepted at the border and sentenced to serve nine months in a Viennese police detention center. Shortly after his release, in September 1939, Josef H. was once again placed under "protective custody," only this time in the Sachsenhausen Concentration Camp.[23]

One month after his arrival there, orders were issued to transfer the prisoner to the Buchenwald Concentration Camp.[24] Before this order could be executed and just three days after the Oranienburg police had issued their letter of complaint regarding Josef's proper identification, the Sachsenhausen Camp authorities reported that prisoner 13129 had died and the Frankfurt Police Department had already been sent the prisoner's final effects: 1 hat, 1 pair of pants, 1 waistcoat, 2 shirts, 1 tie, 1 pair of shoes, and 1 pair of underwear.[25]

The fact that Josef had provided the authorities with the forename which he had always used throughout his adult life was of no consequence to the Oranienburg inspector[26]; nor the fact that Josef had always been careful to use the obligatory name *Israel*. The only point of interest was the discrepancy between the prisoner's birth certificate and his arrest record. Ironically, it does appear that the authorities did have some confusion where Josef H.'s identity was concerned. In a letter from the Frankfurt am Main Police department, dated December 27, 1939, it is recorded that "the Jew <u>Emanuel</u> Israel H. [emphasis added]" was currently located in Sachsenhausen Concentration Camp. At some later unspecified date, a camp employee seems to have spotted the recording error and placed a large question mark behind the name *Emanuel*. It would take some time before the confusion was resolved. Despite their notorious record-keeping, someone in the chain of command had obviously confused the records of the father and the son—both of whom were held in police custody. Emanuel H., Josef H's father, was also arrested by the Nazis four years after his son had been caught during his attempt to reach Israel. According to the German National Archives [Bundesarchiv], on September 1, 1942, Emanuel H. was deported to the Theresienstadt Ghetto where he died six months later, on February 16, 1943. In this family tragedy, the authorities sought to punish a prisoner for failing to use a "Rufname" despite assiduously using the compulsory name *Israel*. In the following case, just the opposite occurred.

In the winter of 1939, during Kristallnacht, the Hahn family's automotive repair shop was utterly destroyed by a group of vandals. During the attack, one of the assailants severely injured himself. Incredibly, the court ruled that the Hahn family would have to pay the medical expenses of the man who had vandalized them. In two signed letters to the court, Mr. Hahn formally requested that he be released from making the odious payments. In reviewing the letters sent on February 17 and 27, 1939, the court discovered that on both occasions, Mr. Hahn's signature omitted the obligatory name *Israel*.

In view of the indisputable evidence, the prosecution recommended that the businessman serve four weeks in prison for violating the LAFFN-2 regulations. On May 16, Mr. Hahn sent a handwritten appeal to the federal prosecutor of Gießen and asked that his prison sentence be commuted to a fine. As justification for his request, Mr. Hahn explained that he planned to leave the country imminently. After reviewing the case, on June 2, 1939, the court issued its final ruling: in the name of the German People, Herr Hahn was ordered to pay a fine of 66.37 Reichsmarks for failing to properly identify himself. It is important to stress here that, at no time, did the court take issue with the fact that Mr. Hahn had used his informal nickname of *Fritz* instead of *Friederich*; nor was there any objection raised to the fact that he did not use his full birth name. The sole reason for the prosecution was the fact that the victim had failed to include the prescribed name of *Israel* in his signature.

Although many within the Jewish community strenuously objected to the LAFFN-2 as another form of state-sponsored chicanery, the legislation seemed to hit the oldest members the hardest. Having spent more than half a century writing their signature in one way, many found it nearly impossible to suddenly adjust to writing it in another. Such was most likely the case of a Ms. Martha H., a nearly seventy-year-old woman who found herself facing criminal charges after sending off a simple postcard to her loved ones.[27] According to the official police record, the scrawled signature which Martha placed at the bottom of her message was clearly missing the obligatory identifier 'Sara.' For the crime of having concealed her Jewish identity, the courts imposed a prison sentence of no less than two weeks. As justification for the severity of this ruling, the court indicated that this incident was not the first time that the convict had failed to use the required identifier on signed documents. A short time later, this original sentence was however commuted and the elderly lady was required to pay the court a fine of 300 Reichsmarks.[28] A review of the criminal records reveals that Martha H's case was not at all unusual. For more than one senior citizen, it was simply all too easy to forget to insert the foreign moniker *Israel* or *Sara*—a fact which the corrupt, the nefarious, and generally reprehensible were all too willing to exploit.

In the summer of 1941, an infirmed, eighty-five-year-old Jewish lawyer, Gustav M., received mail from local authorities. The letter ordered the solicitor to either completely vacate his Brandenburg residence or allow half of his living quarters to be converted into rental space. Either option meant that the bedridden lawyer would have little or no space left for his extensive library. That being the case, on September 25, Gustav M. composed a formal letter requesting permission to donate his impressive book collection to a bright young pupil. Upon signing the letter, the solicitor used his official professional signature which was missing the obligatory name *Israel*. A little over a month later, the lawyer was paid a visit by the Gestapo and by January 30, 1942, formal criminal charges had been filed.

While awaiting his arraignment, Gustav M. sent another letter to the financial authorities to request permission to send his remaining relatives the sum of

80,000 Reichsmarks for their care. Once again, the signature appearing at the end of the letter was without the required name *Israel*; and, once again, the Gestapo's response was both immediate and severe. The elderly gentleman's book collection was seized and his bank account was plundered. Gustav M. was then evicted and sent to a concentration camp in Eastern Europe. And the relatives whom he had so wanted to provide for were collectively transferred to Theresienstadt and Auschwitz where they too were murdered.

In the above cases, the "failure" to comply with the new onomastic ordinance appears to have been accidental. In other cases, the non-compliance was purposeful. However, contrary to the rhetoric of the Nazi propaganda machine, the motivations behind this decision were more often than not heart-wrenchingly altruistic. On July 17, 1940, the Hamburg Police Department filed a report on their interrogation of Jewish resident, Herr Berthold B.[29] According to the transcript, the forty-seven-year-old warehouse worker had recently laid to rest his beloved wife, Johanna, a Christian. The two had been married twenty-seven years, defying first the social and then the legal restrictions against Aryan-Jewish marriages. The reason why Berthold had been summoned for questioning was his failure to include the name *Israel* on the paperwork he'd filed to register his wife's death and apply for her burial in a Christian cemetery. Berthold immediately admitted that he had intentionally omitted the stigmatized name from the official papers. When asked why, he gave the following explanation:

> I admit that I did not use the additional name 'Israel' but I ordinarily use this name. I also possess an identification card that includes this name. I am also completely aware of the fact that I am required to use this additional name which is what I always do when I deal with officials. In this particular instance, I did not. I ask, however, that it be taken into consideration that I neither gained nor intended to gain any personal advantage. The omission in question only occurred in connection with the burial of my German-blooded wife, who would not have been lain to rest in Ohlsdorf in the local Christian cemetery, if I had added the name 'Israel' [to the documents] and been recognized as a Jew. In the future, however, I will always use the name 'Israel' for all business and legal dealings and in this way leave no doubt as to my identity.[30]

In the widower's court case, no other evidence was introduced to demonstrate that the accused had violated the LAFFN-2. The decorated World War I veteran's assertion that this omission had been completely atypical was accepted as truthful. Nevertheless, on September 30, 1940, the court sentenced the grieving widower to pay a fine of 20 RM and serve a jail sentence of four days. Initially, this sentencing may appear to be comparatively lenient. However, the records maintained by Yad Vashem indicate that Berthold B. ultimately became one of the thousands of Hamburg Jews who was imprisoned, deported, and finally murdered. His last known residence was the Minsk Ghetto.[31]

*****

The key to establishing and maintaining the Nazis' lethal system of apartheid was to enforce the use of these onomastic markers in all daily activities, both private and public, without exception. In some municipal utility companies, it became standard practice to check the signatures of Jewish customers to make sure that the obligatory *Sara* and *Israel* appeared. Violations were routinely reported to the authorities. On December 21, 1939, for example, the municipal water company for the city of Berlin [Berliner Stadtische Wasserwerk] sent a letter to the Gestapo to report that one of their long-time customers had failed to comply with the LAFFN-2 regulation.[32] According to the letter, "in previous years, Heine had consistently inserted the name 'Israel' in his letters. Recently, however, H. has stopped using this name. We request an investigation into the matter." Shortly after that denunciation, Herr Heine received a fine of 100 RM and prison sentence of ten days.

A year later and nearly 300 kilometers away, the gas company of Hamburg sent a similar complaint to the local Gestapo about one of their customers. On April 25, 1940, the utility company reported that "through sheer coincidence" they had discovered that their customer, a Mr. Heimberg, was not an Aryan.[33] The company further asserted that Mr. Heimberg had purposefully deceived the firm, "about his racial classification through the omission of the additional name 'Israel.'" Once again, the company requested an immediate investigation into the matter. The Hamburg Gestapo happily obliged. Herr Heimberg was given a fine of 50 RM and made to serve a term of ten days in prison.

Importantly, the Heimberg denunciation by the gas company in Hamburg does not appear to have been exceptional but seems to have been a part of a clandestine system. A clue to this network was found in another letter sent to the Hamburg Gestapo from the city gas company. On August 29, 1940, the officials working in the utility company reported that they had conducted their own private investigations in conjunction with the National Socialist Social Welfare Organization [Nationalsozialistische Volkswohlfahrt] of the district of Eimsbüttel. Through this detective work, it had been discovered that one of their customers was in fact a Jew, despite the fact that he had not identified himself as such. "Undoubtedly" the gas company officials wrote, the Gestapo "will easily be able to verify whether the person named is indeed a Jew."[34]

Utility companies were not alone in denouncing their Jewish clients. In the next case identified in the Hamburg municipal archives, a small Jewish family was denounced at a time that should have been an exclusively joyous occasion: the birth of their son. In March 1939, a local house painter, Mr. K. Schmul, registered himself with the Hamburg insurance company, Hammonia.[35] Two years later, after giving birth to a healthy baby boy, his wife, Mrs. L. Schmul, visited the Hammonia Insurance company to file the necessary paperwork for their three-month-old son. She brought with her, her Jewish ID card. In the discussion that followed, Mrs. Schmul revealed that both she and her husband were "Volljude" [completely Jewish]: a fact that the insurance company had, according to the local director, been entirely unaware of until that point. A review of the records revealed that Mr. Schmul had neither shown his Jewish ID card, nor used the compulsory onomastic identifier *Israel* in his signature when he had applied for the insurance in 1939.

In a letter sent to the local police, the Hammonia insurance director reported that Mr. Schmul had obviously attempted to deceive the firm. Herr Schmul was promptly summoned for questioning at the local police precinct. During the interrogation, the twenty-three-year-old father explained that he had had no intention of deceiving the authorities or concealing his Jewish identity to gain "improper" advantage. After a grueling interrogation, he was released. However, a short time later, he was re-summoned by the court for additional questioning. When Mr. Schmul failed to appear at the specified date and time, a missing person's report was filed and a formal investigation was launched. On January 9, 1942, the court was informed that Herr Schmul had disappeared and his exact whereabouts were unknown. An examination of the records kept in the Yad Vashem database sheds light on Mr. and Mrs. Schmul's last known locations: the Minsk Ghetto and the Sachsenhausen concentration camp. No information could be found about the whereabouts of their newborn.

This case underscores the spurious nature of the LAFFN-2. Although the name *Schmul* cannot be said to be exclusively Jewish, as German surnames go, the probability that the bearer of this name was Jewish was not exactly low. In fact, *Schmul* was included in the Nazis' 1938 list of names considered to be so stereotypically Semitic that Jews with this last name were initially exempted from using the extra identifier *Israel*. That being the case, the company's assertion that, had it not been for their hyper vigilance, the Schmuls would have continued to pass as Aryan without raising the slightest degree of suspicion, quite frankly, verges on the ridiculous. It is far more likely that the family's heritage had been pre-emptively investigated precisely because of their last name. To be sure, if the government officials had discovered the Schmul family name on the company's list of clients, the Hammonia executives would have found it difficult to argue that it had never crossed their mind that the Schmuls might have been Jewish.

This was not the only record found in which the Hammonia Insurance company of Hamburg was found to denounce its Jewish clients. On April 1, 1941, the company director made an official report to the police about another one of their clients: this time, a Mrs. Cäcilie M.[36] According to the director, the new mother had sent a letter to the company requesting a family insurance card under her husband Ernst's policy for their newborn child Denny. At the end of the letter, Mrs. M. signed with her last name and her nickname *Cilly*. She apparently "failed," however, to include the compulsory name *Sara*. As evidence for the accusation, the director included not only the original letter featuring Mrs. M.'s signature. He also forwarded the family's address, birth dates, and full birth names, as well as the birth certificate for their child. After law enforcement reviewed the materials provided by the insurance company, Mrs. M. was found guilty of violating the LAFFN-2. She was consequently sentenced to pay a fine of 10 RM. In the event that she was unable to pay this fine, she was ordered to serve two days in prison. A review of the Yad Vashem records reveals that both Cäcilie and her husband Ernst were placed under arrest and sent to the Minsk Ghetto. According to information provided by a friend of the family who survived the war and later immigrated to the United States, Ernst died in the ghetto. It is assumed that his wife suffered the same fate. What happened to their child "Denny" remains unknown.

Onomastic surveillance such as described in the cases above was not only conducted in an effort to comply with the government regulations. Potential violations of the name regulations were frequently sought in hopes of bilking Jewish residents of their last belongings. In the winter of 1941, for example, a property management firm in Hamburg used precisely this tactic to strongarm a family out of their property, their home, and their livelihood. The object of the company's interest was an elegant Jugendstil villa situated in the town of Volksdorf, a picturesque country village nestled in the northeastern corner of Schleswig-Holstein. Located less than 50 kilometers away from the heart of Hamburg, by the turn of the century, Volksdorf was becoming an attractive real estate option for Hanseatic clientele looking for a fast escape from the daily stress and strain of Germany's largest seaport. In contrast to the vibrant metropolis, Volksdorf was a quiet, traditional, tight-knit community with deep Lutheran roots—an excellent spot to raise a family. No doubt, these assets would all have been persuasive selling points for Herr Friedrich Liebermann, a prominent Hanseatic financier who was on the look-out for a safe investment in the increasingly insecure economic times. In 1917, Liebermann purchased an elegant villa along with 4,000 square meters of the surrounding countryside.

Rather than take up residence in the home himself, the banker gave the property away to someone who would appreciate the villa's modern architectural design, and was in desperate need of support. The recipient of Liebermann's generosity was his son. Although an accomplished construction engineer, his son had been unable to find gainful employment in his field ever since the economic crash. The progressive implementation of Hitler's anti-Jewish legislation, made it nearly impossible for the young engineer to financially support himself, his wife, and their son. The new home, it was hoped, would not only offer the struggling family a quiet haven where they could restore their strength. It would also provide them with the means to regain their financial footing. Initially, it seemed this dream would actually come true.

To secure a regular income, the Liebermanns neatly divided their home into three separate parts. The first section was reserved for the family's own private quarters. The second was made into a comfortable apartment that they rented out to a local family, the Thilos. In the third section, the Liebermanns offered temporary lodgings to Jewish families in search of a safe refuge as they made their final preparations to leave Germany for good. The fact that the Liebermanns had opened their home to Jews in need would have been reason enough for the local officials to begin to pay special attention to the newcomers. However, this was not the only reason. Despite the fact that both the Liebermanns were practicing Lutherans, only Mrs. Liebermann was officially considered an Aryan under the new Party regulations. As a convert, Mr. Liebermann was classified as a Jew. The other reason for the heightened scrutiny was the Liebermann's stylish villa had been earmarked for "Aryanization."

The Liebermanns received repeated offers to sell their property to the city; and each time the family politely but firmly refused. With each refusal, the pressure placed by the authorities increased. Soon the home was being regularly targeted by local members of the Hitler Youth chanting slogans like "Juden RAUS!" [Jews OUT!] Still, the Liebermanns remained steadfast and refused to sell. The authorities did not take "No" for an answer, however. By 1941, they increased the pressure once again. On February 14, the Hamburg Gestapo was sent an official letter of complaint from a property management firm of Hamburg. In the letter, the "Jewish property owner" R. Liebermann was accused of insolently refusing to pay an outstanding bill (for services which Mr. Liebermann staunchly refuted having ordered or received), and failing to include the obligatory identifier *Israel* in his signature. As retribution, the firm requested that the Gestapo take the appropriate correctional steps.

As a part of the ensuing police investigation, the Statistics Bureau for the Hanseatic City of Hamburg reported that the name *Israel* was also frequently missing in the monthly surveys Mr. Liebermann was required to complete and return about the paying guests who had stayed in the family villa. The apparent reason for the omission was that all of the offending documents had been "signed" using a company stamp featuring only Mr. Liebermann's first and last names. Once this discovery was made, it did not take long for the authorities to assemble other official documents where the same stamp had also been used. A review of the Liebermanns' food ration cards, for example, revealed that *Israel* was also routinely missing from the stamped signature. On the basis of this evidence, Mr. Liebermann was formally charged and found guilty of violating the LAFFN on March 21, 1941. As punishment, he was required to pay all of the court fees and serve three weeks in prison.

Given the number of LAFFN-2 violations presented by the state, it would not have come as a surprise had a stiffer sentence been passed. Perhaps in an effort to head off any future criticism or suspicion of impropriety, the presiding judge issued a statement to explain the two mitigating factors which lead to the sentencing leniency. The first was that the accused was a decorated WWI veteran who had earned not one but two Iron Crosses as well as the Hanseatic Cross for his service to his country. The second mitigating factor was that it was considered highly unlikely that the accused had intentionally omitted the name *Israel* with the purpose of passing for an Aryan given that his Jewish identity was well known throughout the tiny community of Volksdorf.[37]

Mr. Liebermann was first remanded to the Fuhlsbüttel police prison. Under the Nazi regime, Fuhlsbüttel was originally erected as a concentration camp in the fall of 1933. By 1936, the prison was used by the Gestapo as a police penitentiary for individuals who had been designated as antisocial and/or detrimental to the welfare of the state (e.g., Seventh Day Adventists, Communists, Roma and Sinti, Social Democrats, Jews, and foreign members of the resistance movement). From 1944 to 1945, it served as a satellite for the larger concentration camp, Neuengamme. After his incarceration in Fuhlsbüttel, Mr. Liebermann was transferred to the Sachsenhausen Concentration Camp where he was held for several weeks. Almost immediately upon his return, the family was made another offer to sell their home. This time, the family acquiesced.[38] In 1941, Mr. and Mrs. Liebermann vacated their home for good. A year later, as Mr. Liebermann was serving as a slave laborer in a local factory, he and his wife received the news that their beloved son had been killed on the Eastern front fighting for the Vaterland that had so betrayed them. As the family grieved, the city of Hamburg was busy making a tidy profit from renting the rooms of the Liebermann villa to Aryans seeking much-needed respite from the tumult of the city.[39]

*****

Initially, the LAFFN-2 only required Jewish residents to identify themselves as such when dealing with public officials. Relatively quickly, however, they were also expected to racially self-identify in private business dealings involving Aryans. During the archival research conducted for this book, it was not unusual to find denunciation letters written by Aryan private business owners who complained about "difficult" Jewish customers who either did not know or refused to accept their newly assigned place. In one such case, a sixty-one-year old Jewish resident was made to realize just how dangerous transgressing this new norm could be.

In the autumn of 1939, Frau Caroline F. contracted a local moving and storage company in Hamburg to transport her few belongings: two boxes and two suitcases.[40] What should have been a straightforward business arrangement revealed itself to be a case of fraud after the Heiser moving company insisted upon receiving additional payment for the indignity of transporting Frau F's "Judengut" [Jewish property]. When subsequent meetings between the two disputing parties failed to bring a mutually satisfactory agreement, Frau F. sent a heated letter to the moving company. In it, the merchant daughter demanded the immediate transfer all of her belongings to a new company she had contracted. She also threatened to file an official report should the company refuse to comply:

> Given our consultation today and your behavior towards both myself and my son-in-law on the telephone, I have enlisted the services of another transport company that will store the goods currently kept on your premises in its storage space. . . . Should you refuse to release my property to the new company I have employed or should you damage or break the import seal of my property, I will bring charges against you with the state prosecutor, the regulatory trade authorities [Gewerbepolizei], and the association of transporters to make sure that a stop is put to your criminal dealings. You are well aware of the fact that this property is to be shipped and you are simply seeking an opportunity to serve as an obstacle or more directly said turn an illegal profit. This conduct is contrary to the laws governing removal companies and you have consequently shown yourself to be unreliable for the execution of this contract. Furthermore, given the current situation, I must also assume that it is your intention to unlawfully take my property into your possession and for that reason I must also assume that my property is no longer safe on your premises. I have no choice, therefore, but to take these steps.[41]

Incensed, and quite likely more than a tad bit alarmed, the owner and director of the family-owned business, A. Heiser, sent a letter to the state police requesting that something be done about the impertinent Jewess. "Once you have reviewed the information," the Director wrote, "I dare say you will have to concede that, under no circumstances, can a Jew be allowed to dare to write an Aryan enterprise such a shockingly offensive letter." Heiser was careful to note that he had no desire to press charges in a court of law—a wise decision given

Frau F.'s justified charges of misconduct. Instead he requested that the matter be discreetly handled by the Gestapo and the necessary punishment be exacted for the obstreperous woman's insolence. As before, the secret police were all too happy to oblige. In their subsequent review of the correspondence sent from Frau F. to the Heiser company, they soon discovered that the lady in question had neglected to include the name *Sara* in her signature.

Frau F. was called into the 70th police precinct for questioning. In the official protocol that was later filed, she readily admitted that she had written the letter of complaint to the Heiser company and that she had signed the letter with only her first initial and surname. When asked why she had not included the onomastic marker, she answered that she had not been aware that the requirement to use the name *Sara* also applied to correspondence between private citizens. Up until the time of her interrogation, she claimed, she had been under the assumption the onomastic regulation only applied to interactions with authorities.

This explanation was evidently not enough to convince the court to issue a simple warning. Instead, Frau F. was formally prosecuted and pronounced guilty on February 21, 1940. As punishment, the court ruled that the elderly widow would have to pay a penalty of 20 RM or serve two days in prison. Rather than face the personal ignominy and physical danger of going to jail, the sixty-one-year-old disabled widow attempted to pay the fine. However, given that she reportedly only received 23.90 RM per month to survive on, she appealed to the court to allow her to pay the fine in monthly installments of 2 RM. Miraculously, this request was granted. Nevertheless, the additional expense paired with the perpetual fear of defaulting soon proved to be too much.

The archival records show that she faithfully made the monthly installments, even sending her elderly mother to bring the payment to the police precinct in her stead on those rare occasions when she was unable to appear herself. The only interruption came in early December. In a handwritten postcard to the court, Frau F. explained that with the onslaught of winter in the northern coastal city of Hamburg, she had simply had to have her shoes repaired. As a result, she had no money left to pay the 2 RM penalty. But, she gave her solemn word that she would immediately resume payment the following month and begged the court to show mercy. Evidently, the court had none to show for according to the records she paid yet another 2 RM on December 16, 1940.

A few months later, she threw herself on the mercy of the court once again after receiving notification that her arrest was imminent if she did not keep up with her payments. She frantically implored:

> I respectfully request that the court waive the fine, as I have no idea how I am to spare 2 Reichsmarks per month from the meager monthly pension of 23.90 Reichsmark. I would also like to add that, aside from this fine, I have never incurred a single debt. I would be

exceedingly grateful to receive the message that the court had laid
this issue to rest. If, however, it is impossible to bring this matter to
a close without further payment, I request that the monthly amount
due be reduced to 50 pf [cents]. I pray that you inform me of the
decision made in this matter as soon as possible, for otherwise I may
be placed under arrest.[42]

Rather than forgo the remaining debt of about 6 Reichsmarks, the court offi-
cials granted Frau F. permission to reduce her monthly installments to 50 cents.
According to the receipts, she was able to pay for the months of May, June,
July, and August when the payments stopped again and mass deportations of
Jewish residents from Hamburg began. An examination of the Yad Vashem
Central Database of Shoah Victims revealed that, in all likelihood, Frau F. was
transported to and murdered in "Jungfernhof," a makeshift concentration camp
in Latvia.[43] As this case demonstrates, the widespread success of this LAFFN1/2
legislation was due to the rabid diligence of the NS officials who were zealously
assisted by everyday citizens. All across the Reich, Aryans took it upon themselves to see to it that these (and other) regulations were rigorously followed.
Part of the motivation for this public scrutiny was the desire to demonstrate
one's enthusiastic support of Hitler's totalitarian regime. At the same time, the
seemingly irresistible attraction of being able to exercise existential power over
others most certainly served as a strong motivator for denunciation as well.
In the new world created by the Nazis, all Aryans were automatically allocated
superior status through no action or achievement of their own, while all non-
Aryans were systematically relegated to an inferior social position, irrespective
of their occupation, age, gender, education, wealth, or experience. An Aryan
gentleman was no longer compelled to open the door for a lady if she was called
Frau Anna Sara Morgenstern. Aryan teenagers were no longer expected to give
up their seats on a crowded tram for a man old enough to be their grandfather,
if his name was *Herr Dr. Josef Israel Rosenbaum.* And, as Frau Caroline F. from
Hamburg was made to learn, no Aryan business owner was obligated to follow
the law or moral conscience when his customer's middle name was *Sara.*

*

Herr H. Gottschalk was a highly successful and affluent businessman whose
stock and trade was the international import and export of fine leathers and
furs.[44] As is still commonplace today within the fashion industry, the registered
name of Gottschalk's Hanseatic company was composed of his own first and
last name. Consequently, all of his products, be they for the domestic or foreign
market, bore this company/personal name. And, not surprisingly, Gottschalk
also signed or stamped all of his business correspondence with that name.

On February 13, 1940, Herr Gottschalk was called in for questioning by the Hamburg police for his alleged failure to include the name *Israel* in the papers and telegrams he routinely sent to his foreign clients. Was he not trying, the police officer asked, to conceal his Jewish identity? In answer to the question, the senior entrepreneur responded:

> I would concede that in seeing my signature any businessman would have to assume that I am Aryan or more to the point that my company is Aryan-owned because the name 'H . . . Gottschalk' on its own wouldn't indicate that the business is Jewish. However, I completely reject the notion that I consciously attempted to give my company the appearance of not being Jewish.[45]

Mr. Gottschalk's steadfast assurance that he had had no intention of deceiving his business partners held little weight with his interrogators; nor evidently did the fact that a significant segment of the "deceptive" correspondence had been sent to Israel, where it can be reasonably assumed that his Jewish identity, had it been explicitly made clear, would not have been negatively received by his business partners. Nevertheless, on March 13, 1940, Mr. Gottschalk was found guilty as charged and sentenced to serve six weeks in prison. On that very same day, his legal counsel formally appealed the decision.

The appeal was placed by Dr. Manfred Zadik. Once a highly successful lawyer with his own practice, by 1938, with the introduction of the National Citizen Act [Reichsbürgergesetz], Dr. Zadik had become one of approximately 20,000 Jewish lawyers formally banned from practicing their profession as an attorney. Instead, Zadik was given the designation "Konsulent." The Nazis resurrected this seventeenth-century, previously archaic occupational name, to describe the new, highly restricted, professional powers of many demoted Jewish lawyers.[46] Despite this public debasement, Zadik continued to use his superior skills and intellect to tenaciously defend his clientele.

In his appeal of Mr. Gottschalk's conviction, Zadik pointed out with piercing eloquence, that in point of fact the third paragraph of the LAFFN specifically and explicitly excluded businesses. He then went on to argue that had his client used the name *Israel* in his business correspondence, he would have been in direct violation of the paragraph of Germany's commercial law which stipulates that the name and signature used in business transactions for a firm must be identical to the registered name of the firm. Given the fact that the registered name of Mr. Gottschalk's was in fact made up of his client's first and last name, the insertion of the name *Israel* would have been unlawful.

Upon reviewing Dr. Zadik's reasoning, the judge presiding over the case agreed. "I am of the opinion," the judge wrote, "that the arrest order is to be lifted. As a tradesman, G. is allowed to sign with his company name, and that

does not include the additional name 'Israel.'" With that decision, Mr. Gottschalk's conviction was overturned. Dr. Zadik was officially notified that, as far
as the court was concerned, nothing stood in the way of Mr. Gottschalk's release
from prison. When, however, the Konsulent arrived at the Gestapo detention
center to take his client home to his family, he was informed that there must be
some mistake. The Gestapo refused to set Gottschalk free.

Undaunted, Dr. Zadik filed again for his client's immediate release. This
time, his argumentation included the fact that Mr. Gottschalk was an elderly
man with an impeccable reputation and a hitherto spotless criminal record; and
if the authorities could not be moved by the character of his client, then certainly
some mercy could be bestowed on his client as a German veteran of World War
I. Dr. Zadik even went so far as to note that the Reich's governor of Hamburg
[Reichsstatthalter], Karl Kaufmann, had himself neglected to use the name *Israel*
when referring to H. Gottschalk in a letter granting the businessman permission
to continue to run his company until the issue had finally been resolved. Surely,
if such a respected member of the Nazi government could be forgiven for this
oversight, so too could a simple businessman.

Before Dr. Zadik could strengthen his appeal, he received word that his
client was no longer being held by the Gestapo in Hamburg but had been deported from the city. Subsequent research of Yad Vashem's database revealed
Mr. Gottschalk's new location: Theresienstadt. From there, he was apparently
sent to the Chelmo Concentration Camp, where he was murdered.[47] As each of
these stories poignantly demonstrates, from the very beginning the LAFFN was
effectively used by both private citizen and public official alike, to label, control,
humiliate, and ultimately destroy millions of people's lives.

*****

On January 6, 1939, the Reich's Minister of the Interior, Wilhelm Frick,
issued an internal governmental directive[48] which imposed even more onomastic restrictions. The circular proclaimed, for instance, that Jewish residents
of the Reich should no longer be permitted to carry family names which
contained the word "Deutsch" [German] (e.g., Deutschland, *Deutschländer,
Deutsch, Deutscher, Deutschmann*, etc.). All such cases were to be immediately
reported to the local police as well as the responsible district commissioner.
Whenever officials identified Jewish residents within their district who had one
of these surnames, they were instructed to have the offending party apply for
an official name change. Governmental officials who received such "requests"
were instructed to change the applicant's name to either an ancestral, readily
identifiable Jewish surname; or when such family names were unavailable, the
word *Deutsch* could simply be removed from the applicant's former last name.

Thus, a Jewish resident whose last name had been *Deutschmann* could be given the name *Mann*.

The historical records are accordingly filled with reports from local civil servants to their immediate supervisors detailing on their progress in seeing that this ordinance was followed. For example, on March 8, 1939, the then Burgermeister of the town of Rimbach reported that the recent review of the Jews registered in his community had uncovered none with a surname containing the word "Deutsch." The Jews in his area were named *Aschenbrand, Hamburger, Marx, Weichsel, Westheimer,* and *Wetterhahn* and therefore did not fall under the new restriction.[49] Similarly, the Burgermeister of Heppenheim dutifully mailed in his official response dated March 17, 1939.[50] In his report, he assured his supervisors that his office had carefully reviewed the records and had not been able to locate a single Jewish resident with the family name of *Deutschland, Deutsch,* or the like. On March 14, 1939, the Burgermeister in the nearby town of Birkenau im Odenwald reported that in his district there was only one Jew remaining and his name was *Schack*.[51] However, not to be undone, the official ends his letter with the assurance that he would remain ever mindful of this new and important regulation and promised that he would not hesitate to enforce it should his community experience an influx of Jews in the future.

The 1939 Frick circular also contained new instructions for processing name-change petitions filed by people with partial Jewish heritage. Effective immediately, these applications were to be handled in the same way as those received from applicants with complete Jewish parentage.[52] This meant that the names *Sara* and *Israel* were now also compulsory for all residents of the Reich with Jewish ancestry. The only permissible exceptions were cases involving persons with extremely distant Jewish ancestry. Exactly what constituted "distant ancestry" was largely left unspecified. When in doubt, officials were instructed to remand the case to the Reich's Ministry of the Interior in Berlin.

As with any alteration in policy, this change caused some initial confusion among German officials who were anxious to properly apply the law. To ensure that their office was following proper protocol, the city council director of Hamburg consulted directly with Dr. Globke on March 14, 1939. In an internal report issued to Hamburg officials afterward, it was explained that exemptions to the law requiring Jews to carry special ID cards and use the compulsory names *Sara* and *Israel* would no longer be granted to anyone of mixed Jewish heritage, even those who had been awarded special commendations for service to the Fatherland or those who had fought on the front during World War I or World War II (i.e., Frontkämpfer).[53]

One resident directly affected by this policy change was E. Heß.[54] A Catholic-convert, Heß had not one but four Jewish grandparents. Ordinarily, this parentage would have required him to add *Israel* to his official name. However, Heß was initially spared this indignity by none other than the Führer himself. During World War I, the war veteran had not only served in the same company as the Adolf Hitler, he had also for a time been his commanding officer. In the summer of 1940, Heinrich Himmler wrote to the Dusseldorf police and informed them that Heß, in accordance with the Führer's express wishes, was to be exempted from carrying the name *Israel* and was to be afforded every courtesy. Just one year later, however, in 1941, Heß was informed that his special status had been revoked. Heß was later sent to Milbertshofen, a forced labor camp from which deportees were routinely transferred to eastern Europe for extermination. Heß's changing status and fate were indicative of a palpable shift in the Nazi policy. Exemptions and privileges previously allowed to persons of mixed Jewish heritage began to disappear. Military service, no matter how distinguished or decorated, was no longer a protection. From now on, even a single drop of Jewish blood was enough to disqualify someone from claiming protected status.

During World War I, approximately 100,000 men of Jewish faith fought on the battlefield for Germany. More than one-third of these soldiers were decorated for their service to their country and more than 2,000 were officers. At the end of the war, some 12,000 Jewish servicemen lost their lives. One of the fallen was twenty-nine-year-old infantryman Josef Zürndörfer. Shortly before his death in an airplane crash, the double recipient of the Iron Cross wrote: "I came to this field of battle as a German to protect my Fatherland from threat. But, I also came as a Jew, in the hope of securing complete equality for my religious brethren"[55] Sadly, Zürndörfer's fervent hopes to be recognized for the sacrifice he and so many others like him had made were left largely unfulfilled. Indeed, long before the war had come to an official end and the reviled Versailles Treaty had been signed, hate-mongers were blaming the imminent defeat upon the cowardice and treachery of "the Jews" in their rank and file. Adding insult to injury, when the National Socialists came to power, it was ordered that the names of Jewish World War I soldiers be completely removed from public monuments and memorials that had been erected throughout the Reich. In the introduction to a collection of personal letters written by fallen Jewish soldiers of World War I to their loved ones, Frank Josef Strauß, former Chair of the Christian Social Union in Bavaria and a veteran of World War II, laments this contemptible treatment of his compatriots—their names, their service, their memories simply blotted out, obliterated, forgotten.

> And why? In the official Hitlerian ideological doctrine, Jews were not allowed be shown as brave. They were not even permitted, as crazy as this may sound, to die for Germany. The names of the fallen must therefore, the National Socialists decreed, disappear from all of the

memorials. Himmler then unleashed his terror upon the German Jewish soldiers who had fought upon the frontlines. He drove them out the country, he ordered that they be thrown into Jewish concentration camps, internment camps, ghettos, and gas chambers; or he made them stand before the wall of an impromptu firing range.[56]

In the winter of 1940, Officer Newmann, a Jewish World War I veteran and holder of the Iron Cross, discovered just how committed the National Socialists were to erasing the memory of those who had served their country. On February 8, 1940, the soldier sent what was his second letter to the Hamburg branch of the Medical Association, once again imploring the physicians for their assistance.[57] The decorated serviceman was quite literally starving to death. He hoped that, with the Association's intervention, he might be allowed to receive a bit more food. As fate would have it, at the end of his desperate message, the forty-one-year-old omitted to include the name *Israel*, an oversight which was immediately reported to the Hamburg police.

A formal police report written on March 5, 1940, indicated that the veteran excused himself for the mistake and explained that in his nervous state he had simply forgotten to include the compulsory name. The officer conducting the interview noted that the veteran had been issued artificial limbs but, due to his weakened state, was completely unable to use them. As a result, he was unable to leave his room and was essentially bedridden. Despite the soldier's exemplary military record and demonstrated service to his country of birth, the court found him guilty of violating the LAFFN-2 and imposed a fine of 20 RM. In the event that he was unable to pay the fine, it was ordered that the veteran be remanded to prison to serve a sentence of four days. Given his desolate condition, it is reasonable to assume that he was neither able to pay the fine nor survive imprisonment. During the course of this research, no record was found to determine what precisely happened to Officer Neumann.

For many people of mixed Jewish parentage this policy change must have come as a complete shock. At a time when names such as *Dachau, Sachsenhausen, Buchenwald, Flossenbürg, Mauthausen,* and *Ravensbrück* had already become a part of the German lexicon, it was clear what this change in status meant for themselves and all those around them. In some cases, residents of the Reich with mixed Jewish heritage willingly followed the new regulation. The reasons for this compliance are manifold. Some saw it as a matter of personal pride and honor to officially recognize their Jewish ancestry; others felt it was a matter of their civic duty to obey the laws of their country; still others hoped that following the laws, no matter how ridiculous or insulting they might have been, might help to ameliorate the situation and demonstrate that Jews were not the congenital miscreants the NSDAP insisted on portraying them to be.

On July 19, 1940, a Mr. A. Rothstein, a Danzig-born veteran who had been bestowed the Iron Cross for extraordinary military service, submitted his application to have the name *Israel* added to his name. The application was filed less than two weeks after the injured soldier's discharge but still after the official deadline. As a result, the war hero with two maternal Jewish grandparents was charged with violating the LAFFN-2. In a <u>highly</u> unusual act of mercy, however, [in fact the only one encountered during this research] all of the charges against the solider were dropped and the case was closed.[58] Why this leniency was shown toward Officer Rothstein could not be determined. Certainly, it was not the veteran's military service alone. In fact, in one case after another, one could not help but gain the impression that Jewish military veterans were seen as a special threat to the NSDAP vision and as such were treated with marked disdain and cruelty. Such was the case of Lieutenant Julius Holz from Berlin-Charlottenburg.

During World War I, Officer Holz earned the Iron Cross for his outstanding bravery before falling in France in June 1918. Some twenty-four years later, his surviving brother and eighty-one-year-old mother were forced to flee Germany to avoid the ensuing deportations. The Officer's mother was given refuge in a Jewish hospital in Holland. Shortly after her arrival, she learned that the family members of Jewish soldiers might be granted an exemption to the round-ups if they could provide evidence of their loved one's service. In hopes of protecting herself and her remaining son, Officer Holz's mother applied for a deportation exemption. To strengthen her petition, she included notarized copies of her deceased son's service papers as well as detailed information about her own person. Her application was rejected with a single sentence: "Your petition for an exemption for a work-assignment is rejected." Fourteen days later, the elderly woman received a follow-up answer. Using all of the biographical details she had provided in her application, a police squad arrived at the Jewish hospital in the dead of night and located Frau Holz's hospital ward. Once there, they arrested the entire floor of elderly patients, loaded them into police wagons, and drove their frail human cargo to the train station in Amsterdam. From there the senior citizens were shoved into trains and sent to Auschwitz where they were immediately liquidated.[59]

*

In a 1940 letter written to the Office for Racial Policy, Herr R. Harder explained that he was the son of a "Jewess" and an Aryan. Despite his mother's ancestry, according to Herr Harder, there was nothing in his upbringing which was remotely Jewish. He was neither given a Jewish education nor made to observe Jewish traditions such as Bar Mitzvah or circumcision. When he entered adulthood, he severed all formal ties with the Jewish community and requested that his name be removed from the register of Israelites in Hamburg. During World War I, he served his country on the frontlines and was awarded an Iron Cross for uncommon bravery on the battlefield. After World War I, he became politically active and joined the National Socialist Society for the Volk's Welfare [Nationalsozialistische Volkswohlfahrt].

In his letter, he also recounted a recent dispute with a local police officer. What began as a discussion over a radio license ended with an argument over Mr. Harder's proper racial classification. While the officer insisted that Mr. Harder fell into the category of "Volljude" [completely Jewish], Mr. Harder rejected this categorization and appealed to the Berlin office for assistance. An excerpt from his letter of appeal appears below:

> Hamburg 23rd January 1940
>
> If this classification should remain, I fear that the consequences for me would befit neither my true character nor my station. . . . I am a completely upstanding character and within National Socialist Germany, I have fulfilled my duty in every respect. Nevertheless, under the current circumstances, I may even have to fear that I will not be able to keep my job in a machine manufactory. For these reasons, I request that I be issued documentation that I am NOT a 'Volljude,' but a 'Half-Israelite.'
>
> Heil Hitler![60]

Mr. Harder is completely aware of the privileges and perils which go with the racial ethnonyms used by the Nazis. It is only too clear why he might prefer the label of "Half-Israelite" to the highly stigmatized designation "Half-Jewish." After reviewing his case, the courts denied Mr. Harder's request and ordered him to pay a fine of 20 Reichsmarks and serve four days in prison for the double-crime of failing to use the obligatory onomastic marker *Israel* and failing to carry the ID card required of all Jewish residents. In short, Mr. Harder's request to maintain his previously self-chosen classification of "Aryan" was summarily denied: the consequences of which were potentially lethal.

A similar dire reality was faced by fifty-three-year-old E. Lüllemann.[61] In 1941, she was also charged with failing to use the identifier *Sara*, despite the fact that both her paternal and maternal grandparents had Jewish ancestry. The fact that these very same progenitors had officially converted in the nineteenth century and Mrs. Lüllemann had been raised as a Christian was immaterial in the eyes of the Reich's office for racial genealogy. In complete disbelief, Mrs. Lüllemann implored the officials to reconsider their decision. Rescinding her Aryan status would have lethal consequences both for herself, and her twenty-one-year-old son who had already served two years on the Front, fighting for his country. In a desperate effort to save herself and her child, she requested that her ancestry be reviewed. Mrs. Lüllemann's request was honored but the result was the same. In April 1942, her Jewish ancestry was confirmed, her previous Aryan status was revoked, and the courts found her guilt violating the LAFF2. Just three months later, on July 19, 1942, according to a follow-up report filed by the Gestapo, Mrs. Lüllemann was forced to join one of the seventeen convoys of Hamburg residents who were "evacuated" from the city. Their destination: Theresienstadt. In the case of Mrs. Lüllemann, her "failure" to use the required onomastic marker was based on her previous self-identification as an Aryan. In that sense, there does not seem to have been any intention to "hide" her Jewish identity. In the next case, however, that is precisely the intention.

*

In August of 1942, the Hamburg police filed a report on one of their many lengthy interrogations. The target of their attention was a Mr. Hermann B. During the course of the intensive questioning, Mr. B. revealed that his official first name was not *Hermann* but *Salomon* and that he was the illegitimate son of a "Jewess" and an unknown soldier. According to his statement, shortly after his birth, his mother had given him up for adoption by a Christian family in Hamburg. His adoptive parents renamed him "Hermann" after their first son. From that point on, the two boys were referred to as *Big Hermann* and *Little Hermann*. As Mr. B. revealed during the police questioning, this name change was not only undertaken to better integrate him into his new family. The change was also made to spare his new parents the social embarrassment of having a son with Jewish ancestry.

Eventually, the name *Salomon* was buried and Mr. B. became exclusively known as *Hermann*. That was until the spring of 1942, when a district leader of the NSDAP knocked on his door to ascertain his racial ancestry. In the conversation that followed, Mr. B. revealed that he was a half-Jewish [Mischling 1. Grad] but without personal affinity or official association with the Jewish faith. The district leader recorded Mr. B's response in his racial census and filed his final report with the local authorities. Shortly thereafter, a criminal investigation was opened regarding Mr. B's identity and status. When asked by the police why he felt he might have been pulled in for questioning, Mr. B. replied that he assumed the investigation had been triggered by his membership in the local chapter of the National Socialist Welfare Society [NSV], where he had been repeatedly asked about his ancestry. Based on the interrogation transcript, however, the reasons were far more complicated. It seems that the police were merely interested in not only getting to the bottom of Mr. B's charitable activities, but also his business dealings and sexual relations.

Unbeknownst to him, on June 3, 1942, a letter of complaint had been sent to the Hamburg police department from one of the city's most affluent businessmen, a Mr. J. Busch, owner of one of Hamburg's largest bread factories. In the letter, Busch alleged that despite repeated warnings, one of his female employees had continued to have relations with the 'Half-Jew,' Mr. B. The baker then reported that this same female employee had recently given birth to an illegitimate child with an unidentified father. As Mr. Busch went on to explain, it was clear to him that "from the perspective of racial politics such relations are clearly undesirable." For that reason, he had already taken the step of informing the Office for Racial Politics and upon their recommendation had decided to inform the local Gestapo to be absolutely sure that "the necessary preventative steps could be taken."

Why exactly the wealthy businessman had taken such a keen interest in the love-life of this particular female employee remains a mystery. Perhaps, as an ardent Party member, Herr Busch truly took personal offense to the forbidden relationship; or perhaps, the NS industrialist's motivation was simply to protect his business interests. With more than sixty slave laborers working in his factory, he may have seen the letter as a way to simultaneously distance himself and his business from his employee's actions while re-asserting his personal and professional allegiance to the Party.[62] In the city of Hamburg alone, no less than a half a million men, women, and children worked as slave laborers in approximately 1,000 companies, factories, farms, and private residences between the years 1939 and 1945. According to archival records, the Busch bread company used approximately twenty-six slave laborers in its Convent Street location; and less than a half a mile away, another thirty prisoners were forced to work in the factory's Anger Street location within the district of Hohenfelde. With three different slave labor camps, Hohenfelde was a local stronghold of radical anti-Semitic political activity. According to statistics presented by the city of Hamburg, as early as 1932, the NSDAP received 47.5 percent of the vote in Hohenfelde. This percentage was roughly 10.2 percent higher than for the entire Reich. Whatever the motivation(s) for the denunciation may have been, the consequence for Mr. B. was devastating.

Although the authorities were never able to conclusively ascertain whether Mr. B. had indeed had an extramarital affair with Busch's Aryan employee, they did conclude that the accused's use of the name *Hermann* rather than his birth name *Salomon*[63] had ultimately concealed his true Jewish identity. The court subsequently ruled that Mr. B.'s onomastic subterfuge constituted an intentional act of deception that had ultimately made it possible for him to illegally avail himself of rights and privileges exclusively reserved for Aryan residents of the Reich (e.g., flying the German flag, having sexual relations with an Aryan woman, and clandestinely running a laundry delivery which served Aryan customers). As punishment, Mr. B. was sentenced to three months in prison.

The relative severity of this sentencing was most probably due in part to the court's assumption that Mr. B.'s motivation had been personal advantage. However, during the course of the interrogation, Mr. B. gives a very different accounting of the events. "The reason I never presented myself as a Jew was to protect the welfare and well-being of my family. For their sake, I simply did not want to risk the disadvantages that a Jew could have suffered." Judging by the events that transpired, it is clear that this fear was more than justified. Once Mr. B's Jewish heritage became public, both his friends and family were targeted for interrogation by the Nazis. Just how much of a toll this questioning took was revealed in one of the transcripts taken during his wife's interrogation. In the middle of the questioning, Mrs. B. was informed that her husband had been discovered during a foiled attempt to take his own life. Rather than break off the session, the questioning relentlessly continued, until Mrs. B. offered a complete confession.

The interrogation which Mrs. B. underwent was routine for Aryan spouses who refused to divorce their partners. The anti-Semitic legislation affected people who were connected to Judaism by birth as well as through marriage. On March 14, 1939, for example, Dr. Globke instructed Hamburg officials in a lengthy telephone consultation that Aryan wives of Jewish husbands were no longer automatically allowed to exchange their spouse's surnames for their original maiden names.[64] Only AFTER the wife in question had filed and obtained a divorce would her request to return to her maiden name be taken into consideration. This policy alteration was presumably put in place to prevent mixed couples from living under the cover and protection of a non-Jewish surname. On May 14, 1942, an internal memo of the Gestapo in Mainz addressed a related irritation among Nazi lawmakers:

> It is an act of impertinence when an Aryan wife in a mixed marriage places her name and the label 'Aryan' upon the marital door front and completely omits the name of her husband. Mixed-marriages that have not been given special official dispensation are required to display the name of the Jewish husband as well as the Jewish star on their door fronts. . . . Failure to follow this regulation will be considered an act of identity concealment and falsification and is therefore absolutely illegal.[65]

The memo goes on to charge that this form of racial concealment had become commonplace among many mixed marriages in the city of Mainz. Before National Socialism, Mainz was home to one of the largest and oldest Jewish communities in Europe. After National Socialism, the community was almost entirely eradicated through a series of deportations. To facilitate this regional genocide, the Nazis utilized the network of the Reich's Association of Jews in Germany [Reichvereinigung der Juden in Deutschland]. More specifically, leaders of the organization were required to assist in compiling name lists of Jewish residents for the NS purposes. In Mainz, from 1943 to the end of the war, this ignominious task fell to Michel Oppenheim.

A local Jewish lawyer, Michel Oppenheim had lost his post in the district government after the introduction of the NS anti-Jewish laws that permitted only Aryans to practice law and hold government positions. In March of 1941, Oppenheim's services were re-enlisted by the Nazi authorities. He was to serve as an intermediary between the Gestapo and the Reich's Association of Jews in Germany [Reichvereinigung der Juden in Deutschland].[66] His principal duty was to oversee the production of comprehensive lists of Jewish residents according to the Nazis changing specifications. These name lists were then used in the subsequent waves of relocation and deportation throughout Hessia and much of the Rhineland. According to an official report issued by the chief of police in Mainz on August 15, 1938, historically, the information that the police had been able to obtain regarding residents' Jewish identity was neither accurate nor complete.

In an effort to correct this security problem, as of January 1, a card index system had been initiated to capture all Jewish residents. Copies of this index were housed in the passport office as well as in the main registry office of every police district. Despite the fact that the idea of this index had initially encountered considerable resistance, in the meantime, the name index had proven to be an invaluable and reliable tool for locating Jewish residents.[67] Nevertheless, the Gestapo demanded that Oppenheim and his team created separate sets of name lists based on the information assembled by the Reich Association of Jews. By manually cross-checking and consolidating the records found in these sources, the Gestapo could ensure that the final name lists generated for the deportations were as comprehensive and correct as possible. In the following passage, Oppenheim describes the work he and his team faced in the compilation of these name lists:

> Since these rosters were usually demanded at short-notice, it was often necessary for 4, 5, or even 6 people to work on a compiling a single list. . . . Demands were not only made for name lists organized by place of residence, but also by age or degree of health. Lists of war veterans, and recipients of military honors also had to be compiled. Then, they ordered the compilation of lists of people who were younger than 65 years old; lists of people who were in their twenties, thirties, forties, fifties, children, the injured and infirmed, the bed-ridden; and on, and on, and on. . . . We often worked the whole night through . . . in order to finish on time. When the lists were completed, I was required to deliver them to the Gestapo upon my very next trip. The first large transport from our region took place in March of 1942. Right before that deportation, we had to prepare a great many lists.[68]

The people whose names appeared on the deportation lists had three hours to pack a small suitcase of belongings and then report to a local school gymnasium with a cardboard sign hung around their necks. The signs were to have both their names and identity numbers. Outside of the high school were machine-gun carrying police officers with orders to shoot to kill anyone resisting orders.[69] The deportees were required to stay in the high school until the day of the transportation to unfamiliar places named *Lublin, Theresienstadt, and Auschwitz*. According to Oppenheim (who managed to escape the deportation rounds along with his wife and son) in two instances he refused to compile the lethal lists demanded by the Nazis. The first involved listing individuals with one-quarter or more Jewish heritage.[70] The second involved naming married couples where one partner was Aryan and the other Jewish. To justify his refusals, Oppenheim reasoned with his Nazi overseers that creating such lists would require him to report on persons of Aryan blood. Such a task was outside of the legal jurisdictional scope of the Reich Association of Jews. Finally, he argued, were he to compile these requested lists, he would be essentially forced to report on racially superior residents which would constitute an untenable violation of the National Socialist order, would it not?[71] It was no doubt this last argument which carried the most sway: the Gestapo recused Oppenheim from compiling these rosters.

In his report to the Allies after the War, Oppenheim explained that his resistance was a part of his personal credo: he would do all he could to avoid providing the names of persons whom the Nazis would not have otherwise have had access to. "It is very important," he wrote, "to stress the following point: I never named Jews who were not on the lists of the Association of Jews or who had managed to live in Mainz without their true identity being known."[72] While some applauded Oppenheim for his acts of resistance, others criticized that his motivation was not purely altruistic. The husband of a Catholic Aryan wife and the father of a boy who was then one-half Jewish, had Oppenheim agreed to the Gestapo's demands, he would have been required to place his own name and those of his immediate family members on the lists as well.

A review of the archival records reveals that Oppenheim's role during the mass deportations was a source of criticism during the Third Reich as well. In a letter written on May 11, 1943, Oppenheim himself describes an unpleasant encounter in Mainz. According to his own account, a Jewish woman who was in a state of extreme agitation publicly accused both him and his team of creating name lists of Jewish residents who were to be arrested or deported by the Nazis. Oppenheim described that he had been so incensed by the woman's charges that he could barely control himself. Indeed, as he readily conceded, had he not been a gentleman, and the woman not a lady, he may well have forgotten himself. What Oppenheim evidently was unable to forget, however, was the public affront. He therefore demanded that the lady in question provide him with the name of the person(s) who had spread such hurtful untruths.[73] Although it would be inaccurate to say that Oppenheim ordered the arrests and deportations, it would be naive to assume that the name lists which he and his team created played no role at all in the plight of the Jews of Frankfurt, Darmstadt, and Mainz under the Nazis.[74]

It is important to stress that Jews who drew up all those name lists were by no means automatically protected. The original regional head of the Hessian Division of the Reich's Association of Jews in Germany was Fritz Löwenberg. A leading member of the Jewish community and the owner of a successful whole-sale granary in Mainz, at the age of sixty-four years, Löwenberg had been the first one chosen to assemble a team to attempt to satisfy the Gestapo's insatiable desire for name lists. Löwenberg continued in this position until the winter of 1943, when his own name and the names of two of his female colleagues, a Fraulein Schetowitz and a Frau Trczeciak, were placed on the "migration lists." On February 10, 1943, the three joined one of the last transports from Mainz to Theresienstadt where Löwenberg died nearly a year later, on February 25, 1944.[75] His successor was Michel Oppenheim.[76] A month after the February 1943 deportation, Oppenheim and his team took up residence in their new Mainz headquarters: Grabenstraße 12—Fritz Löwenberg's vacant home.[77]

Notes

1. Christian Goeschel, *Suicide in Nazi Germany* (Oxford: Oxford University Press, 2009).

2. F. Neureiter, F. Pietrusky, and E. Schütt, *Handwörterbuch der gerichtlichen Medizin und naturwissenschaftlichen Kriminalistik* (Berlin: Springer Verlag, 1940), 403.

3. Goeschel, *Suicide in Nazi Germany*, 180.

4. Nathanja Hüttenmeister, *Jüdische Friedhöfe in der NS-Zeit.* http://spurensuches teinheim-institut.org/pdf/NSZeit.pdf.

5. Hamburg Staatsarchiv, 213–11–2535/40.

6. Hamburg Staatsarchiv, 213–11–3945/40.

7. Clemens Schwender, *Wie benutze ich den Fernsprecher? Die Anleitung zum Telefonieren im Berliner Telefonbuch 1881–1996/97* (Frankfurt am Main: Peter Lang Verlag, 1997).

8. As of 1935, Jews were officially banned from using any and all electrical devices including public and private telephones. By 1940, Jewish telephones were to be confiscated. For more on anti-Jewish decrees during the Third Reich, see http://www.bl.uk/lea rning/histcitizen/voices/info/decrees/decrees.html.

9. Darmstadt Stadtsarchiv, G15 Dieburg Nr I46 Aufbew., Ort 116/24–29.

10. In the city of Mainz, an announcement made by the Reichvereinung der Juden in Deutschland indicated via police order that the obligatory yellow stars to be worn by Jewish residents were to be sold for a price of 10 Pfenning a piece. Stadtarchiv Mainz 52.30.

11. Landeshauptarchiv Koblenz, Bestand. 655, 213. Nr. 715, 1–792; Nr. 463.

12. Staatsarchiv Marburg, Gladenbach B 431, Bl. 8r.

13. The only exception were those Jews whose birth or marriage had been cataloged in a church record or in a governmental registry logged between 1847 and 1849. However, even in those exceptional cases, the residents were still required to provide that the official declaration of the adoption of the names be made with the local police authorities. Hessisches Hauptarchiv Darmstadt, "Generalakten des Generalstaatsanwalts bei dem Oberlandesrericht zu Darmstadt," Dok 25, Best G. 24 N2. 1823.

14. Stadtarchiv Worms, Abteilung 13, Nummer 1894.

15. Detailed record of L. Rawinsky can be found in an online archive devoted to the history of the Jewish community in Weinheim, Germany, www.juden-in-weinheim.de

16. Staatsarchiv Marburg, 330 Gladenbach B431 Bl. 47.

17. Henry Friedlander, *Der Weg zu NS-Genozid: Von Euthanasie zur Endlösung* (Berlin: Berlin Verlag, 1997), 426.

18. Suzanne Evans, *Forgotten Crimes: The Holocaust and People with Disabilities* (Chicago: Ivan R. Dee Publisher, 2004), 92.

19. Landeshauptarchiv Koblenz, Bes. 806, Nr. 2, Unr. 189.

20. Landeshauptarchiv Koblenz, Bes. 806, Nr. 2, Unr. 189.

21. Landeshauptarchiv Koblenz, Bes. 256;Nr. 2; Unternr.:191.

22. Landeshauptarchiv Koblenz, Bes. 806, Nr. 2, Unr. 191.

23. Landeshauptarchiv Koblenz, Bes. 806, Nr. 2, Unr. 173.

24. In this document, dated October 21, 1939, Josef H. is identified with the prison number 7962. The order states that Josef H. is to be transferred to Buchenwald during the next planned mass deportation. Landeshauptarchiv Koblenz, Bes. 806, Nr. 2.

25. Landeshauptachiv Koblenz, Bes. 806, Nr. 2, Unr. 165.

26. In the list of Shoah victims maintained by both Yad Vashem and the national German archives (Bundesarchiv), the name "Josef" and not "Ludwig" is used. In the national German archives (Bundesarchiv), both forenames "Josef" and "Ludwig" are listed.

27. Ernst Noam and Wolf-Arno Kropat, *Juden vor Gericht 1933–1945, Band I* (Wiesbaden: Kommission für die Geschichte der Juden in Hessen, 1986).

28. This sum would be roughly the equivalent of 1,500 US dollars.

29. Hamburg Stadtarchiv, File: 213–11_4660/40.

30. Hamburg Stadtarchiv, File: 213–11_4660/40.

31. http://www.yadvashem.org/.

32. Hamburg Stadtsarchiv, 213–11_1231/40.

33. Hamburg Staatsarchiv, 213–11_4921/40.

34. Hamburg Staatsarchiv, 213–11_6115/40.

35. Hamburg Stadtsarchiv, 213–11_070144.

36. Hamburg Staatsarchiv, 213–11–4923/41.

37. The German original: "In der kleinen Gemeinde Volksdorf war er als Jude bekannt, so dass eine Tarnung wohl kaum möglich war" Hamburg Staatsarchiv, File: 213–11_2108/42.

38. Hamburg Staatsarchiv, File: 213–11_2108/42. For detailed information about the history of the villa, see U. Pietsch, "Die Geschichte der Liebermann-Villa in Volksdorf," *De Spieker Jahrbuch* (2014), 74–75. http://www.heimatecho.de archiv/sonder_pdf/2014–10–01.pdf.

39. In 1945, the city of Hamburg offered to return the villa to the Liebermanns who had miraculously survived. After the couple declined the offer, the villa became the shared residence of the Volksdorf Police and the International Police Association. In 2006, a commemorative plaque was placed in front of the villa in memory of the Liebermann family. The house is still known today among villagers as "The Liebermmann Villa."

40. Hamburg Staatsarchiv, File: 213–11_2881/41.

41. Hamburg Staatsarchiv, File: 213–11_2881/41.

42. Hamburg Staatsarchiv, File: 213–11_2881/41.

43. Further research also revealed that the Heiser moving company appears to still be in operation in Hamburg.

44. Hamburg Staatsarchiv, 213–11_4956/40.

45. Hamburg Staatsarchiv, 213–11_4956/40.

46. On August 7, 1942, the Reichvereiningung der Juden in Deutschland sent a communique to the regional and local heads of Jewish congregations throughout the Reich. The notice was regarding the use of titles in dealings with officials. Leaders of the Jewish community were warned that it was no longer desirable for Jews to use their previous academic and/or professional titles in written correspondence with Aryan officials. In cases where this suggestion was ignored or forgotten, it was warned that reprisals could result. They were further warned against using such increasingly popular forms of self-reference as *Fritz Israel Meyer, Legal Advisor,* Jude [Fritz Israel Meyer, Justizrat, Jude] in either the letterhead or signature of their business letters. The letter was signed by a *Paul Israel Eppstein*. Stadtarchiv Mainz, "Reichvereinigung der Juden im Deutschland an die Jüdischen Kultusvereinigung." August 7, 1942, StdAMz: 52.30.

47. Dr. Zadik, for his part, continued to fight against the Nazis on behalf of his many other clients, until February of 1941, when he and his wife made their escape from Nazi, Germany, and began their new life in the United States. His decision to leave Germany was made right in the nick of time. By that date, the Nazis were closing down on the lawyer and all who surrounded him. Just four months after his emigration, his stenographer, Anna Rosenberg, was deported to the Chelmo Concentration Camp where she was murdered. http://www.stolpersteine-hamburg.de/?&MAIN_ID=7&BIO_ID=3765.

48. RMBliB 1938 Nr. 2.

49. Hauptstadtarchiv Darmstadt, G15 Heppenheim I113 116/52–64.

50. Hauptstadtarchiv Darmstadt, G15 Heppenheim I113 116/52–64.

51. Hauptstadtarchiv Darmstadt, G15 Heppenheim I113 116/52–64.

52. This change in regulation reflected an overall shift in the government's policy on residents defined as having non-Aryan lineage.

53. Hamburg Staatsarchiv, "Staatsverwaltung Hansestadt Hamburg," March 16, 1939, 213–11_2669/42.

54. Sven Kellerhoff, "Hitler schützte jüdischen Frontoffizier." *Die Welt*, July 7, 2012, https://www.welt.de/print/die_welt/politik/article108013899/Hitler-schuetze-juedischen-Frontoffizier.html.

55. *Kriegsbriefe gefallener deutscher Juden* [with an introduction by Franz Josef Strauß] (Stuttgart: Seewald Verlag, 1935), 135.

56. *Kriegsbriefe gefallener deutscher Juden*, 8.

57. Hamburger Staatsarchiv, 213–11_1895/41.

58. Hamburger Staatsarchiv, 213–11_28887/41. Although it could not be definitively confirmed, it may be that the soldier's luck did not completely run out after this ruling. A search for him among the list of Shoah victims in the Yad Vashem database did not yield a match. It must be remembered of course that the database is not exhaustive. Nevertheless, one hopes that he was able to survive.

59. *Kriegsbriefe gefallener deutscher Juden*, 18–20.

60. Hamburg Staatsarchiv, File: 213–11_3965/40.

61. Hamburg Staatsarchiv, File: 213–11_7036/42.

62. According to archival records, the Julius Busch Bread Company used ca. twenty-six slave laborers in its Convent Street location; and less than a half a mile away, another thirty prisoners were forced to work in the factory's Anger Street location within the district of Hohenfelde. With three different slave labor camps, Hohenfelde was a stronghold of radical anti-Semitic political activity. According to statistics presented by the city of Hamburg, as early as 1932, the NSDAP received 47.5 percent of the vote in Hohenfelde. This percentage was roughly 10.2 percent higher than that for the entire Reich.

63. The name *Salomon* was initially one of those forenames which excluded its bearer from having to use the otherwise obligatory marker *Israel*.

64. Hamburg Staatsarchiv, File: 113–5_DVA1.

65. Stadtarchiv Mainz, "Aktentennotiz über eine Besprechung auf der Geheimen Staatspolizei," May 14, 1943. Oppenheim. 49, 3.

66. Birthe Kundrus and Beate Meyer, eds. *Die Deportationen der Juden aus Deutschland: Pläne-Praxis-Reaktionen 1938–1945* (Göttingen: Wallstein Verlag, 2004).

67. Stadtarchiv Mainz, ZGS/E3,15.

68. Stadtarchiv Mainz, "von Oppenheim getippte Bericht," August 17, 1946, 51, 19 Oppenheim.

69. Kundrus and Meyer, *Die Deportationen*, 78.

70. Kundrus and Meyer, *Die Deportationen*, 80.

71. Kundrus and Meyer, *Die Deportationen*, 78.

72. Stadtarchiv Mainz, 51.19 Fasc. 19Oppenheim.

73. Stadtarchiv Mainz, 52.27 Oppenheim.

74. In hearings held by the Allies after the war, it was found the Oppenheim's activities encompassed far more than assembling name lists for the Nazis. He also regularly assisted the Gestapo in interrogations of Jewish residents. For more, see Beate Meyer, *Tödliche Gratwanderung: Die Reichsvereinigung der Juden in Deutschland zwischen Hoffnung, Zwang, Selbstbehauptung und Verstrickung (1939–1945)* (Göttingen: Wallstein Verlag, 2011), 319.

75. Stadtarchiv Mainz, "Rundschrieben Nr. bV 2/42," 52, 29 Oppenheim.

76. After the war, Michael Oppenheim worked with the US American military government. He devoted the rest of his life to helping to rebuild the city of Mainz and was particularly active in supporting education and the arts. Oppenheim died in 1963. www.bundsarchiv.de/gedenkbuch/directory.html.en.

77. Stadtarchiv Mainz, "Rundschreiben Nr. bV 2/42," 51, 19 Oppenheim.

CHAPTER 5

Denazification in Name Only?

In 1945, the four Allied nations assumed "supreme authority" over the occupation zones of Germany and Austria in the form of the Allied Control Council.[1] Through this governing body, many of the administrative policies introduced by the National Socialist Party were finally abrogated "to restore to the German people the rule of justice and equality before the law."[2] This sweeping process of legislative revision even included the Aryanized personal names in the former Reich's telecommunication code: *Siegfried* went back to *Samuel*, *Ypern* back to *Ypisoln*, and *Zeppelin* to *Zacharias*.[3] Of course, the most significant onomastic change was the immediate reversal of the LAFFN1 and 2 laws. Effective immediately, personal name choices were no longer segregated and the use of *Sara* and *Israel* was no longer obligatory for residents of Jewish heritage. In addition, by virtue of the Control Council Law No. 1 that was ratified on September 20, 1945, German and Austrian officials were ordered to remove the compulsory onomastic markers from all the governmental records; and to report back to the responsible Allied officials when this order had been carried out.

In some jurisdictions, this directive was followed with comparatively little resistance. For example, along the Mosel River, in the tiny town of Zell (pop. approx. 4,000), the police reported in November of 1949 that the previous practice of writing in the identifiers *Sara* and *Israel* beside the names of Jewish residents had been discontinued and the compulsory names had all been systematically crossed out whenever they appeared in the town's administrative records.[4] In the neighboring town of Montabaur, officials reported that as of October 23, 1946, they had already completed their review of all birth, marriage, and death records and had identified twenty-three cases in which the compulsory names had been added into the margins beside the names of Jewish residents. In each one of these cases, the officials had reportedly deleted the offending notation. To verify that this directive had been properly followed, the officials responsible included a notarized letter listing the twenty-three personal names and accompanying records that had been expunged of the onomastic markers.[5]

Not all German officials were as conscientious or compliant, however. In Frankfurt am Main, Hessian administrators argued that instead of removing the offending names from the records, it would be far more expedient if they concentrated on cleansing those files belonging to residents who had expressly requested this service.[6] On the surface, this strategy may seem entirely reasonable—perhaps even exemplary of excellent customer service. However, upon closer reflection, nothing could be farther from the truth. Aside from the gall of complaining about the burden of having to remove all of those notations which bureaucrats had so diligently and enthusiastically placed in the records themselves, the time and energy that their counter-proposal promised to save was ultimately based on a grotesque calculation: namely that the number of surviving Jews who could actually request this service was far lower than the number of those Jews who, having lost their lives and families, would never make such a request. Thus, the very people who had suffered the most under the Third Reich would actually stand to gain the least from this proposal.

On September 14, 1947, Erich D., a twenty-seven-year-old registrar for the city of Frankfurt, listened to the impassioned speeches held in honor of Day of Remembrance for the Victims of Fascism.[7] Among the speakers were prominent Jewish Holocaust survivors such as theater critic and essayist Alfred Kerr; writer and political activist Max Zimmering; and political commentator, historian, journalist, and best-selling book author Eugen Kogon. The speech which fascinated Erich the most, however, was held by Auschwitz survivor, Dr. Philipp Auerbach, who warned against smoldering pockets of anti-Semitism.

Emboldened by these words, the young registrar wrote an impassioned letter to the Lord Mayor of Frankfurt, Dr. Walter Kolb. In that letter he questioned the moral efficacy of requiring Jewish residents of Hessia to apply to have the names *Sara* and *Israel* from their records. According to him, such a policy unfairly shifted the onus of responsibility for complying with the Allies' directive onto the very people the measure had been designed to protect. Erich admitted that the administrative task of expunging all of the records of these dreaded names would be considerable but in view of the injuries the Jewish community had been made to suffer, this investment of resources was the least he and his colleagues could do. He went on to warn that the failure or resistance of German public officials to deny their ethical responsibility would only serve to strengthen the "blood-stained hands" of reactionary circles eager to once again take possession of Germany.

Less than a month later, the enthusiastic government worker received an answer from the Lord Mayor's office. According to an internal memo, "in no uncertain terms" the young man had been instructed that a decision against the automatic removal of the names in question could not be misconstrued as an expression of malice on the part of government policy-makers. Rather, it was a question of personal and technical resources. The note went on to indicate that the upstart bureaucrat had further been instructed to provide detailed information about the dangerous, anti-government groups about which he seemed to be surprisingly well-informed. Obviously intimidated, Erich reportedly expressed his sincere and unqualified apologies to his superiors. He had had no intention of questioning or criticizing the operational policies of the government, he explained; and, despite his unfortunate wording, he, in fact, knew of no such "reactionary powers."

While this instance of civil courage was effectively shut down, others would not be so quickly or easily intimidated into silence. An outspoken and powerful opponent of the Hessian plan was found in the Minister of Justice, Georg-August Zinn. According to him, the very idea of forcing Jewish residents to send in written requests for the removal of the names *Sara* and *Israel* was nonsensical, unnecessary, excessive, and unjust.[8] Opposition to the plan also came from the Jewish community that bombarded the registrar's office with incensed letters of protest. One such complaint came from a Mr. E. Cahn.[9] In his letter, Mr. Cahn detailed how he recently applied for and received an official death certificate for his father who had never returned home after being deported to Theresienstadt.[10] In the space reserved for the name of the deceased, the certificate listed his father's name without the name *Israel*. Mr. Cahn had thought nothing of it until he had read an article in the September edition of the city newspaper, *Die Frankfurter Rundschau*. In that article, it was reported that the omission of this hated moniker might cause some German officials to call into question the authenticity of official documents. In disbelief, Mr. Cahn waited to see if the paper would later print a retraction. When no such disclaimer appeared, the outraged son wrote to the government in Frankfurt:

> Should the article be correct in asserting that this view actually exists within the Registry Office, this attitude would, in my opinion, be complete recognition of the Hitlerian system of violence and confirmation of strong identification with Antisemitism. . . . If indeed there is some regulation of this type that has truly been issued by some official in the Registry Office, I want to know this individual's name immediately so that I can bring a public lawsuit against this person. . . . All this shows, once again, is that Jews and their surviving relatives are being treated by some people as second-class citizens merely because they are numerically very weak. I am not, by any stretch of the imagination, willing to tolerate this state of affairs! The very same authority that would require the inclusion of those Jewish

names for verification purposes [. . .] could also be used to enforce other laws of the Third Reich.[11]

Despite such complaints, the fraction in support of the Hessian proposal remained steadfast, even defiant. In an internal memo written on October 11, 1947, evidence of some of the attitudes that motivated this wall of administrative defiance was expressed by a civil servant who was obviously deeply niggled by the entire debate. According to him, the wave of criticism lodged against the governmental decision-makers in Hessia was entirely unwarranted:

> For technical reasons, it simply cannot be expected that the Registry Office look up each and every place where these names might appear. The office has repeated time and time again that such an action would place a disproportionately large burden upon administrative resources. I am therefore of the opinion that the racially persecuted, who have had to endure far greater unpleasantries, take on the very the small task [of applying for the removal of the names *Sara* and *Israel*]. If they truly attach such great importance to having these entries <u>immediately</u> removed, then surely, they can file an application. They only need send two or three lines to the Registry Office.[12]

Granted, the removal of all instances of *Sara* and *Israel* from all official administrative records could not be accomplished overnight. However, the insinuation that the resistance to this application process was based on an underlying laziness on the part Jewish residents who were unwilling to take on "such a small task" coupled with the all too familiar portrayal of the German worker as being unfairly burdened by Jewish indolence reeks of the very anti-Semitic thinking the civil servant denies the existence of. Although the wording may be different, the message is reminiscent of Goebbels's declaration: "the Jew is the nascence and beneficiary of the German's slavery."[13] To top it all off, the shocking equation of the catalog of atrocities committed during the Holocaust with "unpleasantries" [Unangenehmigkeiten] speaks volumes. The policies may have changed, but the mentality of some German administrators clearly had not.

*****

On October 22, 1949, a postwar name-change petition was filed by forty-seven-year-old Ms. H. Goldschmidt. She requested permission to either shorten her surname to the non-descript *Schmidt* or alter her surname completely. Her preferred substitutions were *Pfudel*, the name of her deceased father; or *Herz*, the surname of the family who had once attempted to adopt her.[14] As reason for the name-change request, Ms. Goldschmidt indicated that she had been the repeated target of anti-Semitism in response to her name. The charge of anti-Semitism seems to have sparked a great deal of attention among the German officials, who were still being closely monitored by the Occupational Forces. Within a month's time, the petition had been sent from the office of the Bürgermeister in the town of Schwalbach am Taunus to the desk of the Chief Administrator for all of Hessia [Regierungspräsident]. It is from this office that Ms. Goldschmidt received the following official answer to her request:

> I am afraid that I will not be able to grant the name change request which you filed on the 22nd of October 1949. According to the law governing the alteration of family and first names from January 5, 1938, a name change can only be granted when an important reason has been presented. . . . You have grounded your petition with the statement that you believe you have encountered difficulties in your forward advancement because of your name. This reason cannot be considered either valid or sound. . . . Nevertheless, I have taken the liberty of foregoing the customary administrative fee for processing your request. Enclosed is the documentation you submitted along with your petition.[15]

In an internal memo sent to the district office in Schwalbach, the following note was included along with the Goldschmidt file: "In the petition from October 22, 1949, the notion that the requested name change was justified by prejudices against Judaism in this new state cannot be recognized. A name change is not permissible upon this basis" (emphasis added).[16] In a very real sense, this petition had inadvertently placed the authorities in a real political conundrum. Although the law clearly permitted name changes to be granted in instances where the petitioner had suffered ridicule or abuse, accepting this request or others like it would have been tantamount to an official acknowledgement that anti-Semitism existed in their jurisdiction. Rather than admit that, the officials took the circuitous but familiar route of reducing the petitioner's request as an attempt to gain socioeconomic advantage: a reason which was expressly mentioned in the 1949 laws as being both insufficient and unacceptable. Ironically, in recasting's the petitioner's motivation as being purely pecuniary, the officials seem to have (un)knowingly resorted to the same anti-Semitism Ms. Goldsmith claimed to have been made to suffer.

One need not look far, however, to find further, more direct, and tangible substantiation of Ms. Goldsmith's claim of discrimination. On November 8, 1949, just eleven years after the anniversary of Kristallnacht, the Frankfurt and Wiesbaden branches of the Society for Christian-Jewish Cooperative Action [Gesellschaft für Chistlich-Jüdische Zusammenarbeit] wrote a joint letter to the Minister of the Interior, Heinrich Zinnkann, to complain about the alarming rise of anti-Semitism in Hessia. They demanded that "every government official and employee take responsibility for not only exposing crimes of this type, but also actively assisting in their punishment."[17] The impetus for this letter was a spate of anti-Semitic crimes in Hessen. Between January and July of 1947 alone, some thirty-five Jewish cemeteries were desecrated in the region. In reaction to such public pressure, on July 20, 1950, Christian Stock, the Ministerpräsident of Hessia, felt compelled to write an official letter to the US authorities, assuring them that every step would be taken to promote tolerance and combat anti-Semitism in his region.[18] Interestingly, that same year, Ms. Goldschmidt received word that her petition to have her surname changed had been granted. She could now officially adopt the last name *Herz*.

Despite this reversal in decision, there is some reason to believe that the underlying political sympathies of some government officials remained relatively unchanged. Evidence of this ideological resilience can be seen ten years later. On September 12, 1960, a distraught mother, Gertrud H., sent Frankfurt officials a letter detailing her son's onomastic plight:

> On the 11th of October, 1949, when my little boy came into the world, I unfortunately found myself in the middle of a divorce . . . my father made many sacrifices and took both me and my small son in. Motivated by feelings of gratitude, but without a great deal of thought, I named my child 'Adolf' after his grandfather. There is no way that I could have imagined what that decision would lead to. Ever since the boy has attended school (some 4 ½ years now), he has been teased, beaten, and incessantly bullied. We even tried switching schools not once but twice! Despite all my hopes, there has been no change. And it is not only the children but also adults who react to my child's name with derision and ridicule. For this reason, I am forced to request that my son's name be changed from *Adolf* to *Dolf*.[19]

On September 26, Ms. H. received a rather salty reply from the Police Department:

> In my opinion, the name *Adolf*, despite the coincidental association with the name *Hitler* could never burden the bearer of this first name. There are countless numbers of people with this name who have never had any difficulty because of it . . . the fact that the boy, thanks to his first name, is associated with <u>past men of greatness</u> is only temporary and will certainly not last his whole life long.[20] (emphasis added)

Just two years after the war, the thinly veiled praise of the Führer is as striking as was the decision-maker's complete rejection of any pain the boy might have suffered as a result of carrying the Führer's first name in postwar Germany. The fact that the mother had documented her son's torment with an official letter from his pediatrician was also completely ignored. Despite the official guidelines stipulating that names that cause the name-bearer offense, injury, or ridicule may be changed, the petition was rejected. And this despite the fact that granting the request change would only have entailed the removal of a single letter (*Adolf* → *Dolf*).

Livid, Ms. H. sent another letter: this time to the mayor's office imploring him to intercede. A few days later, she received a similar rejection. In a form letter, the Burgermeister stated that much to his regret, the issue was beyond his discretionary control and the original rejection could not be overturned. A few days before Christmas, Ms. H. penned her final letter of protest to the authorities. After politely thanking the Burgermeister for his time, she wrote:

> I can't help but mention my great disbelief that the authorities have rejected my request because "the grounds are not sufficiently important." I take it that when an already sensitive child is being tormented and is suffering emotional torture so great that one fears for his health, that it is customary for us to dismiss a mother's call for help as being "unimportant."[21]

As explained earlier, the overall frequency of the name *Adolf* was never allowed to reach the inflationary portions it might have had the Führer's office not issued a prohibitory edict. Nevertheless, the name was still relatively common in Germany before and during the Nazi period. However, as the tides of war began to change and it became clear that the Reich would crumble, the popularity of the name plummeted. By the war's end, it had naturally become inextricably tied to National Socialism and the crimes committed in its name. To avoid this stigmatization, most German-speaking parents after the war understandably avoided this name choice for their newborns. For those men (and women) who had been named during or before the war, two basic options were available to them. The first was simply to retain the name *Adolf* on official records but to use a nickname such as *Dolf, Dolfie,* or *Addie* in everyday life. Given the commonality of elderly Germans with one of these nicknames and the fact that remarkably few formal name-change requests for individuals named *Adolf* were uncovered in the archives, it seems that many chose this unofficial option. The second option was, of course, to apply for an official name change as Mrs. H. had done.

Given the fact that both inside and outside of Germany, the name *Adolf* is unquestionably stigmatized; it is remarkable that the decision-makers in this case staunchly refused to grant the name-change petition, even in the face of medical evidence that the name-bearer was suffering. Ironically, on the other side of the country, a different set of officials came to precisely the opposite conclusion.

After the war, Hamburg authorities had received a name-change petition from a local citizen who claimed that the unfortunate similarity between his name and that of the late Führer had become unbearable.[22] Not only had it had a negative impact upon his employment opportunities, it had also put a decided damper on his personal life.[23] For that reason, he respectfully asked the authorities for permission to slightly alter the spelling of his name. The applicant's arguments were carefully reviewed along with the petitioner's supporting biographical data. The case, however, seemed to be quite straightforward. A name change was clearly warranted. It was therefore concluded that "nothing had been found that would speak against the name change."[24] So, on May 5, 1947, after paying the processing fee of 50 RM, the petitioner's personal name was officially changed from *Alois Hitler* to *Alois Hiller*.

Without a shadow of a doubt, the similarities between the Führer and the petitioner were irrefutable. Both men were born in Austria. Both had a father named *Alois*. Both immigrated to Germany. Both were involved in politics. Simply a coincidence? The truth is there was an excellent explanation for all of the biographical overlap between the two: *Adolf* and *Alois* were brothers.[25] What's more, the Hamburg authorities who granted the remarkably speedy name change were perfectly aware of this fact for the sixty-three-year-old half-brother had explicitly mentioned his blood-tie to the Führer in his petition.[26]

What makes this case particularly striking is the contrast it builds with the other cases presented. While other petitioners were chastised for mentioning that their name had been the cause of socioeconomic hardship, psychological distress, and/or unpleasant ties with National Socialism, in this case the mention of all those factors had a favorable impact upon his petition. Moreover, for all of the concerns about granting name changes to petitioners who might wish to use the onomastic "fresh start" to hide past crimes or commit new ones, there seems to have been little concern that someone who was actually a member of Hitler's immediate family might pose a threat. This is not to say that assumptions should be made about a person's character or potential for criminality merely on the basis of their name (although this type of profiling is far more common than most people are consciously aware). The point is that the authorities in charge of adjudicating this case either overlooked or ignored the evidence that clearly spoke against granting this request.

At the time of his application, Alois Hitler had already been convicted of numerous acts of identity fraud in Great Britain, the United States, and Germany. He was a three-time bigamist who had physically assaulted all of his wives and children. That was not all. Contrary to his repeated claims that he'd never been politically active or had any real contact with his brother, Alois was, in fact, a well-known personality in Nazi circles—both before and after the war. According to a 1955 issue of *Der Spiegel*, Alois' political interests were alive and well. Although he obviously never obtained the notoriety of his half-brother, after the war, he did manage to become a leading member in a local branch of a political party.[27] Called the *Nationaldemokratische Partei* [the National Democratic Party] (NDP), the organization's abbreviation was just a few letters shy of its big-brother the NSDAP—not unlike *Alois Hitler* turned *Hiller*.[28]

*****

In 1955, the civil registry in Frankfurt am Main received a letter from a local housewife who requested a name change on behalf of her sixteen-year-old daughter, *Rosemarie*. In a comparatively terse reply, the naming authorities stressed that such changes would only be granted in cases where an extremely important reason could be provided. At the end of the month, the mother provided her reason for the request. While her husband was away serving the country in the Wehrmacht, she was forced to give birth to and select a name for their daughter on her own. A few weeks later, her husband returned home for a short furlough. The soldier was horrified when he learnt what name his wife had selected: the decidedly un-German name *Rosemarie Amanda*. When asked what name he would have preferred, her husband replied: *Edda*. Before the couple had a chance to apply for a name change, they received confirmation that the mother's original choice had been officially registered. Still, out of respect for her husband's wishes, their daughter was always and only referred to as *Edda*.

Ten years after the war's end, the mother, now a war-widow, sought to officially change their daughter's name out of respect for her husband's original wishes. Initially, the responsible authorities seemed to express doubt over whether this posthumous dedication truly constituted a "significant reason." On the first of July 1955, however, the local Burgermeister sent an official letter urging them to honor the request of the woman whom he described as a "struggling warrior-widow [Kriegerwitwe] who had been forced to raise three teenage children on her own." Within a few weeks, the applicant received word that her petition had been granted. Her daughter's official name would now be *Edda*.[29] Not every petition filed to honor the memory of fallen soldier was automatically granted, however, as the next case illustrates.

At first glance, this application appeared to be fairly run-of-the mill. A postwar widow petitioned to have her child's first name changed to that of her deceased husband. What made this request rather unusual were two seemingly contrary facts: (1) the child in question was a girl; and (2) the name desired was *Günter*. Although the mother conceded that her request was indeed out of the ordinary, in her opinion, there was nothing wrong or offensive about wanting to give a daughter the name of her beloved father. She buttressed her argument with the fact that there was ample historical precedent for cross-gendered naming in Germany.

The petitioner was indeed correct. In the South of Germany, for example, among staunch Catholic families, there is a long tradition of giving male children the name *Maria* (e.g., *Carl Maria von Weber, Rainer Maria Rilke*; and *Hans Josef Maria Globke*). And in the primarily Protestant regions of North Germany, there is a similar tradition where Friesian daughters may be given the forenames of favored male relatives or figures from the Bible (e.g., *Jacob, Jost, Peter,* and *Thomas*).[30] Despite the factual strength of the petitioner's argumentation, the request was denied. Evidently, the officials felt the motivation for the unusual name-change request was simply not compelling enough. The fact that the mother made multiple appeals did not persuade the officials to change their decision, nor did it endear her to them. In fact, judging from the internal notes, her tenacity was perceived as a sign of extreme mental instability: a proclamation which could well have had dire consequences a few years earlier.

The ghosts of the not too distant past were also apparent in another case discovered in the archives of Hessia. In the fall of 1953, authorities in the small township of Nieder-Woellstadt were presented with the curious case of *Dieter Hauser* (name completely anonymized).[31] A check through the records revealed that all of the fifteen-year-old's biographical details were identical to those of another boy, *Dieter Horvat*, including full names and birthdates of the boys' mothers and the fathers. When the mother was confronted with these commonalities, she confirmed that both *Dieter Hauser* and *Dieter Horvat* were one and the same person. However, she denied having any knowledge about when, how, or why her son's surname had been changed. Continued investigation into the case by the German authorities revealed that the boy also had an Austrian ID card that apparently had been issued in the Austrian district of Steiermark. Requests for further information from the Austrian authorities failed to shed additional light on the matter, however. In a letter written on February 8, 1954, to the district authorities, the Chief Administrator for Hessia [Regierungspräsident] admitted that attempts to obtain satisfactory answers to "questions surrounding the discrepancies in the family surnames from the authorities in Graz, Austria" had failed. Nevertheless, "in his opinion, there was nothing to speak against Dieter Horvat using the name Dieter Hauser."[32]

Today, there are many aspects of this case that point to the possibility that the mysterious case of Dieter Horvat/Hauser may have been related to a secret Lebensborn adoption. The fact that the child had a Slavic name *Horvat* and had been issued an Austrian passport from the Steiermark, for example, is immediately conspicuous when one considers that "racially desirable" children from

Slovenia were routinely kidnapped and sent to the Old Reich [Altreich] in secret adoptions as a part of the Lebensborn program.[33] Although the names of these children were often Germanized[34] by express order of the Race and Settlement Main Bureau of the SS [*Rasse- und Siedlungshauptamt der SS*], every effort was made to ensure that the new German name resembled the child's original name in sound and form.[35]

Examples of verified name changes enacted for children kidnapped for secret adoption by loyal Party members include *Marian Gajewy* → *Marian Gawner*; *Alexandra Grusinski* → *Alexandra Grusinger*; *Helena Fornalczyk* → *Helene Former*; *Henryk Wojciechowski* → *Heinrich Wochinger*; and *Stefan Slazak* → *Stefan Schlager*.[36] Notice that in each of these cases, the initials of the children's original names were retained. Here again is another striking similarity between the *Dieter Horvat/Dieter Hauser* case (i.e., both of the young boy's names had the initials "D.H."). This case raised many intriguing questions. Could it be that the parents truly did not know that their son had a second official name or was their ignorance merely feigned to maintain an oath of secrecy given during an illegal adoption? Was the similarity between the boy's names merely a coincidence? How could it happen that the boy was issued two different sets of official identification papers without any record of either being filed? And perhaps most curious of all, why was it that the otherwise fastidious German authorities simply decided to close the case without finding the answers to any of these questions.

*****

During World War I, the Ministry of Justice issued an edict that allowed the fiancées of fallen soldiers to ask the Kaiser to grant both themselves and their illegitimate children the right to carry the surnames of deceased soldiers. This onomastic privilege was only to be granted, however, in cases where it could be proven that the father had planned to marry the mother and/or acknowledge the mother's child as his own. Applicants also had to show that no legitimate children would be disadvantaged by the bestowal of the deceased's surname and that the soldier's death was a direct result of his providing military service to the country, be it on the battlefield or off. In cases where all these pre-requisites were fulfilled, the petitioners could also be granted the right to carry the title "Mrs." instead of "Miss" ([Frau] instead of [Fräulein]) along with the deceased's surname.[37]

In the autumn of 1941, the fifty-five-year-old Fräulein Frieda availed herself of this policy. In a personal letter sent to local authorities, she officially requested permission to take on the last name of her deceased fiancé who had died shortly before Christmas of 1914. When the authorities asked why it had taken her so long to apply for the name change, the Fräulein explained that she had only just learnt about this possibility that summer in a public announcement about World War II soldiers. To support her petition, the would-be bride presented her Burgermeister with the engraved wedding rings she had kept all those many years in memory of her lost love. On September 10, 1942, almost thirty years after her engagement, Frieda was finally granted permission to carry the last name of her long-ceased deceased betrothed. Soon thereafter, law makers began to discuss the feasibility of extending such status-changing policies beyond name-only.[38] On June 15, 1943, the Ministry of the Interior issued an internal edict declaring that, upon the express wishes of the Führer, the fiancées of fallen soldiers could be posthumously married to their intended.[39] After an official wedding ceremony where the role of the groom was symbolically to be taken by an iron helmet, the now widowed bride would be allowed to carry her husband's last name. According to this regulation, the couple's official wedding day would be recorded as the groom's official death date. During the research conducted for this book, no cases could be uncovered where such a marriage ceremony had actually been documented. If such ceremonies did take place, they were most likely limited to an extremely small circle of the military elite such as the SS. Be that as it may, the average citizen does not appear to have been afforded this special postmortem matrimonial service.

The judicial undesirability of extending this privilege to the general public was already the subject of discussion in a memo issued to the central Reich's Deputy Office in Hamburg on January 5, 1940. In this communique, it is explained that, from a legal point of view, it was simply not possible to posthumously declare a marriage as having been consummated, even when the soldier in question had left his grieving fiancée with child. The directive goes on to indicate that in the opinion of the highest authorities of Wehrmacht, such a regulation would also be counter to the very principles of marriage.[40] For that reason, women who could prove that they had been engaged to a fallen soldier should still be allowed to apply for permission to adopt their intended's surname for both themselves and any shared children. However, the change in status would be limited to a name change only. Ironically perhaps, the potential to file such petitions ceased as the number of fallen soldiers radically increased. To help fill the growing void on the battlefront, January 25, 1942, saw the release of a new edict. It called for the deployment of male government workers to the German Wehrmacht and the defense industry. In response to this policy, many government offices experienced critical shortages in administrative personnel. As the war waged, name-change petitions were increasingly considered to be of low priority and were processed sparingly, if at all. For example, in 1944, a directive was issued to all of the administrative heads throughout the Rhineland-Palatinate. The mandate called for the immediate suspension of all petitions for personal name changes until the war's end.[41]

When the war finally did come to an end, as a part of the Allied Control Council's mandate to expunge National Socialist doctrine from the German legal system, the statutes and guidelines that had been used during the Third Reich to adjudicate applications for personal name changes were placed under review.[42] In September 1947, for example, a government official from the Rhineland-Palatinate carefully examined the above-mentioned policy that allowed the women to adopt the surnames of their deceased fiancés, provided they had died serving their country. At the end of his review, the administrator declared that the January 1938 policy was no longer valid as it "clearly corresponds with Nazi ideology" and was "unseemly." He further argued that the policy was without legal-grounding as it contradicted the Laws on Marriage (§79) that had been enacted on February 20, 1946.[43]

The overall reaction to this decision was evidently less than positive. So much so that less than a year later, the very same administrator did a complete about-face and announced a reversal of his previous decision. In a government memo issued on February 25, 1948, he stated that the practice of granting unmarried women the right to adopt the surnames of their fallen fiancés and call themselves "widows" had historical precedent before the NS period. Consequently, he formally reversed his previous decision.[44] A little over six months later, he returned to the subject once again and announced that this naming policy could also be applied to petitions involving the surviving partners and children of the death head organization, civil servants, emergency service personnel, the SS, and all such similar organizations. As justification for this expansion, the administrator declared that in cases where a man has made the ultimate sacrifice in service to his country "the bestowal of his surname upon his intended bride and child(ren) cannot be considered a National Socialist regulation."[45] Furthermore, such requests could even be granted in cases where the family of the deceased groom objected.[46]

Part of the reason for the administrator's confusion lay in the fact that many of the policies that were championed by the NSDAP were not actually developed by them but were rather resurrected from obscure and often long-since forgotten legal practices and folk traditions. The fact that this naming practice pre-dated the National Socialism would seem to explain, at least in part, why the Control Council Law No. 1 was not used to reverse this and other policies that had been enthusiastically supported by the Party. This temporal loophole helps to explain how the next case came to pass. It involves one of the most reviled war criminals of the Third Reich, the Butcher of Kraków.

*

A year after World War II came to an official end, Amon Göth, the Butcher of Kraków, was executed.[47] Approximately a year later, his former mistress[48]

Ruth Irene Kalder, applied for permission to adopt his surname. According to an interview conducted on January 28, 1983, Ruth first met Göth during a business meeting with her former employer, Oskar Schindler. Schindler, hoping to exploit the SS officer's infamous weakness for beautiful, young women, had requested that Ruth accompany him. The ploy worked. Schindler left the meeting with Göth's promise to deliver a large contingent of slave workers. As far as Ruth was concerned, the encounter had also proved profitable. She left with the officer's private telephone number and a promise to stay in contact. The two quickly became a couple and Ruth moved into the SS officer's new villa, conveniently located in the Płaszów concentration camp where Göth was Commandant.

When asked how she felt about Göth, Ruth declared, without hesitation: "I loved him. . . . He was a very good-looking man."[49] The incredulous interviewer, who had already spoken to several camp survivors about Commandant's legendary sadism, pressed her about this depiction. He asked what she thought about the fact that survivors had described Göth as an unusually cruel, brutal killer, in fact. Seemingly taken aback, Ruth resolutely replied:

> No, he wasn't a brutal killer. No. Not . . . no more than other people . . . other SS people. He didn't kill just for the fun of it, you see. He wasn't a brutal killer.[50]

As the interview pressed on, Ruth eventually admitted that the man she still affectionately referred to with the nickname *Mony* did not like the Jews. However, she immediately relativized the admission with the assertion that "no one liked the Jews then." It was, according to her, "just how everyone felt, how they had all been raised." The Jews, she said, were there to work and when they didn't, they were punished. It was as simple as that. When the interviewer asked her who dealt out those punishments and how, she immediately shrank back behind her resilient wall of denial. In her memory, Amon was a handsome, charming, benevolent, hard-working man who was liked and respected by everyone.

In interviews with the few surviving Jewish prisoners who labored in the Göth villa and concentration camp, the only point of agreement with Ruth's depiction related to the Commandant's physical attractiveness. The disparity between Göth's outer appearance and his inner nature was addressed by Helen Horowitz, one of the survivors whose story was embodied in the composite character of "Helen" in Spielberg's "Schindler's List."[51] When asked to describe what kind of man Göth was, she did not hesitate:

> A murderer . . . he was a sadist. But in a very handsome body. I would never have believed that such a good-looking person could have satan [sic] within him. A murderer! Bloodthirsty . . . if he was

going out-he had a "3 corner hat," and if he went out in this hat all
of us in the kitchen trembled—"today there will be a sacrifice"—and
in truth this was how it was. If he went out in this hat he had to kill
2 or 3 people. And then he came back sated with blood.[52]

Although his pattern of sadism was so regular that the house servants were able
to predict his killing sprees by the clothing he wore, the woman who lived with
him side-by-side stubbornly maintained that she never noticed anything unusual
about her paramour. Indeed, until the day she committed suicide, she insisted
that she had known nothing about the atrocities being committed directly inside
and outside her home.

In September 1946, Commandant Amon Göth was executed by hanging.
Approximately a year later, *Ruth Irene Kalder* applied for permission to adopt
her deceased lover's surname. Her request was granted. In 1947, she officially
became *Frau Göth* and her baby girl, the daughter the Commandant had never
lived to see, became *Monika Göth*. Many years later, Monika met a charismatic
Nigerian with whom she too had a daughter. She named the little girl *Jennifer*
before giving her up for adoption. In 2013, that daughter published a remarkable book about her family's complex history: *Mein Grossvater hätte mir erschossen,* [My grandfather would have shot me]. Like her biological mother, it was
not until she was an adult and had had children of her own that she finally
discovered the truth about her family's NS history. And like her mother, she
discovered this truth quite by accident when she, on whim, picked up at random
a book on a library shelf: *I Have to Love My Father, Don't I?* As fate would have
it, the book detailed how her biological mother, Monika, tried to come to terms
with being the daughter of Nazi war criminal Amon Göth. From that moment
on, Jennifer began to research not only her grandfather and the horrible crimes
he'd committed. She also examined her grandmother and the many truths she
had so vehemently resisted.

Like millions of people the world over, Jennifer had also seen Steven Spielberg's cinematic masterpiece, *Schindler's List;* and like everyone else she had been
revolted by the insatiable bloodlust of the concentration camp commandant.
But unlike so many other moviegoers, the atrocities committed on that screen
were not simply the depraved acts of a historical figure, but those of a family
member, only a few generations removed from her own children. How could it
be that the man whom her grandmother had so openly adored was the same man
as that corpulent SS officer who had matter-of-factly shot Jewish concentration
camp prisoners in the head from the balcony of his private villa. In her book,
Jennifer describes her feelings before and after visiting that infamous villa:

> How much did my grandmother know? Before my visit to the villa
> I had convinced myself that she probably wasn't aware of everything

that was going on. Before going to Krakow, I had imagined rambling grounds, a massive house. The shots fired in the camp would have been too far away, the screams of the maids being terrorized by my grandfather too quiet to hear. Only it wasn't like that. My grandmother was right in the thick of it. The house was small, the camp not far away. . . . Where was my grandmother's compassion? People were dying a few hundred yards away, and there she was reveling with Amon Goeth.[53]

In an interview I conducted with her, Jennifer nee Göth Teege described her fight to resolve the dramatic schism between the grandmother she knew and loved with the woman who remained loyal to a mass murderer her whole life long. That struggle was magnified by her grandmother's postwar decision to adopt the surname *Göth* after the war had ended: a step which had profound consequences for the rest of the family line. When asked how she interpreted her grandmother's decision, she offered the following answer:

Yes, . . . I consider that to be something completely different than if you are born with such a name. . . . I believe, in her case, in my grandmother's case, it was an expression of her desire to demonstrate the connection, both inwardly and outwardly, not necessarily to the period of time but to the man who was "lost" to her, a man who was now no longer with her because of death and maybe she wanted to somehow keep this connection alive. . . . I can't say with 100 percent assuredness but one might even suspect that this decision also came from a sense of defiance on her part . . . as if to say, "I'll show you!" . . . . But that is really purely conjecture. It might be accurate but then again, perhaps it's not at all. The name change came almost immediately after the war. At that time, my grandmother was still in contact with Göth's father, my great grandfather. She convinced him that his son had promised to marry her and that because of that, a name change would be possible. And, of course, it was possible. But on the other hand, it was already after the war and he had already been executed. I mean, was it really necessary to take on the last name of a <u>convicted war criminal</u>?!?[54]

It may come as a surprise that such name changes were still possible even after the war. However, in comparison to other legislation, the Allied Control Council did not devote a significant amount of attention to reviewing the name laws and policies that had been in place during the Third Reich. Instead, the reformation primarily consisted of demanding the removal of all overtly fascist terminology. The basic underlying structure of the original guidelines remained, however, largely unchanged. For example, even after the revisions, provision

Ic29 of the 1949 laws still stipulated that non-German forenames should not, as a general rule, be granted to German citizens and refugees. In addition, Part VIII of the onomastic guidelines stated that requests to adopt foreign or un-German-sounding names were also to be denied. However, petitions to Germanize [Verdeutschung] names that were either foreign or "un-German-sounding" were to be granted. Examples of germanization that are specifically mentioned include the translation of a foreign name into German (e.g., *Orlowski* → *Adler*) and clipping (e.g., *Borkowski* → *Bork*). These were not the only instances where policies congruent with NS ideology were allowed to remain in the "new regulations." The overall lack of definitional clarity regarding what precisely constituted sufficient and compelling grounds for granting a name change also made it that much easier for decisions to be made on the basis of lingering ideologies.

*****

In 1915, the governments of France, Great Britain, and Russia signed a joint declaration condemning the genocidal atrocities committed against the Armenian people.[55] It would be another three decades before an international military tribunal would formally prosecute the systematic genocidal acts against civilian populations in Europe. On August 8, 1945, France, Northern Ireland, the United Kingdom of Great Britain, the Union of Soviet Socialist Republics, and the United States signed an historic agreement for the "prosecution and punishment of the major war criminals of the European Axis."[56] This agreement, also known as the "London Charter," specifically encompassed the prosecution of three types of criminal action: *crimes against peace*; *war crimes*; and *crimes against humanity*.

The last category specifically pertained to "murder, extermination, enslavement, deportation, and other inhumane acts committed against any civilian population, before or during war, or persecutions on political, racial or religious grounds."[57] On the basis of this prosecutorial mandate, twenty-two leaders of National Socialism were put on trial before the International Military Tribunal (IMT) before a panel of four judges representing the United States, Great Britain, and the Soviet Union. These landmark trials began in November 1945 and were conducted in the Palace of Justice, in the city of Nuremberg.[58] The prosecutors representing these nations faced the herculean task of assembling evidence and gathering witnesses amidst the chaos of a continent devastated by six years of war. As Chief Prosecutor Robert H. Jackson explained in his opening statement before the IMT, "never before in legal history has an effort been made to bring within the scope of single litigation the developments of a decade, covering a while continent, and involving a score of nations, countless individuals, and innumerable events."[59] Added to these logistical obstacles were the psychological challenges posed by the shocking catalog of crimes to be tried—atrocities so unimaginable in their scale and savagery that entirely new vocabulary had to be invented (e.g., the Holocaust).

At the same time that Jackson took on the role of the Chief Prosecutor during the Trials, he also served on the US Supreme Court, where he had often found himself at loggerheads with his colleagues over the importance of preserving civil rights in times of war. For example, in the landmark case *Korematsu v. US* (1944), the US Supreme Court ruled in a 6–3 decision to uphold the arrest of Mr. Fred Korematsu, a native-born Californian of Japanese-American descent who intentionally defied the order to remain within the confines of his assigned internment camp. According to the majority opinion, Mr. Korematsu's arrest was lawful under Executive Order 9066. In his dissent, Jackson argued that the arrest was clearly unconstitutional, as the supposed illegality of Korematsu's presence in the locality in question was not based on "anything he did, said, or thought . . . but only in that he was born of different racial stock. [and] if any fundamental assumption underlies our system, it is that guilt is . . . not inheritable."[60] It was, opined Jackson, both erroneous and dangerous to assume that all actions taken during times of war are rendered legal and just by military expediency. It was this belief that became his guiding principle during his work as the Chief Prosecutor of the Nuremberg Trials.[61]

One of the primary functions of these proceedings was to bring to justice individual offenders who had committed heinous crimes. However, this was not the only purpose. Another was to bear formal witness to the reality of the atrocities committed, lest the follies of time and politics seek to diminish or even deny their existence. This potential was specifically addressed in a classified letter sent to General Marshall by future US President General Dwight D. Eisenhower after his 1945 tour of a German internment camp near Gotha:

> The things I saw beggar description. . . . The visual evidence and the verbal testimony of starvation, cruelty and bestiality were so overpowering as to leave me a bit sick. In one room, where they were piled up twenty or thirty naked men, killed by starvation, George Patton would not even enter. He said he would get sick if he did go. I made the visit deliberately, in order to be in a position to give first-hand evidence of these things, if ever, in the future, there develops a tendency to charge these allegations merely to "propaganda."[62]

With that acute danger in mind, instead of holding closed sessions, the international press was given considerable access to the graphic testimony and evidence presented during the Nuremberg Trials. Great care was therefore taken to present both the men accused and the regime for which they stood as not only the foes of the Allied Forces, but also enemies of the German people. As the

US American Chief Prosecutor Jackson stated during his opening statement, "The Nazi nightmare has given the German name a new and sinister significance throughout the world which will retard Germany a century. The German, no less than the non-German world, has accounts to settle with these defendants."[63] For certain portions of the Reich, this strategy appears to have worked. For others, the Trials were perceived as a vicious attempt to (yet again) humiliate and subjugate the dignity of the German Volk, with exaggerations and fabrications. Indeed, to the loyal National Socialist (then as now), the proceedings were a shameless attempt to defile the honor and memory of those brave men and women whose only crime had been to serve their Fatherland.

Precisely this attitude was expressed by Dr. Fritz Fischer who was prosecuted for his participation in sadistic bone, muscle, and nerve regeneration and transplantation experiments. The research was conducted on scores of Polish women held prisoner in Ravensbrück Concentration Camp. As revealed in graphic detail during the trial, these experiments frequently involved, for example, the deliberate fracture of a woman's limbs in not one but several places to test the effect of experimental treatments. In other instances, women were forced to undergo surgical procedures in which large segments of muscle or entire limbs were removed without anesthesia. Rather than deny his participation in the studies, Dr. Fischer sought to explain his actions as being a difficult but laudable sacrifice for his people. In his final statement before the Court, he stated:

> In my young life I have tried to be a faithful son of my people, and that brought me into this present miserable position. I only wanted what was good. In my life I have never followed egotistical aims, and I was never motivated by base instincts. For that reason, I feel free of any guilt inside of me. I have acted as a soldier, and as a soldier I am ready to bear the consequences. However, that I was born a German, that is something about which I do not want to complain.[64]

By providing a public forum in which such self-serving deception could be exposed by irrefutably incriminating pieces of forensic evidence as well as a long line of highly credible first-hand witnesses, it was believed that the Trials could help to dispel public concerns over the propriety or the credibility of the proceedings.

Concerns over the public reception of Court Tribunal were not unfounded. During the course of the Trials, the IMT staff were in constant danger of being attacked by diehard Party members. In her memoirs, Court Reporter, Vivian Spitz describes an incident in the summer of 1947, when Nazi terrorists threw a bomb through the plate-glass window of the Grand Hotel, where most of the senior members of the IMT staff resided.[65] Although no one was killed, the bombing left many severely injured from the projectiles of glass and flying debris. Despite these risks, the Trials continued until April of 1949 and have since come to stand alone in international public's memory. However, additional trials were also held against leading members of the NSDAP by France, Great Britain, Russia, and the United States in each of their respective zones of occupation. In the British-controlled zone of Germany, the United Kingdom alone held 358 different trials which resulted in the conviction of 1,085 people, 200 of whom were given the death sentence[66] and executed by one of Britain's most prolific hangmen, Albert Pierrepoint.[67]

In each of these proceedings, the Allies made a concerted effort to widely publicize the scope and magnitude of the crimes that had been committed. It was believed that this shock therapy would somehow help to jolt one-time supporters of National Socialism into recognizing how far they had strayed from the universal concepts of justice, humanity, and compassion. This push for collective self-awareness paired with mass atonement was motivated with an eye to the past and the future. Immediately after the war, there was broad consensus among the Allied leadership that if the German people themselves did not come to realize just how inherently evil National Socialism was, they would forever pose a threat to the international peace.[68] Not more than a decade later, however, commitment to this strategy of re-education through confrontation had begun to weaken. In May 1948, during a spirited debate before the UK Parliament, Lord Jowitt pronounced what many of his colleagues had been thinking: "the indefinite prolongation of the trials is not performing a useful or desirable purpose."[69] In fact, there was ample evidence that the Trials may be having the opposite desired effect. Immediately after the war, 1945 polls indicated that nearly 80 percent of the German population expressed support for prosecuting the leaders of National Socialism for their crimes. Just five years later, only 38 percent of the population were in favor of the Trials with an increasing majority suspected that the Allies were more interested in exacting revenge than seeking justice (i.e., Siegerjustiz).[70] Precisely, this suspicion was raised by Dr. von Keller, counsel for the defense, during his closing statement at the Nuremberg Trials. At the end of the day, the Trials, he charged, were conducted by "a tribunal of victors over the vanquished, with laws and procedures which victors created to apply to a defeated people."[71]

The legality of the trials was questioned in not only Europe but in the United States as well. Chief Supreme Court Justice Harlan Fiske Stone, for example, was extremely critical of both the proceedings and Justice Jackson's participation in them. Aside from his belief that the Justices should be singularly devoted to the duties of the US Supreme Court, he also questioned the propriety of proceedings that seemed to have conviction as their primary goal. With great distain for both Jackson's role as Chief Prosecutor and the Trials themselves, Stone mockingly referred to the Trials as "Jackson's lynching expedition."[72]

To be sure, a certain degree of the skepticism surrounding the trials and tribunals was fueled by glaring hypocrisies. Just as the racial segregation and euthanasia had large numbers of supporters throughout Europe and the US, anti-Semitism and anti-Communism were also strongly rooted in many Allied nations. Ugly evidence of this prejudice can be found in General Patton's personal diaries where he complained bitterly about the sentimentalism of US Commissioner of Immigration, Earl G. Harrison: "and his ilk" who believed "that the displaced person is a human being, which he is not, and this applies particularly to the Jews, who are lower than animals."[73] Although Patton's virulent hatred was generally frowned upon in some polite circles, the end of World War II saw the resurgence of conspiracy theories about a subversive secret communist plot led by powerful Jews who'd concealed their true identities through nefarious name changes. One of the leading voices of hatred during the US Red Scare was Mississippi Congressman, John R. Rankin. In the fall of 1947, during hearings held before the House Un-American Activities Committee, the incensed Rankin railed against letters of complaint the Committee had received:

> I want to read you some of these names. One of the names is June Havoc. We found out from the Motion Picture Almanac that her real name is June Hovick. Another one was Danny Kaye, and we found out his real name was David Daniel Kaminsky. Another one here . . . is Eddie Cantor, whose real name is Eddie Iskowitz. There is one who calls himself Edward Robinson. His real name is Emmanuel Goldberg [actually Goldenberg]. There is another one who calls himself Melvyn Douglas, whose real name is Melvyn Hesselberg. There are others too numerous to mention. They are attacking the committee for doing its duty to protect the country and save the American people from the horrible fate the Communists have meted out the unfortunate Christian people of Europe.[74]

Of course, the name-changing that Rankin claimed was clandestine, fraudulent, and uniquely Jewish was in fact quite well known, completely legal, and widely practiced by people of all faiths and creeds. In Hollywood (then as now), many aspiring actors and actresses altered their birthnames to something they and/or the studios felt would have more "star allure." In table 5.1 are just a few Tinsel town favorites whose birthnames underwent similar, more or less drastic, cosmetic changes.[75]

As the list illustrates, during Hollywood's Golden Age, one would have been hard put to find any onscreen personality whose professional name matched the one on their birth certificate. The insinuation that this practice was somehow limited to people of Jewish ancestry with Communist and/or Anti-American

Table 5.1 Stage Names (SN) and Birthnames (BN) of Stars during Hollywood's Golden Age

SN	BN	SN	BN	SN	BN
1. Fred Astaire	Frederic Austerlitz Jr.	11. Judy Garland	Francis Gumm	21. Veronica Lake	Constance Ockleman
2. Jack Benny	Benjamin Kubelsky	12. Greer Garson	Eileen Garson	22. Jerry Lewis	Joseph Levitch
3. Milton Berle	Milton Berlinger	13. Cary Grant	Archibald Leach	23. Peter Lorre	Laszlo Lowenstein
4. George Burns	Nathan Birnbaum	14. Greta Garbo	Greta Gustafsson	24. Dean Martin	Dino Crocetti
5. Mel Brooks	Melvin Kaminsky	15. Rita Hayworth	Margarita Cansino	25. Marilyn Monroe	Norma Mortensen
6. Joan Crawford	Lucile Fay LeSueur	16. William Holden	William Beedle	26. Gregory Peck	Eldred Peck
7. Claudette Colbert	Emilie Chauchoin	17. Gene Kelly	Eugene Kelly	27. Tony Randall	Leonard Rosenberg
8. Tony Curtis	Bernard Schwartz	18. Boris Karloff	William Pratt	28. Ginger Rogers	Virginia McMath
9. Doris Day	Doris Kappelhoff	19. Hedy Lamarr	Hedwig Kiesler	29. Mickey Rooney	Joe Yule
10. Kurt Douglas	Issur Demsky	20. Stan Laurel	Arthur Jefferson	30. Shelley Winters	Shirley Schrift

sentiments was preposterous but sadly effective during a time when fears of yet another world war ran so high.

Adding to the very real concern that continuing the war trials in Europe may be contributing more to the re-nazification than the denazification of the former Reich[76] was the growing conviction that the considerable financial and logistical resources that were being spent to first hunt down and then prosecute leading members of the Nazi Party might be better spent in other ways (i.e., in addressing the new threat posed by the rising conflict between the East and the West).

Even before World War II had come to an end, the tepid relations between the Soviets and the US Americans had gone from cool to icy. Less than six months after the sentences handed down during Nuremberg Trials were affirmed by the Office of the Military Governor,[77] the IMT staff watched in panic as the Soviets erected a military blockade that severely restricted all movement into and out of their military zone. For their part, the US Americans interrupted supplies of coal, steel, and food to the Soviet zone.[78] The Cold War had begun. Under these circumstances, many western leaders argued that the resurrection of Germany as an economic and military world-power that could serve as a future bulwark against Soviet expansionism must take priority over continuing to punish crimes committed in the past.

Operating under the logic that the enemy of my enemy could become an essential ally, strategists within the international intelligence community argued that it would be far more expedient to recruit rather than to prosecute former Nazi leaders before the Soviets did. A 1985 report issued by the Comptroller General of the United States officially acknowledged that "as the Cold War began, US intelligence units knowingly employed alleged Nazis and Axis collaborators in order to obtain information about Soviet intentions and capabilities."[79] Moreover, as the report goes on to detail, US intelligence officials even went so far as to alter the "names of several members of the SD and Abwehr in order to protect them from the German authorities and the occupation authorities."[80] Included among those whose names and identities were protected in exchange for their special services was Nikolaus 'Klaus' Barbie,[81] the Butcher of Lyon.

*****

On March 5, 1946, the "Law for Liberation from National Socialism and Militarism" was introduced. This law called for the establishment of a system of German-operated tribunals throughout the US-controlled zones of Germany. The express purpose of these people's courts was to facilitate "removal and exclusion of National Socialists and Militarists from public administration and other positions." Towards that end, all Germans above the age of eighteen were required to complete and submit a registration form or "Meldebogen"

(MGR 24–500–11). The information provided on this form was to be used by the tribunals to determine each German's level of complicity with the NSDAP. The Law provided for five different levels of responsibility: (1) *Hauptschuldige*—major offenders; (2) *Belastete*—offenders (activists, militarists, and profiteers); (3) *Minderbelastete*—lesser offenders; (4) *Mitläufer*—followers; and (5) *Entlastete*—persons exonerated.

To facilitate this classification process, German authorities were ordered to provide the Allies with detailed lists of any and all persons either known or suspected to have been active members of the Nazi Party. Although this foreign-gathered intelligence was of great importance, clearly the accuracy and completeness of that information was by definition questionable given that it was provided by the former enemy. Concerns over the integrity of these intelligence sources was further magnified by fast eroding relations with the Soviets and the very real potential for infiltration and sabotage. For that reason, even before the war had properly come to an end, the United Kingdom and the United States had already allocated personnel and resources to locate and confiscate NS documents containing classified information about both the Soviets and the National Socialists.[82] That was the plan. In practice, the bi-lateral intelligence-gathering teams were often significantly undermined by competing national interests, mutual distrust, and outright hostility. The resulting "failure to communicate" almost resulted in the loss of one of the largest sources of intelligence.[83]

The term "large" is used here to describe not only the significance of the find, but also its sheer physical size (50 tons). Hidden in the barn of German paper mill owner, Hans Huber, were almost 13 million index cards.[84] Each card contained the personal names and activities of nearly every single member of the NSDAP.[85] Despite the obvious value of these records, were it not for the repeated efforts of Herr Huber to inform the Allies about his treasure, the Nazi Party Membership Files might never have been secured by Western Forces in April of 1945. It seems that the US and British recovery teams were far more pre-occupied at the time with trying to figure out what the other one was up to. Even after Huber sent three sacks of index cards to US authorities to convince them of the value of his secret collection, it still took several months before the Counter Intelligence Corps of the Seventh Army finally responded.[86] And thank goodness they did. During the entirety of the Allies' denazification efforts (and long thereafter), those classified records were used, for example, to cross-check the information being provided by German sources.[87] The advantage of this registry was also its disadvantage. Given the sheer volume of the data,[88] it was simply impossible to obtain the information desired within the timeframe it was desired. For that reason, the denazification process still had to rely heavily upon the information they obtained from German sources.

To generate name lists of known and suspected threats, the Allies relied upon membership records of Nazi organizations. For example, in the city of Worms, membership rosters containing the names and addresses of all Party members from the following NS organizations were used: the NS Aryan charitable alliance, the "Nationalsozialistische Volkswohlfahrt" (NSV); the NS Women's League, the "Nationalsozialistische Frauenschaft" (NSF); the NSDAP's paramilitary wing, the "Sturmabteilung" (SA); and the protective squadron or "Schutzstaffel" (SS). Based on this internal data, authorities in Worms prepared a detailed list of more than fifty women who had been official members of the NSF[89] and over thirty who had been members of the NSDAP.[90] As shown, for example, in table 5.2, the list contained the members' full names, birth dates, and the year that they became official NSF or NSDAP members (MbrY).

On the basis of this information, subsequent interrogations were conducted by denazification committees. The committee in Worms concluded, for example, that NSF members *Katharina B.* and *Wilhemine P.* (numbers 6 and 13, respectively, on table 5.2) were not particularly politically conspicuous. By comparison, a number 75, *Katharina S.*, was described as being "an enthusiastic member of the NSDAP till the very end." Such reports were then used to generate new name lists of people who warranted further investigation. For example, on July 31, 1948, the Bürgermeister of Abenheim, a small town located just outside of the city of Worms, sent local officials a name list of individuals whose right to vote had been revoked.[91] Interestingly, Katherina S's name does not appear on this roster. Neither does the name *A. Feick*, whom the Denazification Committee had described as being a leading member of the NSF who had energetically "pressured a large portion of the women to join the NSF." Feick was reportedly a zealous leader whom the Committee described as being "dangerous." Given these red flags, the absence of her name from the list of persons barred from voting was curious.

Also missing from the 1948 name list of prohibited voters was *Ludwig L.* who was described in the Worm's tribunal report as being an "extremely active and dangerous Nazi" who had joined the NSDAP extremely early on (a so-called Alter Kämpfer). Ludwig L. served as a local block warden (Blockleiter) during the Third Reich and therefore benefitted greatly during the war from his Party connections. Also conspicuously absent was *W. Raffel*. Like the other "Alter Kämpfer," Raffel was also a high-ranking district leader who had been deeply involved in promoting party propaganda before the war's end. He was described as being "feared as a dangerous Nazi."[92] It is possible of course that the absence of these names could be explained by the fact that they appeared on other, earlier, watchlists; and, in an effort to avoid duplication, the administrators decided not

Table 5.2 Postwar Name List of Nazi Organization Members Compiled for Possible Denazification

#	NAME	MbrY	ORG.	#	NAME	MbrY	#	NAME	MbrY	ORG.
1.	Katharina A.	—	NSF	26.	Katharina H.	—	51.	Wilma A	1944	NSDAP
2.	Elisabeth A.	1935	NSF	27.	Katharina H.	1934	52.	Lidia A.	1943	NSDAP
3.	Eliese B.	1935	NSF	28.	Margarete H.	1933	53.	Elise B.	1943	NSDAP
4.	Emmi B.	1934	NSF	29.	Anneliese I.	1942	54.	Anna B.	1937	NSDAP
5.	Eva B.	1936	NSF	30.	Eliese I.	1934	55.	Franziska C.	1941	NSDAP
6.	Wilhemine B.	1938	NSF	31.	Katharina J.	—	56.	Susanne D.	1938	NSDAP
7.	Franziska B.	1943	NSF	32.	Magd. K.	1932	57.	Katharina D.	1943	NSDAP
8.	Magdalene B.	1940	NSF	33.	Barbara K.	1936	58.	Lieselotte E.	1941	NSDAP
9.	Maria B.	1943	NSF	34.	Maria K.	—	59.	Martel G.	1937	NSDAP
10.	Margarete A.	1937	NSF	35.	Rosina K.	—	60.	Johanna G	1943	NSDAP
11.	Appollonia B.	—	NSF	36.	Maria K.	—	61.	Katharina G.	1943	NSDAP
12.	Selma B.	—	NSF	37.	Margarete L.	1938	62.	Christel G.	1942	NSDAP
13.	Katharina B.	—	NSF	38.	Christine L.	1930	63.	Erika G.	1943	NSDAP
14.	Christina B.	—	NSF	39.	Christel L.	—	64.	Katharina H.	1940	NSDAP
15.	Liesel D.	1934	NSF	40.	Elisabeth L.	1935	65.	Barbara H.	1941	NSDAP
16.	Maria D.	1934	NSF	41.	Elise L.	—	66.	Lore H	1943	NSDAP
17.	Eliese E.	—	NSF	42.	Elise L.	1934	67.	Hildegard H	1942	NSDAP
18.	Lore F.	—	NSF	43.	Margarete L.	1935	68.	Gretel H.	1937	NSDAP
19.	Margarete F.	1936	NSF	44.	Barbara M.	1937	69.	Katharina K.	1924	NSDAP
20.	Maria F.	—	NSF	45.	Kath. M.	1935	70.	Hedwig K.	1943	NSDAP
21.	Philippine G.	—	NSF	46.	Lydia M.	—	71.	Erika M.	1943	NSDAP
22.	Herta G.	—	NSF	47.	Maria M.	—	72.	Lisie N.	1942	NSDAP
23.	Eliese G.	1935	NSF	48.	Anna N.	—	73.	Emmy N.	1944	NSDAP
24.	Lotte, G.	1938	NSF	49.	Maria N.	—	74.	Liesel R.	1944	NSDAP
25.	Katharina J.	—	NSF	50.	Maria P.	1935	75.	Katharina S.	1944	NSDAP

to include these names on later lists. It is also possible, however, that the absence of these names was due to an oversight, be it accidental or purposeful. Whatever the reason(s), such blatant inconsistencies were by no means unusual and were the cause of great criticism among the German public. By 1949, as US denazification was drawing to a close, 71 percent of Germans polled felt that program had not been carried out effectively or fairly.[93]

The citizen's tribunals had proven themselves to be deeply flawed. From bribery and corruption to intimidation and cronyism,[94] a major source of these flaws was no doubt to be found in the underlying design. Using the Anglo-American judicial principle that allows the accused to be tried by "a jury of peers," Chapter II, Article 25 of the "Law for Liberation" required that the members of the citizens' tribunals be: "familiar with local conditions within their area of jurisdiction. The occupational group to which the respondent [the person being assessed by the tribunal] belongs, or a related group, shall be represented, to the extent possible, among the assessors."[95] Just one year after the end of World War II, it was perhaps more than naïve to believe that such a codicil would not open the door to gross abuse wherein those who had been terrorized during the Third Reich were re-victimized and those who had wielded unlimited power during the Reich were exonerated. Thus, for all the good intentions that went into their conception, the local tribunals seemed to have a very disconcerting knack of trapping the little fish and letting the big ones get away.

*****

In the weeks and months immediately before and after the war's end, the only intact economy was the Black Market where people attempted to sell what little they had left to buy what little someone else had been able to steal. Among the most sought-after commodities were new names. Even before the war ended, the purchase of a new name was considered a wise investment in one's future. This meant that by the time the Allies had seized over control of the Reich, a not insignificant number of Nazis were living under assumed names in the hopes of escaping prosecution.

Although no precise statistic can be determined, it has been estimated that between 10,000 and nearly 100,000 people were illegally living under an assumed name during this period.[96] To many experts on both sides of the Ocean, the fact that the whereabouts and activities of so many violent offenders remained unknown constituted an unacceptable, international security risk. Clearly something had to be done. In hopes of encouraging at least some of these so-called "submarines" to resurface, the German government took a momentous and exceedingly controversial step. In 1949, just four years after the war's end, in

one of its first official legislative acts, the fledgling West German government announced plans to issue an amnesty to residents living under an assumed name.[97]
In his inaugural address to the Bundestag on September 20, 1949, the newly
named Bundeskanzler, Konrad Adenauer, addressed this plan:

> The war and the chaos of the postwar period brought with them so
> many tests and temptations that one can only but understand some
> of the resulting failings and mistakes. It is for this reason that the
> German government is reviewing the possibility of an amnesty.[98]

Among supporters of the plan, it was argued that this act of generosity would
not only provide much-needed relief to the overburdened, understaffed justice
system. It would also help to ease some of the societal tensions that had amassed
in a show of good will.[99] To help guard against abuse, certain restrictions and
conditions were imposed. For example, only those people who willingly turned
themselves into their local police department on or before March 31, 1950, and
then gave complete disclosure about their true identity would be considered eligible. In addition, amnesty would only be given to those offenders whose crimes
carried a prison sentence of six months or less and/or accompanied a financial
penalty of not more than 5,000 DM or less (§2.1).

As the drafters of the legislation argued, such conditions effectively excluded
dangerous criminals who were living under assumed names to escape rightful
prosecution. At the same time, the plan showed mercy to basic law-abiding citizens who had committed comparatively minor crimes such as fraud, drug use,
theft, bigamy, and prostitution during the general pandemonium that erupted
immediately before and after the general cease fire. To provide further legal
assurance that the legislation would not be misused, §10.2 explicitly excluded
any persons whose offense included murder, manslaughter (i.e., §§211–213 of
the German Criminal Code) or any other crime that had been committed for
the sake of cruelty greed, and/or dishonor.[100] During the parliamentary debate
over the proposed Amnesty that took place on December 9, 1949, Dr. Gebhard
Müller maintained that the proposal had been drafted with such uncommon
diligence and care that very little deliberation was needed. And, if the members
of the Bundesrat moved quickly enough, the proposal could be ratified and presented to general public by the Christmas holidays.

While skeptics of the legislation agreed that the above-mentioned conditions were important, they reasoned that the lack of precision in the legal
formulations left many unsettling contradictions and unsavory loopholes. For
example, hypothetically speaking, an ex-soldier living under an assumed name
could conceivably take advantage of the Amnesty even if he admitted to having

severely beaten, raped, and threatened to kill a female civilian if she ever revealed his true identity. The only two major stipulations were that these offences had to have occurred AFTER May 8, 1945; and the soldier's confession must have come on or before the March 31, 1950, deadline.

The danger of such scenarios was raised by Bavarian lawyer and Bundesrat member Dr. Johann Ehard. In his opinion, the piece of legislation was almost irredeemably poorly written and shockingly ill-conceived. "The way this text is formulated," Dr. Ehard raged during the parliamentary debate in the Bundestag, "short of murder, a person could be excused from committing any crime, if it were perpetrated to keep his true identity a secret. . . . Now just imagine how far some people would be willing to go to protect themselves from being caught out and put in prison!"[101] Dr. Ehard's reservations were echoed by a number of other delegates.

Representative Robert Leibbrand, member of the Communist Party of Germany and survivor of the Buchenwald Concentration Camp, argued that in its present form, the proposal did nothing to protect individuals who had broken the law during the war to fight against National Socialism and/or protect its victims. To make sure that members of the resistance who had been forced underground were also protected under the proposed Amnesty, more time would be needed to adjust the wording of the legislation. If this were not done, Leibbrand declared: "In the next few years, we will see opponents of National Socialism being dragged before courts. . . . because in 1942 or 1943, they had perjured themselves to protect either themselves or someone else from persecution by the NS."[102] In view of these and other grave concerns about the wording of the amnesty, many representatives felt that more time should be taken to more carefully review and craft this important piece of legislation.

Based on the parliamentary record, Mr. Viktor Renner (Württemberg-Hohenzollern), Dr. Dr. Günther Gereke [he had a double doctorate] (Niedersachsen), Dr. Beyerle (Württemberg-Baden), and Dr. Katz (Schleswig-Holstein) all lobbied to temporarily table the discussion until December 19. To the charge that such a delay might endanger the originally envisioned holiday timetable, Renner snapped: "I truly do not believe a satisfactory argumentation can be made with: 'Christmas is right around the corner, so let's just accept this thing as is!'"[103] Dr. Müller, realizing that the opposition was far too great, begrudgingly acknowledged that the only agreement that could be reached was postponing the debate. Although supporters of the Amnesty may have lost that first battle, thanks to behind the scenes lobbying, they were ultimately able to win a thin majority. The legislation was passed by the Bundesrat by a hair's breadth: twenty-two votes in favor and twenty-one against. Five days before Christmas, the Amnesty was delivered to the Allied Occupation Government.

Not surprisingly, the proposal raised more than a few eyebrows among the Western government officials. Many of the same concerns that had been raised by the Bundesrat were voiced once again. In the end, though, the German lawmakers were given the green light.[104] In retrospect, it is difficult to say why the Allies decided to allow this controversial legislation. Perhaps, it was hoped that granting the West German legislature this degree of latitude would show good faith and would thereby help to improve strained diplomatic relations. Or maybe, it was believed that given the mounting public resentment towards the Occupational Forces, especially in light of the extreme postwar socioeconomic tumult, the Amnesty would help to ameliorate the public sentiment and dampen growing animosities. Possibly it was even hoped that the legislation would successfully encourage large numbers of Nazis to come out from hiding and either face justice and/or become productive members of the democratic process. Whatever the reason(s), on December 31, 1949, just in time for New Year's Eve, the Amnesty became law. All that was left to do now was to wait and see whether the supporters or the critics had been right.

After the deadline for registration had passed, both sides of the argument were shocked. Contrary to expectations, the public response to the Amnesty could best be described as wan.[105] In total, no more than 250 people living with a false name under an assumed identity took advantage of the governmental peace-offering.[106] One possible explanation for this dismal turnout might well have been §5.2 which contained the following codicil: a previously granted amnesty could be lifted in the event that new, incriminating, evidence came to light that would increase the severity of the crime(s) and thereby extend the prescribed imprisonment to beyond the six-month limit and/or increase the financial fine to more than 5,000 DM. Certainly, for criminals who knew full well that their offenses extended far beyond mere misdemeanors, this eventuality would most certainly have diminished the attractiveness of the Amnesty offer. This might help to explain the curious case of Fritz Rössler.

Fritz Rössler was born on January 17, 1912, in the mountainous region of Swiss Saxony. As soon as he came of age, he joined the National Socialist Party. With a mixture of charisma, arrogance, and ruthlessness, the young Party member rose relatively quickly through the ranks to become a district leader in Saxony before joining the Reich's Ministry for Propaganda. By 1945, as the war came to an end, Rössler had completely vanished, leaving behind his young wife, Ruth, and their children. The next official sign of Rössler did not come until some twelve months later, when a Dr. Franz Richter reported that he had personally witnessed Rössler's heroic death on the field of combat. According to his account, the professor had gotten to know Rössler sometime between the years 1940 and 1945 when he had served as a simple foot soldier. Unlike Rössler, the professor had never joined the Nazi Party. Nevertheless, the two men had become very close. And given their comradery, the professor considered it his duty to take care of his fallen friend's wife. What began as a promise between men quickly became a vow between a bridegroom and a widow.

On November 7, 1946, Dr. Richter married Ruth in a small civil ceremony in Hannover. He later went on to adopt her children and raise them as his own. The start for the new patchwork family was by no means easy. Like millions of others, all of the professor's documents had been lost during the war. His birth certificate, for example, had been destroyed in calamitous fire in Smyrna, Turkey.[107] In addition, all record of his academic degrees and accomplishments had disappeared in the postwar chaos which erupted in the Sudetenland, where he had reportedly served as a lecturer after completing his studies in Prague. Thankfully, the professor was issued replacement identification papers and degrees on the basis of the information he was able to provide the authorities.

Shortly after receiving this documentation, Dr. Richter applied for and was offered a teaching position in a local community college. Despite the desperate teacher shortage, he was quickly fired from this position. That failure was short-lived. It did not take long before the ever-resourceful Dr. Richter had found his calling: politics. His inflammatory unapologetic speeches soon caught the attention of many high-ranking arch-conservatives who hoped for return of the Third Reich. In no time at all, Richter was elected to represent to the German Conservative Party [Deutsch Konservative Partei]. What the DKP called "conservatism" others recognized as National Socialism. Joining forces with other right-extremist political parties, the DKP eventually found its way into the Bundestag. No sooner had they entered the Parliament, did Dr. Richter take steps to increase his political influence.

On September 15, 1949, during the third meeting of the German Bundestag, it was announced that he had joined forces with five leading members of other right-extremist parties to form the "Gruppe Nationale Rechte."[108] Together, this new political force lobbied against what they perceived as the tyranny of the Allies' occupation. On November 2, 1949, delegates von Thadden, Dr. Meissner, Dr. Leuchtgens, Frommhold, and Dr. Richter submitted a proposal for an unconditional amnesty. Leading the parliamentary charge was Dr. Richter.[109]

Upon failing to receive sufficient parliamentary support for a general amnesty, Dr. Richter and his colleagues threw their full weight behind the more restricted amnesty described above. During the parliamentary debates that took place on December 9, 1949, for example, the professor explained that it was imperative that the Amnesty be passed with all posthaste as there were "still Germans who remained in danger of being placed by the Allies' before War Tribunals because of their alleged crimes against humanity, which," he cynically added, "the Allies were naturally in no way guilty of having committed themselves!"[110] Dr. Richter's incendiary commentary was not reserved for the halls of parliament. Throughout what would prove to be a long political career, he was repeatedly sanctioned for espousing National Socialist ideals in public. In the winter of 1953, for example, during a local chapter meeting in Hildesheim, Germany, he reportedly asserted that the political leaders of the major parties had wormed their way into highest offices only so that they could ruin Germany. During that same meeting, he was also quoted as saying that the reparations for Israel also constituted a betrayal of the German Volk. When confronted with these allegations, Dr. Richter refused to either confirm or deny having made them. What he did do, however, was ardently defend the ideas behind them.

With regard to the charge that he had spoken against Germany paying reparations to Israel, he retorted: "If Israel's demand for reparations were legitimate," he asked, "why are so many of their people still walking around in our country?" And as for his criticism of his fellow elected officials, the professor quipped: "As I have said many times before, my understanding of the category 'Führer' is altogether different than the men who currently lead our political parties." On July 21, 1951, not one but four different ministers brought formal suit against Dr. Richter for slander. Still, the representative kept on, undeterred, until the winter of 1952. On February 20, the German parliament's official usher approached Dr. Richter with the attendance list. As usual, the professor added his signature to the roster. No sooner had he done so was he promptly placed under arrest. It would not take long before the Parliament was officially informed about the incredible circumstances surrounding the professor's arrest.

> Ladies and Gentlemen. The committee for order and immunity has submitted a report in the case of Dr. Franz Richter. It is my duty to inform you that, with my official approval, Representative Dr. Franz Richter has been taken into custody under the charge of falsifying his identity. He is neither a credentialed secondary-school teacher nor in possession of a doctoral degree. Indeed, his name is not even 'Franz Richter' but NSDAP member, Fritz Roeßler, district leader of Saxony.[111]

Slowly but surely, the full story emerged. With the complicity of his wife and family, Rössler had faked his own death, married his own wife, adopted his own children, and conferred upon himself a doctoral title which he then used to establish a completely new career. The only thing it seems that he had not managed to camouflage was his original bellicose, belligerent, racist personality.

On February 21, 1952, the then President of the Bundestag, Dr. Hermann Ehlers, announced amid derisive laughter and jeers, that *Mr. Fritz Rössler* had officially resigned his position in the German Bundestag. This announcement marked one of the first times that the former *Dr. Richter* was referred to using his real name. It also marked the last time that the former representative was mentioned in theWest German parliament at all. Rössler was sentenced to eighteen months for illegally presenting himself as having a doctoral title and falsifying documents for the purpose of disguising his true identity. Neither Rössler's conviction nor his public outing as a former local leader of the Nazi Party destroyed his political career, however. Up until his death on October 11, 1987, in Salzburg, Austria, he continued to be a welcomed and respected public speaker.

Incredibly, neither the embarrassment of the *Rössler/Richter* scandal nor the lackluster response of the first Amnesty deterred German government officials from introducing another pardon. In 1954, a second amnesty was introduced.[112] As before, many in the international community reacted to this legislation with a mixture of horror and outrage. And as before, despite great international media attention, the number of people who took advantage of the amnesty was far lower than expected. By the end of 1954, it was estimated that only 954 people had taken advantage of the offer and admitted to the authorities that they had been living under a false identity to avoid prosecution. By 1955, an additional ninety-seven people had re-surfaced.[113]

After the introduction of the second Amnesty, the Central Council of Jews in Germany [Zentralrat der Juden] contacted the Department of Justice and requested that a similar piece of legislation be introduced to protect the surviving victims of the Nazi regime who had taken on a false name and a new identity in a desperate attempt to save their lives and not to commit a crime. Now that the war was over, without the benefit of an amnesty to protect them, these survivors were being forced to remain under their non-Jewish masks, lest they be made to face prosecution for falsifying their identification records. In support of this proposal, the Head of the Association of German Rabbis offered the following argumentation: if all sides can agree upon bestowing a pardon to war criminals, could not the same be done for their victims? The answer to that question was given by the then German State Secretary Walter Strauß: "It appears questionable whether after only three years, yet another amnesty would be accepted." Whether or not "poor timing" was the real or only reason for this rejection cannot be determined. However, Minister Strauß's seeming refusal to actively follow up on this proposal is particularly intriguing given his personal history.

Although a baptized member of the Protestant Church, both of Strauß's parents were Jewish, making him a "Volljude" in the eyes of the Nazis. However, in March 1927, years before the National Socialists had managed to take over complete power, the aspiring young doctor of jurisprudence married his Russian-German fiancée, Tamara Schneider.[114] The fact that Tamara was non-Jewish meant that their marriage afforded Strauß a certain degree of protection against the onslaught of anti-Jewish laws later introduced by the Nazis. In addition to the initial shield his mixed marriage offered him, Strauß was also protected by a number of powerful officials within Reich. Chief among them was none other than Dr. Hans Globke, the chief architect of the anti-Jewish naming laws and other treacherous legislation designed to protect "Aryan bloodlines."[115] Thanks to such influential connections within the government and law enforcement, Strauß and his wife Tamara were successfully able to dodge the Gestapo and avoid being placed under arrest. He was also able to arrange to have his Jewish identification papers "lost."[116]

Strauß's parents were, however, completely defenseless. In 1943, they were both deported to Theresienstadt. His father, Professor Hermann Strauß, an internationally recognized doctor of internal medicine at the Jewish hospital of Berlin and a decorated World War I veteran, died from a heart attack a year after his deportation.[117] His mother, Elsa Strauß, who also worked in the same hospital as her husband, lived just long enough to see the liberation of Theresienstadt.[118] In the meantime, Strauß and his wife had managed to reach the Russian forces who offered them protection until the end of the war.[119] This personal history meant that Strauß knew full well how hiding one's true identity could mean the difference between escape and capture, survival and death. In view of this history, it is remarkable that in his later capacity as State Secretary, he helped to author portions of the second amnesty. In an impassioned speech made on March 18, 1954 before the Bundestag, he announced that he categorically rejected any discussion of a General Amnesty for crimes committed before May 8, 1945, "there were events that took place which cannot remained unatoned for."[120] Nevertheless, he did support the restricted amnesties.

Although the turnout for the second amnesty was greater than the first, the results were still disappointingly small in comparison to the numbers of people who were presumed to have taken on an alias to escape detection and possible conviction. This low turnout may have (and has) been taken by researchers as an indication that the original estimates of the number of Nazis who were actually living underground were grossly exaggerated. However, this is only one possible reason. Another may be the simple fact that, then as now, comparatively few criminals voluntarily decide to turn themselves in to authorities, no matter how enticing the legal inducements might be. In this respect, the case of Richter/ Rössler is an excellent example. As one of the officials who actually helped to push through the legislative pardon, he was well aware of the potential rewards that might have been his if he had only stepped forward. However, he chose to continue his subterfuge. Why? The answer was certainly not ignorance. He, like many other Nazis who were living under a false identity, was well aware of the Amnesty and yet he did not come forward. Ultimately, there is probably no one, single reason, why Richter/Rössler and others like him chose to remain on the other side of the law.

For some people living under an alias, the fear of losing the new lives they had managed to build up in postwar Germany was simply too great. After all, even if the new government was willing to pardon them, there was no guarantee that their family, friends, and colleagues would do the same. For others, the main reason for not turning themselves in may have had precious little to do with shielding their loved ones and everything to do with protecting their (im)material assets. As will be described in the next chapter, after the war, a surprising number of Nazis managed to re-amass a shocking degree of power, wealth, and prestige. Even among those who failed to achieve the same status in their second lives as they had in their first, after having had the power over life and death, the thought of voluntarily placing themselves in a position where their fate would be decided by others may well have been a completely alien, if not entirely repugnant. For still others, the secret thrill of hiding in plain view combined with the knowledge that revelations about their past would most certainly lead to their immediate incarceration and/or execution might have been motivation enough to remain silent. In most cases, however, it was in all probability, a complex combination of all these and other factors that explain why so few took advantage of this opportunity.

Importantly, as will be shown in the following chapters, in many cases discovered as a part of this research, offenders living under an assumed alias only turned themselves in AFTER they had either been identified by a curious colleague, a disgruntled lover, or a courageous survivor; or AFTER they had been offered personal freedom and political protection in exchange for classified information. At no time during this research was a single case uncovered where an offender had turned himself/herself in out of sense of true remorse. Instead, this elusive set of criminals remained convinced of the necessity, if not the legitimacy, of their actions. Precisely this lament was expressed by Chief Prosecutor, Robert Jackson, during an impromptu speech delivered during a Roosevelt Commemorative Ceremony held in Prague, on the first anniversary of FDR's death.[121]

> Because his [FDR's] feeling and determination were shared by President Truman, I was sent to Europe, and that gives me the opportunity to be here tonight. I shall not speak of the fate of the Nazi war criminals on trial at Nuremberg. The guilt and punishment, of course, is for the court to judge not for me. But I would like to remind you of something that impressed me strongly as we have proceeded with the trial at Nuremberg. I speak of it because it concerns the attitude of the German people and the future dealing with them in the interests of the peace of Europe. I have yet to hear one of these

men say that he regretted he had a part in starting the war. Their only regret is at losing it. Not one sign of contrition or reform has appeared, either in public testimony or private interrogation of the twenty-one men in the dock. Not one of them has condemned the persecution of the Jews or of the Church—they have only sought to evade personal responsibilities. Not one has condemned the creation of concentration camps; indeed Hermann Goering testified they are useful and necessary. Not one has indicated that, if he were free and able, he would not do the same thing over again. From their testimony, it is apparent that they would expect the support of more of the German people in the same program again.[122]

Sadly, as opinion poll after opinion poll conducted after the war confirmed, the major war criminals seem not to have been alone in their refusal to acknowledge the criminality inherent in National Socialism. In repeated surveys conducted by the US High Commission for Germany (HICOG), it was determined that only about one-third of respondents "rejected National Socialism outright" and almost half "thought it merely a good idea badly carried out."[123] Within that postwar climate, far too often, those who continued to call for justice found themselves being publicly condemned as vengeful, ruthless, utterly without mercy or basic human compassion; whereas those who had committed unspeakable crimes were increasingly viewed as hapless victims whose loyalty and bravery were first betrayed by Himmler and Hitler during the War only later to be besmirched by de Gaulle, Churchill, and Truman after the war. As the legendary Nazi hunter Fritz Bauer lamented, to his great chagrin, the criminals of the past had suddenly become the heroes of the present.[124]

The general consensus in the 1950s seemed to be that military actions required during times of war may not necessarily coincide with the political sensibilities that prevail during times of peace; however, that discrepancy negated neither the situational necessity nor ethical justifiability of doing one's duty to protect one's family, village, or homeland. Following that logic, in HICOG surveys conducted between August 26 and 31, 1952, in the zones controlled by the Americans, the vast majority of German respondents (63 percent) felt that the German soldiers who had been placed on trial for war crimes were not guilty and that the sentences passed against them were acts of revenge or fear of German military might.[125] Moreover, the general sentiment among HICOG survey-takers was that by refusing to "prosecute Allied officer accused of war crimes, the entire notion of justice was aborted." Had not the Russians slaughtered thousands in the forests of Katyń?[126] How many had died in the firestorms of Dresden? And what of the Americans who dropped the atomic bomb on Hiroshima? If these brutal acts were to be considered the heavy price of war, then surely the same courtesy could be afforded Austria, Italy, Japan, and Germany?[127] From the local pub to the halls of parliament, many in the German public seemed to feel that one of the spoils of victory was having the luxury to hide one's country's own crimes. As the vanquished nation, they were willing to bear a certain degree of humiliation.[128] But enough was enough. Of course, they conceded, there were a few like Eichmann and Barbie who had escaped the hangman's noose, but in all probability, the vast majority of the NSDAP big wigs were either dead or so well hidden that it was questionable whether they would ever be found.

In the meantime, Germany, Austria, and Italy had finally rejoined the international community; and through their miraculous industry, they were helping to build a stronger, more united, Europe. Now was the time to look forward not back. Many of these sentiments were encapsulated in a speech given on September 17, 1952 before the Bundestag by Dr. Mende, representative for the Free Democratic Party (FDP):

> One might ask why the German people have been so intensively concerned with these issues. Ladies and Gentlemen, it is because the Germans have experienced for themselves how darkness and lightness are meted out and that international law, unfortunately, in an unbridled "total" war, is violated on both sides. The rubble and ruin of Dresden, Hamburg, and Cologne . . . just to name a few names . . . why, the evidence is in our very hands, that the other side, in many cases, did precisely that for which Germany was condemned; and ladies and gentleman, seven years would appear to be the time to finally draw the line. . . . We want to turn our gaze to the future. But we have to expect, that the other side is also ready to demonstrate good will as well.[129]

Thanks to international agreements millions of POWs were finally returning home. These broken fathers, sons, brothers, and husbands could not be compared to evil the likes of Hitler, Himmler, Heydrich, Göring, and Goebbels, their loved ones argued. The majority of Germany's soldiers, the postwar public reasoned, were honorable people who had simply done their duty, no more and no less. It was finally time to move on, the majority felt. There was nothing more to be learnt and no more secrets to be discovered. Just two years after Representative Mende was frenetically applauded for his emboldening speech before the Bundestag, a series of coincidences would take place that would show Germany and the world that there were indeed many more secrets to be discovered and so much more to learn.

Notes

1. Michael Wagner-Kern, *Staat und Namensänderung* (Tübingen: Mohr Siebeck, 2002).

2. "Law No. 1: Abrogation of Nazi Law," Laws and Orders of Military Government: Complete Collection up to June 30, 1945 (Wiesbaden: Vieweg and Teubner Verlag, 1945).

3. Clemens Schwender, *Wie benutze ich den Fernsprecher? Die Anleitung zum Telefonieren im Berliner Telefonbuch 1881–1996/97* (Frankfurt am Main: Peter Lang, 1996).

4. Landeshauptarchiv Koblenz, "Der Amtsbürgermeister," Kreisverwaltung Zell/ Mosel. 21 and 24 November 1949 Az:040/8 Best. 500 Nr. 32.

5. Landeshauptarchiv Koblenz, October 23, 1946, Best.655, 256 Nr. 138 [VK].

6. Stadtarchiv Frankfurt am Main, September 15, 1947 Magistratsakten Zugang III/2–1979.

7. Stadtarchiv Frankfurt am Main, October 3, 1947, Magistratsakten Zugang III/2–1979.

8. Stadtarchiv Frankfurt am Main, Stadtkanzlei II Gu; Document 7.

9. Stadtarchiv Frankfurt am Main, Stadtkanzlei: Standesamt Ander. "Von Fam. u. Vornamen," Magistratsakten Stadtkanzlei II Gu; Document 13.

10. Stadtarchiv Frankfurt am Main, Stadtkanzlei II Gu; Document 13.

11. Stadtarchiv Frankfurt am Main, Stadtkanzlei: Standesamt Ander. "Von Fam. u Vornamen, " Zugang II/2-1979 987; Document B.

12. Stadtarchiv Frankfurt am Main, "Brief an Herrn Stadtrat Dr. Reinert," October 11, 1947. Stadtkanzlei II Gu; Document 5.

13. Joseph Goebbels, "Warum sind Wir Judengegner?," in *Der Angriff* (Munich: Zentralverlag der NSDAP, 1935), 329.

14. Hessisches Hauptstaatsarchiv Wiesbaden, "Namensänderung," HHStaW: 656 Nr. 779.

15. Hessisches Hauptstaatsarchiv Wiesbaden, "Namensänderung," January 18, 1950. HHStaW:656 Nr. 779.

16. Hessisches Hauptstaatsarchiv Wiesbaden, "Namensänderung," December 7, 1949 – December 18, 1950. HHStaW:656 Nr. 779.

17. "Gesellschaft für Christlich-Jüdische Zusammenarbeit beklagt Antisemitismus in Hessen," Frankfurter Allgemeine Zeitung. November 8, 1949. Available from the *Hessian Regional History Information System* (LAGIS) (online), http://www-lagis-hessen. de/de/subjects/idrect /sn/edb/id/3406.

18. "Minister Präsident Stock sagt Toleranz und Bekämpfung des Antisemitismus zu." Frankfurter Allgemeine Zeitung. July 21, 1950. Available from the Hessian *Regional History Information System* (LAGIS) (online), "Zeitgeschichte in Hessen" (Contemporary History in Hessan) http://www-lagis-hessen.de/de/subjects/idrect/sn/edb/id/3552.

19. Stadtarchiv Frankfurt am Main, Magistratsakten, Zugang: 111/2–1979 Signatur: 987.

20. Stadtarchiv Frankfurt am Main, Magistratsakten, Zugang: 111/2–1979 Signatur: 987.

21. Stadtarchiv Frankfurt am Main, Magistratsakten, Zugang: 111/2–1979 Signatur: 987.

22. Kristina Festring-Hashem Zadek, "Wie Hitlers Halbbrüder im Hamburg untertauchte," *Der Norddeutsche Rundfunk*, May 20, 2016: 1. https://www.ndr.de/kultur/geschichte/schauplaetze/Wie-Hitlers-Bruder-in-Hamburg-untertauchte,hitler178.html.

23. Kristina Festring-Hashem Zadek, "Hitlers Halbbrüder," 4.

24. Staatsarchiv Hamburg, 332–4_IV B 7 116/45.

25. For an intriguing review of the Hitler brothers, see Volker Ullrich, *Adolf Hitler, Die Jahre des Aufstiegs* (Frankfurt am Main: S. Fischer Verlag, 2013).

26. Peter Ulrich Meyer, "Wie Adolf Hitlers Halbbruder in Hamburg untertauchte" (How Adolf Hitler's half-brother submerged in Hamburg), *Abendblatt*, March 23, 2016, 1. https://www.abendblatt.de/hamburg/article207266299/Wie-Adolf-Hitlers-Halbbruder-in-Hamburg-untertauchte.html.

27. "Personalien: Alois Hiller," *Der Spiegel*, February 23, 1955, http://magazin.spiegel.de/EpubDelivery/spiegel/pdf/31969320.

28. A year after the *Spiegel* article was published, Alois Hiller/Hitler died and was buried in a cemetery in Hamburg. See Festring-Hashem Zadek, "Hitlers Halbbrüder," 1.

29. Hessisches Hauptstaatsarchiv Wiesbaden, "Namensänderung," July 19, 1955, 656 Nr. 779.

30. Manno Peters Tammena, *Namensgebung in Ostfriesland Personennamen Patronymische Namen: UrSpring, Entwicklung, Niedergang* (Hamburg: Verlag Saltau-Kurier-Norden, 2009), 113–14.

31. Hessisches Hauptstaatarchiv Wiesbaden, September 30, 1953, 656: 779.

32. Hessisches Hauptstaatarchiv Wiesbaden, July 19, 1955, 656: 779.

33. Isabel Heinemann, *Rasse, Siedlung, deutsches Blut: Das Rasse- und Siedlungshauptamt der SS und die rassenpolitische Neuordnung Europas* (Göttingen: Wallstein, 2003), 520.

34. Volker Koop, *Dem Führer ein Kind Schenken: Die SS-Organisation Lebensborn e.v.* (Cologne: Böhlau Verlag, 2007), 154.

35. Ines Hopfer, *Die gewaltsame Eindeutschung' von polnische Kindern in der NS-Zeit* (Graz: Böhlau Verlag, 2010), 55.

36. Hopfer, *Geraubte Identität*, 295–99.

37. According to an official edict issued by the Reich's Ministry of the Interior from June 24, 1941 (Id 21 III/40–5504 gen), brides whose fiancés had died before the wedding were entitled to carry the title "Mrs." even in cases where the union had not produced a child. In the same decree, it was also ruled that women who found themselves in this position would also be allowed to carry a double name formed from their maiden name and their fiancé's surname. Stadtsarchiv Flensburg, ID 0176 (1933–1975).

38. Stadtsarchiv Ludwigsburg, Bestand: FL20/14, Bestell: Bü135.

39. Elisabeth Berger, *Erwerb und Änderung des Familiennamens* (Berlin: Peter Lang, 2001), 166.

40. Hamburg Staatsarchiv, 113–5_DVA1.

41. Landeshauptarchiv Koblenz, "an die Herren Landräte des Bezirks Herrn Ober-burgermeister in Koblenz," March 20, 1944, Best. 655, 203 Nr. 268.

42. Wagner-Kern, *Staat und Namensänderung*, 358.

43. Landeshauptarchiv Koblenz, "Landesregierung Rheinland-Pfalz" Koblenz, September 1947, Best 500 Nr. 30.

44. Landeshauptarchiv Koblenz, "Landesregierung Rheinland-Pfalz" Koblenz, February 25, 1947, Best 500 Nr. 30.

45. Landeshauptarchiv Koblenz, "Landesregierung Rheinland-Pfalz" Koblenz, August 28, 1947, Best 500 Nr. 30.

45. Ministerialblatt, "Änderung und Feststellung von Familiennamen sowie Änderung von Vornamen III Familienrechtliche Gesichtspunkte." No. 7, May 28, 1949, 458.

47. In 1944, Amon Göth was dismissed from his position as commandant for having stolen from the store of possessions stolen from people imprisoned in the Płaszów concentration camp. After the war, he was extradited to Poland where he was sentenced to death and hanged. For more, see Michael J. Bazyler and Frank M. Tuerkheimer, "Chapter 4: The Trial of Amon Göth in Postwar Poland," *Forgotten Trials of the Holocaust* (New York: New York University Press, 2014), chapter 4, "The Trial of Amon Göth in Postwar Poland," 101–28.

48. During the entirety of their relationship, Commandant Göth was married. His second wife, Anna Göth nee Geiger, lived with their two children *Werner* and *Inge* in Austria. In 1945, his wife finally filed for divorce. It is not clear, however, if the divorce had been granted by the time Göth was executed.

49. Oral history interview with Ruth Göth. Accession Number: 1995.A.1284.4. RG Number: RG-50.147.0004. Unites States Holocaust Memorial Museum. Time: 49:08–49:34. https://collections.ushmm.org/search/catalog/irn510760.

50. Oral history interview with Ruth Goeth. Accession Number: 1995.A.1284.4. RG Number: RG-50.147.0004. Unites States Holocaust Memorial Museum. Time: 49:08–49:34. https://collections.ushmm.org/search/catalog/irn510760.

51. Helen Horowitz, SCHINDLER. Department of Sound Records. Imperial War Museum. United States Holocaust Memorial Museum. https://collections.ushmm.org/oh_findingaids/RG-50.147.0005_trs_en.pdf

52. Helen Horowitz, SCHINDLER, 3.

53. Jennifer Teege, *My Grandfather Would Have Shot Me: A Black Woman Discovers Her Family's Nazi Past*. With Nikola Sellmair (New York: The Experiment, 2015), 95.

54. Telephone interview with author. March 2, 2017.

55. Thomas Weatherall, *Jus Cogens: International Law and Social Contract* (Cambridge: Cambridge University Press, 2015).

56. United Nations, "Treaty Series No. 251. Agreement for the Prosecution and Punishment of the Major War Criminals of the European Axis," August 8, 1945. http://www.un.org/en/genocideprevention/documents/atrocity-crimes/Doc.2_Charter percent-t20of percent20IMT percent201945.pdf.

57. United Nations, "Treaty Series 251: II Jurisdiction and General Principles," August 8, 1945, 288.

58. Aside from the symbolic value of conducting the trials in the former site of the infamous *Reichsparteitag* spectacles, Nuremberg's court building and accompanying jail

system had remained largely intact and therefore offered the ideal setting. Frederick Taylor, *Exorcising Hitler: The Occupation and Denazification of Germany* (New York: Bloomsbury, 2011), 234.

59. Robert H. Jackson, "Opening Statement before the International Military Tribunal," *Trial of the Major War Criminals before the International Military Tribunal* (Nuremberg: IMT) November 11, 1945, vol. 2, para. 6. https://www.roberthjackson.org /speech-and-writing/opening-statement-before-the-international-military-tribunal/.

60. Randy Barnett and Josh Blackburn, *Constitutional Law: Cases in Context* (New York: Wolters Kluwer, 2017), 592.

61. On September 1, 1949, in an address before the Canadian Bar Association, Jackson offered the following reflection about the Nuremberg Trials: "It is much too early to appraise the influence of Nuremberg. . . . But I do think that we have forever laid to rest in the minds of the statesmen the vicious assumptions that all war must be regarded as legal and just, and that while the law imposes personal responsibility for starting a street riot, it imposes none for inciting and launching a world war." Robert H. Jackson. "Nuremberg in Retrospect: Legal Answer to International Lawlessness." para. 60. Robert H. Jackson Center. https://www.roberthjackson.org/speech-and-writing/nuremberg-in-retrospect-legal-answer-to-international-lawlessness/.

62. Dwight D. Eisenhower, "Letter, General Eisenhower to General Marshall Concerning his Visit to a German Internment Camp near Goth (Ohrdruf)," April 15, 1945. Dwight D. Eisenhower's Pre-Presidential Papers, Principal File, Box 80, Marshall George C. (6): NAID'12005711.

63. Robert H. Jackson, "Opening Statement before the International Military Tribunal," para. 18.

64. "W. Final Statement of Defendant Fischer," *Trials of War Criminals Before the Nuernberg Military Tribunals Under Control Council Law No. 10*. Volume II: The Medical Case. (Washington DC: U.S. Government Printing Office, 1949), 170.

65. Vivien Spitz, *Doctors from Hell: The Horrific Account of Nazi Experiments on Humans* (Boulder, Colorado: Sentient Publications, 2005).

66. Bazyler and Tuerkheimer, *Forgotten Trials of the Holocaust*.

67. Brian Bailey, *Hangmen of England: A History of Execution from Jack Ketch to Albert Pierrepoint* (Lyndhurst, New Jersey: Barnes and Noble, 1994).

68. Anna Merrett and Richard Merrett, *Public Opinion in Semisovereign Germany: the HICOG Surveys, 1949–1955*. (Urbana: University of Illinois Press, 1980).

69. Bazyler and Tuerkheimer, *Forgotten Trials of the Holocaust*, 153.

70. Georg Bönisch, "Amnesie und Amnestie," *Der Spiegel*, February 21, 2006. para. 12.

71. *Trials of War Criminals before the Nuremberg Military Tribunals: The High Command Case and the Hostage Case*. Volume XI (Washington, DC: US Printing Office): 397.

72. Ann Tusa and John Tusa, *The Nuremberg Trial* (New York: Skyhorse Publishing, 2010), 69.

73. Taylor, *Exorcising Hitler*, 273.

74. John Trumpbour, *Selling Hollywood to the World: US and European Struggles for Mastery of the Global Film Industry, 1920–1950* (Cambridge: Cambridge University Press, 2002), 85.

75. Names taken from Justin Kaplan and Anne Bernays, "Names in the Melting Pot," *The Language of Names: What We call Ourselves and Why it Matters* (New York: Simon and Schuster, 1997): 50–64; and the Internet Movie Database IMDb: http//www.imdb.com.

76. Eugon Kogon, "Das Recht auf den politischen Irrtum," *Frankfurter Hefte: Zeitschrift für Kultur und Politik*, July, 1947. Vol. 7. http://www.ikvu.de/fileadmin/u ser_upload/PDF/Eugen_Kogon_Das_Recht_auf_den_politischen_Irrtum_1947.pdf.

77. *Trials of War Criminals*, "XIV: Affirmation of Sentences by the Military Governor of the United States Zone of Occupation," 327.

78. Spitz, *Doctors from Hell*, 271.

79. According to a postwar US governmental report, "Nazis and Axis Collaborators were used to further U.S. Anti-communist Objectives in Europe—Some Immigrated to the United States" US Government Accountability Office.GAO/GGD-85–66 June 28, 1985 (Washington, DC: Comptroller General of the United States), ii.

80. US Government Accountability Office, "Nazis and Axis Collaborators," 10.

81. US Government Accountability Office, "Nazis and Axis Collaborators," 19.

82. Astrid Eckert, *The Struggle for the Files: The Western Allies and the Return of German Archives after the Second World War* (Cambridge: Cambridge University Press, 2004), 22.

83. Eckert, *The Struggle for the Files*, 44.

84. Bundesarchiv, "Berlin Document Center: Hintergründe zu Geschichte und Hauptbeständen," (June 15, 2013). https://www.bundesarchiv.de/DE/Content/Artikel/Ueber-uns/Aus-unserer-Arbeit/berlin-document-center.html.

85. Today, the records form the basis of the German Document Center at the National Archives. Along with the NSDAP membership lists, this collection also includes hundreds of thousands of individual records for members of the SA as well as the SA. There is also a repository with over 1 million pieces of Party correspondence. The information contained in these records is only searchable by personal names.

86. Eckert, *The Struggle for the Files*, 45.

87. Sven Kellerhoff, "Brisante Papier aus dem Müllhaufen," *Die Welt*, (November 2, 2005, para. 12, https://www.welt.de/print-welt/article174881/Brisante-Papiere-aus -dem-Muellhaufen.html.

88. Kellerhoff, "Brisante Papier," para. 9.

89. Stadtarchiv Worms, "N.S. Frauenschaftsmitglieder," Abt. 42 Nr. 917.

90. Stadtarchiv Worms, "Liste der Frauen, die in der NSDAP waren," Abt. 42 Nr. 917.

91. Stadtarchiv Worms, "Gemeinderats- und Kreistagswahlen," July 31, 1948, Abt. 48-N Nr. 375.

92. Stadtarchiv Worms, "Spruchkammer Worms," Abt. 42 Nr. 917.

93. Richard Merrett, *Democracy Imposed: US Occupation Policy and the German Public, 1945–1949* (New Haven, CT: Yale University Press, 1995), 198.

94. Merrett, *Democracy Imposed*, 198.

95. Neil Kritz, ed. *Transitional Justice: How Emerging Democracies Reckon with Former Regimes. Volume III: Laws, Rulings, and Reports*. (Washington, DC: United States Institute of Peace, 1995), 400.

96. Jörg Friedrich, *Die kalte Amnestie: NS-Täter in der Bundesrepublik* (Frankfurt am Main: Fischer Verlag, 1984), 220.

97. The conditional amnesty offered to people living under an assumed name was part of a larger piece of legislation offering residents immunity from criminal prosecution.

98. Fritz Bauer, *Die Humanität der Rechtsordnung: ausgewählte Schriften*, eds. Joachim Perels and Irmtrud Wojak (Frankfurt am Main: Campus Verlag, 1998), 97–101.

99. Norbert Frei, *Vergangenheitspolitik: Die Anfänge der Bundesrepublik und die NS-Vergangenheit* (München: Deutscher Taschenbuch Verlag, 2003): 51.

100. Frei, *Vergangenheitspolitik*, 51.

101. Deutscher Bundestag, Bundesrat, 9. Session, December 9, 1949, http://pdok.bundestag.de.

102. Deutscher Bundestag, Bundesrat, 22. Session, December 9, 1949, http://pdok.bundestag.de.

103. Deutscher Bundestag, Bundesrat, 9. Session, December 9, 1949, http://pdok.bundestag.de.

104. The introduction of the amnesty in Germany was not an international anomaly. By 1957, the British had also released all convicted war criminals who had been held in custody and a year before that, the US American had already released their last German war prisoner. Michael J. Bazyler and Frank Tuerkheimer, *Forgotten Trials of the Holocaust*, 154.

105. Despite the low response among people living under an alias, as a direct result of this amnesty, approximately 500,000 people were released from prison and another 250,000 had their court cases terminated as a direct result of the first amnesty. Volker Zimmerman. *NS-Täter vor Gericht. Düsseldorf und die Strafprozesse wegen nationalsozialistischer Gewaltverbrechen* (Düsseldorf: Justizministerium des Landes NRW, 2001), 36.

106. Manfred Görtemaker and Christoph Safferling, *Die Akte Rosenburg: Das Bundesministerium der Justiz und die NS-Zeit* (Munich: C. H. Beck, 2016), 188.

107. Often referred to today as the "Great Fire of Smyrna," the inferno erupted in September 1922, shortly after Turkish forces wrested control of Izmir from the Greek army. The fire claimed the lives of tens of thousands, with particularly heavy losses in the Greek and Armenian sections of the city. Suspicions still linger today over whether the fire was accidental or a politically motivated act of arson. For more, see Lou Ureneck, *The Great Fire: One American's Mission to Rescue Victims of the 20th Century's first Genocide* (New York: Harper Collins, 2015).

108. The other founding members were Dr. Herwart Mießner, Adolf von Thadden, Dr. Fritz Dorls, and Dr. Heinrich Leuchtgas. For more, see Bundestag, 3. Sitzung, Bonn, Donnerstag, den 15 September 1949, 139. dok.bundestag.de.

109. Frei, *Vergangenheitspolitik*, 41.

110. Deutscher Bundestag, 22 Session, December 9, 1949: 662–63.

111. Deutscher Bundestag, 194 Session, Februarx 20, 1952: 8341.

112. This includes offenders who had committed crimes falling under §211–213 of the German criminal law statutes (i.e., murder, voluntary, or involuntary manslaughter) as well as crimes motivated by cruelty, immorality, or avarice were exempt.

113. Manfred Görtemaker and Christoph Safferling, *Die Akte Rosenburg*, 190.

114. Friedemann Utz, *Preuße, Protestant, Pragmatiker: Der Staatssekretär Walter Strauß und sein Staat*. (Heidelberg: Mohr Siebeck, 2003), 32.

115. Görtemaker and Safferling, *Die Akte Rosenburg*, 94.

116. Görtemaker and Safferling, *Die Akte Rosenburg*, 95.

117. Görtemaker and Safferling, *Die Akte Rosenburg*, 94.

118. Görtemaker and Safferling, *Die Akte Rosenburg*, 94.

119. Utz, *Preuße, Protestant, Pragmatiker*, 51.

120. Utz, *Preuße, Protestant, Pragmatiker*, 355.

121. John Barrett and Jackson, *That Man: An Insider's Portrait of Franklin D. Roosevelt* (Oxford. Oxford University Press, 2004), 170.

122. Barrett and Jackson, *That Man*, 171.

123. Anna Merrett and Richard Merrett, *The HICOG Surveys*, 7.

124. "Der Verbrecher von gestern ist der Held von heute," Fritz Bauer, *Die Humanität der Rechtsordnung: Ausgewählte Schriften*, eds. Joachim Perels and Irmtrud Wojak (Frankfurt am Main: Campus Verlag, 1998), 258.

125. Anna Merrett and Richard Merrett, *The HICOG Surveys*, 184–85.

126. The *Katyn Massacres* is the name given to a series of mass murders conducted by the Soviet Security Services (NKVD) against more than 15,000 Poles in the spring of 1940. The massacres first came to light when German soldiers discovered the makeshift graves of some 4,000 Polish officers outside of the Katyn forest. For more, see: George Sanford, *Katyn and the Soviet Massacre of 1940: Truth, Justice and Memory*. (New York: Routledge, 2009).

127. Merrett and Merrett, *The HICOG Surveys*, 11.

128. Merrett and Merrett, *The HICOG Surveys*, 11.

129. Speech by Dr. Mende (FDP), Deutscher Bundestag, 230 Session, Bonn, Wednesday, September 17, 1954: 10502 http://pdok.bundestag.dem.

CHAPTER 6

Names and Aliases of Male Nazi War Criminals

Dr. Reimer Möller is the Director of the memorial archives of the former Neuengamme Concentration Camp. One day, he was approached by a private citizen with an intriguing offer. According to the Director, the gentleman was in possession of an original document that he offered to donate to the archives. The manuscript was the autobiography of one of the Nazi's most highly decorated U-boat captains, Reinhard Hardegen. In his memoirs, the marine officer offers an intriguing account of his encounter with a very different sort of submarine:

> To the north of the Kaiser Wilhelm Kanal [the Kiel Canal], I was given the responsibility of mustering soldiers from the Wehrmacht. With their discharge papers in hand, the majority of these soldiers went to work on farms and in forests in the surrounding area. One day, I received a call from Friedeburg who ordered me to discharge several individuals who would appear in my office on the following day. The eight or nine men were supposedly sailors whose vessel had gone under. According to my orders, I was not to enter these men on the discharge lists. The next day, the men appeared in my office in pristine uniforms and with brand-new military paybooks. The men told me that they had been on a minesweeper that had sunk. Incredulous, I retorted: "You all never spent a single day in the navy or the marines!" But, it was all the same to me. I discharged them because I had been ordered to do so. That was my undoing. When they were arrested, it was my signature that appeared on their discharge papers. It turns out the men were high-ranking SS-generals and other henchmen. When I was later imprisoned in the Neumünster Camp, the man whom I believe was the very last Commandant of the Neuengamme Concentration Camp[1] came to me and gave me his official indictment papers. Because he could not read English, he asked me to translate them. He said: "I know you. You were the one who dis-

charged me!" While translating his paperwork, I read what the man had been charged with. Among other things, he was accused of having had 27 people either hanged or shot. He vehemently refuted the allegations: "It could not have been more than 19!" I gave him back the papers and said: "You're on your own." The man was later executed. If my memory serves me correctly, Höß, the Commandant of Auschwitz, was also among that group of men whom I discharged.[2]

A cross-check of this account with Höß's own postwar autobiography reveals considerable agreement between the two. As the Reich began to crumble, Höß reports that he, along with several other high-ranking officers and their families, made their way north, where the Reichsführer of the SS, Heinrich Himmler, had retreated. Along the way, the group received word that Berlin was lost and Hitler was dead. The new provisional seat of government was now the Harbor city of Flensburg under the newly appointed Reichspräsident, Grand Admiral Karl Dönitz. On May 3 and 4, Himmler met with Höß and his comrades to give his final orders. According to Höß, the meeting was nothing like they had anticipated. Rather than a disconsolate leader who told them that the time had come for them to put their lives to an end, the oddly jubilant Reichsführer gave his men entirely different instructions:

"'Disguise yourselves as members of the Wehrmacht!' That was the final farewell from the man whom I had so admired, in whom I had had unshakeable faith, whose orders and opinions had been gospel to me."[3] Despite their profound dismay, Höß and his comrades followed Himmler's orders to varying degrees of success.

Precisely as Hardeger described in his memoirs, clandestine arrangements were made to provide the officers with the necessary identification papers such as the military paybooks. SS-Gruppenführer and Head of the NS Concentration Camp Inspectorate, Richard Glücks, was issued a new name and brought to the naval hospital in Flensburg-Murwik to recover from his injuries and state of shock. Less than a week later, however, he had committed suicide. According to Höß, a similar fate awaited Dr. Enno Lolling, the former chief physician of the Concentration Camp Inspectorate. After being transferred to a military hospital in Flensburg under an alias, Lolling also committed suicide on or about May 27, 1945. Höß hoped his fate would be different.

Under the alias *Petty Officer Frank Lang*, the Obersturmbannführer successfully passed through all of the security checks posted by the British forces after the war. He maintained clandestine contact with his wife and secured work on a farm located on the outskirts of Flensburg. Höß remained undercover there for about eight months, until March 11, 1946, when his true identity was finally discovered. Höß was placed under arrest, put on trial, and executed on April 16, 1947.[4] The Obersturmbannführer's highly publicized capture was seen as tangible evidence that Churchill, Roosevelt, and Stalin were intent on fulfilling their 1945 Yalta

Conference pledge to "bring all war criminals to just and swift punishment and exact reparation in kind for the destruction wrought be the Germans."[5]

During the follow-up conference held in Potsdam from July 17 to August 2, 1945, the three heads of government reiterated their resolve to "destroy the National Socialist Party and its affiliated and supervised organizations"; abolish "all Nazi laws which provided the basis of the Hitler regime or established discriminations on grounds of care, creed, or political opinion"; and bring to justice "war criminals and those who have participated in planning or carrying out Nazi enterprises involving or resulting in atrocities or war crimes."[6] Those pledges were easier said than done. By the time the Allies had been able to establish firm control over the former Reich, many of the war criminals had gone deeply underground with new names and new identities.

As a group, fugitive NS offenders demonstrated a great deal of variation in the aliases they employed. While some used only one false name to disguise their identity, others relied upon such a large number of aliases that the academic and legal enforcement communities are still trying to navigate the onomastic labyrinth. Oftentimes, the fugitives had little or no control of their choice of alias. This was particularly the case immediately after the war when the easiest route to a false identity was to steal or illegally purchase the real identity of another person. The identification papers of fallen or missing soldiers was a popular source. Over time, as the postwar infrastructure improved, stolen identities became more of a liability and high-quality synthetic identities became more preferred. Some NS criminals even returned to their original birth names after the statute of limitations had made their arrest and prosecution either highly or completely unlikely. Taken all together the aliases examined during the course of this research displayed a startling degree of heterogeneity. At the same time, careful comparison did reveal a few, strong linguistic patterns.

The most radical strategy involved the adoption of an alias that was completely different than the fugitive's original birth name. The discovery of this pattern is not surprising as it offered maximum camouflage. Among the NS war criminals identified used this method was SS Hauptsturmführer *Alexander Riesle*. During the war, Riesle participated in the Massacre of Babij Jar[7] where more than 33,000 Jewish men, women, and children in the Ukraine were murdered in a thirty-six-hour frenzy.[8] After the war, Riesle became *Bernd Claasen*, the manager of a small-scale taxi company. Another war criminal who entirely changed his name was SS Obersturmführer *Herbert Andorfer*. The former Commandant of the Sajmiste Concentration Camp in Belgrade, Andorfer oversaw the murder of Jewish prisoners via gas-filled trucks. By 1946, he had secured a passport with the name *Hans Meyer* and immigrated to South America.[9] And then there was NSDAP district leader, *Erich Koch*. Before finally being captured, tried, and found guilty of being an accessory to the murder of 400,000 Poles, he spent nearly fifteen years as a free man under the alias of *Rolf Berger*.[10] Table 6.1 offers many other examples of fugitive Nazis who adopted aliases that were completely different than their birthnames.

One might assume that this strategy was the best, most logical, choice. However, this subterfuge came with a number of formidable obstacles. First and foremost was the immediate challenge involved in obtaining entirely new, high-quality, documents with the desired names for not only oneself but also one's family members. Given the high demand and limited supply, this documentation was neither easy to find nor inexpensive to purchase. Added to these logistical and financial challenges was the exceedingly robust psychological attachment many people have to their birthnames. The strength of this tie might help to explain why some NS offenders either consciously or unconsciously retained the initials of their original name in their aliases (e.g., *Hartmut Pulmer* → *Hans Petersen*; *Karl Heller* → *Kurt Hanz*).

This combination of pragmatic and psychological factors might also help to explain why some Nazi war criminals borrowed from the store of family members' names to re-invent themselves. An example here is SS Untersturmführer *Anton Streitwieser*. During his time as a concentration camp guard in Dachau (1934), Sachsenhausen (1936) and Mauthausen (1938), "Handsome Toni" [der schöne Toni] had amassed a long list of gruesome crimes, including his penchant for commanding his beloved German shepherd *Hasso* to maul camp prisoners to death. After the war, the fugitive took his wife's maiden name *Krug* to form his alias *Klaus Werner Krug*. By the time authorities determined what his real name and identity were, he had spent twenty-two years as a free man.

Despite the role that Streitwieser had played in the misery and murder of thousands of Holocaust victims, the media attention given to the discovery of his final whereabouts on October 30, 1967 was meager in comparison to an earlier case. Although three years had passed since that arrest, the fallout of that explosive case was still being felt. Even today, over six decades later, the case still triggers public outrage, particularly in Northern Germany where the fugitive lived and worked in plain view for decades. In this case, it was not a clever alias that explained this war criminal's getaway but the systematic willingness of community leaders to hide the killer's names and crimes. His story begins with a doctor's visit.

*

It had only taken a few sessions, but the therapist was already fairly sure of his diagnosis.[11] The symptoms displayed by the middle-aged wife and mother of two were not due to some underlying physiological disease but rather a deep-seated nervous disorder that seemed to have its origins in an unresolved, psychological conflict. The woman's husband would have to be informed of course. This part of the therapy was never easy, given all of the prejudices the general public still held about mental illness. The husband might prove to be resistant. Despite his obvious intelligence, there was something off-putting about this bullish looking

Table 6.1   Alias Formation Strategy 1:
            Alias Completely Different than NS Criminals' Birth Name

	BIRTH NAME	ALIAS
1.	Herbert Andorfer	Hans Meyer
2.	Johann Paulus Appler	Saleh Shafar
3.	Richard Baer	Karl Neumann
4.	Gerhard Bast	Franz Geyer
5.	Otto Bradfisch	Karl Evers
6.	Anton Burger	Wilhelm Bauer
7.	Theodor Christensen	Fritz Ramm
8.	Otto Adolf Eichmann	Riccardo Klement
9.	Hans Fischböck	Jakob Schramm
10.	Claus Peter Volkmann	Peter Grubbe
11.	Wilhelm Heinrich Fortenbacher	Walter Schwenger
12.	Anton Hafferl	Heinrich Hartmann
13.	Karl Hass	Rudolfo Giustini
14.	Berthold Heilig	Hans Richwitz
15.	Karl Heller	Kurt Hanz
16.	Otto Hellmuth	Hans Oster
17.	Werner Heyde	Fritz Sawade
18.	Aribert Ferdinand Heim	Tarek Hussein Farid
19.	Rudolf Franz Ferndinand Höß	Franz Lang
20.	Gustav Jürges	Frederico Pahl
21.	Søren Kamm	Peter Müller
22.	Robert Karrasch	Karl Schedereit
23.	Friedrich Katzmann	Bruno Albrecht
24.	Erich Koch	Rolf Berger
25.	Hans Wilhelm König	Dr. Ernst Pelz
26.	Robert Ley	Dr. Ernst Distelmeyer
27.	Julius Levy	Jaac Van Harten
28.	Josef Mengele	Helmut Gregor Fritz Hollmann
29.	Wilhelm Bruno Meiert	Ulrich Herbert Schlichting Grevner
30.	August Moritz	Ralf Müller
31.	Erich Müller	Francesco Noelke
32.	Rudolf Oebsger-Röder	O.G. Röder

(Continued)

Table 6.1   (continued)

	BIRTH NAME	ALIAS
33.	Erich Priebke	Otto Pape
34.	Hartmut Pulmer	Hans Petersen
35.	Alexander Riesle	Bernd Claasen
36.	Eduard Roschmann	Frederico Wegner Fritz Wegner
37.	Fritz Rößler	Dr. Franz Richter
38.	Hans-Ulrich Rudel	Jose Pedro Mattels
39.	Hans-Ulrich Rudel	Hans Meier
40.	Karl Schedereit	Robert Karrasch
41.	Baldur Benedikt von Schirach	Richard Falk
42.	Friedrich Schwend	Venceslav Turi
43.	Franz Alfred Six	Georg Becker
44.	Reinhard Nikolaus Karl Spitzy	Andres Martinez Lopez
45.	Anton Streitwieser	Klaus Werner Krug
46.	Fritz Suhren	Herbert Pakusch
47.	Kurt Waldemar Tank	Dr. Pedro Matthies
48.	Max Thomas	Dr. Karl Brandenburg
49.	Günther Karl August Venediger	Paul August Schaller Nieder
50.	Robert Jan Verbelen	Peter Mayer Alfred Schwab
51.	Horst Wagner	Peter Ludwig
52.	Gerhard Wenzel	Martin Rhodus
53.	Heinrich Wessel	Werner Bierbaum
54.	Hellmuth Willich	Kurt Krause
55.	Paul Zapp	Friedrich Böhm
56.	Eugon Zill	Willi Sonntag

man.[12] His was a strange mixture of clawing ingratiation with that unpleasant whiff of condescension. The therapist resolved to pay particular attention to the husband's reactions when he explained his initial diagnosis.

During the next scheduled session, Dr. Glatzel decided to pose a provocative question and monitor the pair's reaction: Could it be that Frau Sawade's condition might be explained in part by some underlying marital strife? Much to his surprise, the husband not only enthusiastically agreed with the therapist's conjecture but went on to proffer his own thoughts on the possible psychogenic origin of his spouse's adjustment disorder. Completely taken aback by the patient's astounding understanding of psychology and medicine, the therapist asked his patient to explain himself. Triumphantly, the husband declared: "The source of the problem is me. I am not who I appear to be." With that *Dr. Sawade* revealed his true identity: Professor Dr. Werner Heyde, the "Lunatic Murderer" (Irrentöter).

From the very beginning, young Werner seemed predestined to leave his mark on the world. After graduating at the very top of his high school class, the son of a textile manufacturer decided against following in his father's footsteps as was the tradition at the time. Instead, he chose a career that would take him far away from the family home in eastern Germany. What Heyde may have lacked in family connections, he more than made up for with intelligence and cunning. With prodigal speed, he successfully completed his university studies and was awarded his doctorate at the age of twenty-three. Approximately a year later, he earned his medical license and landed a lecturer position at the University of Würzburg. From there, he procured a post as a ward physician in Würzburg's Clinic for Psychiatry and Neurology. By 1932, he had earned the highest German academic degree, the "Habilitation," and was given a professorship for Psychiatry and Neurology at the University of Würzburg. Now Professor Dr. med. habil., Heyde's duties expanded to include providing detailed patient evaluations at the Würzburg Clinic.[13]

During Heyde's tenure (1930–1934), the Clinic made quite a name for itself in the burgeoning field of psychiatric assessment. It was that reputation which no doubt helps to explain the sudden arrival of a man who would later prove to be one the Clinic's most infamous patients: SS officer Theodor Eicke. Eicke had been remanded to the Clinic for psychiatric observation after being charged with and convicted for illegally constructing approximately eighty homemade pipe bombs.[14] According to the court records, Eicke admitted to building and stockpiling the explosives with other members of the SS, but stressed that their motivation was not to endanger but protect the public from violent social democrats and communists. How exactly pipe bombs would keep the peace is difficult to imagine. However, it seems the court at the time found the SS officer's explanation at least partially convincing. Eicke was remanded into protective custody on March 7, 1932 to await formal sentencing. In mid-July, his sentence was formally passed. He was to serve time in prison.

In an act of desperate legal maneuvering, Eicke sent a letter to the court explaining that he was in no fit state to serve jail time. His prolonged stay in protective custody had resulted in a severe nervous disorder. Accompanying Eicke's letter was a medical report issued by a Dr. Raush who confirmed that Eicke was on the brink of a prison-induced psychosis.[15] Rather than sparing himself further public indignity, this maneuver had precisely the opposite effect. It laid the foundation for Eicke's committal to the University of Würzburg's Clinic for Psychiatry and Neurology for prolonged observation and assessment. During the NS reign, this turn of events might well have meant the figurative and literal death of Eicke had it not been for the intervention of a very powerful mentor. For reasons that remain the source of historical speculation, none other than Reichsführer Heinrich Himmler himself had taken a strange liking to Theodor Eicke.

Much to Eicke's relief and Himmler's satisfaction, Professor Heyde issued a series of extremely positive assessments about Patient Number 1098's model comportment in the clinic. In an April 1933 letter sent directly to the Reichsführer, the doctor wrote that "Herr E. has manifested no sign whatsoever of a psychological or neurological illness. Nor was there any evidence of an abnormal personality disorder that might be indicative of an underlying psychopathy. In fact," the doctor added, "the patient demonstrated exemplary comportment and had only pleasantly distinguished himself through his quiet, controlled manner."[16] In response to a formal inquiry by governmental authorities in Ludwigshafen as follow-up to Eicke's impending court case, the physician once again stated that even the most detailed examination and observation had failed to reveal any evidence of mental disorder. Indeed, in Professor Heyde's considered opinion, from a medical standpoint, there was no reason at all for the patient to remain in a psychiatric clinic or convalescent home.[17]

It is not possible to determine to what extent the then thirty-one-year-old doctor may have been influenced by Eicke or his powerful connections while writing these assessments. However, in view of Eicke's future position, one could argue that the young psychiatrist had been correct in asserting that the SS officer had _exactly_ the psychological constitution necessary for the role Himmler had envisioned for him. Some three months after his discharge from the clinic, SS-Obergruppenführer Eicke became Commandant of the Dachau Concentration Camp.[18]From there, he went on to become the Chief Inspector of the Reich's Concentration Camp system[19] and the Head of the SS-Death Head Units. Upon his departure from the clinic, Eicke encouraged his psychiatric-benefactor to consider making a career within the NSDAP. The Party had many exciting opportunities for a young man with his skill set. Heyde apparently followed Eicke's advice and in May 1933 became an official member of both the NSDAP (Number: 3, 068, 165) and the NS Association of Physicians.[20] With that step and Eicke's endorsement, Heyde's career went from fast to meteoric. In 1935, he was appointed the district director for Würzburg's Department of Race Policy and the Hereditary Health Court. Within this capacity, he was chiefly responsible for selecting suitable candidates for the government's sterilization program.[21] In 1938, he was chosen to lead a division on the SS-Medical Corps (SS-Sanitätsamt). In 1939, he was named the Director of the Würzburg University's Clinic for Psychiatry and Neurology.[22] At the same time, he served as a medical evaluator on behalf of the Gestapo and assisted in the selection of patients and prisoners for medical experimentation[23]. This cumulative professional profile made the professor a perfect choice for a new top-secret project that was being initiated by the Chancellery of the Führer (Kanzlei des Führers) or KdF.

In August 1939, Heyde was invited to join an exclusive circle of physicians, lawyers, and politicians who had been chosen to design and implement an innovative, aggressive eugenics plan for the entire Reich. With the assistance of the hand-selected set of experts, the Reich planned to move beyond compulsory sterilization and castration, and allow the systematic extermination of persons deemed unworthy of living. Though radical, this idea was nothing new. Since the Weimar Republic, the idea had been hotly debated in medical and judicial circles.[24] In scientific conferences such as the International Eugenics Congress hundreds of delegates from Belgium, Denmark, England, France, Germany, Italy, Japan, Norway, Spain, and the United States converged to discuss strategies for persuading governments to support their plans with funding and legislation.[25] Around the world, powerful forces were being gathered. To protect the social order, they argued, bold steps were required. One supporter of this view was Supreme Court Justice Oliver Wendell Holmes. In delivering the majority decision which upheld the constitutionality of compulsory sterilization in an 8 to 1 decision, he made the following argument:

> We have seen more than once that the public welfare may call upon the best citizens for their lives. It would be strange if it could not call upon those who already sap the strength of the State for these lesser sacrifices, often not felt to be such by those concerned, in order to prevent our being swamped with incompetence. It is better for all the world, if instead of waiting to execute degenerate offspring for crime, or let them starve for their imbecility, society can prevent those who are manifestly unfit from continuing their kind. . . . Three generations of imbeciles are enough.[26]

At the time of this landmark decision, advocates of the eugenics movement in Germany could only dream of receiving such powerful institutional support. Admittedly, the Germans were highly regarded for their philosophical treatises examining the ethics surrounding eugenics. However, in comparison to many other nations around the world, Germany lagged far behind in putting theory into practice. That is until the National Socialists came to power. Suddenly, concrete steps were being taken to put those theories into practice.[27] The KdF had developed a revolutionary plan to help put Germany at the head of the international eugenics race.[28] The institutional home selected for the operation was a luxurious West Berlin villa that had been seized in 1934 from the Jewish industrialist Georg Liebermann, brother of the world-famous German impressionist painter Max Liebermann.[29] The postal address of the villa, Tiergartenstrasse 4, served as onomastic inspiration for the KdF operation, "Aktion T4."[30] Officially, however, the program was known under a different, more formal, academic-sounding name that would inspire trust among both the lay and scientific community:[31] *Reichsarbeitsgemeinschaft Heil und Pflegeanstalten* [Reich's Working Group of Sanatoriums and Convalescence Clinics]. On the surface, the purpose of this working conglomerate was to identify persons most in need of state-of-the-art healthcare. In reality, the group was designed to do precisely the opposite.

The legal foundation for the clandestine T4 operation came in the form of several key ministerial decrees. One of the first and most important was the September 1, 1939 directive issued by the Führer himself. In this directive, Hitler empowered his personal physician, Dr. Karl Brandt, along with the KdF leader Philipp Bouhler to authorize a selection of physicians to end the lives of the incurably ill.[32] A second decree was issued a month later, on October 9, 1939. With this edict, all medical facilities were required to complete and return detailed questionnaires on all of their patients. The surveys required information pertaining to not only the patients' medical history and prognoses, but also an array of biographical details (e.g., names, gender, marital status, address, employment history, military service record, date of birth, nationality, race, religion).[33] Once returned, the completed forms were copied and sent to three separate T4 consulting evaluators or *Gutachter* who independently of one another assessed whether the patient should be selected for "special treatment."

To maximize the speed of the assessment process, the evaluators used a color-coded system of elementary signs to indicate their decision. A plus-sign marked in red was used if the candidate was recommended for the program; a blue negative-sign if the candidate was rejected; and a blue question mark if the evaluator was undecided. In cases where there was strong disagreement between the initial three consultants, a fourth medical expert was consulted. The decision of this senior evaluator or *Obergutachter* was final. While a cadre of approximately fifty physicians served as consultants, for the first round of decisions, there were less than five official *Obergutachter*. Between May 1940 and December 1941, one of them was Professor Dr. Werner Heyde.[34]

The files of patients selected for the T4 program were then sent to the T4 ambulance transport service known under another deceptively benign name: *Gemeinnützige Krankentransport* [the charitable ambulance transport for the sick and infirmed] or *Gekrat* for short. Using a fleet of grey buses, the Gekrat personnel then picked up and delivered their charges to one of six different killing centers located throughout Germany: Bernberg; Brandenburg/Havel; Grafeneck; Hadamar/Limburg; Hartheim/Linz; Sonnenstein/Pirna. The procedure followed by the local T4 staff once the Gekrat buses arrived was largely invariant. The patients were stripped naked and sent for a last cursory medical examination to identify any potentially interesting features (e.g., gold fillings or unusual physical or psychiatric anomalies of potential scientific interest). They were then photographed from the front, the left, and the right. Once this initial processing was complete, the patients were taken to the basement where large rooms made to look like shower facilities had been erected. Patients who were unable to walk themselves were carried into the room on gurneys and told to wait for further assistance.

As soon as the room was filled to capacity, the attending physician was called in to man the gas valves. Depending on the number of patients in the room, the "kill time" varied. The presence of a peephole made it easier for the physician to check on the progress. Once all of the patients had been murdered, the attendants removed any valuable prostheses and/or organs of interest. The victims were then cremated and a name list of the "disinfected" was sent by the Gekrat officials to the T4 central administration in Berlin. The entire killing procedure, from arrival to cremation, was generally accomplished within the space of a single day.[35]

According to testimony provided by a former T4 administrator in the central Berlin office, once the name lists were received from the various killing centers, the relevant patient files were stamped with the letter code of the relevant killing center and then stored in the basement with the other so-called "plus files" or "disinfection files."[36] In the meantime, the relatives of the murdered were notified in pre-fabricated official condolence letters with fictitious causes of death. Each letter was signed with a pseudonym for each one of the T4 staff members. In 1969 court testimony given by Gerhard S., a former T4 employee at the Grafeneck killing center, to hide their real identities he and his colleagues regularly used different pseudonyms which they rotated depending on the type of letter they needed to send. In correspondence pertaining to the transport of patients' ashes, Gerhard S. used the pseudonym *Police Captain Keil* [Polizeihauptmann Keil]. When sending condolence letters, he used the name *Dr. Ott*; and for generic administration, the name *Dr. Zorn* [Dr. Anger].[37]

The top-ranking KdF officials also routinely used pseudonyms when dealing with T4 matters. Dr. Viktor Brack and Werner Blankenberg, for example, used the code names *Jennerwein* and *Brenner*, respectively. The T4 physicians were also expected to conceal their true identities with a fixed set of aliases. For example, Dr. Aquilin Ullrich, who worked at the Brandenburg an der Havel killing center, regularly used the remarkably unremarkable alias *Dr. Schmitt* when signing T4 forms. By comparison, his Brandenburg colleague, Dr. Heinrich Bunke, used the pseudonyms *Dr. Keller* (Dr. Cellar)[38]—a chilling choice considering the fact that the patients he assisted in murdering were killed in the basement of the clinic where he worked. Even those officials responsible for the transport of the patients to and from the killing centers devised aliases. The secret name for Reinhold Vorberg, one of the Gekrat directors, was based on

**Table 6.2   Cryptic Pseudonyms Routinely Used by T4 Employees
in the Nazi Killing Centers**

KILLING CENTER(S)	T4 EMPLOYEE	PSEUDONYM
Grafeneck, Hadamar	Ernst Baumhard	Dr. Jäger, Dr. Moos
Hadamar	Friedrich Berner	Dr. Barth
Sonnenstein, Bernberg	Kurt Borm	Dr. Storm
Brandenburg, Bernberg	Heinrich Bunke	Dr. Rieper, Dr. Keller
Brandenburg, Bernberg	Irmfried Eberl	Dr. Schneider, Dr. Meyer
Sonnenstein	Klaus Endruweit	Dr. Bader
Hadamar	Hans-Bodo Gorgaß	Dr. Kramer
Grafeneck, Hadamar	Günther Hennecke	Dr. Fleck
Grafeneck, Bernburg	Hermann Holzschuh	Herr Lemm, Herr Boden
Sonnenstein	Curt Schmalenbach	Dr. Palm
Grafeneck, Sonnenstein	Horst Schumann	Dr. Klein, Dr. Blume
Brandenburg	Aquilin Ulrich	Dr. Schmitt
Director of Gekrat	Reinhold Vorberg	Hintertal
Sonnenstein	Ewald Wortmann	Dr. Friede
Grafeneck	Jacob Wögers	Haase

a wordplay of his real surname: [Vor + berg] or 'before' + 'mountain' became
[Hinter + tal] 'behind' + 'meadow.' In table 6.2, just a few of the aliases used by
T4 employees are provided:[39]

Through this system of onomastic subterfuge, in theory, T4 personnel could
identify the person behind the alias, but outsiders were at a loss. In practice, however,
the fact that pseudonyms were strongly recommended but not strictly enforced led
to irregular usage. On January 17, 1947, Viktor Back testified that Philipp Bouhler
had initially insisted that he and his assistants use pseudonyms. However, Brack
reportedly found this practice embarrassingly silly and simply stopped using his assigned alias after a time. Two of his assistants reportedly did the same.[40]

On August 6, 1948, Hermann Holzschuh, a detective at the Stuttgart Police
Department, provided a detailed written statement for the office of the prosecuting attorney in Tübingen about his T4 work. Holzschuh was one of eight
employees to stand trial for the T4 crimes committed at the Grafeneck Killing
Center. During his time there, Holzschuh served as the assistant director and
then director of the center's internal registry office. His duties included overse-
ing the production and distribution of the murdered patients' death certificates
and family condolence letters. He was therefore exceedingly familiar with the
system of aliases used by the T4 staff.

> When they signed the letters of condolences to be sent to the pa-
> tients' families, the doctors used false names like Dr. Keller [Dr.
> Cellar], Dr. Keim [Dr. Pathogen], and Dr. Jäger [Dr. Hunter]. The
> cover names changed. . . . I asked Dr. Bohne for a transfer because
> I suspected that the goings on were not above-board and because I
> preferred to serve as a soldier than an office worker. . . . Bohne told
> me that the only way out of this place was a concentration camp.
> I then told him that I no longer wanted to sign my good name on
> these certificates. His answer was that I should sign with another
> name. I later received that answer once again in the form of written
> order.[41]

Like Brack, Holzschuh also observed considerable inconsistency in the use of the
T4 pseudonyms. Some of the employees used them, some of them did not. Some
of them used the same names, others preferred to mix and mingle. Although
Schuhholz indicated in his statement that he repeatedly expressed grave concerns
over the legality of the serial mass murder taking place in the clinic, in his own
words, his only concern was protecting his "good name." The idea of offering
protection to the disabled patients being gassed in conveyor-belt fashion did not
seem to occur to him at all.[42]

Even when the T4 staff and affiliates did use their aliases consistently,
there was always the possibility that a chance meeting could blow their cover.
In an anecdote related by Joseph T. during the Nuremberg Medical Trials,
a delegation of camp officials was giving a professor from the University of
Vienna a tour of the Dachau Concentration Camp facilities. To protect the
doctor's identity, the Dachau staff was careful to only refer to the physician
using his alias, *Professor Lebersdorfer*. While walking among the prisoners
during the inspection of their quarters, the professor was startled to hear his
real name being called. One of the prisoners was a former medical student at
the University of Vienna. Realizing that there was no use in keeping up the
pretense, the physician, whose real name was Professor Eppinger, stopped
briefly to speak with his one-time protégé.[43] Eppinger's pseudonym of *Lebersdorfer* was no doubt inspired by his research. The Prague-born physician
had written a reference that was broadly considered standard reading for
internal medicine: *Diseases of the Liver* [Die **Leber**krankheiten] The German word for "liver" is "leber."[44] Despite such unforeseen complications, the
overall design and operation of the programs were devastatingly effective.
Hundreds of people were being killed every week. Today, it is estimated
that the T4 operation was responsible for the murder of over 1 million disabled people.

The proven speed, scale, and efficiency of the T4 killing protocol was due in no small measure to the designers' application of the scientific method right down to the utilization of pre-tests to compare and contrast alternative murder methods in real-time under authentic conditions. In preparation for the scheduled killings, two KdF officials requested a meeting with Dr. Heess, the director of the Chemical Division at the Reich's Police Department. As Dr. Heess was absent on that day, his colleague, Dr. Albert Widmann, took the meeting in his stead. According to Widmann, in the closed-door conference, the following conversation took place:

> KdF official: "Widmann, would it be possible for the Criminal Science Institute to procure poison in large amounts?"
>
> Dr. Widmann: "What for? To kill people?"
>
> KdF Official: "No."
>
> Dr. Widmann: "To kill animals then?"
>
> KdF Official: "No."
>
> Dr. Widmann: "Well excuse me, but what precisely would the poison be used for?"
>
> KdF Official: "To kill animals in human form . . . the mentally ill."[45]

According to Dr. Widmann, the men then went on to discuss which poisons should be used to achieve that purpose. Carbon monoxide, morphine, scopolamine, and cyanide were all mentioned.[46] In the end, it was decided that a mixture of all these chemicals would be best as it would assure 100 percent lethality. After this decision was made, orders were placed for the desired poisons and the green light was given to begin the first live trials.

According to testimony given by T4 officials captured and interrogated after the war, in either December 1939 or January 1940, an experiment was run to determine whether gassing or lethal injection yielded the best results (i.e., the highest lethality rates at the lowest financial and personnel costs). To answer the question, two small groups of about eight victims were assembled at the Brandenburg facility for the pilot study. While one group was given an intravenous cocktail of scopolamine, curare, and cyanide; the other group was placed in a small room where the oxygen was gradually replaced with carbon monoxide. Through a peephole, the T4 officials could observe and compare the entire death process. At the end of the experiment, it was decided that in view of the number of people to be eliminated, gassing was by far the most preferable method.[47] Reportedly present during this experiment were Professor Hallervorden, Dr. Renno, and Professor Dr. Heyde.[48]

Using this killing protocol, during Heyde's T4 tenure, approximately 70,000 patients were murdered between January 1940 and August 1941. In addition, in the spring of 1941, Professor Dr. Heyde and other T4 physicians such as Paul Nitsche and Friedrich Mennecke began to tour the various concentration camps (e.g., Sachsenhausen, Buchenwald, Mauthausen, Ravensbrück, Flossenburg, Neuengamme, and Auschwitz) to select prisoners for "disinfection."[49] This expanded program was commonly referred to with the alphanumeric code "14f13."[50] In an affidavit used by the prosecution during the Nuremberg Medical Trials, a Dr. Julius Muthig, concentration camp physician at Dachau and Neuengamme, gave the following description of a prisoner selection he personally witnessed:

> In the fall of 1941 he was informed by Dr. LOLLING that a commission of 4 physicians under Prof. HEYDE would visit Dachau to select prisoners who were unable to work for euthanasia and transfer to Mauthausen for gassing. 4 physicians came shortly after and in a few days examined many hundred prisoners—Jews, German nationals and citizens of other nations. . . . In December 1941 the first transport of prisoners selected by this commission (several hundred) left for Mauthausen and another in January 1942.[51] (emphasis in the original)

In recognition of the professor's contributions to the selection and extermination program, the operation in Dachau was also sometimes referred to by the honorific name *Aktion Heyde*.[52] Through this expanded selection, it is estimated that an additional 15,000 to 20,000 people were gassed in killing centers located in Bernburg, Hartheim, and Sonnenstein/Pirna.[53]

For some T4 physicians, their lethal prolificacy could be explained with a deep-seated satisfaction with being allowed to perform their duty for their Vaterland. For others, the sadistic pleasure of having control over life and death seems to have been the primary motivation. And for still others, there was a much more banal reason to work as quickly as possible. There was money to be made. For assessing 500 cases in a month's time, a T4 physician would receive 100 Reichsmarks. For those who managed to evaluate over 3,500 or more cases, a payment of 400 RM.[54] Such monthly quotas would seem to be impossible to reach until one remembers that the assessments consisted of little more than placing a "+," "-," or a "?" on a form.[55] Eventually, the number of deaths occurring in what were supposed to have been state-of-the-art treatment facilities became suspicious.

This growing incredulity is evident in a 1940 letter addressed to a Mrs. M. Blass, the district leader of the NSDAP Women's Organization in Düsseldorf.[56] In it, the NSDAP representative from the town of Rheydt writes of the need for "clarity and light to be shown in a dark set of events surrounding the Grafeneck Clinic." According to Frau Blass, the mounting number of deaths had led to disconcerting rumors. Many townspeople had even begun to refer to the sanatorium with the nickname *Grafeneck Murder Asylum* [Mordanstalt Grafeneck].

There was even some concern, the writer continued, that all these deaths had been ordered by the government. To allay these fears, Mrs. Blass stressed that it was imperative that certain questions be immediately answered: (1) *What epidemic* was it that had been isolated at the *Grafeneck Clinic*?; (2) *How long* had this *epidemic* waged in the clinic? (3) Who was responsible for *transferring patients* to this clinic?; (4) Who was responsible for *sending notifications* to the patients' relatives?; and (5) Who was responsible for storing and returning the *belongings* of the deceased? [emphasis in the original].[57]

To give additional weight to these concerns, the Rheydt representative went on to detail what she described as an "appalling" case concerning the local pharmacist's wife, Frau C. According to the representative, not only had the woman been transferred from a normal clinic in Weisenau to the specialist clinic in Grafeneck without any compelling medical reason or the prior knowledge of her husband. It seems that Frau C. had also been cremated without the family's permission and none of her belongings had been returned, including two rather valuable rings that Frau C. reportedly never took off.[58] Clearly, as this letter shows, despite the best efforts of the T4 staff to conceal the goings-on, telling "mistakes" were being made, uncomfortable questions were being asked, and information was being leaked. Just how much the public had been able to piece together is chillingly revealed in another letter, this time sent by Arthur Ungewitter, the President of the Regional Court in Frankfurt, to the Reich's Minister of Justice, Franz Schlegelberger,[59] on May 16, 1941. Marked "secret," the Justice describes the talk about town in reaction to the daily business at the Hadamar "Clinic":[60]

> The vehicles with which the infirmed are transported from their original clinics to intermediary clinics and then on to liquidation clinics are well known in the general public. As I have been told, the children have already begun to call out: "Look, they're also gonna be gassed!" Between one to three buses with curtained windows are reputed to travel on a daily basis from Weilmünster to Hadamar. Once there, it is rumored that the newcomers are immediately made to strip naked. They are then given a paper tunic and directly sent to a chamber where they are gassed with hydrocyanic acid. The bodies are then sent to the crematorium in assembly-line fashion and burned 6-deep in an oven. The resulting ash is then divided between six different urns that are sent to the relatives. . . . It is also said that in some cases, the heads and other body parts are removed for anatomical investigation.[61]

After providing this graphic account, Ungewitter goes on to explain that one of the primary sources of these "stories" was none other than the Hadamar employees themselves, who after a long day's work, had developed a penchant for drinking conspicuously large volumes of alcohol in their neighborhood pubs. Although there were (and still are) a few who staunchly dismissed these accounts, for an increasingly large segment of the population, it was more than clear what was really going on in these "special" convalescent homes. Fear began to spread. If a person could be exterminated for being born disabled, what about those who became disabled through injury or illness such as war veterans and senior citizens. Calls to put an end to the state-sponsored murder of Christians began to spread.

Particularly effective were the now famous series of sermons held by Bishop Clemens August Graf von Galen on August 3, 1941, in the St. Lambert Church in Münster. An ardent opponent of the NSDAP since the 1930s, his call to protest was widely reproduced in pamphlets circulated throughout Germany and abroad.[62] Three weeks to the day after his second protest sermon in the St. Lambert Church in Münster, Hitler ordered an official stop to Aktion T4. Some of the T4 staff remained employees in the clinics and continued their activities, only with de-centralized killing schedules.[63] Many other T4 staff members moved on to take on new, challenging, positions in Eastern Europe, where the Reich was steadily erecting a chain of monolithic "special" facilties: Belzec, Sobibór, and Treblinka.[64] Curiously, neither of these options appeared open to the once seemingly omnipotent and ever present, senior T4 official, Professor Heyde.

With the official discontinuance of Aktion T4, Heyde was discharged from his position with the KdF for reasons that remain somewhat unclear.[65] After his removal, he returned to Würzburg where he resumed his university teaching duties and was given an appointment to head the university-run SS-military hospital.[66] However, he never regained his original stature within the NSDAP system. When the war finally came to an end, Heyde was captured by the British forces and placed in the Frøslev prison camp in Denmark.[67] From Heyde's perspective, it was at this point that things quickly turned from bad to dire. On October 29, 1946, the District Court of Frankfurt issued a formal warrant for his arrest on multiple counts of murder. He was also ordered to appear before the Nuremburg Court in the trial against many of his former T4 colleagues. The United States of America had formally charged Karl Brandt, Viktor Brack, and twenty-one others[68] for, among other things, "unlawfully, willfully and knowingly" being principals in and connected with "plans and enterprises involving the execution of the so-called "euthanasia" program of the German Reich, in the course of which the defendants murdered hundreds of thousands of human beings."[69] If found guilty, the penalty was execution. Heyde began looking for an opportunity to escape. Unfortunately, he did not have to wait very long.

In April of 1947, Heyde was called to serve as a key witness in the trial against the KdF personnel and medical staff who had participated in the NS system of killing centers. On the journey he was to be transferred into US custody. Heyde saw his opportunity. The doctor was placed in the back of an open military truck with several other prisoners.[70] For whatever reason, the US soldier in charge of guarding the prisoners decided to sit in the front cabin of the truck with the driver, leaving the prisoners unattended. When the truck passed through the town of Würzburg, Heyde leaped.[71] The date of his escape was July 25, 1947. It would take over a decade before the fugitive was recovered.

Although Heyde was intimately familiar with Würzburg, the city had been decimated and it was the first place that the Allied Forces would look for him. Clearly another, less obvious refuge was needed. Heyde decided to make his way north to the German-Danish border. While the precise moment of Heyde's getaway was spontaneous, his escape plans were anything but. Already during his imprisonment in Denmark, he had taken several steps to establish a new life for himself on the run. It was during this time, for example, that he had letters smuggled out of the camp and mailed to himself under an assumed name, *Fritz Sawade*. While the name *Fritz* was exceedingly popular and therefore entirely nondescript at that time, the surname *Sawade* was and is relatively uncommon.[72] According to Heyde, the inspiration for the name came from a novel he once read.[73] For his new date of birth, he simply shifted his real birthday eight days to help him remember and avoid stupid mistakes in case he were stopped along the way and asked to give his age or birthday.[74] His place of birth, he kept the same: a wise idea considering the difficulty of convincingly maintaining a regional accent that is not your own. He also reported that his wife and two sons had been lost in the war. Here again, Heyde borrowed from the truth. He was in fact married and the father of two sons but all three were alive and well. However, for his new persona he invented completely new identities for his family members, with entirely different names.[75]

Once Heyde reached the northern state of Schleswig-Holstein, he began phase two of his transformation. Using the fake identity he had established by sending himself correspondence from the camp, on September 1, 1951, he applied for and was granted a "replacement" German identity card and refugee pass[76] for those he claimed had been destroyed in the war.[77] On the black market in Kiel, he obtained a forged certificate of military discharge under the name *Dr. Fritz Sawade, M.D.* With these new official documents in hand, the official refugee began looking for suitable employment. He found it eventually in Mürwirk, a small suburb of Flensburg.[78]

The Naval Sports Academy [79] was in desperate need of an onsite physician. Sawade applied for the position and was told the job was his, IF he were willing to accept the meager salary of 30 DM per month. In an interview with the Lord Mayor, Dr. Sawade explained that he would be more than willing to accept that salary IF the administration were willing to hire a fugitive who was compelled to live under a false name to avoid being recaptured by the US Americans and being forced to testify against his comrades in Nuremberg.[80] Both sides agreed to the conditions and Dr. Sawade began his new position with his new name.[81] By the autumn of 1950, the physician had made a solid reputation for himself and was soon asked (again) to serve as an expert medical consultant for the government.[82] With the extra money he received, he was eventually able to move from the tiny room at the Academy and purchase a comfortable brick rowhouse for himself in Flensburg. As his work as a consultant increased, he even had enough money to splurge on a brand-new sports car[83]—and this at a time when owning a car was still a luxury many German families could ill afford. Things were definitely looking up for Dr. Sawade.

Perhaps it was all that sudden good fortune that emboldened him to take another risk: re-establishing contact with his family who was still living under the name of *Heyde* in the South of Germany. With the money he was now earning as a government medical case evaluator, he was finally able to provide some financial support to his wife and two sons. Although this was a definite improvement, it was a far cry from the lifestyle his wife, Erika, had become accustomed to as the spouse of a high-ranking KdF official. Disgruntled and dissatisfied, she had long since begun to take matters into her own hands. She started by having her husband declared dead. Once this status was granted, she applied for and was granted death benefits from the University of Würzburg on behalf of herself and her "fatherless" boys. Given her husband's high-ranking position within the University, the "widow" received quite a tidy sum of money. Within the space of seven years, from April 1, 1952 to November 30, 1959, she had bilked the state out of 65,000 DM.[84]

When Heyde was finally arrested and interrogated by the authorities, he readily admitted to his role in Aktion T4 but remained adamant that he had known nothing about his wife's financial fraud. "I can say most definitively that I neither had any intention nor knowledge of my wife's application for death benefits from the University of Würzburg."[85] The doctor, it seems, was proud of having participated in the murder of approximately 100,000 people as biological waste but took great umbrage at the thought that he might be considered a fraud. Yet for all his attempts to distance himself from his wife's efforts to reclaim at least a bit of their former social-standing, at the end of the day, the professor was no different. He too found himself longing for his previous prestige, power, and recognition. That yearning would be his downfall. No longer satisfied with attending to sprained ankles and pulled hamstrings at the sports school, Dr. Sawade began to attend interdisciplinary conferences where experts in medicine, law, and psychology shared their latest findings. Had he simply sat quietly and passively in the background, this decision would have been fool-hardy enough but Heyde took it <u>much</u> further. First, he drew considerable attention to himself by asking challenging questions of the guest lecturers, the younger of whom must have been taken aback by the simple country doctor's vast scientific knowledge. Later, he even agreed to serve as an invited conference speaker himself on matters of medicine and law. The new notoriety was great for business. Just as before, a lifetime ago, he soon found himself being sent hundreds of requests to serve as a medical consultant on behalf of the government.

In view of Heyde's previous prominence as a top medical consultant for the Reich, one might be tempted to ask whether anyone recognized that *Dr. Sawade* was actually Professor Dr. Heyde. The answer to that question is a resounding: "Yes!" Indeed, as one witness quipped, it would be far easier to count the number of officials who didn't know than those who did. Part of the reason for this conspiracy of silence by professionals who had sworn an oath to protect the society may lie in the unusual political climate of Schleswig-Holstein after the war. Between the years 1950 and 1971, nearly one-half of the Schleswig-Holstein parliament (SHP) was made up of former NSDAP members; and in some electoral periods that proportion was over half.[86] While some of these officials proved to be strong supporters of the West German democratic structures after the war, there were others whose allegiance to the principles of the NS system remained unbroken.[87] Investigations conducted by the University of Flensburg's History Department revealed that more than one closeted NS loyalists in the SHP had committed war crimes themselves.[88] For many decades, this combination of perpetrators and sympathizers made for a nearly impenetrable wall of silence. Therein lies only part of the reason why Heyde's identity was held secret for so long by so many. Other than mutual criminality, there were also other, often more complex, personal motivations for deciding not to disclose the doctor's real identity. Such was the case with the Creutzfeldt Family.

In the 1950s, Professor Dr. Creutzfeldt was also working as an expert medical consultant for the government. In 1954, both he and Dr. Sawade gave their assessment on the same case and came to very different conclusions: a result which was not at all unusual. What was unusual was the manner in which the sport's physician from Flensburg responded to the difference of opinion. Rather than substantiating his assessment with facts from the case, he viciously attacked his Creutzfeldt's competence. That character assassination led Professor Creutzfeldt to investigate his colleague's credentials. Just who was this "Dr. Sawade"? In an official letter sent to Ernst Buresch, the then Director of the Social Welfare Court in Schleswig [Präsident des Landessozialgericht][89], Professor Creutzfeldt stated that the condescension, aggression, and lack of objectivity manifest in his colleague's assessment alone made his continued employment as a medical consultant highly questionable. However, according to the professor's inquiries, this lack of professionalism was not the only problem with Dr. Sawade: "The person you have up there in Schleswig hiding under the name of 'Dr. Sawade' is none other than the 'Lunatic-Murderer'!"[90] Unbeknownst to

Creutzfeldt, Buresch was one of the government officials who already knew full well who and what Sawade truly was.

The situation was very clear. If Creutzfeldt decided to pursue his complaint by bringing a libel suit or making a formal complaint to the prosecuting attorney's office, the results would spell disaster and not only for *Sawade/Heyde*. Protecting the doctor's pseudonymy had now become an acute question of political self-preservation. A solution was needed and fast. That solution came in the form of a mediator who was chosen to speak with the Creutzfelds in person. The person selected for this crisis-intervention was by no means an accident. In a 1964 letter to the editor that was featured in the German news magazine, *Der Spiegel*, the professor's sons, now doctors themselves, gave the following account:

> On the basis of documents at our disposal including diary entries made by our mother and personal correspondence from the year 1954, the following events took place: . . . A mediator secured our father's promise that he would neither pursue the matter privately nor make a formal report to the state attorney's office. Our father agreed to make this promise because both he and our mother felt personally beholden to the mediator. In 1943, political charges had been brought against our mother. That very same mediator had served as a lawyer in this case and helped save our mother from being made to serve a prison sentence in a concentration camp. In memory of the suffering our parents endured after being denounced during the Nazi period, they agreed not to report Professor Heyde in much the same way as they had refrained after the war from denouncing the Nazi acquaintance who betrayed our mother. Instead, they agreed to let the lawyers of the court handle the matter.[91]

The mediator's intervention was a success. However, no sooner had this emergency ended, another emerged: this time in the form of another complaint from a former colleague of Heyde's, Professor Dr. Helmuth Reinwein. Like Heyde, in the 1930s, Reinwein had also been a member of the NS Physicians' Association [NS Ärztebund] and the NSDAP. He had also served alongside Heyde as a faculty member at the University of Wurzburg's Department of Medicine before later moving on to become the director of the University of Gieser's Clinic for Medicine and Neurology. However, unlike Heyde who made his career in the 1940s in the SS and KdF, Reinwein remained in academia. In 1958, as Heyde had just begun to re-establish a career for himself under a false name in Flensburg, Reinwein was being named the President of the German Society for Internal Medicine. Along with this, he awarded a high-paying research position at the University of Kiel. The postwar years were very good for Reinwein. Everything would have been perfect, if it were not for the two infernal fraternity houses in his neighborhood where drunken parties made sleep impossible.

Professor Reinwein began writing letters of complaint, first to the local authorities and then to the Governor's Office in Kiel, the capital of Schleswig-Holstein. In an effort to calm the prominent but querulent professor, the Governor's office sent a representative to speak with Reinwein in person. During the course of that conversation, the professor alleged that one could hardly expect any justice to be done in a state where a criminal was allowed to serve as a medical expert for the government using a false name! Perplexed, the representative returned to the Governor's office and related Reinwein's odd accusation about a "Dr. Sawade" in Flensburg. Inquiries were made and it was discovered that a Dr. Sawade was indeed working as a medical expert for the government and had provided approximately 7,000 case reports for Schleswig-Holstein.

The authorities in Kiel contacted the responsible authorities in Flensburg. A copy of Dr. Sawade's medical license was requested. The doctor's response was short but telling: He regretted that he was unable to produce a medical license under the name *Sawade*[92] The date was November 4, 1959. Critical mass had been reached. Heyde was on the run again. On November 11, a nation wide all points bulletin was posted for the arrest of Prof. Dr. med Heyde, alias Dr. med. Fritz Sawade, for his probable involvement in the so-called Euthanasia Program during the Nazi period. According to the official warrant, the heavy-set, sixty-something, balding man with a grey mustache was presumed to still be in the Bundesrepublik Deutschland and would most probably be driving an ivory colored Borgwald Isabella TS.[93] Just days after the warrant was released, *Heyde/Sawade* turned himself in to the authorities in Frankfurt am Main.

Meanwhile in Schleswig-Holstein, the public exposure of Sawade's true name, identity, and governmental activities both before and after the war had set off a political tsunami. As the December 3, 1959 issue of the local newspaper, *Die Flensburger Presse*, reported, "For everyone who has been following the press, it is as clear as a bell that among those who carry the guilt and responsibility for this set of events are many politicians."[94] In a matter of days, it was revealed that a long line of civil servants, public officials, and VIPs throughout Schleswig-Holstein had known long before his arrest that *Professor Hyde* and *Dr. Sawade* were two names for the very same person.[95]

Hundreds of miles away in Hessia, similar shock waves could be felt. With the capture of Heyde, many hoped that it would be possible to finally obtain the names of large numbers of unidentified people responsible for the NS medical killings as well as their postwar protectors. With that goal in mind, the office of the prosecuting attorney was hard at work building up their case for what promised to be the next great Nuremberg Trial. At the helm of this monumental task was Prosecuting Attorney, Fritz Bauer, who had helped secure the capture and prosecution of Adolf Eichmann. Bauer prepared an 84,000-page dossier of evidence against Heyde. As the Head of the NS-Euthanasia program, Heyde was charged with having maliciously and with deliberate premeditation taken actions that directly led to the murder of over 100,000 people.[96] On February 13, 1964, five days before the mammoth trial was to begin, the psychiatrist strapped a belt around his neck and hanged himself on the radiator of his prison cell—taking with him, the identities and names of untold accomplices.

*

On November 15, 1968, some fourteen years after the second Amnesty was introduced, an elderly gardener made his way to the police department to make an unusual report.[97] In a lengthy interview conducted with the local police commissioner, the senior citizen revealed that he was not the seventy-three-year-old *W. Schwenger* born in Essen on March 15, 1895, but the seventy-year-old Munich-born SS officer *Wilhelm Heinrich Fortenbacher*. According to the official police transcript, Herr Fortenbacher started his military career with the best of intentions. After surviving World War I and living a short time as a POW in France, he returned to Germany to begin a traineeship as a pastry chef.

By the spring of 1934, the ex-soldier realized, however, that he did not want to spend his life in a kitchen. He gave up his position and joined the German ground troops instead. Almost immediately, he was adopted by the Waffen-SS and his military career began. In cloying detail, the ex SS officer described his rise from a simple foot solider to a SS Brigadier general. However, Fortenbacher's memories became conspicuously hazy when he was asked to detail his exact duties during the war. Instead, he frequently downplayed the importance of his actions in the field. For example, although he freely disclosed that he had been a part of the infamous Viking Division of the Waffen-SS, he insisted that his participation had been minimal once the unit had crossed Tarnopol en route to Kiev.

The General's sudden, uncharacteristic, modesty may have had something to do with the fact that the Viking Division committed numerous atrocities in Eastern Europe. In July 1941, the German forces reached the Polish city of Tarnopol or Ternopol. Once there, they engaged in a blood orgy that lasted nearly two weeks long and resulted in the slaughter of several hundred Jewish residents.[98] By September 1941, a ghetto had been established in a tiny quadrant of the city where some 5,000 Jews had originally lived. Within the space of a few weeks, more than twice that number had been forced into the area. Starvation and catastrophic hygiene led to soaring mortality rates and mass burials.[99] Throughout the ghetto's existence, the Nazis and select members of the Ukrainian police force repeatedly entered the ghetto and engaged in mass killing sprees. By the fall of 1942, using name lists forcibly compiled by the local Jewish Council [Judenrat], regular deportations were organized from the ghetto to the Bełżec Extermination Camp.[100] The decimation of Tarnopol was also visited upon Bialytosk, Wilno, Zloczów, and Lvov, where the German *Einsatz* squads and local volunteers murdered tens of thousands of Jews from century-old *shtetlekh* and *shtetl* in frenzied open-air shootings[101] and sent many thousands more to their deaths in Chelmo, Sobibor, Majdanek, Treblinka, and Auschwitz.

When asked what he had done during this time, Fortenbacher stated that during his company's march eastward, he had developed such severe stomach pains that he had been sent to a SS-Lazarett in Dachau to recover. Whether this military hospital was in fact the one located within the Dachau Concentration Camp, Fortenbacher did not say. Instead, his narrative moved rather quickly on to the period after his convalescence when he received a long series of promotions. When directly asked by the police commissioner whether he had ever witnessed or been a part of any criminal activities, Fortenbacher became quite adamant:

> If you're talking about the killings that took place during the war, I have a completely clear conscience. I did nothing of the sort. So that was certainly not the reason why I have concealed my true identity until now.[102]

When asked why then he had chosen to take on a false name after the war, Fortenbacher cited self-protection. As a former SS officer, he explained, he feared maltreatment by the Allies. As soon as it became clear that the war was coming to an end and Germany would be defeated, he made provisions to adopt a new identity. Through his connections with an infantry school where he had previously been employed, in the summer of 1945, he procured the payroll book of a Wehrmacht sergeant named *W. Schwenger*. He then made his way to the Austrian-Germany border. It was there that he met two women who offered him work in their landscaping business. Fortenbacher, now *Schwenger*, readily agreed and served as a gardener there until his retirement. To make his subterfuge complete, he explained that he had taken care to obtain "replacement" identification papers (e.g., driver's license, health insurance cards, etc.) under his new assumed name.

When asked why he had not taken advantage of the two amnesties in 1949 and 1954, Fortenbacher claimed that he had wanted to protect his two benefactresses. According to him, had it become public that their long-time employee was a former SS officer, it would have been a tremendous shock to his two benfactresses. It would also have jeopardized their small gardening business as they were contracted to care for several local Jewish cemeteries. For years, then, he lived secretly under the name *W. Schwenger*. When asked why he had chosen now to reveal his true identity, the ex-soldier's response reveals much about his underlying character.

Once he'd reached retirement, he explained, he quickly realized that the state pension of an ex-gardener was rather paltry in comparison to what he would receive as a former Brigadier General who had served in both world wars. Thus, by Fortenbacher's own admission, his reason for coming forward was not at all to ease a troubled mind. In fact, he was careful to reiterate throughout the interview that his admission had nothing at all to do with a guilty conscience, as he had none. The interview ended with Fortenbacher's fervent request that his case be processed with all haste so that he could immediately get his due.

Careful scrutiny of Fortenbacher's statement revealed several inconsistencies and falsehoods. Unsurprisingly, the former SS officer was not as innocent as he portrayed himself to be. Not only had Fortenbacher served in a division whose commander had been prosecuted during the Nuremberg Trials There was evidence that Fortenbacher himself had participated in war crimes In fact, the United Kingdom had placed Fortenbacher on their official list of sought-after war criminals because of his suspected participation in the execution of ninety British. According to testimony provided by G. Beyer, himself a former SS officer and administrative assistant for the allies after the war, the real reason why Fortenbacher had remained in hiding under a false name for so long after the war was to avoid prosecution. According to Beyer, during the war, Fortenbacher's company commander, a man by the name of *Knöpflein*, had ordered the execution of English pilots who had been forced to parachute from their planes.

> As the battalion commander of the First SS-F, Fortenbacher in all likelihood was attempting to avoid punishment, since his company commander, a man by the name of Knöpflein, had been involved in the shooting of a captured English pilot who had made an emergency parachute landing.[103]

Although subsequent investigation revealed that Beyer had been mistaken in the name of the Company Commander, his recounting of the massacre was largely correct. Fortenbacher's commanding officer, Fritz *Knöchlein*, had in direct violation of the Geneva Conventions ordered the execution of ninety British pilots captured during the war. Were it not for his own greed, Fortenbacher's participation in this and other crimes might never have come to light; and he might well have ended his days as the quiet local gardener.

*****

Another strategy used by NS war criminals to devise an alias involved changing their forename(s) and retaining their surnames. This method was chosen, for example, by NS offender *Reinhold Vorberg*. During the war, Vorberg worked closely with his cousin *Viktor Brack* in the NS's T4 extermination program.

His specific duties involved coordinating the transports to and from the killing centers. While Viktor Brack was made to stand trial at Nuremberg and was executed for his participation on June 2, 1948, his cousin Reinhold obtained false identification papers with the name *Heinz Vorberg* and went to work in a paint factory. Despite the rather unimaginative alias, Vorberg remained a free man until 1962 when he was tried and given a ten-year prison sentence for being an accessory to murder in 70,237 cases.[104] In table 6.3, other Nazis who used this same method to develop their aliases are displayed.

An examination of the names in this list reveals that in many cases, the fugitives simply borrowed or varied one of their previous forenames. Such was the case with the *Bernd Fischer*.

On January 18, 1954, Herr Fischer[105] became the new director of a special refugee camp for displaced persons located in Ulm-Wilhelmsburg. For all intents and purposes, Fischer was a natural for the position. According to his CV, he had served many years as a police officer and was therefore very familiar with enforcing law and order. In a routine review of his employment records, however, certain inconsistencies were discovered. He had curiously given several different dates of birth in his official paperwork.[106] Clearly, such a mistake would be understandable in reporting other sorts of numerical data like one's bank account number or even a telephone number. But it is highly unusual to repeatedly misreport one's date of birth.

This was not the only inconsistency found in his employment data. In some of his records, his official name was not listed as *Bernd Fischer* but *Bernhard Fischer-Schweder*. It was all quite easy to explain, the former police officer assured. As they all knew, *Bernd* was simply a nickname for *Bernhard*. As for his last name, there was a harmless explanation as well. In 1942, he had been given permission to carry his mother's last name "Schweder" along with his father's last name "Fischer." After the war, he reverted to his original last name to avoid

Table 6.3   Alias Formation Strategy 2: Forename Altered, Last Name Retained

BIRTH NAME	ALIAS
1. Gerhard Bohne	Hans Bohne
2. Bernhard Fischer-Schweder	Bernd Fischer
3. Friedrich Wilhelm Siegmund Robert Lorent	Robert Lorent
4. Rudolf Oebsger-Röder	O.G. Röder
5. Hermann Julius Walther Rauff	Abdullah Rauff
6. Franz Paul Stangl	Paul Stangl
7. Johann von Leers	Omar Amin von Leers
8. Reinhold Paul Karl Robert Vorberg	Heinz Vorberg

being persecuted by the Soviets for his loyal service to the Fatherland.[107] That
was the reason why both his wife and his son also carried the last name *Fischer*.
Had the authorities accepted these explanations, the whole story might have
ended there. But it was the mid-1950s, and authorities were immediately un-
easy when such identification irregularities were spotted. If Fischer or Fischer-
Schweder's story were true, they reasoned, it certainly could not hurt to dig a bit
deeper to see if there were any other irregularities, and there were. It seems that
Fischer-Schweder had also failed to mention that, in addition to having worked
for the police force during the war, he also had been a member of the SS.[108] This
omission was the final straw. If it became known that a former SS officer was
the director of refugee camp, the news would be a publicity nightmare. Fischer-
Schweder was offered a compromise. If he simply agreed to quit, the whole unsettling busy would be conveniently forgotten. If he refused, he would be made
to face the social embarrassment of being fired. Confronted with the ultimatum,
Fischer begrudgingly quit.

In no time at all, the resourceful SS officer had landed a position as a salesman in Stuttgart. There was only one problem. It irritated him that he had been
forced out of his position. At the refugee camp, he was a decision-maker with
power and prestige. He was a leader. The people who knew him best, knew
that <u>that</u> was his true calling. Even at a very early age, he had shown leadership
qualities. Hadn't he, he may have thought to himself, successfully completed
six weeks of intensive training at the special leadership academy [Reichsfüh-
rerschule] of the SA at the age of twenty-six? Just two years later, in 1932, he
had been appointed Speaker for the NSDAP in the district of Brandenburg. By
1941, he was an Oberführer in both the SA and the SS. He was even awarded
the coveted golden pin for being one of the earliest to join the NSDAP. He was
member number 17,141. To Fischer-Schweder, it was obvious: a man of his cali-
ber could not accept the indignity of being cheated of his rightful employment.
He decided to take action. He rescinded his letter of resignation and asked to be
returned to his post. His request was denied. Undaunted, he applied for a civil
service position in Baden and sued the state of Baden-Wuerttemberg. Soon what
must happen, did happen.

It did not take long before the story of the former SS officer's lawsuit hit
the newspapers. The officer took the offensive and fought to protect his good
name. In a letter to the editor, he described himself as "a friend to Jews and the
Poles."[109] Unbeknownst to him, though, his past was already catching up with
him. During a security check conducted by the civil service in Baden, a Dr.
Ballweg, the division leader responsible for performing background checks on
potential hires, discovered that his very own secretary had worked with Fischer-
Schweder in the Memel police department. When asked about Fischer-Schweder's performance record, his secretary, Ms. Meta Poneleit, needed no time at all

to recall her former employer. "He was Satan!" she exclaimed. According to her, he was a raging alcoholic who was detested by everyone within the Department. When asked why he was so disliked, Poneleit made the following explosive charge. While serving as the police chief in the Prussian Lithuanian region of Meme or Klaipèda, Fischer-Schweder had actively participated in a series of grizzly village massacres.[110]

The massacres had taken place as a part of the Reich's military push to vanquish Eastern Europe. Four sets of mobile military action units [Einsatzgruppe] were to accompany the German army as it advanced into the Soviet held territories.[111] Making up the Einsatz commandos were members of the German SS, the SA, and police, as well as Nazi sympathizers from the regional communities. The specific task of these units was the rapid execution of people deemed useless for or a threat to the establishment of National Socialism within the East (i.e., Communists, Partisans, the physically and mentally disabled, Roma and Sinti, and the Jews). To heighten their efficiency, the Einsatzgruppen developed newer, faster techniques for killing larger groups of people at one time.

SS Obergruppenführer Friedrich Jeckeln, for example, pioneered a multiphased murder method. In the first phase, a group of victims were made to dig and then lie face down in their own mass graves. This line of victims was then "liquidated" by a row of officers standing above them with machine guns. In the next phase, a second group of victims was made to crawl into the grave and place their heads between the naked feet and ankles of the dead and dying beneath them. The order to fire the machine guns was given again and then the next group of victims was ordered to climb into the grave and position their heads between the feet of those before them—and so it continued, layer for layer, until the grave was finally filled and covered with dirt. Among the members of the Einsatzgruppen, Jecklen's method was given name the "sardine box."[112] This was not the only innovation of the mobile killing units. According to eye-witnesses, one group that murdered with particular efficiency was the Tilsit Einsatzkommando. This group had proven to be extremely effective in liquidating large numbers of villages. Their modus operandi also took place in several phases.

In the first phase of a mission, all of the able-bodied men of a targeted village were informed that they were being evacuated to special work camps. The men were relatively easy to control, once it was made clear to them that the punishments for their disobedience would be exacted upon the families whom they had been forced to leave behind, unprotected. The men were then taken to remote areas where they were given their first work assignment: to dig a deep, long trench. The men were given no time to think but were clubbed mercilessly and ordered to work faster under the constant threat of pistol and machine-gun fire. After the trench had been completed, the men, now physically and emotionally exhausted, were ordered to stand at attention before it, in a line. Then, all at once, the members of the Einsatzgruppe took aim and fired, striking the heads, shoulders, hands, stomachs, and legs of the men standing directly before them. The sheer force of the bullet shower sent the men hurtling backward into the trench that became their mass grave.

Phase two of the liquidation began soon after. The women, children, elderly, and disabled who had been left behind were told that they would finally be reunited with their menfolk. As they would not be returning to their village any time soon, they were instructed to bring all of their valuables. At an appointed time, the families were brought to an area near the original killing site and ordered to disrobe: the adults were to strip down to their underwear and the children were to be completely naked. As the families followed the orders, they were taunted with humiliating jokes by soldiers, many of whom had been drinking themselves into a frenzy. Suddenly, the families were herded into the area where their husbands, fathers, sons, uncles, and brothers had stood before them. Again, seemingly endless volleys of ammunition were fired until the screaming finally came to a jagged end.

At the end of a day's work, once the targeted kill quotas had been reached, it was not unusual for soldiers to strike a triumphant pose next to a body for a souvenir photo.[113] In the meantime, other soldiers in the commando ransacked the victims' clothing for the valuables the womenfolk had been instructed to bring along. At the end of each mission, a careful report was written about the exact number, location, and classification of "undesirables" who had been eliminated that day. These reports were required of all of the mobile killing units for headquarters to document their individual and collective progress, as the land troops moved from one village to the next.

The Einsatzkommando Tilsit was assigned to cleanse the entire border area of between Germany and Lithuania, which brought them to Memel, where Fischer-Schweder had been the police director since January of 1941.[114] The commander of the Einsatzkommando Tilsit, Hans-Joachim Böhme, contacted Fischer-Schweder and requested that he provide a group of police officers to secure the area of Garsden for the commandos coming operation. Fischer-Schweder was not satisfied with taking on such a passive role, however. "It is ridiculous," he complained to the local NSDAP district leader, "that they alone attempt to execute such a large number of prisoners with such a small number of men. I have therefore decided to conduct the executions with the contingent of police officers that had been requisitioned for securing the area."[115] After observing the mass executions perpetrated by his men, he demonstratively strolled up to the trench filled with bodies and fired a few shots to "finish off" victims whom he found still alive.[116]

According to a Russian witness, during the mission, it was frequently necessary to replace police officers who found themselves standing across from people they had grown up with in Memel. "In one case," the witness reported, "the local soap-maker, Feinstein, found himself standing across from his former neighbor and one-time friend, Police Officer Knopens. Feinstein called out to Knopens defiantly: 'Gustav, aim well!'"[117] Although some police officers refused to participate in the killing of their fellow villagers, others had no such compunctions. Having gotten a taste for the action, Fischer-Schweder and those officers who'd follow him voluntarily took part in several subsequent missions—even when the order included executing women and children, the pregnant and the disabled, the elderly and the infirmed. Fischer-Schweder seemed to have no qualms at all: he was in his element.

According to Poneleit's formal police statement, Fischer-Schweder's killing excesses were not limited to the missions. One Sunday afternoon, he reportedly went to the Memel ghetto for a bit of sport and relaxation. He singled out a Jewish man and escorted him to a four-meter-long grave that had been dug out in preparation for another mass shooting. Fischer-Schweder turned to the man and offered him a game of chance. "If you can jump over this grave and make to the other side, I will let you live." As the man leapt, Fischer-Schweder pulled out his pistol and shot him dead mid-air.[118]

Sometime after his time with the Memel police force, Fischer-Schweder found himself wounded and was eventually captured by the US forces. He was sent to an internment camp where he received medical treatment for his injuries and was interrogated about his identity. Well aware that the Allies were especially on the look-out for members of the SS, Fischer-Schweder made sure to hide his true identity. His ruse worked and he was eventually released only to be called up to stand before a local citizen's tribunal for possible denazification. Fischer-Schweder, now an old-hand at hiding his identity, completed the required paperwork and dutifully appeared before the tribunal. After deliberating his case, he was awarded the lowest level of responsibility possible (i.e., *Entlastete*—persons exonerated).[119] This experience most likely emboldened the already cocky SS officer. If he just remained calm and gave plausible, well-reasoned answers, he could quite literally get away with murder. Only this time, it was different.

The government was preparing a strong criminal case against Fischer-Schweder and had begun to dig into the SS officer's past. The prosecution was headed by two district attorneys Erwin Schüle and Erich Nellmann.[120] It did not take long before the duo realized that this case was far more complicated than anyone had originally anticipated. After burying himself in the archival records, Schüle consulted with Nellmann about his preliminary findings. The duo made a bold decision.[121] They streamlined the legal staff working on the case and enlisted the support of military historians who had studied the organization and operation of the Einsatzgruppen in Eastern Europe.[122] In addition, they consulted leaders of Jewish relief organizations, museum directors, and research librarians.[123] Slowly, but surely, the interdisciplinary team was able to piece together evidence documenting thirty different missions of the Tilsit Einsatzkommando.[124]

Meanwhile, the international search for witnesses began: both victims who miraculously had survived the massacres and perpetrators who had taken part in the mass killings. After nearly two decades, it was difficult to find anyone able or willing to testify; and when they were located, there was little assurance that they would survive the entire trial. For example, just one week after giving his deposition about what he had personally witnessed, a detective in the Stuttgart police department hanged himself. In another instance, Artur Gennat, a detective in the Mainz police department,[125] poisoned himself a day after giving his incriminating testimony on the witness stand.[126] Despite these obstacles, the prosecution was able to put together a damning case against Fischer-Schweder and nine other participants in the Einsatzkommandos—many of whom had also managed to make a good life for themselves under false names. For example, *Pranas Lukys*, a Lithuanian police chief who had taken part in the massacres, changed his surname to *Jakys*. SS Sturmbannführer Hans-Joachim Böhme restyled himself as *Dr. jur. Hans-Joachim Böhme*, a law professor with a specialization in economics—a degree he never earned in a field he never studied.[127] Despite that fact, the prosecutorial team found him comfortably employed as a tax consultant and legal advisor for a bank in Karlsruhe.[128]

Over 60 days, the German court was presented with the devastating testimony of 173 witnesses and thousands of pages of evidence, including the photographs the soldiers had taken of themselves next to their victims before, during, and after the mass shootings. There were also reams of official military reports that detailed with sickening accuracy where the mass murders had taken place and how many hundreds had been killed per mission. All the while, the ever-inebriated man whose false name and birthdate had kickstarted the trial, sat in the courtroom—alternately jeering at survivors who recounted their stories and waving to isolated friends and colleagues he'd spotted in the packed courtroom.[129] On August 29, 1958, the sentences were handed down all ten men were found guilty of participating in the murder of more than 5,500 people between Germany and Lithuania.

Almost immediately after the verdicts were read, District Attorney Erich Nellmann seized the moment and announced to the German press that he had made a formal proposal to government officials. Given the enormity and complexity of the crimes that had been committed during the Third Reich and the difficulty in locating the perpetrators—many of whom had gone to great lengths to hide their identities—he proposed that a central investigation agency be formed that would be exclusively devoted to detecting NS crimes.[130] His suggestion received immediate public and political support. Less than six months later, on December 1, 1958, the "Zentrale Stelle der Landesjustizverwaltungen zur Aufklärung nationalsozialistischer Verbrechen" [Central Office of the State Justice Administrative Agencies for the Investigation of National Socialist Crimes] officially opened its doors. Its first appointed director was Erich Nellmann's colleague, District Attorney Erwin Schüle. "In two years," he announced to the press, "we should be able to work through everything."[131] That prediction would prove to be grossly inaccurate. Sixty years after its inception, the Zentrale Stelle is still continuing its work. Its archives now contain millions of records documenting every imaginable criminal offense perpetrated during the Third Reich. This evidence has been instrumental in preparing more than 7,500 NS criminal cases—over 90 percent of which have led to criminal proceedings involving over 100,000 individuals. And still, the work goes on.

*

Johann von Leers was born on January 25, 1902, into a poor but educated Protestant family in a small northeastern village of Mecklenburg. At the age of fifteen, his father, Kurt von Leers, died of a heart attack, leaving his family destitute and the socially awkward Johann embittered but determined. The same year of his father's passing, von Leers graduated from high school with relatively high marks. Less than a decade later, he was awarded a doctorate in law from the University of Rostock and was well on his way to pursuing a career in the German diplomatic service. With that goal in mind, in addition to his legal studies, von Leers had also studied multiple foreign languages, including English, Japanese, Turkish, Arabic, French, etc. His growing political radicalism and increasingly vocal anti-Semitism made him wholly unfit for the diplomatic service. In 1929, he became member of the NSDAP instead. His new path was a perfect match for his increasingly repugnant racism. As von Leers wrote: "Over the course of my entire life, I have studied the Jew, as a bacteriologist studies a toxic bacterium."[132] It was statements like these that soon caught the attention of Joseph Goebbels who put von Leers's seemingly inexhaustible vitriol to use. Among von Leers' growing circle of readers were Darré and Himmler.[133] A prolific writer, between the years 1933 and 1945 alone, he published over twenty books. His signature theme was freeing the world from one of the primal sources of social degeneracy: "the Jew."

By the time the Third Reich had finally been brought to an end, Professor von Leers had risen to become one of the most reviled and virulent propagandists of the Nazi Party. In 1945, he was captured and placed in the American-controlled internment camp in Darmstadt, Germany.[134] His internment was surprisingly short-lived, however. Approximately one year later, von Leers managed to break out of the camp and meld into the human tumult of postwar Europe. After his escape, the most pressing problem for von Leers was getting ahold of new false documents. Ironically, his time in the internment camp held the solution. Through his prison connections, he was able to obtain false identification papers with a new name. For his new moniker, von Leers chose a name with personal and political meaning: *Hans Eule*. While *Hans* was derived from his first name of *Johannes*, the origin of his new surname was inspired by a personal quirk.

From figurines to paintings, the von Leers's household was suffused with images of owls, the pagan symbol for wisdom. The German word for "owl" is "Eule." For outsiders, the onomastic composition *Hans Eule* would have been inscrutable. However, for insiders, the alias was a dead give-away to the name-bearer's true identity. This example illustrates an important point. Among the escaped war criminals, their aliases not only provided them with a means of establishing a new identity. They also served as a secret code that could only be deciphered by like-minded fugitives. To the initiated, a war criminal's choice of alias could indicate whether the fugitive had remained loyal to the cause. In the case of Johann von Leers or *Hans Eule*, the situation was clear: just like his obsession with owls, his allegiance to National Socialism remained unbroken.[135]

By 1947, von Leers had successfully made his way to Argentina where he quickly joined a small but virulent circle of Nazi authors who wrote for the right-extremist publicist Eberhard Fritsch. Von Leers himself published several articles for Fritsch's monthly fascist digest, *Der Weg* [The Way]. Just a few of his provocative titles are "The Tragedy of Democracy" (March 1951); "The Invisible Ball Gag" (January 1952); "A Third of the German Volk's Economic Capital to be given to the Jews" (March 1953); and a "Program for the Jews" (November 1954). As before, von Leers' corrosive writing style attracted a loyal circle of international readers. Within no time, his essays were being published for not only pro-fascist serials within Argentina, but also for more mainstream publications in Europe like "Christ und Welt." The majority of these pieces were published under one of a growing number of aliases. However, in a few instances, the professor's narcissism won out over reason and he published his work under the initials "V. L."[136]

Those small slips were all the international network of Nazi hunters needed. By the start of the 1950s, von Leers had blown his own cover. For his family, the disclosure could not have come at a worse time. The sympathetic Perón government had begun to crumble and so too had their political protection. The family's salvation came from an unexpected place. In the spring of 1956, von Leers received a personal invitation for himself, his wife, and daughter to travel to Cairo, Egypt.[137] The invitation came in reaction to the propagandist's long history of pro-Arab writings in which he repeatedly advanced the idea of natural fraternity between Islam and Fascism born from a shared enemy: Judaism.[138]

As his publication record shows,[139] von Leers's obsession with Islamic extremism had grown simultaneously with his allegiance to National Socialism. As early as 1943 he wrote: "Judaism is a biologically-determined genetic form of criminality, a religious syncretism with a large dose of devil worship. Whosoever battles against Judaism is doing God's work and is waging God's war."[140] It was declarations like these that found powerful resonance in certain sectors of the Middle East. Once in Cairo, Von Leers concretized his anti-Zionist, anti-Jewish, pro-fascist vision of Islam.

In a private ceremony, not unlike the Namensgebung ceremony of the SS, he formally renounced Christianity and converted to Islam. In honor of his conversion, he took on new name: *Omar Amin von Leers.* As before, this name choice was filled with personal and political symbolism. The name *Omar* was chosen in commemoration of Omar bin al Khtaab (ca. AD 592–644), Mohammed's second successor in the line of Islam's spiritual leaders. The second name *Amin* was reportedly inspired by von Leers's religious mentor, the Grand Mufti Amin El Husseini (1895–1941).[141] Despite these onomastic changes, von Leers, ever the snob, chose to maintain his original aristocratic-sounding surname. For him, the conjoining of these two names symbolized his self-appointed position as an ideological, spiritual bridge between the Germanic and Islamic tribes and what he believed was their common struggle to eradicate Jewish people from the face of the earth.[142]

*****

In the cases above, the Nazi war criminals retained their last names but changed their forenames. There were also fugitives who did exactly the opposite (i.e., keeping their forenames and changing their last names). This tactic was particularly useful for criminals whose last names occurred relatively infrequently within the general population. It is one thing to retain the last name *Müller* or *Schmidt*. It is quite another to keep the last name *Schiemanowsky, Renno, Rokita,* or *Barbie.* In table 6.4, some examples of NS offenders who used this strategy are displayed.

A review of these surname switches would seem to reveal a certain penchant for maintaining the sound of the fugitives' original last names. Take, for example, *Richard von Hegener.* During the war, he assisted in the procurement and transportation of injectable and inhalable poisons for the murder of infirmed and disabled children and adults. When seeking an alternative to the name *Hegener,* he chose the similarly sounding surname *Wegner* for his new life underground in the Soviet-controlled zone of Germany.[143] After assisting Eichmann in the deportation of Jewish residents from Austria and Hungary to extermination camp during the war, SS Hauptsturmführer *Franz Novak* adopted the phonologically similar alias *Dolak* in 1945. Then, only two years later, perhaps feeling

**Table 6.4   Alias Formation Strategy 3:
Forename Retained Last Name Altered**

BIRTH NAME	ALIAS
1. Viktor Arais	Viktor Zeibot
2. Fritz Bängert	Fritz Mewes
3. Klaus Jörg Barbie	Klaus Jörg Altmann
4. George Bertagnolli	Georg Greitemberg
5. Werner Blankenburg	Werner Bieleke
6. Kurt Heinz Bolender	Heinz Brenner
7. Friedrick Robert Boßhammer	Fritz Müller
8. Alois Brunner	Alois Schmaldienst
9. Kurt Christmann	Dr. Ronda
10. Josef Didinger	Josef Erich Müller
11. Eugen Dollmann	Eugen Amonn
12. Erich Ehrlinger	Erich Fröscher
13. Otto Adolf Eichmann	Otto Eckmann
14. Friedrich Wilhelm Konrad Siegfried Engel	Friedrich Schotterberg
15. Albert Karl Wilhelm Filbert	Albert Selbert
16. Erwin Gay	Erwin Miller
17. Heinrich Haffner	Heinrich Hartmann
18. August Heißmeyer	August Stuckelbrock
19. Heinrich Luitpold Himmler	Heinrich Hitzinger
20. Hermann Husler	Hermann Munkell
21. Erhard Kroeger	Erhard Koch
22. Franz Novak	Franz Dolak
	Franz Tragbauer
23. Oswald Poche	Oswald Koch
24. Dr. Georg Renno	Dr. Georg Reinig
25. Richard Rokita	Richard Domagala
26. Hans-Ulrich Rudel	Hans Meier
27. Max Schiemanowsky	Max Lengart
28. Hans Ernst Schneider	Hans Schwerte
29. Gotthard Schubert	Gotthard Pietrusky
30. Karl Schulz	Karl Müller
31. Wilhelm Schussen	Wilhelm Frick
32. Josef Schwammberger	Josef Hack(e)l
33. Kurt August Julian Stawizki	Kurt Stein
34. Richard von Hegener	Richard Wegner
35. Wilfred von Oven	Wilfred Oehm
36. Richard Wendler	Richard Kummermehr
37. Richard Wolff	Richard Wolter
38. Marek Wolmann	Marek Krieger
39. Hermann Worthoff	Hermann Josef Schmitz
40. Herbert Zimmerman	Herbert Zöllner

that the names were too similar, he switched to *Tragbauer*. He kept that name for ten years before reverting back to his original name *Franz Novak* and applying for the reinstatement of his Austrian citizenship. Once in Austria, he worked for the next four years as the director of a printing office in Vienna until he finally caught the attention of local authorities in 1961.[144] A year later, in Germany, SS Obersturmbannführer *Albert Filbert* who had been hiding under the nearly homophonous alias *Dr. Selbert* was placed under arrest and eventually sentenced to life imprisonment for war crimes he had committed while he serving as leader of the Einsatzkommando 9 in 1941. In each of these cases, the choice in alias seems to have been partly motivated by phonics.

In other cases, the inspiration for a new last name seemed to have been simply a matter of happenstance. One such example comes from the T4 physician, *Dr. Georg Renno*, who actively participated in the lethal gassing of adults, adolescents, and children in Nazi "medical treatment centers." For some ten years after the war, *Renno* lived under the alias *Dr. Reinig*. After his capture, Renno described in detail how he came to this rather unusual surname. Immediately after the war, the former director of the Hartheim killing center, slowly made his way to the Austrian-German border. As he reached the check-point, the only official documentation he had on his person was his driver's license with the name *Dr. Renno*. To escape detection, he burned the section of his license with his typed name and left only the signature. Then, he carefully altered the shape of the letters in his surname—changing the first "n" to an "i" and the word-final "o" to a "g"—a relatively easy set of orthographic alterations in the antiquated German script, Sutterlin. The simple maneuver worked. *Renno* was now *Reinig*.

Armed with this new surname, the doctor was able to move about with relative ease and quickly obtained new additional identification papers under his self-crafted pseudonym, and began his second lucrative medical career.[145] After a decade of working under his assumed name *Reinig*, the doctor decided to reclaim his original surname, *Renno*. The year was 1955, the very same year in which the statute of limitations forbad prosecution of crimes committed without premeditation during the NS period (e.g., manslaughter, kidnapping, assault, rape, etc.). Renno confessed to his employer that he had been living under a false name. Evidently unperturbed by the deception and uninterested in the motivation(s), his supervisor replied that as long as his medical license was authentic, the name *Renno/Reinig* chose to go by was of no interest to him.

For the next six years, the doctor worked as a representative of the German pharmaceutical company, Schering AG. During this time, he traveled extensively throughout in Homburg, Ludwigshafen, Mainz, and Mannheim under his real name.[146] He was finally placed under arrest and made to stand trial in the fall of 1969, nearly a quarter of a century after the war's end. When confronted with his crimes, he blithely stated that "turning the gas lever had been no big thing."[147] Only seven months into the trial, the court proceedings were stopped due to Renno's apparent ill-health. The allegedly frail doctor was sent home, where he enjoyed the next two decades of his life as a free man.

*

His father was an insurance man whose work was filled with numbers, graphs, and figures. Hans Ernst Schneider was not like his father. He was fascinated by the arts and the humanities. Fancying himself to be a modern Renaissance man, Schneider's semester plan at the Universities of Königsberg, Berlin, and Vienna, Schneider's was filled with courses in theater studies, philosophy, social studies, art history, and his first love—German literature. An excellent student, Schneider graduated summa cum laude before meeting and marrying his second life-long-passion, Annemarie.

Rather than pursue what would have most probably been a very successful and secure career as a university professor, the dynamic new husband made a series of radical life-changing decisions: he left academia, joined the NSDAP, and sent in his application to join the government's elite security force. After passing the prerequisite health, inheritance, and political checks, Schneider was given word of his acceptance and in 1937, he became member 293,691 of the SS.

Initially, it seemed Schneider's career gamble had paid off. After leaving the university, he was soon hired by a newly erected NS-sponsored research institute dedicated to the investigation of Germanic Ancestry [Ahnenerbe]. Schneider quickly ascended the professional ladder, and within a few years after his graduation, he achieved the rank of SS-Hauptsturmführer. He was then made the head liaison for the Nazi's International Alliance of Germanic Volunteers [Germanische Freiwillige]. One of the primary purposes of the Alliance was to strengthen ties between Nazi Germany's Waffen-SS and countries believed to have significant Aryan bloodlines (e.g., Norway, Sweden, Denmark, the Netherlands).[148] Toward that end, one of Schneider's primary functions was to locate exclusive gifts for NS dignitaries on behalf of Nazi luminaries like Reichsführer Heinrich Himmler. Himmler was not the only recipient of Schneider's exclusive requisitions. Schneider also used his international contacts to procure hard-to-find supplies for Dr. Sigmund Rascher's research department at the Institute for Military Science and Applied Research. Dr. Rascher's experimentation included lethal tests on concentration camp prisoners to measure the human body's physiological responses to prolonged exposure to extremes in altitude, air pressure, and temperature. In a report dated April 4, 1942, Rascher excitedly updated Himmler on the results of a high-altitude test involving a concentration camp prisoner:

> The third experiment of this type took such an extraordinary course that I called an SS physician of the camp to serve as witness, since I had worked on these experiments all by myself. It was a continuous

experiment without oxygen at a height of 12 kilometers, conducted
on a thirty-seven-year-old Jew in good general condition. Respira-
tion continued up to thirty minutes. After four minutes, the VP
["volunteer patient"] began to perspire and to wiggle his head; after
five minutes, convulsions occurred; between six and ten minutes,
breathing increased in speed and the VP became unconscious; from
eleven to thirty minutes, breathing slowed down to three breaths per
minute, finally stopping altogether. The severest cyanosis [bluish
discoloration] developed in the meantime and foam appeared at the
mouth. . . . About one-half hour after breathing had stopped, dissection commenced.[149]

Rascher's sadistic human trials continued until nearly the end of the war, when
he was suddenly placed under arrest by the SS and transferred to Dachau concentration camp. On April 26, 1945, Rascher was later executed by an SS firing
squad for embezzlement. Schneider's fate would be a very different one. In the
spring of 1945, as Russian bombs transformed Berlin into a lunar landscape of
rubble and ash, Schneider closed his office doors for the last time. By the end
of April 1945, the SS officer had made his way to Lubeck as rumors of Adolf
Hitler's suicide began to circulate. One month later, the international headlines
were filled with news announcing the suicide of Reichsführer Heinrich Himmler
whom the Allied Forces had captured in his failed attempt to escape under the
assumed alias of *Sergeant Heinrich Hitzinger*. Schneider tried his own luck at
going underground.

Some two years after Himmler's suicide, Frau Schneider reported that her
husband had died along with his SS unit in an effort to pry Berlin from the
Allied Forces. The officer's widow went on to marry a distant relative of her deceased husband, *Hans Werner Schwerte*, whose last name translates into "sword"
in English—a striking similarity to her first husband's surname *Schneider* which
means "cutter" or "slicer." Aside from the similarity in their last names and their
completely identical first names, Frau Schneider's first and second husbands had
another characteristic in common: both men had obtained their doctorates in
German literature. But that, Professor Schwerte, would spend his life insisting,
was where the similarities ended.

While Dr. Schneider had enjoyed power and prominence as a member of
Heinrich Himmler's personal SS entourage, Professor Schwerte had remained
a simple foot soldier. Dr. Schneider was a devoted National Socialist who had
lived and died for the Reich. Professor Schwerte was a highly outspoken leftist
liberal, who had, in his own words, dedicated this life to making sure that the
madness of the Third Reich never repeated itself.

Alongside these differences, there were also several basic, biographical details which clearly separated the two men. Dr. Hans E. Schneider was born on
December 15, 1909, in the northeastern city of Königsberg. Professor Hans W.

Schwerte's papers indicated that he had been born one year later, on October 3, about 350 kilometers away, in the town of Hildesheim. The similarities in their names was, Professor Schneider insisted, no more than coincidence: an assertion which was made easier to believe given the relative commonality of names like *Hans, Schneider,* and *Schwerte* in Germany.

No, Professor Schneider was an entirely different man, a man of culture, of refinement, a modern Renaissance man whose list of accomplishments spanned decades. In recognition of his academic achievements, he was awarded the highest academic degree possible in the German education system: the "Habilitation." In 1981, he was named Northern Rhine Westfalia's scientific liaison for the universities of Belgium and Holland. In 1985, he was awarded the Officier de L'Ordre de la Couronne du Royanne de Belgique. Five years later, he was made Senator and then President of the RWTH University of Aachen. But still, despite all these accomplishments, there were always a few who continued to whisper and wonder. In the spring of 1995, those rumors were finally put to rest.

In an official statement, the then retired professor finally admitted that he, like many of his SS-brethren, had used the chaos and confusion at the end of the war to obtain a new name and identity for himself. Why then after so many years of proclaiming his innocence did the professor finally admit to the life of lies he had spent nearly half a century creating? In all probability, he would have gone happily to his grave with the secret had it not been for a team of journalists in the Netherlands who had investigated all those rumors and finally found evidence that *Schwerte* and *Schneider* were indeed one and the same man. On April 27, 1995, right before the results of the Dutch team's investigation were due to be televised, the professor turned himself in to the German authorities.

Once the news of the subterfuge hit the press, the public reaction was outrage tinged with a not insignificant portion of Schadenfreude. The professor's reaction to all the attention quickly swung from baffled confusion to acidic indignation once people began to contemplate removing his titles and stripping him of his academic degrees. After all, he reasoned, he had legitimately earned both his doctoral and post-doctoral degrees; and he had been properly elected the President of the University. The fact that the names on his birth certificate were slightly different than the ones that appeared on all those honors must surely be inconsequential, he argued. When asked why he had not taken advantage of the amnesty in 1954, Schwerte-Schneider explained that at the time he had learnt of it, he was in the final stages of completing his post-doctoral degree. Had he disclosed his true identity, he exclaimed, he would have ruined his career. In addition, he argued, there would have been nothing to gain by turning himself in. He had, after all, already put himself through a very personal and highly effective denazification program. Wasn't that enough? he protested.

Yielding to tremendous public pressure, the university and governmental officials ultimately decided that the answer to that question was "no." One by one, *Schwerte/Schneider's* status and pension as a civil servant were revoked, and his long list of national and international honors was rescinded. Although the decision was made to allow him to keep his doctoral title, he was informed that an official investigation was being opened into whether there was a legal mandate to prosecute him for his activities during the war. Despite the fact that there was clear evidence that Hauptsturmführer Schneider had indeed gathered supplies that were later used in lethal medical experiments conducted on concentration camp prisoners, it could not be established that he had procured these instruments with the knowledge and intent that they be used to commit murder. For that reason, it was ruled that there was insufficient evidence to convict the professor of either accessory to murder or murder. In 1996, the investigation was officially closed. Three years later, on December 18, 1999, the professor died, leaving his wife a widow for the second and last time.

*

One year after the second amnesty was issued, a Berlin housewife reported the death of her husband, SA Oberfürher *Werner Blankenburg*. According to her, her spouse had died a heroic death along with his comrades on the field of battle in a desperate effort to save the German Reich. Four months later, Frau Blankenburg received official notification that her husband had been officially declared dead on March 15, 1956. He left behind him two sons, a daughter, and a widow—at least on paper, that is.[150]

While Mrs. Blankenburg was busily collecting her widow's pension, her husband was steadily making plans in Stuttgart to marry his long-term mistress, a young nurse by the name of Margarete. Werner was devoted to Margarete. So much so that he named her his sole heir in the event of his death. He even went so far as to include in the document that he left it entirely up to Margarete's own discretion and generosity to decide if she wanted to share that good fortune with anyone else. To make the last will and testament complete, he was careful to provide his signature at the bottom. However, instead of the last name *Blankenburg*, Werner used another surname: *Bieleke* his wife's maiden name.

Whether Margarete eventually found out her fiancé's true identity and marital status remains unclear. What is clear is that he did not add bigamy to his long list of crimes. According to intelligence gathered after *Blankenburg/Bieleke's* actual death, there were two probable reasons for his marital restraint. The first was quite simply the fear that filing all of that paperwork would draw unwanted attention to himself and his false identity. The second reason was his allegiance to his wife. This loyalty may not have so much been due to shared affection as it was mutual benefit.

While Werner's wife had provided him with a new name and new life, through his continued death, Werner provided her with a pleasant social-standing, financial support, and a level of freedom which she could never have had were she a divorcee. Mrs. Blankenburg did not live a life of solitude while her husband enjoyed his life with Margarete. For many years, the would-be widow kept a lover—a US soldier, with whom she had a child. This comfortable arrangement came to an abrupt end in November of 1958, when *Blankenburg/ Bieleke* died from throat cancer. Soon thereafter, his wife and mistress would have even more in common than their shared significant other. Both women were formally investigated for having knowingly assisted in the concealment of the Nazi officer's true identity. Despite repeated interrogation, neither woman ever freely admitted to having known the true extent of their paramour's crimes.

At the height of his career, Blankenburg was the chief administrator of Section II of the Führer's Chancellery (KdF). Within this capacity, he was responsible for overseeing the identification and distribution of suitable equipment and personnel to be used in the government's top-secret program, "Aktion Reinhardt."[151] The official purpose of this program was to safeguard the Reich's Aryan bloodlines by eliminating all persons deemed unworthy of living through mass sterilization and/or extermination. According to military intelligence gathered long after the war's end, several former Aktion Reinhardt employees continued to maintain close ties with one another, despite having assumed new names and new lives. Much to his mistress's alleged surprise, Blankenburg's funeral was remarkably well attended by a host of strangers who explained that they had worked with her fiancé in the early days. Subsequent investigation revealed that among the funeral attendees were the lawyer August Dietrich Allers, chief administrator of the NS T4 euthanasia program in Berlin; and NSDAP Erwin Lambert, who was charged with overseeing the erection of the gas chambers and crematoria in death camps like Treblinka. In Blankenburg's case, his selection of the alias *Bieleke* was most probably a question of simple pragmatics. In the next case, the choice seems to have been motivated by secret semantics.

*

At the end of the nineteenth century, the Austrian Prince Starhemberg donated the largely dilapidated Hartheim Castle and surrounding lands to a local charitable society to be converted into a sanatorium for the severely mentally disabled. For nearly half a century, the patients in the clinic were cared for by nuns in a local order. However, with the annexation of Austria, the property came under control of the National Socialists. In the spring of 1940, the castle underwent another renovation for its newest function: the systematic collection, torture, and murder of tens of thousands of patients. It was here that *Kurt Heinz Bolender* found employment which perfectly suited his interests and temperament. He became a corpse burner [Leichenbrenner]. It was thanks to this avocation he was given the nickname *Heinz Brenner* or [Heinz Burner] by his Hartheim colleagues.

In the spring of 1942, Bolender was transferred along with several of his colleagues to work in the recently completely Nazi death camp, Sobibor. The camp had a relatively small but highly trained staff who shared one single ambitious goal: the complete extermination of the entire Jewish population located in the Lublin, Poland. In May 1942, one month after his arrival, the gassing facilities were ready for operation and Bolender was put to work doing what he did best. By the end of the war, approximately 1.7 million people had been murdered in Sobibor. Starting in August 1942, the swelling mass graves surrounding the camp were exhumed and the rotting corpses of thousands of victims were set alight to dispose of the mounting evidence. The attempt was futile.

Once the war ended, the majority of the Sobibor staff, including Kurt Bolender, went underground. Incredibly, the first false name that Bolender chose for himself was the nickname he had been given at the Hartheim Killing Center: *Heinz Brenner*. In the 1950s, perhaps recognizing the folly in this onomastic choice, he took on a new, less conspicuous, alias: *Wilhelm Kurt Vahle*.

In direct opposition to the experiences of *Heinz Brenner*, the biography of *William Vahle* was striking only in its mundanity. Who would have suspected that the aging porter who passed out customer keys was a mass murderer who had assisted in the murder and incineration of a quarter of a million people.[152] The man's real identity was not revealed until the 1960s. On September 6, 1965, *Bolender/Brenner/Vahle* was put on trial for murder in some 360 cases and accessory to murder in nearly 90,000 cases. Before his final sentence could be passed, however, he committed suicide on October 10, 1966. In his apartment, the authorities found a tiny metal shield that had once adorned the wooden handle of a whip used in the concentration camp. Upon the shield was the engraved monogram "K.B."[153]

*****

For NS war criminals whose names and faces were especially well known, multiple aliases were often utilized. Consequently, the escape route of many high-ranking Nazis is frequently marked by a series of name changes, each one selected to help the fugitive blend into his/her onomastic surroundings. One such an onomastic chameleon was *Otto Heninger*.[154] Born on March 19, 1906, the unemployed salesman from the Silesian city of Breslau was lucky enough to find work in Altensalzkoth, a remote northern German village located deep within the Lüneberger Heide. Among his fellow workers, *Heninger* was known as well-mannered yet oddly aloof. When the other men would gather together in the evenings to share stories, a beer, and a friendly game of cards, Heninger always politely declined, preferring instead to play his violin or listen to the evening news on his radio—the only one in the village at the time. Heninger seemed to prefer his own company and avoided talking about his life during or before the war. But that did not seem to worry the villagers of Altensalzkoth. In postwar Germany, almost everyone had a secret they wanted to keep or a past they wanted to leave behind. What mattered most was that Heninger was hard-working and reliable; if you gave him a task, no matter the size, you could be sure that he would get the job done.

That uncommon work-ethic paid off when the local factory closed and left many of the local men without a job. Without missing a beat, Heninger found a new source of income. For a few marks a month, he rented a local chicken farm and began to sell fresh eggs and chicken to the locals. Soon, he was delivering his produce throughout neighboring towns, like Celle, where survivors of the Bergen-Belsen Concentration Camp counted among his growing list of customers. As the Altensalzkoth residents later recalled, Heninger had an unexpected real knack for handling his chickens. Although as one resident recounted, in retrospect it was odd that he never called out to them when it came time to feed. Instead, he ordered them aggressively about the yard. Be that as it may, in no time at all, Heninger had become a well-respected member of the community. It must then have come as somewhat of a surprise when he suddenly decided to shut down his business and move away. Just as quickly and mysteriously as he had arrived, *Otto Heninger* disappeared. When they thought about it though, before he had left, he had mentioned more than once that he wanted to leave Germany and maybe try his luck as a machinist in Norway.

Based on what is known today, the one-time chicken breeder did leave Germany, but he did not go north as he had hinted. Instead, he went South, to Austria, and then later on to Italy, where he took on a new identity and name, *Ric(c)ardo Klement*.[155] In the following excerpt, he recounts how he came to his new name:

> From there we travelled to Meran. This was—according to my new c.v.—my birthplace, and it was here that I received my "*libro desembargo*," the landing permit for Argentina. I was given it from someone who to my great surprise didn't want a single lira. Until then I had had to pay dearly for the services of the "U-boat agents," With my new entry permit in my pocket, made out in the name of *Riccardo Klement*, I reached Genoa.[156]

From Italy, the elusive traveler made his way to Argentina, where he eventually found work at a German automotive plant of Mercedes Benz. As before, Klement quickly established useful ties. Many of these contacts were also German-speaking ex-pats, many of whom he'd either known of or worked alongside during the war. Once settled in Argentina, Klement sent for his German wife, Vera, to join him. In 1955, they had their fourth son, "Ricardo." Just five years later, the man known as *Klement* found himself on a plane destined for Israel, where he would live out the final days of his life before being executed for the crimes against humanity he had committed under his birthname, *Otto Adolf Eichmann.*

*

During the war, the Austrian-born SS Hauptsturmführer was known by his NS colleagues as a deportation specialist. In a four-month period between September 6 and December 18, 1943, he coordinated the deportation of 10,067 people to Auschwitz from Theresienstadt where he served as a Commandant for seven months. Of those original deportees, only 765 survived.[157] It was during his time in Theresienstadt that Burger first demonstrated an uncommon talent for using names to cover his crimes. In 1944, Himmler granted permission for a delegation of the International Red Cross to inspect Theresienstadt.[158] In preparation for the inspection, the thirty-three-year-old Commandant replaced the ghetto's alphanumeric military grid markers with everyday street names one might encounter in any normal town. In a secret diary, Otto Pollak, a prisoner of Theresienstadt, noted the changes:

> July 31, 1943. Evacuation of the Sudeten Barracks. Forty-five hundred people to be resettled. A whole city breaking camp. People packing what little they have, all in a great commotion. . . . Waves of people, unlike any I've seen. . . . The Germans are having even more homes evacuated. Every street has been given a name. Some are called lanes, some streets. . . . New street names: L1 = See Strasse [Lake Street]; L1A = Kurze Strasse [Short Street]; L2 = Bahnhof Strasse [Railway Station Street]; L3 = Lange Strasse [Long Street]; L4 = Hauptstrasse [Main Street]; L5 = Park Strasse [Park Street]; L6 = Wall Strasse [Wall Street]; the road to Bohušovice = Sud Strasse [South Street] . . . SS *Obersturmführer* Anton Burger had begun his work.[159]

The onomastic facelift helped to create a veneer of normalcy for both the Red Cross inspectors as well as for the friends and family members who sent valuable care packages to loved ones who had been deported to Theresienstadt.

It was strategies like this that helped to capture the attention and admiration of NSDAP leaders. As Eichmann once said when describing Burger, "He is the kind of guy you start reading out an order to and before you're finished, he's already gotten the job done!"[160] After his service in Theresienstadt, Burger assisted in the identification and deportation of Jews residing in Athens, Korfu, Kos, Rhodos, and Saloniki, Greece.[161] And 90 percent of these deportees also met their deaths in the gas chambers of Auschwitz.[162] After the war, Burger's talent for using names as camouflage demonstrated itself again, only this time the object to be hidden was himself.

In 1945, Burger found himself imprisoned in the US internment camp "Glasenbach" in Austria. In no time at all, he managed to escape and purchased a fake passport with the alias, *Johann Anton Burger*.[163] Alternating between the nicknames *Toni* and *Hans,* Burger used this alias for the next three years as he worked as a low-level employee in an Austrian lumber company. The only major risk which the wanted war criminal took during this time was taking the daughter of a local pub owner as his wife. The marriage did not last long, however. By 1952, his wife filed for divorce on the grounds that she no longer wished to live her life under an alias. It seems that during their much-abbreviated wedded bliss, the former concentration camp commandant had changed his name at least two more times from *Toni Steiner* to *Franz Bauer.*

By the end of the 1950s, even Burger seemed to have become tired of his name-game. He began to inquire discretely whether it would be possible for him to return to his hometown under his real birth name. In hopes of expediting matters, he even wrote a formal letter of appeal to the Bürgermeister of his village, describing himself as a forlorn native son who wanted nothing more than to come home. "As a so-called 'war criminal,'" he lamented, "I have been forced to live under a false name in Germany. The Austrian people can barely conceive that that would still be possible or even necessary in this day and age. . . . I can assure you, however, that the accusations made against me are based on nothing more than lies, hatred, and revenge."[164] To his great chagrin, his letter did not achieve the desired effect.

In fact, through his lawyer, Burger learned that Austria had extended the search for him in hopes of trying him for murder, accessory to murder, theft, and extortion. The final charge was based on the fact that, for exorbitant sums of money, Burger promised to give a reprieve to several of the Jewish residents whom he immediately sent to the gas chambers after receiving payment. Upon learning that he would not be allowed to simply resume his life as *Anton Burger* from Neuenkirchen, Austria, he continued his onomastic merry-go-round, adopting a host of new fake surnames (e.g., *Dolezel, Fasching, Katzerowsky, Kralik, Riedel, Schützenauer,* and *Steiner*)[165] combined with a set of alternating collection of forenames and accompanying nicknames (e.g., *Franz, Hans, Toni,* and *Willy*).[166]

The onomastic merry-go-round only found an end in 1991, when the impoverished Burger, now known under the name *Wilhelm Bauer*, checked into a hospital in Essen, Germany, for an operation on his sciatica. The routine surgery took an unexpected turn for the attending medical team and patient. *Wilhelm Bauer* was suffused with cancer. By the time the authorities made their way through the international labyrinth of aliases, it was too late. The man whom so many hoped they would live long enough to see executed had already died, on Christmas Day, 1991.

*

Where were you born? What is your date of birth? What is your name? For most people, the answers to these three questions remain relatively stable over the course of their lifetime. For that reason, most people are able to answer questions about their birthplace, birthdate, and name automatically, without any conscious attention or strenuous effort. It is this automaticity that makes these questions such a favorite among interrogators. If given enough physical and/or psychological pressure, even the most accomplished liars can find it extremely difficult to refrain from automatically giving a truthful answer to these basic questions regarding their identity. To avoid such potential blunders, resourceful criminals often select aliases that are either extremely similar to their original name; or have some personal significance to them, such as the name of a close friend or distant relative. In the case of one of the Reich's most prolific and dedicated mass murderers, a combination of these two strategies was used.

Born on April 8, 1912, in Austria, Alois Brunner quickly distinguished himself as an over-achiever among murderers. After a less than lackluster start as a window-dresser and salesman in a local department store, at the age of nineteen, the farmer's son made a radical career change and became member 510,064 of the National Socialist Party. Initially, this decision must have seemed anything but promising to Brunner's conservative family—especially when the young Brunner lost his job after terrorizing a local Jesuit Priest who had spoken out against the Nazis.[167] Two years later, however, when Austria became an official part of Hitler's Reich, Brunner's professional gamble paid off. He was not only one of the early members of the largest, most powerful political forces in Austria; he was also increasingly recognized as one of its future leaders.

In 1938, just seven years after taking on Party membership, he was called to become a member of the Central Office for Jewish Emigration [Zentralstelle für jüdische Auswanderung] in Vienna. Unlike what the euphemistic label portends, the true purpose of this agency was to establish an administrative hub for the systematic identification, demarcation, expropriation, collection, and final deportation of the entirety of the city's Jewish population. At the time of agency's establishment, Vienna was home to nearly a quarter of a million people with direct or mixed Jewish ancestry. By the fall of 1939, that number had fallen to under 100,000. Still, the idea that such a large mass of people could be "disposed of" without causing a massive revolt must have seemed completely ridiculous. Only a madman would consider taking on such a task. In 1938, the head of the agency, SS Obersturmbannführer Adolf Eichmann, believed he had found just such a man—Alois Brunner.

Eichmann's instincts proved to be correct. Brunner excelled in his new position. In seemingly no time at all, he established a shockingly effective system of intimidation, collusion, and terror that seemed to penetrate every corner of Vienna. In a 1939 memo signed by Alois Brunner, an agreement reached between Alois Brunner; Adolf Eichmann; the head of the Viennese Gestapo, Dr. Karl Ebner; and Dr. Becker of the Reichskommissar is recorded. According to the document, Eichmann stressed the necessity of accelerating the deportation of the Viennese Jews to Poland. With that goal in mind, Dr. Ebner gave his personal assurance that the entirety of his logistical resources would be made available for processing the deportation of the city's Jewish population and seizing all ensuing goods and properties. Dr. Becker indicated that he would not only help to coordinate the work of the district leaders and the Central Office for Jewish Emigration. He also assured that he would personally see to it that the living quarters that had been made available via the deportations were properly registered for future Party use.

On the basis of these assurances, it was determined that two transports containing 1,000 Jewish residents could be organized every week, starting on October 20, 1939, at 10 pm.[168] To meet this quota, Alois Brunner worked closely with his assistant Anton Brunner. Although the two men were unrelated and looked nothing alike, the similarity between their names made for frequent confusion. Finally, to keep the two "A. Brunners" apart, co-workers resorted to using the nicknames *Brunner I* and *Brunner II*. The Brunners worked with the Gestapo and local police, rounding up Jewish residents from anywhere and everywhere they could find them: hospitals, nursing homes, schools, synagogues, convalescent homes, hospices. The rich, the poor, the young, the old, the healthy, and the ill, the famous, the cooperative, and the defiant—no one was safe from the "two bloodhounds" as they were sometimes called.

What exactly took place during this phase was detailed in a deposition offered by Mr. Ernst Weiss, a disabled Roman Catholic, who, despite having a Jewish mother, was able to survive six-week's detention and the subsequent threat of deportation thanks to his marriage to an Aryan Austrian. On August 13, 1945, Mr. Weiss gave the following statement to the Viennese police:

> The roundups followed this procedure. Approximately 100 people were brought in and made to stand in lines. Then in smaller groups of ten, the people were brought into the examination room. In one hand, they were told to hold all of their cash and in the other hand, their documentation. B [Anton Brunner] examined both. If he discovered that someone had complete Jewish ancestry, a so-called "Volljude," and was married to someone of the same faith, he ripped apart that person's documents (e.g., their citizenship papers) with the mocking comment: "These documents won't be of any value to you anyway in Poland!" Then the Jewish identification card was stamped with "evacuated" and everyone was assigned a number. . . . The money as well as all other valuables were seized. . . . In cases where someone had attempted to hide something of value, everything was taken from them and they were placed in the bunker.[169]

Those who were able to survive the subsequent torture and starvation of the bunker were eventually herded into trains traveling to unfamiliar destinations: Theresienstadt, Kaunas, Riga, Minsk, Lublin, Belzec, Sobibor, Lodz, Chelmno, Treblinka, and Auschwitz.

By October 1942, Brunner I reported that the Austrian metropolis had been ostensibly freed of all Jews (i.e., "judenfrei"). Now considered an undisputed "deportation expert," Brunner was quickly sent to other European cities to apply his "Viennese method" on other Jewish communities (Berlin, Germany; Paris, France; Salonica, Greece). Assisting him along the way was one of his favorite henchmen. Overtime, the two Brunners had discovered that they shared not only similar names, but also similar appetites for the perverse and the profane.

During the war, Anton may have felt somewhat flattered by the association drawn between himself and his boss. As soon as the war ended and the Allied Forces took control, people's tendency to confuse the two men became anything but flattering. For nearly a year after Germany's official surrender, Anton Brunner had been able to avoid capture by the Allied Forces. His luck, however, ran out on February 20, 1946, when he ran into Police Officer Wilhelm Pollak in Bavaria. Perhaps Officer Pollak might have let the stranger go had it not been for the sack of jewelry and money he had in his possession. In no time, Brunner II was facing trial before the District Court of Vienna for his actions during his employment in the Central Office for Jewish Emigration—actions which led to the deportation and death of tens of thousands of Austrians.[170] The trial captured national and international attention, as one survivor after another testified to unspeakable acts of sadism.

During the trial, Anton Brunner entered a plea of "not guilty" and repeatedly insisted that it was in fact the fugitive Alois who was ultimately responsible for the crimes perpetrated via the Central Office for Jewish Emigration.

Although he admitted that there might have been times when he had been guilty of overreacting here and there by on the rare occasion slapping a Jewish interviewee across the face, he insisted that he never committed any act which could be considered an atrocity. Nor, he stressed, was he personally aware of any such crimes having been committed. The deportations, he protested, were as far as he had been informed at the time, simply that: deportations. Miraculously, there were enough eye-witnesses who gave convincing evidence to the contrary. In less than a week, from May 6 to 10, 1946, the Viennese prosecuting attorney's office called more than fifty witnesses who detailed how the accused had routinely, directly, and ofttimes independently participated in the systematic expropriation, and brutalization of some 49,000 Austrians before sending them on to their certain deaths. On May 10, 1946, Anton Brunner was found guilty. His entire stolen wealth was made forfeit and he was sentenced to be hanged by the neck until dead. The sentence was carried out two weeks later.

Whereas the trial reached a personally calamitous end for the one Brunner could, it not have been more fortuitous for the other. With the final execution of his underling, the circle of eye-witnesses who could directly tie Alois Brunner to his wartime crimes was made that much smaller. Further, the fact that the identities of the two men had gradually become so enmeshed in the minds of many officials was a stroke of luck for the fugitive. Like their former colleagues, the names, identities, and deeds had become so co-mingled during the proceedings that the court transcript errantly used the blended name *Anton Alois Brunner*. After the trial many came to believe that the authorities had gotten their man. The time and attention that was spent on interrogating, prosecuting, and executing Brunner II gave Brunner I just enough of a lead to establish a new life for himself under a completely new name.

After his final trip to the Theresienstadt concentration camp, it is postulated that Alois Brunner managed to evade the incoming Russian troops and make his way to Vienna where he picked up his heavily pregnant wife, Anni, and brought her to Lembach im Muehlkreis, a small Austrian town roughly 130 miles outside of Vienna. In Lembach, he entrusted his wife with the sympathetic wife of a local butcher. She promised to hide Anni, until Brunner could send for her and the baby. Brunner then quickly made his way eastward to Prague where he exchanged his officer's uniform for civilian clothing and joined a group of displaced women and children traveling West. Along the way, the group was intercepted by Partisans who arrested the strange male traveler and handed him over to the US forces in the area. In the subsequent interrogation, Alois Brunner was asked for his first and last name. In response, he supplied the alias: "Alois S-c-h-m-a-l-d-i-e-n-s-t" [limited + service/duty].

Initially, one might be tempted to assume that this last name was Brunner's attempt at an inside joke. However, the surname *Schmaldienst* was not Brunner's private creation. It was the real last name of his maternal first cousin. In appropriating a real person's name, Brunner was not only able to continue to hide his true identity. He also ensured that any preliminary background check with Austrian officials would confirm that a "Herr Schmaldienst" did in fact exist but was not currently being sought for questioning or prosecution. The onomastic ruse worked—so well in fact that after a period of "good behavior," Brunner was first used by the US to transport prisoners to and from containment camps located in Austria and Germany. He was later hired on by US forces to serve as a chauffeur for high-ranking officers.[171]

Approximately ten months after Anton Brunner was executed for war crimes, Alois Brunner must have decided it was too dangerous to continue hiding directly in the midst of the very people charged with locating him. In the winter of 1947, he left his position with the US forces and made his way northward. In his possession were the official release papers issued by the US military to *Alois Schmaldienst*. For the next several years, he remained a registered resident of Essen, where he took on a several different jobs: everything from coal mining to waitering. Then, in 1950, Brunner made a critical tactical error. He was caught trying to renew a conspicuously obvious false passport. When called in by authorities in Essen to answer questions about the falsified document and verify his identity, Brunner demonstrated his criminal prowess once again, shamelessly mixing lies with the truth. He claimed, for example, that to the best of his knowledge, the photograph appearing in the fake passport was that of his cousin, the NS war criminal "Alois Brunner." The supplier of Brunner's counterfeit passport was put on trial and sentenced to prison, but Brunner, alias *Schmaldienst*, was allowed to go free.

Perhaps that brush with the authorities was simply too close for comfort. Maybe the fact that two military courts in France had sentenced him in absentia to death for war crimes rattled him.[172] Or perhaps it was the fact that the long sought-after Amnesty came with an exclusionary clause for cases involving maliciousness, cruelty, avarice, and/or dishonor. Whatever the reason(s) was or were, by the early 1950s, Brunner decided to make a radical change in his life. Even now, over six decades later, the information available on Brunner's activities during this period of his life remain largely fragmentary and frustratingly contradictory. One source of this continuing confusion is no doubt Brunner himself, whose labyrinth of lies, half-truths, and exaggerations were key in his eluding capture, extradition, and execution. Another reason for the ongoing difficulty in piecing together Brunner's postwar biography has been the remarkable reluctance and at times outright refusal of leading international government agencies to release intelligence gathered on Brunner's post–World War II activities. However, thanks to unrelenting pressure from organizations working on behalf of Shoah survivors and their descendants, previously classified files have been gradually released to the general public. The information contained in these files sheds some light on Brunner's movements as of the 1950s.

For example, according to intelligence gathered from the General Consulate of Damascus and released in a 2015 report issued by the German Bundestag[173], sometime between 1953 and 1954, Alois Brunner left Europe, his family, and the name *Alois Schmaldienst* behind and made his way to Egypt. Once there, he assumed the alias *Ali Mohammed* and met with fellow ex-pat and Party Loyalist, *Omar Amin von Leers*. Present at their meeting was the Palestinian Arab political and religious leader, Grand Mufti al-Hajj Amin al-Husaini. From 1941 to 1945, the exiled al-Husaini had lived in Europe where he gradually established strong political ties with the Hitler regime. On behalf of the SS, for example, al-Husaini actively recruited and trained Muslim soldiers from the Middle East and the Balkans to serve in special, segregated military units such as the Thirteenth. SS-Freiwillligen-Gebirgsdivision (Kroatien) or "the Handschar."[174]

Based on evidence gathered by the United States Holocaust Memorial Museum, al-Husaini also received funding from the German Foreign Office and the SS to establish an espionage network with contacts in Egypt, Turkey, Palestine, and Syria.[175] When the Hitler regime crumbled, al-Husaini first escaped to Switzerland where he was immediately denied asylum. On his way back to Germany, he was intercepted and arrested by the French. In a clandestine act of Western appeasement, French, British, and the US officials decided against prosecuting al-Husaini for war crimes and quietly released him in 1946. Once set free, al-Husaini immediately flew to Egypt where he assisted other National Socialists on the run. In the case of the fugitive Alois Brunner,[176] al-Husaini advised his colleague to relocate to Syria. There, he would find the necessary protection and support. Al-Husaini's prediction was correct. Operating under a new alias, *Dr. Georg (Waldemar) Fischer*, the infamous specialist for interrogation and liquidation, was able to establish a new life and career for himself. According to research conducted by German journalist Christoph Sydow, Brunner borrowed the new alias from a former SS comrade, a Georg Fischer.[177] Along with the new name, Brunner was also supplied with a new identity. According to his fraudulent identification papers, *Dr. Georg Fischer* was an official member of the security escorts assigned to West Germany's first Bundeskanzler, Konrad Adenauer. With this new cover, Brunner was able to travel relatively unencumbered.

To outsiders, *Dr. Fischer* was a successful entrepreneur with several small-sized import and export businesses. A few of the most well-known include "the Kathar Office[178]"; the "Orient Trading Company"; and "The Arabian Medical Company."[179] The last two enterprises are better known by their acronyms OTRACO and THAMECO. Contrary to the differing company names, the principal commodity bought and sold by these businesses was the same: arms and intelligence. Other notable Nazis living who have been identified as being key participants in Brunner's lucrative death trade include Otto Ernst Remer,[180] who was a commander of the Berlin Wachbatallion, self-styled body-guard of Adolf Hitler and co-founder of the fascist Socialist Party of the Reich [Sozialistische Reichspartei] (SRP); Ernst Wilhelm Springer, another SRP co-founder; and former SS Obersturmführer Franz Rademacher who assisted in the deportation of 6,000 French Jews to Auschwitz. Springer was also convicted of participating in the forced deportation of 6,000 French Jews to the Auschwitz concentration camp.[181] And, last but not least, there was the mysterious businessman who answered to a number of different aliases (e.g., *Mr. Brinkmann, Mr. Eckmann, Mr. Hirth*) but achieved international infamy under his birthname, *Otto Adolf Eichmann.*

As a part of his business dealings, Brunner also reportedly used a number of other aliases which he seems to have derived from his principal assumed name *Dr. Georg Fischer.* In de-classified CIA reports, he is recorded as using the aliases *Dr. George Fischer; Otto Fischer; Dr. George Smith; G. Rischer; Alois Mohammed;* and *Adlatus Brunner.*[182] Additional aliases listed by a modern report released by the Deutscher Bundestag include *Alois Fescoer; Klaus Fischer;* and *Franz Kolar.*

An examination of international secret service records of Brunner's activities during this period also reveals that the SS officer's stock-in-trade was not merely confined to weaponry. There is also ample evidence that the special skill set Brunner had accumulated during his work with Adolf Eichmann was also much sought after during the Cold War period. In no time at all he became a frequent flier throughout the Arab-Muslim world. In particular, his business saw him fly regularly between Cairo, Beirut, and Damascus. In a 1961 declassified dispatch released by the US Central Intelligence Agency, it is stated, for example, that the former SS major worked as an agent and advisor to the Syrian GID [General Intelligence Directorate].[183] Operating within this capacity, he became an integral part of an clandestine network which involved other fugitive Nazis with alternative names.

For example, there was former SS Obersturmführer Franz Rademacher, who in March 1952 was convicted as an accessory to 1,300 counts of manslaughter. Before he could serve his sentence, Rademacher managed to escape to Spain with a fake passport issued to a *Tomé Rosselle.* Eventually, he was able to leave Europe and re-establish a new life working in Syria in clandestine intelligence and weapons operations under a series of false surnames (e.g., *Rosello, Rozallo, Razello*) and first names (e.g., *Tome, Fio, Fiol*). A close confidante of Rademacher during this time was former SS Hauptsturmführer Wilhelm Beissner who reputedly worked for both the Egyptian and the German secret intelligence under a long chain of false name variants (*Wilhelm Beisner, Heinrich Meissner, Willi Beis(s)ner, Dr. Willy Beis(s)ner, Dr. Willi Beissner, Dr. Jaeger*). In 1958, Beissner, operating under the code name *Betram* helped to recruit a former SS colleague of his, Standartenführer Walter Rauff for the Geman secret service [**B**undes**n**achrichten**d**ienst (BND)]. During World War II, Rauff had been involved in the development and deployment of mobile gas vans used to murder Jewish residents in Tunisia, Milan, Turin, and Genoa. In the Cold War, Rauff became known as a conspicuously wily BND agent with excellent international connections. Alongside the BND cover name *Enrico Gomez*, Rauff also used a number of pseudonyms (e.g., *Walter Rauf, Rauf Walter, Walter Rapp, Walter Rouff, Walter Rouff, Herr Alff, Alfonso Raffo, Adbullar Rauf, Abullah Rauff, Abulahr Rauf, Alfonso Raffo, Dr. Homis, Dr. Holis, Herr Bauermeister*) [184] Together with other war criminals, these operatives formed an intricate espicnage ring.[185]

Brunner's speciality within this Islamofascist network centered around counterintelligence interrogation methods. It is rumored that one of the instruments which Brunner developed for use by the Syrian GID was a special interrogation metal chair which when turned slowly broke the spinal cord of interviewees.[186] This torture instrument is still known today in some circles as the "Kursi Almani" or the "German chair." Brunner's unique expertise made him a popular consultant.

Brunner's uncommon expertise appears to have been particularly on demand between the years 1955 and 1960.[187] Ironically, it was also around this time that public pressure to finally root out the SS fugitive regained international momentum. One of the major factors fueling this new push was, of course, the spectacular capture of Brunner's SS superior officer, Adolf Eichmann. If Eichmann could be brought to trial, why couldn't the same be done with Alois Brunner. In September of 1960, the Attorney General's Office of Austria re-opened the case against the infamous Brunner I and demanded an official re-examination of the trial records from fifteen years earlier. The hope was that new evidence might be identified.[188] Then in November 1961, the district attorney issued a request to the Syrian government for Brunner's extradition. The authorities in Syria replied that to the best of their knowledge, the fugitive was no longer to be found in their country. A similar answer was given to the Israeli government in response to their formal request.

When diplomacy failed to produce Brunner's extradition, some Nazihunters decided it was time to take matters into their own hands. In 1961, a pipe bomb was delivered to his home during Purim. The date for the bomb was in all probability no accident. According to a letter written by Brunner's friend and confidant, Franz Rademacher, the explosive was sent during Purim, a Jewish holiday commemorating Queen Esther's rescuing the Jews of ancient Persia from an extermination plot.[189] The explosion severely damaged one of Brunner's eyes and destroyed the other. Brunner's ego, however, remained intact. It was not long before he was publicly gloating about his homicidal exploits with seeming impunity. He even agreed to give in-depth face-to-face interviews with Western reporters brave enough to travel to Syria to meet with the infamous *Dr. Georg Fischer.* These interviews took place in and around the Dr.'s home residence in Damascus: Rue George Haddat 22, the same address as "the Kathar Office."

Rather than stay underground as so many other NSDAP fugitives did when the international spot light shone too brightly in their direction, Alois Brunner seemed to enjoy all the publicity. In a 1985 tell-all interview with the German Boulevard Magazine, *Bunte,* the former SS officer demonstrated that the man who had been described during the Nuremberg Trials as "the most cold-blooded killer in Adolf Eichmann's retinue" had lost none of his virulence. His unremitting hatred erupted in a compulsive litany of outrageous anti-Jewish/anti-Israeli slurs and taunts. Although the resulting article was freed from the very worst of these epithets, the surviving material still caused an international firestorm. In the article, Brunner unabashedly outed himself as Eichmann's "right hand man." And in stunning act of braggadocio, he allowed himself to be photographed in broad daylight walking the streets of Damascus. That bombshell was soon followed by another.

A year later, in 1986, Brunner agreed to speak with award-winning Austrian journalist, Kurt Seinitz. According to Seinitz, that high point in his professional career marked a low point in his personal life. Brunner was, in Seinitz's opinion, bar none, absolutely the most repulsive human being whom he had ever met. Far from demonstrating personal remorse for his crimes, the then seventy-five-year-old murderer chastised his compatriot for even suggesting that he feel regret: "You should be happy that I freed beautiful Vienna of the Jews for you!"[190]. This explosive interview was followed twelve months later by an equally disturbing exposé with a US American reporter working for the *Chicago Sun Times.* In an exclusive telephone interview, the man responsible for sending over 120,000 people to their certain deaths offered readers the following explanation for his deeds: "All of them deserved to die because they were the devil's agents and human garbage. I have no regrets and would do it again."[191] *The Chicago Sun Times* article went on to report that the Brunner's personal body guards were the courtesy of Syria's First Family, the Al Assads, in gratitude to the SS officer having trained the nation's security forces in torture and intelligence.[192]

Now, some two decades later, it seems that the Syrians may not have been the only power protecting Brunner. Under his various aliases and code names, Alois Brunner is rumored to have worked directly or indirectly with a number of secret service agencies that also availed themselves of Brunner's unique expertise. There is also ample evidence that many of the former SS men who formed Brunner's intimate circle did the same under a host of aliases and cover names. It has been estimated, for example, that approximately 10 percent of the personnel forming Germany's postwar Secret Security Agency (BND) were once high-ranking officials in the NSDAP.

As of 2015, the German government still maintained that no evidence had been uncovered to demonstrate that he had been one of these men. However, this assertion must be taken with a grain of salt in view of the fact that many potentially corroborating records were apparently destroyed just after it was announced that an independent commission of historians would be given access to BND records to clarify what classified actions had been taken. Among those missing and destroyed records were many documents relating to Alois Brunner. Eventually, time exacted its own revenge. Based on its analysis of clandestine reports, the Wiesenthal Center announced that it believed Alois Brunner was dead and buried in an unknown location. There is some irony that a man who spent most of his life with so many different names would be buried in an unmarked, anonymous grave.

Notes

1. The last commandant of Neuengamme was SS Obersturmbannführer Max Pauly. Pauly was sentenced to death by a British Military Tribunal on May 3, 1946. The sentence was carried out on October 8, 1946. Ernst Klee, *Das Personenlexikon zum Dritten Riech: Wer war Was Vor und Nach 1945* (Hamburg: Nikol Verlag, 2015), 452.

2. Manuscript graciously provided by the Neuengamme Concentration Camp Research Archives.

3. Martin Broszat, ed. "10. Nach dem Zusammenbruch (1945–1947)," *Kommandant in Auschwitz: Autobiographische Aufzeichnung des Rudolf Höss* (München: Deutsche Taschenbuch Verlag, 1979), 148.

4. Martin Broszat, ed. "10. Nach dem Zusammenbruch (1945–1947)."

5. Crimea (Yalta) Conference, 1945. Report signed at Yalta February 11, 1945.

6. The Berlin (Potsdam) Conference, Protocol of the Proceedings. https://usa.usembassy.de/etexts/ga4–450801.pdf.

7. For more on the Massacre of Babij Jar and the subsequent trials, see Kalk von den Wänden. "Prozesse: Babij Jar," *Der Spiegel*. October 2, 1967. http://www.spiegel.de/spiegel/print/d-46289911.html; Fritz Bauer Archiv, "Der Darmstädter Einsatzgruppenprozess 1965-1968 und der Massenmord in Babij Jar." http://www.fritz-bauer-archiv.de/index.php/bauers-liste/verbrechen-der-wehrmacht.

8. Klee, *Das Personenlexikon*, 498.

9. Klee, *Das Personenlexikon*, 16.

10. Klee, *Das Personenlexikon*, 322.

11. Uwe Danker and Astrid Schwabe, *Schleswig-Holstein und der Nationalsozialismus* (Neumünster: Wachholtz Verlag, 2005), 174.

12. Jobst Böning, "Der hauptverantwortliche NS-Euthanasie-Täter und Leiter der T4-Aktion Werner Heyde alias Fritz Sawade-Ein jahrzehntes verdrängtes 'offenes' Geheimnis in Umgang mit der 'Banalität des Bösen,'" *Geheimnis: Psychologische, Psychopathologische und künstlerische Ausdrucksformen im Spektrum zwischen Verheimlichen*

und Geheimnisvollem, eds. Daniel Sollberger, Jobst Benning, Erik Boehlke, and Gerhard Schindler (Berlin: Frank and Timme, 2016), 203–20.

13. Niels Wiese, *Eicke: Eine SS-Karriere zwischen Nervenklinik, KZ-System und Waffen-SS* (Zürich: Ferdinand Schönigh, 2013), 206.

14. Klee, *Das Personenlexikon*, 130.

15. In Dr. Rausch's report to the court, Eicke was reportedly suffering from severe neurosis and was on the brink of a full-blown prison-induced psychotic break. Wiese, *Eicke*, 126.

16. Klaus-Detlev Godau-Schüttke, *Die Heyde/Sawade-Äffare: Wie Juristen und Mediziner den NS Euthanasieprofessor Heyde nach 1945 deckten und straflos blieben*. 3rd ed. (Hamburg: Nomos, 2010), 14.

17. Wiese, *Eicke*, 196.

18. SS-Obergruppernführer Eicke would go on to become the Chief Inspector of the Reich's Concentration Camp system as well as the Head of the SS-Totenkopf division. He died in an airplane crash on February 26, 1943. Klee, *Das Personenlexikon zum Dritten Riech*, 130.

19. Robert Jay Lifton, *The Nazi Doctors: Medical Killing and the Psychology of Genocide* (New York: Basic Books, 1986), 118.

20. Many researchers have inferred that Heyde's decision to join the NSDAP was upon the direct advice of Eicke (e.g., Godau-Schüttke, *Die Heyde/Sawade-Äffare*, 13; Henry Friedlander, *The Origins of Nazi Genocide*, 201; Lifton, *The Nazi Doctors*, 118). Niels Wiese, however, contends that Heyde most probably had already applied for Party membership before his fateful encounter with Eicke. This supposition is supported by the fact that Heyde demonstrated violent right-extremist tendencies well before meeting Eicke. According to his sister, Käthe Heyde, already at the age of seventeen, he had actively participated in the Kapp-Lüttwitz Putsch along with their brother. Käthe Heyde, "Leser Brief," *Der Spiegel* 1964, Nr. 13, 10. Named after the action's leaders, Wolfgang Kapp and Walter von Lüttwitz, the putsch was a failed "attempt by right-wing paramilitary and military organizations to overthrow the Weimar Republic in March 1920," Lifton, *The Nazi Doctors*, 117. It is clear then that Heyde had already shown not only an interest in, but a willingness to participate in right-extremist violence, like his patient, Theodor Eicke. It is perhaps this commonality which helped to forget the bond between the two men. Rather than instilling, it may be more accurate to say that Eicke helped to channel Heyde's interest in a Party career. Wiese, *Eicke*, 196.

21. Wiese, *Eicke*, 209.

22. Godau-Schüttke, *Die Heyde/Sawade-Äffare*, 15.

23. Ulf Schmidt, *Hitlers Arzt Brandt: Medizin und Macht im Dritten Reich* (Berlin: Aufbau Verlag, 2009), 204.

24. Heyde completed part of his coursework at the University of Freiburg am Breisgau. It is here that he is believed to have been influenced by the works of Psychiatry Professor Alfred Erich Hoche and Law Profesor Karl Lawrence Binding. Godau-Schüttke. *Die Heyde/Sawade-Äffare*, 16. According to Robert Jay Lifton, the young Heyde "was said to have attended Hoche's psychiatric lectures as a medical student during the early 1920s." Lifton, *The Nazi Doctors*, 117. Throughout the 1920s, Hoche and Binding were outspoken proponents of applying negative eugenics to segments of the population whose psychological or physical ailments were considered to place an untenable burden

upon the larger society's financial and genetic well-being. Their seminal work, "Die Freigabe der Vernichtung lebensunwerten Lebens" [The Permission to Destroy Life Unworthy of Living] was praised internationally by leaders of the eugenics movement and was later used by the Nazis as scientific and legal justification for the mass murder of millions. For more, see Edward Seidler, "Die medizinische Fakultät zwischen 1926 und 1948," *Die Freiburger Universität in der Zeit des Nationalsozialismus*, eds. Eckhard John, Bernd Martin, Marc Mück, and Hugo Ott (Freiburg: Freiburg Verlag, 1991), 73–90.

25. Edwin Black, *War Against the Weak: Eugenics and America's Campaign to Create a Master Race* (Washington, DC: Dialog Press, 2003), 213.

26. Harry Bruinius, *Better for all the World: The Secret History of America's Quest for Racial Purity* (New York: First Vintage Books, 2007), 71.

27. On June 11, 1930, Cora Hudson, the British director of the International Federation of Eugenic Organizations wrote: "I used to say, when asked, that I thought probably Germany was taking Eugenics most seriously, but I am quite sure that now the American Eugenics Society leads the world." Black, *War Against the Weak*, 229.

28. After hearing the plans, only one of the invitees politely declined to participate. The others enthusiastically set about transforming the Führer's vision into lethal reality.

29. The villa was originally built as a private residence for the German banker and fine arts patron, Valentin Weisbach. In the summer of 1909, Weisbach sold the residence for 1 million Reichsmark to Georg Liebermann. After Liebermann's death in 1926, his children transformed the villa into one of Berlin's most prestigious art and auction houses. Annette Hinz-Wessels, *Tiergartenstrasse 4: Schaltzentrale der nationalsozialistischen 'Euthanasie-Morde'* (Berlin: C. H. Link, 2015).

30. Among some members of the SS, the program for killing the mentally ill was referred to using a different name, "IT" for "Irrentötungsaktion" Ernst Klee, *Deutsche Medizin im Dritten Reich: Karrieren vor und nach 1945* (Frankfurt am Main: S. Fischer Verlag, 2001).

31. KdF official Hans Hefelmann helped organize the extermination of children and adolescents. According to him, great care was given to select highly technical-sounding names to give the lethal operations the air of scientific legitimacy. Thomas Beddies, "Die Tötung 'Lebensunwerter' Kinder im Nationalsozialismus': Die Kinderfachabteilung," *Tödliche Medizin: Rassenwahn im Nationalsozialismus*, ed. Margret Kampmeyer (Gottingen: Wallstein, 2009), 78.

32. The German original: "sind unter Verantwortung beauftragt, die Befugnisse namentlich zu bestimmender Ärzte so zu erweitern, daß nach menschlichem Ermessen unheilbar Kranken bei kritischster Beurteilung ihres Krankheitszustandes der Gnadentod gewährt werden kann." Goddau-Schüttke, *Die Heyde/Sawade Affäre*, 35.

33. Klee, *Dokumente zur "Euthanasie,"* 95.

34. In the T4 medical hierarchy, Heyde was second only to Brandt. According to postwar testimony given under oath by Dr. Muthig, a physician at the Dachau Concentration Camp, in the fall of 1941, a team of medical specialists traveled to the camp to select prisoners whom they deemed unfit for labor. After several hundred were selected, the prisoners were transferred to the Mathausen Concentration Camp where they were immediately put to death. The entire operation was named after Professor Heyde who was the head medical expert in charge of the selection process. Cornelia Schmitz-Bening, *Vokabular des Nationalsozialismus* (Berlin: Walter de Gruyter, 2000), 218.

35. Georg Lilienthal, "Wie die T4-Aktion organiziert wurde: Zur Burokratie eines Massenmordes," *Lebensunwert zerstörte Leben: Zwangsterilisation und 'Euthanasie,'* ed. Magret Hamm (Frankfurt am Main: Verlag für akademische Schriften, 2006), 143–157.

36. Klee, *Dokumente zur 'Euthanasie,'* 98.

37. Klee, *Dokumente zur 'Euthanasie,'* 138.

38. Willi Dreßen, "NS-'Euthanasie'-Prozesse in der Bundesrepublik Deutschland im Wandel der Zeit," *NS-'Euthanasie' vor Gericht: Fritz Bauer und die Grenzen juristischer Bewältigung,* eds. Hanno Loewy and Bettina Winter (Frankfurt am Main: Campus Verlag, 1996), 35–58, 49.

39. This list of pseudonyms was compiled from two main sources: Klee, *Das Personenlexikon zum Dritten Reich* and Friedlander, *The Origins of Nazi Genocide,* 103. It should be noted that these sources contain certain contradictions. For example, while Klee lists Schmalenbach's first name as Curt and his pseudonym as "Dr. Palm," Friedlander spells Schmalenbach's first name with a 'K' and asserts that his pseudonym was "Dr. Keim." In the case of Ewald Worthmann, Klee spells the T4 employee's last name without an "h" as Friedlander indicates and asserts that his pseudonym in Sonnenstein was "Dr. Friede." Frielander speculates that the name "Dr. Ott" was used by Günther Hennecke in Grafeneck and Hadamar. Friedlander, *The Origins of Nazi Genocide,* 49. However, in 1969, a Grafeneck office-worker by the name of "Gerhard S." reportedly gave sworn testimony before the Frankfurt Criminal court that he sometimes used the pseudonym "Dr. Ott." Klee, *Dokumente zur 'Euthanasie,'* 138.

40. Harvard Law School Nuremberg Trials Project, January 17, 1947, http://nuremberg.law.harvard.edu/, 7574.

41. Landesarchiv Baden-Württemberg, "Amtsgericht: Anschrift der angeschuldigte Hermann Holzschuh" (August 5, 1948). Abt. Staatsarchiv Sigmaringen, Wü 29/3 T 1 Nr. 1758/03/01, 1–23.

42. Today, it is estimated that the T4 staff at Grafeneck was responsible for the murder of over 70,000 people. The industrial method developed at Grafeneck and the other T4 facilities laid the foundation for the extermination camps.

43. Harvard Law School Nuremberg Trials Project, December 16, 1946, http://nuremberg.law.harvard.edu/, 500.

44. In the 1940s, Eppinger turned his attention to other areas of sadistic research, including the infamous sea-water experiments in which Roma and Sinti concentration camp prisoners were deprived of all nutrition aside from chemically processed sea water. Vivien Spitz, *Doctors From Hell: The Horrific Account of Nazi Experiments on Humans* (Boulder, CO: Sentient Publications, 2005), 157–74.

45. Klee, *Dokumente zur 'Euthanasie,'* 69–70

46. Klee, *Dokumente zur 'Euthanasie,'* 69–70.

47. "Die 'Euthanasie-Anstalt' Brandenburg an der Havel," Gedenkstätten Brandenburg/Havel. http://www.stiftung-bg.de/doku/neues/doku2.htm. For more, see Norbert Jachertz, "Brandenburg: 9000 Opfer, 8000 Namen," *Arzteblatt* 11 (December 2012): 564.

48. Klee, *Deutsche Medizin im Dritten Reich.*

49. Schmidt, *Hitlers Arzt Brandt,* 263.

50. This name is derived from the Concentration Camp Inspectorate which used several alphanumeric codes to indicate the manner of death. Other codes include 14f2 for suicides or accidental deaths, 14f3 for prisoners who were shot during an escape attempt, and 14f1 for death by execution. Lifton, *The Nazi Doctors*, 135.

51. Harvard Law School Nuremberg Trials Project. Document 2799 http://nuremberg.law.harvard.edu/.

52. During the Nuremberg Trials both Viktor Brack and Dr. Muthig assert that the 14f13 operation in Dachau was referred to as "Aktion Heyde." Harvard Law School Nuremberg Trials Project. May 16, 1947 (p. 7712). http://nuremberg.law.harvard.edu/.

53. This initiative was also referred to by the name "Aktion 14f13." Schmidt, *Hitlers Arzt Brandt*, 263.

54. Godau-Schütke, *Die Heyde/Sawade Äffäre*, 47.

55. Despite the grotesque simplicity of this system, in 1945, one of the T4 physicians was reprimanded for having mistakenly used the "+" symbol to indicate the patient in question should be kept alive. The error was spotted after the physician had already mis-marked several thousand cases. *Der Spiegel*, 1961, Nr. 19, 39.

56. For more on the structure, activities, and leaders of this organization, see Claudia Koonz, *Mothers in the Fatherland: Women, the Family, and Nazi Politics* (New York: St. Martin's Press, 1987); Nicole Kramer, *Volksgenossinnen an der Heimatfront: Mobilisierung, Verhalten, Erinnerung, Schriftenreihe der Historischen Kommission* Band 82 (Göttingen: Vandenhoeck & Ruprecht, 2011).

57. Klee, *Dokumente zur 'Euthanasie,'* 224.

58. Klee, *Dokumente zur 'Euthanasie,'* 225.

59. After the war, Dr. Franz Schlegelberger spent his retirement in Flensburg. *Der Spiegel*, Nr. 8, 1964, 33.

60. In that secret memo, the Court Justice makes explicit reference to state-sponsored mass murder occurring in the local killing center Hadamar. More specifically, he writes that his letter is in reference to the destruction of lives unworthy of living "Vernichtung lebensunwerten Lebens." Although it is not clear how and when the Oberlandesgerichtspräsident learned of this action, it has been established that Kurt Wackermann, the district attorney of Frankfurt am Main, attended a meeting held by Victor Brack and Werner Heyde in Berlin from April 23 to 24, 1941. The topic of that meeting was Aktion T4 and the efforts of Schlegelberger to provide at least the semblance of legality to the program. Klee, *Das Personenlexikon zum Dritten Riech*, 647. It is quite conceivable that upon his return to Frankfurt, Wackerman informed Ungewitter about that meeting, and Ungewitter, knowing of Schlegelbberger's involvement, evidently felt free to write about the information leaks in Hessen with unusual candor.

61. Klee, *Dokumente zur ,Euthanasie,'* 229.

62. Annette Hinz-Wessels, "Die Halten der Kirchen zur 'Euthanasie im NS-Staat" in *Lebensunwert zerstörte Leben: Zwangssterilisation und 'Euthanasie,'* ed. Margret Hamm (Frankfurt am Main: Verlag für akademische Schriften, 2006), 177.

63. Kurt Novak, "Widerstand, Zustimmung, Hinnahme. Das Verhalten der Bevölkerung zur 'Euthanasie,'" *Medizin und Gesundheitspolitik in der NS-Zeit*, ed. Norbert Frei (Munich: Oldenbourg Verlag, 1991), 235–52.

64. Ute Hoffmann, "'Wir haben nur unsere Pflicht getan . . .': Täter und Täterinnen in den Gasmordanstalten der 'Euthanasie,'" *Tödliche Medizin: Rassenwahn im National-sozialismus*, ed. Margret Kampmeyer (Gottingen: Wallstein, 2009), 118.

65. It has been speculated that Heyde's sudden loss of favor among the KdF leadership was due to the discovery of his alleged homosexuality. For more, see Schmdt, *Hitlers Arzt Brandt*, 204; Bönning, "Der hauptverantwortliche," 210. In 1939, the SS appears to have launched an investigation into allegations of Heyde having made "inappropriate" advances towards a SS Untersturmführer in the 1920s. The investigation ended without charges being levied. Weise, *Eicke*, 208. Another possible reason for Heyde's replacement may have been professional and personal disputes with Karl Brandt. Henry Friedlander, *Der Weg zum NS-Genozid: Von Euthanasie zur Endlösung* (Berlin: Berlin Verlag, 1997), 326.

66. The construction of the facility was accomplished by a group of fifty-eight prisoners sent from the Flossenbürg concentration camp. Niels Wiese, *Eicke*, 212. For the duration of the construction, a satellite prison camp was established near the building site. The prisoners were forced to remove the bombs and bodies that had fallen during the city air raids. KZ-Gedenkstaette Flossenbürg: Außenlager engl. Würzburg. http://www.gedenkstaette-flossenbuerg.de/en/history/subcamps/subcamps/wuerzburg/.

67. The SS-military hospital was transferred from Würzburg to Denmark after a twenty-minute bombing raid by the British Airforce on March 16, 1945. Nearly 90 percent of the city's infrastructure was destroyed, 90,000 residents lost their homes, and 4,000 people were killed during that attack. The air raid was considered to be retribution for the German Luftwaffe's destruction of Coventry in 1940. Oliver Das Gupta, "Das kleine Gluck im Inferno," *Süddeutsche Zeitung*, March 16, 2015, http://www.sued deutsche.de/bayern/zweiter-weltkrieg-in-unterfranken-das-kleine-glueck-im-inferno-1.2 393963.

68. The list of the accused included the following: Hermann Becker-Freyseng, Kurt Blome, Viktor Brack, Karl Brandt, Rudolf Brandt, Fritz Fischer, Karl Gebhardt, Karl Genzken, Siegfried Handloser, Waldemar Hoven, Joachim Mrugowsky, Herta Oberheuser, Adolf Pokorny, Helmut Poppendeck, Hans Wolfgang Romberg, Gerhard Rose, Paul Rostock, Siegfried Ruff, Konrad Schaefer, Oskar Schroeder, Wolfram Sievers, and Georg August Weltz. *The United States v. Karl Brandt et al.*, Nurnberg Military Tribunals, Indictments, Office of the Military Government for Germany (November 21, 1946–August 20, 1947), 3–5, https://www.loc.gov/rr/frd/Military_Law/pdf/NT_Indictments.pdf.

69. *The United States v. Karl Brandt et al.*, 11.

70. *Der Spiegel*, 1964, Nr. 8. Page 37; Godau-Schüttke, *Die Heyde/Sawade-Äffare*.

71. Ronnen Steinke and Andreas Voßkuhle, *Fritz Bauer: Oder Auschwitz vor Gericht* (Berlin: Piper Verlag, 2015), 191.

72. As of the writing of this book, there are only a little over 200 entries in the German telephone book for residents with the last name *Sawade*. In a country of 80 million people, that makes the name extremely rare. Verwandt.de, http://www.verwandt.de/ka rten/absolut/sawade.html.

73. Godau-Schütke, *Die Heyde/Sawade Äffare*, 62.

74. Godau-Schütke, *Die Heyde/Sawade Äffare*, 62.

75. In the official records, Heyde reported that his wife's maiden name was *Maria Lossow* and his sons were *Hans* and *Gerd Sawade*. Stadtarchiv Flenburg, "Meldeangelegenheit Sawade/Heyde. Vertrauliche Brief an den Herrn Oberburgermeister, Flensburg,"

[The Circumstances surrounding the registration Of Sawade/Heyde. Classified letter sent to the Office of the Lord Mayor of Flensburg], December 7, 1959, IIE 02871. However, in actuality, their names were *Erika, Achim,* and *Werner.* Godau-Schütke, *Die Heyde/Sawade Äffäre*, 78–79.

76. Heyde claimed that he was a refugee from the former German territories in the east and was subsequently issued a "Flüchtlingsausweis A." With these papers, Heyde became a part of an unprecedented refugee wave to hit Schleswig-Holstein after the war. According to official statistics, the crest of this wave occurred in 1949 at precisely the time when Heyde reached the area. "Das Flüchtlingsgeschehen in Schleswig-Holstein infolge des 2. Weltkriegs im Spiegel der amtlichen Statistik" (Kiel, Statistische Landesamt Schleswig-Holstein, 1974: 16). An indication of the dimensions of postwar refugee population is made clear by the following fact: in 1949, the total population of Schleswig-Holstein equaled 2.6 million. Of that number, 1.8 million or ca. 44.25 percent were either refugees or asylum-seekers. Godau-Schütke, *Die Heyde/Sawade Äffäre*, 90.

77. Stadtarchiv Flensburg, StAFL: IIE 08271. "Meldeangelegenheit Sawade/Heyde."

78. Lifton somewhat incorrectly identifies the school as being just outside of Kiel which is nearly 100 km away as opposed to Flensburg which is only 5 km away. Robert Jay Lifton, *The Nazi Doctors*, 119.

79. In German, the institution has various names: the "Marinesportschule," "Marine-Sportschule," and the "Sportschule Flensburg-Mürwik."

80. Godau-Schütke, *Die Heyde/Sawade Äffäre*, 63.

81. By comparison, several of Heyde's closest T4 colleagues had already been tried, convicted, and executed (e.g., Paul Nitsche, executed March 25, 1948; Viktor Brack, June 28, 1948; Karl Brandt, June 2, 1948). Klee, *Das Personenlexikon zum Dritten Riech.*

82. Heyde apparently was recommended by Professor Dr. Hans Glatzel. A dietary physiologist at the University of Kiel, Glatzel had served as an expert medical consultant on insurance cases for Schleswig-Holstein. During the war, he had been a member of the NSDAP and the SA. Klee, *Deutsche Medizin im Dritten Reich*, 259–61.

83. A Borgward-Isabella TS or the 'the triumphant Isabella' [siegreiche Isabella], as it was called in the 1959 advertising, was a mid-sized roadster. Today, the car is considered a classic among collectors.

84. On April 26, 1962, she was found guilty of fraud and sentenced to one-year imprisonment. Godau-Schüttke, *Die Heyde/Sawade-Äffare*, 78.

85. Godau-Schüttke, *Die Heyde/Sawade-Äffäre*, 80.

86. Schleswig-Holsteinischer Landestag, "NS-Kontinuitäten in der Landespolitik: Schleswig-Holstein ist ein Extremfall," April 27, 2016. https://www.sh-landtag.de/aktuell/panorama/Beitraege_2016/16_04_27_danker.html.

87. Uwe Danker, Sebastian Lehmann, and Stephan Glienke, "Geschichtswissenschaftliche Aufarbeitung der personellen und strukturellen Kontinuität nach 1945 in der schleswig-holsteinischen Legislative und Exekutive." Präsentation der Ergebnisse im schleswig-holsteinischen Landtag und auf der Landespressekonferenz am 27.04.2016. https://www.sh-landtag.de/export/sites/landtagsh/homedata/kat1/data/Danker_LPK_Text_20160427.pdf.

88. An excellent example is the lawyer Heinrich or "Heinz" Reinefarth. During the Nazi period, the SS-Gruppenführer was known as the "Executioner of Warschau." He was responsible for helping to orchestrate the military massacre of some 200,000 civilians

in Poland's capital. After the war, Reinefarth was elected the Bürgermeister of Wester-land on the Island of Sylt and in 1958, he became an official member of the Schleswig-holstein Parliament until 1967. "1958: Ein SS-General zieht in den Landtag ein: Junger Beamter protestiert—und tritt Debatte über Nazi-Vergangenheit und Zivilcourage los." *Der Landtag: Der Parliamentzeitschrift für Schleswig-Holstein*, Nr. 02 (June 2016), 6–8.

89. Klee, *Das Personenlexikon zum Dritten Riech*, 85.

90. Godau-Schüttke, *Die Heyde/Sawade-Äffare*, 135.

91. "Professor Dr. Werner Creutzfeldt and Dr. Otto Creutzfeldt, Ein Leserbrief," *Der Spiegel*, Nr. 13, 1964, 11.

92. *Der Spiegel*, Nr. 19, 1961, 38.

93. Staatsarchiv Ludwigburg, EL48/2I Bestell # Bü138.

94. Bericht des Untersuchungsausschusses II in der Angelegenheit Prof. Heyde/Dr. Sawade. Schleswig-Holstein Landtag 4. 1958. Drucksache Nr. 445.

95. To get to the bottom of just who knew what when, a parliamentary inquiry was opened on November 30, 1959. The first formal question asked was "Which civil servants, public officials, and public figures in Schleswig-Holstein knew before November 10, 1959, that Professor Hyde was one and the same as Dr. Sawade?" Less than a month after the fugitive's capture, the following list of people were identified as having known that the physician was living under an alias: (1.) Dr. Buresch, Präsident des Landessozial-gerichts; (2.) Professor Dr. med. Creutzfeldt; (3.) Medizinaldirektor, Dr. med. Delfs; (4.) Prof. Dr. med. Doerr; Sozialgerichtsdirektor Gerstenhauer; (5.) Prof. Dr. med. Glatzel; (6.) Prof. Dr. med. Hallerman; (7.) Dr. med. Knolle; (8.) Senatpräsident Dr. Meister-ernst; (9.) Senatpräsident Michaelis; (10.) Obermedizinalrat Dr. Osteram; (11.) Prof. Dr. med. Reinwein; (12.) Obermedizinalrat Dr. Rischer; (13.) Landgerichtsrat Schlüter; (14.) Bundesrichter Sonnenberg; (15.) Frau Dr. med. Spallek; and (16.) Sozialgerichtsrä-tin Frau Stumpf. Schleswig-Holstein Landtag 4, "Bericht des Untersuchungsausschusses II in der Angelegenheit Prof. Heyde/Dr. Sawade," D rucksache Nr. 4441958.

96. Steinke and Voßkuhle, *Fritz Bauer*, 191.

97. Stadtsarchiv Ludwigsburg, Bestell:EL 48/2I; Bestand: Bü 1965.

98. Simon Wiesenthal states that "on the day of the German invasion of Ternopol, Poland [. . .] a pogrom against the Jewish population of 18,000 is organized and 5,000 Jews are killed with the help of the Ukrainians." *Everyday Remembrance Day: A Chronicle of Jewish Martyrdom* (New York: Henry Holt Company, 1985), 150.

99. Yad Vashem, "Tarnopol: Historical Background," http://www.yadvashem.org/righteous/stories/tarnopol-historical-background.html.

100. Yad Vashem, "Tarnopol: Historical Background," http://www.yadvashem.org/righteous/stories/tarnopol-historical-background.html.

101. Maurice Zeitlin, "The Last Stands of Jews in the Small Town Ghettos of German-occupied Poland, 1941–1943," *Society, History, and the Global Human Condition: Essays in Honor of Irving M. Zeitlin*, eds. Baber Zaheer and Joseph M. Bryant (London: Lexington Books, 2010), 33–70.

102. Stadtsarchiv Ludwigsburg, Bestell: EL 48/2I; Bestand: Bü 195, Number 21. Betr. Fortenbacher.

103. Stadtsarchiv Ludwigsburg, Bestell:EL 48/2I; Bestand: Bü 1965, Number 21.

104. Klee, *Das Personenlexikon zum Dritten Riech*, 645.

105. For more, see Patrick Tobin, *Crossroads at Ulm: Postwar West Germany and the 1958 Ulm Einsatzkommando Trial.* Unpublished Doctoral Dissertation. University of North Carolina at Chapel Hill. 2013.

106. Nicholas Kulish and Souad Mekhennet, *The Eternal Nazi—from Mathausen to Cairo: The Relentless Pursuit of SS Doctor Aribert Heim* (New York: Random House, 2014), 69.

107. Tobin, *Crossroads at Ulm*, 92.

108. Adalbert Rückerl, *Die Strafverfolgung von NS-Verbrechen 1945–1978* (Heidelberg: CF Müller Juristischer Verlag, 1979), 49.

109. Andreas Mix, "NS Prozesse: Als Westdeutschland aufwachte," *Der Spiegel*, April 27, 2008.

110. Tobin, *Crossroads at Ulm*, 119.

111. There were four different Einsatzgruppen, each with a different geographical killing assignment: (1.) Einsatzgruppe A for the Baltic States and White Russia; (2.) Einsatzgruppe B for Central Russia; (3.) Einsatzgruppe C for the Ukaine and White Russia; and (4.) Einsatzgruppe D for the southeastern perimeter of the Soviet Union.

112. Alfred Streim, "Zum Beispiel: Die Verbrechen der Einsatzgruppen in der Sowjetunion," *NS-Prozesse Nach 25 Jahren Strafverfolgung: Möglichkeiten, Grenzen, Ergebnisse*, ed. Adalbert Rückerl (Karlsruhe: C. F. Muller Verlag, 1971), 65–106.

113. Mix, "NS Prozesse," para. 10.

114. Helmut Langerbein, *Hitler's Death Squads: The Logic of Mass Murder* (College Station: Texas A & M University Press, 2003), 164.

115. Jörg Friedrich, *Die kalte Amnestie: NS-Täter in der Bundesrepublik* (Munich: Piper Verlag, 1984), 338.

116. Langerbein, *Hitler's Death Squads*, 164.

117. Friedrich, *Die kalte Amnestie*, 339.

118. Tobin, *Crossroads at Ulm*, 120.

119. Rückerl, *Die Strafverfolgung*, 49.

120. Irmtrud Wojak, ed., *"Gerichtstag halten über uns selbst": Geschichte und Wirkung des ersten Frankfurter Auschwitz Prozesses* (Frankfurt: Campus Verlag, 2001).

121. Wojak, *"Gerichtstag,"* 100.

122. *Der Spiegel*, "Ein Toter gleich zehn Minuten Gefängnis": Die Ro le der bundesdeutschen Justiz bei der Aufarbeitung von NS- Verbrechen," Nr. 28/1979, 46–55.

123. Claudia Fröhlich, "Der Ulmer Einsatzgruppenprozess, 1958: Wahrnehmung und Wirkung des ersten großen Holocaust Prozesses," *NS Prozesse und deutsch Öffentlichkeit: Besatzungszeit frühe Bundesrepublik und DDR*, eds. Jörg Osterloh and Clemens Vollnhals (Göttingen: Vandenhoeck and Ruprecht, 2011), 232.

124. Fröhlich, "Der Ulmer Einsatzgruppenprozess, 1958," 234.

125. Tobin, *Crossroads at Ulm*, 282.

126. *Der Spiegel*, "Ein Toter gleich zehn Minuten Gefängnis," 46.

127. Tobin, *Crossroads at Ulm*, 96–97.

128. Klee, *Das Personenlexikon zum Dritten Riech*, 59.

129. Fröhlich, "Der Ulmer Einsatzgruppenprozess, 1958," 240.

130. Wojak, *"Gerichtstag,"* 100.

131. Andreas Mix, "50 Jahre Zentrale Stelle zur Verfolgung der NS-Verbrechen: Wir dürfen nicht zulassen, dass sie straffrei ausgehen," *Berliner Zeitung*, November 11, 2008. https://www.berliner-zeitung.de/50-jahre-zentrale-stelle-zur-verfolgung-der-ns-v erbrechen--wir-duerfen-nicht-zulassen--dass-sie-straffrei-ausgehen--15723302.

132. Martin Finkelberger, "Während meines ganzes Lebens habe ich die Juden erforscht, wie ein Bakteriologe eine gefährlichen Bazillus studiert—Johann von Leers (1902–1965) als antisemitischer Propaganda experte bis 1945," *Bulletin des Deutsches Historisches Institut Moskau* (2008): 88–99.

133. Finkelberger, "wie ein Bakteriologe," 89.

134. Civilian Internment Camp 91 or "CI Camp 91" was established in the spring of 1945 and served as one of the primary collection centers after the war. At its peak, the camp held almost 26,000 prisoners, representing a broad cross section of NS society. In the tumult after the war, the US interned a wide range of suspicious persons from Party sympathizers to high-ranking NS dignitaries. Some of the most prominent internees include the Austrian-born SS-Obersturmbannführer Otto Skorzeny who helped to free Mussolini on September 12, 1943; and SS-Sturmbannführer Kurt Lindow, a member of the Gestapo who was placed on trial for the murder Soviet prisoners of war. The camp remained under the authority of the United States, until November 1946 when control was officially turned over to the West German government. Four years later, CI Camp 91 was officially closed.

135. "Die Tragödie der Demokratie," *Der Weg* 5, no. 4 (1951): 295–99; "Der unsichtbare Knebel," *Der Weg* 6, no.1 (1952): 64–68; "Ein Drittel des deutschen Volksvermögens – den Juden," *Der Weg* 7, no. 1 (1953): 56; "Ein Programm für die Juden," *Der Weg* 8, no. 11 (1954): 795.

136. Marco Sennholz, *Johann von Leer: Ein Propagandist des Nationalsozialismus* (Berlin-Brandenburg: Be-Bra Verlag, 2013).

137. According to the US government declassified file on von Leers from August 8, 1956, the professor relocated to Cairo, Egypt, on April 1956. While there, he reportedly maintained excellent contact with leaders of the Arab League. For more, see https://www.cia.gov/library/readingroom/docs/LEERS percent2C percent20JOHANNES percent-20VON_0035.pdf.

138. David Motadel, *Islam and Nazi Germany's War* (London: The Belknap Press of Harvard University Press, 2014), 66.

139. Just a few of the early publications that fall into this category are the following: "Mustafa Kemal Pascha," *Zeitschrift für Politik* 24, no. 1 (1934): 4–27; "Der Weg der modernen Türkei," *Die Tat* 25, no. 12 (1934): 923–38; "Frankreich und der Islam," *Der Türmer* 39, no. 4 (1937): 382; "Die arabischen Argumente gegen die Neufestigung der Juden in Palästina," *Der Weltkampf* 15, no. 172 (1938): 146–60; "Islam und Judentum im Laufe der Jahrhunderten," *Der Deutsche Erzieher* 5, no. 17 (1938): 427; "Islam und Judentum-Zwei unversöhnliche Gegensätze. Teil 1 & 2," *Der Weltkampf* 16 (1939): 8–20, 64–71, 181–82; "Judentum und Islam als Gegensätze," *Die Judenfrage* 6, no. 24 (1942): 275–78.

140. Finkelberger, "wie ein Bakteriologe," 99.

141. One of the most important NS allies in the Arab world was al-Husseini who also fled to Cairo where he continued to call for the annihilation of the Jews.

142. For this reason, von Leers argued that the term "anti-Semitism' was actually inappropriate and preferred to use the name "anti-Judaism."

143. Klee, *Das Personenlexikon zum Dritten Riech*, 237.

144. Klee, *Das Personenlexikon zum Dritten Riech*, 439.

145. Ernst Klee, "Den Hahn aufzudrehen war ja keine grosse Sache: Vergassungsärzte während der NS-Zeit und danach." *Dachauer Heft* 4. Medizin um NS-Staat: Täter, Opfer, Handlungen. 1993, 1–21.

146. Klee, *Den Hahn aufzudrehen*, 11.

147. Klee, *Den Hahn aufzudrehen*, 1.

148. Schmitz-Berning, *Vokabular des Nationalsozialismus*, 267.

149. Vivien Spitz, *Doctors from Hell*, 68, 65–83.

150. Staatsarchiv Ludwigsburg Bestand, EL48/2I; Bestellnummer Bü158.

151. There is some dispute over the origin of the name "Operation Reirhardt." Some assert that it is derived from the surname of the State Secretary at the Reich's Ministry of Finance, Fritz Reinhardt. Others indicate that the namesake of the operation was Reinhard Heydrich. This lack of agreement may also account for the difference in spelling used for the mission during and after the Third Reich. Jules Schelvis, *Sobibor: A History of a Nazi Death Camp* (New York: Bloomsbury, 2007), 5.

152. Ferdinand Ranft, "Ohne Scham und ohne Reue," *Zeit Online*, March 25, 1966, para. 2. https://www.zeit.de1966/13/ohne-scham-und-ohne-reue/.

153. *Der Spiegel*. "NS Verbrechen. Peitsche bewahrt," December 19, 1966. http://www.spiegel.de/spiegelprint/d-46415595.html.

154. For more, see Eike Frenzel, "Mein Nachbar, der Massenmörder: Ungetauchter Kriegsverbrecher," *Der Spiegel*, August 6, 2010. http://www.spiegel.de/einestages/un tergetauchter-kriegsverbrecher-a-946564.html.

155. There appears to be some disagreement on the exact spelling of Eichmann's alias. While Klee reports the spelling *Ricardo*, Steinacher records the spelling *Ficcardo*. Klee, *Das Personenlexikon zum Dritten Riech*, 130; Gerald Steinacher, *Nazis on the Run: How Hitler's Henchmen Fled Justice* (Oxford: Oxford University Press, 2012), 49.

156. Steinacher, *Nazis on the Run*, 53.

157. Karla Müller-Tupath, *Verschollen in Deutschland: Das heimliche Leben des Anton Burger, Lagerkommandant von Theresienstadt* (Hamburg: Konkret Literatur Verlag, 1994), 14–15.

158. Otto Dov Kulka, "Ghetto in an Annihilation Camp: Jewish Social History in the Holocaust and Its Ultimate Limits," *The Nazi Holocaust.: The Victims of the Holocaust*, ed. Michael Robert Marrus, Volume 2, Part 6, 1133–1150 (London: De Gruyter, 1989), 1149.

159. Hannelore Brenner, *The Girls of Room 28: Friendship, Hope, and Survival in Theresienstadt* (New York: Schocken Books, 2009), 112.

160. Müller-Tupath, *Verschollen in Deutschland*, 101.

161. Eva Holpfer, "Ich war nichts anderes als ein kleiner Sachbearbeiter von Eichmann: die justizielle Ahndung von Deportationsverbrechen in Österreich," *Holocaust*

Kriegsverbrechen vor Gericht: Der Fall Österreich, eds. Thomas Albrich, Winifried Garscha, and Martin Polaschek (Innsbruck: Studien Verlag, 2006), 155.

162. Müller-Tupath, *Verschollen in Deutschland*, 15.

163. Müller-Tupath, *Verschollen in Deutschland*.

164. Müller-Tupath, *Verschollen in Deutschland*, 149.

165. According to Müller-Tupath, in 1960, after learning that he was still being sought by the authorities, Burger took on the alias *Josef Weiszl* and returned to Austria. If this is indeed true, Burger's choice was a poor one, for the name belonged to a former Viennese colleague of his who had been convicted for his role in the deportation of Jewish residents from Paris. According to Eva Holpfer (2006), after Weiszl's conviction in France, the Austrian authorities decided to suspend their indictment (161). Nevertheless, the selection of such an alias might well have drawn unwanted attention, particularly in Austria.

166. Müller-Tupath, *Verschollen in Deutschland*, 13.

167. Georg M. Hafner and Esther Schapira, *Die Akte Alois Brunner: Warum einer der größten Naziverbrecher noch immer auf freiem Fuß ist* (Frankfurt am Main: Rowohlt, 2002), 26–36.

168. A reproduction of the original memo can be found in Georg M. Hafner and Esther Schapira, *Die Akte Alois Brunner: Warum einer der größten Naziverbrecher noch immer auf freiem Fuß ist* (Frankfurt am Main: Rowohlt, 2002), 37–93.

169. Holpfer, "Ich war nicht anderes," 153–54.

170. Anton Brunner was also charged and found guilty of assisting in the round-up, abuse, and murder of Jewish Viennese residents in collection centers [Sammellager] located throughout the city. The centers were erected in buildings that had been seized by the Nazis for processing Jewish residents earmarked for deportation. The intentional combination of desperate overcrowding, unhygienic facilities, malnutrition, and torture led to high rates of disease and death, many via suicide. LG Wien Vg 1 g Vr 4574/45.

171. After his arrest by the US American troops, Burger, prisoner number 10579, was sent to CIC Internment Camp. "Marcus W. Orr" in Glasenback bei Salzburg. For more on this period, see Müller-Tupath, *Verschollen in Deutschland*, 107.

172. On January 5, 1954, Alois Brunner was found guilty and sentenced to death for war crimes in absentia by a court in Marseille, France. On May 3, 1954, he was once again sentenced to death by a second French court, this time in Paris.

173. Deutscher Bundestag, 18 Wahlperiod, January 20, 2015, "Antwort der Bundesregierung auf die Kleine Anfrage der Abgeordneten Jan Korte, Sevim Dagdelen, Ulla Jelpke, weiterer Abgeordneter und der Fraktion DIE LINKE," Drucksache 18/3599.

174. Peter Longerich, *Heinrich Himmler: Biographie* (Berlin: Pantheon Press, 2010), 667–716.

175. For a brief summary of al-Husaini's anti-Jewish and anti-Israel activities before, during, and after the war, see https://www.ushmm.org/wlc/en/article.php?ModuleId=10007667. A very detailed investigation of al-Husaini and other Islamists with strong ties to the Nazi regime can be found in Barry Rubin and Wolfgang G. Schwanitz, *Nazis, Islamists, and the Making of the Modern Middle East* (New Haven, CT: Yale University Press, 2014).

176. This appears not to have been the first meeting between al-Husaini and Brunner. Already in the early to mid-1940s the two had encountered one another numerous times

in France, Hungary, and Poland. It is even suspected that Alois Brunner was among the small SS entourage that accompanied al-Husaini on his specially arranged tour of a Nazi concentration camp. Rubin and Schwanitz, *Nazis, Islamists*, 225.

177. Christoph Sydow, "Judenmörder Alois Brunner starb in Syrien: Eichmanns Stellvetreter," *Der Spiegel*, December 12, 2014. http://www.spiegel.de/politik/ausland/ nazi-verbrechen-alois-brunner-stellvertreter-eichmanns-ist-tot-a-1005980.html.

178. Unbelievably, the "Kathar Office" happened to be run out of Alois Brunner's home residence in Damascus. Company executives who traveled from German affiliates in Cologne, Munich, Duesseldorf, and Dortmund were knowingly or unknowingly visiting the home of one of the world's most sought after World War II war criminals.

179. Brunner's apparent attraction to names based on acronyms might well explain one of his many aliases: *Fescoer*. In German, the suffix -er is often added to a company name to designate people who work for that company. For example, the name Thyssianer is given to an employee of the Thyssen Company. Following Brunner's penchant for onomastic wordplay, the surname *Fescoer* could have been derived from [**F**ar **E**ast **S**hipping **Co**mpany]+ -er. Meaning one who works for /belongs to the Far East Shipping Company.

180. Oliver Schröm and Andrea Römpke, *Stille Hilfe für braune Kameraden: Das geheime Netzwerk der Alt- und Neonazis* (Berlin: C. H. Links, 2001), 55.

181. A copy of the secret memo written by Franz Rademacher confirming the evacuation order to Auschwitz can be found in the United States Holocaust Memorial Museum archives. This document became a key piece of evidence during the 1961 trial of Adolf Eichmann. http://collections.ushmm.org/search/catalog/pa1069605.

182. In declassified CIA files, one of Brunner's aliases is listed as being *Adlatus*. However, this could have come from a mistranslation. In a 1960 issue of the popular German news magazine, "Der Spiegel," the following is written about Alois Brunner: "Ehemalige prominente SD-Leute, die heute in Damaskus und Kairo leben, wissen indes, das Eichmann—genauso wie sein Frühere Adlatus Brunner—den 'römischen SD-Weg' eingeschlagen hat, um dorthin zu kommen, wo man alle Judenfeinde mit offenen Armen aufnahm: nach Syrien." [Former, prominent security service people who are now living in Damascus and Cairo, know that Eichmann as well as his earlier loyal assistant Brunner followed the so-called "Roman Security Forces Route" to arrive where all enemies of the Jewish people were welcomed with open arms: Syria.]

183. Central Intelligence Agency, "CIA Dispatch EGMA-54517, Willelm Beissner." Declassified CIA Report. April 20, 1961. https://www.cia.gov/library/readingroom/doc ument/519a6b2f993294098d5120f6.

184. For more on Walter Rauff's activities as an agent of the German Secret Service, see Bundesnachrichtendienst, "Walter Rauff und der Bundesnachrichtendienst. Mitteilungen der Forschungs- und Arbeitsgruppe Geschichte des BND, Nr. 2," September 23, 2011. http://www.bnd.bund.de/DE/Organisation/Geschichte/Geschichtsaufarbeitu ng/MFGBND_Uebersicht/MFGBND_pdf_Dateien/MFGBND2_Hauptdokumen t.pdf;jsessionid=A7B350CC16F192497687E635FF80E174.1_cid377?__blob=publicati onFile&v=1.

185. Detailed information on the aliases and cover names of these and other Nazis who worked internationally as operatives for secret service agencies can be found in the

now declassified name files of the CIA. Detailed discussion of the role played by Nazi war criminals in developing secret police and secret service operations in the Middle East can be found in the following references: Richard Breitman and Norman J. W. Goda, *Hitler's Shadow: Nazi War Criminals, US Intelligence and the Cold War* (Washington, DC: National Archives, 2014); Rubin and Schanitz, *Nazis, Islamists*.

186. Sydow, "Judenmörder Alois Brunner starb in Syrien.

187. Hafner and Schapira, *Die Akte Alois Brunner*.

188. Staatsarchiv Wien, September 19, 1960, "Letter from the Attorney General's office to the District Attorney's office" Record 51 St 109560/99. For more, see Holpfer, "Ich war nichts anders," 151–82.

189. Bettina Stangneth, "Warum tilgte der BND die Akte des Eichmann-Helfers?" *Die Welt*, August 21, 2011, https://www.welt.de/kultur/history/article13554689/Warum-tilgte-der-BND-die-Akte-des-Eichmann-Helfers.html.

190. Kurt Seinitz, "'Krone' Journalist Seinitz interviewte Brunner in 1986 in Damaskus," *Tiroler Tagezeitung Online*, http://www.tt.com/home/9333392–91/krone-journalist-seinitz-interviewte-brunner-1986-in-damaskus.csp, accessed on 20.11.2016.

191. Declassified CIA report from November 1987. Document ID: 127425708.

192. In response to the mounting international pressure to extradite Alois Brunner, the Syrian government repeatedly replied that to its knowledge no such person lived within its jurisdiction. According to a 2015 report issued by the German government, "The Syrians staunchly deny that Dr. Georg Fischer's identity is Alois Brunner and maintain that the charge that Brunner resides in Syria to be a 'myth' created by the press" (13). Official confirmation of Brunner's residence in Syria has, to this day, never been confirmed by the Syrian government. However, the German report goes on to say that the Damascus Embassy has indeed reported that personal security was arranged for Alois Brunner after a second attempt was made on his life in 1980. For details, see Deutscher Bundestag. 18 Wahlperiode. January 20, 2015. "Antwort der Regierung auf die Kleine Anfrage der Abgeordneten Jan Korte, Sevrim Dagdelen, Ulla Jepke, und weiterer Abgeordneter und der Fraktion DIE LINK. Such nach dem Kriegsverbrecher Alois Brunner" [Drucksache 18/3777] http://dip21.bundestag.de/dip21/btd/18/037/1803777.pdf.

Top, SS Untersturmführer Otto Bachschneider, the first head administrator at the Hohehorst Lebensborn Facility (February 1938 to March 1940); *bottom*, Bachschneider with his dog, "Ranko." Photos courtesy of Hans-Werner Liebig, Hohehorst Archive.

Lebensborn: Nurses with babies in a Lebensborn facility in Zdunska Wola in Lodz, Poland (May 18, 1942). Photo courtesy of Hans-Werner Liebig, Hohehorst Archive.

Top, the Hohehorst Lebensborn Facility; *bottom*, mothers and nurses during free time at the Hohehorst Lebensborn Facility. Photos courtesy of Hans-Werner Liebig, Hohehorst Archive.

Top, Eve Line's father, Abraham Cherchevsky; *bottom*, Eve Line's mother, Germaine Cherchevsky. Photos property of the family, used with permission of the survivor.

Abraham Cherchevsky and his daughter, Eve Line.
Photo property of the family, used with permission of the su⁻vivor.

Top, Etja's paternal relatives, the Gross Family; *bottom*, Etja's other European relatives, the Weiss Family. Photos property of the family, used with permission of the survivor.

Top, Henri and his parents; *bottom*, the identification cards of Henri's parents.

Fanny/Joan
Paris 1941

Top left, Fanny/Joan in Paris, 1941; *top right*, Fanny/Joan's mother in Paris, 1938; *bottom*, Fanny/Joan's birth certificate. Photos property of the family, used with permission of the survivor.

Mugette's family, Paris, 1940: (*left to right, standing, back row*) Aunt Deeneh; Muguette's mother, Bella; and Muguette's brother, Jojo; (*left to right, seated, front row*) Muguette (age 9) and her grandmother, Gromeh. Photo property of the family, used with permission of the survivor.

CHAPTER 7

Names and Aliases of Female Nazi War Criminals

Many popular accounts of the Holocaust focus their attention upon the individuals who directly participated in war crimes and crimes against humanity. However, without the oversight and organization offered by legions of administrators sitting behind their office desks, these crimes would not have been executed with such devastating efficiency over such a large geographical and temporal expanse. The recognition of this deadly contribution led to the prosecution and conviction of several so-called office-desk offenders [Schreibtischtäter] like Adolf Eichmann.

The administrators of the Holocaust did not act on their own, however. Every step of the way, they were assisted by an army of complicit administrative assistants. All across the Reich, thousands upon thousands of typists, stenographers, archivists, receptionists, translators, bookkeepers, interpreters, file managers, and telephonists (etc.) all played their part in the Final Solution.[1] Many of those executive assistants were women. Women, therefore, not only had first-hand knowledge of the atrocities. Their labor was also integral to first perpetrating and then concealing these crimes. In addition to these administrators of death, there were also many thousands of women who directly participated in the atrocities in a wide range of professional environments. In hospital wards and research laboratories, psychiatric clinics and open fields, factory floors and extermination camps, women voluntarily pulled the triggers, inserted the injections, cracked the whips, held the scalpels, wielded the cudgels, ordered the dogs, administered the poisons, dissected the bodies, and built their careers as dealers of death. And this is to say nothing of those women whose denunciations and exultations facilitated in the ostracization, persecution, and annihilation of millions of men, women, and children.

Despite these lethal contributions, the primary investigative focus of research into the role of women during National Socialism has nevertheless

291

remained stubbornly trained upon their actions as mothers and wives, mistresses and daughters. And when the actions of female NS perpetrators are examined, their legal culpability and even moral responsibility are often so diminished that they frequently appear to be victims of either their own pathology or that of the system they "found themselves" in.

Even in modern examinations of the Holocaust, one still finds descriptions that dismiss, belittle, or outright deny the actions of female perpetrators relative to their male counterparts. For instance, in an otherwise outstanding 2015 examination of the NS concentration camp system, the author maintains that despite the existence of concentration camp matrons and the erection of Ravensbrück, a predominately female concentration camp, the NS system of terror remained "gender-specific as the most violent abuses were still reserved for the male prisoners."[2] The author goes on to give the following assessment of the Ravensbrück concentration camp:

> Although whippings were introduced as an official form of punishment, most of the other excesses including pole-hanging [being suspended from a pole by the wrists] were excluded. Instead of brutal mistreatment, the SS camp personnel in Ravensbrück utilized guard dogs because Himmler believed that women would be especially afraid of them.[3] (emphasis added)

As even a cursory of the camp archives in the concentration camp quickly reveals, the assertion that savage brutality was rare in Ravensbrück is entirely counterfactual.[4] Further, when one reads the accounts of survivors who either witnessed or experienced dog maulings, be it in Ravensbrück or elsewhere, the notion that the use of SS attack dogs was somehow less brutal than other torture methods is simply ludicrous. In the following excerpt, a survivor of Majdanek describes just how horrific such dog attacks were:

> I heard a woman start to scream. It was Wladka, a Polish woman . . . I looked over and saw that 'Brigida' had set her large German shepherd on the girl. The dog bit her hands, which the girl was holding in front of her face to protect herself. Then the dog began tearing her clothes; at that point, the rhubarb the girl had hidden under her clothes started to show. The dog grew more and more agitated, and 'Brigida' kept spurring him on. He tore off all her clothing. Then 'Brigida' assembled us for a kind of roll call; we were forced to stand in a triangle-formation, with the girl in the middle, to watch her punishment. I found out later that the girl had become pregnant by an SS soldier, a man whom 'Brigida' also liked. That was the first time in my life I saw what an umbilical cord looked like, and a fetus. Two girls had to carry Wladka away on a stretcher. . . . After the dog

had torn the clothing from her body, she was covered in blood. You could see shredded bits of flesh hanging down, and the long umbilical cord.[5]

As this and many other first-hand accounts show, there were women who actively and avidly participated in the twelve years of butchery known as the Holocaust. Despite that fact, in the trials held immediately after the war, women were relatively infrequently prosecuted. When they appeared in court, it was typically to testify as a witness. Even in cases where it was clear to the court that the women had actively participated in the crimes for which their male counterparts were being tried, they were frequently spared prosecution themselves.

The historical misconception that women played only peripheral roles in the NS atrocities has reduced the amount of incriminating evidence collected on their crimes and decreased the quality of intelligence gathered on the known or suspected whereabouts of female perpetrators. These factors, in turn, have compromised the ability to build strong prosecutorial cases, as the amount of time and resources needed to fill in the evidentiary gaps are artificially heightened. As a result, the majority of female NS offenders have been allowed to re-enter society and resume outwardly normal lives as daughters, wives, and widows. And as the years pass and the female fugitives' legal status and names change, it becomes harder and harder for authorities to locate these women and bring them to justice. As Judy Feigin of the Department of Justice explained in a 2008 report for the Office of Special Investigation (OSI):

> There were a significant number of female camp guards and women who served in other capacities as well. It is very difficult to determine whether a notable number of women persecutors emigrated, however, since INS could only identify émigrés by the name on their travel documents; if a woman married before emigrating, INS would have no record of her maiden name.[6]

And therein lies a striking gender difference discovered in this research. While the male NS war criminals often were forced to resort to illegal means to obtain a change of name and identity, female perpetrators were often able to take advantage of pre-existing laws that allowed them to easily and serially alter their names without drawing any undue attention to themselves. Just how many women are we talking about? More than many might imagine. FAR more in fact. Table 7.1 presents the names of a small sampling of the approximately 4,000 women who served as camp guards at Ravensbrück.[7]

As a group, the women who worked in the NS concentration camp system were fairly young.[8] This demographic was no accident. Given the physical and emotional demands of the position, only women who were between the ages

Table 7.1   Concentration Camp Matrons and their Legal Name Changes

MAIDEN NAMES	CAMPS EMPLOYED	MARRIED SURNAMES	
		FIRST	SECOND
Erika Belling	Ravensbrück Neu Rohlau Genthin	Koch	Bergmann
Gertrud Brandenburg	Ravensbrück Neubrandenbur	Schlosser	Walt
Hermine Braunsteiner	Ravensbrück Majdanek	Ryan	
Hermine Brückner	Ravensbrück	Böttcher	
Gertrud Dipner	Ravensbrück	Rabenstein	
Hertha Girgdies	Ravensbrück	Sobotta	
Hildegard Glimpel	Ravensbrück	Dahl	
Ruth Göcke	Ravensbrück	Hühnerbein	
Ruth Hartmann	Ravensbrück Neudeck	Closius	Neudeck
Elfriede Lina Huth	Ravensbrück	Rinkel	
Margot Kunz	Ravensbrück Wittenberge ARADO Factory	Pietzner	
Hertha Ließ	Majdanek Plaszow Auschwitz Raisko Sachsenhausen	Ehlert	Neumann
Heide Lieswicz	BergenBelsen	Michina	
Margarete Mewes	Ravensbrück	Labuda	
Erna Pfannsteil	Majdanek	Wallisch	
Friede Radoy	Ravensbrück	Pinske	
Hildegard Seibt	Ravensbrück	Beck	
Hildegard Schröder	Ravensbrück	Mahler	Kroponicki
Ingeborg Schultze	Ravensbrück	Laier	
Ida Schwarzkopf	Ravensbrück	Leinweber	
Charlotte Wollert	Ravensbrück	Mayer	
Margarete Wolter	Ravensbrück	Kässner	Albrecht
Erna Zietelman	Ravensbrück Bergen-Belsen	Hentschel	Kula

of twenty-one and forty-five were eligible to apply for a guard position.[9] This meant that even before the war ended, a significant portion of this female work force had taken on a husband and changed their last name. Although intimate relationships between staff members were officially discouraged, it was not uncommon for camp matrons to meet and marry one of the male SS officers assigned to the same camp.[10] It has even been reported that some couples even chose "their" camp as their wedding venue.[11] Although it was not prohibited for wives or mothers to work in the camps, when it was financially feasible, marriage and childbirth were often accompanied by a professional scission. As a result, the names women had while working in the camps frequently altered at least once after their contract ended. The same is true, of course, for women working in other professional NSDAP settings where murders were committed as well.

To make matters even more complicated, the naming laws immediately before, during, and after the Third Reich permitted women considerable latitude in the surnames they used to designate their change in legal status. Brides were allowed to take on the surname of their husbands, either instead of or in combination with their maiden names. A woman who divorced or became widowed could revert to her original name at birth or maintain her marital surname. A woman who remarried was allowed to adopt her new spouse's name or retain the surname of her previous husband(s), again, either in place of or in combination with any one of her previous last names.

For those who decided to use a double last name, there was also a great deal of freedom in the sequence in which those surnames could appear. If one combines these legal permutations with the variations possible in the forename (e.g., shortenings, nicknames, initializations), the possibilities for female NS offenders to create new and completely legal names are considerable. In practice, this onomastic variability has made it extremely difficult for authorities to isolate these fugitives on their internal watchlists. Historically, the US Office of Special Investigations has had to search the databases maintained by the Department of Homeland Security to search for NS offenders.[12] This means that law enforcement officials have had to shift through all of the murderers, rapists, kidnappers, and right-wing extremists who have committed a crime in the recent US history to find a handful of murderers, rapists, kidnappers, and right-wing extremists whose crimes were committed over half a century ago in Europe.[13] All that background noise has made finding female offenders extremely difficult and has allowed the majority of them to quite literally get away with murder.

*****

In the early autumn, an elderly gentleman drove his sister to the international airport in California. Their conversation, the brother would later recall, was nothing out of the ordinary. Elfriede was simply taking a trip back to Germany to visit their other sister.[14] Thinking back, perhaps the flight did come as a bit of a surprise, especially since she had just finished renovating her apartment. But, there again, *Elfriede* had been through quite a lot recently. She had just buried her husband of over forty years. His death could not have come as a complete surprise, though. After working so many grueling hours as a waiter in the Bay Area, he had gradually developed a serious heart condition. Still, after so many years of marriage, her husband's death devastated Elfriede. The couple, according to friends and relatives, had always been inseparable. Although generally well-liked and respected in their community, the two rarely socialized and preferred to keep to themselves. They could often be seen together arm-in-arm strolling through their adopted city, enjoying an evening of ballroom dancing, or attending synagogue in their tight-knit Jewish community.

The Jewish faith had been particularly important to Elfriede's husband. He did his best, despite his long work hours, to regularly attend B'nai B'rith meetings. The couple also made an effort to give as generously as they could afford to Jewish charities. In the years before his death, Elfriede's husband had even considered taking up lessons to become a cantor—that is, if he could find the time. But, there never seemed to be enough time. The funeral was held at Sinai Memorial Chapel and the burial took place in a local Jewish cemetery. The two had a double plot, adorned with both their names and a star of David above. When it was her time to go, Elfriede would be buried next to him. That was her plan. But things rarely turn out the way we plan them.

In 1959, Elfriede, like millions of other European immigrants after the second great war, came to America to start a new life. The unexpected combination of homesickness and loneliness eventually led her to go to a local German-American Dance Night. It was a decision she would never regret, for it was on that night that she met the man who would become her husband. His name was *Fritz* or *Fred* like the famous American dancer from the Hollywood films. Fred had also immigrated fairly recently from Germany to the United States. His journey to the Golden State had not been an easy one. Before his arrival in California, Fred had been one of the thousands of Jewish immigrants who had fled to Shanghai to escape the Nazis. From there, he made it to the United States, where he and three of his brothers settled. The fact that they were not alone must have made the transition easier but the boys had suffered terrible losses during the War. Both of their parents had been murdered in the Holocaust. When Elfriede and Fritz married, they resolved to leave their pasts behind them and never look back. And from all reports, it seems that the couple did precisely that. That is until Fred's death.

Almost immediately, the already quiet and somewhat reclusive Elfriede became even more withdrawn. It was a depression, some of her friends said. So, although people might have been surprised when Elfriede suddenly announced that she was going back to Europe, perhaps they thought it might do her some good to get away for a while. Maybe the trip was just what she needed to stop dwelling on the past and start to think about her future. What they did not know then was that Elfriede's past had finally caught up with her.

During World War II, Fräulein Elfriede Huth, as she was called then, was one of the millions of young German women supporting the war effort by working in a factory. Although the position was fairly secure, it was, according to the story Elfriede would later tell, rather poorly paid. For that reason, she was overjoyed when she discovered a newspaper advertisement for a new governmental position in one of the Reich's modern facilities. She immediately applied and was thrilled when she learned that her future employers felt she had just the profile they were looking for. Elfriede accepted the job offer and began her new position as a female guard in the Reich's new penal institution, Ravensbrück.

Constructed in 1939 by prisoners from the Sachsenhausen Concentration Camp, Ravensbrück was the largest concentration camp ever erected on German soil for female prisoners [Frauenlager].[15] Unlike Auschwitz, where the primary purpose was mass extermination, Ravensbrück was originally designed as a large-scale forced labor camp.[16] Around the camp perimeter, major companies like Siemens established satellite production facilities to harness slave labor directly from the camp.

To ensure that the grueling work schedules were kept and that none of the prisoners managed to escape, Ravensbrück became one of the first concentration camps to employ a specially trained team of prison guards who patrolled the camp with highly trained attack dogs. Although Elfriede freely admitted to being a part of Ravensbrück's canine unit, in repeated statements made to international law enforcement and journalists, she adamantly rejected the notion that she had participated in any of the brutality that took place in the camp. Her only responsibility, she claimed, was simply to make sure that no one escaped. However, considerable evidence casts doubt on the credibility of Elfriede's claims. One the strongest sources of contradiction comes from none other than Reichsführer Heinrich Himmler himself. In a letter written to SS Obengrüppenführer Oswald Pohl and SS Brigadierführer Richard Glücks of the SS's Main Office for Economics and Administration [Wirtschafts- und Verwaltungshauptamt] (WVHA),[17] Himmler provided a chilling description of the attack dogs' function in the concentration camps:

> Dogs that patrol the outside perimeter of the camp must be raised to be vicious, tearing beasts, like the attack dogs used in Africa. They must be so well-trained that they will attack anyone other than their master. They must also, of course, be accordingly handled to make sure that no misfortune takes place.[18]

Written on February 8, 1943, the letter also goes on to order that the dogs only be allowed to patrol the camp unaccompanied during the evening when the camp was closed. This regulation was imposed to not only protect the prison staff and invited visitors. It was also designed to help guard against the dogs becoming accustomed to and friendly with any of the camp prisoners.

In a postwar account, a Belgian survivor of the Wiener Neudorf Concentration Camp[19] recounted what happened when a dog was perceived as being too weak. During his time in the camp, the prisoner had been charged with caring for and feeding the personal guard dog of the Camp Commandant, Karl Emil Schmutzler. One day, the dog lay his head gently on the knee of the prisoner. As luck would have it, at that very moment, Commandant Schmutzler happened by and saw what had happened. Enraged, the Commandant ordered that his dog be immediately shot and told the prisoner: "If you ruin another dog of mine, I will destroy you."[20]

The guard dogs used in Ravensbrück were far from being docile pets. They were sentient weapons that were systematically used by camp officials to control and terrorize, torture and kill.[21] In her postwar memoirs, Ravensbrück survivor, Germain Tillion describes how the attack dogs were used during the type of work details that Elfriede admitted to having guarded:

> For a pre-arranged fee, managers of businesses and corporations could place orders for 500 to 1,000 women along with female guards equipped with clubs and their specially trained attack dogs. Together these units made sure that the already exhausted and starving women worked twelve-hour days until the day they died. And when one worker died, the guards saw to it that another woman took her place—all without any additional costs to the contractor. Through the continual use of the attack dogs and beatings, the female guards made sure that the prisoners had given even last drop of their energy before they died and were replaced with someone else—within this perfect cycle, there was no toleration for material waste.[22]

The crimes committed by *Elfriede Huth* in a German concentration camp stand in glaring contrast to the life enjoyed by *Elfriede Rinkel* a devoted wife and member of California's Jewish community. Were it not for an odd twist of fate, the fact that *Elfriede Huth* and *Elfriede Rinkel* were in fact one and the same might never have been discovered.

The OSI authorities were finally able to pinpoint Elfriede's whereabouts thanks to the obituary of her husband—the man who apparently never knew his wife's true identity.[23] As is still the custom in German obituaries, Fred's death notice listed his widow with both her married and maiden names.[24] With that information, officials were finally able to close in. When US law enforcement confronted Rinkel with her past, she made no effort to deny the truth. In an official report released by the Department of Justice,[25] authorities working on the case indicated that she freely admitted her previous employment as a guard at the Ravensbrück Concentration Camp. On the basis of this admission and the collection of incriminating evidence, Rinkel was informed that a court order directing her removal to Germany had already been issued and that she had until September 30, 2006 to leave the country. Rinkel agreed to leave the United States immediately.[26] In exchange for her cooperation, US authorities agreed not to release the story of her discovery until after she had left the country.

When the news about Elfriede broke, the people who knew her fell into two groups: those who felt angry and betrayed; and those who felt sympathetic, even protective, towards the elderly woman whom her lawyer described as having devoted her life to atoning for her past. No doubt the size and strength of that second group shrunk considerably when the next shock wave hit. It seems that, even after her departure from the United States, the former concentration camp guard still continued to collect widow's benefits from her deceased Jewish husband; and over the years those checks added up to the tidy sum of 120,000 US dollars. To make matters worse, Elfriede s case was by no means isolated. According to a report issued in 2015 by the Office of the Inspector General, "Between February 1962 and January 2015, SSA [Social Security Administration] paid $20.2 million in benefits to 133 individuals alleged, or found, to have participated in Nazi persecution."[27] Thus, to the outrage of many a survivor, the US government was well aware of the fact that NS perpetrator, *Elfriede Rinkel nee Huth*, was still receiving US benefits. However, as SSA officials explained, before the passage of the "No Social Security for Nazis Act"[28] signed by President Obama on December 18, 2014, the government had no legal authority to terminate benefits paid out to known or suspected NS perpetrators.[29] The only recourse which the government had at the time was to expedite Rinkel's removal from the US, making her the first woman in US history that the OSI had ever brought suit against in connection with World War II war crimes.

As soon as *Rinkel/Huth* returned to Germany, deliberations began in earnest over whether a formal trial was in order. Certainly, there was some historical precedent for doing so. Immediately after the war, a nest of former concentration camp guards was convicted, imprisoned, or executed for crimes during the war (e.g., Dorothy Binz, executed May 1947; Greta Bösel, executed May 1947; Ida Schrieter, executed September 1948; Emma Zimmer, executed September 1948; Ruth Naudeck, executed July 1948). The successful prosecution of these female offenders may seem to be in direct contradiction to the previous assertion that female NS offenders were rarely brought to justice: that is until one remembers the tens of thousands of women who assisted in the persecution, deportation, imprisonment, exploitation, torture, and murder of tens of millions of people across Europe during the Third Reich.

Despite this fact, by the time Elfriede Rinkel nee Huth returned to Germany, public interest in prosecuting former NS offenders had largely dissipated and the statute of limitations had passed for all crimes excluding murder. In an interview conducted with the German news magazine, *Der Spiegel*, Kurt Schrimm, the Chief of the German Bureau responsible for investigating and prosecuting the NS crimes, reported that his office would not be pursuing her case.[30] According to Schrimm, the only NS crime that German authorities would be bringing to court was murder. And given that no evidence had been uncovered to demonstrate that *Elfriede Huth* had <u>directly</u> committed a murder, there were no official plans to prosecute her—much to the disappointment and dismay of many survivors and their families. However, according to Efraim Zuroff, the Simon Wiesenthal Center's Chief Nazi Hunter, it is important to see things pragmatically. German authorities would be very busy if they prosecuted everyone like Elfriede Huth. After all, Zuroff quipped, "Germany is full of people like her."[31]

*

On April 15, 1943, a *Fräulein Erika Belling* reported to duty as a concentration camp guard in Ravensbrück. During her employment, she would serve as an overseer on several different work details or "commandos." She was also a part of the camp's canine unit. It was there that she made a name for herself. One episode in particular left a lasting impression on the surviving prisoners. It was the summer of 1943. Belling had been assigned to supervise the "forest commando." During that detail, she spotted a young Sinti woman who seemed to be moving more slowly than the rest. Belling's punishment was swift. She gave her German shepherd the attack command. Already in issuing this order, Belling had stepped outside of the official protocol which mandated that in cases where prisoners were found to be shirking, the dogs were to be ordered to confront, corner, and bark at the prisoners until they raised their hands in surrender.[32]

According to the court testimony, however, Belling, like so many of her colleagues, ignored the official procedure and immediately ordered her dog to maul the prisoner without restraint. The dog tore at the woman's ankles, knees, and calves pulling her to the ground and tearing away chunks of flesh. The women of the work detail formed a small circle around the scene, too terrified to help too heart-broken to turn away, they all watched in silent horror. The only sounds to be heard were those of the dogs' incessant barking and Belling's shrieks as she repeatedly kicked the woman's body with her black leather boots. In the wave of injuries, the prisoner lost unconsciousness.

Instead of ending the attack, Belling ordered her dog to attack once again. This time, the shepherd sank its teeth into the soft skin and muscle of the unconscious woman's groin. As the dog yanked back its head from the woman's shredded torso, it reportedly ripped away part of the woman's bladder and uterus. According to the postwar witness reports, there was surprisingly little blood: instead a thick yellow substance gushed forth from the woman's gaping wound. Just as quickly as the frenzy started, it came to an end. Belling ordered a handful of the prisoners to take the young woman back to the camp but not to the hospital. They were to take her to the prisoners' barracks. Once there, the women gently laid their injured comrade on the wooden planks, before rushing back to their work detail in the woods. In the evening, when the women returned to the main camp, they found their comrade, dead. What remained of tattered body was later tossed into the camp wagon that transported the daily collection of corpses to the camp crematorium.[33] That same summer, Belling reportedly repeated this scenario, commanding her dog to mercilessly maul at least two other female prisoners of the forest detail. The prisoners survived but received serious injuries to their ribs and feet.[34]

After the war, Belling slipped quietly into civilian life, becoming an official member of the German Democratic Republic's Socialist Unity Party [Sozialistische Einheitspartei Deutschlands] (SED). She made ends meet as a health care worker in various East German hospitals and clinics. For some ten years, she was able to hide her true identity—a task made that much more easy by her changing her maiden name not once but twice.[35] In 1955, however, she finally came to the attention of authorities when she was reported on for having mistreated elderly patients placed under her care in a state-run geriatric facility. Like so many other offenders, she had successfully changed her name but not her personality.

Once her true identity had been exposed, she soon found herself facing trial for crimes against humanity. According to witnesses called to testify before the court, the aforementioned events were by no means isolated. It was scenes like this that earned the young Berlin-native the moniker "the demon in human skin." During the trial, Belling first denied the crimes, claiming that the most she had ever done was slap one of the prisoners in the face. After listening to testimony given by eye-witness survivors like M. Horn who recounted in detail what they had seen that day, the former camp guard eventually broke down and admitted the truth: "The prisoners knew me then under the name Erika Koch and Belling. . . . I worked in Ravensbrück from April 1943 to May 1944. My previous testimony was false. I wanted to prevent the truth from coming to light."[36] In November 1955, an East German court sentenced *Belling/Koch/ Bergmann* to life imprisonment in a women's prison.[37]

*

One can only imagine what he went through, how he suffered. There are times when the laws of the Church and the laws of the land come into direct conflict and one must decide which calling is higher. That was the question that must have tortured the Bavarian priest's conscience. One of his flock had confessed a secret . . . about her name and what she had done so many years ago. It was up to the law enforcement now. The wheels of justice turn slowly but they do turn. One simply had to have faith. But, there she was again, on yet another Sunday, sitting in the pews in front of him, torturing his conscience again.

Finally, the priest decided that he might just have to give the authorities a gentle nudge in the right direction. Not disclose all of what he had learnt. Only a name. That would be enough, if her story were true. And maybe it was even divine intervention that of all the people in the world, she had chosen to tell him, a man of God, about her unholy acts. Whatever the reason was, it was now time for him to confess about the parishioner with the impossibly innocent name: *Rosa Süß* or *Rosa Sweet* in English. Her story was anything but.[38] At first, there might have been a few discrete inquiries made by the authorities to see if there was any real interest in pursuing the matter. There was.

Rosa's story began innocently enough. Almost forty years ago, long before she was married and the mother of three, her name had been *Rosa Reischl*. Fraulein Reischl was just eighteen years old when she completed her training to be a pediatric nurse. She had gone to the employment office in hopes of receiving another vocational placement. After all, it was dangerous in Hitler's Germany to be unemployed for too long. She was assigned a position almost immediately but not in a hospital or a clinic where she could use her newly gained skills. She was to work as a matron in one of the newly erected labor camps. If she had worries about never having worked in such a place before, she might have been reassured by the fact that she would first receive intensive training in the fall of 1942 at a special facility, called Ravensbrück. There she would become one of the more than 3,000 women to graduate from the new vocational program for female guards.[39] After completing this intensive training, she was sent to her first assignment in Lublin; and a few weeks later, she received another assignment: Majdanek.

She arrived in Majdanek in January 1943. Her fellow male guards seemed friendly enough. They invited her and four other new female colleagues for a drink. When the atmosphere became a bit too friendly for her tastes, she and one of the other female recruits, Herta Ehlert, decided to try to find their quarters but soon they became lost in the sea of barracks. They eventually came upon a building and entered, hoping to find their sleeping quarters. Instead they found a room with three SS officers who also showed them a human skull. According to Süß, she was so terrified at the sight that she ran through the nearest door, thinking it was an exit. What she found on the other side was a wall of corpses.[40] Despite these sights, she reportedly did not question the system. As she testified in court, "I had no doubt that the prisoners were there for good reason. . . . The only thing that really bothered me was the hair shaving."

Despite her initial shock, Reischl apparently fit right in to the camp daily routine. In no time, she had even earned herself a nickname among the prisoners. She was called the *Bavarian laundress*. The nickname had been motivated by her most salient features. She was the big-boned girl with the heavy Bavarian accent who supervised the laundry-detail. Other prisoners preferred another nickname inspired by her facility with the cat-of-nines: *the Beast*. One example of her savagery that stayed in both the prisoners' and Reischl's memory involved a detail of Jewish women prisoners from Greece. During her inspection, Reischl immediately spotted that the women had incorrectly sewn their prisoner numbers onto their uniforms. Reischl reportedly had a sharp eye for such details and no tolerance for what she perceived as wanton sloppiness. Enraged, she whipped the prisoner in charge of the detail so savagely that she had been unable to walk for weeks afterward. Shortly thereafter, Rieschl found herself in the hospital with a case of typhoid fever.

As she lay in her sickbed, she was plagued with the memory of how mercilessly she had beaten that woman. Even after her fever broke, she simply could not forget what she had done, although her colleagues assured her that it was nothing. When she finally returned to work, she asked two of her colleagues to bring her to the prisoner she had almost whipped to death. Once there, she did something that few would forget: she apologized. The story of the apology was corroborated by none other than the prisoner herself. Aside from this single moment of humanity, Reischl's behavior in the camp fit her reputation as a killer.

Once the war ended, Reischl returned to Bavaria where she landed a job in a factory that produced uniforms for the German military. In no time, she rose to a position of respect as quality control officer. She evidently had an uncommon eye for detail and could immediately spot when a uniform did not meet the regulations. She later married, took on her husband's last name, and went from *Rosa Reischl* to *Rosa Süß*. Afterwards the children followed. She had a simple life, a good life, a quiet life in Bavaria until her priest had denounced her, and landed her in Duesseldorf before a criminal court filled with cameras. *Reischl/Süß* was charged with 100 counts of accessory to murder.

Right from the very start, the trial created a media frenzy. Part of the attention was due to a completely serendipitous event. In the late 1970s, as the trial was well underway, German television aired for the first time a four-part US American mini-series. Called "Die Geschichte der Familie Weiss" [The History of the Weiss Family] in Germany, in the States, the made for television film was known by the title "Holocaust." After some initial concern among television executives that the series might damage the budding political relations between Israel and Germany or even re-ignite a wave of Nazism, the decision was made to air the US docudrama. The mini-series hit like a bombshell. At 9 pm, on January 22, 23, 25, and 26, the 1979 series captured an audience of around 20 million viewers.

Nearly every second adult living in West Germany watched the series in part or in its entirety. Among those who chose not to watch, the number one reason given was it would have been too upsetting. In national polls conducted after the series aired, two-third of viewers reported that the film had left them devastated.

The overwhelming response was nevertheless extremely positive. Despite some historical inaccuracies, the mini-series started a much-needed public discussion over the questions of guilt and responsibility. The German word of the year for 1979 was "Holocaust." Not all reactions were positive, of course. In an effort to stop the series from continuing to air, approximately twenty minutes before the third segment began, a Neo-Nazi group successfully exploded two bombs that destroyed essential television cabling.[41] The initial result was that around 100,000 homes were unable to see the episode "The Final Solution" on the scheduled night for broadcasting. The ultimate consequence of the bombing attack, however, was to stimulate even more public interest in watching the mini-series. The next evening, when the episode finally re-aired, the number of viewers around the country significantly increased. Much to the terrorists' chagrin, the bombing backfired by helping to increase public awareness that the specter of National Socialism had by no means disappeared.

With all of the ensuing publicity, the women on trial did their best to keep their faces out of the media. They never appeared in court without large scarves or dark glasses; and during the short breaks, they routinely huddled together in the hallways of the courthouse under a wall of large umbrellas to shield themselves from the aim of the reporters' cameras. But, it was naturally impossible to keep their guard up all of the time. The photojournalists were eventually able to get their shots. The reaction of the reporters and the general public was the same: shock.

Perhaps in memory of the spectacular trial against the beautiful blonde concentration camp guard, Irma Grese,[42] many people had expected to see a parade of seductive she-devils. Instead what they saw was a strange hodgepodge of heavy-set, white-haired, elderly women dressed in frumpy, ill-fitting, polyester jumpsuits.[43] These women seemed more like grandmothers than murderers: that is until the witnesses began detailing what they had seen. Suddenly, the courtroom was transported more than thirty years back into the past. Some of the survivors who came to testify admitted that it was difficult to recall which female guard had committed which crimes. As one eye-witness explained:

> We did not register any particulars. We had no hope that we would be able to use them outside of the camp. We had no hope that we would be able to make them pay for what they had done. Back then, the only things that interested us were our fellow suffering comrades. We tried to help one another through our desperation. That was the focus of our attention, not our executioners. At that time, we did not

think about categories liked trials and courts. We were only trying to survive.[44]

In June 1981, the 17th criminal court of Duesseldorf issued its final judgment. After listening to the testimony of 350 witnesses, inspecting the Majdanek concentration camp twice, and reviewing 100 case files filled with 20,000 pages of court evidence, the trial that lasted twice as long as the extermination camp had been in operation came to an end.[45] A court reporter who had attended every day of the proceedings described the public's reactions to the verdict:

> [T]heir sentences left a bad taste in the mouths of so many people who been following the trials. One life-time sentence and seven received time in prison. Those would remain the only punishments to be handed down in West Germany for the murder of over a quarter of a million people in Majdanek.[46]

Ironically, perhaps, one of the very few people who seemed to feel a deep sense of vindication after the trial was *Frau Reischl/Süß*. That sensation did not come from the verdict. In her opinion, the trial had been a horrific waste of her time and energy. At the end of the day, *Reischl/Süß's* contentment came from something else—something she had recently learned. It seems that the priest who had tipped off the police had died from cancer. That bit of news made her feel a lot better. Maybe, she mused, there was some justice in the world after all.

*

On September 14, 1948, thirty-six-year-old *Gerda Sonntag* wrote her husband a love letter. "Our time together in Ravensbrück was and will forever remain the most beautiful time in my life. No one will ever be able to take these memories away from us." Three days later, her husband, Walter, was executed before a British military tribunal putting an abrupt end to their seven-year marriage. Gerda and Walter, like many modern young couples today, met one another at their place of work. Gerda joined the small medical staff of the Ravensbrück Concentration Camp in the fall of 1939 after completing her medical studies at the prestigious Universities of Heidelberg and Nuremburg.

According to eye-witness accounts given by camp survivors after the war, *Gerda Weyand*, as she was then called, was not like the other NS officers on staff. In the beginning, the talented, young gynecologist seemed to genuinely care for her patients, asking detailed questions about their ailments and offering what rudimentary medical care she could. She was never seen to verbally or physically abuse her patients and she staunchly refused to participate in the medical selections of patients deemed fit for extermination. That is until Dr. *Walter Sonntag* joined the staff. A member of the NSDAP and the Waffen-SS, Dr. Sonntag was well-familiar with the concentration camp system. Between 1939 and 1940, he had already worked as a camp physician in the Sachsenhausen Concentration Camp where he had conducted lethal mustard gas experiments on male prisoners. In Ravensbrück, the eager doctor would have a chance to broaden this expertise to include a new area of interest, gynecology.

Later described as an arrogant eccentric with an unquenchable need for alcohol and sadism, SS-Hauptsturmführer Sonntag would also be remembered by survivors for his unusual bedside manner.[47] As one survivor recounted, Dr. Sonntag often struck the sick and infirmed with his riding crop or used the leather tip of his whip to bore deeply into the painful open wounds and sores of his patients.[48] That same survivor went on to detail how the dentist frequently misdiagnosed prisoners as having a sexually transmitted disease, before sending them off for "special treatment." Given the differences between the two doctors, to many Ravensbrück prisoners, it must have come as quite a surprise when Weyand and Sonntag started to spend a conspicuous amount of time together; and it must have been positively shocking when it became clear that their relationship went far beyond professional collegiality. The evidence was undeniable. As one survivor reported, no sooner had Dr. Sonntag arrived did prisoners begin to find used condoms in the corners of the camp where the doctors had been seen in private consultation;[49] and on at least one occasion, the two were discovered in flagrante.[50]

No sooner had their affair become public did the prisoners begin to notice unsettling changes in Dr. Weyand's behavior. Not only did her tone and demeanor towards the prisoners change, but for the first time, she began to participate in the camp brutalities including the selections of prisoners to be sent for immediate deportation and extermination.[51] Despite this pathological shift in personality, there was no evidence uncovered to indicate that she had participated in Dr. Sonntag's perverse medical experiments in which he attempted, for example, to sterilize female prisoners or terminate their pregnancies. However, there was also no evidence that she ever tried to stop him either. What does appear to be clear is that, at least in the beginning of their affair, Dr. Weyand was devoted to Dr. Sonntag. So much so that in the summer of 1941, the couple married and moved into one of the spacious Bavarian-style villas located along the camp's perimeter.

Within no time, the newlyweds were expecting their first child. While the pregnant *Dr. Weyand-Sonntag* began to cut back on the number of hours she spent working in the camp, her husband seemed to become all the more present. Prisoners assigned to the camp infirmary began to notice that the increasingly inebriated doctor would show up at odd hours in the evening to make unscheduled visits with patients whose corpses were found abandoned on the premises on the following day.[52] By the end of the summer, several women had fallen prey to Sonntag's private evening murder series.

After the war, Dr. Sonntag slipped into the general public and opened his own dental practice. On the surface, his life had returned to normalcy. Nothing could be farther from the truth, however. According to testimony provided by trial witness Rosa Jochmann, the dentist often lamented that his time in the camp was over. His only regret was that he had not been able to kill more. The irony of that testimony was that Jochmann had been originally called to testify on Dr. Sonntag's behalf.[53] She had been contacted by the dentist's wife in her vain attempt to find eye-witnesses willing to vouch for her husband's good character. After hearing the evidence, the court found Dr. Sonntag guilty of war crimes and sentenced him to death by hanging. The sentence was carried out two days later. For her own role in the camp activities, *Frau Doktor Weyand* was never made to stand trial. After the execution, the widowed physician dropped her husband's surname and quietly slipped away into the general population herself.

*

In looking back, there was one thing that everyone seemed to remember about *Hermine*. She loved dogs. All dogs. Large, small, old, or young, it did not matter to her. Even as a frail old woman, she would always take the time to stop and pat the head of a dog passing by. She even reportedly asked her neighbors if she could take their dogs out for a walk.[54] It relaxed her, she said. Dogs did not ask difficult or annoying questions. They were loyal, obedient, and ever anxious to please their masters. They did not get getting caught up in the right or wrong of things. They simply did as they were told and were always looking for a way to show their loyalty—all traits that Hermine appreciated, all qualities that she also possessed in abundance and that had helped her climb the career ladder as a young woman, all those many years ago.

After working in a series of low-paying, manual jobs, in 1938, the ambitious nineteen-year-old daughter of an Austrian butcher decided it was time for a radical change. Although she only had the equivalent of an eighth-grade education, what Hermine lacked in formal education, she more than made up for in enthusiasm and commitment. In the autumn of 1939, she left her job in a Berlin munitions factory and began her service as a female prison camp guard at Ravensbrück.

For Hermine, this new position was definitely a step in the right direction. Advertised as being a progressive workplace for women in the Reich, Ravensbrück offered its female employees a number of attractive benefits: room and board, round-the-clock childcare, a smart uniform with a flamboyant cape, impressive leather boots, a smart cap, a pistol, and a whip to help maintain order. For industrious employees interested in making a career in the NSDAP, the job even offered a number of advanced vocational courses (e.g., "The Tasks and Duties of the Concentration Camp Guard," "The Basics of Guard Duty in a Concentration Camp"; and "Weaponry").[55] This intensive on-the-job training was provided by seasoned camp matrons who drilled the new recruits in proper concentration camp decorum. Despite this rigorous training and intense mentorship, not every woman who put on the uniform was suited to the life of a concentration camp guard. As archival records reveal, a few of the new recruits proved to be completely unable or unwilling to conform to the camp hierarchy.

To maintain this order, guards who were discovered showing kindness toward prisoners could be brought up on charges. For example, in the winter of 1944, one year before the War came to an end, a female prison guard working in an all-female facility in Cottbus was formally reprimanded for unseemly behavior. According to the official report, it seems that the guard, a Ms. Ella P., had been caught giving a female prisoner a few cookies, a tiny wedge of dried chicken broth, and an apple. In the ensuing disciplinary report, Ms. P's supervisor wrote that the prison guard's action was in all likelihood motivated by a completely misplaced sense of mercy during the Christmas season. The infraction, the supervisor noted, might therefore appear to be minor. However, the fact that this guard had already been warned in August about incorrect behavior toward the very same prisoner showed, in the opinion of her supervisor, a completely unacceptable pattern of willful disobedience. Instead of demonstrating the expected degree of distance, the young matron had proven herself to be obstinate and recalcitrant. The report ends with the supervisor's declaration that a repeat of such behavior would not be tolerated and would be met with severe disciplinary action.[56] Camp guards who treated prisoners with cordiality or respect were considered a liability to camp operations and could be formally reprimanded, punished, transferred, or fired outright.[57]

No such disciplinary action was ever needed with regard to Hermine's service. In no time at all, she had made an impressive name for herself among both her colleagues and the prisoners. But, Hermine did not find her one true calling until she joined one of Himmler's canine units. After successfully completing the obligatory intensive training with the head of the local police's canine unit, Hermine was finally issued her very own, specially bred, SS attack dog that, like her service revolver, no one but she was allowed to handle. Hermine learned to use both with deadly precision. After less than six months of service, she had been promoted to become one of the highest-ranking female guards in the camp and was awarded a military medal of honor for her service to the Reich's war effort.[58] Then in 1942, just three years after she had begun work at Ravensbrück, Hermine was chosen for another professional honor reserved for the NS female elite. She was one of approximately thirty female guards selected to serve in the ultra-new SS-run penal facility being erected in a small suburb on the outskirts of Lublin, Poland.

The camp had been originally envisioned by Himmler to be a large-scale prison camp for the hundreds of thousands of Eastern European POWs the Nazis had planned to use as slave labor after the surprise invasion of the Soviet Union in the early summer of 1941. This new facility, therefore, opened under the name *POW Camp of the Waffen-SS Lublin* [Kriegsgefangenenlager der Waffen-SS Lublin]. Once it became clear that the anticipated masses of captured Soviet POWs would not be coming,[59] on February 16, 1943, the camp's name was officially changed to the more mundane title "The Lublin Concentration Camp." This official moniker was eventually replaced, however, by the popular nickname derived from the name of the Polish suburb where the camp was located: *Majdan Tatarski*. Today, the camp is still principally known by the nickname *Little Majdan* or *Majdanek*.

Unlike Ravensbrück's prison population which was principally made up of women and adolescents, Majdanek housed thousands of male prisoners. As such, the female guards enlisted to work there were expected to come already equipped with the commensurate skills and attitude.[60] From the very start, Hermine once again proved that she was more than able to handle to the horrendous physical and psychological camp conditions. Indeed, even decades later, her uncompromising brutality made her stand out among the faceless, nameless sea of officers. In particular, she was remembered for the thick iron plates she had had added to the tips of her leather boots. In the following excerpt, Lola Givner, a Majdanek survivor describes why:

> I still have the scars today. She stomped upon me several times. It would happen whenever she would walk through the barracks or over the field. Whenever anyone stood in her way, she simply lifted her foot and kicked. That was precisely what happened to me. Our paths crossed in the field and I did not have enough time to get out of her way. She kicked me so hard that I fell to the ground. As I lay there, she continued to kick me. When I finally managed to stand up, she kicked me in my back and I fell back down upon my stomach. She kicked me again and then walked away, leaving me to lay there.[61]

In recognition of her penchant for tripping, kicking, and trampling her emaciated victims, the Polish prisoners of Majdanek soon bestowed upon Hermine the secret nickname (cryptonym) of *Kobyla* or in English, *The Mare of Majdanek*.[62] Although her boots and dog appear to have been her two favorite weapons of choice, according to another Majdanek survivor Sofia Skibinska, *Kobyla* was not averse to using other weapons:

> The guard woman was a terror for us. . . . Every time, anytime, she would appear, we were in danger. She would hit prisoners with a riding crop made of ox leather as well as with the handle of a spade. And when she was angry, she would strike out with anything she could get her hands on. As I recall, she also always had a whip with her.[63]

One day, when a male prisoner was crossing the camp grounds, *Kobyla* noticed something unusual about his gait. Perhaps it was the way that he gently shifted the rucksack on his back, or maybe it was the way he nervously avoided eye-contact. Whatever it was that caught her attention, she immediately descended upon the prisoner, savage whipping at the tiny rucksack on his shoulders and whatever it was he had hidden inside it. The rucksack began to seep blood. When it was opened, a small boy was discovered. As Barbara Steiner, a survivor of both the Warsaw Ghetto and the Madjanek Concentration Camp reported, in a desperate attempt to save his two-year-old son, the prisoner had attempted to carry the boy away with him to the fields where he had been assigned to work. The child was finally taken away to "Area 5" where truckloads of children and infants were regularly stripped naked, beaten, whipped, bayonetted, shot, or gassed before being incinerated in one of the camp ovens. Some thirty years later, this was one of the more horrific events recounted in the Düsseldorf courtroom over a five-year-period, as a fifty-four-year-old Hermine sat rigidly alongside the other Majdanek officials also accused of crimes against humanity. The fact that the infamous *Mare of Majdanek* was forced to stand trial for her crimes was far from a matter of course. Had it not been for the combined detective work and dedication of survivors, she, like the majority of Nazi camp matrons, may simply have disappeared under the nearly impenetrable cloak of mundanity. A look at her life after the war would lead one to believe that that was exactly her plan.

During the progressive liberation of the Nazi network of concentration camps, the then Chief Camp Matron [Oberaufseherin] *Hermine Braunsteiner* managed to escape capture by the Soviet forces. She eventually made her way back to Austria to rejoin her mother, who was now living in the American sector of Vienna. Relatively soon after her arrival, Hermine was arrested and made to stand trial for suspected war crimes. On November 22, 1948, she was found guilty of contributing to the torture and manslaughter of prisoners in Ravensbrück.[64] However, the Viennese court ruled that it did not have sufficient evidence to convict her of crimes against humanity committed during her time in Majdanek. For that reason, she was sentenced to three years imprisonment from which her time in pre-trial detention was subtracted. By 1950, she was a convicted criminal but was free to leave the country. And leave she did.

In 1958, right before her fortieth birthday, the still single *Fraulein Braunsteiner* met a US soldier by the last name of *Ryan* who would offer her the chance to leave the war and Europe behind her. Four months after that chance meeting, the two found themselves together on an airplane bound to Halifax, Canada. One week after their arrival, the two were married; and one year after that, in April 1959, the newlyweds relocated once again, only this time to New York City, where Mr. Ryan's brother owned an automotive repair shop. It was there that the two finally settled down and made a life for themselves. In 1963, Mrs. Ryan applied for and was granted US citizenship. On all the many forms she had to complete, it seems she always neglected to mention her conviction and imprisonment in Austria for NS war crimes. These omissions ultimately became her undoing.

Just one year after Mrs. Ryan had become a bona fide American, the famed Jewish Austrian Nazi hunter Simon Wiesenthal had successfully tracked down the whereabouts of the infamous "Kobyla" and contacted *The New York Times*.

Joseph Lelyveld was a freshman reporter, at the time, who was working the general assignments desk.[65] Lelyveld was given the task of checking out whether a former SS camp matron was actually living as an American housewife in Maspeth, a blue-collar neighborhood of Queens. The reporter's first step was to compile a list of all the "Ryans" residing in Maspeth, no small task given the large number of the Irish-Americans living in that area. Armed with his name list, Lelyveld began the second arduous step of knocking on people's doors and asking uncomfortable questions. As luck would have it, the very first "Mrs. Ryan" he spoke with said that, although she was not the one he was looking for, she might very well know which one was. She suggested the young reporter try the "Mrs. Ryan" on 72nd Street. She had a foreign accent that sounded like it could be German.

Lelyveld followed the tip, found the address, rang the doorbell, and found himself confronted with a middle-aged woman wearing a decidedly 1960s pink-and-white striped jumpsuit and a headful of curlers. Wasting no time, Lelyveld took a deep breath and asked his first question: "Mrs. Ryan, I need to ask about your time in Poland, at the Majdanek camp, during the war."[66] Many years later, Lelyveld recounted her reaction: "Oh my God, I knew this would happen. . . . You've come." Years later, Lelyveld recounted his thoughts, when he realized that he had found the woman who assisted in the murder of nearly half million people in the Majdanek Concentration Camp:

> There was nothing frightening about her. If you had passed her on
> the street you wouldn't have seen anything frightening in her. That, I
> guess, is the whole horror of the Holocaust; perfectly ordinary people
> turning into psychopathic killers.[67]

A few days after that doorstep encounter, on July 14, 1964, *The New York Times* ran an article with the provocative title "Former Nazi Camp Guard is now a housewife in Queens." Almost overnight, the story was picked up by the international press and soon US government officials were being forced to confront a lot of very uncomfortable questions themselves like how was it possible for a convicted war criminal to not only enter the United States, but also apply for US citizenship. US officials did not face the resulting public condemnation alone. Not long after the story broke, law enforcement in Europe was facing similarly uncomfortable questions. How could it happen that the *Mare of Majdanek* had slipped through their fingers?! Both the Polish and the German governments made formal applications for the extradition of Mrs. Ryan to stand trial for crimes against humanity. There was one major problem, however. Mrs. Ryan was now a US citizen.

An official hearing was opened in the United States to establish whether there were sufficient grounds for revoking Mrs. Ryan's US citizenship and forcibly deporting her should she refuse to leave voluntarily.[68] Eye-witnesses were sought.

One such survivor was Danuta Medryk. In the summer of 1940, the Polish teenager had been placed under arrest by the Gestapo for the crime of having attended school as a non-Aryan.[69] Nearly two decades later, she positively identified *Mrs. Ryan* as being the *Mare of Majdanek*. Mrs. Ryan's US American citizenship was officially revoked. On August 7, 1973,[70] *Hermine Braunsteiner-Ryan* flew from Kennedy Airport to Duesseldorf,[71] where she and seventeen others were put on trial for the murder of 200,000 people in Majdanek Concentration Camp. During the trial, the judge asked one of the 350 witnesses how she had come to learn Hermine Braunsteinter's real name. The witness explained that as a general rule, their torturers remained nameless. However, in the case of *Braunsteiner*, she remembered precisely the moment when she had learnt the accused name:

> We were standing in lines for the roll call [Appell]. She [Braun-steiner] suddenly pulled a woman from one of the rows and began to kick and hit her. The girl fell to the ground, unconscious. Someone doused her with cold water but she did not stand up. She was carried away and I never saw her again. A Polish woman said: "Look what Hermine did." It was then that I learned that Kobyla was called Hermine.[72]

Thanks to such eye-witness testimony, *Braunsteiner-Ryan* was found guilty and sentenced to life imprisonment for having participated in the selection of 1,000 prisoners who were sent to their deaths; and for having been an accessory to the systematic murder of over 100 imprisoned children.[73] Once again, however, that justice was short-lived. In 1991, the then German President Johannes Rau signed papers permitting Braunsteiner's early release upon compassionate grounds. The by then grossly overweight seventy-nine-year-old inmate had developed an advanced case of diabetes and gout. Hermine Braunsteiner-Ryan died thirty-six months later in Bochum, Germany. She was survived by her husband, who never left her side. When news of her death and identity hit the German newspapers again, neighbors were shocked to discover that the elderly woman who so loved dogs was a war criminal.

One of the keys to Hermine Braunsteiner's conviction was the fact that eye-witnesses were available who could specifically name her as a perpetrator. In most other cases, however, the real names of the perpetrators remained a mystery. The army of defense lawyers enlisted by people accused of war crimes has routinely been able to use this lack of information to help establish reasonable doubt. Given the abundance of documentation, it would have been fruitless to argue that heinous crimes had been not committed. Instead, they argued that it was impossible to determine without a reasonable degree of doubt that their clients had been the one to commit them.

Unlike the T4 staff members whose real names and pseudonyms had been partially recorded in official internal NS documents, the informal nicknames assigned to the camp staff by the prisoners in Majdanek were usually only orally transmitted and kept secret upon pain of death. This was not the only obstacle to making a positive identification. As a general rule, these covert nicknames were based upon some salient physical or behavioral feature.[74] One survivor described how this naming process worked using the example of concentration camp matron, Alice Orlowski:

> At that time, Orlowski was a particularly beautiful woman, healthy, statuesque, and imposing. She was so tall in fact that none of the Ravensbrück concentration camp uniforms that she was to wear during her service in July 1943 fit her. Her size and her muscular build were the reason for her nickname 'Krowa,' the cow.[75]

Of course, what may have been striking to some prisoners might not have been to others. Such differences in perception helped to introduce a certain degree of inconsistency in the nicknames devised. A single camp guard could be issued multiple nicknames (in several different languages), particularly if the guard had worked in more than one different camp. By the same token, a single nickname (e.g., "the beast," "the bitch") might be used for many different camp guards. Further complicating the matter was the fact that the native language of the perpetrator and that of the victim did not always match. This meant that even in cases where the name of a perpetrator had been overheard, subsequently recalling and accurately reproducing to the satisfaction of the court that name was often difficult. In table 7.2, some of these nicknames that were reportedly used for some of the camp matrons in Majdanek Concentration Camp are presented.

As can be seen above, in many cases, it is still not completely clear which person(s) lay behind the camp cryptonyms. Defense teams have been able to use this insecurity to their advantage. For example, Marthe Lächert, the woman accused of being *Blütige Brygida,* started off the proceedings by vociferously denying that she was the person known as *Bloody Bridgit.*[76] When she finally acquiesced and admitted that that had in fact been her nickname, she protested that the entire trial was so unfair. She admitted that she had not been an angel back then but in her opinion, dragging everything up from so long ago was simply cruel. According to her, had she been placed under arrest right after the war, even a few years after the war, she would have understood. But now? "[It] is completely incomprehensible to me that people are coming NOW with all of these things. . . . I mean, I never changed or hid my name!"[77] Why now? Why not sooner? It would probably be very fair to say that Lächert was not alone in asking those questions.

*

On February 9, 1902, the future Reichsfrauenführerin, *Gertrud Emma Treusch,* was born. At the age of eighteen, she married the district leader of the NSDAP,

Table 7.2 Secret Nicknames Used by Concentration Camp Prisoners for Female Guards

NICKNAMES			REAL NAME
POLISH	GERMAN	ENGLISH TRANSLATION	
Krwawa Brygida	Blütige Brigitte	Bloody Bridgit	Marthe Luise Hildegard Lächert
Drabina	Leiterin	The Director	Alice Elisabeth Minna Orlowski
Kobyla	Stute	The Mare	Hermine Braunsteiner-Ryan
Kogut	Hahn	The Rooster	—
Krowa	Kuh	The Cow	Alice Elisabeth Minna Orlowski
Perelka	Perlchen	Little Pearl	Hermine Böttcher
Sloma	Stroh	Straw	Charlotte Mayer
Sloneczko	Mäuschen	Little Mouse	Anna David
Myszka also Muschka	Die Zigeunerin	The Gypsy	Lina Hillebrecht
	Die Güte	The Good One	Hermine Brückner
	Mutti	Mommy	Emilie Macha

Friedrich Klink, and adopted his surname. Four children and nine years later, she also adopted his Party. In September 1929, she became an official member of the NSDAP. Her passion for the Party did not begin, however, until one fateful event. "During the 1920s I had all I could do to keep house, raise the children, and provide a good home. But one day my husband, who was an ardent SA man, did not return from a rally."[78] During the event, her husband suffered a fatal heart attack.

Perhaps in an effort to channel her grief, Frau Klink approached a colleague of her deceased husband and asked if there was anything she might do to continue her husband's good work. Not wishing to disrespect the widow's desires to get involved, but also most likely somewhat bemused by the notion of her taking her husband's place, he suggested that Frau Klink try her hand at bringing the various women's groups of Baden into the NSDAP fold—a task ripe for Sisyphus given the strength of the Church in the region and the animosities that existed between the various women's groups.

Either unaware of or unfazed by these challenges, the widow set about the task and achieved the impossible: she created a unified network of fourteen women's chapters in a single unit or *Gauzelle*,[79] all loyal to the National Socialist ideals. It was that organizational talent that would lead her to become one of the most prominent women in the NSDAP. In the autumn of 1933, she was called to Berlin to use her organizational talents on the national level. By the winter of 1934, she had become the head of several large-scale organizations: the women's division of the German Labor Front [*Deutsche Arbeitsfront*] with 5 million members; the NS Women's Organization [*Nationalsozialistische Frauenschaft*] (NSF) with approximately 2 million members; and the Women's League of the German Red Cross.[80] Within just a few years, she had been able to edge out women who had been members of the Party for far longer and whose cadre of male supporters had at least initially been far larger. This meteoric advancement was not a question of simply being in the right place at the right time. It was also directly attributable to her natural ability to outmaneuver her female competitors while disarming most of her potential male detractors.

As she stated before a hall filled with delegates at a 1934 International Conference of Domestic Sciences, "A German woman must always be able to do joyfully anything and everything that is demanded of her."[81] It was no doubt precisely this rare combination of unrelenting ambition and natural servility that led the Führer himself to officially name Frau Scholtz-Klink the "Reichsfrauenführerin," making her the highest-ranking woman in the Third Reich.[82] As the Party increased in power and prominence, so did she. In 1936, she became one of less than 1,500 female recipients of the NSDAP Golden Party Pin [*Goldenes Ehrenzeichen der* NSDAP], an exclusive medal of honor devised by Adolf Hitler himself to recognize those who had demonstrated extraordinary service and uncompromised loyalty to the Party. These major developments in her professional life were accompanied by a significant change in her personal life. She met Dr. Günther Scholz, the man who became her second husband. She adopted his surname and became *Gertrud Scholtz-Klink.*

During a speech delivered during a party rally in 1936, she declared that the National Socialism had "given back honor to the housewife, which she had lost during the Marxist era."[83] Despite extolling the virtues of motherhood and wifedom, neither this second marriage nor the birth of two additional children spelt the end of her political career. She evidently saw no hypocrisy in leaving her family at home while she traveled from one venue to the next to proclaim, that the role of the National Socialist woman was to use all of her strength to support the man at her side and provide him a home "where he can come at any time and find an understanding partner and comrade."[84] She also seemed to see no conflict in calling her female followers to stand steadfastly beside their men, at the same time that she filed for divorce in 1938.

She did not remain single for long. In December of 1940, she married Obergruppenführer August Heißmeyer, the future head of the National Socialist Alliance of Educational Institutions [**Nationalpol**itische Erziehun**gsa**nstalten] (Napolas). With this third wedding, she became an official member of the SS-fold as her newly betrothed was also a General in the Waffen-SS. Theirs was a perfect match. Although each of them brought their own children into the marriage (she four and he six), the couple consummated their union with a son, bringing their grand total of Aryan offspring to eleven and earning *Scholtz-Klink* yet another NS award: the coveted Golden Mother's Cross. Gertrud Scholtz-Klink had more than answered Himmler's call for every healthy German to contribute generously to the perpetuation of the Aryan bloodline. To help ensure that young women in the Reich also fulfilled this duty, Gertrud Scholtz-Klink stressed that women must be taught their proper place within the NS order.

Towards that end, in 1936, the Reichsfrauenführerin reached an agreement with the Reichsführer Heinrich Himmler. Every woman who was engaged to marry a member of the SS would first have to provide certification that she had successfully completed a course in motherhood from one of the elite SS schools for prospective brides.[85] Her aim in this and all of her Party endeavors was the same: "Using the good stock of German women to form an instrument, for the Führer to be able to use at a moment's notice."[86] Interestingly, though happy in her third marriage, she did not adopt her husband's the surname *Heißmeyer,* but continued to go by the name *Scholtz-Klink.* Having reached international notoriety, she no doubt was loathe to surrender the fame and power associated with her unusual surname. However, after the war, the notoriety of that double name quickly became a liability. The two needed a new name and identity and they needed it fast.

Though convenient, the surname *Heißmeyer* would have been a poor option for two reasons. First, by the war's end, her husband had also reached a certain degree of notoriety as the head of the National Political Institutes of Education [Nationalsozialistischen Erziehungsanstalten (Napolas)]. Secondly, the last name *Heißmeyer* was already held by the General's nephew, Dr. Kurt Heißmeyer, the pulmonary specialist who had performed a ghastly series of medical experiments on more than one hundred adult prisoners from the Neuengamme Concentration Camp and twenty children from Auschwitz.[87] During these medical trials, *Heißmeyer* infected each patient with tuberculosis bacilli through a tube forced directly into the lungs through a chest incision. After the disease had taken hold, the lymph glands of each patient were removed and examined for antibodies. Those patients who did not die during the course of the experiment were subsequently murdered.

The children, the youngest of whom was reportedly only five years old, had been told they were being taken to rejoin their parents. Instead, they were transported to the boiler room of a school in Hamburg, where the Nazis had established satellite camp of Neuengamme. One by one, the children were injected with morphine but not enough to induce immediate death. A rope was then tied around each of their necks and they were hanged from metal hooks posted along the basement wall. When death did not come quickly enough, SS Unterscharführer Johann Frahm[88] reportedly wrapped his arms around the children's waists and hung his full weight upon their tiny bodies until their necks snapped. After all of the patients had been murdered, the handful of adult prisoners who had been forced to serve as nursing assistants in the experiments were hanged as well.[89] The killings took all night and most of the morning. The bodies were returned to Neuengamme where they were cremated and their ashes spread over the cabbage fields of the camp, as fertilizer. Two weeks later, the Neuengamme Concentration Camp was liberated by the British. By the time the details of his fatal experiments had been discovered, Heißmeyer had managed to escape with his family.[90] Two sets of *Heißmeyers* on the run was simply too much. The Reichsfrauenführer and her spouse would have to find another solution.

Immediately after the war, she and her husband obtained false identity papers. *Gertrud Scholtz-Klink* became *Maria Stuckelbrock* and her husband, August Heißmeyer became *Heinrich Stuckelbrock*. The name was not chosen by accident. *Stuckelbrock* was the maiden name of August Heißmeyer's mother. Under cover of this name, the couple obtained work in a village bakery in the middle of the Black Forest. The new identities might have worked. Already in 1946, the press had begun to report that Scholtz-Klink had committed suicide in a fit of despair over the defeat of Nazi, Germany. This rumor played directly into the hands of the fugitive pair; and for a while it must have seemed to *Mr.* and *Mrs. Stuckelbrock* that they might just have gotten away with it all. But, in the winter of 1948, the Allies received a tip.

During the night of February 28, the couple was surprised by the authorities and placed under arrest. In the interrogation that followed, the two were asked about their possible ties to the NSDAP. The General vehemently denied all connections to the Party.[91] When her turn came, Frau Scholtz-Klink took another route. "Of course, I told the Americans I had belonged to the Nazi Party. I made a choice when I joined and I'm not ashamed."[92] On April 14, a French court sentenced Gertrude Scholtz-Klink to eighteen months of imprisonment: the charge? Falsifying her identity.

After the German courts assumed jurisdiction for trying German war criminals, Scholtz-Klink's original sentence was placed under judicial review. This time she received a stiffer sentence of thirty months in a labor camp.[93] In 1978, inspired by the memoirs of Albert Speer, the Reichsfrauenführerin published her own autobiography. For those readers who might have hoped that she would express some sort of shame, some degree of sorrow, or modicum regret after completing compulsory denazification, being sentenced to nearly three years in prison, and having over three decades to reflect upon her life, the book was a major disappointment. She remained unquestionably loyal to the Party and all that had been done to its name. She devoted her last publication, *The Woman in the Third Reich* [*Die Frau im Dritten Reich*],[94] to the martyrs of the Nuremberg Trials. This defiance did not come from ignorance or denial of the Holocaust. In fact, she freely and rather proudly admitted to having personally visited a concentration camp herself during the war:

> Yes, once I visited a camp near Berlin. You know, just a normal inspection visit. Some of my women worked there as social workers. They had been sent to care for the anti-social women inmates. As I toured the premises, everything appeared quite normal. In good order.[95]

In the face of such declarations, the once celebrated female leader found herself an outcast in the nation she still considered her Fatherland. Her only source of acceptance and appreciation came from the network of (Neo-)Nazis who applauded her unrepentant allegiance to the Third Reich. On March 24, 1999, the heroine of National Socialism finally followed her beloved Führer to the grave.

Notes

1. Wendy Lower, *Hitlers Helferinnen: deutsche Frauen im Holocaust* (Munich: Carl Hansen Verlag, 2013), 132.

2. Nikolaus Wachsmann, *KL: Die Geschichte der Nationalsozialistischen Konzentrationslager* (Munich: Siedler Verlag, 2015), 161.

3. Wachsmann, *KL*, 161.

4. In addition to dog maulings, female camp guards whipped, kicked, trampled, shot, gassed, starved, and worked prisoners in Ravensbrück to death. Katrin Kompisch, *Täterinnen: Frauen im Nationalsozialismus* (Cologne: Böhlau Verlag, 2008), 179.

5. Elissa Mailänder, *Female SS Guards and Workaday Violence: The Majdanek Concentration Camp, 1942–1944* (East Lansing: Michigan State University, 2015).

6. Judy Feigin, *The Office of Special Investigations: Striving for Accountability in the Aftermath of the Holocaust.* Department of Justice (December 8, 2008), 307 https://www.justice.gov/sites/default/files/criminal/legacy/2011/03/14/12-2008osu-accountability.pdf.

7. Fotini Tzani, *Zwischen Karrierismus und Widerspenstigkeit-SS-Aufseherinnen im KZ-Altag* (Bielefeld: Lorbeer Verlag, 2011), 6.

8. Ino Arndt, "Das Frauenkonzentrationslager Ravensbrück," *Dachauer Heft 3: Frauen, Verfolgung, und Widerstand* (November 1987): 125–57.

9. Ino Arndt, "Das Frauenkonzentrationslager Ravensbrück," 134.

10. Kompisch, *Täterinnen*, 181.

11. Kompisch, *Täterinnen*, 181.

12. The Office of Special Investigations watchlist "contains approximately 80,000 names of SS officers, concentration camp guards, members of mobile killing units (Einsatzgruppen)." Feigin, *The Office of Special Investigations*, 297. It has been estimated that between 1948 and 1956 more than 600,000 refugees entered the United States. Included in this number were an unknown number of Nazi war criminals. For more on the OSI's search for these offenders, see Michael MacQueen, "Das 'Office of Special Investigations' beim US-Justizministerium: Die Verfolgung von NSVebrechern in den Vereinigten Staaten," *Dachauer Heft* 13: Gericht und Gerechtigkeit (1997): 123–34.

13. Feigin, *The Office of Special Investigations*, 297.

14. Demian Bulwa, "Her Secret Past as a Nazi Guard: S.F. Immigrant Married Holocaust Survivor, Attended Synagogue." *SF Gate*, September 2006, para. 5.

15. In point of fact, the term "Frauenlager" is inaccurate as the camp not only housed female prisoners. According to official estimates provided by NAME, between 1939 and 1945, the camp held approximately 132,000 women, 20,000 men, and 1,000 female adolescents.

16. By 1942, the camp's purpose began to shift and by 1943, prisoners were being murdered in increasing numbers. To keep up with the mounting pressures in corpse disposal, in 1943, a crematorium was established on the camp grounds. From this point on, it was no longer necessary to use the crematoria in the neighboring town of Fürstenberg.

17. DI/6, the Department for Schutz- und Suchhunde [Guard and Search dogs] was sub-divided into five different units: (1.) the procurement and documentation of dogs; (2.) the training and documentation of canine personnel; (3.) the training of guard

and patrol dogs; (4.) breeding; and (5.) Veterinary Services. Bertrand Perz, "müssen zu reißenden Bestien erzogen werde: Der Einsatz von Hunden zur Bewachung in den Konzentrationslagern," *Dachauer Heft* 12 (1996):143, 139–58.

18. Helmut Heiber, *Reichsführer! Briefe an und von Reichsführer Himmler* (Munich: deutscher Taschenverlag, 1993), 256.

19. Located near Vienna, Austria, the Wiener Neudorf camp was established in 1944. It was one of forty forced labor satellite camps located around the Mauthausen Concentration Camp. Approximately 600 prisoners were held in this location between 1944 and 1945 before it was evacuated by the SS on March 30, 1945. For more, see the Mauthausen Memorial website: https://www.mauthausen-memorial.org.

20. Perz, *Dachauer Heft*, 156.

21. In an official directive issued by the SS-WVHA's Unit DI/6, from May 28, 1943, all concentration camp commandants were given the following instruction regarding the proper use of guard dogs: "In cases where prisoners are found to be shirking their duties, the dog should be ordered to confront the offender and bark until given the command to stop. If the prisoner ceases to remain still with upraised hands, tries to flee, attacks the dog, or makes any movement—the dog should be given the order to bite the prisoner with abandon." Perz, *Dachauer Heft*, 139–58.

22. Germaine Tillion, *Frauenkonzentrationslager Ravensbrück* (Fernwald: zu Klampen Verlag, 1998), 243.

23. Michael J. Bayzler and Frank M. Twerkheimer, *Forgotten Trials of the Holocaust* (New York: New York University Press, 2014).

24. Bayzler and Twerkheimer, *Forgotten Trials of the Holocaust*.

25. Department of Justice, "San Francisco woman who served as Nazi Concentration Camp Guard is Deported to Germany." September 19, 2006 (06–633-USDOJ).

26. US authorities face a considerable legal hurdle when Nazi war criminals have obtained US citizenship before their past is discovered. In such cases, the government is forced to initiate denaturalization proceedings. Feigin, *The Office of Special Investigations*, 307.

27. Office of the Inspector. Social Security Administration. "General Congressional Response Report. Payment of Social Security Benefits to Individuals Who May Have Participated in Nazi Persecution." A-09–15–50013 (2015), 3. https://oig.ssa.gov/sites/default/files/audit/full/pdf/A-09–15–50013.pdf.

28. No Social Security for Nazis Act, Public Law No:113-270. HR 5739. (December 18, 2014). https://www.congress.gov/113/plaws/publ270/PLAW-113publ270.pdf.

29. The original bill was introduced to Congress for approval on November 19, 2014 by Republican Representative Sam Johnson of Texas. The bill was unanimously passed by the House of Representatives and became Public Law No: 113–270. The law prohibits individuals identified as Nazi persecutors from receiving Old-age, Survivors, and Disability Insurance (OASDI) as well as Supplemental Security Income (SSI). In a May 2015 report was released by the Office of the Inspector General (OIG), the results of an in-depth investigation of security benefits paid out to known or suspected Nazi persecutors. According to the OIG findings, in more than one case, the benefits continued to be paid even when the beneficiary had left the United States after legal actions like denaturalization proceedings had been initiated (A-09–15–50013). As Representative Johnson explained in a December 15, 2014 letter to US Attorney General Holder, clearly this was "never Congress's intention."

30. Michael Scott Moore, "Former Nazi Guard Deported: US Send Elderly Widow Back to Germany," *Der Spiegel*, September 12, 2006. http://www.spiege..de/internat ional/former-nazi-guard-deported-us-sends-elderly-widow-back-to-german y-a-438234 .html.

31. Moore, "Former Nazi Guard Deported."

32. According to Perz's review of the training instructions given to NS canine units, the dogs were only told to attack without restraint in situations where prisoners either attacked NS personnel (including the dog itself) or attempted to defend themselves from the dog's attack. *Dachauer Heft*, 139–58.

33. Ravensbrück Concentration Camp Archive. Bericht 568: M. Mason. SlgBu-Bd_05 SS-Strafen.pdf.

34. Ravensbrück Archive, SlgBu_Bd_05 SS-Strafen.pdf Seite 155/316.

35. Ravensbrück Archive, SlgBu_Bd_05 SS-Strafen.pdf Seite 155/316.

36. Ravensbrück Archive, SlgBu_Bd_30Ber.568.pdf.

37. Ravensbrück Archive, Bericht 568: M. Mason.

38. For a detailed description of Rosa Suß during the Majdanek Trials, see Ingird Müller-Münch, *Die Frauen von Majdanek: Vom Zerstörten Leben der Opfer und der Mörderinnen* (Hamburg: Rowohlt Verlag, 1983), 112–16.

39. According to Fritz Suhren, one of the Commandants at Ravensbrück Concentration Camp, approximately 3,500 women were trained as wardens in the camp between the years 1942 and 1945. Simone Erpel, *Im Gefolge der SS: Aisfseherinnen des Frauen KZ Ravensbrück* (Berlin: Metropol Verlag, 2018), 22.

40. Mailänder, *Female SS Guards and Workaday Violence*, 114.

41. *Der Spiegel*, "'Holocaust': Die Vergangenheit kommt zurück," no. 5 (1979): 17–28.

42. Irma Grese was a female prison guard at Ravensbrück, Auschwitz-Birkenau, and Bergen-Belsen. Nicknamed the "Hyena of Auschwitz" and "the Bitch of Belsen," she was remembered by the prisoners for both her savagery and beauty. Immediately after the war, she was sentenced to death by a British Military Tribunal and hanged on December 13, 1945. Her executioner was the famous English hangman Albert Pierrepoint. For more, see Daniel Brown and Wendy Lower, *Das Personenlexikon zum Dritten Riech: Wer war Was Vor und Nach 1945*. (Hamburg: Nikol Verlag, 2015), 200.

43. *Der Spiegel*, "Blutige Brgyda," no. 48 (1975): 86–87. http://magazin.spiegel.de/ EpubDelivery/spiegel/pdf/41392711.

44. Müller-Münch, *Die Frauen von Majdanek*, 152.

45. Of the some 1,300 employees who worked at the Majdanek Concentration Camp, only 15 were put on trial. Thorsten Schmitz, "Die Stüte von Majdanek." In *Hitlers Schatten: Deutsche Reportagen*, edited by Helmut Ornter, 50–68 (Frankfurt am Main: Nomen Verlag, 2013), 56.

46. Müller-Münch, *Die Frauen von Majdanek*, 59.

47. Hamburg Staatsarchiv, Bericht 36 Grossmann, Bericht 15 Buchmann; Bericht 39a Grossmann, SlgBu_Bd_06 SS-Ärzte.pdf.

48. Ravensbrück Archive, Bericht 16: Buchmann.

49. Ravensbrück Archive, Bericht 39a: Großmann.

50. Hamburg Staatsarchiv, Bericht 39a: Grossmann, SlgBu_Bd_06 SS-Ärzte.pdf.

51. According to witness testimony, the selected patients were sent to "Bernberg," a city in Saxony-Anhalt which was home to several T4 clinics that specialized in the gas-

sing, dissection, and cremation of more than 10,000 people between 1940 and 1943. Hamburg Staatsarchiv, Bericht 500 Dolanska, SlgBu_Bd_06 SS-Ärzte.pdf.

52. Sarah Helm, *Ohne Haar und Ohne Namen: In Frauen-Konzentrationslager Ravenbrueck* (Darmstadt: Theiss Verlag, 2016).

53. Ravensbrück Archive, Bericht 381: Wiedmaier.

54. Schmitz, "Die Stüte von Majdanek," 54.

55. Tzani, *Zwischen Karrierismus*, 43.

56. Hamburg Staatsarchiv, File: 242–7_187.

57. Fotini Tzani (2011) documents a few cases where female camp supervisors requested the replacement of guards who were found to be unfit for service thanks to their refusal to alter their original friendly demeanor towards the camp prisoners. Such cases appear to have been the exception rather than the rule, however. For more, see Tzani, *Zwischen Karrierismus*.

58. Schmidt, *Hitlers Arzt Brandt*.

59. On January 26, 1942, Himmler sent word to Richard Glücks, the head of the Inspectorate for the Reich's System of Concentration Camps, about this turn of events. In it, Himmler stated that he intended to fill the camps with Jews and Jewesses in lieu of the Russian POWS. He then indicated that within the next four weeks, Glücks should be prepared to "process" 100,000 Jewish men and up to 50,000 Jewish women. Heiber, *Reichsführer!*, 125.

60. Elissa Mailänder Koslov, "Going East: Colonial Experiences and Practices of Violence Among Female and Male Majdanek Camp Guards (1941–1944)," *Journal of Genocide Research* 10, no. 4 (2008): 563–82.

61. Dieter Ambach and Thomas Köhler, *Lublin-Majdanek: Das Konzentrations- und Vernichtungslager im Spiegel von Zeugenaussagen*, Justizministerium des Landes Nordrhein-Westfalen. Band 12 (Düsseldorf: Ministerium der Justiz, 2003), 111.

62. Volker Zimmerman, *NS-Täter vor Gericht: Düsseldorf und die Strafprozesse wegen nationalsozialistischer Gewaltverbrechen* (Düsseldorf: Justizministerium des Landes Nordrhein-Westfalen, 2001), 274.

63. Ambach, *Lublin-Majdanek*, 195.

64. Feigin, *The Office of Special Investigations*, 14.

65. Joseph Lelyveld provides a detailed account of his search for the "Mare of Majdenek" in his autobiography, *Omaha Blues: A Memory Loop* (New York: Picador Press, 2006).

66. Joseph Lelyveld remained a reporter at *The New York Times* for almost four decades and was later appointed the paper's executive editor. In 2005, he provided *Times* readers with a detailed account of that prophetic meeting. In it, he described not only his first encounter with the "Mare of Majdanek," but also the reaction of her husband, who insisted for the first but certainly not the last time that he had known nothing of his wife's war crimes. See Lelyveld, "Breaking Away," *The New York Times*, March 6, 2005. http://www.nytimes.com/2005/03/06/magazine/breaking-away.html.

67. Terence McHale, "But the Thing Will Still Remain," *California Conversations* (Summer 2011), para. 55. http://www.californiaconversations.com/index.php/current_issue.

68. Ryan's US citizenship was revoked for having failed to disclose her conviction as a war criminal. Schmitz, "Die Stüte," 54.

69. In her memoirs, Danuta Medryk describes vividly how she was arrested by the Gestapo in the middle of taking her oral exams for her high school diploma. After the invasion of Poland and the enforcement of NS laws prohibiting non-Aryans from attending schools and universities, an underground movement began to hold secret classes for knowledge thirsty pupils. Even after her imprisonment, Ms. Medryk continued her resistance and was one of the founding members of a radio program broadcast by word-of-mouth in Majdanek Camp. She survived imprisonment in three concentration camps: Majdanek, Ravenbrueck, and Buchenwald. After her liberation, Ms. Medryk married and resumed her childhood dream of studying medicine. She later opened up her own dentistry practice. After thirty years, she turned to writing and became one of Poland's celebrated postwar authors. Between 1998 and 2003, she served on the memorial committee of former prisoners of Buchenwald and was a member of the High Commission for the Investigation of NS crimes perpetrated in Poland. In 2015, she passed away in Warsaw, Poland. For more on Ms. Medryk and her lifestory, see Danuta Brzsoko-Medrk, *Der Himmel ohne Vögel* (Warsaw: Verlag des Ministeriums für National Verteidigung, 1968); Ingrid Müller-Munch, *Die Frauen von Majdanek*.

70. This made her the first person in US history to face denaturalization and deportation for being a suspected NS war criminal.

71. Despite international public outrage, the denaturalization and extradition of Ryan was anything but automatic given prohibitions against double-jeopardy, especially in death-penalty cases.

72. Müller-Münch, *Die Frauen von Majdanek*, 162.

73. Feigin, *The Office of Special Investigations*, 14.

74. Müller-Münch, *Die Frauen von Majdanek*, 46.

75. Müller-Münch, *Die Frauen von Majdanek*, 116.

76. Zimmerman, *NS-Täter vor Gericht*, 173.

77. Zimmerman, *NS-Täter vor Gericht*, 174.

78. Claudia Koonz, *Mothers in the Fatherland: Women, the Family, and Nazi Politics* (New York: St. Martin's Press, 1987), xxvii.

79. Kompisch, *Täterinnen*, 53.

80. Robert Wistrich, *Who's Who in Nazi Germany* (New York: Routledge, 2002), 228.

81. Wolfgang Schneider, *Frauen unterm Hakenkreuz* (Munich: Knaur Taschenverlag, 2003), 62.

82. Kompisch, *Täterinnen*, 55.

83. Randall L. Bytwerk, *Landmark Speeches of National Socialism* (College Station, Texas: Texas A & M University Press, 2008), 59.

84. Randall L. Bytwerk, *Landmark Speeches of National Socialism*, 57.

85. Kompisch, *Täterinnen*, 204.

86. Klee, *Das Personenlexikon*, 557.

87. For a detailed account, see Günther Schwarberg, *Der SS-Arzt und die Kinder: Bericht über den Mord vom Bullenhuser Damm* (Hamburg: Stern Verlag, 1979).

88. For his participation in the murder of child and adult victims of the tuberculosis experiments, Frahm was sentenced to death and executed on October 11, 1946. Klee, *Das Personenlexikon*, 160.

89. Günther Schwarberg, "Inferno und Befreiung: Zwanzig Kinder erhängen lange," *Die Zeit*, April 6, 2005, http://www.zeit.de/2005/15/A-Kinder.

90. Kurt Heißmeyer fled to Magdeburg where he opened up a successful clinic for pulmonary patients. It would take another twenty years before his crimes were discovered. In December of 1963, he was arrested and put on trial. For his crimes against humanity, he was sentenced in 1966 to life imprisonment. In 1967, he died in prison of a heart attack. Neuengamme Offenes Archive: Kurt Heißmeyer, BstU, Ix/11, ZUV 46. Bd. 162. http://media.offenes-archiv.de/ss1_2_3_bio_1986.pdf.

91. After his capture, August Heißmeyer was given a prison sentence of three years. After his release, he lived in Schwäbisch Hall, Germany. He died on January 16, 1979. Klee, *Das Personenlexikon*, 241.

92. Koonz, *Mothers in the Fatherland*, xxxi.

93. Klee, *Das Personenlexikon*, 556.

94. Gertrud Scholtz-Klink, *Die Frau im Dritten Reich: Eine Dokumentation* (Tübingen: Grabert, 1998).

95. Koonz, *Mothers in the Fatherland*, xxxii.

CHAPTER 8

Namestories of Shoah Survivors

The strict enforcement of naming laws that differentially marked Jewish and Aryan residents had devastating and direct consequences. At the same time, that onomastic division also offered an opportunity, however small, to survive. By adopting an Aryan name and constructing an Aryan identity, Jewish residents could hide themselves, often in plain sight. The Nazis were, of course, well aware of this potential escape route and instituted exceedingly rigorous regulations to control the distribution and use of official identification papers. The penalties for violating these regulations, either by illegally carrying or dispensing "safe" aliases, were lethal. Despite these risks, within the insanity of the Third Reich, there were still a few individuals whose humanity and bravery triumphed over the evil that surrounded them.

In this chapter, the personal namestories of Shoah survivors and their descendants are told. These individual histories provide first-hand information about the impact of the naming laws on the day-to-day lives of the Jewish community during the Third Reich. In addition, they explore the complex relationships which survivors and their families developed to their names and identities after the Holocaust. Most of the stories presented here are in the original words of the Shoah survivors themselves. In a few cases, however, at the behest of the survivors, I have written the stories myself on the basis of the information they provided me. In all cases, the stories are real. Each name story ends with the names of loved ones lost but never forgotten.

*****

Etja

I was split into two names at birth. For America, I was named *Evelyn*; for my parent's lost world, I was named *Etja*, after my father's mother, burned at Auschwitz. Evelyn never felt like my real name. Maybe it was the way my mother broke her teeth saying "Eh- va -lin." Maybe it was the confusing chasm of grief at the bottom of every joy.

My parents were Holocaust survivors from the Carpathian mountain region of the Ukraine, then Czechoslovakia. Mom was the fourth of eleven children, daughter of *Esther Sheyndl* and *Avram Shia*. She grew up in the mountains, part of a little town famous for its mineral waters. My grandfather, *Avram Shia*, had a little grocery. When the peasants came to drink their paycheck at the end of the week, my grandfather would send for their families before all the money was gone. This kindness was repaid during my mother's daring escape from Communist Czechoslovakia with my father after the war.

Their store was confiscated by the Hungarian/Nazi occupation in 1939. The family began a long slow road towards starvation until they were taken to a concentration camp in the spring of 1944. Once the Hungarians took over, each of the older children left home to find work. My mother held out as long as she could, but there wasn't enough food. So, at the age of fourteen years, she left home to work for an aunt in Romania. She was abused and after a year, escaped and returned home.

Drought had come along with the horrors of war, and the family was truly starving. Mother told of her twin baby sisters waking in the night, crying piteously from hunger. She began saving her daily ration of one slice of bread to feed her sisters at night. Her father stopped her, telling her she could not starve herself for her sisters.

She left again to join another sister in Hungary to apprentice as a quiltmaker to another aunt. She and her sister were forced into the ghetto, along with the relatives. Mother was in several concentration camps before she was finally liberated from Auschwitz by the Russians. Mother said going from Camp to the Russians was like going from the frying pan into the fire.

After the war, Mother met Father at her sister's wedding. The story goes that Dad had a girlfriend, but danced with Mother. Shortly after the wedding, she made the decision to escape from Communist Ukraine into free Czechoslovakia. My father surprised her at the train station and they made a daring escape to freedom and marriage.

My father's family were tailors. His father, *Chaim Akiva*, had a bustling shop in Polanak, a suburb of Munkascz, a thriving small city. He was the fourth of six boys and a sister. His mother, Etja, was surrounded by a sea of boys (her own six and four live-in apprentices) until her last child, *Rosalyn,* was born. The

Grosses were well-fed and well-dressed. They owned a little property where their grandfather lived.

The Hungarian Nazis took away their shop during the occupation and sent the older boys and men to labor camps. Father escaped after a couple years only to find his family had been taken to concentration camp and their home stolen. He went into hiding for the remainder of the war. My grandparents died in a concentration camp, but the siblings all survived.

After their escape to free Czechoslovakia, my parents lived in Ash for three years; they then emigrated to America, sponsored by my father's uncle in Elwood City, Pennsylvania. When they came to America, they kept their last name, *Gross*, but my mother's first name *Rifka* was changed to *Ruth* and my father's name, *Baruch Bendit*, was changed to *Bernard*. Diversity was not welcome in Mid-western America at that time. Taking an American name was part of becoming American, heavy accents notwithstanding.

Their American aunt forbade them to speak Yiddish, keep kosher, or talk about the Holocaust. She told them it was not the American Way. My mother insisted on keeping kosher, but they did speak English to their children. Stories of the Holocaust were not talked about openly, although they were part of the fabric of my life. When I was ten, Mother started telling me the stories.

I was the youngest of four children. My sister was named after my mother's mother and I was named after my paternal grandmother. Several of Father's siblings named their daughters after their departed mother with variations. Only one cousin, however, had a consistent Hebrew/Yiddish and English name. It is no longer the fashion to give children separate Hebrew and English names in the Jewish communities.

Everyone called me *Evey* or *Evelyn*, except *Uncle Freddy*. He and *Aunt Mae* were our next-door neighbors. Their house was a refuge from the pain and grief that was a permanent fixture in mine. Uncle Freddy, a two-pack-a-day-unfiltered-Marlboros smoker, had a voice stuck permanently between first and second gear. When he called me, *Evie*, everything seemed to be set right in a world mostly askew. My older brother, *Marvin*, also called me *Evie* to alternately tease and endear. Marvin died suddenly at the age of sixty-two years, a few months after my marriage of thirty-two years cracked open. These two events intensified my desire for a new name, new identity. Bittersweet memories of my raspy-voiced Uncle Freddy calling me *Evie* brought on the decision to call myself *Evie Ruth*. *Etja* whispered her name from the sidelines, but she felt too daring, too radical, too different. My training was to blend in, not stand out.

The last name, Ruth, was chosen after the Biblical figure. But it was my mother's name, too. Ashkenazi Jews have a prohibition against naming children after the living and Mother died a few years later. In his nineties, my Father became talkative after her death. I asked him questions about Etja, my namesake.

In all the stories I had heard about her, she was always so good and kind. But still, it was difficult for me to get a real sense of her.

I interviewed my Aunt Rosalyn, my father's only sister. She gave me a sense of the strength it took to raise so many children and be responsible for so many others. My aunt told me a devastating story of Etja's courage and sacrifice in the last two weeks of her life. When they were taken to Auschwitz, Etja and Rosalyn were put together at first. Their bunk "beds" were slatted boards. Until she was finally separated from her daughter and sent to the gas chamber, Etja sat up every night, all night, so that Rosalyn and her best friend could lay their heads on the pillow of her legs. Over and over, Etja made Rosalyn promise that she would live no matter what. That promise, Rosalyn says, is what kept her alive.

My missing grandparents were a gash in my world. I longed for them in my childhood. Out of the devastation of my divorce and my older brother Marvin's death, that old pain re-emerged. It took a lot to go against that old prohibition, but once I owned her name, I felt more loss, more longing, and more love for the family I would never be able to know.

> *This family name story was shared in honor of*
> *My Mother, Rifka/Ruth*
> *My Father Baruch Bendit/Bernard*
> *And my maternal grandmother, Etja.*

*****

Shlomit

My parents came from Chasidic communities. They were named according to the Chasidic tradition of naming newborns in honor of their family elders (paponymy). The tradition was established when the Greek conquered the Holy Land in the middle of the fourth century BC. Their culture influenced the Jews severely, including their naming practices.[1]

My father was born in 1910 in Oraseny, a small village near Czernowitz. At the time, it was located in the Austro-Hungarian Empire, though today it is part of Ukraine. He was named *Avner Zeav*, after his great grandfather on his mother's side, who died in 1907 in Jerusalem. The name is a combination of two Hebrew Biblical names: אבנר זאב. The tradition of paponymy, naturally, caused a proliferation of the same set of names within families and communities. To better differentiate, people were referred to by unique nicknames. My father acquired the nickname *Vove*, which also belonged to his grandfather. *Vove* is also the Russian nickname for *Vladimir*. In civilian documents, though, my father's registered name is *Wolf*, which is the German translation of the Hebrew name *Zeav*.

After World War I, Romania conquered my father's village of birth. At the age of eighteen, he was conscripted into the Romanian army, where he was known by his German name: Wolf. In 1941, he was transported by Romanian soldiers, along with all the Jews of his village, to Trasnistria, a region located in today's Moldova. More specifically, the village is located behind the Dniester River, where Romania, and later on the Wehrmacht as well, established concentration camps for the Jews. My father ended up in a camp called "Bersad."[2]

When the Russians liberated the camp in 1945, they imprisoned 1,000 Jewish men. They were used for purposes such as digging trenches on the battlefield and assisting in communication with German prisoners. This fact is not surprising since only the Jews were familiar with both languages at the time. During his time in the Russian military, my father was known as *Vladimir Lazarowitz Landman*.

I do not know when exactly he escaped the Russian army to return to Czernowitz. However, I do know he left the village once he received a message informing him of his sister's survival. As soon as he received the news, he immediately set off for Israel, which was under the British control at the time and was known as "Palestine." He arrived in Israel in 1949 and registered himself as *Zeav Landman*. I do not know why he neglected to include his second name *Avner*, though he later regretted doing so. A cousin of his, who had been given the same name at birth as my father, registered himself as *Avner*. My father, within the family circle, was usually named *Vove*. While at work and in the neighborhood, he was referred to by his formal name, *Zeav*.

My mother was born in 1916 within the Austro-Hungarian Empire boarders, in a large village named "Borsa," located in the region of Transylvania which is today located in northern Romania. At birth, she received her paternal great grandmother's name: *Chaya Rachel* (חיה רחל). The name is a combination of the talismanic name *Chaya* (meaning "alive" in Hebrew) and the Biblical name *Rachel*. She was the oldest of five female cousins who all went by the same exact name. Thus, like my father, she too went by a unique nickname: *Chacze* (חאטשה).

After the First World War, when the Romanian regime conquered her village, she was forced to register in the municipality, this time under the rather uncommon name *Hermina*. The way she got this name is a part of our family lore. When my mother was born, in her village as in many other communities, the principal naming registry was the synagogue, where within the first month following birth, the names of all girls had to be recorded. I assume her father did so.

All Jews were also required to take on an additional civilian name that was neither Hebrew or Jewish. In order to perform the irritating bureaucratic task, my grandparents sent my mother's ten-year-old aunt, *Edith*, who spoke Romanian. Unfortunately, they neglected to select a name, leaving the decision in the hands of her young aunt. She named my mother after her favorite teacher:

Hermina. The unfortunate incident later became a family joke. The few people I recall ever using this name pronounced it in a Hungarian accent, making it sound like *ERmino*.

During the Second World War, the Hungarian army conquered her village. In 1944, she was sent to Birkenau Concentration Camp where she was stripped of her name and given a number. Later on, she was selected, among others, to work in Uber Hohen Elba,[3] one of the camps of Gross-Rosen, where she was slaved, still nameless, to repair communication machinery for planes produced by the Lorentz company.

My mother immigrated to Israel in 1949 alongside my father. I do not know how my parents met in some location along the path of the Jewish Exodus. Was it in Poland or Austria or Italy? I don't know precisely where it was but in 1949, they got married in Haifa, Israel. At first, she registered herself as Chaya Rachel. Later, she proceeded to apply only her first name, *Chaya*. Her family called her by two nicknames. Most referred to her using her nickname, *Chacze*. Our Israel-born relatives pronounced it differently, though, as *Chaiczu* (חייצ׳ו).

This family name story was shared in honor of Avner Zeav and Chaya.

*****

Eve Line

My great grandparents were originally from Lithuania. My great grandmother was born in Grodno and my great grandfather in Rujany (today in Byelorussia). They lived in the Vilnius area. In the mid-nineteenth century, like a lot of Jewish families of that country, my great grandparents left the country and emigrated to Palestine to escape the conscription of twenty-five years of military service. As my great grandparents had several sons, they chose to leave the country to save their boys. That is how that side of my family came to Palestine. My grandparents were married in a little synagogue in the ghetto of Hebron (Palestine) around 1880. My grandmother, *Haya Hava Pecha Lazinsky*, was only sixteen at the time. My grandfather, *Shmuel (Samuel) Cherchevsky*, was eighteen. They had several children of whom only six survived. One of those survivors was my father, *Abraham Cherchevsky*. My father was the sixth and last child of the family. He was born in Hebron on March 6, 1901, and lived his early childhood in Jerusalem. Between 1909 and 1910, his family successively immigrated to Paris. My father and grandmother were the last two to arrive.

My father did not speak French when they arrived but he learned our language during his education at the Lucien de Hirsch School in Paris. Some ten years after his arrival in France, my father applied for and obtained French citizenship. It was 1924 and my father was twenty-three. Soon thereafter, my father became a journalist and worked in a Jewish office in Paris. It was there that he would meet the woman who would become his wife, *Germaine Bernard*. As luck would have it, my mother had been a secretary in the office where my father worked as a reporter.

In accordance with the family tradition, my parents had a religious ceremony and were married by Rabbi Henri Schilli on December 9, 1930, in the Parisian synagogue on Rue Chasseloup-Labat. In 1932, 1935, and 1938, they had three daughters. I am the eldest.

When it came time to name me, my father very much wanted me to have the name *Eve*, in memory of his mother who had died four months before my birth. But my mother thought that *Eve* was far too harsh-sounding for a baby name. In the end, the two reached a compromise. My father agreed to the name *Eve Line*, as long as it was written without a hyphen or comma. He wanted to keep *Eve* quite free, in memory of his mother's Hebrew name *Hava*. So *Eve Line Cherchevsky* I became.

In the same year of my birth, my father created a little bimonthly Jewish newspaper. Entitled *Grégoire*—not to be confused with the infamous anti-Semite Gringoire—the paper unfortunately, only had five issues, the first dated November 15, 1938 and the last March 30, 1939. In these five publications, one could already feel his uneasiness with the rise of Nazism.

My family had been no stranger to the dangers of National Socialism. My mother, you see, was one of the nieces of Bernard Lazare which allowed my father access to the archives by B.L. about the Dreyfus affair[4]. My mother was born in Paris as *Germaine Bernard*. Her family had called France home for many, many generations. My mother was a very educated and hard-working woman. In addition to working as a secretary, she was also an accomplished translator for French, English, and German. Even after the Germans forbade Jews from most occupations, my mother and my father continued to work in the administration of Jewish children's homes for the Union of French Jews or *Union General des Israelites de France* (UGIF).

Looking back, our family life was the same as everybody else's. We lived in the Parisian suburbs in Issy-les-Moulineaux. And my parents did all they could to keep their concerns about the changing tides away from us children. But, as the number of Jews being arrested increased, my parents decided that Paris was no longer safe. Between 1940 and 1941, as the Germans invaded, we, like many other families, left Paris area and tried to find refuge in several different cities, notably in Eure-en-Loir, then in Royan. Our journey was long and I can't recall all of the different cities we traveled along that journey. It did not take long for my parents to conclude that they had to find another answer for us children. A life-on-the-run was simply too dangerous.

It was July 1943 and our parents told me and my second younger sister that we would be going "on holidays" at the home of a very nice lady who had been a maid at my maternal grandparents' for many years. The lady had since retired and had married a kindly widower in the countryside. I remembered the woman very well. From my birth to the age of around three, she had looked after me very often. My parents told us that the couple was very much looking forward to welcoming me and my eight-year-old sister. My baby sister, though, who was only five at the time, would have to remain with my mother because she was too young to leave "her Mummy" and because the woman who was to be our caretaker was too old to look after three children. So, we lived in the countryside near Châteauroux (Indre) and my parents returned to Paris with my baby sister.

A few days after our departure, my mother was arrested in Paris while she was at work at the offices of the UGIF. My father narrowly avoided the roundup. As soon as he heard that my mother had been arrested, he rushed home, grabbed my baby sister and a few clothes he picked up at random in her bedroom, and fled to a close female friend of our family. Along with her, they deliberated quickly and found a solution. They decided it would not be safe for my baby sister and my father to hide in the same place in case there was another raid. Our lady friend knew a woman living in another Parisian suburb. She was sure her friend would be willing to take in my sister.

As I wrote above, my sister was only five at the time. My father and our family friend told her several times that she was to tell no one that she was Jewish. Afterwards, they delivered her to the safe house. All of the adults hoped for the best but they had underestimated the power of children to interrogate. On the very first Sunday, my sister was bombarded with the fateful question: "So, why don't you go to mass?" Two minutes later, the entire neighborhood knew: the new little girl is a Jew! In a panic, the woman called my father and asked him to come and take his daughter immediately, for not only my sister's, but also for her own sake as well. If the Germans heard that she was hiding a Jewish girl, she would be arrested too.

All was not lost, our family's lady friend reassured my father. She had another idea: she knew a neighbor who had family in the countryside, far from Paris. Within a few hours, my sister was in a train with a small suitcase and a brave adult stranger who volunteered to escort her. A short while later, she arrived in her new family and there she stayed. In the meantime, my second sister and I knew nothing of these events. In our minds, our parents were safe in Paris with our baby sister and we were on holiday in Levroux.

Our mother had removed the yellow stars from our coats, and my sister and I had changed our surname to *Bernard*, our mother's maiden name. I don't remember exactly how they explained to us that we would have to change our last name. Thinking back, they probably explained it to me, because I was the eldest, and I was probably then told that I should explain everything to my younger sister, with my own words. I understood very well that the Germans were dangerous people and that my sister and I had to change our name so that nobody would recognize us. Given that *Bernard* is simpler and shorter than *Cherchevsky*, I imagine we were very glad to make the change. It was far easier to go to *Bernard* from *Cherchevsky* than the opposite!!!

It was wonderful to be with Mr. and Mrs. Couagnon, our rescuers. Some of the most important memories I have concern the food. In Paris, there was nothing to eat. The only vegetables we had were vile Jerusalem artichokes and disgusting rutabagas and I hated them both (actually, I still hate them!!). There was never enough bread and on those rare occasions when our family did have bread, it was loathsome. There was barely any butter to be found, to say nothing of fruit and milk. In the countryside with the Couagnons, we suddenly had EVERYTHING!!! Butter, milk, cheese, fresh from the nearby farm. Eggs from the hens; grapes from the vineyard; all sorts of vegetables from the garden; chickens and rabbits; and fruit direct from the trees that grew right in the middle of the vineyard. At the beginning of the new school year, in October 1943, they even enrolled us in the village's school. It was like a fairy tale for us! Madame Couagnon never ever asked us to work. We just had to play and to live. Still today, I often describe this period as the best time of my life because we were completely innocent, naïve, confident, and safe.

We were happy—thanks to the loving adults all around us, family and friends who, at the request of our father, had not told us about our mother. We only learnt that she had been taken away, one day when one of our guardians accidentally mentioned in front of us that our mother had been "arrested." At that time, they did not talk about "deportation." Since we didn't know exactly what it meant to be arrested, we calmly awaited her return. Our father had tried to calm everyone and said over and over that we should simply "wait and see."

Then, one day, quite unexpectedly, a cousin of ours arrived at the farmhouse from Paris while we were at school. He was still there at noon, when we came home for lunch. He had come to tell us that our father had also been "arrested," and that we had to leave our guardians for a few days in case the Germans came looking for us. We didn't really understand the seriousness of the situation. All we knew was that we would spend two or three weeks on a farm, a few kilometers from where we had been living. They told us that the farm where we were being sent had many animals and that we would not have to go to school while we were there. We were delighted! When the adults felt that the immediate danger had passed, we went back to our beloved refuge and stayed there until December 1944.

A little before Christmas 1944, our maternal grandfather and aunt had us return to Paris. They did what they could to welcome us in their home. Finally, we three sisters were together again. Our youngest sister had returned to Paris before us, after being hidden for a year by the family whom my father had entrusted her. It turns out that she had been very unhappy there and had been mistreated. But at least she had been saved. By contrast, my other sister and I left the Couagnons with great sadness. The eighteen months we had spent there were wonderful.

Many years later, in 1998, I formally requested that they be honored as "Righteous Gentiles—Righteous among the Nations." I had to look for witnesses from the time when my sister and I had been in hiding in Levroux. Eventually, fifty years after losing contact, I was able to locate some classmates. Jeanne, Monique, and Jean-Paul were glad to give me their assistance. Thanks to them, Françoise, like Alain, will receive the award in the name of his great-aunt and great-uncle, Mr. and Mrs. Couagnon, my rescuers. Although I was always appreciative of the loving care that the Couagnons had given me and my sister, I don't think I truly realized <u>just</u> how brave these people had been until very recently, after I heard the personal stories of other survivors during a commemorative trip to Lithuania. They literally risked their lives to save my sister and me.

As of 1944, our aunt became our new "guardian." Our aunt was an admirable woman. She had entered the Resistance very early on and her bravery earned her Medal of the Resistance and the Cross of War (1939–1945). Our aunt raised us with much tenderness and devotion. She never ever complained about the sudden arrival of three little girls aged seven, ten, and thirteen years who completely changed her life.

My sisters and I owe her a lot, indisputably, for all she did for us. She was always there for us, long after she stopped serving as guardian. When we left her home, she continued to come to the aid of each of us three, in one way or another, anytime we need her. And when we had children, she was there for them as well. Even when they hit those difficult teenage years, she was there, until age and illness prevented her. She left us in May 1997, at the age of ninety-three.

It was only after her death that I learnt more about my Aunt Madeleine and what she had done during the war as a member of the French Resistance. While we children were in hiding, she moved to the South of France with our grandfather. To keep their identities hidden, they changed their surname from *Bernard* two or three times and moved several times. She survived because she was lucky and brave. She never told though about what exactly she had done during this period.

She did tell me though what had happened to my mother. After being arrested on July 31, 1943, my mother was forced to stay several weeks in Drancy. On September 2, 1943, she was deported to Auschwitz on Convoy No. 59. According to someone who was arrested at the same time and who survived, our mother was immediately sent to the gas chambers on her arrival.

Looking back, my aunt never spoke about our father to us, and we never asked questions. There was a tacit silence, which lasted fifty years. After her death though, I would discover that my aunt had obviously tried to locate my father. In her belongings, I discovered information about Convoy No. 73 and list of names she had noted on a card. Over the years and after much intensive research, I have been able to put the pieces of my father's end together.

In Paris, my father hid at a friend's apartment. I am sure that he was aware that he should never leave the safety of that apartment. But this voluntary confinement would have weighed very heavily on him, and on Tuesday, April 11, 1944, he went out into the street. In a document we located many years later, we learnt that it was on that day that decision spelt the end for our father. According to the records, toward noon, a thirty-five-year-old Frenchman who operated as a Nazi collaborator, an *André H.*, saw my father on a sidewalk. My father's face appeared suspect to this André, who later made a report to the authorities. The subsequent identification check proved fatal and my father was immediately placed under arrest. He was taken to Drancy, where he remained until May 15, 1944. He was then deported on Convoy No. 73.

This convoy of deportees was the only one which left the Paris-Bobigny Railway Station and traveled to Lithuania. Of the 878 men in that convoy, only twenty-three came back after the camp was finally liberated. After the war, André H., the French traitor who had had my father arrested, went underground. In 1944 and 1949, he was sentenced in absentia to death for treason and conspiring with the enemy. Based on what we learnt, he later escaped to Germany in August 1944. The person who gave us the police report detailing our father's arrest informed us that André H. was acquitted in 1957. He is probably walking around today as a free man.

In 1952, totally by chance, I met the man who a year later would become my husband, André Blum. André's father had been deported to Auschwitz in Convoy No. 35 on September 21, 1942. He had been placed under arrest on September 2, André's birthday. The similarity in our fathers' destinies helped me, without a doubt, endure more calmly and less painfully the disappearance of my parents when I finally learned what happened to them.

Thanks to the tireless work of people like Serge Klarsfeld, we now have at our disposal the name lists that were carefully prepared by the Germans for each convoy just before they left for the internment camps. Through these lists we have been able to learn what happened with each one of these poor souls. However, concerning my father's convoy from May 15, 1994, there is still much uncertainty and many painful, unanswered questions for the surviving families. What we do know is that Convoy No. 73 was made up of fifteen wagons. After leaving Paris, the Convoy traveled for three days and three nights; it made a temporary stop in Kaunas (Kovno), Lithuania, where a part of the convoy was left behind. The remaining deportees were taken to Reval in Estonia.

In 1992, during genealogical research that my husband and I had begun that year, I learned by chance of the existence of *Mémorial de la Déportation des*

Juifs de France [Memorial of the Deportation of the Jews of France] by Serge Klarsfeld. In this work, I finally learned what had happened to my father. In a terrible twist of fate, his life ended about a hundred kilometers from the city where his grandmother was born, in the very region of Lithuania from which his grandparents and parents had fled a century earlier.

On the fiftieth anniversary of the Drancy departure (May 15, 1944 to May 15, 1994), a small group of families who had a loved one in that convoy came together and placed an anniversary notice in "Le Monde" about our lost family members. Shortly afterward, in 1995, a "memorial trip" was organized for the surviving families in Lithuania and Estonia, the two main destinations of that fatal convoy. I was among the survivors who made this journey. In honor of my father, *Abraham Cherchevsky*, in May of 1995, I traveled to the very place where he spent his last hours.

We had to be at Roissy-Charles de Gaulle Airport, in front of Air France/ Lithuanian Airlines on Wednesday, on May 24, 1995 at 8:30 am. Takeoff was at 10:25 am and arrival in Vilnius was scheduled for 14:05 pm (Vilnius time). One after another, we arrived at the meeting place. By the time we had checked in our luggage and made our way to the waiting room, we were already close friends and using the "tu" form with one another.

The average age of our group was sixty: some of us were retired, and others were still working. As for our professions, our group was very diverse—senior manager, secretary, psychologist, shopkeeper, physician—all of us belonged to the same immigrant generation, that is, to the first generation born in France, at least as far as our paternal families were concerned. Our group was composed of Sephardic as well as Ashkenazi Jews. Except for Dominique, the director of the travel agency, none of us were orthodox. Some of us attended the main celebrations, most of us took no part in any ritual whatsoever.

During the trip, another detail impressed me very much: several members of our group knew Yiddish (not me). That linguistic knowledge became a real bonus on our journey, as those who had the privilege of being able to speak Yiddish were able to communicate easily with our Lithuanian and Estonian fellow Jews. Despite their different nationalities, they were able to establish a natural, familiar, international, universal mother tongue, which the non-initiated of our group didn't understand any more than Lithuanian, Estonian, or Russian. The magical effect of that language connection repeatedly shone in the happy and moved faces of those Yiddish speakers.

The whole trip had been prepared with much care, although the timetable was physically and emotionally grueling given all that we wanted to see. For that reason, our trip leader and organizer—also a survivor who was making the trip with her daughter *Françoise* in the name of Louise's mother and her brother,

Lucien, who was twenty-two when he was deported—had made sure to allow time for relaxation and recovery.

After our three-and-a-half hour flight, we arrived in Vilnius. At the airport, a lovely young Lithuanian woman named *Jurate* greeted us. A fluent speaker of French, she would be our interpreter. Jurate welcomed us quickly with some words, slipped a ribbon with Lithuania's colors round Louise's neck, and gave each of us a small pin with a little bit of amber, explaining that amber has been a national treasure since ancient times. Jurate was a marvelous interpreter! Although she wasn't Jewish herself, she was very interested in Jewish issues in general, and had prepared herself intensively for our trip. In no time, she became an integral part of our group.

After a quick stop at the hotel, Jurate took us to the French Embassy in Vilnius, where the ambassador's assistant was waiting for us with two members of the Jewish community. Then we visited the old town of Vilnius which was once nicknamed "The Jerusalem of Lithuania" because of the importance of the Jewish population. We walked in the streets of the ancient ghettos. Before World War II, Vilnius had around 80,000 Jews. During the war, 90 percent were exterminated. Today, there are a few thousand Jews left. At the end of the day, we went to the synagogue, where we were very warmly welcomed. A short service was given in memory of our departed loved ones. Each one of us tearfully read aloud the name(s) of his/her lost family member(s).

The next morning, we traveled by train to Kaunas, the former capital of Lithuania. Once we arrived, Mrs. Preiskeliene, a member of the Jewish community of Kaunas, was waiting for us. She stayed with us until the evening as we made our distressing pilgrimage. Before World War II, Kaunas had about 150,000 inhabitants, one-third of which were Jews. Today, there are 430,000 people who live in Kaunas. Only a few thousand of those residents are Jewish. Here again, the Nazis and their Lithuanian collaborators decimated the original Jewish community in a series of horrific massacres.

Our small group took "le Chemin de la Mort," the Path of Death. The narrow path wound its way upwards between large green fields that stretch as far as the eye can see. It was not difficult for us to imagine the conditions in which a portion of the doomed men from Convoy No. 73[5] were made to climb that path after a terror-filled three-day train ride. Exhausted with thirst and hunger, ill from the horrible hygienic conditions, the prisoners were made to march on until they reached an ancient Kaunus fortress. It was here that the Nazis murdered their Jewish captives: our sons, brothers, uncles, cousins, husbands, and fathers.

A few days later, after we had had some time to recover, we continued our journey. We flew some 560 kilometers to the north of Vilnius to reach Tallinn, where the rest of Convoy No. 73 met their death. We arrived at where the Kloga concentration camp once stood, hidden by the forest. A memorial plaque had the following inscription: "In the memory of the victims of fascism. Here lie nearly 2,000 Jews from the Kloga concentration camp, who were shot on September 19, 1944." Our journey was now complete. We had been to both Kaunas and Tallinn, where our loved ones had met their deaths.

When our plane landed in Paris and we collected our luggage, we turned and kissed one another and bid everyone a safe journey home. All of us were deeply moved. But we promised to meet again soon to look at all of the photos taken during the trip. We also wanted to see the film Louise shot on her camcorder. As we finally took our leave of one another, Esther smiled and said: "We are all cousins now. We are family." Shortly after returning from the trip, an amazing coincidence occurred.

On the occasion of the fiftieth anniversary of the "Vélodrome d'Hiver Raid" in Paris, a special stamp was presented by "La Poste" (Post Office), in France, and the "Musée de la Poste" took the opportunity to hold a small historical exhibition between July 1, 1995 and August 27, 1995, to commemorate what had happened to the Jews during World War II. Esther went to the exhibition at the beginning of July with her husband. He hadn't been on our trip but Esther had told him all about it and had mentioned all of the names she'd heard during the readings of the kaddish.[6] Suddenly, Esther's husband, called out:

"Look ! There is an identity card with the giant red stamp 'Jew' on it !"
"Really?," Esther replied.
"What name is on the card?"
"Cherchevsky," he answered.
"What did you say!?," said Esther, walking quickly to the part of the exhibit
      where her husband was standing. "Was it 'Abraham'?," she asked, excitedly.
"Yes. How did you know?," her husband replied.
"But . . . that's Eve Line's father!!"

As soon as she returned home, Esther called me. My astonishment and my emotion were overwhelming. I couldn't understand how this card could be there. I asked friends of mine to investigate. Through their detective work, I learnt that this card had been part of a folder "offered" to the "Centre de Documentation Juive Contemporaine" in Paris by my uncle, my father's own brother.

When my two sisters and I contacted the Centre, the Director became very annoyed. He was not willing to give us the card back because it was an important historical document verifying that not only foreign but also French Jews had been deported. Moreover, he testily asked what we three sisters would do with this document: "What's the use of having this one card for the three of you? Which one of you would get it?," he scoffed. As a compromise, he made me a color copy of the card.

I believe that fate played a hand in my discovering that document. Thanks to that incredible journey, I met a woman named Esther; a woman whom I hadn't even known longer than a few months; a woman whose father died with mine; a woman who led me to one of the last pieces of identification with my father's name on it: *Abraham Cherchevsky.*

> *This family name story was shared in memory of*
> *Germaine Cherchevsky nee Bernard and Abraham Cherchevsky,*
> *as well as all those lost on Convoy No. 73.*

*****

Michel

My father was *Grisha Siritsky.* He was born in Sebsatopol, in the Crimean Peninsula. My mother was born in Odessa and was called *Judcovici.* My parents married in France where my father was in the movie business. He owned seventeen movie theaters in France. His road to the cinema started in the most unlikely of places: the Middle East. When he and his brother left Russia in 1925, their journey took them to Turkey.

Once there, they noticed that all of the movie houses were for men only. So, the two rented a tent with fifty-nine chairs and started showing feature films for women only—an idea which no one before had either thought of or dared to act on. Whatever the reason, the brothers' business was a huge success: so much so that the government informed them that it might be better for them to leave Turkey before they caused any more upset. So, the two continued their journey and landed in France. There they quickly made use of their movie contacts and acquired permission to show Hollywood films. Before long, they had a very successful network of cinemas. Just at the time when we all thought things could not get any better, they became unimaginably worse. The Nazis were on their way to France and there was nothing to stop them.

My parents went to the Secretary General of the Mayor of Cannes, André Chataignier. He was a Protestant who risked his life to save French Jews by giving them new identity cards with false names. Thanks to Chataignier, we no longer existed as the *Siritsky* family but the *Steva* family. I did not have any difficulty in adapting to our new name. It was easy to remember to use because our lives depended on our ability to play this charade. What made it even easier for me as a child was the fact that my assumed name and my birth name had the same initials: M. S. Only when we were in the company of other Jews did we feel at ease. Otherwise, we were always on our guard. As difficult as that time was for me as a child, for the adults, the games of deception were far more dramatic, particularly for those who tried to leave the country and escape to Spain, for example.

In 1942, my teacher informed my mother that the police had begun picking up the Jewish children in the schools. He explained it would be better for me if

I did not go back to school. Instead, he offered to hide both of us in the village of his parents. My mother thankfully accepted his offer. The next day, at 2 am in the morning, he arrived with his car and drove us 500 kilometers to a little village where he left us with his parents. Then he quickly drove the entire way back before anyone noticed he'd been gone.

After three weeks, the gendarmes came to inform us that next day they would come to pick us up. We were lucky as the gendarme were less inclined to murder the Jews than the police. Upon hearing the news, the papa of my teacher advised us that it would be better for us to get out of the village. So, at 3 am he took us to one of his friends. It was completely dark and we walked for easily five or six hours until we reached the farm of Vincente Navarro, a Spanish farmer who had escaped to France during the Civil War in which close to half a million Spaniards died between 1936 and 1939. Vincente Navarro took us in. The story we told people was that we were Vincente's cousins. The story was convincing because mama and me look Spanish. I could also speak a little Spanish and my mother could understand a little Spanish.

The farm was very rudimentary. There was no electricity. That meant that there was no radio and very little news from the outside world. We only received mail once or twice a month. No electricity also meant that we had no way of preserving our food. So, when you had bread, if you did not eat it the same day, the next day, it was covered with a green fungus.

Once I turned ten years old, I began to work on the farm. I was in charge of looking after the twenty-four goats and cleaning after ten pigs. I worked from 6 am to 6 pm. There was always work to be done. We wasted nothing. It was very hard living. But we were protected and had food to eat.

For two years we lived on that farm. One day, we heard the sound of a motor. It was completely different from the sound of the other engines we knew. Suddenly, three Jeeps emerged from the forest with twelve US soldiers. They were scouting the area for German troops. We did not know it but the day before the Americans had landed in the South of France! Alleluia! I cannot describe that moment! Suddenly we could breathe! My teacher came to bring us back to Cannes and there we learned that my father had been exterminated at Auschwitz.

Later, when I moved to Canada, I made sure that my teacher's name "Jean Monge" was inscribed on a memorial list of non-Jews who risked their lives to save people like me and my mother. Unfortunately, Monsieur Monge had already died by the time this honor took place. But I know his children appreciated this small gesture to recognize their father's name.

After the occupation of France ended, General Secretary Andre Chataignier was interviewed about his activities during the War.[7] According to him, he and his colleagues worked feverishly to save as many as they could:

During the entire period of the occupation we delivered no fewer than 4,000 false cards for food and identity. I never wanted to know the real names of the people to whom I gave these papers. I said to myself, "If one day you are taken: you believe now that you would not talk, but how to foresee the effect of the torture: it is better to know nothing, it is more sure for the others."[8]

As Chataignier went on to explain, once the false identification papers with the aliases were complete, he generally passed them on to a colleague, Joseph Bass, who in turn passed them on to a Catholic priest who saved the lives of thousands of French Jews from the Holocaust. That priest's name was Father Pierre-Marie Benoît (1895–1990). Today, he is listed among Yad Vashem's "Righteous among the Nations."[9]

This family name story was shared in memory of Grisha Siritsky.

*****

Muguette[10]

The new German law instructed all Jews to register at the nearest police station. As foreigners, we took the laws very seriously. To break the law as a foreigner is quite different than breaking the law as a citizen. We were Polish Jews living in Paris, France, and although we had done our best to blend in to the massive city around us, this new regulation placed us before a true dilemma. If we obeyed the law, who knew what would happen. If we disobeyed the law, who knew what would happen. These were the kinds of questions that my Maman had to face at that time. She did not have a husband to rely on to help her with these difficult decisions, as my father, *Abraham Szpajzer*, had died many years earlier from a lung infection, leaving her alone with two small children, my older brother and myself. I was three and a half at that time. My Maman was not completely alone, though. She had her sister, my Aunt Deeneh whom I called *Meeneh*[11] *Deeneh;* and my *Gromeh* [from "grand-mère," in French]. And she also had a few very good girlfriends as well. After talking with everyone, my Maman finally made her decision. As I had contracted a severe lung infection, I would go to a convent where I would be kept safe and would have time to recover. In the meantime, Maman, Gromeh, and my brother would leave the city until things hopefully improved. They three traveled deep into the French countryside to a small, remote village by the name of Champlost.

Once there, my Maman and another Jewish woman from Paris, who was also seeking refuge, met with the town mayor. He informed the women that there was a house where they could stay. It was a small home on the outskirts of the village. A retired, elderly sea captain lived there. According to the Mayor, the captain was a kindly old man whose health was failing. If the women agreed to look after the gentleman, prepare his meals, and clean up a bit, they would be allowed to stay free of charge. The house was not luxurious, the mayor warned, but it was safe and with the vegetable gardens and fruit orchards nearby; there was more than enough to eat. The women eagerly agreed and made their way to the sea captain's house.

When they arrived, they discovered that both the house and the captain were in a pitiful state. Maman immediately made the elderly gentleman a warm meal and when he was finished, she and her new companion from Paris set about cleaning the kitchen. While Maman was busy working her way through what must have been years of clutter, she heard the woman behind her shriek. Maman turned and discovered that the woman was holding a wooden box. Inside that box were jewels and gold coins. "We're rich!," the woman exclaimed. "What do you mean 'WE'RE rich'?!," Maman retorted angrily. "That does not belong to us!." "But—," the woman sputtered. "No. That does NOT belong to us," said Maman resolutely closing the box shut. The woman replied, meekly: "Yes, but of course, you are right." But Maman had already seen the way she had looked at the box. The next day, Maman arrived at the Mayor's office and quietly placed the box upon his desk. Not wanting to get her companion in trouble, she simply said: "I think it would be better if you kept this in your office . . . for safe keeping. We found this in the sea captain's kitchen last night." The mayor, baffled, opened the box. Maman watched his face as the Mayor's chin fell. "You found THIS in the kitchen?" "Yes." "And you are bringing it to me—for safe keeping?" "Yes, I think that would be best." A heavy silence fell between the two. You see, the Mayor knew all too well what that treasure could have meant to someone who was as desperate as Maman was. And still, despite what would have been a horrible temptation for anyone, Maman brought the box to him. The Mayor then explained that the sea captain was a distant cousin of his. "Madame? Please stay as long as you wish. You are welcome here. You are now an official citizen of this town. And should you ever need us, we will be here for you."

As it turns out, that promise was probably worth more than all of the jewels in that box. A few weeks or months later, when things had died down in Paris, Maman decided it was safe enough to return home to our apartment. And things were quiet for a time. That was until July 15, 1942, when there was a sudden un-expected knock at the door. It was one of Maman's gentile sisters-in-law. Like Ma-man, she also worked as a secretary. But unlike Maman, her sister-in-law worked for the Nazis. You see, she was tall, blonde, and beautiful and those were exactly the qualifications the Nazis were looking for in their French secretaries. In that position, she was able to gain information about what the Nazis were planning. The fact that she had shown up so unexpectedly did not bode well then. Maman ushered her into the apartment and her sister-in-law hurriedly explained that the Nazis were planning to start rounding up all of the Jewish women and children, TOMORROW! After delivering the message, she explained that she must hurry to warn the others.

Maman turned to Madame Dumas, a dear friend of hers who had been visiting us at the time. "Bella? What are you going to do?," Mde. Dumas exclaimed. Both women were in a panic now. Suddenly Mde. Dumas made a decision. "Bella? You and the children will stay with me tonight." That may seem like nothing. But in times like those, opening her home to a Jewish family meant risking her life. "You and the children will stay with me." She repeated; and with that, she stood up and walked across the room, and retrieved a pair of scissors. Then without saying a word, she took each of our coats and cut away the three yellow Stars of David away. She then hid them in the only place she could think of, her brassiere. "No one will think of looking here!," she exclaimed. With that both women, laughed as much out of relief as out of fear. A decision had been made. We had crossed the line and gone underground.

Maman and Mde. Dumas gathered the two of us and we left our small apartment. "We have to warn Aunt Deeneh and Gromeh," Maman said. And once again we were confronted with one of those horrible dilemmas. Do we walk or should we take the train? If we walked, it would take much longer and we did not dare to be on the streets that long, as there were Nazis everywhere. If we took the train, it would be faster but it was illegal for Jews to take the train and if we were caught out, the results would be disastrous. Maman decided. We would take the train. It had been such a long time since we had ridden the train. I had completely forgotten how crowded it was. There was only one seat available. Maman motioned for me to sit down as she and my brother stood next to the door. Seated directly across from me was an old man who kept staring at me, looking up and down from my face to my lap. "What are you looking at, you OLD GOAT!?!?," I thought, defiantly. As his face darkened into a horrible, hate-filled scowl, I followed his gaze downward to my coat and to my horror I discovered that on my coat were small pieces of yellow thread that together made the outline of a star. I was sure that the man was about to yell out "JEWS!," when suddenly Maman called my name. It was our stop. I don't even remember my feet touching the ground, I sprang that quickly from my seat to the sidewalk. I did not dare look back at the train lurched forward and surged away towards its next stop. While Mde. Dumas took us back to her apartment, Maman dove into the tumult of the street again to reach the apartment where *Aunt Deeneh* and *Gromeh* lived together. It was only a few blocks away on the third floor, but it was terrifying to be on the streets now, knowing about the upcoming deportations.

When Maman finally reached the apartment building, she bounded up the staircase. Suddenly she was stopped by the sound of thundering boots and scuffling shoes racing down the staircase. What happened next changed my mother's life forever. It was the sound of her sister being dragged down the staircase with a French police officer on either side of her. As the three roared past, my aunt said in Yiddish as if speaking to the heavens: "You see, I am doomed!"[12] And then, just as quickly as they had appeared, there were gone . . . out the front door of the apartment building into a waiting car below. Maman never forgave herself for that moment . . . for not having shouted out. Instead in her shock, she had said nothing. . . . When the door below slammed shut, Maman raced upstairs to the apartment and discovered Gromeh in a horrible state. In her terror and grief, as she watched the police take her daughter away, she had suffered a massive heart attack. Maman summoned a doctor came and Gromeh was taken to the hospital. After only two days, she was ordered to leave. When Maman protested that her mother was far too weak to leave the hospital, the medical attendant exploded with rage. "You should be happy that I did not call the police to tell them who you!" Two days later, Gromeh died. Now we were alone and Maman remembered the promise she had been given. We were on the train again. Back to Champlost.

Once there, we went straight to the Mayor's office. And true to his word, he informed us that we were more than welcome to stay as long as we wished. We were given a small house on the outskirts of town. A few days later, the local priest arrived and said he must speak to our mother. "Bella?," he said, very gravely. "The Mayor and I have been speaking and the present arrangement is simply too dangerous. It is your names, you see. If the Germans come, they will know straight away that you are not from here. You need new names." The Priest thought for a moment and then declared that Maman could use her first name as her surname. "But what will my first name be?," Maman asked. "Isabelle.," The Priest declared. "And what about my son and my daughter?" Maman asked, looking at the two of us. "Hmm, yes." The Priest thought again. And then he named us what I imagine any Priest would. I became *Marie* and my brother, whom we all called *JoJo* would become *Joseph*. It was decided. We were now *Isabelle Bella*, *Marie Bella*, and *Joseph Bella*.

It was also decided on that day that our family would attend church every Sunday like the rest of the village; and my brother and I, like all of the other children in the village, would begin to study for the catechism. This was not done so much to convert us. That really wasn't the point. It was to integrate so much into the village that when and if the Nazis came, they would not be able to tell us apart. And one day that day did come.

Suddenly, a tank arrived and with a man in a black uniform. I remember how he was waving his arms about. I screamed to Maman: "The Germans are coming! The Germans are coming!," Maman rushed to where I had been sitting next to the window and closed all of the shutters. Through the slats we watched them slowly make their way into the center of the village. When they arrived, the leader immediately started yelling wildly at everyone to do this and to do that! The problem was no one understood a single word he was saying. Then one of the villagers thought that perhaps it would be a good idea to call for Maman. "Yes, get Bella!," they decided. You see, because Maman came from the city and was educated, they assumed that she had the best chance of being about to understand what it was that the man was yelling about. So, they sent for Maman. What could she do? She went and listened to what the officer was shouting. By this time, he had become quite red in the face with fury and frustration. "The animals are everywhere!" You see when the Nazis came, many of the farmers in the local areas abandoned their farms in an attempt to escape. That meant that all over the countryside, there were animals roaming everywhere. The commander was quite beside himself and ordered Maman to tell all of the women in the town square to gather the cows and milk them.

Well, Maman had never milked a cow before in her life. She did not know the first thing about them, coming from the city. But, she realized on that day she had better act as if she could. And don't you know, she was the only one who managed to get a drop of milk out of those cows on that day. From that point on it was settled. Maman would serve as the commander's official translator. On more than one occasion, he would praise Maman for her excellent German. What he never seemed to realize is that Maman did not speak a word of German. The entire time that she worked as his translator, she was using Yiddish. German to Yiddish and Yiddish to French and then back again until suddenly the Nazis were gone just as quickly as they had come. The war was suddenly over. The American soldiers had come and the French Resistance had broken through. France was liberated.

Maman thanked our fellow villagers for their bravery and their generosity. They had literally saved our lives. We then traveled back to Paris to see if we could find some of our friends. When we returned, every day was filled with more news about someone who was missing and another one who had been carted away. I soon became quite depressed. Maman hoping against hope to cheer me up, declared one day that we were going to the movies—like we used to do before the war.

As we sat in the darkened movie theater, I remember feeling quite happy and then the newsreel began. Back then, there was always a newsreel before the picture started. The next thing I knew, I found myself on the sidewalk with Maman slapping me in the face as someone was shrieking. I was quite shocked to discover that the person who was screaming was me. Maman later told me that the newsreel had been made up of footage taken by the soldiers who'd liberated the concentration camps. And as soon as the image of all those bodies came on the screen, I apparently started screaming and would not stop.

Maman had immediately taken me out of the theater but it had taken quite some time for me to regain my senses. Even now, this many years later, I have no memory of it. None at all! All I remember was sitting in the theater, waiting for the film to start. It was horrible back then. . . . We were alive but we had all lost so much. Everyone was grieving . . . it hung over the entire city.

One day, a neighbor of my Gromeh came by our tiny apartment. In her hands she held a winter coat. She said, "Your mother made me swear that I would make sure that you got this coat!" Maman was quite astonished. "Thank you," Maman said, not wanting to be rude. "But I don't need a winter coat. It is really much too small. Please, you, take it." But the woman, absolutely refused. "No. I'm afraid. I really must insist. Your mother made me promise to deliver this coat." She then resolutely placed the coat in Maman's arms, turned, and walked away.

Maman held the coat up. "What am I going to do with this? It is FAR too short. We'll have to let the hem out." She strode across the room, found the scissors, and began to snip away the tiny stitches. It was then that she discovered that sewn into the hem of that coat was a tiny wisp of paper with two names carefully penned in my Gromeh's handwriting. *Morris* and *Harry Szpajzer.* These were the new English names of Maman's two older brothers whom she had known as *Moysche* and *Hartzke.* The boys had immigrated many, many, years ago to Canada to seek their fortune. Over the years and with the War, the family had lost touch. With the help of these two English-versions of their names, we were able to track down my uncles in Canada. They were ecstatic to hear from us. "We heard all the horrible news over there and we thought everyone in the family was dead!" The two arranged everything for us and within no time at all we were on our way from Europe to Canada. I have lived here ever since. So, you see names saved my family twice. Those two names that my Gromeh hid in that Winter coat and those three names given to us in our honorary town of Champlost. On June 8, 2005, I returned to our French village for a special ceremony to honor the townspeople of Champlost and recognize their heroism for collectively protecting us from 1942 to 1945. The ceremony was attended by Mr. Victor Kuperminc, a delegate of the French committee for Yad Vashem who bestowed posthumous medals, including "the Righteous Among the Nations."[13]

This family name story was shared in dedication of my mother, Bella Fridberg, and my brother, George Spiner, and in loving memory of Gromeh Fiszman and Deeneh Fiszman.

*****

Henri

My father, *Abraham Obstfeld*, was born in 1896 in Krakow, now Poland. Before the war, my father and a younger brother of his ran a slipper factory in Amsterdam. The factory had been started by their father (my grandfather) before 1930. My mother, *Jacoba Vet*, was born in 1906 in Amsterdam My mother had been a secretary since she left secondary school, and worked, for instance, for the Hoover vacuum cleaner company in their Amsterdam branch. My parents met one another while taking dancing lessons in Amsterdam. On November 21, 1934, they were married in Amsterdam. After their marriage, my mother continued to do some secretarial work and my father worked on in the family factory. During the rise of Nazism, my parents attempted to carry on with their lives as they had done before but they were well aware of the changes taking place for Jews (and other groups) in Germany.

I was born on April 11, 1940, one month before the German invasion of the Netherlands (and Belgium and France) on May 10, 1940. When the time came to select a name for me, my parents had two different ideas. My father, who had spent his formative years in Vienna, wanted to call me *Hans*. But my mother was a Francophile and preferred to call me *Henri*. The outcome was that I was called *Hans*, but my birth certificate listed my name as *Henri*. My Hebrew name is *Tswi* which translates into German as *Hirsch*.

Before the danger for Jews in Amsterdam became completely unbearable, my parents were able to secure false identity cards. I still have them today. My father's ID card lists him as *Hendrik Oom*, born in Leeuwarden (the Netherlands) on May 29, 1900; and my mother's ID card indicates that she is *Berendina de Groodt*, born in Amsterdam on July 5, 1906. The next obstacle facing my parents was to somehow bring me to safety.

The story is as follows. My mother had had a boyfriend from her secondary school time. He lived in a small village near the city of Arnhem. He was prepared to look after me. However, since he was unmarried, the three agreed that it would be strange if a small child suddenly appeared in his life. Clearly, another solution had to be found. My mother's old boyfriend, I believe, was a member of the Free Masons just like the man who would ultimately became my gentile foster-father, Mr. Klerk.

When Mr. Klerk brought me home to his gentile wife and family, I was told that at home I would be called *Hans*. But, if ever asked for my "official" name, I was to say *Hendrik Klerk*. The "cover up" story to explain where I had come from was that I was a nephew who had lost his parents in the bombardment of the city of Rotterdam in May 1940.[14] I was not yet three years old. I was looked after by the Klerks for the rest of the War.

I was never called either *Hendrik* or *Henri,* but always *Hans,* until I left the Netherlands and moved to Great Britain to study.[15] I have lived for more than fifty years in England. Initially, I went by the name *Hans* here too. However, pronouncing and spelling *Hans* caused real problems for the British. So, to make matters easier for them and simpler for me, I decided to go by the name *Henri. Henri* is more easily recognized here. But, I do use the French spelling on my birth certificate. My parents and I all survived the War. But so many other members of our family were murdered.

> *This family name story was shared in memory of Esther Obstfeld, Selig Obstfeld, Joseph Vet, Henriette Vet nee Emmering, Loebel Obstfeld, Marguerite Obstfeld nee Mahler, Izaak Obstfeld, Marco Obstfeld, Kitty Bed nee Vet, Meyer Bed, John Bed, and Henriette Bed.*

*****

Joan/Fanny

My passport identifies me as *Joan Frances Salter,* British citizen. I have had this persona for so long that in my everyday life I never think twice about it. Indeed, there is nothing to distinguish me from my fellow Londoners. Nothing except for a slight inflection in my voice which no one can quite place. Because of my fair skin, deep-blue eyes, and once very dark hair, some people assume I am Irish while others place my accent as West Country. In fact, it is the now faint remnant of an American accent. Only that is not my country of origin, but that of a child named *Joan Farell.*

Hidden away in the jumble of my filing cabinet is a file marked "Certificates: Birth, Death, Marriage, Insurance etc." Inside is a green document written in French bearing the title and seal *Ville de Bruxelles.* It states that a daughter, Fanny, was born to *Jakob Zimetbaum* (born in Zabno, Poland) and to *Sprynca* nee *Perelman* (born in Warsaw, Russia) in Brussels on February 15, 1940. This is my birth certificate. Although Warsaw was Russian when my mother was born there at the beginning of the last century, by the time I was born, it had become a part of Poland. Today Poland is a member of the European Community and its citizens are free to travel and live all over Western Europe. But times were very different then. Indeed, had I been issued a Polish passport back then, it would not have identified me as Polish, but as a child of Jewish or Hebrew nationality. With this identification, the only journey I would have been entitled to make would have been direct to a concentration camp.

When the Germans invaded Belgium on May 10, 1940, one of their first acts was to round up all male aliens over the age of fifteen. I was barely three months old when my father was arrested. Having lived in Western Europe most of his adult life, my father used the first name *Jacque*, the French equivalent of *Jacob* at this time, with his surname *Zimetbaum*. At the time, Germany was busy moving troops down into France and the logistics of supplying an invading army meant that diverting resources for the deportation of the Jews was initially given low priority. So, instead of being sent straight to the "East" as the extermination camps were euphemistically described, Jacque was taken over the border into France and interned first in an ordinary French prison in Angouleme and subsequently in another prison, in Bordeaux. The previous occupants of these prisons were, no doubt, freed to commit more of the same crimes for which they had been convicted in order to facilitate the incarceration of those deemed to have committed the worst crime of all: being born Jews.

Jacque languished in prison for approximately six months before being put on a train with a group of fellow Polish Jews, bound for a camp in the East. It was an ordinary train, but they were placed in a carriage separated from "normal" travelers. They were guarded by only a handful of young German soldiers, who soon settled into a game of cards. Jacque tried to persuade some of his friends that their best bet was to slip out unseen and jump off the train as soon as it slowed down outside of Paris. But they all thought he was just making trouble. "Why endanger yourself? A labor camp is better than being on the streets without papers!," they said. Unable to convince them, he slipped away quietly by himself and then jumped. He lay on the tracks watching the train move painfully slowly away, expecting it to squeal to a halt when the others alerted the guards. The lives of his companions would be safer if they informed on him. But surprisingly the train continued on its way without stopping. Whether their final destination was truly a labor camp, my father was never able to determine but, ultimately, it is unlikely that any of his fellow deportees survived.

Jacque's decision to jump may have been made easier by the fact that he knew his way around Paris. Before moving to Belgium, he had lived there many years. His journey from the family home in Tarnow, in the southeastern region of Poland, to Western Europe started in 1920. His father, my paternal grandfather, was *Moses Spielman*. The fact that my grandfather and father had two different surnames is an interesting window into the lives of the Jews who lived in that part of the world. *Zimetbaum* was actually the surname of my father's mother. How or when my grandmother's family had acquired the surname *Zimetbaum* is lost to memory. Records of the name appear from the mid-1700s, all in the area round when my father comes from.

When my grandparents married at the end of the nineteenth century, they would have had a traditional wedding under the "authority" of their own rabbi; and in accordance with Jewish law at the time, the children born of that marriage would have first carried the surname of their mother. Hence my father's surname

Zimetbaum. Only after the children were registered would the name of the man who recognized them as his own be entered into the official records. However, under the Nazi occupation, many of those official documents were destroyed.

It is family legend that all Zimetbaums come from the same ancestor. Despite that real or imagined connection, there is no consensus about what "zimet" actually means. Some say it is a type of citrus fruit; others insist that it means "cinnamon." What everyone agrees on though is that "baum" definitely means "tree." When I think about our family name *Zimetbaum,* I picture some great-great-great-great grandfather sitting under a tree studying his Talmud when a local official came to register people's names. I imagine that the two men would not have had a common language. So when the official asked my great-great-great-great-grandfather for his name, my ancestor, not understanding him, would simply have shrugged his shoulders and held his arms up in the air towards the sky. The official, thinking he was intentionally pointing to the tree, would have jotted down *Zimetbaum.* It is probably as good a guess as any.

As it turns out, my grandfather and my father differed not only in their last names. *Grandfather Moses* was, according to my father, a very tolerant man. But that patience soon ran out when his second son showed a distinct preference for playing cards over working in the family-run garment factory. In hopes of setting him straight, at aged seventeen, my father was sent to Antwerp to be apprenticed to a distant cousin as a trainee gemstone cutter. This apprenticeship didn't suit him at all. For one thing the cousin was ultra-Orthodox and their days were punctuated by frequent prayers and punctilious adherence to the minutiae of religious observance.

Although Jacque's ideology diverged sharply from that of his younger siblings, who were both active in the Communist Party, he shared their non-religious outlook. So, to him prohibitions like not smoking on the Sabbath were clearly meant to be broken. His other problem was the long hours he was expected to work. After about six months, he decided he knew all he needed to know about precious stones and moved on, causing yet another rift with his parents. This period of my father's life remained of little interest to him. He never spoke of the cousin by name, so I have no knowledge of this branch of the family. I suspect he may have been from the *Spielman* side of the family as the impression given was that my father's paternal side were much more religious than his maternal side. Whether any of them survived the Holocaust, I do not know.

After leaving the diamond cutting business in Antwerp, Jacque settled in Paris, first as a gemstone salesman. He found the nightclubs and casinos a good source of income. He always had something in his pocket to offer a man on a winning streak for the attractive lady on his arm. And his prices always were wholesale! A gregarious, flamboyant personality, Jacque's entrepreneurial skills enabled him to diversify. He soon took to attending fashion shows put on by the Paris couture houses to make surreptitious copies of their designs. By then, he had not only made peace with his parents but had a winning business idea.

On his regular trips back to the family garment business in Tarnow, he would bring the latest designs he had discovered in France. Then, on his return to Paris, he would have with him a consignment of "ready to wear" fashions. At a time when only the wealthy had access to haute couture, the sale of these stylish copies made for a very profitable business. My father spoke with pride of his parents' factory. I have been back to Tarnow to try to find some evidence of the family business but I found no mention of a *Zimetbaum* or *Spielman* owning a factory in Tarnow in any of the business journals. Whether this absence was due to missing records, or the business having been registered under a different name, or my father's need to embellish and transform what amounted to a tiny sweatshop into a grander enterprise, I will probably never know. My father took that truth with him to his grave. I do know that, together with many others who lost everything in the Holocaust including their pride, my father did tend to speak in superlatives when reminiscing about the past.

By the 1930s, Jacques had become a very rich man with a wide circle of friends. Their lives were a continual round of social events. In 1937, still a bachelor, he met my mother who was known by her Polish name, *Bronia*. Though only in her mid-thirties, she had already known much sorrow. In 1932, she was twenty-eight and still living in her parents' home in Warsaw. A marriage was finally arranged for her, after which she moved to Paris with her new husband. The seventh of eight children, most of whom had also moved to Paris, Bronia adapted happily to her new life. But her good fortune would soon change.

Her first child, born in 1933, died after only a few months. Then, while she was pregnant with her second child (my half-sister *Liliane*), her husband died of tuberculosis. Two of her older sisters, themselves already grandmothers, took her under their wing, and she stayed on in Paris with her baby daughter. At age thirty-three, her fortune was about to change again. She met my father, Jacque. Bronia was a very attractive woman and Jacque was a very charismatic man. It did not take long before romance blossomed though her sisters opposed the match.

Both sisters were married to professional men and considered themselves quite genteel. Jacque and his entrepreneurial ways seemed very déclassé to them. Although I was told that none of my mother's immediate family—her parents, her seven siblings, their children, and, even in some cases, their grandchildren—survived the Holocaust, I do not know much about the exact circumstances. *Perelman* is a common name in Warsaw where my mother came from. I know my maternal grandparents' names were *Bluma* and *Isaac Perelman* but I do not know my mother's siblings' first or married names. I can only guess that my grandparents, if they survived that long, would have been sent to the Treblinka death camp along with most of the other Warsaw Jews. My aunts who lived in Paris were probably sent to Auschwitz, but as I do not know their married names, I have no way of verifying that either.

The only one whose death was spoken about by my mother was her younger brother. He was a pediatrician who lived with his wife in Warsaw. The photo I have is of a young couple, without any obvious signs of their religious background. My parents were told by a survivor of the Warsaw ghetto, that during the uprising, my uncle had been working in the hospital before he was pulled out onto the street and shot. But that was sometime in 1944. In the late 1930s, when my parents first met one another, no one could have known that so many members of our family would be so utterly destroyed in just a few short years.

In February 1938, my parents traveled to Tarnow to be married. The celebrations were nearly spoilt when my grandmother and an extremely religious aunt accompanied my mother to the *mikvah*.[16] This ritual was essential for orthodox Jewish brides at that time and meant purification by total immersion. Although my mother was originally from Warsaw, she had spent most of her life in Paris. So assimilated was she that she had never heard of this celebratory ritual and, thinking they were trying to drown her, she fought against the dunking. In her panic, she grabbed the two women by their hair, tearing their *sheitles* (wigs) from their heads.

After this slight hiccup, the marriage went ahead, the festivities lasting seven days as tradition demanded. The newly weds had planned to travel to Vienna, but delayed their departure to stay with Jacque's family for the festival of *Purim*. This was the first of many strokes of luck with which they were blessed. On March 11, the first detachment of German troops crossed the Austrian border. Had they been in Vienna as they had planned, they would probably have been among the first deportees to the concentration camps.

Instead they were able to return to Paris and resume their society life. Photographs of them taken at this time show a very attractive, cosmopolitan couple. But in spite of their virtual assimilation, the shadow of Nazism increasingly blighted their lives. Non-Jewish friends, with whom they had previously shared their social life, became ever more reluctant to be seen with them in public, simply out of fear. The Nazis were everywhere and there was a growing expectation that Germany would soon invade France. Being seen with Jewish friends was tantamount to having your card marked.

Jacque thought the Germans would not bother with Belgium,[17] but would march straight on into France. So, at the end of 1939, the family moved to Brussels where I was born a few months later. Before leaving Paris, Jacque converted all his wealth into easily negotiable currency, mainly gold coins, jewelry, and precious stones. He squirreled away small caches in a number of different places: in an unsuspecting friend's cistern, under floorboards, even under a churchyard headstone. The rest he carried to Belgium. When he jumped from the train in 1941, he headed straight for the churchyard and retrieved one of his nest-eggs.

As an escaped Jew without papers, he was in grave danger on the streets of Paris. But he had other resources which helped him to survive these dangers. One of his greatest strengths was his ability to merge into any environment; another of his advantages was the fact that he had always had an eclectic circle of friends. As long as he could play a fair hand of cards, he was happy to spend time drinking with anyone. Some of these friends came through his sister *Salle*.

Although before the war the two had frequently found themselves embroiled in heated arguments thanks to their sharply diverging political views, Jacque and Salle had always been very close. During the 1920s and the 1930s, Salle had attended many Socialist and Communist rallies in France and Belgium. She introduced her brother to many of her young activist friends who later became stalwarts of the French and Belgian resistance movements. With the combined benefit of his hidden jewels and his sister's contacts, he was able to get us smuggled back into Belgium.

Brussels was a small city compared to Paris. Even if we stayed hidden in our apartment, a chance remark by my seven-year-old sister Liliane could endanger all our lives. My father decided it was safer for us to move to Paris during such dangerous times. The question was how to get the family safely back to Paris without arousing the attention of the Nazis. Here my mother's ingenuity came into play.

My mother bravely went to the authorities. She explained that she was no longer able to support herself and her two children since her husband had been deported. So, she was seeking permission to travel to Paris to stay with her sisters. We were given the necessary travel permits. My mother hid her jewelry in my feeding bottles and we left Brussels by train to move into her elder sister's home. Part one of my parents' plan was accomplished. The second was to somehow unite our family again in Paris—a goal that came with its own risks and obstacles.

Jacque had to travel clandestinely and it was several weeks before he arrived in Paris. Because he was effectively an escaped criminal, my aunts considered him a danger to their families and they refused to have him in their homes. He stayed hidden with a cousin of his who had an apartment in Boulevard Voltaire in the *11e Arrondisement*. My aunts were so terrified that my mother would be putting the whole family at risk that she had to visit him in secret. Eventually she fell out with her sisters and moved into a small hotel in the *Place des Foires* run by a Madame Roux, a contact of my Aunt Salle.

By this time Salle had risen in the ranks of the Communist party. Somehow, she had escaped the ruthless purges of the Polish Communist party and had gone to Russia as a party official. Salle was the only member of my father's immediate family who survived. After the war, she returned to Tarnow and married a concentration camp survivor, who had lost his wife and most of his family except for one son who lived in France. Poland was behind the iron curtain and they remained in Poland until they were given permission to leave in 1955. They then re-settled in Paris with their young son, *Mark Fiterman*. My first cousin Mark, my sister Liliane, and I are the only descendants of both sets of grandparents. The others all died in the Holocaust. Looking back, the fact that any of us survived at all verges on a miracle.

During the night of June 22, 1941, my father woke up to a surprising silence. The window of his bedroom faced a busy road where there was always traffic noise, even throughout the night. During his months in hiding, he had whiled away his time by playing cards and sharing a drink or two with the concierge. Jacque awakened the concierge and asked him to find out if anything was going on. The man came back with bad news. The road was blocked and army trucks were moving from house to house, rounding up the Jews. Jacque's cousin, a French national, was certain the only danger he personally faced would be if he were discovered harboring Jacque. Therefore, he ordered his cousin to leave immediately. My father, always a fast thinker, pointed out that if he were caught without papers, he would be tortured into revealing who had hidden him. Realizing the reality of this risk, his cousin reluctantly agreed to Jacques's plan. Passing over a few brightly colored gemstones, Jacque asked the concierge to board up the door, the custom when families left the city for their summer vacations. "When the soldiers come, tell them that Monsieur Ada left earlier tonight to join his family in the country."

The two cousins hid under the bed waiting for the lorry to pull up outside their block. They listened as the soldiers knocked on the door of the apartment below and heard someone being escorted away. Their knees knocking and their teeth chattering, they heard the soldiers return and head for their apartment. They had no confidence that the porter would put his own life at risk for them. But to their surprise they heard him turn the soldiers away. When, later that afternoon, my mother made her usual visit, the concierge intercepted her and told her what had happened. Through her landlady, Madam Roux, arrangements were made for all of us to be smuggled out the next morning. It has become such a cliché, the laundry van smuggling out potential victims under the noses of the Gestapo but that's exactly how it happened.

We joined Jacque and his cousin at a "safe" farm on the outskirts of Paris. My father's cousin, still certain he was in no personal danger, joined his own family at their summer home. Jacque felt that it would be much too risky if he traveled with us to the unoccupied part of France. At that time, it was still commonly believed that only men would be deported to the Nazis' labor camps and the women and children would be spared. So, my father acquired false papers and traveled alone by train towards unoccupied Vichy France. Fifteen miles before the boundary between occupied and unoccupied France, he got off the train and walked over fields and hills unnoticed. In July 1941, he arrived safely in Lyon. In the meantime, we returned to Paris.

Each week my mother took us to the local police station for the required registration of aliens. This took place in a small room manned always by the same two policemen. One was a kindly young man; the other was known for his hostility and rudeness towards foreigners. One week in the summer of 1942, there was as usual a long queue for the "nice" policeman. As my mother was in a hurry, she took her place in the shorter queue for the other officer. My sister's constant demand that my mother picks her up and put me down resulted in the pair of us screaming at once, causing the man behind the desk to erupt in absolute fury. Terrified, my mother took us both outside and waited for hours until everyone else had registered. She then took her place in front of the gentler of the two men. She announced our name: "Zimetbaum." The policeman perused his list but insisted, in spite of my mother pointing to our names, "No," he said, "you are not on my list." He turned to his senior officer and asked him to search in another room for another list. When the assistant left the room, the friendly officer turned quickly to my mother and warned her, "Madam, tomorrow they are starting the round up of the women and children. Your name is on that list. If you have anywhere to hide, go."

Frantic, my mother returned to the boarding house. Again Madame Roux arranged for us to be collected by the Resistance. The van turned up at 5 am, an hour before expected. It is a measure of my mother's innocence, that in spite of everything, she insisted on taking the time to wake us gently and give us breakfast before the journey. She was told in no uncertain terms that either she bundled us into the back of the laundry van immediately, or they would go without us. Miraculously, we were safely smuggled over the occupation border into Vichy France where we were told to wait until a guide came for us. Madame Roux wrote later to say that the Gestapo had turned up for us at 5 50 am. Little more than half-an-hour stood between our life and death.

The first round-up of women and children in Paris is well-documented. They were initially kept in a sports' stadium [Velodrome d'Hiver][18] for several days in blistering heat with inadequate sanitation, no shade, and virtually no food or water. By the time transport had been arranged to the internment camp at Gurs, many were dead, dying, or seriously ill. The conditions at Gurs were little better and those who survived were soon deported to the death camps in the East. Children fifteen and under were sent to the camp at Drancy. There is little doubt that at barely two years old, I would not have survived. Luck was again on our side, however.

Eventually, we were able to join my father, Jacques, in a little village near Lyon. Despite the Vichy Government's declared "independence," the Nazi influence was steadily increasing and the internments had started. Jacques was the first of our little family to be rounded up and taken to a camp near Annecy.[19] Here he spent each day working with other Jews building a railway track for the transportation of the Jews to the concentration camps as soon as the Nazis occupied the whole of France. In his usual way, my father played cards with his guards, who were Corsicans; he sympathized with their complaints of being treated like second-hand citizens by the French. We were allowed to visit my father at the perimeter fence and bring food to the prisoners. At my father's instructions, my mother smuggled in a few of their remaining jewels. Although uncertain as to how much trust he could put in them, Jacques passed the stones on to his Corsican "friends." They helped him to escape and he was taken by motorbike to Perpignan, at the foot of the Pyrenees.

Dressed roughly, like any other French worker, Jacques sat in a cafe, drinking coffee and smoking cigarettes, studying the activities of what were clearly groups of refugees bartering with locals to take them to safety over the mountains into Spain. He stayed in the shadows and witnessed the "guide" returning and bragging to their friends about how they had stripped the Jews of their possessions before turning them in. This was clearly not a place to trust anyone, so Jacques headed off to a small town further along the base of the Pyrenees.

I believe it was St. Girons where he found someone prepared to take him over the mountains and across the border into Spain. In fact, the guide took him down as far as Barcelona where the Quakers,[20] acting as agents for the Joint Distribution Committee, were supplying food and shelter for the refugees. My father handed over the guide virtually the last of his wealth as advanced payment for smuggling his wife Bronia and their two daughters into Spain.

The Quakers advised him that he was still in danger, as all adult male Jews were being interned in a camp at the town of Miranda de Ebro, in anticipation of a German occupation of Spain. The only help they could give was a piece of advice: if he managed to get to Lisbon, as a Polish national he might be able to join the Polish Free Forces, by then part of the British Armed Forces. It seemed that that was his best and only option. Jacques headed straight toward Portugal.

For several weeks he hopped on and off trains, hid in bushes, and stole what little food he could find. At Vigo, he talked a friendly fisherman into smuggling him down the coast into Porto. From there, he made his way down to Lisbon and the British Embassy. Diplomats informed him that they could do nothing for him without proper documentation, including an exit visa from his own Embassy. Jacques, by now, was completely discouraged and broken. Three years of running and hiding like a sewer rat had taken its toll on his health, but far more importantly, on his spirit. He was a penniless Jew in a hostile world; and his family, he assumed, had all been deported to the camps in the East. Frankly, he no longer cared what happened to him.

Eventually, Jacques found himself being ushered into an interview room with an official who was seated at the opposite side of a table. Jacques did not raise his eyes from the ground.

"Name?" the official asked.
"Isaac Jakob Zimetbaum," my father replied.
"Home address?"

"20 Urszulifska, Tarnow," my father replied.

There was silence.

The man spoke again. "You're Gerry Zimetbaum's brother, aren't you?"

The voice was shockingly friendly. Amazed, my father looked up. Sitting opposite him was the son of Tarnow's Chief of Police. He and my uncle, Jacques's oldest brother, had been close childhood friends. Many a time the three of them had broken all the rules, skipped school, and enjoyed a clandestine game of cards together. Now, years later, where the stakes could not have been higher, the rules were secretly broken again. My father received the necessary documents to enable him to return to the British Embassy.

On January 1, 1943, my father arrived in Gibraltar. From there a military ship carried him to Scotland. In London, he informed the relevant officials that he had no wish to join the Polish Free Forces because he believed them to be as anti-Semitic as the Nazis. Instead he was drafted into the Pioneer Corps and spent the rest of the war in England. And what became of us? True to his word, the guide had returned for us and after Vichy fell, sometime in the winter of 1942/1943, we made the hazardous journey across the mountains. We were captured at the border but luckily by the Spanish police. My sister was put into a convent and I was allowed to stay with my mother in prison in Figueres. Although history puts Spain politically in the Fascist camp, everyone I know who was a refugee there—my mother included—spoke highly of the Spaniards they encountered and their kindness. The guards allowed the children to wander freely, and local people brought my mother food and cigarettes. This was a very kind and generous gesture, given that their own people were suffering appalling food shortages. Moreover, it was clear that the Spaniards who helped us Jews would be suffering themselves when the Nazi occupation took hold. I did not witness what happened then. Instead, in June of 1943, I was put on a ship from Lisbon to the United States.[21]

When the deportations started in France, Polish parents whose children had been born in France were offered the choice of either taking their children with them or leaving them behind. Approximately 5,000 children were being kept in children's villages in unoccupied France, and pressure was applied on the United States to give visas to these "orphans." The Vichy government promised safe passage for the children and guaranteed that they would be allowed to exit France under the care of the Red Cross. The pressure worked. In November 1942, a relief team left the United States and headed out for the neutral port of Lisbon with visas for 500 children. However, when their ship arrived in Lisbon, Vichy France had fallen and the majority of the children remained trapped by the German occupation.

The Americans bringing the visas were informed that approximately 100 child refugees had managed to reach Spain and Portugal. As it was expected that

Spain would soon be occupied, it was agreed that these children would be allowed to travel on the visas and those in Spain would be transferred into the care of the Portuguese Red Cross. Although a handful of children—like me—were not orphans, no such concessions were given for our parents. Indeed, the US authorities made it clear that the children's entry to the United States was only a temporary measure. Parents were only being given the opportunity to send their children to safety in anticipation of Spain's occupation and their likely deportation. But many skeptical US officials took additional measures to make sure that the children's arrival could not be used as "anchors" that would enable their surviving relatives to gain entry to the United States at a later date. I can only guess at what my mother must have felt as she agreed to let us go while she remained in Europe.

Our sea voyage was not without danger. Though she was flying the flag of a neutral country, our ship, the "Serpa Pinto,"[22] was stopped by a German submarine which surfaced silently beside her: a vast grey shape with an enormous logo on its fin. Our ship was boarded and one of the older children later recalled hearing a splash. As we stood, silent and terrified on deck, the submariners returned to their ship which rapidly submerged and vanished. The Serpa Pinto continued safely across the Atlantic; one person on board, the cook, had disappeared.

On arrival in the United States, we had health checks and were sent to an orphanage. My sister, Liliane, was thought to have tuberculosis, which was later correctly diagnosed as pneumonia. She was sent immediately to hospital where she stayed for a long time. A report at the time notes that I was the youngest child the local Committee had received into their care. The description on the report read, "Fanny is a very winsome little girl, lovable and responsive and is well developed physically and mentally who speaks flawless French."

Dr. and Mrs. Farell, a local physician and his wife, became my foster parents. Another field staff report concerning me from the US Committee for the Care of European Children describes the scene where I met my foster parents:

> This little girl walked into the arms of her foster parents and has a very secure place in their affections. The foster parents are middle class people living in a suburban community and have fine standards of living. Fanny fits into such a home, whereas Liliane has to strive very hard to meet their standards.

Sometime after this scene, a report of an interview conducted with my mother in Barcelona included the following comment: "Mrs. Z. makes an excellent impression. Although obviously very much moved by news of her children, she was restrained and intelligent in speaking of them." Although our situations were different, our reactions were rather similar. Hysteria, tears, and other shows of strong emotion were given short shrift in those days. The classic symptoms of the as-yet-unrecognized "Post-Traumatic Stress Disorder" might also have been misinterpreted as ungovernable, recalcitrant, or disobedient. Instead, gratitude, acceptance, and a smile were what was expected of all of us.

I was young enough to adapt to my new life, but my sister, like many of the older children, was too traumatized to be able to cope with the expectations placed on her. She was first returned to the orphanage as being "unmanageable" and subsequently passed onto a series of foster homes. My name was changed by my foster parents to *Joan*, my language from French to American. Over the next few years, little Polish *Fanny Zimetbaum* morphed into all American *Joan Farell*.

Eventually, the war ended. It took the refugee agencies time to locate splintered families and to untangle the bureaucratic demands necessary to unite them. It was not until 1947 that I was reunited with my parents in London. This might seem like the "fairytale ending" but it was anything but.

I remember being taken onto the plane by the man I regarded as my father. He settled me into my seat, told me to be a good girl, and kissed me goodbye. He then returned to the tarmac and stood there waving until the plane took off. I looked down at the document he had put into my hand. It had my picture on it and identified me as *Fanny Zimetbaum*, "Stateless Person." What on earth was that about? People had tried to explain this to me before, but how much meaning could this concept have for a seven-year-old? As far as I was concerned, I was *Joan Farell* and this was the person I wanted to be. The last thing on earth I wanted was to be a refugee.

When I met my parents, things were no better. Both of them were severely traumatized—I think beyond any possibility of recovery—by what they had lived through in the preceding seven years. To me, looking through the eyes of a child, their behavior seemed irrational, incomprehensible. My mother was the sole survivor of her family. Her parents, her seven siblings, their spouses, and their children had all perished. Even my aunts' grandchildren whose toys I had shared were all dead. It is most likely that those of my mother's family who remained in Warsaw were murdered in Treblinka; and those who lived in Paris were deported and perished in other camps. The only trace of their lives survives as a handful of sepia photographs which my mother carried with her wherever she went. Of my father's family, only Salle survived. All of the rest—his parents, two brothers, and their families—all of them died in the camps.

My parents were broken in health, spirit, and mind. And the hardships did not stop with the end of the war. Now destitute, they were forced to work all hours of the day and night to try and pick up the pieces of their lives. In short, they were utterly ill-equipped to deal with the return of their angry and alienated children.

Among his new acquaintances, my father was now known as *Jack*, the Anglicized version of *Jakob*. Although on my birth certificate my mother's name was *Sprynca*, she never used this name. She had two names, *Sophie* and *Bronia*. Apparently, *Sophie* was the name her Jewish family had used for her; and *Bronia* was her Polish name. In the tower of Babel which comprised their circle of friends after the war, all of these names became interchangeable.

I would elect to keep my American name, *Joan*. My surname, however, changed several more times. My father, in an attempt to help him and us become more British, changed our surname, first to *Roberts* and then to *Bennett*. Given that he spoke with a very strong foreign accent to his dying day, this name change had little effect as a camouflage. I have no idea when, how, or why he chose these particular aliases. It is fascinating to note that in Britain, there was no law requiring names to be changed officially by deed poll.[23] I believe that when you changed your name, all that was required on official documents was for your former name to be kept in brackets next to your new name for a certain period of time.

Nobody's adolescence is easy; mine was a nightmare. I would stand for hours by the window of our flat in London watching passers-by. All I wanted to be was "normal" like them. I spent the next ten years shuttling between my two families, becoming more and more confused as to who I really was. In the United States, notwithstanding what was on my passport, I was *Joan Farell*. In England, I became someone else. When I received my first British passport in 1949, it had the surname *Zimetbaum*. A later one was documented as, "Bennett (formerly known as Zimetbaum)." I was embarrassed to be identified as a foreigner and as soon as I was issued a passport without the name *Zimetbaum*, I destroyed the earlier ones. This was in keeping with the attitudes of many survivors of the time. The past was behind us.

In 1956, I was offered the opportunity of studying at a college for Youth Workers in Israel. I jumped at the chance to get away from the never-ending tug-of-war between my two families, my two personae. Israel itself meant very little to me; it could have been China for all I cared. I had very little affection for my Jewishness. I felt that everything terrible which had ever happened to me was because of it, and I certainly was no Zionist. In the States, at the Reform Synagogue we attended, I was taught that I was an American of Jewish faith. In England, at the ultra-Orthodox school my parents sent me to, more out of an intense fear of the outside world than any religious inclinations, we were taught that it was only when we were redeemed by the Messiah that we would be returned to the land of Israel. Until such time it was not for us to take matters into our hands. The Anglo-Jewish Community was grappling with the hostility the British Mandate in Palestine had brought down on them and, in the main, was leaning over backwards to identify as being British and to play down their

Jewishness. In fact, I was the first candidate from the American Jewish Youth—at that time a strongly non-Zionist Youth Organization—to go on the course.

We sailed from Marseilles in January 1957, on a rickety old ship. The passengers were an oddly assorted bunch, many of them refugees. These were what remained of European Jewry who, more than a decade after the liberation of the concentration camps, still remained in Displaced Persons' camps waiting to be offered a permanent home. There was an amazing hotchpotch of languages and cultures. I became friends with a group of young and very secular Israelis. We steadfastly remained seated as the blessing was said over the Friday night candles, arms folded across our chests, ignoring hostile demands to show respect for the Sabbath.

On the morning of our final day onboard ship, an excited wave of emotion rippled through the passengers. Not understanding a word, I followed the others up onto the deck. There, just coming into view over the horizon, were the green hills of Haifa, the golden dome of the Baha'i Temple reflecting the sun. Suddenly these brash young Israelis and the motley bunch of refugees all broke into spontaneous song: *Ha' Tikvah.* There were many tears; the refugees' knuckles white as they clung to the rail as if letting go would make the mirage vanish. It was a heart-stopping sight, but I still could not identify with them. Then the Israelis joined hands, singing *Hinei Mah Tov*—how good it is for brothers to join together—pulling all the refugees into their circle as they danced round the deck in a spontaneous show of unity. To me it all seemed very strange and terribly un-British.

The year in Israel was important for me. The country, like me, was young and enthusiastic. It radiated idealism and great optimism for a future where all Jews would live in harmony, not only with fellow Jews but with their Arab neighbors. After the year ended, I returned to England and began making plans for my upcoming marriage. During the preparations, I had one of my first brushes with official ignorance about Jewish names and naming. My fiancé's family were nominally orthodox Jews who have very strict rules. For example, for them, a Jew can only be a Jew if his/her mother was also a Jew. Another one of their conditions of Jewishness is that one's parents had to have been married in a traditional Jewish ceremony. The gatekeeper at the Beth Din was called *Reverend Sunshine.* I have yet to meet a person whose name was more ironic

When he demanded that I produce my parents' marriage certificate, I explained that we were Holocaust survivors and I had no such certificate. His reply was dismissive: "Well go back to Poland and find one." His lack of insight into the recent history of his own people was only equaled by his lack of humanity. I have since been to the archives in Tarnow and was only able to find the birth certificate of my father's younger brother, *Yerucham (Gerry).* No other documentation pertaining to the births, deaths, or marriages of my paternal family remain. This is common for Jewish families that come from that region and can be a source of frustration for people trying to find information about their heritage and incredulity for officials in the "modern" world who cannot comprehend why proof of origins is not available on demand.

The stumbling block to being married under the authority of the United Synagogue was ultimately bypassed by a technical loophole. A person of standing in both the Jewish and civic society swore an affidavit stating that she had been present at my parents' traditional Jewish wedding in Poland in 1938. The fact that she had never stepped foot in Poland, worried neither her nor the Jewish Q. C. who, never having met either myself or any of my relatives, countersigned the document. They were more concerned with moral principles than Jewish law. With the signature of such esteemed personages on this counterfeit document, the Reverend Sunshine allowed me to pass through the gates of the United Synagogue, much to the relief of my future mother-in-law. As of this newest identification paper, my marriage certificate, *Joan Bennett* became *Joan Salter* on September 13, 1959.

My husband and I had two daughters and this became my family. At this stage of my life, the past was truly another country I hardly remembered, let alone visited. Only when my daughters had grown up and my foster-father died, was I able to take the first tentative steps back into my origins. My birth parents were still living, and though my mother found the past too painful to revisit voluntarily, my father and I were at last able to find some peace in our relationship in our travels back through his memories.

It was not only what he told me which recreated the past for me. I also visited many countries and trawled through reams of archive material to find the documentation which verified the truth of his reminiscences. I researched the archives of the American Friends' Service Committee (The Quakers) in Philadelphia, and the Joint Distribution Committee in New York. Among the papers I unearthed were the social workers' reports on my sister and me as well as a telegram reporting that the US Ambassador to Barcelona had refused me a visa because I did not have a passport. I also discovered many original documents concerning the plight of children in France, including a letter dated June 25, 1941, from Albert Einstein in his role as Honorary President of the Oeuvre de Secours Aux Enfants or Children's Aid Society, the organization in France which was responsible for caring for children in need. In the letter, Einstein urged to "keep the problem of the evacuation of the refugee children in the forefront of your attention."

There also was, as my father had described, evidence of the internment camp at Miranda de Ebro in Spain,[24] of which very little has been reported. I found the ship's manifest of the SS Serpa Pinto which arrived in Philadelphia on June 22, 1943. On this document, the name *Fanny Zimetbaum* is stamped:

REFUGEE. My nationality is listed as Polish, my race as Hebrew. The most poignant reminder of all from the past was a photograph I found at the Portuguese Red Cross archive. It is of a group of fourteen children; the trauma they lived through was etched on their faces. At the front is a skinny little girl of three-and-a-half. This is Fanny Zimetbaum—the child I once was.

I found no records of what happened to my parents' families. When, postwar, my Aunt Salle returned to Poland from Russia, no one from the family was at their home. Despite registering with all the agencies, no contact has ever been made. I can only assume that my father's parents and his brothers, along with all the other Tarnow Jews, either died in the massacres in the town or nearby forest or were exterminated in Belzec in the spring of 1942.

I returned to Warsaw several years ago to try to find out about my maternal grandparents. The only documentation I could find was a pre-war telephone directory. It featured the name and address of my mother's youngest brother, a pediatrician, just as she had told me.

Only now, sixty years on, am I able to open the door behind which I left *Fanny*, locked firmly away, for so many years. Perhaps the biggest irony of all is that there is no paper trail to link *Fanny Zimetbaum* with *Joan Salter*. This has been a stumbling block with the claim I lodged with "The Claims Conference." Several years ago, an agreement was made with the German government that a special fund would be set up for child survivors in recognition of the trauma they had gone through during the Holocaust. We were each to be allocated 2,500 euros. To date, (the summer of 2017), I have received nothing. It would be comforting to think that no other mother would have to make the choices my mother did; no child would have to take the journeys that Fanny took. But you only have to turn on the news to know that the lessons of history are never learnt.

In 2005, I "returned" to Tarnow. I use the term loosely. Born in Belgium in 1940, before I had only been a visitor to my father's bittersweet memories of the town he had grown up, the lively family he had loved, the friendships he had valued with his Jewish and Christian school friends. Tarnow was that safe place he had left as a young man to seek his fortune in first Belgium and then later in France. Tarnow was the secure place he had frequently returned to over the years, just barely escaping the Nazi invasion; the place where my grandparents, aunts, uncles and cousins had lived until their lives were extinguished. Postwar he had been unable to return; and now I felt it was my duty as his proxy to return to pay homage to my ancestors; to bear witness that they had existed, to say Kaddish.

I had no idea what to expect. My first shock was on the hour-long journey by train from Krakow. In the train yard, I saw rusting cattle trucks, one after another. My first instinct was to tell myself that they couldn't possibly be the same ones used then. But then my logic retorted: "Why not? What does a railway do with redundant stock, no matter how horrendous its past?"

At the hotel, I was warmly welcomed and handed a booklet, "In the Footsteps of the Jews of Tarnow," written by Adam Bartosz,[25] the director of the Regional Museum in Tarnow. It was this pamphlet which guided me through the streets as I, literally, walked in my father's footsteps. In the Plaza of "The Auschwitz Prisoners" is a relief mural depicting the citizens of Tarnow. Some were Jews, some were not; all were considered political dissidents and were sent to Auschwitz in June 1940. These "Tarnovian inmates," as they became known, were tattooed with the numbers 31 to 758, signifying they were among the first at this camp. I looked across to a magnificent Moresque style building where on June 13, 1940, these men were locked up before they were forcibly transported. This building was erected in 1904 as the Jewish ritual bathhouse (Mikvah). Another image of this building came into my head. This was the place where my mother had been brought by my father's mother and aunt on the eve of her wedding to my father in February 1938. Today the building is used as a retail outlet. How does one make sense of all these contradictory images?

Adam Bartosz could not have been more helpful. He handed me the key to the local cemetery. As I unlocked the gate I noticed I was not alone. In the distance, someone was taking photographs. Much of the cemetery is overgrown and a work party was busy clearing the brambles. Later, I learnt from Adam that these were local prisoners "released" to do useful community work. I walked among the 4,000 tombstones looking in vain for a family name. But time and the wind made this search a thankless task. I stopped in silent contemplation at the site marking the mass grave of the 3,000 Jews shot in the cemetery in June 1942. The monument is a broken column excavated from the ruins of Tarnow's largest synagogue. At the top is an inscription: "And the sun was shining and it wasn't ashamed." At the base of the monument, there is a commemorative to the 25,000 Jews who were murdered by German thugs between June 11, 1942 and September 5, 1942, and are now resting in this grave. There are no records of names, so I don't know if this cemetery or Belzec or the local woods is the final "resting" place of my family.

The next day I traveled to Bełżec. Started in November 1941, this camp was purely and simply a factory of death, the first to use stationary gas chambers. Here over a period of a few weeks in June 1942, the remaining 10,000 Jews of Tarnow were transported and taken straight from the trains to the "showers." In June 1943, the Nazis attempted to obliterate all traces of this camp, even grinding the bones into dust. There remains no significant physical evidence or records of the people murdered here. The site is now marked by a huge mound of volcanic rock, surrounded by steps—each of which marks the date of a specific transport.

At the stone commemorating the transport from Tarnow, I lit a candle and said Kaddish. In the Jewish tradition, only the men are permitted to say Kaddish. However, from what I know of my paternal roots, it is a family of strong women. So, if there were any ghosts with me on that day, I believe they would have approved and recognized me as one of their own. Before I left, I walked to the back of the site where some of the original trees still stood. I scooped up some of the leaf mold and placed it in a plastic bottle. Afterwards I traveled to Warsaw and then onwards to Treblinka. There, alone, I walked through the monuments commemorating the murdered Jews. Again, there are no records of the individuals, only the places they came from. So, I lit a candle at the Warsaw stone and said Kaddish for my mother's family. Again, I collected a handful of soil. Back in England, I visited the graves of my mother and father and told them I had honored our past and my heritage. I scattered the earth gathered from Poland over their graves. The souls of my ancestors are now left to rest in peace.

In June every year, the Regional Museum in Tarnow in cooperation with the Committee for the Protection of Monuments of Jewish Culture organizes a week-long series of events to commemorate the fate of its Jews. I returned to Tarnow the following year to join in. The main event is held in the nearby Buczyna woods where about 6,000 Tarnow Jews, including 800 children, were massacred in June 1942. A middle-aged woman wearing a large Star of David joined us. Sadly, she spoke no English and I no Polish, but through the universal language of hand gestures, I learned that she was from Tarnow.

Surrounded by an Honor Guard of Cadets and children from the local schools, Adam Bartosz led a most moving ceremony which included speeches by the local Bishop and the Israeli Ambassador. Both emphasized that Jewish and Polish history, with all their painful twists and turns, are irrevocably entwined. A rabbi recited Kaddish. Later in the week, we joined a Kletzmer concert held at the site of the oldest Tarnow synagogue. The original wooden building dating back to 1581 was replaced in the seventeenth century and it is the fire scarred Bimah of this building which is the sole remainder of all the prayer houses and synagogues of this town.

There must have been an audience of over 1,000 local residents, with others hanging out of windows and balconies from the buildings in surrounding streets who listened to the haunting traditional melodies, but only one person—the same lady I had met earlier in the week—wore a Star of David. Possibly there were others there of Jewish descent, probably without any knowledge of the Jewish blood flowing through their veins. We told the band how much their music had moved us. They humbly thanked us, explaining that while the music was Jewish, they were not; an apt symbol for the whole of post-Holocaust Poland.

Since then, a booklet and accompanying leaflet about the Jewish Cemetery has now been published. Among the photos of tombstones, there is one showing a woman standing before the monument placed at the site of the mass murder of ghetto Jews. In my distinctive black leather coat, with white collar and cuffs, that woman is irrefutably me.

This family name story was shared in memory of my paternal Grandparents Moses & Perla; my uncles Samuel Zimetbaum & Gerry Zimetbaum, their wives and children. They lived in Tarnow, Poland, and are believed to have perished in Belzec Death Camp in 1942.

This memoir is also shared in memory of maternal Grandparents, Bluma and Isaac Mendel Perelman, from Warsaw, Poland, all my mother's siblings, my seven aunts and uncles, their husbands, wives, children and grandchildren. Some lived in Warsaw and are believed to have perished in Treblinka, others lived in Paris and are believed to have perished in Auschwitz.

Some of my aunts gave us shelter in Paris where I played with my cousins. Forgive me that your faces have vanished from my memory and that your names are forgotten. But the fact that you lived, and the manner of your deaths, I remember.

Notes

1. The tradition was established when the Greeks conquered the Holy Land in the middle of the fourth century BC. Their culture greatly influenced Jewish traditions, including their naming practices.

2. The Bersad or Bershad Ghetto was established in September 1941 in the Vinnitsa District of the Ukraine. Initially, the ghetto contained around 500 Jewish residents. However, very quickly, through the combined deportation efforts of the Nazis and Romanian forces under Ion Antonescu, the number of ghetto inhabitants soon reached into the thousands. In the meantime, marauding Einsatzgruppen decimated Jewish villages in the surrounding areas. According to Yad Vashem on March 10, 1942, nearly 2,000 Jews were slaughtered in the Vinnitsa District. Yad Vashem, "January 1943, Partisans in the Vinnits District, Ukraine," http://www.yadvashem.org/holocaust/this-month/january/1943–4.html.

3. Located in Rogoźnica, Poland, the Gross-Rosen Concentration Camp was originally designed to be a satellite of the Sachsenhausen Concentration Camp. During the height of its operation, over 125,000 people were held prisoner in Gross-Rosen. That number is probably an under count, however given the large number of unregistered, unnamed prisoners of war who were transferred there as well. It is estimated that at least 40,000 people died in the camp due to starvation, catastrophic hygiene conditions, and crippling work hours. One of the primary industries there was granite mining. Gross-Rosen Museum in Rogoźnica: http://de.gross-rosen.eu/.

4. "The Dreyfus Affair" is the name given to a spectacular trial in which a Jewish officer in the French military was wrongfully sentenced by a military court to live his life in exile on Devil's Island. After international protests, the case was reexamined and it was

determined that Officer Dreyfus had been framed. For an in-depth examination of this historic miscarriage of justice, see Erich Cahm, *The Dreyfus Affair in French Society and Politics* (London: Routledge, 1994).

5. In its collections, The United States Holocaust Memorial Museum (USHMM) has archived testimony from Henri Zajdenwergier, the last survivor of convoy 73. The interview was conducted in French in Paris, France on December 18, 1996. USHMM Oral History: VHA Interview Code: 23517, https://collections.ushmm.org/search/catalog/vha23517.

6. The Kaddish is the traditional Jewish prayer said by mourners after the death of a close relative.

7. Susan Zuccotti, *Pierre Marie-Benoît and Jewish Rescue: How a French Priest Together with Jewish Friends Saved Thousands during the Holocaust* (Bloomington: Indiana University Press, 2013).

8. Zuccotti, *Pierre Marie-Benoît*, 93.

9. Yad Vashem, "The Righteous Among the Nations." Rescue Story. File 201. http://db.yadvashem.org/righteous/family.html?language=en&itemId=4057268.

10. This namestory is based on a personal interview conducted with the survivor as well as a published account. In places where there was a slight deviation in the two accountings, the transcript from the 2018 interview was used. For the survivor's story, see Muguette Myers, *Where Courage Lives* (Toronto, ON: The Azrieli Foundation, 2015). The telephone interview was conducted March 28, 2018.

11. "Memeeh" is Yiddish for "Aunt." Myers, *Where Courage Lives*, 7.

12. The family later determined that Deeneh was taken to Drancy before being deported to Auschwitz. Myers, *Where Courage Lives*, 32.

13. Myers, *Where Courage Lives*, 97.

14. In an effort to force the surrender of the Dutch, Nazi Germany bombed Rotterdam relentlessly destroying 24,000 homes, killing nearly 100 civilians, and leaving nearly 80,000 homeless. For more, see David Zabecki (ed.) *Germany at War: 400 Years of Military History* (Boulder, CO: ABC-CLIO, 2014), 1114.

15. For more on Jewish Immigration to Great Britain after the Holocaust, see: Caroline Sharples and Olaf Jensen, eds. *Britain and the Holocaust: Remembering and Representing War and Genocide* (London: Palgrave Macmillan, 2013).

16. A "mikvah" or "mikweh" is a ritual bath for purification.

17. Despite declaring a state of armed neutrality, Belgium was invaded by Nazi, Germany, on May 10, 1940. After resisting for more than two weeks and suffering heavy civilians losses, the King of Belgium formally surrendered. For more see Zabechi (ed.) *Germany at War*, 1114.

18. Velodrome d'Hiver Raid. From July 16, 1942 to July 17, 1942, the Vichy government in France arrested more than 13,000 Jewish men, women, and children. The majority of them were kept prisoner in the Velodrome d'Hiver Raid stadium without food, water, or sanitary conditions. The victims were eventually deported to Auschwitz. For more, see Robert Paxton, *Vichy France: Old Grand and New Order, 1940–1944* (New York: Columbia University Press, 1972); and Susan Zuccotti, *The Holocaust, the French, and the Jews* (London: University of Nebraska Press, 1993).

19. The Camp Annecy Internment Camp was located at the northern tip of Lake Annecy of eastern France and approximately 30 km from Geneva, Switzerland. Convoys from this region sent French Jews to their deaths in Auschwitz. For more see Geoffrey P. Megargee, ed. *Aligned with Nazi Germany* (Bloomington: Indiana University Press, 2018).

20. For more on the Quakers and the Holocaust, see Ira Zornberg, *Jews, Quakers and the Holocaust: The Struggle to Save the Lives of Twenty Thousand Children* (Middletown, DE: Ira Zornberg, 2016).

21. For more on US adoptions of Jewish child survivors of the Holocaust, see Hasia Diner, *We Remember with Reverence and Love: American Jews and the Myth of Silence after the Holocaust, 1945–1962* (New York: New York University Press, 2009).

22. The SS *Serpa Pinto* was one of the last ships carrying European refugees that was allowed to enter the United States during World War II. Included among its passengers were nearly sixty refugee children from Belgium, Czechoslovakia, France, Germany, and Hungary. The transport was sponsored by the US Committee for the Care of European Children. For more, see Walter Laqueur ed. *The Holocaust Encyclopedia* (London: Yale University Press, 2001).

23. A "deed poll" or deed of change of name is used in Britain to formally declare one's intention to alter one's name.

24. Located in northern Spain, the Miranda de(l) Ebra Concentration Camp was the primary internment facility for foreign prisoners. The camp was erected during the Spanish Civil War and was initially designed to hold political opponents of Franco. Although documentation pertaining to this camp remain sparse, there are a few eye-witness accounts published by survivors. For example, in his personal memoirs, Reuben Ainsztein, a Jewish medical student in Brussels, recounts in vivid detail his experiences in the camp, after his internment in January 1942. For more, see Reuben Ainsztein, *In Lands Not My Own: A Wartime Journey* (New York: Random House, 2002). A reasonably detailed discussion of the camp foundation and operation can be found in the following sources: Bernd Rother, *Spanien und der Holocaust* (Tübingen: De Gruyter, 2001); Wolfgang Benz and Barbara Distel (eds.) *Der Ort des Terrors: Geschichte der nationalsozialistischen Konzentrationslager*, vol. 9 (Munich: C. H. Beck, 2009).

25. Adam Bartosz, "In the Footsteps of the Jews of Tarnow" (Tarnow: Tarnow Regional Museum, 2007).

CHAPTER 9

Naming Names
and Recovering Identities

In view of the progress that was being made in attempting to annihilate the world's Jewish population, the scientific community of the Reich began to consider the importance of preserving a few specimens for future generations to study. The idea was to have a collection of prepared skulls and skeletons that would demonstrate the enormous breadth and variety of the Jewish race for teaching and research purposes. The collection would be housed in the newly established Reich's University in Strasbourg. On October 1, 1941, the person appointed to head the Anatomical Institute of that university was the renowned anatomist and researcher Professor August Hirt.[1] Born in Mannheim to Swiss parents in 1898, Hirt served as a soldier in World War I, where he received a near fatal injury to his upper and lower jaw that resulted in life-long facial disfigurement. After his discharge at the end of the war, Hirt studied medicine at the University of Heidelberg and received his license in 1921 at the age of twenty-three.[2] Four years later, he had earned his doctorate and was awarded a postdoctoral degree in Anatomy.

By the mid-1920s, the young anatomy professor had begun a fruitful collaboration with professor of pharmacology, Philipp Ellinger. The two achieved international fame with a break-through invention: a microscope which finally allowed researchers to clearly view living cells. Named "the intravital fluorescence microscope," this revolutionary invention became an indispensable tool in the biological and medical sciences. The microscope was patented on July 13, 1933 under the names of both researchers, although Ellinger had served as the senior investigator on the project.[3] This invention seemed to herald the start of two extraordinary careers in which both men would leave a lasting mark upon their fields. That prediction came true, however, in two very different ways.

In 1932, Ellinger was awarded a professorship in Pharmacology at the University of Düsseldorf's Medical School and Hirt was awarded the same in the

Anatomical Institute of Heidelberg.[4] A year later, the similarities between the one-time colleagues abruptly ended. As a Jewish academic, Ellinger was forced to surrender his position at the University of Düsseldorf. After fleeing to Turkey where he was able to continue his scientific research for a brief period,[5] he and his wife eventually relocated to England.[6] In the meantime, Hirt, now a member of the SS, continued to advance in Nazi, Germany. Eventually accepting full credit for the invention of the microscope, Professor Hirt was awarded a number of leading positions in the Anatomical Institutes at the Universities of Greifswald and Frankfurt am Main,[7] before being offered the Directorship of the Anatomical Institute for the Reich's University in Strasbourg. He immediately accepted.

From the very start, the Director made his mark upon the Institute. Under his leadership, the Institute began many new, innovative scientific projects. One of them was to be the collection of Jewish specimens. In a letter sent to top Nazi officials, Hirt stated that the easiest method would be to select suitable specimens during the Eastern offensive. As he detailed in his letter, the army could simply send back "material" to the institute where it would be properly prepared and preserved for display and analysis. He emphasized that the collection would be of terrific importance after the war's end:

> There are extensive collections of skulls of almost all races and peoples. Of the Jewish race, however, only so few specimens of skulls stand at the disposal of science that a study of them does not permit precise conclusions. . . . By procuring the skulls of the Jewish Bolshevik Commissars, who personify a repulsive, yet characteristic subhumanity, we have the opportunity of obtaining tangible scientific evidence.[8]

The real-life logistics of collecting and transporting untarnished bodies from the battlefield was probably considered unnecessarily complex however. Therefore, the decision was made to harvest the specimens from another source: Auschwitz. The development of the collection would take place in four steps. On June 7, 1943, step one of the plan began. A scientific delegation entered Auschwitz to search for subjects for the skeletal collection. Professor Hirt was accompanied by anthropologist and SS-Hauptsturmführer Dr. Bruno Beger; anthropologist and SS-Obersturmführer Professor Hans Fleischhacker; and Wilhelm Gabel, a laboratory technician experienced in tissue preparation and preservation.[9] Their goal was to locate a set of individuals who would collectively represent the anatomical breadth of the Jewish race. After reviewing the camp prisoners, individuals with striking features were selected and removed to special quarters which had been set aside as examination rooms for the potential candidates. The prisoners selected were then subjected to a grueling and dehumanizing set of evaluations, designed to measure and document every aspect of their bodies. On the basis of these measurements, the preliminary set of people for the collection was chosen.

Before final decisions for inclusion were made, each candidate was required to undergo blood tests conducted by the SS Hygiene Institute of Auschwitz to determine whether they had contracted typhus or some other deadly contagious disease. Possibly one reason for the extra screening came from a highly publicized incident that had recently occurred at the Reich's University in Posen (Poland). In April of 1941, the Baltic-German Gustav Adolf Hirschheydt became the lead forensic illustrator, dissectionist, and preparator for the anatomist, Professor Hermann Voss.[10] With Hirschheydt's assistance, Professor Voss had established a booming business in selling the body parts of Gestapo murder victims to anatomical institutes throughout the Reich.[11]

In particular, Voss and Hirschheydt specialized in providing human skulls, skeletons, tissue samples, and death masks to the clamoring scientific community. For a single skull of a Polish or Jewish victim male or female—the team charged 25 Reichsmarks; for a death mask, 15 RM; and for a plaster bust, 30 to 35 RM.[12] The duo guaranteed their growing client list first-class preparations with precise information about the decedent's place of birth and age at the time of death.[13] Among their customers were anatomical institutes in Breslau, Leipzig, Königsberg, and Hamburg as well as the anthropology department of the Museum of Natural History in Vienna.[14] The death masks and skulls of Jewish NS victims purchased from Voss and Hirschheydt by the Viennese museum were put on display in a 1939 exhibit, "The Physical and Psychological Appearance of the Jew" [Das körperliche und seelische Erscheinungsbild der ˉuden].[15] The collection remained in museum's anthropological holdings until 1992 when the remains of the Jewish NS victims were finally given a proper burial.[16] It would take another seven years before the skulls of the executed Polish citizens were returned to their homeland.[17]

Based on Voss's personal diaries entries, it can be inferred that his motivations for selecting this financial sideline were not simply scientific or even pecuniary. Indeed, his entry for May 24, 1941, offers disturbing insight into the psyche of the anatomist and his complicity with the NS killing machinery:

> Here in the basement of the institute building there is a crematorium for bodies. It now serves the Gestapo exclusively. The Poles shot by the Gestapo are brought there at night and cremated. If one could only incinerate the whole Polish pack! The Polish people must be exterminated, or there will be no peace here in the East. It is terrible that we are still dependent on Polish labor here at the Institute.[18]

Voss was, of course, not alone in his sentiments. NS researchers had no compunction against purchasing body parts harvested from NS murder victims. Soon Hirschheydt was struggling to meet the demand. In his attempt to keep up with the incoming orders, Hirschheydt evidently failed to follow standard safety procedures and had reportedly contracted typhus while preparing the body of a Jewish concentration camp victim for transport. As Voss recounted in his diary:

> On Sunday, Herr von H[irschheydt] told me he had gotten lice on Saturday from a louse-ridden Jewish corpse. He has been making plaster casts of Jewish heads for the Vienna anthropological museum.[19]

On June 4, 1942, the prolific dissectionist died from his infection. Given the comparatively small circle of fascist faculty and staff employed at the elite Reich Universities (e.g., Prague, Posen, Strasbourg, Graz) also known as Combat Universities [Kampfuniversitäten],[20] it stands to reason that the cause of Hirschheydt's death quickly made the rounds and other institutes that also dealt in body parts began to take extra precautions. It was also generally well-known that the abysmal sanitation conditions of the camps were perfect breeding grounds for contagious diseases. In fact, thanks to an outbreak of typhus in early September 1942, Hirt and Beger had been forced to cancel their scheduled trip to Auschwitz until June 7, 1943.[21]

Approximately a week later, on June 15, 1943, the typhus blood tests came back. The medical report with the names and tattooed numbers of all eighty-six test persons confirmed that none had the dreaded disease.[22] This was welcome news to Hirt and his associates. It meant that their selectees were healthy enough to be murdered. Phase three of their plan could begin. Immediately after the test results were received, preparations were made to progressively transport the group to the Alsace. Once there, the prisoners would be sent to the Natzweiler Concentration Camp for "processing." The prisoner transport from Auschwitz was documented on yet another list.[23] At the end of August 1943, their final journey began.

The group was loaded once again into train cars, only this time they were taken away from Auschwitz. The journey took approximately three days. To keep the anxious men and women calm and compliant, they were told that they were being released to work in a factory. Before they could start their new assignments, however, they would have to undergo a final set of medical examinations and measurements as well as a precautionary delousing.[24]

When they reached their final destination, the prisoners were divided into smaller, more manageable groups. Each set was forced into a gas chamber that had been established in an annex of the Natzweiler camp, in Struthof. As panic erupted in the completely darkened room, the gas was added. The exact poison used for the killings was hydrogen cyanide or prussic acid, better known as "Zyklon B." Thus, the prisoners who had managed to escape the gas chambers of Auschwitz had traveled over 1,000 kilometers from Poland to France only to meet their deaths with Zyklon B days later. In less than ten minutes, all of the people placed in the chamber were dead. Their bodies were load onto trucks and transported to Hirt's Institute. Stage three of the plan was complete and stage four could begin.

The person assigned to perform the corpse preparation was not the famed anatomist Professor Hirt but his assistant, Henri Henripierre.[25] After being placed under arrest by the Nazis in Paris and deported to a series of concentration camps, Henripierre was eventually released. The trained pharmaceutical assistant traveled to Strasbourg where he sought employment in local hospitals.[26] As there were no positions available there, he was sent to the Anatomical Institute at the newly opened Reich University of Strasbourg.[27] On June 20, 1942, Henripierre was formally hired as a technical assistant. After being forced to Germanize his name to *Heinrich Heinzpeter*,[28] the new hire was given extensive training in the dissection and preparation of human corpses for use by the staff and students. While Henripierre was assigned to duties in the morgue, Professor Hirt concentrated on procuring new corpses for the research and teaching curriculum for the anatomy and medical students at the University.

At a time when there were so many dying throughout Europe, the anatomical institute, according to Professor Hirt, had extreme difficulty in securing satisfactory corpses for the students and faculty, despite multiple requests to the local hospitals and hospices.[29] Soon, Hirt hit upon a solution. In and around Strasbourg, there were multiple POW internment camps (e.g., in Ludwigsburg, Villingen, and Offenburg). He contacted the responsible authorities and requested that the corpses collected there be sent directly to his facility for scientific use.[30] On August 5, 1942, Professor Hirt received confirmation that Soviet prisoners who perished in those camps would be sent to the Institute.[31]

The use of unclaimed bodies from prisons, psychiatric clinics, hospices, and hospitals had long since been a widespread practice within the scientific community. Already in the nineteenth century, many jurisdictions in Germany permitted the use of cadavers who had either not been claimed by surviving family members or had been released by their relatives for such use. With the onset of National Socialism, prior permission was no longer required for the use of non-Aryan corpses. Research and teaching facilities eagerly accepted this new supply of corpses. Just a few of the institutions of higher education that accepted the cadavers of those who'd fallen prey to the Nazis included the Universities of Bonn, Cologne, Freiburg, Giessen, Göttingen, Greifswald, Halle, Hamburg, Heidelberg, Marburg, Tübingen, and Wurzburg.[32]

Soon after Hirt's special arrangement with the surrounding POW camps, the Anatomical Institute at the Reich's University of Strasbourg began to receive special deliveries. Henripierre, who by that time had become an expert in preparing corpses, immediately noticed the difference. According to the testimony he provided during the Nuremberg Trials, without exception, the bodies of the Russian and Polish POWs had been in extremely poor shape, providing tangible evidence of prolonged torture, long-term illness, and extreme stages of starvation. The deliveries the Institute received in the late summer of 1943, were noticeably different. The first was, for example, entirely made up of female bodies. Gender was not the only difference, however. In comparison to the other medical "donations" the Institute had routinely received from the military camps, these bodies had blood seeping from the noses, ears, and eyes. In addition, the eyes were all wide open and shiny—not dull and half closed or closed as was normally the case with the POW corpses they received. Furthermore, none of the bodies evidenced rigor mortis. In fact, many were quite warm to the touch. In addition, on the left arm of each body was a five-digit tattoo. A former concentration camp survivor himself, it did not take long for Henripierre to recognize that these persons were in all likelihood camp prisoners who had been poisoned or asphyxiated. As Henripierre later testified, it was then that he decided to deviate from protocol and do something that could have cost him his life: "I made a note of the serial numbers that the women had tattooed on their loft [sic] forearm. I made a note of them on a piece of paper, and I kept them in secret in my house."[33]

Over the next few days, several more deliveries arrived, this time the bodies were all from men who displayed the same tell-tale signs. In total, the cadavers of twenty-nine women and fifty-seven men were received between August 11, 1943 and August 19, 1943. In all eighty-six cases, Henripierre followed the same procedure, carefully and secretly noting down the numbers of all of the people who had entered the institute. Aside from this secret deviation, Henripierre was careful to prepare each of the bodies precisely as Professor Hirt had ordered. The internal organs were excised, the heads were removed, and the limbs were severed. In a few cases, under Hirt's instructions, the torsos were also cleaved into quarters. Once dissected, the body parts were placed in large vats filled with preservatives. There they waited until further instructions were received and the fourth and final stage of the plan could begin.

Over a year later, the body parts of those eighty-six victims were still being stored in the Anatomical Institute. Since their murder, the tide of the war had finally turned against the Nazis. The Allied Forces were gaining ground. Through the combined efforts of the French 2nd Armored Division and the US 4th Infantry Division, Paris had already been liberated on August 25, 1944. It was just a matter of time before Strasbourg was reached. In anticipation, orders were sent from Berlin demanding the immediate destruction of the Hirt collection before it fell into enemy hands. In September 1944, the Managing Director of the Institute for Ancestral Heritage [Reichsgeschäftsführer des SS-Ahnenerbe], Wolfram Sievers, wrote to Dr. Rudolf Brandt to assure him that the collection would be "defleshed and rendered unrecognizable."[34] The fact that the response came from Sievers and not from Hirt may be explained in part by the fact that during this period, the professor had experienced a crippling loss. As he was busy scrambling to find a new, safe location for his anatomical equipment, his wife Marie and son Rainer died in a bombing raid that destroyed their family home in Strasbourg.[35] The date was September 25, 1944, the birthday of his only daughter, Renate, who also survived.

On November 23, 1944, the French Second Armored Division reached Strasbourg. Although Himmler's office had ordered that the collection be destroyed, in the growing chaos of the war, there was neither enough time nor willing manpower to complete the gruesome task. Instead, priority was given to destroying those parts which were considered to be the most useful for possible identification. Many of the severed heads and torsos were accordingly sent to the local crematoria where they were incinerated.[36] Beforehand, the gold teeth of the victims were removed and given to Professor Hirt. The remaining body parts were then intentionally mixed in with the regular holdings of the Anatomical Institute, in an attempt to hide the evidence. By the time the Allies reached the bowels of the Anatomical Institute on December 1, the original set of eighty-six corpses had been rendered into seventeen mangled bodies and 225 body parts.[37] While the staff of the Institute were busy attempting to assure the soldiers that the specimens were no different from what one would expect to find in any institution where future doctors and nurses were taught how to save lives, Hirt's secretary managed to slip into the Institute and destroy many of the most incriminating reports and files. The subterfuge still remained unsuccessful, however.

Long before the war's end, the Allies had already received credible reports of monstrous medical experiments being conducted by the Nazis. The soldiers were given instructions to secure any evidence that might substantiate these claims. Even to the untrained eye, the grisly collection of jumbled body parts was more than suspect. If there were any doubt, their suspicions soon found immediate and powerful confirmation. It seems that in their haste to destroy as much evidence as possible, the Nazis had overlooked one important point: the presence of an eye-witness who had not only seen everything, but had also unbeknownst to them, documented everything. Technical Assistant, Henri Henripierre, greeted the Allied troops and readily offered his assistance in gathering the photographic evidence of the Institute's criminal holdings. He later provided detailed testimony at the Nuremberg Trials. His secretly made list of the eighty-six tattooed numbers was also entered into evidence.

Initially, the Allies made an effort to re-assemble the bodies, but the attempt was soon abandoned as hopeless. Without the benefit of DNA testing available today, the task of trying to put back together the anatomical jigsaw was deemed impossible. Instead, the decision was made to bury the recovered remains in a mass grave in a special ceremony. As the Allies were busy documenting the horrors of the Nazi "racial science" in Strasbourg, the Director of the Anatomical Institute had already made his escape to the Black Forest, some 90 kilometers away. Perhaps concluding that escape was impossible, on June 2, 1945, he walked into the woods and shot himself. Hirt's body was later identified thanks to his tell-tale facial deformity. News of the horror laboratory was quickly spread by the Allies as an example of the atrocities committed in the name of National Socialism. However, very little attention was given to trying to uncover the names and identities of those eighty-six victims. Over time, they simply faded into the estimated 6 million Jewish victims of the Holocaust.

It would take half a century before their story was re-discovered by researcher, journalist, and Professor Dr. Hans-Joachim Lang. In January of 1995, Lang took it upon himself to give the victims back their names. After years of intensive research, he was able to compare a copy of Henry Henripierre's clandestine list[38] to the names and tattooed numbers contained on the transportation lists and typhoid blood tests. Through this cross-comparison, he was finally able to identify the names of all eighty-six victims.[39] Though momentous, determining the victims' names was only Lang's first step in this memorialization. The second was to piece together the story of each person's life. Based on his research and help from the general public, Lang has determined that the eighty-six victims came from seven different countries: Belgium, France, Germany, Greece, Norway, Poland, and the Netherlands. For some of the victims like *Albert Isaac*, *Mordochai Saul*, and *Martha Testa*, this search has proven to be extremely challenging; for others, Lang has been able to recover quite a bit of information. One example is *Alice Simon*.

Born *Alice Remak* on August 30, 1887, Alice was the eldest daughter of three children. Before the age of ten, her parents separated and her mother decided to build a new life for herself and her children away from the growing anti-Semitism of Poland. She moved her family to Charlottenburg, a district of Berlin, Germany. Alice adjusted well to life in the dynamic metropole. By the time she had reached her early thirties, she, like her mother, had become an unusually independent single woman. She worked as a secretary for a prominent lawyer's office, Dr. Herbert Simon. Herbert, like Alice, was also a Polish immigrant who had come to Berlin in his youth.

The two eventually fell in love and decided to marry. But before they did, they converted to Protestantism and got baptized. They took their wedding vows on August 2, 1920. One year later, on February 25, Alice gave birth to twins, *Carl* and *Hedda*. When the time came, the two were also baptized. Conversion to Christianity did little to protect the new family from the mounting discrimination. At the age of fifty-five, after witnessing the spread of National Socialism, Dr. Simon died. Before his passing, he made one final request of his wife: to look after his aging mother who was rapidly losing her eye-sight. Alice gave and kept her word.

Now, a single-parent of twins, Alice, like her mother some thirty years before her, found herself alone in a world that was growing more and more hateful. By 1936, she had had enough. She made the excruciating decision to send her children away to London where she hoped they would finally be able to live their lives in safety. Just two years later, as Jewish businesses, homes, and places of worship were set ablaze during Kristallnacht, she must have felt a deep sense of relief that her children were in England. Her children no doubt felt precisely the opposite. Desperate to save their mother as she had rescued them, Hedda and Carl prevailed upon her to stay with them in Britain during one of her short visits. Although sorely tempted, Alice remained true to her promise and made the agonizing decision to return to Germany to protect her late husband's disabled mother.

By the end of December 1942, her mother-in-law passed away and less than six months later, Alice received notification that she would have to vacate her apartment and report for deportation. In the middle of May, she was loaded onto Transport 38 which travelled from Berlin back to her country of birth. Only this time, the destination was a place called "Auschwitz."[40] Less than two months after her arrival, she found herself on another train, this time to Natzweiler. During that last journey, perhaps she made the acquaintance a fellow countryman who shared a remarkably similar fate. His name was *Max Menachem Taffel*.

Born on July 21, 1900, in Sedziszow, Poland, Max had also immigrated to Berlin, where he met and married the Polish immigrant *Klara Schenkel*. On May 3, 1928, the couple had their first and only child, *Ester Ottilie*. As the family dairy-delivery business collapsed under the weight of the Nazis' anti-Semitic laws, the young family was forced to move in with Klara's parents. On March 12, 1946, Klara, Max, and Ester were placed on Transport 36 from Berlin to Auschwitz.[41] Immediately upon their arrival, the three were separated. While Max was chosen to labor in the camp, his Klara and Ester were sent directly to the gas chamber. Some four months later, Max was chosen for a new work assignment. On July 30, 1943, he, along with eighty-five others, became a part of Hirt's death detail. Unlike the other victims whose butchered bodies would take decades to name, Max's cadaver was discovered nearly intact with his tattooed concentration camp number clearly visible on his left forearm. For this reason, his identity was already recovered in the 1970s.[42] Years later, his name would become a key to solving another criminal mystery.

During Hirt's tenure, the Anatomical Institute at the Reich's University of Strasbourg had procured an extensive collection of human tissue samples from World War II POWs. Sometime after news broke that the names of the eighty-six men and women murdered for the skeletal collection had been recovered, a young physician in Strasbourg was contacted by relatives of a missing Soviet World War II soldier who had been held prisoner in the Alsace. According to the family's research, their grandfather's last known whereabouts had been an anatomical institute in Strasbourg. The family asked the physician if he would be willing to help them discover what had finally become of their grandfather. That was the beginning. Dr. Raphaël Toledano, himself a former student of the University of Strasbourg, had heard the rumors of the Hirt era and had avidly followed the news surrounding the recovery of the eighty-six victims' names and identities. Inspired by Lang's work, Toledano agreed to do what he could to help the family in their search for their missing relative.

A general physician with a small practice in Strasbourg, Toledano spent his free time searching through the international archives to find helpful clues. According to an interview given to a German newspaper, Toledano simply found it intolerable that people who had been murdered were further defiled by being put on display as a part of anatomical exhibit.[43] Eventually, the young doctor's research led him to search the documents contained in a military archive in France. It was there that he found a clue left by Camille Simonin, a medical examiner, who had investigated Hirt's crimes after the war. According to notes left by Simonin in 1952, biological samples from Hirt's "work" had been secured at the Anatomical Institute of the Reich Universität Strasbourg—the current site of the Institute for Forensic Medicine at the University of Strasbourg.

Toledano immediately contacted the University and asked permission to view the Institute's holdings. His request was repeatedly rejected by the then President of the University, Professor Alain Beretz, who categorically denied that any such samples were to be found on the university premises.[44] Toledano remained unconvinced, however; and he was not the only one. A similar theory was advanced in the 2015 French best seller *Hippocrate aux enfers, les médecins des camps de la mort* [Hippocrates in Hell: The Crimes of the Concentration Camp Doctors].[45] Written by Parisian physician, Michel Cymè, the book detailed the life and crimes of Professor Hirt, and suggested that part of the NS collection might still be found in the Anatomical Institute. This assertion was strenuously rejected by Strasbourg University President Beretz.[46] In an interview with *Spiegel Magazine*, Beretz made the following statement in response to Cymè's book: "The claim that remains from the Jewish victims are or could be stored somewhere here at this University or in the Institute, as Michel has done, is quite simply false and wrong."[47] In the meantime, Dr. Toledano patiently repeated his requests to view the Institute's holdings.

Suddenly, his request was granted. In July 2015, it seems that a new director, Dr. Jean-Sebastien Raul, had been appointed to the Institute of Forensic

Medicine. Raul gladly granted the local physician a tour of the tiny anatomical museum.[48] According to Dr. Toledano, he was led by Dr. Raul to a small locked storage room with dozens of jars, bullets, and gas masks on display.[49] Within just a few minutes, the two laid their hands on irrefutable evidence of Hirt's crimes: jars and test-tubes filled with human remains. The labels indicated that the samples had been taken from the Natzweiler-Struthof Concentration Camp where the eighty-six victims had been murdered. Also found were glass containers with several skin samples with the number 107969: the same number that had been tattooed on the forearm of Max Menachem Taffel. Despite his years of intense research Toledano later admitted in an interview with *Haaretz*, "It was a shock to discover that these jars were still there, that we put in a museum display a part of these Jews who were murdered by the Nazis."[50]

In an agreement made between the Institute, the medical faculty, and the University of Strasbourg, the remains were returned to the Jewish community and buried on September 6, 2015.[51] Through his continued research, Dr. Toledano has since then been able to uncover the names of the 232 Russian POWs who were murdered by the Nazis and used for "research." Like Lang, Toledano's work is far from over, however. According to him, in all probability, the corpses of several hundred more POWs were delivered to the Institute. Moreover, if one stops to consider the fact that the Reich's University of Strasbourg was one of many institutions on the European continent that regularly received the cadavers of people murdered during the reign of National Socialism, the number of victims whose names and identities have yet to be reclaimed expands significantly.

*****

Shortly before joining the expedition to Auschwitz for the Hirt collection, SS Obersturmführer Hans Fleischhacker presented the findings of his post-doctoral investigation of hands. The research was based on a series of palm prints that had been made in the Lodz Ghetto. Fleischhacker had not taken these prints himself. They were provided to him by a female colleague who had served as an assistant to his doctoral supervisor, Professor Theodor Mollison.[52] That colleague's name was Sophie Ehrhardt.[53]

Born in Russia in 1902, Ehrhardt obtained her MA in Zoology at the age of twenty-eight. On November 1, 1935, she took on a position at the University of Berlin, where she assisted the infamous racial theorist, Professor Hans F. K. Günther, one of the architects of the infamous "Law for the Prevention of Genetically Disabled Offspring" [*Gesetz zur Verhütung erbkranken Nachwuchs*]. It was during this assistanceship that Ehrhardt's scientific methodology and political ideology became inextricably bound. Evidence of this evolution is found in a number of her scientific publications. For example, for a journal devoted to continuing education in the medical sciences, she declared that it was the inalienable right of the German Volk to follow a selective program of racial politics to prevent Jewish blood from continuing to seep into the superior German racial stock.[54]

In the fall of 1938, Ehrhardt left Günther's team and joined the scientific staff of the Racial Hygiene Research Center of the NS Department of Health [Reichsgesundheitsamt]. Her supervisor was Professor Robert Ritter. Ritter's area of specialization was the investigation of what he believed to be the biologically determined criminality and moral degeneracy of the Roma and Sinti. Ehrhardt shared Ritter's fascination and took a special interest in the Roma and Sinti from Eastern Prussia. In the 1940s, Ritter was awarded funding to identify, measure, and categorize thousands of people with partial or complete Roma and Sinti heritage.[55] A significant number of these individuals were later deported and murdered in concentration camps.

Ritter's team conducted numerous field studies in remote villages to collect their anthropological measurements. However, as Ritter later reported, their data collection was greatly facilitated by the fact that so many members of these traditionally nomadic peoples were increasingly to be found in densely concentrated locations such as Auschwitz-Birkenau.[56] In addition, between 1933 and 1939, large pockets of study subjects could be located in smaller "Gypsy camps" that had been set up in German cities like Cologne, Düsseldorf, Essen, Frankfurt am Main, and Hamburg.[57] According to Ehrhardt's travel journals, in 1938 and 1939, she conducted anthropological measurements of concentration camp prisoners in Sachsenhausen and Dachau as well as in the Lodz Ghetto in 1940.[58] Ehrhardt was an active and avid participant in racial survey-taking.

In the spring of 1940 and 1941, she alone completed measurements on approximately 1,000 Roma and Sinti from Eastern Prussia who had been been forced to take part in her research by police troops.[59] The majority of these unwilling study participants were also later deported and murdered. It was during this time that Ehrhardt had contact with Professor Voss about the supply of skeletal collections he had on offer.[60] In April of 1942, she accepted a position as a research and teaching assistant at the Institute for Racial Biology at the University of Tübingen. One of her primary responsibilities in this position was to write racial assessments of people suspected or known to have either so-called "Jewish or Gypsy" ancestry. The information supplied in these reports was sent to the Reich's Department for Family Ancestry and Heritage [Reichssippenamt][61] and was used later by officials to determine whose names would be placed on the lists for interrogation, incarceration, deportation, sterilization, and/or extermination. After the war, when many of her male colleagues went into hiding or were taken into custody for possible war crimes,[62] Ehrhardt was able to continue her career relatively unfettered.

By 1950, she was awarded a post-doctoral degree, in Anthropology for her investigation of human handprints;[63] and in 1957, she was offered a professorship in Anthropology at the University of Tübingen.[64] Over nearly four decades, she established herself as a leading expert in the physical anthropology of the Roma and Sinti. She published papers in scientific journals on the basis of the measurements taken during the NS period and taught the next generation of students using a unique collection of human skulls. Sometime after the war, many of the materials from Ritter's research institute were eventually transferred to the University of Tübingen, in the Department where Ehrhardt worked. Ironically, Ritter had tried unsuccessfully to obtain a professorship at the University of Tübingen, given his activities during the NS period.[65]

Between 1966 and 1970, she even received a grant from the German Research Foundation [Deutsche Forschungsgemeinschaft] to examine the data that had been collected by Ritter and his team.[66] Her research did not go unnoticed. On September 1, 1981, a delegation of the Central Council of German Sinti and Roma [Zentralrat der Deutschen Sinti und Roma] organized several highly publicized marches, hunger strikes, and sit-ins to draw attention to their continued discrimination and exploitation. One of these protest actions included a demonstration at the University of Tübingen, where a delegation from the Council demanded the immediate transfer of the Ritter files to the national archives.[67] That evening, a portion of the documents was surrendered to the protesters who saw to it that the materials were delivered to the German Federal Archives in Koblenz for future generations to study the persecution of their peoples during the Third Reich.[68] Encouraged by this success, they continued their fight for recognition of the horrific injustices inflicted upon their community.

In 1981, criminal charges were filed against Ehrhardt for accessory to murder on behalf of the Central Council of German Sinti und Roma. The charges were eventually dropped and Ehrhardt continued on as a faculty member in Anthropology Department at the University of Tübingen until her retirement.[69] Today, as a part of its historical collection of scientific artifacts, the University is still in possession of a controversial cranial collection gathered during the first half of the twentieth century and organized into the archaic system of racial classifications such as "Gypsy."[70] For many years, the names of the people whose bodies made up a part of this collection were held secret. However, in recent years, the University of Tübingen has undergone a significant policy shift from secrecy to transparency, from rigid denial to critical examination.

With that shift, the University has investigated and reported upon the history of the Anthropological Institute, its founding, its administration, and its holdings. Research into the institute's cadaver records has provided a wealth of information.[71] Between the years 1933 and 1945, the institute reportedly received a record-breaking number of cadavers: 1,083 to be exact.[72] Based on an analysis of the names listed for each of the cadavers, it has been determined that, during this same period of time, there was a steady increase in the number of non-German Eastern Europeans who died a violent death (e.g., decapitation, hanging, and shooting).[73] Moreover, a significant number of these corpses were recorded as having been prisoners of war, forced laborers, or concentration camp prisoners. As a general rule, once the Institute finished utilizing the bodily remains, they were transferred to the city cemetery where they were discretely buried in a remote, anonymous segment of the graveyard—named "Sector X."[74] However, in accordance with the University's modern policy of transparency, there has also been a change in this burial practice. As has been increasingly recognized, anonymization was systematically used during the NS period to dehumanize victims, decriminalize the perpetrators, and deceive the general public. In an attempt to work directly against the resulting conspiracy of silence, as Dr. Edgar Bierende, museum curator at the University of Tübingen, explains, a conscious decision was made to publicly name the NS victims listed in the University cadaver records and buried in Sector X.

Sadly, this courageous policy of honesty and transparency remains the exception rather than the rule. By and large, the names and identities of those who murdered and were murdered for the sake of NS science remain a well-kept secret. Admittedly, as the work of courageous pioneers like Professor Lang attests, finding this information is no easy task, especially when one considers the millions of NS victims whose bodies lay in unmarked mass graves across Europe. These logistical challenges are further compounded by the widespread assumption that doing so could violate, injure, or impinge upon the privacy of both groups and their descendants. In many countries, this belief has dictated official institutional policies, making it illegal to reveal the full personal names until so much time has transpired that the persons involved are all dead. Even after this period of time, the ethics of publishing the personal names of persons who are unable to grant or deny their permission is considered by some to be questionable at best.

Given this controversy, publishing the full names of the eighty-six NS victims found at the University of Strasbourg's anatomical institute revealed not only an awe-inspiring degree of personal and scientific dedication. It also constituted a daring break with previous conventions. When I asked Professor Lang in an interview whether he had been criticized by colleagues for publishing the names and identities of the victims, he had the following response:

Naturally, I deliberated at length whether I should publish the names. . . . And, up to now, no one has ever criticized my decis on. In fact, precisely the opposite has been the case. Almost immediately after it was published, my book was reviewed by multiple literary critics and my intention was always understood. We cannot allow the victims to be forgotten. That was exactly the point which the Jewish Community in Strasbourg made, when they had a stone erected to mark the mass grave where the victims were buried in the Jewish Cemetery in Strasbourg-Cronenbourg. On that gravestone, the names of each of the victims appear. I have had personal contact with approximately thirty family members of the eighty-six victims. Without exception, they have also expressed agreement with my decision and have given me positive, encouraging feedback. And where naming the names of the perpetrators is concerned, I consider that to be completely acceptable as long as the legal regulations and professional journalistic standards are followed.[75]

The process of full public onomastic reclamation serves as a powerful act of resistance against the attempt to blot out all memory of millions of men, women, and children murdered in the past. It also offers additional irrefutable evidence to all those who still—despite everything we know today—seek to deny the significance, enormity, or even reality of the Holocaust. It is with these goals in mind that Holocaust memorial and research organizations around the world have worked tirelessly to gather the names and recognize the identities of those people whose lives were cut short during the Third Reich.

*****

The International Tracing Service in Bar Arolsen, Germany, is one of the world's largest and oldest Holocaust-related archives. Established by the Allied Powers immediately after World War II, for the past seven decades, the ITS has served as an essential document repository for helping to identify or "trace" missing persons. In the year 2017 alone, the ITS processed more than 150,000 tracing requests from NS survivors and their relatives.[76] On average, the ITS receives approximately 1,000 requests each month from more than sixty different countries.[77] In addition, the ITS also routinely provides key evidence to be used in indemnification cases involving victims of NS persecution. As Hugh Elbot, the US American Director of the ITS, declared during the opening of the agency's new headquarters in August 1952, "This service is dedicated to millions of innocent victims of war, dictatorship and intolerance and to their families. We serve the dead and the living. . . . We serve. Period!"[78]

The documents housed within the ITS collection include a vast range of administrative records kept on the national, state, regional, and local levels during

National Socialism. From concentration camp prisoners, slave laborers, to displaced persons, the ITS records contain data on more than 17.5 million NS victims.[79] In addition, it is estimated that the ITS also holds more than 190 million digital images. Given the sensitive nature of the information contained in the archive, for most of its history, the ITS has strictly restricted its usage to authorized staff only. This closed-door policy was legally based on the international agreements made in 1955. In postwar Europe, when public records had been so flagrantly misused to destroy the lives of millions of people, the initial impetus for placing such highly restrictive controls over record access and use can be appreciated.

However, the fact that the ITS policy often prohibited direct access by official governing bodies, public institutions, Holocaust researchers, and survivor organizations was much less understood. In particular, critics questioned the legitimacy of the ITS' restrictive policy when other German-based institutions that also house highly sensitive materials had long allowed individual and institutional use after careful vetting. For example, the German National Archives (Bundesarchiv) in Berlin is an institutional partner of the ITS with an open-door policy that allows usage by authorized institutions and members of the general public. The continued refusal of the ITS to change its policy was not only criticized for its perceived lack of logic. To the extent that the refusal to share information might have thwarted the retrieval of vital information needed to substantiate thousands of survivor restitution claims, the morality of the ITS's closed-door policy was also sharply questioned as well. This position was powerfully expressed by Alcee Hastings, Chair of the Commission on Security and Cooperation in Europe.

In a prepared statement made before the House of Representatives' Committee on Foreign Affairs, Hastings declared: "It is a moral and humanitarian imperative to permit Holocaust survivors and their families' immediate access to the millions of Holocaust records housed there. The issue is as clear cut as right and wrong, moral and immoral, just and unjust."[80] This sentiment was echoed by the Honorable Elton Gallegly, a congressional representative from California, who further emphasized the temporal imperative of changing the ITS policy:

> [t]he time for waiting with respect to the Bad Arolsen archives is over. Every day, there are fewer and fewer Holocaust survivors left among us. The United States should do everything in its power at the upcoming ITS annual meeting to push for the immediate opening of the archives. In the interest of justice and for the sake of those who have already suffered so much in the Holocaust, we should demand nothing less.[81]

In 2006, the German Minister of Justice, Brigitte Zypries, announced a groundbreaking development. After ratification by the eleven country-strong governing board of the ITS in Luxemburg, the archive would be officially ending its previous policy and would be providing digital copies of its records to the non-German member nations.[82] Although the ITS had already agreed to ease its restrictions in 1999, continued resistance by certain officials had severely hampered the implementation of this policy change. According to the Zypries announcement, the internal and external policies of the ITS had finally reached a turning-point. "Our point of view," explained Zypries, "is that the protection of privacy rights has reached by now a standard high enough to ensure . . . the protection of privacy of those concerned."[83] Since that announcement, the ITS has slowly but surely accelerated and expanded its services to allow authorized users access to its 50 million references; 232 thousand meters of microfilm; and 107 thousand microfiches.[84]

According to Gideon Taylor of the Conference on Jewish Material Claims against Germany, this change in policy and practice is to be applauded: "These records have been awaited for years by Holocaust survivors and scholars of this terrible period. Their release while survivors are still alive will enable these documents to be enhanced and explained through personal testimony of those who lived through the Nazi era."[85] One of the institutions that has been particularly supportive of the ITS's policy development is Yad Vashem. Like its institutional partner in Bad Arolsen, since the end of World War II, Yad Vashem has also been dedicated to the victims of National Socialism. However, right from the beginning, the policy followed by Yad Vashem has been radically different.

*

One of the first to think of establishing an everlasting Holocaust memorial in *Eretz Israel* was Mordechai Shenhavi, a member of Kibbutz Beit Alfa in the Jezreel Valley. In 1942, as the news spread about thousands upon thousands of European Jews being sent to their deaths, Mordechai had a vision. He saw a place in Israel where the spirits of the dead could lay their souls to rest and the souls of the living could come to remember, grieve, and honor their brethren. Haunted by the horrific reports from Europe, Mordechai soon put pen to paper and drew out a detailed conceptual plan. He named it "The Idea of Commemorating All Victims of the Jewish Catastrophe Caused by the Nazi Horrors and the War."

Once he finished his project sketch, he submitted his idea to the head office of the Jewish National Fund.[86] His was not the only plan being developed, however. The Jewish community in Israel had long demanded its leaders do more to recognize the horrors taking place all across Europe. Although there was support for the basic idea of a place of commemoration, there were also many critical questions posed. Given the devastating events in Europe, wouldn't it be more powerful, some asked, to focus such a monument on Jewish Life, Culture, and Resiliency rather than Jewish death, dying, and suffering? Which names should be commemorated? Those of all the Jews who died during the war or only those who perished as a direct result of National Socialism? How would such an ambitious monument be financed? And where should it be erected? As leaders deliberated over these and other logistical questions, more plans continued to be generated by the general public. Soon, members of government were also taking part in the design process.

In the winter of 1945, another powerful conceptual project had begun to take shape. This project was developed by Baruch Zuckerman, a top administrator of the World Jewish Congress (WJC) and Dr. Jacob Helman, the WJC representative for South America. Together, these men developed a plan for a memorial to be erected on Mt. Carmel. It would feature the names of all the "Jewish martyrs" during the War. They called their project "In Everlasting Remembrance." Important supporters of this idea included Chaim Weizmann, Dr. Stephen Wise, Rabbi Isaac Herzog, Prof. Albert Einstein, and Dr. Nahum Goldmann.[87] This new plan was taken into advisement, along with the other proposals. In the meantime, Mordechai kept working on his original plan. He soon produced a revised proposal that powerfully incorporated many of the best and most popular ideas from the other projects (e.g., "The Everlasting Remembrance" concept). Mordechai also gave his revised project a new name: *Yad Vashem Foundation Memory of the Lost Jewries in Europe.*[88] The new wholistic, integrative, concept was a success; and in 1953, the Israeli Parliament officially established "the Yad Vashem: World Holocaust Remembrance Center."

Right from the very beginning, the official purpose of the center has always been four-fold: to commemorate, document, research, and educate the world about the Holocaust. As Dr. Alexander Avraham, Director of Yad Vashem's Hall of Names, revealed in my interview with him,[89] the accomplishment of that complex intersecting mission required recovering and publishing the names of the 6 million Jews who died during the Shoah. According to Dr. Avraham, the commitment to naming the names of all the Shoah victims serves a double mandate. It allows the families of Shoah victims to commemorate the names of their loved ones in a public space of honor; and it offers the deceased a place where their memories are cherished with reverence. This dual objective was developed out of respect for the last wishes explicitly expressed by many Shoah victims. As Dr. Avraham went on to elaborate, in the Yad Vashem archives, there are literally thousands of "farewell letters" written by doomed Shoah victims who begged their families and friends not to forget them. By naming each and every Jewish victim, Yad Vashem seeks to fulfill its duty and promise to the dead and the living: the past, the present, and the future.

To date, with the public's assistance, researchers working at and with Yad Vashem have been able to recover and publish the names of approximately 4.7 million Jewish victims of the Holocaust. Since 2006, the names of these victims as well as many pertinent identifying biographical details (e.g., date of birth, place of birth, deportation, place of death, death date) have been stored in the Center's Names Database. This database is accessible through the internet and is available in multiple languages. Around the world, this e-archive has become an indispensable tool for Holocaust researcher purposes. It is also a critical source of information for family members who are still searching for their loved ones. The personal and scholarly importance of this resource is reflected in its use. Based on figures provided by Dr. Avraham, it receives millions of visitors each year. In 2017 alone, more than half of the 18 million visitors to the Yad Vashem website used this onomastic repository.

The Names Database is a part of Yad Vashem's "Names Recovery Project." Despite the incredible successes of this project since its inception in the 1990s, the initiative is clearly not without challenges. There are many practical difficulties that come from managing a multilingual onomastic database of this size, scope, and complexity that is available for use by millions of visitors 24-hours-a-day. Added to these common logistical challenges are a host of special issues that are specific to the primary information sources.

Unlike many other modern databases that are constructed using readily available, easily readable, digitalized data, many of the records needed for the Names Database are often only partially or completely unavailable—having been either accidentally damaged during the course of the genocide or purposefully destroyed after the war to hide the atrocities. Even when the necessary name documents are recovered, the previously mentioned legal restrictions can severely or completely limit data access or data use. Furthermore, documents that have been located and made available are frequently not in a digitalized, easily readable format.

Of all the difficulties inherent to the names recovery process, the one that is the most formidable is the absence of written records. Indeed, as Dr. Avraham asserts, "most of the victims (murdered in extermination camps or by the Ensatzgruppen) were never registered." For many readers, this assertion stands in direct contradiction to the widespread media image of the fastidious Nazi who insisted upon recording the name of each and every victim. In point of fact, as the war continued and the killing accelerated in scale, speed, and sadism, the priority was not so much given to identifying <u>who</u> was killed, but <u>how many</u>. From large public institutions (e.g., hospitals, psychiatric clinics, sanatoria for the physically or cognitively disabled) to private gatherings (e.g., "Rabbit Hunts' [Hasenjagd] where emaciated prisoners were forced to dash across fields in a futile attempt to dodge the hail of bullets shot by jovial soldiers, their friends, and families), the names and identities of countless NS victims were never officially registered.

For all these reasons, the Names Recovery Project relies heavily on the information provided by the general public. People who, for example, have information on the survival or death of an individual are strongly encouraged to share these details on so-called Pages of Testimony. These testimonials are then meticulously reviewed by the Yad Vashem staff before the information is added to the museum's databank. Based on the statistics that Dr. Avraham was able to recover, "Over the last few years, the yearly average of new Pages of Testimony was of about 20,000 per year." Thanks in no small measure to those one-page testimonials, the Names Recovery Project collection now includes more than million names.

As critical as this source of information is, Dr. Avraham acknowledges that making these reports is never easy for survivors: "the emotional difficulty of registering one's relatives as murdered." Completing the forms to report a Shoah victim's death necessarily entails re-experiencing the loss and giving up that last vestige of hope that a loved one will somehow miraculously return. Still, despite that pain, Dr. Avraham stresses how essential it is that Shoah survivors and their families share what information they have NOW—before it is too late. In cases, for example, where there is no written documentation of a Shoah victim, the only evidence of that person's name and existence is in the memory of a loved one. If that person dies before sharing that information, the memory of that victim is lost forever. Given the rapidly dwindling number of first-hand Holocaust survivors, the race to rescue the names of those victims is becoming even more pressing with every passing day. This urgency is also keenly felt by another of the world's keeper of names, the United States Holocaust Memorial Museum (USHMM).

*

On November 1, 1978, under President Carter, the Commission on the Holocaust was convened to investigate the state of Holocaust remembrance and education in the United States. One of the recommendations made by that Commission was the establishment of a "living memorial" to honor the Shoah victims and the survivors and to help ensure that the lessons of the Holocaust would be taught in perpetuity.[90] Nearly ten years later, on October 16, 1985, the groundbreaking ceremonies for the memorial began and on April 26, 1993, the USHMM finally opened its doors to the public.[91] Since then, the USHMM has welcomed over 41 million visitors to view its more than twenty-thousand art pieces and historical artifacts. However, the USHMM is not simply a museum. It is also a modern interactive research center equipped with a world archival collection.

The repository includes 190 million digital images from the ITS; over 100,000 historical photographs and images with more than 1,000 hours of film and video footage; over 16,000 Holocaust testimonials; over 100 million pages of historical records; and an in-house library with an excess of 110,000 items in over fifty different languages.[92] All of these resources provide essential assistance to the USHMM research staff in their attempt to recover the names of Shoah victims and survivors. The importance of this initiative is described by Sara-Joelle Clark, an ITS Researcher at the USHMM's Holocaust Survivors and Victims Resource Center: "History comes alive when you put a name to a victim. The Nazis tried to take away any and all human virtues from their victims. By restoring their names, we are in a sense correcting history—history that the Nazis tried to erase."[93]

To accomplish this goal, the Center's researchers systematically comb through an incredible volume and variety of historical documents. These records include deportation and arrival lists for the various processing centers, ghettos, concentration camps, and satellite factories; the transportation, and medical records produced by the killing centers established for the mentally and physically disabled, the injured and the infirm; the assignments and military reports issued by the Einsatzgruppen; arrest and detention records; society, club and party membership rosters; registers of residents, immigrants, and displaced persons. Before the names can be extracted from these documents and formally added to the USHMM official repository in the Central Name Index (CNI), the entries must be scrupulously cross-checked. Some of the difficulties that regularly present themselves in this verification process are exemplified by the three hypothetical case records presented in table 9.1.

In RECORD 1, a transportation list from 1939, there is an entry for a *Johanna Pavlak* who was registered as having been born on January 1881. According to this record, under the Nazis, she was issued the identification number of 48759. Both of these details are identical to those listed for *Hanna Sara Pavlakova*, the entry that appears on the death listings in RECORD 3. Curiously, in the second record, a hospital list from 1944, there is also a listing for a *Hanni Sara Pavlakova*. However, this person's birth year is recorded as 1912 and her identification number as 33658. There is a patient in this record, however, with the number "48759": a *Hayim Hirsch*. A careful comparison of details listed for these two patients might lead one to infer that their names may simply have been switched by mistake. Such an accident would explain the presumably erroneous gender classifications entered for *Hayim* and *Hanni*. The question remains whether *Johanna Pavlak*, *Hanni Sara Pavlakova*, and *Hanna Sara Pavlakova* are one and the same person.

If the entries are for the same person, the onomastic differences in the first names could be easily explained by the fact that *Hanna* and *Hanni* are common nicknames for *Johanna*. The fact that the middle name *Sara* is absent in the 1939 transportation list might be a simple oversight. Alternatively, it might reflect a change in status. For example, the location of a Jewish grandparent might have caused the person's classification to change from Aryan to Jewish. Such a re-classification would also explain why the 1944 entries for this individual contained the onomastic marker *Sara* but the earlier 1939 entry did not.

With regard to last name *Pavlakova* vs. *Pavlak*), if the entries are for the same individual, these onomastic deviations could be accounted for by differences in the native language of the record-keepers. For example, as ITS Researcher Sara-Joelle Clark, explains, during the war, it was not at all uncommon for Czech officials to add automatically add the "'ova' ending to women's surnames even when they were not Czech themselves. According to Clark, "The 'ova' is traditionally added to the end of the last name of a married Czech woman."[94] If it were discovered that the woman in question had been kept a prisoner in camp like Theresienstadt where Czechs regularly worked as record-keepers, it might be possible that "officials used the ova to distinguish marital status." In order to determine if that factor played a role in the case being examined, it would be necessary to conduct more research to help in the record-matching and disambiguation process. Though time-consuming, this background check is essential. After all, despite the many similarities and plausible explanations for the differences, it is still possible that the names *Johanna Pavlak*, *Hanni Sara Pavlakova*, and *Hanna Sara Pavlakova* actually belong to two or even three entirely different people.

Other common onomastic challenges reproduced in the fictitious records shown in table 9.1 include cross-linguistic name variants (e.g., *Chaim* vs. *Hayim*); (un)intentional spelling differences (*Rosner* vs. *Roesner; Zidkowsky* vs. *Zidkowski*); recording errors/omissions (*Barlewin* vs. *Lewin*); transposition of name elements (*Zelig Abraham* vs. *Abraham Zelig*); nicknames (*Heinrich* vs. *Heinz; Charlotte* vs. *Lotte*); missing name elements (*Charlotte-Magdalena* vs. *Magdalena*); and phonetic approximations (*Zelig* vs. *Zelisch*). Adding to these linguistic challenges is the fact that many records documenting the Holocaust are incomplete, damaged, faulty, and/or highly illegible due, for example, to aging or the handwriting of the record-keeper. Further compounding the complexity of the record-management task is the sheer volume of names to be recovered.

Technical Information Specialist at the USHMM, Sarah Kopelman-Noyes adds another factor that can complicate the Shoah names research and recovery process. The extraordinary number of the records that have been assembled since the end of the War means that "there are literally millions of names of survivors and victims hidden within the millions of pages of archival documents." To help facilitate the effective and rapid search-and-recovery task, the USHMM has continually pioneered new strategies. For example, for years, the staff had been working on the compilation of an in-house names index, but the process involved was both laborious and slow. Sarah Kopelman-Noyes describes how and why the USHMM decided to explore other information gathering approaches:

> With the survivor generation shrinking every day we knew we needed to increase the number of names appearing online and do it quickly. Crowdsourcing seemed to make the most sense. We teamed up with Ancestry.com, one of the most experienced crowdsourcing companies out there. Our partnership with them has been going on since 2011.[95]

Like Yad Vashem then, the decision of USHMM to actively liaison with the general public has always been a cornerstone of the institution's successful

Table 9.1   Fictitious Records of Biographical Data from Three Different Types of Holocaust Documents

RECORD 1: TRANSPORTATION RECORD (1939)

ID#	BIRTH DATE	ADDRESS	LAST NAME	FIRST NAMES	RACE
48759	January 1881	Weyhe	Pavlak	Johanna	—
52149	April 1901	Stuhr	Barlewin	Aaron Israel	J
33568	June 1912	Bremen	Roesner	Heinrich Israel	J
95874	September 1940	Wilhemshaven	Zidkowski	Lotte Sara	—
111547	December 1942	Bremerhaven	Abraham	Zelig Israel	—

RECORD 2: HOSPITAL RECORD (1944)

PATIENT #	NAME	SEX	BIRTH YEAR	RACE
33658	Hanni Sara Pavlakova	M	1912	J
625811	Aaron Israel Lewin	M	1907	J
111547	Abraham Israel Zelisch	M	1941	J
958974	Magdalena Sara Zidkowsky	F	1940	J
48759	Hayim Hirsch	F	1881	J

RECORD 3: DEATH RECORD (1944)

ID#	NAME	DOB	RACE	CAUSE OF DEATH	DATE OF DEATH
48759	Hanna Sara Pavlakova	1881	1/8 J	Heart attack	June 26, 1944
52149	Aaron Israel Lewin	1902	1/2 J	Pneumonia	June 26, 1944
11154	Abraham Israel Zelisch	1941	J	Appondicitis	June 26, 1944
95874	Magdalena Sara Zidkowsky	1940	J	Tuberculosis	June 26, 1944
652811	Hayim Hirsch	1907	J	Pneumonia	June 26, 1944

operation. Evidence of this successful partnership can be clearly seen in the USHMM names recovery initiative where interested members of the public are actively invited to help compile the names index via the World Memory Project (WMP).[96] The WMP is an online resource that allows visitors to search for and contribute to information about individual victims of the Holocaust. So far, over 4 million records have been added to the USHMM repository via this project. Only in its seventh year, the WPM has already proven to be a tremendous aid to families seeking to discover and/or provide information about their loved ones.

*****

Support for the ongoing fight to keep the memory of the Holocaust alive has come not only come from Shoah survivors and their descendants. It has also come from a small but dedicated circle of people whose relatives were directly responsible for the carnage. It has been estimated that Concentration Camp Commandant Amon Göth singlehandedly killed 500 people and tortured many more. In a 2005 interview given to the German newspaper, *Frankfurter Allgemeine*, his daughter, Monika Hertwig nee Göth, explained why she has chosen to speak out publicly about the depravity of her father and the complicity of her mother.[97] "I can't undue [*sic*] or make up for the past. But I can show the survivors, that I hear their pain and suffering."[98] Hertwig is one of a handful of descendants of NS perpetrators who have chosen to directly confront and help to publicly expose the crimes committed in the name of National Socialism.

To do so, she, like so many of other descendants of Nazis, has had to break through formidable walls of family secrets. In her case, it was her grandmother who finally told her that her father had been a member of the SS and had served as a commandant of a labor camp in Poland. However, it was not until she saw Spielberg's film *Schindler's List* that she truly comprehended who and what her father was. Since then, she has devoted herself to researching and exposing her father's atrocities. In her opinion, the descendants of NS perpetrators have a moral responsibility to all those people whose lives were lost and/or destroyed.

Ironically, at about the same time that Hertwig saw Spielberg's film and learnt the truth about her father, the Afro-German daughter whom she had given up for adoption was also viewing the film several thousand miles away in Israel. A short time after the film made its debut in US theaters, it was shown on Israeli television where Hertwig's daughter, Jennifer, then a university student, watched the film alone in her shared apartment in Tel Aviv. Several years later, after getting married, having two sons, and building a successful career as a journalist, she would discover that the psychopath she had seen portrayed in Spielberg's film was none other than her grandfather.

Since then, she too has publicly denounced the crimes of her grandfather and others like him. In 2014, she chronicled her experiences in the book *Mein Großvater Hätte Mich Erschossen* [My Grandfather Would Have Shot Me: A Black Woman Discovers Her Family's Nazi Past].[99] Her activism has not only made her a welcomed international speaker. She has also become a target. "If you look in the internet, you can find a lot of racist comments about me. Even in response to the interviews I have given. That's a part of society. . . . These people express themselves in the safe anonymity of the internet." There are people, for example, who categorically refuse to believe that Teege is the granddaughter of Commandant Göth because her skin color and surname differ from his. Such self-proclaimed internet experts seem to have missed the fact that her birth name *Jennifer Göth* changed after she was put up for adoption by her German mother and her Nigerian father; and then altered once again after she married.

In my interview with her, Teege stressed how important it is to make distinctions when dealing with people who make such racist comments. According to her, "there are always a few who are completely rigid" but there are many, many others "who have simply naively or ignorantly babbled what they have heard others and those people can be reached." The best way to do that, Teege believes, is talking with one another. "Dialogue, dialogue, dialogue. . . . I believe firmly that people have to talk with one another." Through her writings and speeches, Teege hopes to serve as a positive catalyst for this open, constructive, exchange. Talking with one another to find common ground does not, however, mean compromising one's principles, she stressed. People have both the right and the responsibility to raise their voices when they witness injustice, immorality, or cruelty.

In the Göth family line, both daughter and granddaughter have taken on this mammoth task, albeit independently of one another. In other families with a NS perpetrator, this role has been principally shouldered by one single member. Such was the case with Katrin. After completing her degree in Political Science at the University of Berlin, Katrin began work as a writer and researcher. One day, she received an unexpected call from her father asking her if she would please check the national archives to see what files, if any, she could find about his father, her grandfather, *Ernst*. She made an appointment at the German National Archives and several months later found herself seated at a desk with a single file before her. The file was surprisingly thin. Nevertheless, its contents would radically contradict much of what she had been told about *Grossvater Ernst*.

She discovered, for example, that he had not, as she had always been told, joined the Party extremely late. In fact, he became an official member of the NSDAP in November of 1931 and a member of the SS in 1933. And contrary to the family lore that had always portrayed her grandfather as a technology-obsessed engineer who had very little if any interest in politics, she discovered that in actuality he had served as the Head Engineer and Technical Director of the Reich's broadcasting system before dying under mysterious circumstances shortly before the war's end.[100] If she were a different type of person, she could have simply returned that file to the archivist that day and closed the chapter on her family's past. There were certainly many in the family who would undoubtedly have been far happier if she had done. But, Katrin decided to take another path.

Slowly, she began to piece together the story of her family. In 2005, she published that story in the best-selling book, *The Himmler Brothers: A German Family History.* Translated into more than ten different languages, the family saga traces the lives and crimes of all three Himmler brothers: Ernst, Gebhard, and Heinrich. As she explained in my interview with her, one of the most painful yet historically significant findings of her research was the fact that *Uncle Heinrich* was not the only relative who had been complicit. Other members of her family had been active as well in supporting the NSDAP.

Some ten years later, with coauthor German historian Michael Wildt, she coauthored another book: this one featuring the private correspondence of her great-uncle, Heinrich Himmler. *Himmler Privat: Brief eines Massenmörders* [Himmler: The Private Letters of a Mass Murderer]. In between these two publications, she lectured around the world and was featured in a number of documentaries. What began then as a personal favor to her father has turned into a life's project. In an interview with the author, she admitted that it was not an easy decision to so publicly confront generations of family secrets and national myths that had been stockpiled under decades of silence and shame, fear and guilt. When I asked her if she had ever considered simply changing her name and leaving the family history behind her, she gave the following response:

> As children, my sister and I longed so much to be finally freed from the burden of our last name, because we felt guilty, although we personally had not done anything. That was one of the reasons why we desperately wanted to get married. Once that happened, there would be no one left in our family line to carry on that last name. When my sister and I finally did get married, though, we both decided to keep the last name Himmler . . . because it had become a part of us, because it was the name we were born with, it was the name of our parents . . . and because it is no longer simply expected that a wife automatically takes on the last name of her husband, we realized we had a choice. Since then, it has become easier for me to live with the weight of this name and this family history, and that is because for many years, I have intensively investigated our family history. And

> my decision not to hide my name has enabled me to have contact
> with people whom I never would have had the opportunity to meet
> like Holocaust survivors and their relatives.[101]

Some of those Shoah survivors became members of her immediate family, when
she met and married an Israeli man whose father managed to survive the horrors
of Nazi-occupied Warsaw by securing identification papers that listed him as
Aryan.[102] The marriage ultimately ended in divorce, but not before the two had a
son together: a German-Israeli child to whom she would one day have to explain
how just three generations ago, one part of his family had tried to annihilate the
other.[103] To do that, she would have to learn the truth herself: all of it.

When the time came, Katrin Himmler kept that promise and told her son,
about their family's history. She has also helped others who want to research
their family history during the Third Reich. Not everyone, of course, has the
emotional fortitude to take the path that Katrin Himmler did. Some children
of well-known Nazis decided to change their name in an attempt to build a
new identity for themselves. While this onomastic disassociation may work for
some, for Katrin Himmler, what worked best was an uncompromisingly honest
confrontation with the crimes committed by her family in the name of National
Socialism. This approach has not only earned her public praise, however. It has
also made her the target of Neo-Nazis.

> Naturally, I do receive those kinds reactions, most of the time from
> people who remain anonymous, from fascists around all of Europe. I
> have been charged, for example, with sullying my "Aryan race" and
> of "bringing shame" upon the name of Himmler. There has also been
> the occasional violent threat and I was stalked once.[104]

Katrin is not alone in being accused of sullying the memory and name of a Nazi
leader still revered by ideological followers, both old and new. Still this has not
stopped her or other descendants from continuing to speak the truth no matter
how ugly or dangerous it may be.

One individual who has spent more than five decades doing precisely
that is German journalist and book author, Niklas Frank, the son of Nazi
war criminal Dr. Hans Frank. Frank obtained his law degree and joined the
NSDAP in 1923. In 1928, he founded the National Socialist Association of
German Legal Professionals [Nationalsozialistischen Juristenbundes].[105] When
three lieutenants (Hanns Ludin, Richard Scheringer, and Hans Wendt) were
tried for attempting to convince fellow officers at the Ulm garrison not to draw
arms against revolting members of the NSDAP it was Frank who served as

their defense lawyer. During the course of the trial, Frank called his star witness, Adolf Hitler.[106] Although the three officers were found guilty as charged, the trial succeeded in drawing national attention to Hitler and the NSDAP.[107] Frank would go on to represent the Führer in more than fifty different trials. By 1939, he had been appointed the Governor General of Nazi-occupied Poland and was involved in the administration of all the ghettos and death camps erected there.

After the War, "The Butcher of Poland" was placed under arrest by the US Americans and put on trial in Nuremberg. He was charged with helping to orchestrate the murder of almost 18 percent of the Polish population and approximately 6 million people.[108] On October 16, 1946, Hans Frank was executed. He left behind a wife, several mistresses, and five children: *Sigrid, Brigitte, Michael, Norman,* and *Niklas.* The last of these sons, Niklas Frank, has spent much of his adult life chronicling the crimes of his father. Frank could have published this material under a pseudonym or even anonymously. However, as he revealed in my interview, for him, that option would have been impossible. Although he was born into the Frank family through no fault of his own, he would have considered it cowardly to have hidden behind anonymity:

> Especially in the face of the maddening fact that, year after year, there is this growing tendency in Germany to remain silent and to try to worm around the fact that the crimes committed in this country between 1933 and 1945.[109]

That trend, Frank asserts, has continued to drive him to take a clear and defiant stand against this trend and against his father. In 1987, that crusade culminated in the publication of his book, *The Father: A Reckoning* [*Der Vater: Eine Abrechnung*], a scathing and relentless indictment of his father. That book was followed by several others in which he morally excoriates other relatives who carry the Frank family name. For many, Niklas Frank is applauded and honored for his unflinching refusal to minimize, relativize, diminish, or avoid the atrocities under his father and millions of others like him. For others, he is reviled for what they consider to be his unforgivable betrayal of his father and Vaterland.

Niklas Frank's defiant refusal to forgive the unforgivable has often resulted in his being greeted with hatred, repulsion, bewilderment, and apathy. Of these reactions, the only one which seems to truly gall him is the last. When asked why that is the case, he explained:

> the Germans who are alive today are for the most part innocent of the crimes committed by the generations before them, but they must still acknowledge that these atrocities took place, without qualification or

> excuses. What you have called apathy, I call a lack of empathy. The silent majority of Germans don't spend any real time trying to put themselves into the roles of the innocent victims. . . . If they did, that would give them a very different vantage point when looking at the crimes of our forefathers and foremothers.[110]

According to Frank, it is the failure or refusal to adopt the victim's perspective that prohibits a truly empathetic response.

In my opinion, Frank makes an excellent point. Far too often, people are asked: "If you were suddenly transported back seventy years, what would you have done if you were ordered to kill someone else? How would you feel? Would you have had the courage to take a stand against the regime and perhaps risk the life of your loved ones?" The fact that so few people can honestly say without a shadow of a doubt that they would have resisted against the NS system of killing leads almost automatically to feelings of sympathy towards the perpetrators. Imagine, what would happen, however, if people were invited to answer the same questions but this time from the victims' point of view. "If you were suddenly transported back seventy years, what would you have done if someone had been ordered to kill you? How would you feel? Would you have had the courage to take a stand against the regime and perhaps risk the lives of your loved ones?" This set of questions also tends to provoke feelings of empathy, only this time for the victim rather than the perpetrator. It is precisely this depth of insight that Frank's work brings.

Armed with his surname, Niklas Frank's writing simultaneously indicts and condemns Germans of the past for their actions while warning and castigating Germans of the present for their inaction. From his vantage both of these Germany's co-exist together, side-by-side, inextricably bound together in much the same way as the two sides of his father were inseparable.

> I see us Germans and I am afraid. I see the letters that they write with your spirit, your ideology, and I think to myself, here they are: two people in one German. There is the one—well-mannered, hard-working, officiously conservative; but just beneath, immediately behind, that one, as if composed of negative charges, there is the other one, the murdering one. And the killers are growing in number from one day to the next. Oh yes, I am afraid of the Shadow German . . . made of your [Niklas Frank's father] spirit, your thoughts, your ghost.[111]

The fact that Niklas Frank insists upon addressing the collective responsibility of modern Germany for the widespread guilt of its forebearers (including his own) has led some to conclude that his warnings are exaggerated, outmoded, unnecessary. National Socialism, some say, may have been a danger seventy years ago, but today, the world faces many other enemies that are far more menacing than the NSDAP.

In January of 2017, people championing this opinion were given a powerful boost from the Germany's Supreme Court. After much deliberation, the Court ruled against a petition to outlaw the modern political successor of the NSDAP, the National Democratic Party of Germany [Nationaldemokratische Partei Deutschlands] (NPD). The primary reason the court offered for its judgment was that the Party had become so weak that it no longer represented a serious threat to German democracy.[112] While the numerical size and financial wherewithal of the NPD may have indeed radically decreased, there is every indication that their political ideology has remained remarkably resilient and deadly.

Indeed, during the final stages of writing this book, the news has been filled with reports about the increase in anti-Semitic crimes in Germany. According to the latest statistics assembled by Germany's Ministry of the Interior, in the first six months of 2016, there were 654 registered cases of hate-motivated crimes against Jewish residents in Germany.[113] In 2017, during the same period of time, that number had risen to 681. Of these cases, around 93 percent were committed by offenders who were right extremists.[114] What is particularly alarming is the increase in not only the number, but also the naked aggression displayed.

Statements that years ago might have been condemned as fascist are now being openly declared by people who would describe themselves as being politically moderate to extremely left of center. Anti-Semitism is no longer being whispered or sneered at behind closed doors in private conversations. It is now being openly, defiantly, and proudly declared in everyday, public forums.[115] From football stadiums to doctors' offices, university lecture halls and street cafes, Friday night talk shows, Sunday night family dinners, townhall meetings, to the floors of German parliament, anti-Semitism has risen in frequency, vehemence, and in more than a few circles, acceptability. And expressions of this prejudice are by no means limited to words. On the eve of Kristallnacht in 2016, for example, a Neo-Nazi group publicized the names and addresses of seventy Jewish-owned businesses and establishments on a map of Berlin on a right-extremist Facebook page. The map was accompanied with the phrase "Jews amongst us."[116] According to yearly surveys conducted by the Amadeu Antonio Stiftung, an independent non-profit organization dedicated to promoting democratic principles in Germany, the consequences of such actions for members of the Jewish community have been more than tangible:

> All those who reveal themselves to be Jewish live dangerously in Germany. It is now commonplace to be yelled at, spit on, and threatened,

in response to wearing a yarmulke. Without warning, they are attacked in the streets when they openly show their Jewish identity.[117]

These findings echoed a 2017 online opinion poll conducted by the Institute for Interdisciplinary Research in Conflict and Violence [Institut für interdisziplinäre Konflikt- und Gewaltforschung] at the University of Bielefeld.[118] According to this survey, 70 percent of respondents reported that they intentionally avoid any outward signs of their Jewish identity in public for safety reasons.[119] The study also found that within the last twelve months, 62 percent had experienced an indirect form of anti-Semitism; 29 percent had been the target of direct verbal assault; 3 percent had been the victim of a physical attack; and 85 percent of those asked indicated that they feared that anti-Semitism would increase in Germany.[120]

Startling support for this conjecture came during the recent trial of what is left of the National Socialist Underground (NSU) Trio: Uwe Böhnhardt, Uwe Mundlos, and Beate Zschäpe. After participating in a series of attacks on Jewish residents in 1996, the three made preparations for expanding their homicidal binges to include paramilitary attacks.[121] Between 1998 and 2011, the three Neo-Nazis went on a killing spree which resulted in the murder of at least nine German immigrants (Enver Şimşek; Abdurrahim Özudoğu, Süleyman Taşköprü, Habil Kılıc, Yunus Turgut, İsmail Yaşar, Theodoros Boulgarides, Mehmet Kubaşık, Halit Yozgat). In addition, the trio is credited with having murdered a German policewoman (Michèle Kiesewetter) and severely injuring her partner (Martin A.).[122] Investigation into the NSU's operation has also uncovered evidence that the group perpetrated fifteen armed robberies and two bombings: one of which was detonated in a predominantly Turkish-German quarter of Cologne and resulted in the injury of twenty-two people. In addition to stockpiling a ready arsenal of weapons, a central activity of the trio consisted in compiling the names of organizations and people whom they deemed to be desirable political, religious, and/or social targets. German law enforcement has recovered detailed computerized lists containing the names of 10,116 people and institutions which the NSU contemplated targeting.[123]

In November 2011, Böhnhardt and Mundlos died together in an explosion. It is suspected that the detonation was an act of suicide to avoid capture by the police. The remaining member of the trio, Beate Zschäpe, has been on trial for her suspected active and willing participation in the crimes. In addition to the victims' families' hope that the proceedings would finally shed some much-needed clarity on the events surrounding the group's seven-year-long crime spree, government authorities announced that the trial would provide important information regarding the genesis and operation of the NSU. However, both sets of desires have been deeply disappointed. Worse yet, the case has raised deep concerns that the group might have been aided through the (in)actions of undercover agents working for the German government's central intellgence agency, the **B**undesamt für **V**erfassungsschutz (BfV), Germany's domestic intelligence service. In response to public pressure, on July 12, 2012, the BfV issued an official statement in which it declared that the failure of isolated employees was in no way representative of the work performed by the agency's staff of some 2,700 people.[124] Nevertheless, the NSU case has left a cloud of doubt over the sincerity of some German officials to acknowledge and neutralize the very real threat posed by right-extremist groups. Such criticism was strengthened by the fact that authorities were relatively slow in recognizing and responding to the emergence of other potentially dangerous groups with strong right-extremist ties or tendencies.

Recently, for example, Germany has seen the emergence of a network of residents who categorically reject the legitimacy of the **B**undesrepublik **D**eutschland (BRD) and consider themselves citizens of the German Reich. Such "Reichsbürger," as they call themselves, refute the authority of the German constitution and refuse to adhere to any laws, policies, or regulations established by the German government. From parking tickets to voter registration, they see themselves as separate, unique, and immune. Many even have their own forms of identification papers. One of the reasons for their widespread refusal to carry the standard German ID card is the requirement that the carrier's name be written in upper-case letters. Some particularly suspicious Reichsbürger have construed this regulation as a holdover from Rome where slave names were written in block letters.[125] The fact that all names were written in block letters in Roman antiquity, be they free or slave, seems to have been ignored; as has the simple fact that block lettering is generally far more legible than cursive.

With conspiracy theories like these, it is easy to see why initially, people within this loosely connected network were dismissed as querulous, eccentric, and slightly paranoid, but ultimately harmless. That evaluation has gradually changed, however, as the prevalence and violence of Reichsbürger have radically increased. According to information released by the German federal bureau of investigations, the **B**undeskriminalamt (BKA), Reichsbürger have committed approximately 771 crimes.[126] These offenses include arson, violent assault, threatening grievous bodily harm, disturbing the peace, resisting arrest, attempted murder, and murder.

In October 2017, for example, a fifty-year-old Reichsbürger shot and killed one police officer and severely wounded two others when they approached his home on a routine call. According to the offender's lawyer, when he saw the officers approach his home, he believed the world was literally coming to an end. While it is difficult to assess with a high degree of certainty, the most recent statistics released by the BKA estimates that there are approximately 16,000 people active in this movement. Of this group, some 900 are right extremists. Among the many conspiracy theories popular within this network is the idea that the Holocaust is an elaborate hoax fabricated by Jewish controlled capitalists who seek to keep the German Volk in a perpetual state of socioeconomic servitude.

One of the early expounders of this theory was Manfred Roeder. Roeder is also commonly considered a founding father of the Reichsburger movement. Born the son of an SA Obersturmführer in 1929, from his very earliest days, Roeder was completely immersed in Nazi ideology.[127] After the war, he earned a law degree and briefly joined the Christian Democratic Union (CDU) but soon left in protest over what he felt were the Party's overly liberal policies. Disenfranchised with the political panorama of the postwar period, he ultimately rejected the legal legitimacy of the Federal Republic of Germany and proclaimed that he was a citizen of the German Reich. In the late 1970s, early 1980s, he established his own political party based on the principles of the NSDAP: the "Deutsche Aktionsgruppen" (DA).[128] In 1980, Roeder and other members of the DA were charged with setting several public shelters for asylum-seekers on fire.[129] In the ensuing blaze, two Vietnamese asylum-seekers were killed. Roeder received a thirteen-year sentence but was granted early release for good behavior.[130] Once a free man, he continued his anti-Semitic and anti-foreigner campaign and maintained that the Holocaust was a total fabrication.

Thus, once dismissed as a phenomenon of fringe groups which ultimately posed little real danger to the society, there has been increasing awareness that the basic ideologies of these hate-groups have already leached into organs of governance. In response to a formal query posed by the Left Party, a 2017 governmental report examined the prevalence of right extremism in the German military. The report made mention of several troubling instances in which soldiers illegally greeted comrades with the words "Sieg Heil!" Other instances involved the discovery of soldiers who were clandestine members of right-extremists groups.[131] According to the German military counterintelligence service [Militärische Abschirmdienst], there has been a record increase in the number of disciplinary cases involving right-extremism. Since the 2011 replacement of compulsory military service with a professional volunteer military, there have been 300 such cases. In the year 2017, an additional 400 cases were reported.[132]

There are several potential explanations for these findings. Optimists have attributed them to positive changes in German military. Right-extremist actions are no longer as likely to be tolerated, downplayed, excused, ignored, or even condoned. As a result, such misconduct is simply more often reported than it was before. Pessimists have warned that this increase could also be explained by disturbing demographic shifts towards nationalism and populism. As the military is drawn from the general public, political trends in the general public are being manifested in the attitudes and behavior of military personnel. A realist position would, in my opinion, assert that these two explanations are not mutually exclusive.

Be that as it may, the increase in right-extremist ideology can also be detected in other sectors of the establishment. Evidence of this assertion can be seen in the shifting electoral landscape. The year 2017, for example, marked the first time in a half a century that a far-right political party had won seats in Parliament. Called the "Alternative for Germany" or AfD, this party won more than 13 percent of the popular vote, making it the third largest party in the nation. After the final results of the national election had been announced, party leader Alexander Gauland declared to an ecstatic crowd of AfD supporters: "We will change this country! We will chase them down, Angela Merkel and whoever else, and we will take our country back!"[133] Such provocative statements from representatives of this party are nothing new. Right from the very beginning, AfD leaders have continued to capture the headlines with slogans and policy proposals borrowed from days gone by. In 2015, for example, Björn Höcke, the AfD Party leader in Thuringia, made direct allusion to Hitler's 1933 declaration that the Reich would last a thousand years. "I want Magdeburg and Germany to have a not only a thousand-year past," Höcke crowed with his hair combed conspicuously to the side, "I want them to have a thousand-year future! And I know you all want that as well!"[134]

No sooner had the AfD taken seats in Parliament did they begin to introduce petitions to begin to collect names. In 2017, for example, AfD representative Dr. Matthias Manthei requested that the parliament of Mecklenburg-West Pomerania create a list identifying all those asylum-seekers who had been given refuge in Protestant churches within the parish of Anklam. That list was to include not only such biographical details as age, gender, nationality, ethnicity, ancestry, and religion.[135] It was also to include the full name of each individual. On June 12, 2017, that information was officially provided to the AfD as required by law. However, in the subsequent parliamentary debate that took place on July 13, 2017, the MWP Minister of the Interior, Lorenz Caffier, lambasted the AfD and Representative Manthei:

> In a formal petition for information submitted by the AfD, a request was made for the names of the asylum-seekers who have been given refuge by the church. My dear Mr. Manthei, you were the one who submitted this position. Tell me: What is the meaning of asking for the names? What—in God's name are you trying to achieve with this request? Do you wish to publicly denounce these people? Is it your desire to pass these names on to some shady figures? What are you going to do with the names that we, regrettably, were constitutionally required to give you? Unfortunately, we were compelled by law to list these names. I have to say that I sometimes am taken aback

by the things that data protection officials take issue with but in this case it is different. . . . In all honesty, such requests literally make me shudder. You truly need not be surprised, in fact, you should not be shocked in the least, that the AfD is said to have a particular closeness with the NPD [National Democratic Party of Germany, the political successor of the NSDAP].[136]

During the course of the ensuing debate, representative Manthei refused to disclose why this private information had been requested and what precisely he and his party planned to do with it. Unfortunately, in today's political landscape such incidents are neither isolated nor novel. Already in September of 2015, AfD representative, Corinna Herold, made national headlines with her petition to the parliament of Thuringia for a census of the gays, lesbians, bisexuals, transsexuals, transgender, and inter- and intragender persons living in the state.[137] Similar shock waves were set off by AfD representative Ralph Weber who proposed that all persons who tested positive for HIV should have their names placed on an official government registry.[138] In response to this proposal, Sven Warminsky, the Head of AIDS Foundation of Saxony-Anhalt, retorted that unless the goal is to increase people's reticence to take an HIV test, the utility and necessity of such a name registry were completely beyond his comprehension. "Perhaps Mr. Weber," Warminsky rebutted, "would like to suggest next that people with HIV wear a special identifying marker or would he simply prefer to start right now with the internment camps?!"[139]

On February 14, 2018, AfD representative Wolfgang Gedeon, from Baden-Württemberg, sent an open letter to the Lord Mayor calling for the immediate stop of the Stolpersteine art project in the town of Singen. Developed by German artist Gunter Demnig[140] in 1996, the project involves setting a small brass plaque into the cobblestones of European streets to mark the last known residence of Holocaust victims before they fell into the hands of the Nazis. Each stone contains important information about the victim (e.g., birthdate, date of arrest or deportation, place of internment, death date, and full name). As of April 2017, over 61,000 stones have been lain in over 1,100 locations throughout Europe. In October 2017, the first Stoplersteine was lain outside of Europe, in Buenos Ares.

The project was conceived as an interactive way to commemorate the names and identities of Holocaust victims in a manner that encourages people, as they go about their daily activities, to take a moment to remember the past whenever they stumble upon one of the stones. The stones provide a way to remind people who live in peace and freedom today about all those people who walked these very same streets during the terror of the Third Reich.

According to AfD delegate Dr. Gedeon, however, the commemoration of the victims' names in public spaces foists "an inflationary culture of memorialization" upon the people and "prescribes when, what, and on about whom people should focus their thoughts" in a manner that is reminiscent of a dictatorship.[141] Although such incendiary comparisons have been broadly condemned, the brazenness of this Party's actions is more than unsettling.

What's more, the AfD is not the only right-extremist party with members occupying elected positions in government. In 2014, for example, Dennis Giemsch, a leading member of the Neo-Nazi party "Die Rechte," became a member of the municipal government of Dortmund. While in this position, he also submitted a formal petition on behalf of his party for an official census to be taken of all persons of the Jewish faith living in and around the city of Dortmund.[142] As might be imagined, this request was also met with widespread outrage and disbelief. Once again, the very same groups that had been persecuted by the National Socialists of the past were being purposefully and systematically targeted by the political descendants of the NSDAP.

*****

The tie between Holocaust denial and xenophobia is sadly all too familiar. It is for that reason that, from the very beginning, the USHMM has stressed the importance of viewing the Shoah as a warning for all of humankind. The importance of this admonition is expressed in the USHMM's Strategic Plan (2013–2018):

> The Holocaust is a warning that the unthinkable is possible and that human nature makes all of us susceptible to the abuse of power, a belief in the inferiority of "the other," and the ability to justify any behavior—including inaction. Its significance is not only that it happened, but that it occurred in one of the most educated, advanced regions of the world and was led by a nation—albeit a struggling one—with a democratic constitution, a rule of law, and freedom of expression.[143]

One of the most powerful means of honoring the memory of the millions of lives that were destroyed during the Holocaust is to help prevent such atrocities from ever being repeated. It is this idea that underlies the international call to action "Never Again!" Tragically, during a 2014 visit to the USHMM, Canon White, the chaplain of the only Anglican church in Iraq and the innovator of the Foundation for Relief and Reconciliation in the Middle East, declared during an impassioned invited speech at the Museum: "What we dreamt would never happen again IS happening again." In Iraq, Bangladesh, Burma, Zimbabwe, Cambodia, the Sudan, the Democratic Republic of the Congo, the Central African

Republic, South Sudan, and Syria. Across all seven continents, there are horrific atrocities being committed. In recognition of the moral mandate to help prevent the killings and protect the innocent, from the very start the USHMM had always invested heavily in a wide variety of anti-genocide projects—"from memory to action." The importance of supporting genocide research for families affected by the Shoah was addressed by Cynthia Simon Skjodt:

> My parents were teenagers during the Holocaust, and while they were born in the United States, they were deeply impacted by what was happening in Europe. The questions of how and why—how human beings could commit such crimes and why so many others were complacent—lingered throughout their lives.[144]

In hopes of finding answers to these questions and applying that knowledge to help prevent acts of genocide in the future, Cynthia Simon Skjodt and Paul Skjodt provided a 20-million-dollar endowment for the establishment of "The Simon-Skjodt Center for the Prevention of Genocide." The research conducted at this center will no doubt make a substantive contribution to the international study of the phenomenon of large-scale atrocity.

The importance of such research cannot be overstated. Contrary to popular opinion, there is nothing mystical or predestined about genocide. Precisely this point is made by Holocaust researcher and award-winning author, Dr. Daniel Goldhagen. Himself the son of a Shoah survivor, Goldhagen states that, at the end of the day, it simply "boils down to a series of choices. Leaders choose to initiate the killing. Ordinary people make a conscious choice to participate and those with the power to prevent or stop it choose to do nothing."[145] According to him, the key to stopping the killing lies in the early identification of and decisive action against the various means genocidal human agents use to target and attack the people they have defined as undesirable.[146] Two of the most powerful tools for facilitating genocidal acts are names and naming practices. Ample evidence for this assertion is found in both the history of the Holocaust as well as in other modern-day genocides.

*****

In a multicultural society where groups have discernibly different onomastic practices, names can be used to identify and select intended genocide victims. This is precisely what happened when violence erupted in the multiethnic society of Bosnia. In 1991, the Bosnian population was made of three large groups: (1) Muslim Bosniaks (44 percent), (2) Orthodox Serbs (31 percent), and (3) Catholic Croats (17 percent). Before the war, these groups lived in relative peace over many centuries. All that changed when nationalist forces began a systematic program of genocide. Armed militia began picking out their victims by name. A heart-wrenching example of this onomastic segregation which made international news occurred in 1992. As the number of killings saw a dramatic increase, a multinational team of politicians, relief workers, and social activists helped broker a deal to evacuate children from a local orphanage in Ljubica, to Germany.[147]

Initially, the idea was completely against the better judgment of the orphanage director, Vera Zoric. However, in view of the rapidly deteriorating situation, Zoric made the agonizing decision to allow a small group of children all under the age of four to make the perilous journey. After securing agreement from all of the necessary government officials, a temporary cease-fire was reached, just long enough to give the children safe passage. Close to fifty children, many of whom were too small to sit on their own, were strapped into their seats and the bus began the journey to what everyone hoped would be safety.[148] Approximately four kilometers along the journey, as the bus entered an area locals called "Sniper's Alley," automatic gun fire suddenly erupted. Two children were fatally wounded: *Roki Sulefmanovic* and *Vedrana Glavas*.[149]

The bus was brought to a halt. Serbian guerillas entered the vehicle and read through the transport roster of children's names. Nine of the children were identified as having what the gunmen felt were Serbian names. These children were unstrapped from their seats and taken from the bus. The rest of the children were allowed to travel on, until the bus was stopped once again—allegedly to give the children medical attention. After much behind the scenes negotiating, the orphanage director was finally able to locate the hospital where the children had been taken and reach the doctor who had assumed responsibility for their care. Much to Director Zoric's outrage, the children had been "ethnically culled" again.[150] When she asked how on earth the medical staff presumed to be able to determine which child was Serbian, the doctor-in-charge retorted: "By the names, of course!" In an interview conducted afterwards, the Director summed up her reaction: "Trying to divide up children like this is simply wicked."[151] A total of thirty-eight children survived that harrowing four-day trip to Germany. Upon their arrival, five of them had to be rushed to the hospital to treat them for exhaustion, dehydration, and pneumonia.[152]

Throughout the war, as Serbian forces continued their efforts to "cleanse" the area of Bosniak and Croatian residents, Director Zoric and her staff continued their efforts to bring the rest of their tiny wards to safety. In 1991, award-winning British journalist, Michael Nicholson, traveled with a camera team to the Ljubica Ivezic orphanage.[153] At the time, some 2,000 children were still being housed there.[154] While conducting interviews with the staff and underage residents, a ten-year-old little girl, *Jelena Natasha Mihalijicic*, wandered up to the

British reporter and asked where he was from and what he was doing. When the interpreter explained that the man came from a place called "England," Jelena cheerfully replied that she would like to visit there one day. Nicholson was immediately struck by Jelena and was devastated when he learnt that her name was not among those listed for the next rescue attempt, this time organized by a French relief agency. It was then that Nicholson made a life-changing decision.

After securing Director Zoric's permission, he decided to bring Jelena to safety himself. As the camera team left the orphanage and boarded the bus back to Croatia, Nicholson was there, with Jelena at his side. By the time he arrived at the airport, Jelena was still with him. In hopes of getting her onto his flight to England, he added an alias to his passport: *Natasha Nicholson*.[155] When questioned, he told the passport check authorities that the little girl was his daughter and that it was customary in England to simply write-in the names of children on UK passports.[156] The authorities believed him and a few hours later, he and Jelena landed in Great Britain. Nicholson and his wife later officially adopted Jelena as their own. In 1992, the journalist published a book chronicling the entire experience called *Natasha's Story: How a Nine-Year-Old Orphan was Rescued from War in Sarajevo*. That story later became the basis for the award-winning film "Welcome to Sarajevo."

Around the time that the film was being released in US theaters, news of more mass killings began to hit the international media. The site was Kosovo. From June to October 1999, a human rights fact-finding mission was conducted by the Organization for Security and Co-operation in Europe (OSCE). In a final report, detailed statements from eye-witnesses testified about the sickening panorama of atrocities committed against people known or believed to be Kosovo Albanian by Yugoslav and Serbian forces, assisted by paramilitary units, local police, and willing civilians.[157] In many of these testimonies, survivors detailed how perpetrators used personal names to identify their victims for "special treatment."

In a case that reportedly took place in April of 1999, a survivor related how four policemen interrogated a Kosovo Albanian family who, despite having been ordered to vacate the area, were still living in their home. The family members explained that they had tried to leave the area but had been stopped at the border and forced to go back. Upon checking the residents' identification papers, one of the officers discovered that the fifteen-year-old girl, whom they had originally assumed was a member of the family, had a different surname than the others. According to the witness, the officers then ordered the frightened teenager to leave the house with them. She was taken to a nearby abandoned house where all four officers proceeded to gang rape her.[158]

In this case, the perpetrators' use of personal names to select their victims seems to have been somewhat haphazard. In other cases, the use of names was organized in advance. For example, during the widespread deportation of the civilian population, survivors reported that it was common for militia forces to use name lists of villagers to identify Kosovo Albanians who were made to pay special taxes. A survivor from the town of Letance, Podujevo gave the follow description:

> When we arrived in Podujeve we were immediately surrounded by VJ [the Armed Forces of Yugoslavia], police, paramilitaries and local Serbs from the town. They opened a list with the names of [Kosovo] Albanians. When they came to our surname they immediately said they knew that my seventy-five-year-old uncle had money and they gave him twenty minutes to find DM 30,000. They ordered one member of my family to collect the gold from the women. My uncle told them he did not have it, he only had DM 12,000. They took this money and proceeded to beat him severely with rifle butts. They brought two trucks, looted the home, and took one Mercedes truck and three cars. The process was repeated in other houses.[159]

Along with cases of extortion, name lists were also used by the perpetrators to identify individuals for execution. Numerous survivors, for example, told OSCE officials that members of the police had assisted the Serbian paramilitary forces in locating "intellectuals" whose names had been placed on lists for immediate elimination.[160] On April 13, 1999, one survivor testified that he personally observed four members of a paramilitary unit enter a school in the town of Gllogofc or Pristina with just such an execution list. Upon locating two male Kosovo Albanian teachers whose names were included on their list, the soldiers escorted the men out of the building. In the words of the eye-witness, the teachers "were killed metres away from the school. I heard the shots and saw the bodies later."[161] It was also during this time that so-called military "cleansing units" reportedly traveled from village to village in search of anyone whose surname happened to be identical to the leaders of the Kosovo Liberation Army or Ushtria Çlirimtare e Kosovës (UCK). Persons with these last names were summarily eliminated, whether they were confirmed members of the UCK or not.[162]

Some ten thousand kilometers away and a few years earlier, on the African continent, name lists had also been used in another genocide. Even now, almost a quarter of a century later, the name of that country still conjures up images of that mass depravity: Rwanda. Within the space of approximately 100 days in 1994, between 150,000 and 250,000 women were raped and between 800,000 and 1 million people were slaughtered by strangers, acquaintances, co-workers, neighbors, friends, and family members. The targets of the butchery were primarily people known or believed to be members of the Tutsi community, who made up about 14 percent of the country's population before the killings began. As in so many other cases of genocide, one of the primary methods of victim selection utilized by the perpetrators was name lists.[163] Listeners to the hate-radio station RTLM, "Radio Television Libre des Mille Collines" [Free Radio and Television of the Thousand Hills], for example, were fed daily messages of anti-Tutsi propaganda.[164] The predaceous programs also regularly announced the full names of people described as being sub-human "cockroaches" who must be eliminated.

A lethal example came on May 28, 1994, when a broadcaster told listeners about a man named *Aloys* who had been hiding from armed Hutu extremists. After announcing Aloys's full name, occupation, and last known location, the broadcaster warned listeners that the fugitive, who "is afraid of being killed," may well identity himself as a Hutu and produce an ID card with that ethnic designation. According to the radio announcer, his Hutu audience members were not to allow themselves to be deceived by this man for "his mother is a Tutsi." The announcer then went on to issue the following threat:

> If you are a cockroach you must be killed, you cannot change anything. . . . No one can say that he has captured a cockroach and the latter gave him money, as a price for his life, this cannot be accepted. If someone has a false identity card . . . don't accept anything in exchange, he must be killed.[165]

Thanks to reports such as these, RTLM, or "Radio Machete," as it came to be known in Rwanda, helped the marauding death squads select and locate their victims by broadcasting the full names, addresses, license plate numbers, and suspected hiding places of Tutsis on their daily most-wanted lists.[166] According to one person who was targeted for attack, soon the killers were not the only ones who became avid RTLM listeners. The potential victims also tuned-in because, as the survivor explained, "We wanted to know if we were on the list of people selected to be hunted."[167]One witness of a neighborhood massacre described in detail how these name lists had been used by the paramilitary he'd witnessed on the morning of April 7, 1994:

> I saw nine soldiers of the paracommando battalion . . . and a civilian who was apparently guiding them. He held a list of names in his hand. It was a list of people to be killed. They went to another neighbor and threw grenades and shot open the door of the house. They killed the people inside. They left on foot.[168]

According to the survivor, after leaving his neighborhood, that same battalion moved on to another neighborhood and attacked another four families, presumably also on the same name list the soldiers had been handed that morning.[169]

One of the most popular and incendiary guests on RTLM was Hassan Ngeze. Ngeze was the owner and editor-in-chief of the Hutu extremist French-Kinyarwanda newspaper, *Kangura*. *Kangura*, which means essentially "Wake Up!," also regularly featured name lists of so-called traitors for its primarily Hutu readership. For example, in February 1993, issue number 40 of the propagandist newspaper published the names of 123 individuals.[170] In the provocative article accompanying the list, readers were warned to take pre-emptive action against these "people who are going to use the gun to exterminate you . . . organize your self-defense, as the security services seem to have lost their nerve."[171] The infamous 1993 list included the names of entire families, children as well as adults.

After the bloodshed subsided, the International Criminal Tribunal for Rwanda opened criminal proceedings to investigate the role of the media in inciting crimes against humanity and acts of genocide. According to witnesses and documentary evidence presented during the trial, people whose names had appeared in the *Kangura* lists were routinely murdered. The same was true of the people named in the RTLM broadcasts. After reviewing the case, the Court ruled that Jean-Bosco Barayagwiza, Ferdinand Nahimana, and Hassan Ngeze had all egregiously abused their position and power in the public media in a conspiracy to commit genocide and perpetrate crimes against humanity. As part of its reasoning for the final judgment, the Court cited the many parallels between the three Rwandan media moguls and the Nazi publisher Julius Streicher, whose hate-mongering publication, "Der Stürmer," also regularly featured the names of enemies of the Reich. At the end of World War II, Streicher was "convicted of crimes against humanity for his incitement to murder" by the International Military Tribunal in Nuremberg.[172] On November 28, 2007, the three Rwandan media titans were also found guilty and were given prison sentences of between thirty and thirty-five years.[173]

*

In the 1971, US psychologist Dr. Philip Zimbardo conducted what would become known as the "Standford Prison Experiment." During this innovative and highly controversial social psychological research project, a group of college students with no known history of psychological disorder were randomly assigned to play the role of either a guard or prisoner in a mock jail. Zimbardo was forced to prematurely terminate the elaborate experiment for ethical and safety reasons. Within a just few days' time, the research participants had begun to engage in unexpected acts of shocking psychological and physical abuse.[174]

According to Zimbardo, one of the most essential insights to be gained from this study was how important language is for first denying and then violating human rights. Language can be used to create extraordinary works of literature that elevate and enrich the soul. At the same time, Zimbardo warns, "that very same creativity can be perverted into inventing torture chambers and torture tactics, into paranoid ideologies."[175] And, more often than not, names and naming play an essential role in realizing both of those creative potentials. To a certain extent, one need not have locked up a group of college students in a mock prison to recognize that fact.

As history has shown time and time again, the perpetrators of atrocity and genocide frequently use personal names to mark, identify, and select their victims during the slaughter. Then by suppressing, erasing, or ignoring the names of their victims, the offenders are able to disguise, diminish, and/or deny their crimes. It is important to stress that the discussion of the Holocaust alongside these other genocidal events is not meant to invite comparisons according to size, magnitude, importance, impact, perversion, or pain. In my opinion, such comparisons are wholly inappropriate, injurious, and not infrequently grotesque. Instead, my purpose in introducing other large-scale atrocities is quite different. Although all acts of genocide have unique characteristics, they also share certain similarities. By the same token, the specific manner and extent to which personal names may be used in genocidal acts may differ. However, the systemic, deliberate, and organized use of names and naming policies as a tool of mass destruction is commonplace.

During the Third Reich, from the very beginning, the Nazis systematically used personal names to implement their program of genocide. Well before they began to distribute the name lists to killing agents (e.g., soldiers, nurses, doctors, prison guards, midwives, police officers), they had already taken many other crucial steps. They had begun to continuously compile and refine name lists of individuals and groups whom they had designated as inherently and incorrigibly threatening, unwanted, alien, and subhuman. They had implemented obligatory comprehensive naming policies which marked the names of those targeted individuals and groups. These policies were presented to the public as a necessary and safe means for identifying, registering, and monitoring dangerous elements of the society. In reality, however, they were used for pinpointing, isolating, deporting, and ultimately annihilating millions of people in a carefully orchestrated campaign of terror. At the same time, onomastic markers were also used to designate the chosen few who were given privileged access to sociocultural and economic power and privilege. This differential treatment is important as it helped to buy the silence, complicity, acceptance, and/or loyalty of non-targeted segments of the society. To further promote feelings of unity among the power-elite, the Nazis also championed preexisting naming traditions or practices that eased the determination of probable group membership.

The effects of these top-down policies upon the general public are also of great importance. As the power of the Party spread, there was a palpable increase in the inflationary increase in the prominence and popularity of the names associated with Party leaders, organizations, or events. Supporters of the National Socialist ideology and policies adorned themselves and their perceptual world with names designed to demonstrate their support and allegiance to the Party. At the same time, potential targets of the Nazis were strictly prohibited from using these now deified monikers.

Once these steps of onomastic apartheid had been taken, it was relatively easy to move on to the next: re-labeling and thereby re-classifying the already marginalized with names that denied, revoked, diminished, or negated their status as fellow human beings. This re-labeling process involved assigning victims names that are normally reserved for non-humans (e.g., the names of animals, insects, diseases, environmental disasters). At the pinnacle of this onomastic dehumanization came the complete prohibition against referring to marginalized people with any human names. Instead, identification was only to be achieved through the compulsory use of labeling systems such as (alpha-)numerical codes and graphic symbols typically reserved to brand inanimate objects or species designated as non-sentient and fit only for exploitation, consumption, or termination.

Long after the active genocide ended, vestiges could still be detected, for example, in the official rejection of survivors' attempts to regain control over their names; in the clandestine retention of pejorative onomastic tags in government files; in the refusal to provide the names of the perpetrators; and with the erasure of the names of their victims. Added to this list is the staunch rejection of legal names broadly accepted by the international community as appropriate labels for genocidal acts in favor of euphemistic onomastic creations that diminish, negate, or even promote atrocities. At the same time, one can see the gradual resurrection of names strongly associated with past genocidal acts and actors to show allegiance to and agreement with that history.

Importantly, many of these same onomastic trends can be found around the globe. That ubiquity does not however negate the importance of these onomastic signs, rather it speaks to the point made earlier. Genocide is an international phenomenon that can occur anytime, anywhere. That does not mean to say that genocide is inevitable. Murder is not inevitable. Rape is not inevitable. Forced starvation is not inevitable. Sterilization is not inevitable. Kidnapping is not inevitable. Hatred, ignorance, and cruelty are not inevitable. There are certain factors that will tend to inhibit these violent acts, just as there are factors that will tend to promote them. The keys to prevention are vigilance and action. By monitoring the ways in which names and naming policies are being used within our communities, it may just be possible to intervene before the killing begins—again.

Notes

1. Julien Reitzenstein, "Abteilung H-Anatomie und Menschenversuche," *Himmlers Forscher: Wehrwissenschaft und Medizinverbrechen im "Ahnenerbe" der SS* (Paderborn: Ferdinand Schönigh, 2014), 105–68.

2. Reitzenseiten, "Abteilung H-Anatomie," 105–6.

3. Barry Master, "The Development of Fluorescence Microscopy," *The Encyclopedia of Life Sciences* (Chichester: John Wiley & Sons, 2010).

4. Benno Müller-Hill, "Human Genetics and the Mass Murder of Jews, Gypsies, and Others," *The Holocaust and History: The Known, the Unknown, the Disputed and the Reexamined,* eds. Michael Berenbaum and Abraham J. Peck (Indianapolis: Indiana University Press, 1998), 103–14.

5. In the 1930s, the Turkish Republic became a popular destination for scholars of Jewish descent. Kemal Atatürk welcomed these outstanding professionals from the West to bolster his modernization efforts. The majority of these Jewish refugees were given professorships at the Universities of Istanbul and Ankara as well as leading positions in the nation's growing number of research institutes. For more, see Stanford J. Shaw, *Turkey and the Holocaust: Turkey's Role in Rescuing Turkish and European Jewry from Nazi Persecution, 1933–1945* (New York: Palgrave Macmillan, 1993).

6. In the spring of 1933, Ellinger took on a position at the Lister Institute for Preventative Medicine in London. Reitzenstein, "Abteilung H-Anatomie," 353.

7. Angelika Uhlmann and Andreas Winkelman, "The Science Prior to the Crime: August Hirt before 1941," *Annals of Anatomy* 204 (2016): 118–26.

8. Nuremberg Medical Trials 1: Medical Case. Letter from SS Hauptsturmführer Professor Hirt to SS Officer and Law Professor Rudolf Brandt regarding the procurement of Jewish skulls for the Strasbourg Reich University (p. 697) Nuremberg Trials Project. Harvard Law School, http://nuremberg.law.harvard.edu/documents.

9. Hans-Joachim Lang, *Die Namen der Nummern: Wie es gelang, die 86 Opfer eines NS-Verbrechens zu identifizieren* (Hamburg: Fischer Taschenbuchverlag, 2004), 107.

10. Sabine Hildebrandt, *The Anatomy of Murder: Ethical Transgressions and Anatomical Science During the Third Reich* (New York: Berghan: 2016), 136.

11. Aly, "Ein Arbeitsunfall: Rassenkunde, Nebenerwerb und Versicherungsrecht," *Rasse und Klasse: Nachforschungen zum deutschen Wesen* (Frankfurt am Main: S. Fischer, 2003), 145–54.

12. Aly, "Ein Arbeitsunfall," 150.

13. Klee, *Deutsche Medizin im Dritten Reich* (Frankfurt am Main: S. Fischer Verlag, 2001) 139.

14. Hildebrandt, *The Anatomy of Murder*, 136.

15. Aly, "Ein Arbeitsunfall," 152.

16. Götz Aly, "Der anthropologische Ehrgeiz des Oberpräparators Gustav von Hirschheydt und dessen tödliche Begegnung mit einem toten Juden: Ein Arbeitsunfall," *Berliner Zeitung*, March 2, 2015, https://www.berliner-zeitung.de/der-anthropologische-ehrgeiz-des-oberpraeparators-gustav-von-hirschheydt-und-dessen-toedliche-begegnung -mit-einem-toten-juden-ein-arbeitsunfall-16699166.

17. Aly, "Ein Arbeitsunfall," 154.

18. Hildebrandt, *The Anatomy of Murder*, 137.

19. Hildebrandt, *The Anatomy of Murder*, 138.

20. Hartmut Lehman and Otto Gerhard Oexle, eds. *Nationalsozialismus in den Kulturwissenschaften* (Göttingen: Vandenhoeck & Ruprecht, 2004).

21. Paul Weindling, *Victims and Survivors of Nazi Human Experiments: Science and Suffering in the Holocaust* (London: Bloomsbury, 2014), 156.

22. Lang, *Die Namen der Nummern*, 161.

23. Lang, *Die Namen der Nummern*, 228.

24. Lang, *Die Namen der Nummern*, 173.

25. His name sometimes appears with the alternative spelling *Henry Henrypierre*.

26. Nuremberg Medical Trials 1: Medical Case. *Testimony of Henri Henripierre*, 710.

27. Strasbourg was one of several cities with a university opened by the Reich's Ministry for Science, Education, and Culture [Reichserziehungsministerium] or REM. Other cities include Posen, Prague, and Dorpat. Specifically regulated by the ideology and principles of the Führer, these Aryan institutions were dedicated to perpetuating the scientific theories and martial practices of the NSDAP.

28. Raphaël Toledano, "August Hirt and the Supply of Corpses at the Anatomical Institute of the Reichsuniversität Straßburg," *From Clinic to Concentration Camp: Reassessing Nazi Medical and Racial Research, 1933–1945*, ed. Paul Weindling (New York: Routledge, 2017), 102.

29. Toledano, "August Hirt," 104.

30. For more on this issue, see: Gretchen Schafft, *From Racism to Genocide: Anthropology in the Third Reich* (Chicago: University of Illinois, 2004).

31. Toledano, "August Hirt," 104.

32. Hildebrandt, *The Anatomy of Murder*, 355–56.

33. Nuremberg Medical Trials 1: Medical Case. *Testimony of Henri Henripierre*, 715.

34. Vivien Spitz, "Jewish Skeleton Collection," *Doctors from Hell: The Horrific Account of Nazi Experiments on Humans* (Boulder, CO: Sentient Publications, 2005), 233, 231–33.

35. Reitzenstein, "Abteilung H," 165.

36. Bärbel Nückles, "Mediziner spurt die Sammlung des Nazi-Arztes August Hirt auf," *Badische Zeitung*, July 24, 2015. www.badische-zeitung.de.

37. Nückles, "Mediziner spurt die Sammlung," para. 6.

38. In my interview with Professor Lang, he indicated that one of the greatest challenges of this research was attempting to gain access to the original note written by Henrypierre. According to him, the document is a French military archive and has been restricted from all public view for a period of 100 years. During his research, Professor Lang tried repeatedly to gain special permission to view the document. However, even with the assistance of the German Minister of Justice, Herta Däublie-Gmelin, and the

world-famous Holocaust researcher/activist, Serge Klarsfeld, the French authorities refused to allow an exception. Hans-Joachim Lang, interview with author, February 2018.

39. Lang, *Die Namen der Nummern*, 271–301.

40. Yad Vashem, The Central Database of Shoah Victims' Names.

41. Yad Vashem, The Central Database of Shoah Victims' Names.

42. Lang, *Die Namen der Nummern*, 264.

43. Nückles, "Mediziner spurt die Sammlung," para. 11.

44. The repeated refusal to allow Dr. Toledano access to the archives of the Institute stands in sharp opposition to one of the main resolutions of the 2012 Resolution passed by the German Medical Association [Deutsche Äztekammer]. This resolution stated that the Association would actively work to ensure unlimited access to archives for the purposes of shedding light upon crimes committed in the name of medical science during the Third Reich, http://www.bundesaerztekammer.de/aerztetag/aerztetage-ab-200 6/115-deutscher-aerztetag-2012/beschlussprotokoll/top-i-gesundheits-sozial-und-aerztl iche-berufspolitik/nuernberger-erklaerung/.

45. Michel Cymè, *Hippokrates in der Hölle: Die Verbrechen der KZ-Ärzte* (Trier: Thiess Verlag, 2016).

46. Yvonne Schymura, "Morden im Namen der Wissenschaft," *Der Spiegel*, March 9, 2016, http://www.spiegel.de/einestages/ns-aerzte-experimente-an-kz-_nsassen-a-108 0450.html.

47. Schymura, "Morden," para. 15.

48. Reinhard Reck, "Der Professor Hirt und seine Todestransporte," *Mittelbadische Presse*, June 14, 2016, https://www.bo.de/nachrichten/nachrichten-regional/der-profe ssor-hirt-und-seine-todestransporte.

49. Lindsey Bever, "Remains of Holocaust Experiment Victims Found at French Forensic Institute," *Washington Post*, July 22, 2015, https://www.washingtonpost.com /news/morning-mix/wp/2015/07/22/remains-of-holocaust-victims-used-as-guinea-pigs -found-at-french-forensic-institute/?utm_term=.ed518421f9e2.

50. *Haaretz*, "French Lab Discovers Remains of Jews Experimented on by Nazi Anatomist," https://www.haaretz.com/jewish/french-lab-discovers-remains-of-jews-ex perimented-on-by-nazi-anatomist-1.5376988.

51. Toledano, "August Hirt," 109.

52. The influential mentor was Professor Theodor Mollison. An anthropologist with a medical degree and a license to practice, Mollison's academic interests were unusually diverse for that period, as reflected in the specializations of his students. While Fleischhacker's early work centered in investigating the genetic influence of eye colour and the structure of handprints among people of Jewish and Polish ancestry; another of Mollison's graduates conducted countless experiments on prisoners in Auschwitz to investigate blood proteins. His name was Joseph Mengele. Klee, *Deutsche Medizin im Dritten Reich*, 164.

53. Weindling, *Victims and Survivors of Nazi Human Experiments*, 155.

54. Bernd Grün, "Sophie Ehrhardt (1902–1990)," *100 Jahre Frauenstudium an der Universität Tübingen 1904–2004: Historische Überblick, Zeitzeuginnenberichte und Zeitdokumente* (Tübingen: University of Tübingen, 2007), 398, https://publikationen.uni -tuebingen.de/xmlui/handle/10900/44021.

55. Annegret Ehmann, "From Colonial Racism to Nazi Population Policy: The Role of so-called 'Mischlinge,'" *The Holocaust and History: The Known, the Unknown, the Disputed, and the Reexamined*, eds. Michael Berenbaum and Abraham Peck (Bloomington: Indiana University Press, 2002), 115–33.

56. Klee, *Deutsche Medizin im Dritten Reich*, 193.

57. Sybil Milton, "Holocaust: Gypsies," *Century of Genocide: Critical Essays and Eyewitness Accounts*, eds. Samuel Totten, William Parsons, and Israel Charny (New York: Routledge, 2004), 133–70.

58. Grün, "Sophie Ehrhardt," 400.

59. Grün, "Sophie Ehrhardt," 399–400.

60. Weindling, *Victims and Survivors of Nazi Human Experiments*, 265.

61. Grün, "Sophie Ehrhardt," 400.

62. In the spring of 1945, Fleischhacker was placed under arrest and sent to an internment camp, where he stayed for three years. During the same period of time, Ehrhardt's immediate supervisor at the University of Tübingen, Professor Wilhelm Gieseler, was also taken into custody. During Gieseler's absence, Ehrhardt ipso facto assumed his supervisory position. Grün, "Sophie Ehrhardt," 403.

63. Grün, "Sophie Ehrhardt," 396.

64. Melanie Stelly and Corinna Schneider, "Mit beschränkter Aufenthaltsberechtigung Frauen an der Universität Tübingen in der Nachkriegszeit," *100 Jahre Frauenstudium an der Universität Tübingen 1904–2004: Historische Überblick, Zeitzeuginnenberichte und Zeitdokumente* (Tübingen: University of Tübingen, 2007), 74.

65. Volker Harms, Gottfried Korff, and Anette Michels, eds., *Achtunddreissig Dinge: Schätze aus den Natur- und Kulturwissenschaftlichen Sammlungen der Universität Tübingen* (Tübingen: Museum der Universität Tübingen, 2006).

66. Klee, *Deutsche Medizin im Dritten Reich*, 193.

67. Günter Levy, *The Nazi Persecution of the Gypsies* (Oxford: Oxford University Press, 2000), 215.

68. *Die Zeit*, "Nichts gewußt: Wie kam die 'Zigeneurkartei' nach Tübingen?" September 11, 1981, http://www.zeit.de/1981/38/nichts-gewusst.

69. Grün, "Sophie Ehrhardt," 404.

70. https://portal.wissenschaftliche-sammlungen.de/SciCollection/6232.

71. Edgar Bierende, "Kriegsgefangene, Zwangsarbeiter und KZ-Häftlinge in den anatomischen Leichenbüchern," in *Forschung Lehre Unrecht: Die Universität Tübingen in Nationalsozialismus*, ed. Ernst Seidl (Tübingen: Museum Universität Tübingen, 2015), 223–27.

72. Bierende, "Kriegsgefangene, Zwangsarbeiter und KZ-Häftlinge," 223.

73. Bierende, "Kriegsgefangene, Zwangsarbeiter und KZ-Häftlinge," 223.

74. Bierende, "Kriegsgefangene, Zwangsarbeiter und KZ-Häftlinge," 223.

75. Hans-Joachim Lang, email interview with author, February 1, 2018.

76. Andreas Mix, "Akten von Millionen NS-Opfern in Bad Arolsen werden Forschern geöffnet," *Berliner Zeitung*, November 11, 2008, https://www.berliner-zeitung.de/akten-von-millionen-ns-opfern-in-bad-arolsen-werden-forschern-geoeffnet-druck-aus-washington-15777118.

77. The International Tracing Service (ITS). "Fact Sheet," *ITS*, June 2017, https://www.its-arolsen.org/fileadmin/user_upload/Metanavigation/Presse/Englisch/ITS_Fact_Sheet.pdf.

78. Jennifer Rodgers, "'Humanity's Ancestral Inheritance': The International Tracing Service, 1942–2008," *ITS*, https://www.its-arolsen.org/fileadmin/user_upload/images/Ueber_ITS/content/Englisch/Humanity_s_Ancestral_Inheritance_Rodgers.pdf.

79. Mix, "Akten von Millionen NS-Opfern," n.p.

80. US Congress, "Prepared Statement of the Honorable Alcee Hastings, Chairman, Commission on Security and Cooperation in Europe, US House of Representatives." Opening Up of the Bad Arolsen Holocaust Archives in Germany. Hearing Before the Subcommittee on Europe of the Committee on Foreign Affairs House of Representatives. 110 Cong., 1st sess., March 28, 2007. Serial No. 110–31.

81. US Congress, "Prepared Statement of the Honorable Elton Gallegly, a Representative in Congress from the State of California." Commission on Security and Cooperation in Europe, US House of Representatives." Opening Up of the Bad Arolsen Holocaust Archives in Germany. Hearing Before the Subcommittee on Europe of the Committee on Foreign Affairs House of Representatives. 110 Cong., 1st sess., March 28, 2007. Serial No. 110–31.

82. Sven Kellerhoff, "Arolsen liegt bald in elf Staaten," *Die Welt*, https://www.welt.de/print-welt/article211499/Arolsen-liegt-bald-in-elf-Staaten.html.

83. *Deutsche Welle,* "Germany to Allow Opening of Huge Holocaust Archive," April 19, 2006, http://www.dw.com/en/germany-to-allow-opening-of-huge-holocaust-archive/a-1973870.

84. ITS, "Fact Sheet," *ITS*, June 2017, https://www.its-arolsen.org/fileadmin/user_upload/Metanavigation/Presse/Englisch/ITS_Fact_Sheet.pdf.

85. Deutsche Welle, "Germany to Allow Opening of Huge Holocaust Archive," April 19, 2006, http://www.dw.com/en/germany-to-allow-opening-of-huge-holocaust-archive/a-1973870.

86. Mooli Brog, "In Blessed Memory of a Dream: Mordechai Shenhavi and Initial Holocaust Commemoration Ideas in Palestine, 1942–1945," SHOAH Resource Center, The International School for Holocaust Studies, Yad Vashem, http://www.yadvashem.org/odot_pdf/Microsoft percent20Word percent20- percent205423.pdf.

87. Brog, "In Blessed Memory of a Dream," 22.

88. Brog, "In Blessed Memory of a Dream," 25.

89. Dr. Alexander Avram, interview with author, January 21, 2018.

90. Yad Vashem, "The President's Commission on the Holocaust," https://www.ushmm.org/information/about-the-museum/presidents-commission.

91. United States Holocaust Memorial Museum (USHMM), "Frequently Asked Questions," https://www.ushmm.org/collections/ask-a-research-question/frequently-asked-questions#2.

92. USHMM, "Facts and Figures," https://www.ushmm.org/information/press/press-kits/united-states-holocaust-memorial-museum-press-kit/.

93. Sara-Joelle Clark of the USHMM, interview with author, February 8, 2018.

94. Clark 2018.

95. Author interview with Sarah Kopelman-Noyes of the USHMM, February 8, 2018.

96. USHMM, "The World Memory Project," https://www.ushmm.org/online/world-memory-project/.

97. Simone Kaiser, "Den charmanten Sadisten entlarven," *Frankfurter Allgemeine*, March 25, 2005, http://www.faz.net/aktuell/gesellschaft/menschen/ns-verbrechen-den-charmanten-sadisten-entlarven-1214328.html.

98. Kaiser, "Den charmanten Sadisten entlarven," 4.

99. Jennifer Teege and Nikola Sellmair, *Mein Vater Hätte Mich Erschossen* (Hamburg: Rowohlt, 2013).

100. For more, see Katrin Himmler, *Die Bruder Himmler: Eine deutsche Familiengeschichte* (Frankfurt am Main: Fischer Verlag, 2005).

101. Katrin Himmler, interview with author, March 7, 2017.

102. Markus Werner, "Einer mußte es tun: Katrin Himmler, Großnichte des SS-Führers, gräbt in der Familiengeschichte," *Frankfurter Allgemeine*, Nr. 42 (October 23, 2003), para. 5. https://www.katrinhimmler.de/wp-content/uploads/2013/07/FAS_Okt05.pdf.

103. Werner, "Einer mußte es tun," para. 7.

104. Himmler, interview 2017.

105. Ernst Klee, *Personen Lexikon zum dritten Reich: Wer war was vor und nach 1945* (Hamburg: Nikol Verlag, 2016), 160.

106. William L. Shirer, *The Rise and Fall of the Third Reich: A History of Nazi Germany* (New York: Simon & Schuster, 2011), 139.

107. Shirer, *The Rise and Fall of the Third Reich*, 140.

108. Michael Sontheimer, "When We Finish, Nobody Is Left Alive," *Spiegel*, May 27, 2011, http://www.spiegel.de/international/europe/germany-s-wwii-occupation-of-pol and-when-we-finish-nobody-is-left-alive-a-759095.html.

109. Niklas Frank, interview with author, February 15, 2018.

110. Frank, interview 2018.

111. Niklas Frank, *Der Vater: Eine Abrechnung* (Erben: Eigenverlag Brigitte Frank unsel, 2014), 295.

112. Bundeszentrale für politische Bildung, "Bundesverfassungsgericht lehnt NPD-Verbot ab," January 1, 2017, http://www.bpb.de/politik/hintergrund-aktuell/222103/npd-verbotsverfahren.

113. Bundesministerium des Innern, *Antisemitismus in Deutschland: Aaktuelle Entwicklungen*, https://www.bmi.bund.de/SharedDocs/downloads/DE/publikationen/201 7/expertenbericht-antisemitismus-in-deutschland.pdf?__blob=publicationFile.

114. Ansgar Graw, "Zahl der antisemitischen Delikte in Deutschland steigt," *Die Welt*, September 8, 2017, https://www.welt.de/politik/deutschland/article168436745/Zahl-der-antisemitischen-Delikte-in-Deutschland-steigt.html.

115. Amadeu Antonio Stiftung, *Lagebild Antisemitismus 2016/2017*, https://www.amadeu-antonio-stiftung.de/w/files/pdfs/aktionswochen/lagebild-deutschland-internet.pdf.

116. *Der Tagesspiegel*, "Neonazi-Gruppe listet jüdische Geschäfte auf: Staatsschutz ermittelt," November 11, 2016, http://www.tagesspiegel.de/berlin/polizei-justiz/berlin er-facebook-gruppe-neonazi-gruppe-listet-juedische-geschaefte-auf-staatsschutz-ermitt elt/14819364.html.

117. Stiftung, *Lagebild Antisemitismus 2016/2017*, 16.

118. Andreas Zick, Andreas Hövermann, Silke Jansen, and Julia Bernstein, *Jüdische Perspektiven auf Antisemitismus in Deutschland: ein Studienbericht für den Expertenrat Antisemitismus*, April 2017, https://uni-bielefeld.de/ikg/daten/JuPe_Bericht_April2017.pdf.

119. Zick, et al., *Jüdische Perspektiven*, 4.

120. Zick, et al., *Jüdische Perspektiven*, 8.

121. Deutscher Bundestag. Beschlussempfehlung und Bericht des 2. Untersuchungsausschusses nach Artikel 44 des Grundgesetzes. "Überblick über die dem NSU zugerechneten Straftaten," 17. Wahlperiode. Drucksache 17/14600, 71.

122. Bundestag, "Überblick," 73.

123. Bundestag, "Überblick," 74.

124. Bundesamt für Verfassungsschutz, "Aufklärung des NSU: Fehlverhalten Einzelner nicht repräsentativ für die Arbeit des Bundesamt für Verfassungsschutz." Press Release. July 12, 2012.

125. Christoph Elzer, "Reichsbürger: Was sie glauben, weshalb sie gefährlich sind," *Abendzeitung*, July 21, 2017.

126. *Die Zeit*, "BKA zählte 771 politisch motivierte Straftaten," January 27, 2018, http://www.zeit.de/gesellschaft/zeitgeschehen/2018–01/reichsbuerger-bka-politische-st raftaten.

127. Diether Strothmann, "Der Schlag gegen das Roder-Rudel," *Die Zeit*, Nr. 38, September 12, 1980, http://www.zeit.de/1980/38/der-schlag-gegen-das-roeder-rudel

128. Sven Felix Kellerhoff, "De Vordenker der, Reichsbürger"? Terroristen!" *Die Welt*, October 25, 2016, https://www.welt.de/politik/deutschland/article159036380/Die-Vordenker-der-Reichsbuerger-Terroristen.htm.

129. Strothmann, "Der Schlag gegen das Roder-Rudel," n.p.

130. TAZ, "Manfred Roeder ist tot: Tod eines Neonazis," August 1, 2014, http://www.taz.de/!5036341/.

131. Deutscher Bundestag, "Rechtsextreme Vorkommnisse und Verdachtsfälle in der Bundeswehr im Jahr 2017," 18th Wahlperiode. Drucksache 18/13644, http://dip21.bu ndestag.de/dip21/btd/18/136/1813644.pdf.

132. *Die Zeit*, "Mehr rechtsextreme Verdachtsfälle in der Bundeswehr," January 28, 2017, http://www.zeit.de/politik/deutschland/2018–01/rechtsextremismus-bundeswehr -verdachtsfaelle-2017.

133. Christian Teevs, "The AfD in the Bundestag: A Populist Upheaval on the Right," *Der Spiegel*, September 25, 2017 http://www.spiegel.de/international/germany/g ermany-right-wing-afd-celebrates-entry-into-parliament-a-1169631.html.

134. Justus Bender and Reinhard Bingener, Der Parteiphilosoph der AfD. *Frankfurter Allgemeine*, January 1, 2016, http://www.faz.net/aktuell/politik/inland/marc-jongen-ist-afd-politiker-und-philosoph-14005731-p2.html.

135. Landtag Mecklenburg-Vorpommern, "Kirchenasyl in Anklam: Kleine Anfrage des Abgeordneten Dr. Matthias Manthei, Fraktion der AfD," June 12, 2017, 7. Wahlperiode, Drucksache 7/506.

136. Landtag Mecklenburg-Vorpommern, Plenarprotokoll, 17 Sitzung, 7 Wahlperiode, July 13, 2017.

137. Thüringer Landtag, Kleine Anfrage 492 der Abgeordneten Herold (AfD). "Lesbische, Schwule, Bisexuelle, Transsexuelle und Intersexuelle (LSBTI) in Thüringen." September 1, 2015. 6. Wahlperiode.

138. *Focus*, "AfD-Politiker will Aids-Kranke namentlich registrieren: Experten reagieren schockiert," March 16, 2017, https://www.focus.de/politik/deutschland/diskriminierung-von-menschen-mit-hiv-afd-forderung-registrierung-von-aids-kranken-mit-namen-wird-heftig-kritisiert_id_6800915.html.

139. AIDS Hilfe Sachsen-Anhalt e.V., "Warminsky zur AfD-Forderung einer Namentlichen Meldung von Menschen mit HIV," March 15, 2017, https://www.aids-lsa.org/2017/03/15/warminsky-zur-afd-forderung-einer-namentlichen-meldung-von-menschen-mit-hiv/.

140. Detailed information about the project and how to arrange a stone-laying can be found at http://www.stolpersteine.eu/en/home.

141. Stolperstein-aktion Beenden! Appell an den Oberbürgermeister und den Gemeinderat von Singen: Offener Brief, February 14, 2018, http://www.wolfgang-gedeon.de/2018/02/stolpersteine.

142. Dennis Giemisch, *Anfrage für die Sitzung des Rates der Stadt Dortmund am 13. 11. 2014*. Die Rechte. October 16, 2014.

143. USHMM, "Strategic. Plan Summary: 2013–2018," https://www.ushmm.org/m/pdfs/Strategic-Plan-2013–2018.pdf.

144. USHMM, "Museum Announces $20 Million Gift to Name the Simon-Skjodt Center for the Prevention of Genocide," February 19, 2015, https://www.ushmm.org/information/press/press-releases/museum-announces-20-million-gift-to-name-the-simon-skjodt-center-for-the-pr.

145. Daniel Goldhagen, *Genocide: Worse than War*, (documentary film), directed by Mike DeWitt (Public Broadcasting Service, 2010), 7 min., 46 sec, http://goldhagen.com/worse-than-war-the-film.

146. Goldhagen, *Genocide: Worse than War*, 51 min., 34 sec.

147. Mitteldeutscher Rundfunk, "Ein Akt der Menschlichkeit," https://www.mdr.de/heute-im-osten/sarajevo-100.html.

148. *UPI*, "Orphans Leave Sarajevo after Two Killed by Snipers," August 2, 1992, https://www.upi.com/Archives/1992/08/02/Orphans-leave-Sarajevo-after-two-killed-by-snipers/2277712728000/.

149. Tony Barber, "Snipers Kill Two Fleeing Orphans: As Zagreb Holds its First Independent Elections, Serbian Forces Fire on a Bus Evacuating Bosnian Children from Sarajevo," *The Independent*, August 2, 1992, http://www.independent.co.uk/news/world/europe/snipers-kill-two-fleeing-orphans-as-zagreb-holds-its-first-independent-elections-serbian-forces-fire-1537793.html.

150. John Burns, "'Serbs' Campaign for Ethnic Purity Divides up a Busload of Orphans," *The New York Times*, August 3, 1992, http://www.nytimes.com/1992/08/03/world/serbs-campaign-for-ethnic-purity-divides-up-a-busload-of-orphans.html?pagewanted=all.

151. Burns, "'Serbs' Campaign for Ethnic Purity," para. 24.

152. Tamara Jones, "Orphans' Funeral Shelled in Bosnia: Conflict: Grandmother is seriously wounded. Surviving Children Reach Germany, Four Days after Terrifying Journey Began," *Los Angeles Times*, August 5, 1992, http://articles.latimes.com/1992–08–05/news/mn-5024_1_terrifying-journey.

153. Bartrop, "Michael Nicholson," *A Biographical Encyclopedia of Contemporary Genocide: Portraits of Evil and Good* (Oxford: ABC-CLIO, 2012), 232–34.

154. Bartrop, "Michael Nicholson," 233.

155. Michael Nicholson, *Natasha's Story: How a Nine-Year-Old Orphan Was Rescued from War in Sarajevo* (New York: Macmillan, 1993).

156. Nicholson, *Natasha' Story*, 62.

157. OSCE/OIHR, *Kosovo/Kosova: As Seen, As Told: An Analysis of the Human rights Findings of the OSCE Kosovo Verification Mission* (October 1998 to June 1999), http://www.osce.org/odihr/17772?download=true.

158. OSCE/OIHR, *Kosovo/Kosova*, 552.

159. OSCE/OIHR, *Kosovo/Kosova*, 156.

160. OSCE/OIHR, *Kosovo/Kosova*, 57, 58.

161. OSCE/OIHR, *Kosovo/Kosova*, 260.

162. OSCE/OIHR, *Kosovo/Kosova*, 324.

163. Alison Desforges, *Leave None to Tell the Story*. Human Rights Watch March 1999, https://www1.essex.ac.uk/armedcon/story_id/Leavepercent20Nonepercent20topercent20tellpercent20thepercent20story-percent20Genocidepercent20inpercent20Rwanda.pdf.

164. Radio Télévision Libre des Mille Collines (RTLM). Recording from May 28, 1994. English translation of the original Kinyarwanda broadcast. Transcripts of the UN International Criminal Tribunal for Rwanda. Genocide Archive of Rwanda, http://www.genocidearchiverwanda.org.rw/index.php/RadioTpercentC3percentA9lpercentC3percentA9visionLibre_desMille_Colline.

165. Radio Télévision Libre des Mille Collines, 4.

166. Sharon Lafraniere, "Court finds Rwanda Media Executives Guilty of Genocide," *The New York Times*, December 3, 2003, http://www.nytimes.com/2003/12/03/international/africa/court-finds-rwanda-media-executives-guilty-of-genocide.html.

167. Desforges, *Leave None to Tell the Story*, 158.

168. Desforges, *Leave None to Tell the Story*, 294.

169. Desforges, *Leave None to Tell the Story*, 294.

170. International Criminal Tribunal for Rwanda (ICTR), "The Prosecutor v. Ferdinand Nahimana, Jean-Bosco Barayagwiza, and Hassan Ngeze: Judgement and Sentence," December 3, 2003, http://unictr.unmict.org/sites/unictr.org/files/case-documents/ictr-99–52/trial-judgments/en/031203.pdf.

171. ICTR, "The Prosecutor v. Ferdinand Nahimana," 65.

172. ICTR, "The Prosecutor v. Ferdinand Nahimana," 326.

173. Nahimana et al. (Media Case) International Criminal Tribunal, http://unictr.unmict.org/en/cases/ictr-99–52.

174. For a detailed discussion of this study within the context of atrocities and genocide, see Philip Zimbardo, *The Lucifer Effect* (London: Rider, 2007).

175. Zimbardo, *The Lucifer Effect*, 230.

References

Adam, Uwe Dietrich. *Judenpolitik im Dritten Reich*. Düsseldorf: Droste, 2003.

Afzali, Samira. "How 'Comprehensive' is the Comprehensive Immigration Reform Bill?" *Hamline University's School of Law and Policy* 35 (2014): 296–329.

AIDS Hilfe Sachsen-Anhalt e.V. "Warminsky zur AfD-Forderung einer Namentlichen Meldung von Menschen mit HIV." March 15, 2017. https://www.aids-lsa.org/2017/03/15/warminsky-zur-afd-forderung-einer-namentlichen-meldung-von-menschen-mit-hiv/.

Ainsztein, Reuben. *In Lands Not My Own: A Wartime Journey*. New York: Random House, 2002.

Al-Shuaili, Mazin and Marco Carvalho. "Personal Identity Matching." *Computer Science and Information Technology* (2016): 31–43.

Albrich, Thomas, Winfried Garscha, and Martin Polaschek, eds. *Holocaust und Kriegsverbrechen vor Gericht: Der Fall Österreich*. Vienna: Studien Verlag, 2006.

Allen, L. V. Brown, L. Dickinson, and K. C. Pratt. "The Relation of First Name Preferences to their Frequency in the Culture." *The Journal of Social Psychology* 14 (1941): 279–93.

Aly, Götz. *Rasse und Klasse: Nachforschungen zum deutschen Wesen*. Frankfurt am Main: S. Fischer, 2003.

———. "Der anthropologische Ehrgeiz des Oberpräparators Gustav von Hirschheydt und dessen tödliche Begegnung mit einem toten Juden: Ein Arbeitsunfall." *Berliner Zeitung*, March 2, 2015.

Amadeu Antonio Stiftung. "Lagebild Antisemitismus 2016/2017." https://www.amadeu-antonio-stiftung.de/w/files/pdfs/aktionswochen/lagebild-deutschland-internet.pdf.

Ambach, Dieter and Thomas Köhler, eds. *Lublin-Majdanek: Das Konzentrations-und Vernichtungslager im Spiegel von Zeugenaussagen*. Duesseldorf: Justizministerium des Landes Nordrhein-Westfalen, 2003.

American Civil Liberties Union. "US Government Watchlisting: Unfair Process and Devastating Consequences," 2014. https://www.aclu.org/sites/default/files/assets/wa tchlist_briefing_paper_v3.pdf.

Anderson, Margo. "Public Management of Big Data: Historical Lessons from the 1940s." *Federal History* 15 (2015): 17–34.

Anderson, Timothy. "Unique and Common Names of Males and Females." *Psychological Reports* 57, no. 1 (1985): 204–6.

Arab American Institute. "National Security Entry-Exit Registration System." http://www.aaiusa.org/nseers.

Arndt, Ino. "Das Frauenkonzentrationslager Ravensbrück." *Dachauer Heft* 3: *Frauen, Verfolgung und Widerstand* (1987): 125–57.

Arndt, Nicole. "Politischer Regimewechsel und der Aufstieg und der Fall der deutschen Vornamen." In *Die Moderne und ihre Vornamen: Eine Einladung in die Kultursoziologie*, edited by Juergen Gerhards, 71–86. Berlin: Springer Verlag, 2003.

———. *Die Geschichte und Entwicklung des familienrechtlichen Namensrechts.* Munich: Herbert Utz Verlag, 2004.

Bailey, Brian. *Hangmen of England: A History of Execution from Jack Ketch to Albert Pierrepoint.* Lyndhurst, NJ: Barnes and Noble, 1994.

Barber, Tony. "Snipers Kill Two Fleeing Orphans." *The Independent*, August 2, 1992. http://www.independent.co.uk/news/world/europe/snipers-kill-two-fleeing-orphans-as-zagreb-holds-its-first-independent-elections-serbian-forces-fire-1537793.html.

Barrett, John and Robert H. Jackson. *That Man: An Insider's Portrait of Franklin D. Roosevelt.* Oxford: Oxford University Press, 2004.

Barnett, Randy and Josh Blackburn. *Constitutional Law: Cases in Context.* New York: Wolters Kluwer, 2017.

Bartosz, Adam. *In the Footsteps of the Jews of Tarnow.* Tarnow: Tarnow Regional Museum, 2007.

Bartrop, Paul. "Michael Nichholson: A Biography." In *A Biographical Encyclopedia of Contemporary Genocide: Portraits of Good and Evil.* Oxford: ABC-CLIO, 2012.

Bauer, Fritz. *Die Humanität der Rechtsordnung: Ausgewählte Schriften*, edited by Joachim Perels and Irmtrud Wojak. Frankfurt am Main: Campus Verlag, 1998.

———. "Der Verbrecher von gestern ist der Held von heute." *Die Humanität der Rechtsordnung: Ausgewählte Schriften*, edited by Joachim Perels and Irmtrud Wojak, 97–101. Frankfurt am Main: Campus Verlag, 1998.

Bazyler, Michael J. and Frank M. Tuerkheimer. *Forgotten Trials of the Holocaust.* New York: New York University Press, 2014.

Beddies, Thomas. "Kinder- 'Euthanasie' in Berlin-Brandenburg." In *Dokumente zur Psychiatrie im Nationalsozialismus*, edited by T. Beddies and K. Hübener, 219–22. Berlin: be.bra Verlag, 2003.

———. "Die Tötung 'Lebensunwerter' Kinder im Nationalsozialismus: Die Kinderfachabteilung." In *Tödliche Medizin: Rassenwahn im Nationalsozialismus*, edited by Margret Kampmeyer, 76–83. Gottingen: Wallstein, 2009.

Bender, Justus and Reinhard Bingener. "Der Parteiphilosoph der AfD," *Frankfurter Allgemeine*, January 1, 2016. http://www.faz.net/aktuell/politik/inland/marc-jongen-ist-afd-politiker-und-philosoph-14005731.html.

Benz, Wolfgang. "The Legend of German-Jewish Symbiosis." *The Leo Baeck Institute Year Book* 37, no. 1 (1992): 95–102.

Benz, Wolfgang and Barbara Distel, eds. *Der Ort des Terrors: Geschichte der nationalsozialistischen Konzentrationslager*. Vol. 9. Munich: CH Beck, 2009.

Berenbaum, May. "ICE Breakers." *American Entomologist* 56, no. 3 (2010): 132–33, 185.

Bering, Dietz. *The Stigma of Names: Antisemitism in German Daily Life, 1812–1933*. Ann Arbor: University of Michigan Press, 1992.

Berger, Elisabeth. *Erwerb und Änderung des Familiennamens*. Berlin: Peter Lang, 2001.

The Berlin (Potsdam) Conference. "Protocol of the Proceedings." https://usa.usembassy.de/etexts/ga4-450801.pdf.

Bertelsmann Stiftung. "Deutschland and Israel Heute." https://www.bertelsmann-stiftung.de/fileadmin/files/BSt/Publikationen/GrauePublikationen/Studie_LW_Deutschland_und_Israel_heute_2015.pdf.

Bever, Lindsey. "Remains of Holocaust Experiment Victims Found at French Forensic Institute." *Washington Post*. July 22, 2015. https://www.washingtonpost.com/news/morning-mix/wp/2015/07/22/remains-of-holocaust-victims-used-as-guinea-pigs-found-at-french-forensic-institute/?utm_term=.b3b8bad9d4e6.

Bierende, Edgar. "Kriegsgefangene, Zwangsarbeiter und KZ-Häftlinge in den Anatomischen Leichenbüchern." In *Forschung Lehre Unrecht. Die Universität Tübingen in National Sozialismus*, edited by Ernst Seidl, 223–32. Tübingen: Museum Universität Tübingen, 2015.

Bjelopera, Jerome, Bart Elias, and Alison Siskin. "The Terrorist Screening Database and Preventing Terrorist Travel." *Congressional Research Service*. https://fas.org/sgp/crs/terror/R44678.pdf.

Black, Edwin. *War Against the Weak: Eugenics and America's Campaign to Create a Master Race*. Washington, DC: Dialog Press, 2003.

Bnai Brith Messenger. "Demand Prison for Jew Who Took Hitler's Name." June 30, 1933.

Boehm, Hermann. "Nationalsozialistische Gedanken zum Paragraphen 218." *Nationalsozialistische Monatshefte* 24 (1932): 126–30.

Böltken, Andrea. "Inge Viermetz: Eine weibliche Karriere im Dritten Reich." In *Historische Rassismusforschung: Ideologen, Täter, Opfer*, edited by B. Danckwortt, T. Querg, and C. Schöningh, 179–207. Berlin: Argument Verlag, 1995.

Böning, Jobst. "Der hauptverantwortliche NS-Euthanasie-Täter und Leiter der T4-Aktion Werner Heyde alias Fritz Sawade-Ein jahrzehntes verdrängtes 'offenes' Geheimnis in Umgang mit der 'Banalität des Bösen,'" In *Geheimnis: Psychologische, Psychopathologische und künstlerische Ausdrucksformen im Spektrum zwischen Verheimlichen und Geheimnisvollem*, edited by Daniel Sollberger, Jobst Benning, Erik Boehlke, and Gerhard Schindler, 203–20. Berlin: Frank and Timme, 2016.

Bönisch, Georg. "Amnesie und Amnestie." *Der Spiegel*. February 21, 2006.

Breitman, Richard and Norman J. W. Goda. *Hitler's Shadow: Nazi War Criminals, U.S. Intelligence and the Cold War*. Washington, DC: National Archives, 2014.

Brenner, Hannelore. *The Girls of Room 28: Friendship, Hope, and Survival in Theresienstadt*. New York: Schocken Books, 2009.

Brog, Mooli. "In Blessed Memory of a Dream: Mordechai Shehavi and Initial Holocaust Commemoration Ideas in Palestine, 1942–1945." SHOAH Resource Center, The

International School for Holocaust Studies, Yad Vashem. https://www.yadvashem. org/odot_pdf/Microsoft%20Word%20-%205423.pdf.

Broszat, Martin, ed. "10. Nach dem Zusammenbruch (1945–1947)." In *Kommandant in Auschwitz: Autobiographische Aufzeichnung des Rudolf Höss.* München: Deutsche Taschenbuch Verlag, 1979.

Brown, Daniel and Wendy Lower. *Hitler's Furies: German Women in the Nazi Killing Fields.* New York: Houghton Mifflin Harcourt, 2013.

Bruinius, Harry. *Better for all the World: The Secret History of America's Quest for Racial Purity.* New York: First Vintage Books, 2007.

Bryant, Thomas. *Himmlers Kinder: Zur Geschichte der SS-Organisation, Lebensborn e.V. 1935–1945.* Wiesbaden: Matrix Verlag, 2011.

Brzsoko-Medrk, Danuta. *Der Himmel ohne Vögel.* Warsaw: Verlag des Ministeriums für National Verteidigung, 1968.

Bulwa, Demian. "Her Secret Past as a Nazi Guard: S.F. Immigrant Married Holocaust Survivor, Attended Synagogue." *SF Gate*, September 2006. https://www.sfgate.com/news/article/Her-secret-past-as-a-Nazi-guard-S-F-immigrant-2488370.php#photo-2649802.

Bundesministerium des Innern. "Antisemitismus in Deutschland: aktuelle Entwicklungen." https://www.bmi.bund.de/SharedDocs/downloads/DE/publikationen/2017/expertenbericht-antisemitismus-in-deutschland.pdf?__blob=publicationFile.

Bundesnachrichtendienst. "Walter Rauff und der Bundesnachrichtendienst. Mitteilungen der Forschungs- und Arbeitsgruppe Geschichte des BND, Nr. 2." September 23, 2011. http://www.bnd.bund.de/DE/Organisation/Geschichte/Geschichtsaufarbeitung/MFGBND_Uebersicht/MFGBND_pdf.

Bundesarchiv. "Berlin Document Center: Hintergründe zu Geschichte und Hauptbestände." June 15, 2013. https://www.bundesarchiv.de/DE/Content/Artikel/Ueber-uns/Aus-unserer- Arbeit/berlin-document-center.html.

Bundeszentrale für politische Bildung. "Bundesverfassungsgericht lehnt NPD-Verbot ab." January 1, 2017. http://www.bpb.de/politik/hintergrund-aktuell/222103/npd-verbotsverfahren.

———. "Sophie Scholl und die Weiße Rose." *Dossier.* http://www.bpb.de/geschichte/nationalsozialismus/weisse-rose/.

———. "Widerstand der Weißen Rose: Flugblättergegen Hitler." http://www.bpb.de/geschichte/nationalsozialismus/weisse-rose/61028/flugblat t-vi.

Burns, John. "'Serbs'" Campaign for Ethnic Purity Divides Up a Busload of Orphans." *The New York Times.* August 3, 1992. http://www.nytimes.com/1992/08/03/world/serbs-campaign-for-ethnic-purity-divides-up-a-busload-of-orphans.html?pagewanted=all. Bundesamt für Verfassungsschutz." Aufklärung des NSU: Fehlverhalten Einzelner nicht repräsentativ für die Arbeit des Bundesamt für Verfassungsschutz."

Bytwerk, Randall L. *Landmark Speeches of National Socialism.* College Station, Texas: Texas A & M University Press, 2008.

Cahm, Erich. *The Dreyfus Affair in French Society and Politics.* London: Routledge, 1994.

Cankar, Louise. "Post 9/11 Domestic Policies Affecting US Arabs and Muslims: A Brief Review." *Comparative Studies of South Asia, Africa and the Middle East* 24, no. 1 (2004): 245–48.

Central Intelligence Agency. "CIA Dispatch EGMA-54517, Wilhelm Beissner." Declassified CIA Report. April 20, 1961. https://www.cia.gov/library/readingroom/document/519a6b2f993294098d5120f6.

———. "Nazi War Criminal Alois Brunner's Presence in Damascus." Declassified CIA Report, November 1987. https://www.cia.gov/library/readingroom/docs/EICHMANN%2C%20ADOLF%20%20%28DI%29_0005.pdf.

Christin, Peter. *Data Matching: Concepts and Techniques for Record Linkage, Entity Resolution and Duplicate Detection.* London: Springer Verlag, 2012.

Christmann, Ernst. *Deutsche Rufname! Eine deutsche Forderung auf Grund einer Untersuchung der Verhältnisse im Saarpfälzischen Raum Kaiserlautern.* Kaiserlautern: Pfälzische Gesellschaft zur Förderung der Wissenschaften, 1939.

Cole, David. "Secrecy, Guilt by Association, and the Terrorist Profile." *Journal of Law and Religion* 25 (2000): 267–88.

Cole, David and James Dempsey. *Terrorism and the Constitution: Sacrificing Civil Liberties in the Name of National Security.* New York: The New Press, 2006.

Comenetz, Joshua. "Frequently Occurring Surnames in the 2010 Census." United States Bureau of Census, October, 2016. https://www2.census.gov/topics/genealogy/2010surnames/surnames.pdf.

Cymè, Michel. *Hippokrates in der Hölle: Die Verbrechen der KZ Ärzte.* Trier: Thiess Verlag, 2016.

Dakwar, Jamil. "Not so Safe and Sound." *The SUR File on Migration and Human Rights* 13, no. 23 (2016): 49–60.

Danker, Uwe and Astrid Schwabe. *Schleswig-Holstein und der Nationalsozialismus.* Neumünster: Wachholtz Verlag, 2005.

Danker, Uwe, Sebastian Lehmann, and Stephan Glienke. "Geschichtswissenschaftlich Aufarbeitung der personellen und strukturellen Kontinuität nach 1945 in der schleswig-holsteinischen Legislative und Exekutive." Präsentation der Ergebnisse im schleswig-holsteinischen Landtag und auf der Landespressekonferenz am 27.04.2016. https://www.sh-landtag.de/export/sites/landtagsh/homedata/kat1/data/Danker_LPK_Text_20160427.pdf.

Das Gupta, Oliver. "Das kleine Gluck im Inferno." *Süddeutsche Zeitung.* March 16, 2015. http://www.sueddeutsche.de/bayern/zweiter-weltkrieg-in-unterfranken-das-kleine-glueck-im-inferno-1.2393963.

Davis, Austin. "Anti-Semitism is still alive in Germany as Jews face 'disturbing' discrimination." *USA TODAY,* December 21, 2017. https://eu.usatoday.com/story/news/world/2017/12/21/anti-semitism-germany-jews-discrimination-muslms-right-wing-nationalists/962383001/.

DDR-Justiz und NS Verbrechen: Sammlung ostdeutscher Strafurteile wegen nationalsozialistischer Tötungsverbrechen: Das Urteil gegen Hans Josef Maria Globke. Einzelausfertigung des Urteils des OG von 23.07.1963, 1 ZST (I) 1/63) Band III, Lfd. Nr. 1068. http://www1.jur.uva.nl/junsv/pdf/globke.pdf.

Der Landtag: Der Parlamentzeitschrift für Schleswig-Holstein. Nr. 02. June 2016. http://www.landtag.ltsh.de/export/sites/landtagsh/service/bestellungen/downloads/der-landtag/derlandtag-2016–02.pdf.

Der Tagesspiegel. "Neonazi-Gruppe listet jüdische Geschäfte auf: Staatsschutz ermittelt." November 11, 2016. http://www.tagesspiegel.de/berlin/polizei-justiz/berliner facebook-gruppe-neonazi-gruppe-listet-juedsche-geschaefte-auf-staatsschutz-ermittelt/148193 64.html.

Desforges, Alison. "Leave None to Tell The Story." *Human Rights Watch*, March 1999. https://www.hrw.org/report/1999/03/01/leave-none-tell-story/genocide-rwanda.

Deutsche Welle. "Germany to Allow Opening of Huge Holocaust Archive." April 19, 2006. http://www.dw.com/en/germany-to-allow-opening-of-huge-holocaust-archive/a-1973870.

Deutscher Bundestag. 3. Session, Bonn, September 15, 1949. http://pdok.bundestag.de/.

———. 9. Session. December 9, 1949. http://pdok.bundestag.de/.

———. 22 Session. December 9, 1949. http://pdok.bundestag.de/.

———. 18 Wahlperiode. *Suche nach dem Kriegsverbrecher Alois Brunner.* "Antwort der Bundesregierung auf die Kleine Anfrage der Abgeordneten Jan Korte, Sevim Dagdelen, Ulla Jelpke, weiterer Abgeordneter und der Fraktion DIE LINKE." Drucksache 18/3877. http://dip21.bundestag.de/dip21/btd/18/035/1803599.pdf.

———. "Rechtextreme Vorkommnisse und Verdachtsfälle in der Bundeswehr im Jahr 2012." http://dip21.bundestag.de/dip21/btd/18/021/1813644.pdf.

———. "Überblick über die dem NSU zugerechneten Straftaten. http://dipbt.bundestag.de/doc/btd/17/146/1714600.pdf.

Dewey, Caitlin. "Why Nelson Mandela was on a Terrorism Watch List in 2009." *The Washington Post*, December 7, 2013. https://www.washingtonpost.com/news/the-fix/wp/2013/12/07/why-nelson-mandela-was-on-a-terrorism-watch-list-in-2008/?utm_term=.792f4be51234.

Diederichs, Monika. "Stigma and Silence: Dutch Women, German Soldiers, and Their Children." In *Children of World War II: The Hidden Legacy*, edited by Kjersti Ericsson and Eva Simonsen, 151–64. Oxford: Berg, 2005.

Diekman, Florian and Philipp Seibt. "Wer sind die Quandts?" *Der Spiegel*, August 6, 2015. http://www.spiegel.de/wirtschaft/unternehmen/quandt-clan-wer-sind-die-bmw-erben-und-woher-kommt-ihr-reichtum-a-1046996.html.

Diner, Hasia. *We Remember with Reverence and Love: American Jews and the Myth of Silence after the Holocaust, 1945–1962.* New York: New York University Press, 2009.

Donovan Nuremberg Trials Collection. "Experience Report of Concentration Camp Inhabitant Olga Schaub." Cornell University Law Library. http://lawcollections.library.cornell.edu/nuremberg/catalog/nur:00424.

Dreßen, Willi. "NS-'Euthanasie'-Prozesse in der Bundesrepublik Deutschland im Wandel der Zeit." In *NS-'Euthanasie' vor Gericht: Fritz Bauer und die Grenzen juristischer Bewältigung*, edited by Hanno Loewy and Bettina Winter, 35–58. Frankfurt am Main: Campus Verlag, 1996.

Du Bist Halle. "AIDS-Hilfe Sachsen-Anhalt lehnt namentliche Meldung HIV-Infizierter ab." March 15, 2017. https://dubisthalle.de/aids-hilfe-sachsen-anhalt-lehnt-namentliche-meldung-hiv-infizierter-ab.

Eberle, Henrik. *Briefe an Hitler: Ein Volk schreibt seinem Führer.* Cologne: Bastei Lübbe Verlag, 2007.

Eckart, Wolfgang. "Erster Weltkrieg 1914–1918: Hunger und Mangel in der Heimat." *Deutsche Ärzteblatt* 112, no. 6 (2015): A-230–2.

Eckert, Astrid. *The Struggle for the Files: The Western Allies and the Return of German Archives after the Second World War.* Cambridge: Cambridge University Press, 2004.

The Economist. "A Nation of Immigrants," December 23, 1999. http://www.economist.com/node/346908.

Ehmann, Annegret. "From Colonial Racism to Nazi Population Policy." In *The Holocaust and History: The Known, the Unknown, the Disputed, and the Reexamined*, edited by Michael Berenbaum and Abraham J. Peck, 115–33. Indianapolis: Indiana University Press, 1998.

Eisenhower, Dwight. "Letter, General Eisenhower to General Marshall concerning his Visit to a German Internment Camp near Goth (Ohrdruf)." April 15, 1945. Dwight D. Eisenhower Presidential Library. World War II: Holocaust, the Extermination of European Jews. Dwight D. Eisenhower's Pre-Presidential Papers, Principal File, Box 80, Marshall George C. (6): NAID'12005711. https://eisenhower.archives.gov/Research/online_documents/holocaust.html.

Elkins, Ruth. "Fans Nearly Exterminate 'Hitler' Beetle." *The Independent*, August 19, 2006. http://www.independent.co.uk/news/world/europe/fans-exterminate-hitler-beetle-6232054.html.

Elzer, Christoph. "Reichsbürger: Was sie glauben, weshalb sie gefährlich sind." *Abendzeitung*, July 21, 2017. https://www.abendzeitung-muenchen.de/inhalt.az-hintergrund-reichsbuerger-was-sie-glauben-weshalb-sie-gefaehrlich-sind.a09b178b-1d33-4e51-8dc6-13e276544d36.html.

Engelberg, Stephen. "Greater Access to Terrorism Data is Sought for Immigration Agency." *The New York Times.* February 5, 1987. http://www.nytimes.com/1987/02/06/us/greater-access-to-terrorism-data-is-sought-for-immigration-agency.html.

Erpel, Simone. *Im Gefolge der SS: Aisfseherinnen des Frauen KZ Ravensbrück.* Berlin: Metropol Verlag, 2018.

Evans, Suzanne. *Forgotten Crimes: The Holocaust and People with Disabilities.* Chicago: Ivan R. Dee Publisher, 2004.

The Evening Telegraph. "Ficken's Anniversary." February 13, 1871.

Fahrenkrog, Rolf Ludwig. *Deutschen Kindern—Deutsche Namen.* Berlin: Fritsch Verlag, 1939.

Federal Bureau of Investigation. *Image-Based Matching Technology Offers Identification Intelligence Prospects.* Criminal Justice Information Services, Link 14, No. 3. December 28, 2012. https://www.fbi.gov/services/cjis/cjis-link/image-based-matching-technology-offers-identification-and-intelligence-prospects.

Federal Register. US Immigration and Naturalization Service. Notice. *Registration of Certain Nonimmigrant Aliens from Designated Countries, doc. no. 02–32045.* December 18, 2002. https://www.federalregister.gov/documents/2002/12/18/02-32045/registration-of-certain-nonimmigrant-aliens-from-designated-countries.

———. Executive Order No. 13354. *National Counterterrorism Center.* 69 August 27, 2004: 53589–53592.

———. US Department of Homeland Security. Notice. Privacy Act, Office of Intelligence and Analysis Enterprise Records System, Doc. No. E8–10888, 73, no. 95 May

15, 2008: 28128–28135. https://www.gpo.gov/fdsys/pkg/FR-2008–05–15/html/E 8–10888.htm.

———. *Removing Designated Countries from the National Security Entry-Exit Registration System (NSEERS),* Doc. No.: 2011–10305. April 28, 2011. https://www.federalregist er.gov/documents/2011/04/28/2011–10305/removing-designated-countries-from-t he-national-security-entry-exit-registration-system-nseers.

Feigin, Judy. "Striving for Accountability in the Aftermath of the Holocaust." Office of Special Investigation. December 2008. https://www.justice.gov/saites/default/files/criminal/legacy/2011/03/14 /12–2 008osu-accountability.pdf.

Fergusson, Adam. *Das Ende des Geldes: Hyperinflation und ihre Folgen für dieMenschen am Beispiel der Weimarer Republik.* Munich: FinanzBuch Verlag, 2011.

Festring-Hashem Zadek, Kristina. "Wie Hitlers Halbbruder im Hamburg untertauchte." *Norddeutscher Rundfunk,* May 20, 1016. https://www.ndr.de/kultur/geschichte/sch auplaetze/Wie-Hitlers-Bruder-in-Hamburg-untertauchte,hitler178.html.

Finkelberger, Martin. "Während meines ganzen Lebens habe ich die Juden erforscht, wie ein Bakteriologe eine gefährlichen Bazillus studiert—Johann von Leers (1902–1965) als antisemitischer Propaganda experte bis 1945." *Bulletin des Deutsches Historisches Institut Moskau* (2008): 88–99.

Fleischer, Wolfgang. *Die deutschen Personnennamen: Geschichte, Bildung, und Bedeutung.* Berlin: Akademie-Verlag, 1968.

Focus Online. "Die unsagbaren Grausamkeiten der SS." February 12, 2016. https://ww w.focus.de/wissen/videos/1939-ss-terror-die-unsagbaren-grausamkeiten-der-ss_id_5 277906.html.

———. "AfD-Politiker will Aids Kranke Namentlich Registrieren: Experten Reagieren Schockiert." https://www.focus.de/politik/deutschland/diskriminierung-von-mens chen-mit-hiv-afd-forderung-registrierung-von-aids-kranken-mit-namen-wird-heftig-kritisiert_id_6800915.html.

Frank, Niklas. *Der Vater: Eine Abrechnung.* Erben: Eigenverlag Brigitte Frank Unsel, 2014.

Frankfurter Allgemeine Zeitung. "Gesellschaft für Christlich-Jüdische Zusammenarbeit beklagt Antisemitismus in Hessen." November 8, 1949. Hessian Regional History Information System (LAGIS) (online). http://www-lagis-hessen.de/de/subjects/idrect /sn/edb/id/3406.

———. "Minister Präsident Stock sagt Toleranz und Bekämpfung des Antisemitismus zu." July 21, 1950. *Zeitgeschichte in Hessen* (Contemporary History in Hessian). Hessian Regional History Information System (LAGIS) (online). http://www-lagis-hessen.de/de/subjects/idrect/sn/edb/id/3552.

Frei, Norbert. *Vergangenheitspolitik: Die Anfänge der Bundesrepublik und die NS-Vergan-genheit.* München: Deutscher Taschenbuch Verlag, 2003.

Frenzel, Eike. "Mein Nachbar, der Massenmörder: Untergetauchter Kriegsverbrecher." *Der Spiegel,* August 6, 2010. http://www.spiegel.de/einestages/untergetauchter-kriegs-verbrecher-a-946564.html.

Friedlander, Henry. *The Origins of Nazi Genocide: From Euthanasia to the Final Solution.* Chapel Hill, NC: University of North Carolina Press, 1995.

———. *Der Weg zum NS-Genozid: Von Euthanasie zur Endlösung.* Berlin: Berlin Verlag, 1997.

Friedrich, Jörg. *Die kalte Amnestie: NS-Täter in der Bundesrepublik.* Munich: Piper Verlag, 1984.

Freitag, Thomas. *Niel.* Cottbus: Regia Verlag, 2014.

Fritz Bauer Archiv. "Der Darmstädter Einsatzgruppen-prozess 1965–1968 und der Massenmord in Babij Jar." http://www.fritz-bauer-archiv.de/index.php/bauers-liste/ verbrechen-der-wehrmacht.

Fröhlich, Claudia. "Der Ulmer Einsatzgruppenprozess, 1958: Wahrnehmung und Wirkung des ersten großen Holocaust Prozesses." In *NS Prozesse und deutsch Öffentlichkeit: Besatzungszeit frühe Bundesrepublik und DDR*, edited by Jörg Osterloh and Clemens Vollnhals, 233–62. Göttingen: Vandenhoeck and Ruprecht, 2011.

Gedeon, Wolfgang. "Stolperstein-Aktionen Beenden!" http://www.wolfgang-gedeon.de/ 2018/02/stolpersteine/.

Geller, Jay. "The Scholem Brothers and the Paths of Germany Jewry, 1914–1939." *Shofar. An International Journal of Jewish Studies* 30 (2012): 52–73.

Gerhards, Juergen. "Politischer Regimewechsel und der Aufstieg und der Fall der deutschen Vornamen." In *Die Moderne und ihre Vornamen: Eine Einladung in die Kultursoziologie*, edited by J. Gerhards, 71–85. Berlin: Springer Verlag, 2003.

Godau-Schüttke, Klaus-Detlev. *Die Heyde/Sawade-Affäre: Wie Juristen und Mediziner den NS Euthanasieprofessor Heyde nach 1945 deckten und straflos blieben.* 3rd ed. Hamburg: Nomos, 2010.

Goebbels, Joseph. "finden Sie, daß Isidor sich richtig verhält?" In *Der Angriff: Aufsätze aus der Kampfzeit*, 314–15. Munich: Zentralverlag der NSDAP, 1935.

———. *Der Angriff.* Munich: Zentralverlag der NSDAP, 1935.

Goeschel, Christian. *Suicide in Nazi Germany.* Oxford: Oxford University Press, 2009.

Görtemaker, Manfred and Christoph Safferling. *Die Akte Rosenburg: Das Bundesministerium der Justiz und die NS-Zeit.* Munich: C. H. Beck, 2016.

Goldenhagen, Daniel. "Genocide Worse than War." http://www.pbs.org/wnet/worse-than-war/the-film/about/the-film-about-the-film/17/.

Gräbner, Dieter. *Wer war Hermann Röchling?* St. Ingbert, Saarland: Conte Verlag, 2014.

Graw, Ansgar. "Zahl der antisemitischen Delikte in Deutschland steigt." *Die Welt*. September 8, 2017. https://www.welt.de/politik/deutschland/article168436745/Zahl-der -antisemitischen-Delikte-in-Deutschland-steigt.html.

Gray, David and Stephen Henderson, eds. *The Cambridge Handbook of Surveillance Law.* Cambridge: Cambridge University Press, 2017.

Grün, Bernd. "Sophie Ehrhardt (1902–1990)." In *100 Jahre Frauenstudium an Universität Tübingen 1904–2004: historische Überblick, Zeitzeuginnenberichte und Zeitdokumente*, edited by Gleichstellungsbüro der Universität Tübingen, 396–408. Tübingen: University of Tübingen, 2007.

Grzebyk, Partrycja. *Criminal Responsibility for the Crime of Aggression.* London: Routledge, 2010.

Haaretz. "French Lab Discovers Remains of Jews Experimented on by Nazi Anatomists." https://www.haaretz.com/jewish/french-lab-discovers-remains-of-jews-experimented -on-by-nazi-anatomist-1.5376988.

Hafner, Georg M. and Esther Schapira. *Die Akte Alois Brunner: Warum einer der größten Naziverbrecher noch immer auf freiem Fuß ist.* Hamburg: Rowohlt Verlag, 2002.

Harms, Volker, Gottfried Korff, and Anette Michels, eds. *Achtunddreissig Dinge: Schätze aus der Natur- und Kulturwissenschaftlichen Sammlungen der Universität Tübingen."* Tübingen: Museum der Universität Tübingen, 2006.

Harrell, Erika. "Victims of Identity Theft." United States Department of Justice, Bureau of Justice Statistics. September 2015. https://www.bjs.gov/content/pub/pdf/vit14.pdf.

Harvard Law School Nuremberg Trials Project. December 16, 1946. http://nuremberg.law.harvard.edu/.

———. January 17, 1947. http://nuremberg.law.harvard.edu/.

———. May 16, 1947. http://nuremberg.law.harvard.edu/.

Heiber, Helmut. *Der ganz normale Wahnsinn unterm Hakenkreuz: Triviales und Absonderliches aus den Akten des Dritten Reichs.* Munich: Deutscher Taschenbuch Verlag, 2001.

———. *Reichsführer! Briefe an und von Himmler.* Munich: Deutscher Taschenbuch Verlag, 1970.

Heiber, Beatrice and Helmut Heiber. *Die Rückseite des Hakenkreuzes: Absonderliches aus den Akten des Dritten Reiches.* Munich: Deutscher Taschenbuch Verlag, 1993.

Heinemann, Isabel. *Rasse, Siedlung, deutsches Blut: Das Rasse- und Siedlungshauptamt der SS und die rassenpolitische Neuordnung Europas.* Göttingen: Wallstein, 2003.

Helm, Sarah. *Ohne Haar und Ohne Namen: Im Frauen-Konzentrationslager Ravensbrück.* Darmstadt: Theiss Verlag, 2016.

Hernández-Truyol, Berta. "Nativism, Terrorism, and Human Rights." *Columbia Human Rights Law Review* 31 (2000): 521–59.

Heyde, Käthe. "Leser Brief." *Der Spiegel,* 1964. http://magazin.spiegel.de/EpubDelivery/spiegel/pdf/46163172.

Hildebrandt, Sabine. *The Anatomy of Murder: Ethical Transgressions and Anatomical Science During the Third Reich.* New York: Berghan, 2016.

Hill, Benno. "Human Genetics and the Mass Murder of the Jews, Gypsy, and Others." In *The Holocaust and History: The Known, the Unknown, the Disputed, and the Reexamined,* edited by Michael Berenbaum and Abraham J. Peck, 103–15. Indianapolis: Indiana University Press, 1998.

Hillel, Marc and Clarissa Henry. *Lebensborn e.V.: Im Namen der Rasse.* Hamburg: Paul Zsolnay Verlag, 1975.

Hilmes, Oliver. *Berlin 1936: Sechzehn Tage im August.* Munich: Siedler Verlag, 2016.

Himmler, Katrin. *Die Bruder Himmler: Eine deutsche Familiengeschichte.* Frankfurt am Main: Fischer Verlag, 2005.

Hing, Bill Ong. "The Administration of Immigration Law." In *Immigration Law and Social Justice,* edited by Bill Ong Hing, Jennifrer Chacon, and Kevin Johnson, 153–246. New York: Wolters Kluwer, 2018.

Hinz-Wessels, Annette. "Die Halten der Kirchen zur 'Euthanasie' im NS-Staat." In *Lebensunwert zerstörte Leben: Zwangssterilisation und 'Euthanasie,'* edited by Margret Hamm, 168–82. Frankfurt am Main: Verlag für akademische Schriften, 2006.

———. *Tiergartenstrasse 4: Schaltzentrale der nationalsozialistischen 'Euthanasie-Morde'.* Berlin: C. H. Link, 2015.

Hoffmann, Ute. "'Wir haben nur unsere Pflicht getan': Täter und Täterinnen in den Gasmordanstalten der 'Euthanasie.'" In *Tödliche Medizin: Rassenwahn im Nationalsozialismus,* edited by Margret Kampmeyer, 116–22. Gottingen: Wallstein, 2009.

Holpfer, Eva. "Ich war nichts anderes als ein kleiner Sachbearbeiter von Eichmann: die justizielle Fahndung von Deportationsverbrechen in Österreich." In *Holocaust Kriegsverbrechen vor Gericht: Der Fall Österreich*, edited by Thomas Albrich, Winifried Garscha, and Martin Polaschek, 151–82. Innsbruck: Studien Verlag, 2006.

Hopfer, Ines. *Geraubte Identität: Die gewaltsame Eindeutschung von polnische Kindern in der NS-Zeit*. Graz: Böhlau Verlag, 2010.

Hrabar, Roman, Zofia Tokarz, and Jacek Edward Wilczur. *Kinder im Krieg—Krieg gegen Kinder: Die Geschichte der Polnischen Kinder 1939–1945*. Hamburg: Rowohlt Verlag, 1981.

Hüttenmeister, Nathanja. *Jüdische Friedhöfe in der NS-Zeit*. http://spurer suche.steinh eim-institut.org/pdf/NS_Zeit.pdf.

International Tracing Service Bad Arolsen. "Stiefvater von Magda Goebbels." Code: 1.1.5.3/5893549. ITS Digital Archive. September 30, 2015. https://www.its-arolsen. org/nc/news/news/detailseite/news/stiefvater-von-magda-goebbels/.

Jachertz, Norbert. "Brandenburg: 9000 Opfer, 8000 Namen." *Arzteblatt* 11 (December 2012): 564.

Jackson, Robert H. "Nuremberg in Retrospect: Legal Answer to International Lawlessness." *Robert H. Jackson Center*. https://www.robertjackson.org/speech-and-writing/ nuremberg-in-retrospect-legal-answer-to-international-lawlessness/.

———. "Opening Statement before the International Military Tribunal." November 11, 1945. *Trial of the Major War Criminals before the International Military Tribunal*. Volume II. Proceedings: November 14–30, 1945. https://www.robertjackson.org/ speech-and-writing/opening-statement-before-the-international-military-tribunal/.

John, Eckhard, Bernd Martin, Marc Mück, and Hugo Ott, eds. *Die Freiburger Universität in der Zeit des Nationalsozialismus*. Freiburg: Freiburg Verlag, 2000.

Jones, Tamara. "Orphans' Funeral Shelled in Bosnia Conflict." *Los Angeles Times*, August 1992. http://articles.latimes.com/1992–08–05/news/mn-5024_1_terrifying-journey.

Judt, Tony. *Postwar: A History of Europe Since 1945*. New York: Penguin Books, 2005.

Jungbluth, Rüdiger. *Die Quandts: Deutschlands erfolgreichste Unternehmerfamilie*. New York: Campus Verlag, 2015.

———. *Die Quandts: Ihr leiser Aufstieg zur mächtigsten Wirtschaftsdynastie Deutschlands*. Berlin: Campus Verlag, 2002.

Kaiser, Simone. "Den charmanten Sadisten entlarven." *Frankfurter Allgemeine*, March 25, 2005. http://www.faz.net/aktuell/gesellschaft/menschen/ns-verbrechen-den-char-manten-sadisten-entlarven-1214328.html.

Kampmeyer, Margret, ed. *Tödliche Medizin: Rassenwahn im Nationalsozialismus*. Gottingen: Wallstein, 2009.

Kaplan, Justin and Anne Bernays. *The Language of Names: What We Call Ourselves and Why it Matters*. New York: Simon and Schuster, 1997.

Kater, Michael. *Das 'Ahenenerbe' der SS 1935–1945: Ein Beitrag zur Kulturpolitik des Dritten Reiches*. Munich: R. Oldenbourg Verlag, 2006.

Kean, Thomas and Lee Hamilton. *The 9/11 Commission Report: Final Report of the National Commission on Terrorist Attacks Upon the United States*. New York: St. Martin's Press, 2004.

Kellerhoff, Sven. "Brisante Papier aus dem Müllhaufen," *Die Welt*, November 2, 2005. https://www.welt.de/print-welt/article174881/Brisante-Papiere-aus-dem-Muellhaufen.html.

———. "Arolsen liegt bald in elf Staaten," *Die Welt*, April 20, 2006. https://www.welt.de/print-welt/article211499/Arolsen-liegt-bald-in-elf-Staaten.html.

———. "Hitler schützte jüdischen Frontoffizier." *Die Welt*. July 7, 2012. https://www.welt.de/print/die_welt/politik/article108013899/Hitler-schuetzte-juedischen-Frontoffizier.html.

———. "Die Vordenker der Reichsbürger? Terroristen!" *Die Welt*, October 25, 2016. https://www.welt.de/politik/deutschland/article159036380/Die-Vordenker-der-Reichsbuerger-Terroristen.html.

Kessler, Gerhard. *Die Familiennamen der Juden in Deutschland*. Leipzig: Zentralstelle für Deutsche Personen—und Famliengeschichte, 1935.

Khull-Kholwald, Ferdinand. *Gebt den Kindern deutsche Namen!* Leipzig: Leopold Stocker Verlag, 1939.

Kilpert, Daniel. "Antisemitismus von links." Bundeszentrale für politische Bildung, November 28, 2006. http://www.bpb.de/politik/extremismus/linksextremismus/33604/antisemitismus-von-links?p=all.

Klabunde, Anja. *Magda Goebbels: Annäherung an ein Leben*. Berlin: Bertelsman, 1999.

Klee, Ernst. *Dokumente Zur "Euthanasie."* Frankfurt am Main: Fischer Taschenbuch Verlag, 1985.

———. "Den Hahn aufzudrehen war ja keine grosse Sache': Vergassungsärzte während der NS-Zeit und danach." *Dachauer Heft* 4: Medizin um NS-Staat: Täter, Opfer, Handlungen (1993): 1–21.

———. "Verschonte Medizinverbrecher: Die Professoren Heinze und Hallervorden." *Dachauer Hefte* 13: Gericht und Gerechtigkeit. (December 1997): 142–52.

———. *Deutsche Medizin im Dritten Reich: Karriere vor und nach 1945*. Frankfurt am Main: S. Fischer Verlag, 2001.

———. *Das Personenlexikon zum Dritten Riech: Wer war Was vor und nach 1945*. Hamburg: Nikol Verlag, 2015.

Klemperer, Victor. *LTI: Notizbuch eines Philologen*. Halle a. d. S.: Niemeyer, 1957. Reprinted. 23rd edition. Stuttgart: Reclam Taschenbuch, 2007.

Kogon, Eugen. "Das Recht auf den politischen Irrtum." *Frankfurter Hefte: Zeitschrift für Kultur und Politik*, 7 (July 1947). http://www.ikvu.de/fileadmin/user_upload/PDF/Eugen_Kogon_Das_Recht_auf_den_politischen_Irrtum_1947.pdf.

Koonz, Claudia. *Mothers in the Fatherland: Women, the Family, and Nazi Politics*. New York: St. Martin's Press, 1987.

Koop, Volker. *Dem Führer ein Kind Schenken: Die SS-Organisation Lebensborn e.v.*. Cologne: Böhlau Verlag, 2007.

———. *Himmlers Germanenwahn: Die SS-Organisation Ahnenerbe und ihre Verbrechen*. Berlin: be.bra Verlag, 2012.

———. *Wer Jude ist, bestimmte ich: Ehrenarier im Nationalsozialismus*. Cologne: Böhlau Verlag, 2014.

Kompisch, Kathrin. *Täterinnen: Frauen im Nationalsozialismus*. Cologne: Böhlau Verlag, 2008.

Koslov, Elissa Mailänder. "Going East: Colonial Experiences and Practices of Violence Among Female and Male Majdanek Camp Guards (1941–1944)." *Journal of Genocide Research* 10, no. 4 (2008): 563–82.

Kramer, Nicole. *Volksgenossinnen an der Heimatfront: Mobilisierung, Verhalten, Erinnerung, Schriftenreihe der Historischen Kommission*, Band 82. Göttingen: Vandenhoeck & Ruprecht, 2011.

Kriegsbriefe gefallener deutscher Juden. [with an introduction by Franz Josef Strauß] Stuttgart: Seewald Verlag, 1935.

Kritz, Neil. *Transitional Justice: How Emerging Democracies Reckon with Former Regimes. Volume III: Laws, Rulings, and Reports.* Washington, DC: United States Institute of Peace, 1995, 400.

Kulish, Nicholas and Souad Mekhennet. *The Eternal Nazi—from Mathausen to Cairo: The Relentless Pursuit of SS Doctor Aribert Heim.* New York: Random House, 2014.

Kulka, Otto Dov. "Ghetto in an Annihilation Camp: Jewish Social History in the Holocaust and Its Ultimate Limits." In *The Nazi Holocaust: The Victims of the Holocaust.* Vol. 2, Part 6, edited by Michael Robert Marrus, 1133–50. London: De Gruyter, 1989.

Kundrus, Birthe and Beate Meyer, eds. *Die Deportationen der Juden aus Deutschland: Pläne-Praxis-Reaktionen 1938–1945.* Göttingen: Wallstein Verlag, 2004.

Kunze, Konrad. *Vor- und Familienname im deutschen Sprachgebiet.* Munich: Deutsche Taschenbuch Verlag, 2004.

Lacquer, Walter, ed. *The Holocaust Encyclopedia.* London: Yale University Press, 2001.

Lafraniere, Sharon. "Court finds Rwanda Media Executives Guilty of Genocide." *The New York Times*, December 3, 2003. http://www.nytimes.com/2003/12/03/international/africa/court-finds-rwanda-media-executives-guilty-of-genocide.html.

Lamey, Annegret. *Kind unbekannter Herkunft: Die Geschichte des Lebensbornkindes Hannes Dollinger.* Augsburg: Wißner-Verlag, 2008.

Landtag Mecklenberg-Vorpommern. "Kleine Anfrage des Dr. Matthias Manthei, Fraktion der AfD." Kirchenasyl in Anklam und Antwort der Landesregierung. Plenarprotokolle 17. Sitzung, 2017. https://kleineanfragen.de/mecklenburg-vorpommern/7/506-kirchenasyl-in-anklam.

Lang, Hans-Joachim. *Die Namen der Nummern: Wie es gelang, die 86 Opfer eines NS-Verbrechens zu identifizieren.* Hamburg: Fischer Taschenbuchverlag, 2004.

Langerbein, Helmut. *Hitler's Death Squads: The Logic of Mass Murder.* College Station: Texas A & M University Press, 2003.

Latif, et al. v. Eric Holder, US Attorney General et al. (2013). https://www.aclu.org/sites/default/files/assets/latif_v_holder_opinion_and_order.pdf.

Laws and Orders of Military Government: Complete Collection Up to June 30th 1945. "Law No. 1: Abrogation of Nazi Law." Wiesbaden: Vieweg and Teubner Verlag, 1945.

Lehman, Hartmut and Otto Gerhard Oexle, eds. *Nationalsozialismus in der Kulturwissenschaften.* Göttingen: Vanderhoeck and Ruprecht, 2004.

Lelyveld, Joseph. *Omaha Blues: A Memory Loop.* New York: Picador Press, 2006.

———. "Breaking Away." *The New York Times*, March 6, 2005. https://www.nytimes.com/2005/03/06/magazine/breaking-away.html.

Lenhart, Anne-Maria. *Eine Darstellung der Organisation 'Lebensborn e. V.'* Hamburg: Diplomica Verlag, 2013.

Letau, Hermine. *Wie heißt du? 500 Vornamen und ihre Bedeutung.* Königsberg: Sturmverlag, 1942.

Levine, Marci and Frank Willis. "Public Reactions to Unusual Names." *The Journal of Social Psychology* 134, no. 5 (1994): 561–68.

Levy, Günter. *The Nazi Persecution of the Gypsies.* Oxford: Oxford University Press, 2000.

Levy, Max. *Der Napoleonische Erlass von 1808: Wegen der Vor- und Zunamen der Juden und seine Ausführung in Worms.* Worms: Buchdruckerei Eugen Kranzbühler, 1914.

Liebig, Hans-Werner. "Historie von Gut Hohehorst." December 2013. http://loehnhorst-online.de/hohehorst/HOHEHORST-HISTORIE.pdf.

Lifton, Robert Jay. *The Nazi Doctors: Medical Killing and the Psychology of Genocide.* New York: Basic Books, 1986.

Lilienthal, Georg. "Medizin und Rassenpolitik: Der Lebensborn der SS." *Deutsches Ärzteblatt* B. 85 (1988): 2128–34.

———. *Das 'Lebensborn e. V.': Ein Instrument nationalsozialistischer Rassenpolitik.* Frankfurt am Main: Fischer Verlag, 2003.

———. "Wie die T4-Aktion organisiert wurde: Zur Bürokratie eines Massenmordes." In *Lebensunwert—zerstörte Leben: Zwangssterilisation und 'Euthanasie',* edited by Magret Hamm, 143–57. Frankfurt am Main: Verlag für akademische Schriften, 2006.

Lisbach, Bertrand and Victoria Meyer. *Linguistic Identity Matching.* Wiesbaden, Springer, 2013.

Longerich, Peter. *Heinrich Himmler: Biographie.* Berlin: Pantheon Press, 2010.

Lommatzsch, Erik. *Hans Globke (1898–1973): Beamter im Dritten Reich und Staatssekretär Adenauers.* Frankfurt: Campus Verlag, 2009.

Lower, Wendy. *Hitler's Furies: German Women in the Nazi Killing Fields.* New York: Houghton Mifflin Harcourt, 2013.

Ludwig, Astrid. "Internierungslager mit eigener Zeitung und Universität." *Frankfurter Allgemeine.* March 30, 2005. http://www.fr-online.de/zeitgeschichte/internierungslager-mit-eigener-zeitung-und-universitaet,1477344,2802516.html.

Lutteroh, Judith. "Als ein deutscher Wollbaron die Welt erschütterte." *Spiegel Online.* December 2, 2011. http://www.spiegel.de/einestages/bankenkrise-1931-als-ein-deutscher-wollbaron-die-welt-erschuetterte-a-947408.html.

MacQueen, Michael. "Das 'Office of Special Investigations' beim US-Justizministerium: Die Verfolgung von NS Vebrechern in den Vereinigten Staaten." *Dachauer Heft* 13: Gericht und Gerechtigkeit (1997): 123–34.

Mailänder, Elissa. *Female SS Guards and Workaday Violence: The Majdanek Concentration Camp, 1942–1944.* East Lansing: Michigan State University Press, 2015.

Master, Barry. "The Development of Fluorescence Microscopy." In *The Encyclopedia of Life Sciences,* edited by Yixian Zheng. Chichester: John Wiley and Sons, 2010.

McDonnell, Thomas. "Targeting the Foreign Born by Race and Nationality: Counterproductive in the 'War on Terrorism.'" *Pace Law Faculty Publications* 16, no. 19 (2004): 20–63.

McHale, Terence. "But the Thing Will Still Remain." *California Conversations* (Summer, 2011). http://www.californiaconversations.com/index.php/current_issue.

Megargee, Geoffrey P., ed. *Aligned with Nazi Germany*. Bloomington: Indiana University Press, 2018.

Meier, Thomas. "Konrad Adenauer: Integration." In *Das Wort hat der Herr Bundeskanzler: Eine Analyse der Großen Regierungserklärungen von Adenauer bis Schröder*, edited by Karl-Rudolf Korte, 85–116. Wiesbaden: Westdeutscher Verlag, 2002.

Meissner, Hans-Otto. *Magda Göbbels: eine Lebensbild*. Munich: Blanvalet Verlag, 1978.

Merrett, Anna and Richard Merrett. *Public Opinion in Semisovereign Germany: the HICOG Surveys, 1949–1955*. Urbana: University of Illinois Press, 1980.

Merrett, Richard. *Democracy Imposed: US Occupation Policy and the German Public, 1945–1949*. New Haven: Yale University Press, 1995.

Metzer, Erwin. *Die deutschen Vorname*. Goslar: Blut und Boden Verlag, 1939.

Meyer, Beate. *Tödliche Gratwanderung: Die Reichsvereinigung der Juden in Deutschland zwischen Hoffnung, Zwang, Selbstbehauptung und Verstrickung (1939–1945)*. Göttingen: Wallstein Verlag, 2011.

Meyer, Peter Ulrich. "Wie Adolf Hitlers Halbbruder in Hamburg untertauchte." *Abendblatt*. March 23, 2016. https://www.abendblatt.de/hamburg/article207266299/Wie-Adolf-Hitlers-Halbbruder-in-Hamburg-untertauchte.html.

Migration Policy Organization. "Chronology of Events Since September 11, 2001 Related to Immigration and National Security." http://www.migrationpolicy.org/sites/default/files/source_charts/FE-post911-chronology-2002.pdf.

Milton, Sybil. "Holocaust: Gypsies." In *Century of Genocide: Critical Essays and Eyewitness Accounts*, edited by Samuel Totten, William Parsons, and Israel Charny, 133–69. New York: Routledge, 2004.

Ministerialblatt. "Änderung und Feststellung von Familiennamen sowie Änderung von Vornamen III Familienrechtliche Gesichtspunkte." No. 7, May 28, 1949: 458.

Minkel, J. R. "Confirmed: The US Census Bureau Gave Up the Names of Japanese-Americans in WWII." *Scientific American*. March 30, 2007. https://www.scientificamerican.com/article/confirmed-the-us-census-b/.

Mitteldeutscher Rundfunk. "Ein Akt der Menschlichkeit." https://www.upi.com/Archives/1992/08/02/Orphans-leave-Sarajevo-after-two-killed-by-snipers/2277712728000/.

Mittelstadt, Michelle, Burke Speaker, Doris Meissner, and Muzaffar Chishti. "Through the Prism of National Security: Major Immigration Policy and Program Changes in the Decade Since 9/11." *Migration Policy Institute*. August 2011. http://www.migrationpolicy.org/research/post-9–11-immigration-policy-program-changes.

Mix, Andreas. "50 Jahre Zentrale Stelle zur Verfolgung der NS-Verbrechen: Wir dürfen nicht zulassen, dass sie straffrei ausgehen." *Berliner Zeitung*. November 21, 2008. https://www.berliner-zeitung.de/50-jahre-zentrale-stelle-zur-verfolgung-der-ns-verbrechen--wir-duerfen-nicht-zulassen--dass-sie-straffrei-ausgehen--15723302.

———. "Akten von Millionen NS-Opfern in Bad Arolsen werden Forschern geöffnet." *Berliner Zeitung*. April 21, 2006. https://www.berliner-zeitung.de/akten-von-millionen-ns-opfern-in-bad-arolsen-werden-forschern-geoeffnet-druck-aus-washington-15777118.

———. "NS Prozesse: Als Westdeutschland aufwachte." *Der Spiegel*. April 27, 2008.

Moore, Michael Scott. "Fomer Nazi Guard Deported: US Send Elderly Widow Back to Germany." *Der Spiegel*. September 12, 2006. http://www.spiegel.de/international

/former-nazi-guard-deported-us-sends-elderly-widow-back-to-germany-a-438234 .html.

Motadel, David. *Islam and Nazi Germany's War*. London: The Belknap Press of Harvard University Press, 2014.

Müller-Hill, Benno. "Human Genetics and the Mass Murder of Jews, Gypsies, and Others," In *The Holocaust and History: The Known, the Unknown, the Disputed and the Reexamined*, edited by Michael Berenbaum and Abraham J. Peck, 103–14. Indianapolis: Indiana University Press, 1998.

Müller-Münch, Ingrid. *Die Frauen von Majdanek: Vom zerstörten Leben der Opfer und der Mörderinnen*. Munich: Rowohlt Verlag, 1982.

Müller-Tupath, Karla. *Verschollen in Deutschland: Das heimliche Leben des Anton Burger, Lagerkommandant von Theresienstadt*. Hamburg: Konkret Literatur Verlag, 1994.

Myers, Muguette. *Where Courage Lives*. Toronto: The Azrieli Foundation, 2015.

National Counterterrorism Center. Office of the Director of National Intelligence. "Who We Are." https://www.dni.gov/index.php/nctc-who-we-are.

———. "How We Work." https://www.dni.gov/index.php/nctc-how-we-work.

———. "Terrorist Identities Datamart (TIDE)." https://www.dni.gov/files/NCTC/ documents/features_documents/TIDEfactsheet10FEB2017.pdf.

Neuhoff, Willi. "Die Tochter darf nicht Esther heissen." *Wattenscheid: 600 Jahre Freiheit!* Wattenscheid, 2017.

Neureiter, F., F. Pietrusky, and E. Schütt. *Handwörterbuch der gerichtlichen Medizin und naturwissenschaftlichen Kriminalistik*. Berlin: Springer Verlag, 1940.

Nicholson, Michael. *Natasha's Story: How a Nine-Year-Old Orphan was Rescued from War in Sarajevo*. New York: Macmillan, 1993.

Noam, Ernst and Wolf-Arno Kropat. *Juden vor Gericht 1933–1945 Band I*. Wiesbaden: Kommission für die Geschichte der Juden in Hessen, 1986.

Novak, Kurt. "Widerstand, Zustimmung, Hinnahme. Das Verhalten der Bevölkerung zur 'Euthanasie.'" In *Medizin und Gesundheitspolitik in der NS-Zeit*, edited by Norbert Frei, 235–52. Munich: Oldenbourg Verlag, 1991.

Nuebling, Damaris and Antje Dammel. "Das deutsche Personennamensystem." In *Europäische Personennamensysteme*. edited by Andrea Brendler and Silvio Brendler, 139–52. Hamburg: Baar, 2007.

Nückles, Bärbel. "Mediziner spürt die Sammlung des Nazi-Arztes August Hirt auf." *Badische Zeitung*, July 24, 2015. http://www.badische-zeitung.de/elsass-x2x/mediziner-spuert-die-sammlung-des-nazi-arztes-august-hirt-auf--108263483.html.

Office of the Inspector. Social Security Administration. "General Congressional Response Report. Payment of Social Security Benefits to Individuals Who May Have Participated in Nazi Persecution." [A-09–15–50013], 2015. https://oig.ssa.gov/sites/ default/files/audit/full/pdf/A-09–15–50013.pdf.

Olson, Kåre. *Vater: Deutscher: Das Schicksal der norwegischen Lebensbornkinder und ihre Mütter von 1940 bis heute*. Frankfurt am Main: Campus Verlag, 2002.

Organization for Security and Co-operation in Europe. *Kosovo/Kosova: As Seen, as Told*. https://www.osce.org/odihr/17772?download=true.

Ornter, Helmut. *Hitlers Schatten: Deutsche Reportagen*. Frankfurt: Nomen Verlag, 2013.

Orr, Bob. "Inside a Secret US Terrorist Screening Center." *CBS News*, October 12, 2012. https://www.cbsnews.com/news/inside-a-secret-us-terrorist-screening-center/.

The Palestine Post. "Official List of Names for Jews." August 29, 1938.

Paxton, Robert. *Vichy France: Old Grand and New Order, 1940–1944*. New York: Columbia University Press, 1972.

Perz, Bertrand. "müssen zu reißenden Bestien erzogen werde: Der Einsatz von Hunden zur Bewachung in den Konzentrationslagern." *Dachauer Hefte* 12: Lebenswelt und Umwelt (1996): 139–58.

Pietsch, U. "Die Geschichte der Liebermann-Villa in Volksdorf." *De Spieker Jahrbuch* (2014). http://www.heimatecho.de/archiv/sonder_pdf/2014–10–01.pdf.

Poliokov, Leon and Joseph Wulf. *Das Dritte Reich und seine Denker*. Munich: K.G. Sauer Verlag, 1978.

President, Proclamation Alien Enemies—Germans, No. 2526. http://www.foitimes.com/internment/Proc2526.html.

———. Italians, No. 2527. http://www.foitimes.com/internment/Proc2527.html.

———. Japanese, No. 2525. http://www.foitimes.com/internment/Proc2525.html.

Radio Télévision libre des mille Collines. Broadcast Transcripts from the UN International Crimes Tribunal for Rwanda. http://www.genocidearchiverwanda.org.rw/index.php/Radio_T%C3%A9l%C3%A9vision_Libre_des_Mille_Collines.

Ranft, Ferdinand. "Ohne Scham und ohne Reue." *Zeit Online*, March 25, 1966. https://www.zeit.de/1966/13/ohne-scham-und-ohne-reue/.

———. "Der Professor Hirt und seine Todestransporte. " *Mittelbadische Presse*, June 14, 2016. https://www.bo.de/nachrichten/nachrichten-regional/der-professor-hirt-und-seine-todestransporte.

Redmonds, George, Turi King, and David Hey. *Surnames, DNA, and Family History*. Oxford: Oxford University Press, 2011.

Reck, Reinhard. "Der Professor Hirt und seine Todestransporte." *Mittelbadische Presse*, June 14, 2016. https://www.bo.de/nachrichten/nachrichten-regional/der-professor-hirt-und-seine-todestransporte.

Reichstag Protokolle, Band 425, 96. Sitzung June 26, 1929.

Reitzenstein, Julien. *Himmlers Forscher: Wehrwissenschaft und Medizinverbrechen im "Ahnenerbe" der SS*. Paderborn: Ferdinand Schönigh Verlag, 2014.

Reilly, Kate. "Action is the Only Remedy to Indifference: Elie Wiesel's Most Powerful Quotes." *Time*, July 2, 2016. http://time.com/4392252/elie-wiesel-dead-best-quotes/

Rennick, Robert. "Offensive Names." *Verbatim* 29, no. 4 (2004): 21–26.

Reuth, Ralf Georg, ed. *Joseph Goebbels Tagebücher 1924–1945*. Munich: Piper Verlag, 1999.

Roberts, Sam. "Hispanic Surnames on the Rise in the US as Immigration Surges." *The New York Times*. December, 2016. https://www.nytimes.com/2016/12/15/us/census-data-hispanic-surnames.html.

Rodgers, Jennifer. "Humanity's Ancestral Inheritance." *International Tracing Service*. https://www.its-arolsen.org/fileadmin/user_upload/images/Ueber_ITS/content/Englisch/Humanity_s_Ancestral_Inheritance_Rodgers.pdf.

Roemer, Nils. *German City, Jewish Memory: The Story of Worms*. Lebanon, NH: Brandeis University Press, 2010.

Rosenberg, Eli. "Motel 6 Gave Lists to ICE Agents Looking for 'Latino-Sounding' Names, Lawsuit Alleges." *The Washington Post*, January 3, 2018.

Rother, Bernd. *Spanien und der Holocaust*. Tübingen: De Gruyter, 2001.

Rubin, Barry and Wolfgang G. Schwanitz. *Nazis, Islamists, and the Making of the Modern Middle East*. New Haven, CT: Yale University Press, 2014.

Rückerl, Adalbert. *Die Strafverfolgung von NS-Verbrechen 1945–1978*. Heidelberg: CF Müller Juristischer Verlag, 1979.

Ruth, Georg, ed. *Joseph Göbbels Tagebücher 1924–1945*. Munich: Piper Verlag, 1999.

Sacramento Daily Union. "Shot for leaving a Valentine." February 28, 1870. California Digital Newspaper Collection. Vol. 38. No. 5904. https://cdnc.ucr.edu/cgi-bin/cdnc?a=d&d=SDU18700228.2.20.

Saito, Natsu Taylor. "Internments, Then and Now: Constitutional Accountability in Post-9/11 America." *Duke Forum for Law and Social Change* 2, no. 71 (2010): 72–101.

Sanford, George. *Katyn and the Soviet Massacre of 1940: Truth, Justice and Memory*. New York: Routledge, 2009.

Schafft, Gretchen. *From Racism to Genocide: Anthropology in the Third Reich*. Chicago: University of Illinois Press, 2004.

Scheibel, Oskar. "Ein neuer Anophthalmus aus Jugoslawien." *Entomologische Blätter* 33, no. 6 (1937): 438–40.

Schelvis, Jules. *Sobibor: A History of a Nazi Death Camp*. New York: Bloomsbury, 2007.

Schiff, Vera and Jeff McLaughlin. *Bound for Theresienstadt: Love, Loss, and Resistance in a Nazi Concentration Camp*. Jefferson, North Carolina: McFarland and Co., 2017.

Schleswig-Holsteinischer Landtag. "NS-Kontinuitäten in der Landespolitik: Schleswig-Holstein ist ein Extremfall." April 27, 2016. https://www.sh-landtag.de/aktuell/panorama/Beitraege_2016/16_04_27_danker.html.

Schleswig-Holstein Landtag 4. *Bericht des Untersuchungsausschusses I in der Angelegenheit Prof. Heyde/Dr. Sawade*. 1958. Drucksache Nr. 444.

———. *Bericht des Untersuchungsausschusses II in der Angelegenheit Prof. Heyde/Dr. Sawade*. 1958. Drucksache Nr. 445.

Schmidt, Ulf. *Hitlers Arzt Brandt: Medizin und Macht im Dritten Reich*. Berlin: Aufbau Verlag, 2009.

Schmitz, Thorsten. "Die Stüte von Majdanek in Hitlers Schatten: Deutsche Reportagen." In *Hitlers Schatten: Deutsche Reportagen*, edited by Helmut Ornter, 50–68. Frankfurt am Main: Nomen Verlag, 2013.

Schmitz-Berning, Cornelia. *Vokabular des Nationalsozialismus*. Berlin: Walter de Gruyter, 2000.

Schmitz-Köster, Dorothee. *Deutsche Mutter, bist du bereit: Alltag im Lebensborn*. Berlin: Aufbau Taschenbuch Verlag, 2002.

Schmitz-Köster, Dorothee and Tristan Vankann. *Lebenslang Lebensborn: Die Wunschkinder der SS und was aus ihnen wurde*. Munich: Piper Verlag, 2012.

Schneider, Wolfgang. *Frauen unterm Hakenkreuz*. Munich: Knaur Taschenverlag, 2003.

Schoen Consulting. "Holocaust Knowledge & Awareness Study." May 2018. http://cc-69bd.kxcdncom/wp-content/uploads/2018/04/Holocaust-Knowledge-Awareness-Study_Executive-Summary-2018.pdf.

Scholtyseck, Joachim. *Der Aufstieg der Quandts: eine deutsche Unternehmerdynastie.* Munich: C. H. Beck, 2011.

Scholtz-Klink, Gertrud. *Die Frau im Dritten Reich: Eine Dokumentation* Tübingen: Grabert, 1998.

Schröm, Oliver and Andrea Römpke. *Stille Hilfe für braune Kameraden: Das geheime Netzwerk der Alt- und Neonazis.* Berlin: C. H. Links, 2001.

Schymura, Yvonne. "Morden in Name der Wissenschaft." *Der Spiegel*, March 9, 2016. http://www.spiegel.de/einestages/ns-aerzte-experimente-an-kz-insassen-a-1080450. html.

Schwarberg, Günther. "Inferno und Befreiung: Zwanzig Kinder erhängen dauert lange." *Die Zeit*, April 6, 2005. http://www.zeit.de/2005/15/A-Kinder.

———. *Der SS-Arzt und die Kinder: Bericht über den Mord vom Bullenhuser Damm.* Hamburg: Stern Verlag, 1979.

Schwender, Clemens. *Wie benutze ich den Fernsprecher? Die Anleitung zum Telefonieren im Berliner Telefonbuch 1881–1996/97.* Frankfurt am Main: Peter Lang, 1997.

Seghetti, Lisa and Stephen Viña. "US Visitor and Immigrant Status Indicator Technology (US-VISIT) Program," *Congressional Report Service* [CRS], Report for Congress, February 23, 2005.

Seibert, Winfried. *Das Mädchen, das nicht ESTHER heißen durfte: Eine exemplarische Geschichte.* Leipzig: Reclam Verlag, 1996.

Seibicke, Wilfried. *Die Personenamen im Deutschen.* Berlin: de Gruyter, 2008.

Seidler, Edward. "Die medizinische Fakultät 1926 und 1948." In *Die Freiburger Universität in der Zeit des National Sozialismus*, edited by Eckhard John Bernd Martin, Marc Mück, and Hugo Ott, 73–90. Freiburg: Freiburg Verlag, 1991.

Seinitz, Kurt. "'Krone' Journalist Seinitz interviewte Brunner in 1986 in Damaskus." *Tiroler Tagezeitung Online*, December 1, 2014. https://www.tt.com/ticker/9333392/ krone-journalist-seinitz-interviewte-brunner-1986-in-damaskus.

Sennholz, Marco. *Johann von Leer: Ein Propagandist des Nationalsozialismus.* Berlin-Brandenburg: Be-Bra Verlag, 2013.

The Sentinel. "Jews Forbidden to Adopt Gentile Names." February 2, 1920.

———. "Joshua Not Good Name for Nazi, Court Rules." August 18, 1938.

———. "Israel will not Alter Name." February 23, 1939.

Sharples, Caroline and Olaf Jensen, eds. *Britain and the Holocaust: Remembering and Representing War and Genocide.* London: Palgrave Macmillan, 2013.

Shaw, Standford. *Turkey and the Holocaust: Turkey's Role in Rescuing Turkish and European Jewry from Nazi Persecution, 1933–1945.* New York: Palgrave, 1993.

Shirer, William. *The Rise and Fall of the Third Reich: A History of Nazi Germany.* New York: Simon & Schuster, 2011.

Sigmund, Anna Maria. *Die Frauen der Nazis I.* Vienna: Überreuter, 1998.

———. *Die Frauen der Nazis II.* Vienna: Heyne Sachbuch, 2000.

———. *Die Frauen der Nazis III.* Vienna: Heyne Sachbuch, 2002.

Sontheimer, Michael. "When We Finish, Nobody is Left Alive." *Der Spiegel*, May 27, 2011. http://www.spiegel.de/international/europe/germany-s-wwii-occupation-of-pol and-when-we-finish-nobody-is-left-alive-a-759095.html.

Der Spiegel. "Personalien: Alois Hiller." February 23, 1955. http://www.spiegel.de/spi egel/print/d-31969320.html.

————. "Globke: ein unbedeutende Mann." No. 19, 1961. http://magazin.spiegel.de/EpubDelivery/spiegel/pdf/43159747.

————. Professor Dr. Werner Creutzfeldt and Dr. Otto Creutzfeldt, Leserbrief, Nr. 13, 1964.

————. "Handvoll Asche." *NS-Verbrechen/Euthanasie.* No. 8 (February 19, 1964): 28–38. http://magazin.spiegel.de/EpubDelivery/spiegel/pdf/46163172.

————. "NS Verbrechen: Peitsche bewahrt." December 19, 1966. http://www.spiegel.de/spiegel/print/d-46415595.html.

————. "Blutige Brgyda." *KZ-Prozesse.* No. 49 (December 1, 1975): 86–87. http://magazin.spiegel.de/EpubDelivery/spiegel/pdf/41392711.

————. "'Holocaust': Die Vergangenheit kommt zurück." No. 5 (January 29, 1979): 17–28. http://magazin.spiegel.de/EpubDelivery/spiegel/pdf/40350860.

————. "Ein Toter gleich zehn Minuten Gefängnis. Die Rolle der bundesdeutschen Justiz bei der Aufarbeitung von NS- Verbrechen." No. 28 (July 9, 1979): 46–55. http://magazin.spiegel.de/EpubDelivery/spiegel/pdf/40350042.

————. "Diese Augen." Prozesse. No. 12 (March, 19, 1979). http://magazin.spiegel.de/EpubDelivery/spiegel/pdf/40350194.

————. "Die Kreuzelschreiber." Ärzte. Euthanasie. http://magazin.spiegel.de/EpubDelivery/spiegel/pdf/43160977.

Spitz, Vivien. *Doctors from Hell: The Horrific Account of Nazi Experiments on Humans.* Boulder, CO: Sentient Publications, 2005.

Stangneth, Bettina. "Warum tilgte der BND die Akte des Eichmann-Helfers?" *Die Welt,* August 21, 2011. https://www.welt.de/kultur/history/article13554689/Warum-tilgte-der-BND-die-Akte-des-Eichmann-Helfers.html.

Steinacher, Gerald. *Nazis on the Run: How Hitler's Henchmen Fled Justice.* Oxford: Oxford University Press, 2012.

Steinbock, Daniel. "Designating the Dangerous: From Blacklisting to Watchlist." *Seattle University Law Review* 30 (2006): 65–118.

Steinke, Ronnen and Andreas Voßkuhle. *Fritz Bauer: Oder Auschwitz vor Gericht.* Berlin: Piper Verlag, 2015.

Stelly, Melanie and Corinna Schneider. "Mit beschränkter Aufenthaltsberechtigung: Frauen an der Universität Tübingen in der Nachkriegszeit." In *100 Jahre Frauenstudium an Universität Tübingen 1904–2004: historische Überblick, Zeitzeuginnenberichte und Zeitdokumente,* edited by Gleichstellungsbüro der Universität Tübingen, 70–77. Tübingen: University of Tübingen, 2007.

Streim, Alfred. "Zum Beispiel: Die Verbrechen der Einsatzgruppen in der Sowjetunion." In *NS-Prozesse Nach 25 Jahren Strafverfolgung: Möglichkeiten, Grenzen, Ergebnisse,* edited by Adalbert Rückerl, 65–106. Karlsruhe: C. F. Muller Verlag, 1971.

Strothman, Diether. "Der Schlag gegen das Roder-Rüdel." *Die Zeit,* September 12, 1980. http://www.zeit.de/1980/38/der-schlag-gegen-das-roder-rudel.

Sullivan, Bob. "Identity Theft Hit an All-Time High in 2016." *US Today,* February 13, 2017. https://www.usatoday.com/story/money/personalfinance/2017/02/06/identity-theft-hit-all-time-high-2016/97398548/.

Süß, Winfried. *Der 'Volkskörper' im Krieg: Gesundheitspolitk, Gesundheitsverhältnisse, und Krankenmord im nationalsozialistischen Detuschland 1939–1945*. Munich: Oldenburg Verlag, 2003.

Swarns, Rachel. "Program's Value in Dispute as a Tool to Fight Terrorism." *The New York Times*. December 21, 2004. http://www.nytimes.com/2004/12/21/us/programs-value-in-dispute-as-a-tool-to-fight-terrorism.html.

Sydney Morning Herald, The. "'Perfect Nazi Woman' in London." March 9, 1939. *Trove* (online archive). National Library of Australia. https://trove.nla.gov.au/newspaper/article/17583379/1172693.

Sydow, Christoph. "Judenmörder Alois Brunner starb in Syrien: Eichmanns Stellvertreter." *Der Spiegel*. December 12, 2014. http://www.spiegel.de/politik/ausland/nazi-verbrechen-alois-brunner-stellvertreter-eichmanns-ist-tot-a-1005980.html.

Tammena, Manno Peters. *Namensgebung in Ostfriesland Personennamen. Patronymische Namen: Ursprung, Entwicklung, Niedergang*. Hamburg: Verlag Saltau Kurier Norden, 2009.

Taylor, Frederick. *Exorcising Hitler: The Occupation and Denazification of Germany*. New York: Bloomsbury, 2011.

———. *Inflation: Der Untergang des Geldes in der Weimarer Republik und die Geburt eines deutschen Traumas*. Hamburg: Siedler Verlag, 2013.

TAZ. "Manfred Röder ist tot: Tod eines Neonazis." August 1, 2014. http://www.taz.de/!5036341/.

Teege, Jennifer. *My Grandfather Would Have Shot Me: A Black Woman Discovers Her Family's Nazi Past*. In collaboration with Nikola Sellmair. New York: The Experiment, 2015.

Teevs, Christian. "The AfD in the Bundestag: A Populist Upheaval on the Right." http://www.spiegel.de/nternational/germany/germany-right-wing-afd-celebrates-entry-into-parliament-a-1169631.html.

Tillion, Germaine. *Frauenkonzentrationslager Ravensbrück*. Fernwald: zu Klampen Verlag, 1998.

Thompson, Larry. "Lebensborn and the Eugenics Policy of the Reichsführer-SS." In *The Nazi Holocaust*, vol. 3. edited by Michael Robert Marrus, 601–24. Munich: De Gruyter, 1989.

Tobin, Patrick. *Crossroads at Ulm: Postwar West Germany and the 1958 Ulm Einsatzkommando Trial*. Unpublished Doctoral Dissertation. University of North Carolina at Chapel Hill. 2013.

Toledano, Raphäel. "August Hirt and the Supply of Corpses at the Anatomical Institute of the Reichsuniversität Straßburg," In *From Clinic to Concert: Reassessing Nazi Medical and Racial Research, 1933–1945*, edited by Paul Weindling, 100–120. New York: Routledge, 2017.

Trials of War Criminals Before the Nuernberg Military Tribunals Under Control Council Law. Volume II. "The Medical Case W. Final Statement of Defendant Fischer." Washington, DC: US Government Printing Office, 1949.

———. *Volume XIV. Affirmation of Sentences by the Military Governor of the United States Zone of Occupation*. Washington, DC: US Government Printing Office, 1949.

Trials of War Criminals before the Nuremberg Military Tribunals. Volume XI. The High Command Case and the Hostage Case. Washington, DC: US Government Printing Office, 1949.

Triumpbour, John. *Selling Hollywood to the World: US and European Struggles for Mastery of the Global Film Industry, 1920–1950.* Cambridge: Cambridge University Press, 2002.

Tucker, Spencer, ed. "Military Organization." In *World War II: The Definitive Encyclopedia and Document Collection, 1865-1870.* Boulder, Colorado: ABC-CLIO, 2016.

————, ed. "Rank Structures, Selected World War II Belligerents." In *World War II: The Definitive Encyclopedia and Document Collection,* 1871–1890. Boulder, CO: ABC-CLIO, 2016.

Tusa, Ann and John Tusa. *The Nuremberg Trial.* New York: Skyhorse Publishing, 2010.

Tzani, Fotini. *Zwischen Karrierismus und Widerspenstigkeit: SS-Aufseherinnen im KT-Alltag.* Bielefeld: Lorbeer Verlag, 2011.

Uhlmann, Angelika and Andreas Winkelman. "The Science Prior to the Crime: August Hirt Before 1941." *Annals of Anatomy* 204 (2016): 118–26.

Ullrich, Volker. *Adolf Hitler: Die Jahre des Aufstiegs.* Frankfurt am Main: S. Fischer Verlag, 2013.

United Nations. Treaty Series. No. 251. Agreement United Kingdom of Great Britain and Northern Ireland, United States of America, France union of Soviet Socialist Republic for the Prosecution and Punishment of the Major War Criminals of the European Axis. London. August 8, 1945. http://www.un.org/en/genocideprevention/documents/atrocity-crimes/Doc.2_Charter%20of%20IMT%201945.pdf.

United Nations International Criminal Tribunal for Rwanda. "The Prosecutor v. Ferdinand Nahimana, Jean-Bosco Barayagwiza, and Hassan Ngeze: Judgement and Sentence." December 3, 2003. http://unictr.unmict.org/sites/unictr.org/files/case-documents/ictr-99–52/trial-judgments/en/031203.pdf.

United Press International (UPI). "Orphans Leave Sarajevo After Two killed by Snipers." August 2, 1992. https://www.upi.com/Archives/1992/08/02/Orphans-leave-Sarajevo-after-two-killed-by-snipers/2277712728000/.

Ureneck, Lou. *The Great Fire: One American's Mission to Rescue Victims of the 20th Century's First Genocide.* New York: Harper Collins, 2015.

US Bureau of Census. *Census Confidentiality and Privacy: 1790–2002.* https://www.census.gov/prod/2003pubs/conmono2.pdf.

————. *Frequently Occurring Surnames in the 2010 Census.* by Joshua Comenetz. October 2016. https://www2.census.gov/topics/genealogy/2010surnames/surnames.pdf.

————. "Hello My Name Is: Top 15 Most Popular Last names in the US by Rank." December 15, 2016. https://www.census.gov/library/visualizations/2016/comm/cb16-tps154_surnames_top15.html.

US Congress. "Ensuring America's Security: Cleaning Up the Nation's Watchlists." Hearing before the Subcommittee on Transportation Security and Infrastructure Protection of the Committee on Homeland Security House of Representatives, 110th Cong., 2nd Session, Serial No. 110–35, September 9, 2008, 17. https://www.gpo.gov/fdsys/pkg/CHRG-110hhrg47173/pdf/CHRG-110hhrg47173.pdf.

————. *Immigration and Nationality Act of 1954,* Public Law 414, HR 5678, 82nd Cong., June 27, 1952.

———. *The Commission on Wartime Relocation and Internment of Civilians. Summary Report*. December 1982. https://www.archives.gov/files/research/japanese-americans/j ustice-denied/summary.pdf.

———. The Civil Liberties Act of 1988, Public Law 100–383, 100th Cong., H.R. 442, Sect. 1 (1–2). August 10, 1988.

———. *The Enhanced Border Security and Visa Entry Reform Act of 2002*. House Amendment. HR 1885, 107th Cong., 2nd Sess. March 12, 2002.

———. *Intelligence Reform and Terrorism Prevention Act of 2004*. Public Law 108–458, 108th Cong., December 18, 2004. https://www.gpo.gov/fdsys/pkg/PLAW-108pu bl458/html/PLAW-108publ458.htm.

———. *Fair, Accurate, Secure, and Timely Redress Act*, HR 110–686. 110th Cong., 2nd Sess. June 19, 2008.

———. Senate Select Committee on Intelligence. *Unclassified Executive Summary of the Committee Report on the Attempted Terrorist Attack on Northwest Airlines Flight 253*. May 18, 2010.

———. House. "No Social Security for Nazis Act." 11th Cong., (December 18, 2014): HR 5739. Public Law No: 113–270. https://www.congress.gov/113/plaws/publ270/ PLAW-113publ270.pdf.

US Department of Homeland Security. Homeland Security Fact Sheet. December 1, 2003. http://www2.gtlaw.com/practices/immigration/news/2003/12/01a.pdf.

———. Field Hearing of the Committee on Homeland Security. *The Progress and Pitfalls of the Terrorist Watch list*. H.R. 1st sess., Serial No. 110–84, November 8, 2007. https://www.gpo.gov/fdsys/pkg/CHRG-110hhrg48979/html/CHRG-110hhrg48979 .htm.

———. Subcommittee on Transportation Security and Infrastructure Protection of the Committee on Homeland Security. *Ensuring America's Security: Cleaning up the Nation's Watchlists*. H.R. 110th Cong., 2nd sess., Serial No. 110–35, September 9, 2008.

———. *Privacy Policy Guidance Memorandum 2008–1: The Fair Information Practice Principles*. December 29, 2008. https://www.dhs.gov/sites/default/files/publications/ privacy-policy-guidance-memorandum-2008–01.pdf.

———. *Privacy Impact Assessment for the Watchlist Service*. July 14, 2010. https://ww w.dhs.gov/xlibrary/assets/privacy/privacy_pia_dhs_wls.pdf.

———. *Privacy Impact Assessment for the Neptune Pilot*. DHS/ALL/PIA-046–1. September 25, 2013. https://www.dhs.gov/sites/default/files/publications/privacy-pia-dhs-w ide-neptune-09252013.pdf.

———. *Privacy Impact Assessment for the Cerberus Pilot*. DHS/ALL/PIA-046–3. https:// www.dhs.gov/sites/default/files/publications/privacy-pia-dhs-cerberus-rov2013.pdf.

———. *Guidance for Implementing Section 5 of EO 13636: Privacy and Civil Liberties Protections*. June 10, 2013. https://www.dhs.gov/sites/default/files/publications/NS S%20Guidance%20on%20Section%205%20implementation_0.pdf.

———. *Safeguarding Privacy and Civil Liberties while Keeping and our Skies Safe*. September 18, 2014. https://www.gpo.gov/fdsys/pkg/CHRG-113hhrg93366/html/CH RG-113hhrg93366.htm.

———. *Fiscal Year 2016 Entry/Exit Overstay Report*. https://www.dhs.gov/sites/default/ files/publications/Entry%20and%20Exit%20Overstay%20Report%20%20Fiscal%2 0Year%202016.pdf.

———. *Privacy Impact Assessment Update for the DHS Data Framework: Unclassified Use*. DHS/ALL/PIA-046(e). October 6, 2017. https://www.dhs.gov/sites/default/files/publications/privacy-pia-dhswide-dhsdfunclassifieduse-october2017.pdf.

US Department of Justice. *San Francisco woman who served as Nazi Concentration Camp-Guard is Deported to Germany*. (06–633- USDOJ). September 19, 2006. https://www.justice.gov/archive/opa/pr/2006/September/06_crm_633.html.

———. Office of the Inspector General. *Audit of the US Department of Justice Terrorist Watchlist Nomination Process*. March 2008. https://oig.justice.gov/reports/plus/a08 16/final.pdf.

———. *The Federal Bureau of Investigation's Terrorist Watchlist Nomination Practices: Audit Report*. May 9–25, 2009. https://oig.justice.gov/reports/FBI/a0925/final.pdf.

———. Audit of the Department of Justice's Handling of Known or Suspected Terrorists Admitted into the Federal Witness Security Program. September 2017. https://oig.justice.gov/reports/2017/a1734.pdf.

US Department of State. "The Fiscal Year 2004 Performance Plan." Washington, DC, March 2003. http://www.state.gov/m/rm/rls/perfplan/2004./.

US Government Accountability Office. *Nazis and Axis Collaborators were used to further US Anti-communist Objectives in Europe: Some Immigrated to the United States*. GAO/GGD-85–66 June 28, 1985. Washington, DC: Comptroller General of the United States. https://www.gao.gov/products/GGD-85–66.

———. *Highlights of a Forum: Combating Synthetic Identity Fraud*. Comptroller General of the United States. GAO-17–708SP. July 2017. http://www.gao.gov/assets/690/686134.pdf.

US Holocaust Memorial Museum. *Frequently Asked Questions*. https://www.ushmm.org/collections/ask-a-research-question/frequently-asked-questions.

———. *Strategic Plan 2013*. https://www.ushmm.org/m/pdfs/Strategic-Plan-2013–2 018.pdf.

———. "Facts and Figures." https://www.ushmm.org/information/press/press-kits/united-states-holocaust-memorial-museum-press-kit/.

———. "Museum Announces $20 Million Gift to Name the Simon-Skjodt Center for the Prevention of Genocide." February 19, 2015. https://www.ushmm.org/information/press/press-releases/museum-announces-20-million-gift-to-name-the-simon-skjodt-center-for-the-pr.

———. Henri Zajdenwergier. Testimony. Oral History. VHA Interview Code: 23517. https://collections.ushmm.org/search/catalog/vha23517

———. "The World Memory Project," https://www.ushmm.org/online/world-memory-project/

———. *War Crimes Trials: RuSHA Case; Justice Case Sentencing*. Film. Accession Number: 2001.358.1: RG-60.2986. Film ID: 2383. https://collections.ushmm.org/search/catalog/irn1000383.

US National Counterterrorism Center. Office of the Director of National Intelligence. "Who We Are." https://www.dni.gov/index.php/nctc-who-we-are.

———. "How We Work." https://www.dni.gov/index.php/nctc-how-we-work.

———. *Watchlist Guidance*. March 2013. https://www.eff.org/files/2014/07/24/201 3-watchlist-guidance_1.pdf.

————. *Terrorist Identities Datamart (TIDE).* https://www.dni.gov/files.NCTC/docu ments/features_documents/TIDEfactsheet10FEB2017.pdf.

US Patent Office. Treating Bone Black. Reference Number (US62537) Issue date: March 5, 1867.

US Submission to the United Nations Universal Periodic Review. *The Persistence, in the United States, of Discriminatory Profiling Based on Race, Ethnicity, Religion and National Origin.* November 1–12, 2010. http://lib.ohchr.org/HRBodies/UPR/_layou ts/15/WopiFrame.aspx?sourcedoc=/HRBodies/UPR/Documents/session9/US/USH RN_UPR_USA_S09_2010_Annex19_Racial%20Profiling%20Joint%20Report%2 0USA.pdf&action=default&DefaultItemOpen=1.

Utz, Friedemann. *Preuße, Protestant, Pragmatiker: Der Staatssekretär Walter Strauß und sein Staat.* Heidelberg: Mohr Siebeck, 2003.

Vögle, Jörg, Ulrich Koppitz, and Hideharn Umehara. "Epidemien und Pandemien in Historischer Perspective." In *Epidemics and Pandemic in Historical Perspective*, edited by Jörg Vögele, Stefanie Knöll, and Thomas Noack, 3–34. Wiesbaden: Springer Verlag, 2016.

von den Wänden, Kalk. "Prozesse: Babij Jar." *Der Spiegel.* October 2, 1967. http://www.spiegel.de/spiegel/print/d-46289911.html.

von Horn, Detlef. *Lebensborn-Standesamt Hohehorst.* Bremen: Hohehorst Archiv.

von Leers, Johann. "Der Weg der modernen Türkei." *Die Tat* 25, no. 12 (1934): 923–38.

————. "Frankreich und der Islam." *Der Türmer* 39, no. 4 (1937): 382.

————. "Die arabischen Argumente gegen die Neufestigung der Juden in Palästina." *Der Weltkampf* 15, no. 172 (1938): 146–60.

————. "Islam und Judentum im Laufe der Jahrhunderten." *Der Deutsche Erzieher* 5, no. 17 (1938): 427.

————. "Islam und Judentum-Zwei unversöhnliche Gegensätze. Teil I." *Der Weltkampf* 16, no. 181 (1939): 8–20.

————. "Islam und Judentum-Zwei unversöhnliche Gegensätze. Teil II." *Der Weltkampf* 16, no. 182 (1939): 64–71.

————. "Judentum und Islam als Gegensätze." *Die Judenfrage* 6, no. 24 (1942): 275–78.

————. "Die Tragödie der Demokratie." *Der Weg* 5, no. 4 (1951): 295–99.

————. "Der unsichtbare Knebel." *Der Weg* 6, no. 1 (1952): 64–68.

————. "Ein Drittel des deutschen Volksvermögens—den Juden." *Der Weg* 7, no. 1 (1953): 56.

————. "Ein Programm für die Juden." *Der Weg* 8, no. 11 (1954): 795.

von Miquel, Marc. "Wir müssen mit den Mörden zusammenleben! NS-Prozesse und politische Öffentlichkeit in den sechziger Jahren." In *Gerichtstag halten über uns selbst: Geschichte und Wirkung des ersten Frankfurter Auschwitz Prozesses*, edited by Irmtrud Wojak, 97–116. Frankfurt am Main: Campus Verlag, 2001.

von Reeken, Dietmar. *Lahusen: eine Bremer Unternehmer Dynastie 1916–1933.* Bremen: Edition Temmen, 1996.

von Selchow, Bogislav. *Das Namenbuch: Eine Sammlung Sämtlicher Deutscher, Altdeutscher, und in Deutschland gebräuchlicher fremdländischer Vornamen mit Angabe ihrer Abstammung und ihre Deutung.* Leipzig: K. F. Köhler, 1935.

Wachsmann, Nikolaus. *KL: Die Geschichte der Nationalsozialistischen Konzentrationslager.* Munich: Siedler Verlag, 2015.

Wagner-Kern, Michael. *Staat und Namensänderung.* Tübingen: Mohr Siebeck, 2002.

Weatherall, Thomas. *Jus Cogens: International Law and Social Contract.* Cambridge: Cambridge University Press, 2015.

Weindling, Paul. *Victims and Survivors of Nazi Human Experiments: Science and Suffering in the Holocaust.* New York: Bloomsbury, 2015.

Werner, Markus. "Einer mußte es tun: Katrin Himmler, Großnichte des SS-Führers, gräbt in der Familiengeschichte." *Frankfurter Allgemeine.* October 23, 2003. http://www.katrinhimmler.de/wp-content/uploads/2013/07/FAS_Okt05.pdf.

Widmann, Carlos. "Gefährtin des Bösen." *Der Spiegel.* September 24, 2001. http://magazin.spiegel.de/EpubDelivery/spiegel/pdf/20184307.

Wiese, Niels. *Eicke: Eine SS-Karriere zwischen Nervenklinik, KZ-System und Waffen-SS.* Zürich: Ferdinand Schönigh, 2013.

Wiesenthal, Simon. *Everyday Remembrance Day: A Chronicle of Jewish Martyrdom.* New York: Henry Holt Company, 1985.

Wilson, Stephen. *The Means of Naming: A Social and Cultural History of Personal Naming in Western Europe.* New York: Routledge, 1998.

Wistrich, Robert. *Who's Who in Nazi Germany.* New York: Routledge, 2002.

Wittebur, Klemens. *Die deutsche Soziologie im Exil 1933–1945: eine biographische Kartographie.* Hamburg: LIT Verlag, 1991.

Wojak, Irmtrud, ed. *Gerichtstag halten über uns selbst: Geschichte und Wirkung des ersten Frankfurter Auschwitz Prozesses.* Frankfurt: Campus Verlag, 2001.

Wolffsohn, Michael and Thomas Brechenmacher. *Deutschland, jüdisch Heimatland: Die Geschichte der deutschen Juden von Kaiserreich bis heute.* Munich: Piper Verlag, 1996.

Wulf, Peter. "'Juda ist überall': Antisemitismus in Schleswig-Holstein in der Zeit der Weimarer Republik." In *Ausgegrenzt-verachtet-vernichtet: Zur Geschichte der Juden in Schleswig-Holstein, Landeszentrale für Politische Bildung,* 71–81. Kiel: Landeszentrale für Politische Bildung, 1994.

Yad Vashem. "Tarnopol: Historical Background." http://www.yadvashem.org/righteous/stories/tarnopol-historical-background.html.

———. "January 1943, Partisans in the Vinnitsa District, Ukraine." http://www.yadvashem.org/holocaust/this-month/january/1943–4.html.

———. "The Righteous Among the Nations." Rescue Story. File 201. http://db.yadvashem.org/righteous/search.html?language=en.

Zabecki, David, ed. *Germany at War: 400 Years of Military History.* Boulder, CO: ABC-CLIO, 2014.

Die Zeit. "Mehr rechtsextreme Verdachtsfälle in der Bundeswehr." January 28, 2017. http://www.zeit.de/politik/deutschland/2018-01/rechtsextremismus-bundeswehr-verdachstfaelle-2017.

———. "BKA zählte 771 politisch motivierte Straftaten." January 27, 2018. http://www.zeit.de/gesellschaft/zeitgeschehen/2018–01/reichsbuerger-bka-politische-straftaten.

———. "Bundesregierung bezeichnet Gauland-Äußerung als beschämend." June 4, 2018. https://www.zeit.de/politik/deutschland/2018-06/afd-bundesregierung-alexander-gauland-hitler-nationalsozialismus-vogelschiss.

Zeitlin, Maurice. "The Last Stands of Jews in the Small Town Ghettos of German-occupied Poland, 1941–1943." In *Society, History, and the Global Human Condition: Essays in Honor of Irving M. Zeitlin*, edited by Baber Zaheer and Joseph M. Bryant, 33–70. London: Lexington Books, 2010.

Zick, Andreas, Andreas Hövermann, Silke Jansen, and Julia Bernstein. *Jüdische Perspektiven auf Antisemitismus in Deutschland*. April 2007. https://uni-bielefeld.de/ikg/daten/JuPe_Bericht_April2017.pdf.

Zimbardo, Philip. *The Lucifer Effect*. London: Rider, 2007.

Zimmerman, Volker. *NS-Täter vor Gericht: Düsseldorf und die Strafprozesse wegen nationalsozialistischer Gewaltverbrechen*. Düsseldorf: Justizministerium des Landes Nordrhein-Westfalen, 2001.

Zornberg, Ira. *Jews, Quakers, and the Holocaust: The Struggle to Save Lives of Twenty Thousand Children*. Middletown, DE: Ira Zornberg, 2016.

Zuccotti, Susan. *The Holocaust, the French, and the Jews*. London: University of Nebraska Press, 1993.

———. *Pierre Marie-Benoit and Jewish Rescue: How a French Priest Together with Jewish Friends Saved Thousands During the Holocaust*. Bloomington: Indiana University Press, 2013.

Subject Index

Name Index

Page references for figures are italicized. Alternative names appear in parentheses. Topics are covered in the Subject Index.

Ackermann, Otto, 120
Adenauer, Konrad, 196, 263
Ainsztein, Reuben, 368n24
Akiva, Chaim, 326
Anderson, Margo, 16
Andorfer, Herbert (Hans Meyer), 215–16
Anna K. (one of Poland's "lost children"), 122
Antonescu, Ion, 366
Arlosoroff, Chaim, 55
Atatürk, Kemal, 413n5
Avraham, Alexander, 386–88

Bachschneider, Otto, 115, *281*
Baer, Arthur, 87
Barayagwiza, Jean-Bosco, 410
Barbie, Nickolaus ("Butcher of Lyon," Klaus), 191, 204, 246
Bartosz, Adam, 364–65
Bass, Joseph, 341
Bauer, Fritz, 234
Beger, Bruno, 370, 372
Beissner, Wilhelm, 264
Bella: Isabelle, *289*, 343–45; Joseph, 344; Marie (Muguette), *289*, 341–46

Belling, Erika (Bergmann, "Demon in Human Skin," Koch), 300–301
Benoît, Pierre-Marie, 341
Berger, Rolf (Erich Koch), 216
Bierende, Edgar, 382
Binz, Dorothy, 299
Blankenburg, Werner (Werner Bieleke), 223, 252–53
Böhnhardt, Uwe, 399
Bolender, Kurt Heinz (Heinz Brenner, Heinz Burner, Wilhelm Kurt Vahle), 254
Bonhoeffer, Dietrich, 130
Bormann: Gerda, 79; Martin, 62, 101–2, 130
Bösel, Greta, 299
Boulgarides, Theodoros, 399
Brack, Viktor, 223–25, 229, 238, 272n68
Brandt: Karl, 222, 269n34, 272n68, 273n81; Rudolf, 272, 374
Braun, Eva, 130
Brunner: Alois (Brunner I, Georg Fischer, Ali Mohammed, Alois Schmaldienst), 258–66, 278n174, 279n177, 280n190; Anton (Brunner II), 259–62, 278n168

About the Author

Iman Nick is an American sociolinguist. She holds a PhD in English linguistics (University of Freiburg), an MA in German linguistics (University of Washington, Seattle), a BA in Germanic languages and literatures (University of Maryland), a BSc in clinical and social psychology (University of Maryland), and an MSc in forensic and investigative psychology (University of Liverpool). For each of these degrees, she achieved university and departmental honors. In the summer of 2010, she was also awarded the German post-doctoral degree, the "Habilitation," for her research in English linguistics (University of Cologne). She regularly teaches and publishes within the areas of forensic linguistics, English dialectology, multilingualism, onomastics, language policy, and the Holocaust. She also serves as a linguistics journal editor and reviewer. From 2014 to 2016, she was the elected chair of the Committee for Ethnic Diversity in Linguistics (CEDL) for the Linguistic Society of America. She is currently the president of the American Name Society (ANS), the oldest scholarly society for the scientific investigation of names and naming. Within the area of forensic onomastics, her particular areas of interest include the statistical investigation and detection of criminal aliases.

Lightning Source UK Ltd.
Milton Keynes UK
UKHW051134070619
343879UK00006B/35/P